Computer Modeling:

From Sports To Spaceflight ...From Order To Chaos

J. M. A. Danby

Published By:

P.O. 35025
Richmond, Virginia 23235 USA
(804) 320-7016
www.willbell.com

Published by Willmann-Bell, Inc.
P.O. Box 35025, Richmond, Virginia 23235

Printed in the United States of America

Library of Congress Cataloging-in-Publication Data.
Danby, J.M.A.
Computer modeling : from sports to spaceflight, from order to chaos / J.M.A. Danby.
p. cm.
ISBN 0-943396-51-4
1. Computer simulation. I. Title
QA76.9.C65D36 1997 97-22651
003'.3–dc21 CIP

97 98 99 00 01 02 03 04 05 9 8 7 6 5 4 3 2

Preface

This volume has as its origin the time, many years ago, when North Carolina State University acquired a computer system in which any student could have an account. Then it became possible that many problems that had hitherto only been accessible to graduate students or professional scientists could be investigated by sophomores. I instituted a course, aimed primarily at sophomores, for tackling such problems; the course is now host to many hundreds of undergraduate students each year.

In this volume the problems of concern are those that can be modeled by systems of ordinary differential equations and cannot be solved by mathematical formulas. This includes most models of practical interest, as a glance at the table of contents may show. They contrast with the applications in a traditional course on differential equations, which must be solved briefly and without computational aids, and which have always appeared to me as stifling in their narrowness. The computer has given us a new freedom to explore the fresh air of reality. This text is offered as an advocate for the enjoyment of this freedom.

One of my purposes is that this volume should be accessible for use as a text, especially in mathematics, the natural sciences and engineering. Many university departments are instituting courses on "Computer Applications," and I hope that the diversity of the contents will make the text useful in different curricula. Based on my experience, I contend that most models in the text are accessible to a sophomore; all should be accessible to a senior or a graduate of a scientific or engineering curriculum. Indeed, another of my purposes is that this volume be of interest to those who have graduated, but are interested in using the computer for exploration.

What do I expect of my readers? Every model involves change, so you must know some calculus. Applying calculus need not involve memorization, or the learning of elaborate techniques, but it must involve understanding basic concepts. Combine the concept of the derivative with a physical law, and many models appear instantly. For some models you will need to know some concepts in physics, such as energy, angular momentum and the use of Newton's laws of motion. To follow some derivations you will need to be at home with vector notation. You will need to be at ease in a computing environment. This environment includes computers, "packages" and program code, but, most importantly, other people. If you are a lonely soul, so be it; but you are likely to have fewer difficulties and more profit and fun in company. More than anything else, I want this book to be enjoyed.

The first two chapters are concerned with basic concepts necessary for understanding any numerical computation of solutions of differential equations. The third examines in detail the background, learning and implementation of one excellent method of solution: Fehlberg's RKF4(5). This, with some modifications, is now widely used. An essential feature is automatic stepsize control, so that the user specifies the accuracy desired, and the program chooses and varies the stepsize. I would not recommend any method that does not include this facility.

Many users of this book are likely to skip these opening chapters, arguing that they already use a "package" that takes care of the solution without the need for the user to be aware of details; they may well be correct. When my students interview for jobs, they are mostly expected to be able to work with programming languages, FORTRAN, C, or whatever. Reliance on particular black boxes is unlikely to impress. I would personally be reluctant to teach a course from this text without spending time on these preliminary chapters, because I want my students at least to have some idea about what is taking place in a numerical solution. But if you have a "package" that you like and can control, who am I to argue against playing with the projects immediately?

The fourth chapter attempts to describe concepts to do with modeling on the computer. I recommend that you look at this; if you disagree with much of it, it may still help generate ideas of your own. At least, I hope you will agree with me that modeling should involve discourse and communication.

For the rest, there is no reason for looking at chapters or models in any special order; there are only a few instances where I assume that you have looked at an earlier model. In fact my desire to make most models stand alone has led to some redundancy in discussion that I hope you will tolerate.

Any text of this sort must involve chaotic models. After all, it has been known for some hundred years that chaos is the norm, not the exception. The purpose of chapter five is to describe some of the methods that can be used for exploring chaotic systems. Some of these may be useful in later projects, so this chapter can be dipped into as needed. Some of the concepts and numerical techniques are not easy, but this need not stop you from generating and experiencing chaos. One section is devoted to difference equations; these are useful since many manifestations of chaos that are slow to be seen in computing with differential equations, appear almost instantaneously with difference equations. (By rights, a chapter on modeling with difference equations should have been included; but the book is already long enough!)

The variety of "packages" and of programming languages currently in use makes it impossible to favor any of these specifically in the text. Some models can be run very simply: you might start at one given time and end at another, and a printout of the calculation will tell you what you want to know. In between the two times, you let the program function undisturbed. But in many cases extra coding and maybe some knowledge of numerical analysis may be needed. You may need to intervene – to control the actions of a child on a swing, to find the precise top of a pendulum's swing, or the landing point of an ICBM – taking the stepsize control away from the program. The nature of the intervention will depend on the language or package being used. I discuss it using pseudo-code; this is specific to no language, and is only intended to suggest a way to structure your code, as I have structured mine.

Chapters 6 through 8, involving population change, spread of disease and competition, contain models that are mostly easy to follow, to set up and to run. You should find that many of these can be interpreted in different ways and can be generalized quite simply. They can also be chaotic.

Chapter 9 deals with sports. Since starting to write it I have been amazed at the wealth of excellent science to be found in sports, and surprised at its neglect in teaching. I hope that this chapter will contribute toward using sports in teaching, and in broadening the range of applications in mathematics and physics. Some models are more realistic than others, but I hope that all can provide some insight into the sports involved. Sports can be hard work. Chapter 10 deals with relaxation: travel, jogging, visiting the amusement park or watching fireworks. These models are mostly fairly simple to understand and allow a lot of experimentation.

Chapter 11, on space flight and astronomy, contains some of the most difficult models but also, in my opinion, the most interesting. From a student's point of view, extra guidance is needed for many projects. This is partly because, with the flight of a rocket, for instance, there are so many quantities to vary that it may be hard to get started. The contents of this chapter alone could contain material for a full course.

Pendulums are cool. We all know what they look like and how they behave, and the basic model is simple but not at all trivial. This model can be varied simply in any number of ways. The models for a child on a swing might have been placed in chapter 10. Many models produce chaotic behavior. Some of the models in Chapter 12 can be played with easily but are complicated to run in detail; if possible, view them in animation. We even put pendulums in orbit, when they can model a dumbbell satellite around the Earth, a chaotic satellite of Saturn or the rotation of Mercury.

Chapter 13 deals with springs, or rather with models containing springs. None of the models is particularly difficult, although many are chaotic. Chapter 14, on chemical and other reacting systems, does not involve chaos; the models should be fairly straightforward, although those on enzyme kinetics can be elaborate to run. The model of the "oregonator" involves a "stiff" system of equations that may require a special integration method.

Finally, chapter 15 contains various models that I felt unable to classify, but was also unable to resist. These are mostly simple to run. They certainly don't lack variety.

After the title of each model there appear one to five "computers." These are intended to indicate, subjectively, the degree of difficulty or complication that may be involved. A model with just one computer should be easy to understand, and to run, with the minimum of code. Such a model, the simple pendulum, for instance, is by no means trivial, and merits as much attention and love as any other. Two computers imply a little extra coding, maybe with logical decisions; the equations may be more involved, or special events (the extreme and lowest points in the swing of a pendulum, for instance) may need to be found. Models in these first two categories should be suitable for student projects with little guidance needed.

The appearance of three computers is not intended to indicate a "difficult" model. It will probably involve more detail and also a greater variety of possibilities to be investigated. A student would probably need extra guidance and more time.

Four or five computers warn of a project that may be hard to understand fully and to run, and may involve a lot of coding. But these projects are beautiful and rewarding. The interaction of two galaxies is fairly easy to understand, but not so easy to code; presenting results is not easy unless they can be shown in animation. The model for the white dwarf is not so hard to code, but involves some elementary quantum mechanics, so may be hard to understand. Incidentally, one reason why I include this model of Chandrasekhar, is that it is, in my opinion, the outstanding model of the twentieth century.

A problem in presenting these models is to determine to what extent detailed and specific instructions should be given, and to what extent the reader can be expected to explore unaided. The treatment here is deliberately uneven. I have tried to provide most detail, and the most graphics, for the simplest models, where a novice may need help to get started. (Also a major consideration was to compromise between including many models and limiting the size of the book.)

I have tried to provide adequate and clear derivations of all equations. If these seem too elaborate, then they should not prevent you from playing with a model, provided you have clear definitions of all the variables and parameters. Some derivations of equations for dynamical systems involve the use of Lagrange's equations. There is some prejudice that these are "difficult" and so belong in "advanced" physics courses. Actually, they only require the expression of kinetic and potential energy, and first-year calculus; then the differential equations fall out like magic. An appendix deals briefly with the background and the derivation of these equations.

Software, on a CD-ROM, accompanies this text (inside the back cover). Approximately one-third of the models are represented. Emphasis is placed on user input and control, and on animation. The programs might be used to clarify models, or to look for significant numerical values that might be used in a detailed computation. I hope that they will also be a source of enjoyment.

Over the years I have received help and ideas from many people and many sources—too many for individual acknowledgments. But I would particularly like to thank Gerhard Holtkamp, who read and made hundreds of valuable comments on the manuscript just prior to publication. My thanks are also due to my wife, Phyllis, who provided encouragement and support over many years, and who also made many suggestions to improve the manuscript.

The software uses a set of utilities developed for the Consortium of Upper-level Physics Software, or CUPS. Many of the illustrations in the text were generated using this software. I am indebted to John Wiley and Sons for their kind permission for this use of the CUPS utilities.

J.M.A. Danby

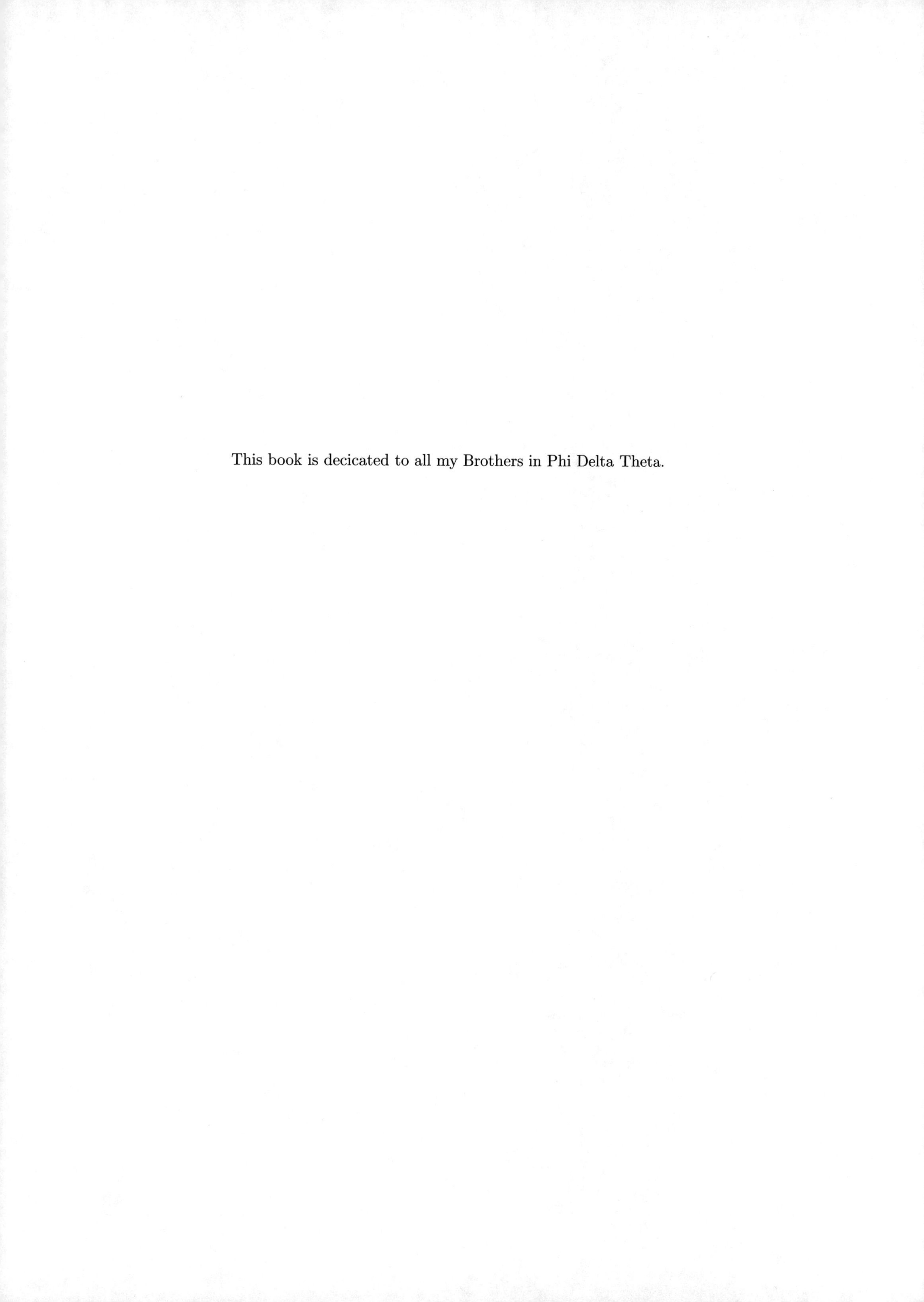

This book is decicated to all my Brothers in Phi Delta Theta.

Table of Contents

Chapter 1

Getting to Know a Differential Equation

1.1 What a Differential Equation Might Mean

Calculus is the science of change and differential equations are the engines of calculus. A differential equation is like a machine that is capable of movement and ready for action. It only requires some activation: pressing a button, inserting a coin, lighting a fuse — or running a computer. Then it will describe and give details of something that is continually changing. A chemical compound is formed or broken up (gradually, one hopes), a mortgage is repaid, a population increases, a disease spreads, a miss-hit golf ball curves away from its intended direction or an orbit is described in space: in each of these cases the changes will be modeled by differential equations. Look at the orbit. The differential equations that we use (a system of them) will be able to control a whole class of orbits, and a particular orbit will depend on the launch conditions: *where* is the launching pad (or the burnout point), *when* does the launch take place, and *what* is the starting velocity? These are the *initial conditions.* Sometimes a differential equation is used to find out about just one orbit, or solution: then we have an *initial value problem.* But usually we want to know about the nature and details of a lot of different solutions, and there is need, in some sense, to *understand* the equation. *In nearly every case that is true to life* (most orbital problems, for example), there is no way to use known mathematical functions to give a precise description of the solution, and the computer must be used. "Understanding" a differential equation and the model that it represents, and using the computer safely and wisely to solve it, require a lot of experience. In this text, we shall make a start.

Even if we have a mathematical formula for a solution, it may be complicated and may not immediately convey much information about what the solution is *like.* Further, it may not be clear how the possible solutions depend on the initial conditions. (Which, for example, among many possible orbits, will actually hit the Moon?) Traditionally, there has been prejudice against the use of the computer and in favor of mathematical methods for approximating solutions, or theorems for providing qualitative information. But these may require an advanced degree; meanwhile, anyone with a little knowledge of calculus can derive similar information — and more — by properly using a computer.

To start, we shall work with differential equations that can be "solved." Knowing the answer, it will be easier to understand what a differential equation can do, and also it will be easier to play with some ideas about the numerical investigation of the equation. Understanding these ideas will give you confidence when you work with equations for which there is no known solution. Also, *never forget* that any program for numerically solving equations should be debugged using special equations having known solutions.

For a start, you must adopt (or you may be assigned) one of the differential equations listed at the end of this chapter in section 1.5. They are all of the form

$$\frac{dy}{dx} = y' = f(x, y). \tag{1.1.1}$$

With most of these there is no physical interpretation (although you might try to work one out, or find a story for what the equation might represent). Get to know the qualitative properties of your equation; don't just see it as a vehicle for computation.

Two equations will be used here for illustration. The first is

$$\frac{dy}{dx} = x + y. \tag{1.1.2}$$

To see how this equation *might* be applied, suppose that you have a savings account on which you are earning interest continuously at the rate of $R\%$ per year, and that (as you become richer) you deposit money into the account at a rate that is steadily increasing in time, so that after t years the rate of deposit is kt dollars per year. Then if the account holds $\$A$ after t years, A will satisfy the differential equation

$$\frac{dA}{dt} = (R/100)A + kt. \tag{1.1.3}$$

This is quite similar to (1.1.2); if we let

$$A = k(100/R)^2 y, \; t = (100/R)x, \tag{1.1.4}$$

then (1.1.3) is transformed into (1.1.2). This sort of transformation can be very useful *before* numerical work is started, so that the equation used in a program is as simple as possible. Such transformations will often be used in the projects.

Equation (1.1.3) is capable of following the histories of many different savings accounts; these depend on *when* the account was opened, the *amount* of the initial deposit (which are initial conditions), and the interest rate R and deposit rate k (which are parameters of the model).

The second equation for illustration is

$$\frac{dy}{dx} = \sin x - y. \tag{1.1.5}$$

Let us see how this equation might be applied. A body has temperature T°C in an environment having temperature U°C. If the temperature of the body changes in accordance with Newton's law of cooling, then

$$\frac{dT}{dt} = k(U - T), \tag{1.1.6}$$

where k is a positive constant. Now suppose that the time t is measured in hours and that the environment has a daily temperature change such that

$$U = U_0 + U_1 \sin(2\pi t/24) \tag{1.1.7}$$

for constants U_0 and U_1. Then

$$\frac{dT}{dt} = k\left[U_0 + U_1 \sin\left(\frac{2\pi t}{24}\right) - T\right]. \tag{1.1.8}$$

So we have a model for the temperature of a body left out in the open. As we know, the maximum temperature of the body occurs some time after the occurrence of the maximum temperature of the environment, and this feature can be confirmed by the model. The delay depends on the value of k, which depends on the thermal conductivity of the body. If we let

$$T = U_0 + U_1 y, \; t = (12/\pi)x, \tag{1.1.9}$$

then (1.1.8) becomes

$$\frac{dy}{dx} = (12k/\pi)(\sin x - y), \tag{1.1.10}$$

which is similar to (1.1.5).

In either case, the ability to associate a story with the differential equation is a considerable help in predicting and interpreting the nature of the solutions.

1.2 What is a Differential Equation Telling Us To Do?

You have just been introduced to an equation of the form

$$\frac{dy}{dx} = f(x, y). \tag{1.2.1}$$

Your equation is special: you can solve it. But *in general*, none of the techniques that you learn for solving first-order equations is going to help you to solve an equation like (1.2.1). You must learn to develop a dialog with the equation, and that means that you must be prepared to listen to what it has to say. We shall talk about "solutions" more carefully in a moment; let us for now assume that there are *some* solutions *somewhere* and see what (1.2.1) has to say about them.

In the first place, for progress to be made, there must be some region in the x-y plane in which the function $f(x, y)$ is defined and is single valued. We assume that there is, indeed, some rectangular region R in which this is true. R might be open or closed, finite or infinite; we want to represent it in a diagram, so let's say it is finite. If $y = y(x)$ is a solution, then it must be differentiable at all points within R, and if it is substituted into (1.2.1), then that must become an identity in x for all x in R. So a solution $y = y(x)$ can be plotted as a curve in R. Suppose that we are walking along a solution and that we come to a point P having coordinates (a, b). In front of us we see the solution path winding away. To take the next step along this path, we must start to move tangent to the path at (a, b). Now the direction of the tangent at (a, b), or the slope of the path through (a, b), is given by the derivative $\dfrac{dy}{dx}$ evaluated at (a, b); using (1.2.1), this slope is $f(a, b)$. See figure 1.2.

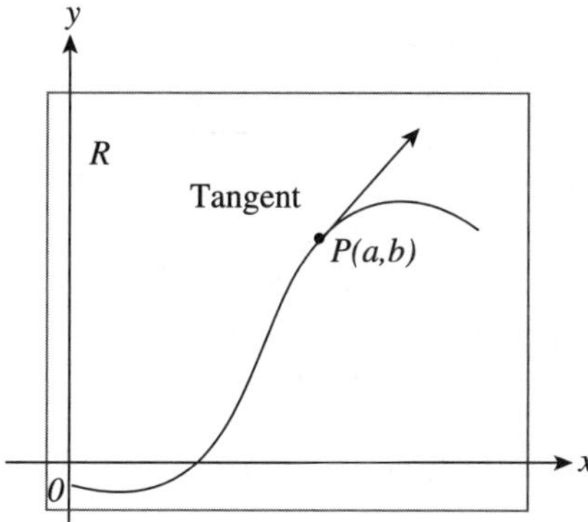

Figure 1.1: *The tangent line to a solution at the point* (a, b).

This slope can also be specified by an angle. If the tangent to the curve $y = y(x)$ at P makes the angle α with the x-axis, then

$$\tan\alpha = \left(\frac{dy}{dx} \text{ at } P\right) = f(a, b). \tag{1.2.2}$$

See figure 1.2.

Now let $P(a, b)$ be any point in the region R. Let us calculate $f(a, b)$ and the angle α (or an equivalent quantity) and then draw a short line starting at P and extending in the direction specified by α. Then we have graphically represented how the solution through P should proceed, or, at least, in what direction it should proceed. If we now do this for a set of points in R, then we have constructed what is called a "direction field" for the differential equation. Direction fields can be fun to look at, and they provide a quick insight into the nature and variety of the solutions of a differential equation. In figures 1.3 and 1.4, there are plotted direction fields for the two

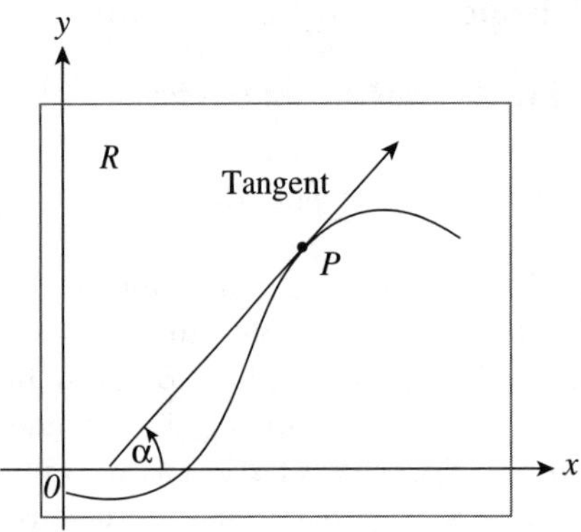

Figure 1.2: *The slope of the tangent line at P.*

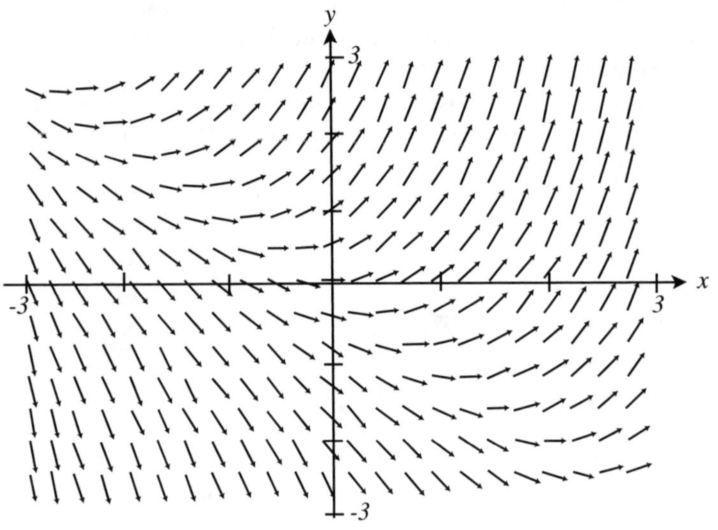

Figure 1.3: *Direction field diagram for $y' = x + y$.*

demonstration equations. Notice that they seem to set up a "flow" for the solutions. Look at the diagrams and see how much you can say about the possible solutions. Remember that you are deriving this information *without* using the actual solutions.

Software for plotting direction fields abounds, and programs are simple to write. Construct a direction field for your differential equation. You will probably need to experiment to find a satisfactory region for the plot. Make several copies. Then describe, in as much detail as you can, the nature of the possible solutions.

1.3 Looking at and Interpreting a Solution

The mathematical definition of a solution is precise and important. For (1.1.2), the *general* solution can be written

$$\frac{dy}{dx} = x + y : \quad y = Ce^{x} - x - 1. \tag{1.3.1}$$

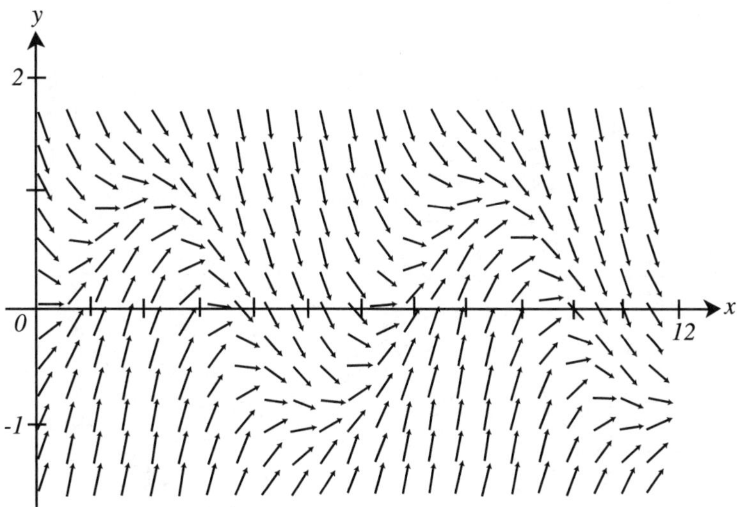

Figure 1.4: *Direction field diagram for* $y' = \sin x - y$.

For (1.1.5), we have

$$\frac{dy}{dx} = \sin x - y: \quad y = Ce^{-x} + \tfrac{1}{2}(\sin x - \cos x). \tag{1.3.2}$$

In each case C is an arbitrary constant. When you *think* that you have a solution to a differential equation, you should check it. To do this, make separate substitutions of the expression for the "solution" into the left and right-hand sides of the equation: then see whether the two are equal. For instance, for the alleged solution, $y = Ce^x - x - 1$ from (1.3.1) we find

$$\left.\begin{aligned} \text{Left}: \quad \frac{dy}{dx} &= Ce^x - 1. \\ \text{Right}: \quad x + y &= x + (Ce^x - x - 1) = Ce^x - 1. \end{aligned}\right] \tag{1.3.3}$$

Are these equal? Yes. So for any value of C, the relation $y' = x + y$ is *identically* satisfied. So the solution is correct.

For $y = Ce^{-x} + \frac{1}{2}(\sin x - \cos x)$ from (1.3.2),

$$\left.\begin{aligned} \text{Left}: \quad \frac{dy}{dx} &= -Ce^{-x} + \tfrac{1}{2}(\cos x + \sin x). \\ \text{Right}: \quad \sin x - y &= \sin x - \left(Ce^{-x} + \tfrac{1}{2}(\sin x - \cos x)\right) \\ &= -Ce^{-x} + \tfrac{1}{2}(\cos x + \sin x). \end{aligned}\right] \tag{1.3.4}$$

Again, the solution is confirmed.

For your equation in section 1.5 a general solution has been provided. YOU MUST NOT BELIEVE IT! Check it, as we have just done, and make sure that it is correct. You may invest some time in that solution. Make sure that the time will not be wasted.

For the project for this section you should plot some solution curves, superimposed onto your direction field diagram. These curves should confirm your conclusions about the nature of the solutions. The solutions should follow the flow of the field exactly. If you find a solution curve crossing a line in the field, then you have probably made an error. If two solutions cross one another, then you have probably made an error. Find it!

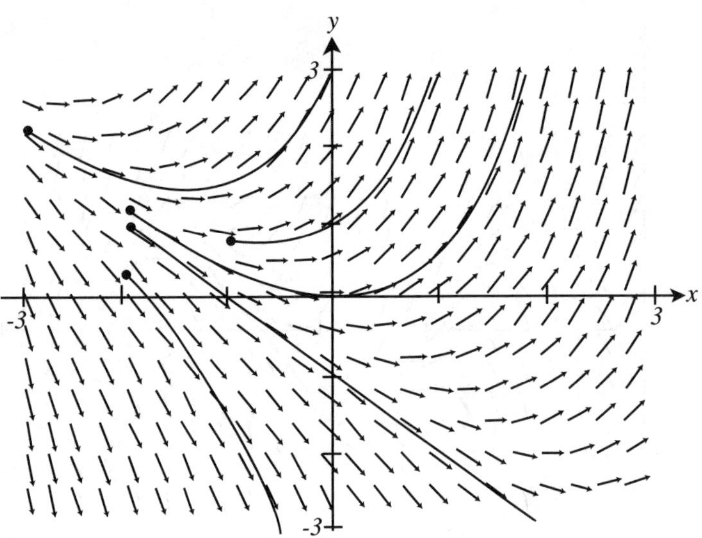

Figure 1.5: *Direction field and solutions for* $y' = x + y$.

Figures 1.5 and 1.6 show solution curves superimposed onto the direction fields 1.3 and 1.4.

Each differential equation in section 1.5 includes the general solution and also a particular solution for a given initial condition. The purpose of this is to remind you how to apply initial conditions to find the value of the arbitrary constant C; the actual initial condition used has no special merit, and can be ignored. For (1.3.1), suppose we choose the initial point $x_0 = -1,\ y_0 = 1$. Substituting into the solution

$$y = Ce^x - x - 1 \quad \text{gives } 1 = Ce^{-1} + 1 - 1, \quad \text{so } C = e.$$

Then the particular solution to be plotted is $y(x) = e.e^x - x - 1 = e^{x+1} - x - 1$. Choose at least five starting points, based on the possible interest of the solutions passing through them. (If your equation contains trigonometric functions, make sure that you use radians in your calculations.)

The two examples given illustrate very different characteristics. The solutions of (1.1.2) all diverge away from one another as x increases. However close two solutions may be initially, the difference between them will eventually become arbitrarily large. This is not encouraging if the equation is to be solved numerically. With finite precision every number in a computation has some round-off error; for (1.1.2) an initial, unavoidable round-off error will become magnified without limit as the computation proceeds, with sufficient increase of x. This will happen regardless of the numerical method that is used; in this work you are ultimately in the hands of the differential equation itself.

The solutions of (1.1.5), however, are quite different: they appear to "funnel" together. Reverting to the illustration of the body exposed to a diurnal (24 hour) temperature change, this funnelling can be interpreted as meaning that whatever the initial temperature of the body may be, its temperature at later times will come to resemble more and more closely that of similar bodies around it. Notice that the maximum values of the solutions (in terms of x) occur $\pi/4$ units later than the maximum value of the forcing term, $\sin x$, in the differential equation. This confirms the time lag mentioned earlier. It is easier to see if we write the solution (1.3.2) as

$$y = Ce^{-x} + \frac{1}{2}\sqrt{2}\sin\left(x - \frac{\pi}{4}\right). \tag{1.3.5}$$

The solution (1.3.2) can also be broken up into the *transient* term Ce^{-x} and the *steady-state* component $\frac{1}{2}(\sin x - \cos x)$. The "funnelling" results from the dying away of the transient term.

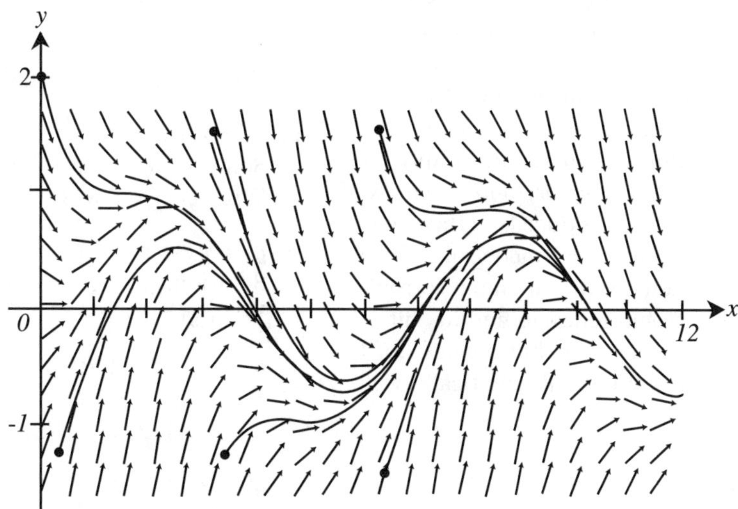

Figure 1.6: *Direction field and solutions for* $y' = \sin x - y$.

When you think of "the solution" or "a solution" of a differential equation, don't be limited by the mathematical definition. Look for qualities of the solution and, where possible, physical interpretation. Without these you will miss most of the fun in the coming projects.

1.4 *When* is there a solution? Or when *is* there a solution? Or when is there *a* solution?

This text is not concerned with mathematical theory; maybe you are getting that elsewhere. And liking it. This is not to say that theory is not important. In particular, there are fundamental theorems about differential equations that are concerned with matters of the *existence* and *uniqueness* of solutions. The key questions are: given a differential equation (or a set of them) and initial conditions, does a solution exist, and, if it does exist, is it unique? These are not trivial questions to ask if you are about to spend time and money in generating sets of numbers that, you hope, will approximate the solution. Computers can be friendly and obliging: if there is no solution, they may still present you with output; if the solution is not unique, and several different ones are possible, the computer is likely to make its own selection, whether or not it is the solution that you actually want. In *fact* the more you become involved in computing, the more you may need the reassurance and background of basic mathematics. These make their presence known in the "theorem." A theorem having to do with existence and uniqueness is likely to give you a checklist of properties that your equations must have. Use it!

Among the equations listed at the end of this chapter, many have places where you cannot put initial conditions and *depend* on finding a solution. For the equation $y' = f(x, y)$, theory tells us that if R is an open region and that if $f(x, y)$ and the partial derivative $f_y(x, y)$ are continuous in R, then there is one and only one solution passing through any point in R. Have a look at some of the equations at points where these conditions are not satisfied, and see what might happen.

Be careful! One of the astronomical projects deals with an approximate model for a star. The initial conditions occur at the center of the star; but the equations have a mathematical singularity at the center, so the mathematical requirements are not satisfied; in a situation like this, extra care is needed in order to start the solution correctly.

This brings us to another point: if a system of differential equations models a physical system, then it is tempting to assume that *because* the problem has a physical background, then the equations *must* be well behaved. This is not the case. The construction of a model inevitably involves approximation and error, and often extraneous problems are introduced. (Have you heard about the mathematical model of a farm involving spherical cows, radiating milk isotropically? I have not yet succeeded in finding differential equations to model this, but when I do, I doubt whether they will be mathematically well behaved.)

1.5 Assignments

These equations are offered for possible use in a class where some of the projects in chapters 1 to 3 may be assigned. The initial conditions are shown only as an example. They have no special significance.

1. $y' = x^2 - 2y/x$.
   Solution: $y = x^3/5 + Cx^{-2}$.
   With $y(1) = -1,\ y = (x^3 - 6x^{-2})/5$.

2. $y' = (y-3)/(2x)$.
   Solution: $y = 3 + Cx^{1/2}$.
   With $y(1) = 2,\ y = 3 - x^{1/2}$.

3. $y' = -(x^2 + y^2)/(2xy)$.
   Solution: $y^2 = -x^2/3 + C/x$.
   With $y(1) = 2,\ y^2 = -x^2/3 + 13/(3x)$.

4. $y' = -y + 3x^2e^{-x}$.
   Solution: $y = (x^3 + C)e^{-x}$.
   With $y(0) = -1,\ y = (x^3 - 1)e^{-x}$.

5. $y' = -y/x + 1/x + 1/x^2,\ x > 0$.
   Solution: $y = 1 + \ln x/x + C/x$.
   With $y(1) = 0,\ y = 1 + \ln x/x - 1/x$.

6. $y' = xy - x^3 + 4x$.
   Solution: $y = x^2 - 2 + Ce^{x^2/2}$.
   With $y(0) = -2,\ y = x^2 - 2$.

7. $y' = 2y + x^2$.
   Solution: $y = -x^2/2 - x/2 - 1/4 + Ce^{2x}$.
   With $y(-1) = -1/4,\ y = -x^2/2 - x/2 - 1/4$.

8. $y' = (2xy - y^4)/(3x^2)$.
   Solution: $y = \left(x^2/(x+C)\right)^{1/3}$.
   With $y(1) = 2,\ y = \left(x^2/((x - \frac{7}{8})\right)^{1/3}$.

9. $y' = 1 + 2y/x$.
   Solution: $y = -x + Cx^2$.
   With $y(1) = -3/4,\ y = -x + x^2/4$.

10. $y' = y\cot x + \sin x$.
    Solution: $y = (x + C)\sin x$.
    With $y(\pi/2) = \pi/2 - 2,\ y = (x-2)\sin x$.

11. $y' = (y^2 - x^2)/(2xy)$.
    Solution: $y = \sqrt{Cx - x^2}$.
    With $y(1/2) = \sqrt{3}/2,\ y = \sqrt{2x - x^2}$.

12. $y' = 2xe^x + y$.
    Solution: $y = (x^2 + C)e^x$.
    With $y(0) = -1,\ y = (x^2 - 1)e^x$.

13. $y' = 3 - 2y/x$.
    Solution: $y = x + C/x^2$.
    With $y(1) = -1,\ y = x - 2/x^2$.

14. $y' = -y\cot x + x$.
    Solution: $y = (x + C)/\sin x$.
    With $y(\pi/2) = 0,\ y = (x - \pi/2)/\sin x$.

15. $y' = -\tan x \cot y$.
    Solution: $\cos x \cos y = C$.
    With $y(0) = \pi/3,\ \cos x \cos y = 1/2$.

16. $y' = x^2 + 2y/x$.
    Solution: $y = x^3 + Cx^2$.
    With $y(1/2) = -1/8,\ y = x^3 - x^2$.

17. $y' = (2 - 3xy^2)/(2x^2y)$.
    Solution: $y = \sqrt{(x^2 + C)/x^3}$.
    With $y(1) = 2,\ y = \sqrt{(x^2 + 3)/x^3}$.

18. $y' = y - x$.
    Solution: $y = Ce^x + x + 1$.
    With $y(-1) = 0,\ y = x + 1$.

19. $y' = 1 + y/x,\ x > 0$.
    Solution: $y = x\ln x + Cx$.
    With $y(1) = -1,\ y = x\ln x - x$.

20. $y' = (x + y)^2$.
    Solution: $y = -x + \tan(x + C)$.
    With $y(0) = -1,\ y = -x + \tan(x - \pi/4)$.

21. $y' = y - 2e^{-x}$.
Solution: $y = e^{-x} + Ce^{x}$.
With $y(0) = 1,\ y = e^{-x}$.

22. $y' = y + xy^2$.
Solution: $y = (1 - x + Ce^{-x})^{-1}$.
With $y(0) = 1/2,\ y = (1 - x + e^{-x})^{-1}$.

23. $y' = y/x - y^2$.
Solution: $y = 2x/(x^2 + C)$.
With $y(1) = 1/2,\ y = 2x/(x^2 + 3)$.

24. $y' = 2y/x + y^2/x^2$.
Solution: $y = x^2/(C - x)$.
With $y(1) = -1/2,\ y = -x^2/(1 + x)$.

25. $y' = 2\sin x - y$.
Solution: $y = Ce^{-x} - \cos x + \sin x$.
With $y(0) = 1,\ y = 2e^{-x} - \cos x + \sin x$.

26. $y' = 2\cos x + y$.
Solution: $y = Ce^{x} - \cos x + \sin x$.
With $y(0) = -1,\ y = -\cos x + \sin x$.

27. $y' = \left((y + 3)/(2x)\right)^2$.
Solution: $y = -3 + 4x/(1 + Cx)$.
With $y(1) = -1,\ y = -3 + 4x/(1 + x)$.

28. $y' = x^3e^{-x} + 3y/x$.
Solution: $y = Cx^3 - x^3e^{-x}$.
With $y(1) = -e^{-1},\ y = -x^3e^{-x}$.

29. $y' = y/x - 2xy^2$.
Solution: $y = 3x/(2x^3 + C)$.
With $y(1) = 1,\ y = 3x/(2x^3 + 1)$.

30. $y' = (y/x)\,(1 + \ln(y/x))\,,\ x > 0,\ y > 0$.
Solution: $y = xe^{Cx}$.
With $y(1) = e^{-1},\ y = xe^{-x}$.

31. $y' = (y/x)\,(\ln(xy) - 1)\,,\ x > 0,\ y > 0$.
Solution: $y = e^{Cx}/x$.
With $y(1) = 1,\ y = 1/x$.

32. $y' = y + e^{x}$.
Solution: $y = xe^{x} + Ce^{x}$.
With $y(0) = -1,\ y = xe^{x} - e^{x}$.

33. $y' = 3x^2e^{-x} - y$.
Solution: $y = x^3e^{-x} + Ce^{-x}$.
With $y(0) = 1,\ y = x^3e^{-x} + e^{-x}$.

34. $y' = y/x + x^2\sin x$.
Solution: $y = -x^2\cos x + x\sin x + Cx$.
With $y(\pi/2) = 0,\ y = -x^2\cos x + x\sin x - x$.

35. $y' = 1/x - y - y/x$.
Solution: $y = (1 + Ce^{-x})/x$.
With $y(1) = 1 + e^{-1},\ y = (1 + e^{-x})/x$.

36. $y' = x + y + y/x$.
Solution: $y = Cxe^{x} - x$.
With $y(1) = -1,\ y = -x$.

37. $y' = (1 + e^{x})^{-1} - y$.
Solution: $y = Ce^{-x} + e^{-x}\ln(1 + e^{x})$.
With $y(0) = \ln 2,\ y = e^{-x}\ln(1 + e^{x})$.

38. $y' = y/x + (y/x)^{1/2},\ x > 0,\ y > 0$.
Solution: $y = x(\ln x + C)^2/4$.
With $y(1) = 1,\ y = x(\ln x + 2)^2/4$.

39. $y' = e^{x-y}$.
Solution: $y = \ln(C + e^{x})$.
With $y(0) = 0,\ y = x$.

40. $y' = 2y/x + x,\ x > 0$.
Solution: $y = x^2\ln x + Cx^2$.
With $y(1) = -1,\ y = x^2\ln x - x^2$.

Chapter 2

Some Fundamental Concepts in the Solution of Differential Equations

2.1 Euler's Method

Before efficiently using numerical methods to solve differential equations, it is necessary to understand some fundamental concepts. The initial approach to be used here is to apply *Euler's method.* Euler's method is not, in my opinion, good enough for useful application today; but it is simple and beautiful, and can be learned as soon as the concept of the derivative is understood. It will enable you to understand concepts that are important in all methods.

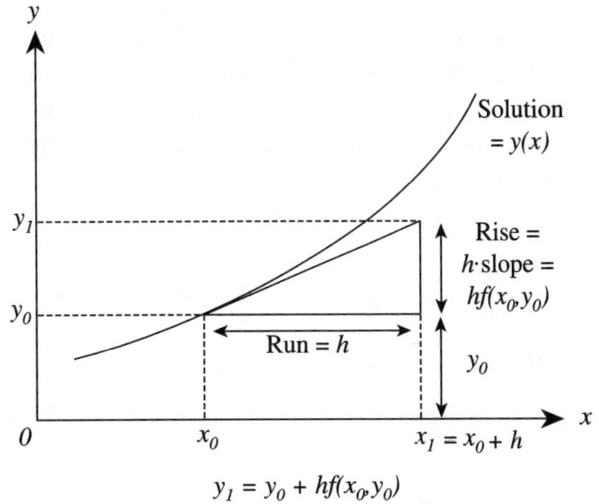

Figure 2.1: *An approximation using Euler's method.*

In essence, we shall use the little arrows in a direction field diagram to approximate a solution. The differential equation with initial condition that we shall discuss is

$$\frac{dy}{dx} = f(x, y); \quad y(x_0) = y_0. \tag{2.1.1}$$

The actions to be taken are illustrated in figure 2.1. First, stand at the initial point, (x_0, y_0). Assuming that the rules governing existence and uniqueness are satisfied, there is just one solution passing through this point; we would like to travel along it. For a start, the direction field will tell us in what direction we should face. So face in that direction and take a step along the field line to reach a new point (x_1, y_1). The x-coordinate has increased by the quantity

$$h = x_1 - x_0, \tag{2.1.2}$$

called the *stepsize*. You are going to be very concerned with this. (h is almost invariably positive; but this is not essential.) Notice that h is not the length of the physical step taken, but is the increment in x. To find the increment in y, note that the slope of the solution curve at (x_0, y_0) is $f(x_0, y_0)$. If this is represented as the *rise* over the *run*, as shown in figure 2.1, then the run is equal to the stepsize, h, and the rise is equal to the increment in y, or $y_1 - y_0$. Therefore at the end of the step we have

$$x_1 = x_0 + h, \quad y_1 = y_0 + hf(x_0, y_0). \tag{2.1.3}$$

We have just taken one *step* using Euler's method.

A beauty of this method is that once we have reached the point (x_1, y_1), we can follow the procedure all over again, with x_1 and y_1 substituted for x_0 and y_0. Let us take another step, using the same stepsize, h. If this brings us to (x_2, y_2), then

$$x_2 = x_1 + h, \quad y_2 = y_1 + hf(x_1, y_1). \tag{2.1.4}$$

Now take another step; you have one guess to see where it takes you!

In general, if we are at (x_n, y_n), then the following position will have coordinates

$$x_{n+1} = x_n + h, \quad y_{n+1} = y_n + hf(x_n, y_n). \tag{2.1.5}$$

With starting conditions $x = x_0$ and $y = y_0$, (2.1.5) is used recursively for $n = 0, 1, 2, ...$ until we have had enough. This is Euler's method. It is as if we were stepping from arrow to arrow in a direction field. It is an example of a *single-step* method where each step taken is similar to the first. (There are also *multistep* methods, where some past history of a solution is used when taking a step. It is as if you were looking back over your shoulder to help you get a smoother path. In single-step methods we do not look back.) Euler's method is extravagant and inaccurate, but it provides a good learning tool, and we shall use it — once.

First, look at some numbers. Consider

$$\frac{dy}{dx} = f(x, y) = x + y; \quad y(0) = -0.5. \tag{2.1.6}$$

Let $h = 0.1$. For successive iterations, we have

$$x_0 = 0.000000, \quad y_0 = -0.500000,$$

so

$$y_0' = f(x_0, y_0) = 0.000000 - 0.500000 = -0.500000,$$

and $\quad x_1 = x_0 + h = 0.100000, \qquad y_1 = y_0 + hf(x_0, y_0) = -0.550000.$

Then

$$y_1' = f(x_1, y_1) = 0.100000 - 0.550000 = -0.450000,$$

and $\quad x_2 = x_1 + h = 0.200000, \qquad y_2 = y_1 + hf(x_1, y_1) = -0.595000.$

Then

$$y_2' = f(x_2, y_2) = 0.200000 - 0.595000 = -0.395000,$$

and $\quad x_3 = x_2 + h = 0.300000, \qquad y_3 = y_2 + hf(x_2, y_2) = -0.634500.$

And so on. Write down x_4 and y_4!

Figure 2.2 shows the flow of this procedure for (2.1.6) with N steps. Here is some pseudo-code for doing the same thing. It is necessary to write a subroutine (procedure) that will take as `input`

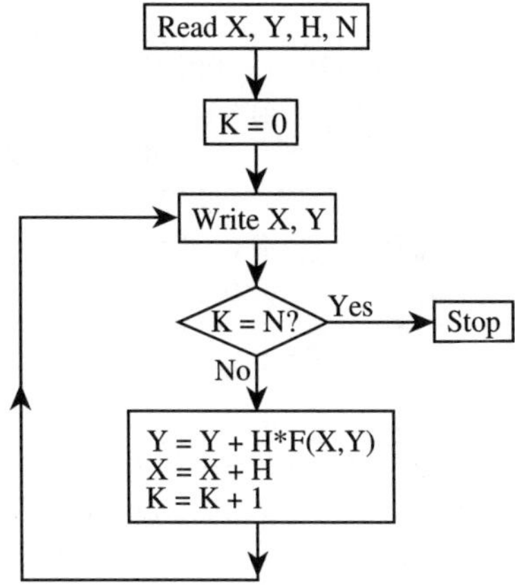

Figure 2.2: *Euler's method for $y' = x + y$, with N steps.*

values of x and y, and give as `output` the value $z = f(x, y)$, the value of the right-hand side of the differential equation. For the example here, we might have:

```
Subroutine Fun(x, y, z)
    z = x + y
Return
End
```

Then the main program might contain the following:

```
Enter initial values of x and y
Enter a value of the stepsize, h
Enter the number of steps to be taken, N
Do K = 1, N
    Call Fun(x, y, F)
    x = x + h
    y = y + h*F
    Write the values of x and y
End Do
```

It is easy to implement the method on a programmable calculator or almost any CAS (Computer Algebra System). Indeed, it is already coded in many systems.

You should use your own equation from Chapter One, pick initial conditions that do not give too great an initial slope (or a straight line solution — even Euler's method can get that correct) and replicate calculations of the sort just described. Take at least ten steps.

2.2 Truncation Error

Corresponding to the initial conditions that you selected for the calculations in the preceding section, you can find the value of the arbitrary constant in the general solution, and then the formula for the particular solution satisfying the initial conditions. For the example given,

$$\frac{dy}{dx} = x + y, \; y = Ce^x - x - 1. \quad \text{For } y(0) = -0.5, \; C = 0.5, \text{ and } y = 0.5e^x - x - 1. \tag{2.2.1}$$

The final formula is the *correct* solution. It was used to construct the following table:

x	y_{Euler}	y_{correct}	Error
0.0	−0.500000	−0.500000	0.000000
0.1	−0.550000	−0.547415	0.002585
0.2	−0.595000	−0.589299	0.005701
0.3	−0.634500	−0.625071	0.009429
0.4	−0.667950	−0.654088	0.013862
0.5	−0.694745	−0.675639	0.019106
0.6	−0.714220	−0.688941	0.025279
0.7	−0.725641	−0.693124	0.032517
0.8	−0.728206	−0.687230	0.040976
0.9	−0.721026	−0.670198	0.050828
1.0	−0.703129	−0.640859	0.062269

$y' = x + y$. Figures have been rounded to six decimal places.

The errors seen here are caused by *truncation error*; a clarification of the word "truncation" will be given shortly.

(A general cause of error in all computations where floating point numbers are used is *round-off error*; for instance, if we are computing to twelve digit accuracy, the product 2.0 multiplied by 2.0 might result in the output 4.000 000 0002. This need not be a major cause of concern if the accuracy required in a computation involves tolerating errors much larger than the expected round-off errors.)

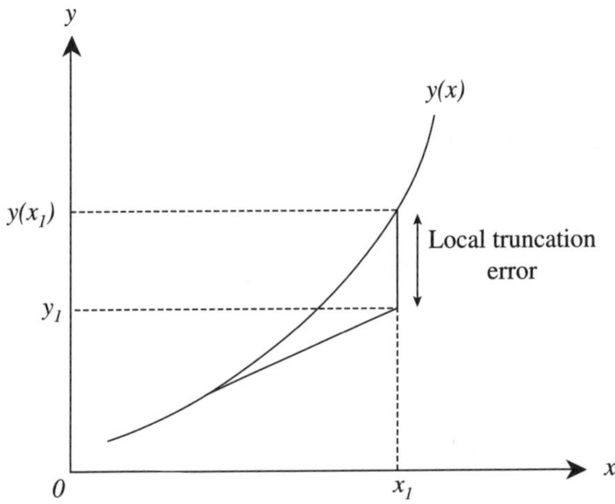

Figure 2.3: *Local truncation error in Euler's method.*

The truncation error of just one step is called the *local truncation error*. It is illustrated in figure 2.3. Consider

$$\frac{dy}{dx} = f(x, y); \quad y(x_0) = y_0. \quad \text{Correct solution} \quad y = y(x). \tag{2.2.2}$$

At the end of one step, with stepsize h, we have reached $y_1 = y_0 + hf(x_0, y_0)$; but we would have preferred to be at the correct value $y(x_1) = y(x_0+h)$. So the local truncation error is $\text{TE} = y(x_1) - y_1$. Using a Taylor series expansion in powers of h, this can be expressed as

$$\left.\begin{aligned} \text{TE} &= y(x_0 + h) - y_1 \\ &= y(x_0) + hy'(x_0) + \tfrac{1}{2}h^2 y''(x_0) + \cdots - y_1 \\ &= y_0 + hf(x_0, y_0) + \tfrac{1}{2}h^2 y''(x_0) + \cdots - (y_0 + hf(x_0, y_0)) \\ &= \tfrac{1}{2}h^2 y''(x_0) + \cdots. \end{aligned}\right] \tag{2.2.3}$$

In approximating $y(x_1)$, the Taylor series expansion of $y(x_0 + h)$ in powers of h,

$$y(x_0 + h) \quad = \quad y_0 + hf(x_0, y_0) + \tfrac{1}{2}h^2 y''(x_0) + \cdots,$$

has been *truncated* after the second term to give Euler's approximation. Since the Taylor series is infinite, then a truncation is bound to happen, however accurate the approximation.

In the numerical example shown above, the correct solution for the given initial conditions is

$$y = Ce^x - x - 1 = 0.5e^x - x - 1.$$

After one step, Euler's approximation gives $x_1 = 0.1$ and $y_1 = -0.55$. If these are taken to be initial conditions, the solution that passes through (x_1, y_1) is found to be

$$y = 0.497661e^x - x - 1.$$

The difference between these two solutions will change whether or not there are further truncation errors. This means that at the end of several steps there is a complicated *accumulated* truncation error. This will depend on the nature of the differential equation as well as the approximating method that is used. A differential equation might, of its own accord, magnify a small initial truncation error into one that was seriously large. So however good the numerical method that you use, you must use it with an understanding of the nature of the differential equations involved.

To get some insight into the possible nature of the accumulation of error, consider it non-rigorously as follows. Suppose we integrate from $x = a$ to $x = b$ taking 20 steps with stepsize h. Now let us cover the same interval using 40 steps with stepsize $h/2$; the error of an individual step is divided by 4, since the local truncation error depends on the square of the stepsize; but we have doubled the number of steps, so, overall, we might expect the total error to be divided by 2. Now cover the same interval in 10 steps with stepsize $2h$; the error of an individual step is multiplied by 4, but with only half the total number of steps, we might expect the total error to be multiplied by 2. This argument is, I repeat, non-rigorous, but suggestive.

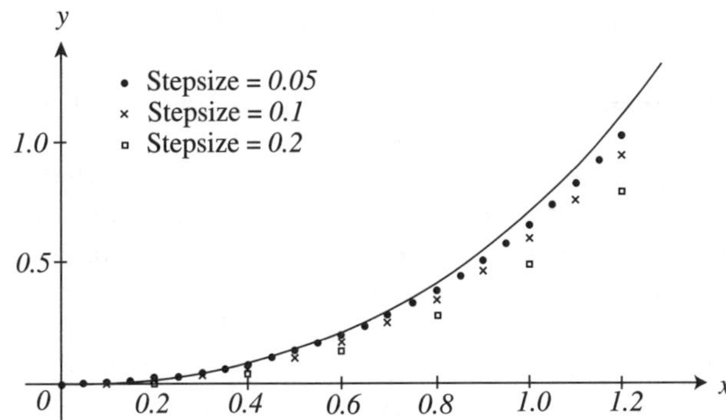

Figure 2.4: *Euler's method, using three different stepsizes, for* $y' = x + y$.

This suggests the following project, illustrated in figure 2.4. For the initial condition $y(0) = 0$, three runs were made covering the interval $0 \le x \le 1.2$, using successively the stepsizes $h = 0.2$, 0.1, and 0.05, with 6, 12 and 24 steps taken. The calculated points were plotted, together with the correct solution for this initial condition. The figure is consistent with the qualitative results just discussed. Perform a similar experiment with your equation. The interval for x can be different, as may be the choice of stepsizes; but the latter should differ by factors of 2. When you plot the points given by Euler's method, do not join them; the method (as will the method that we shall shortly use) provides only isolated points, with no immediate information about intermediate values.

Figure 2.4 looks effective in part because of the nature of the differential equation $y' = x + y$ which has solutions that diverge exponentially from each other. The effects are not so easy to see if the solutions converge, as with an equation such as $y' = x - y$; then you will need to observe the results of the earlier steps used in the experiment.

2.3 The Order of a Method

Local truncation error depends on the stepsize and the method being used, and also on the differential equation. For Euler's method, we found in the preceding section, equation (2.2.3), that

$$\begin{aligned} \mathrm{TE}(h) &= y(x_0 + h) - y_1 \\ &= \frac{1}{2}h^2 y''(x_0) + \cdots . \end{aligned} \tag{2.3.1}$$

The terms omitted on the right all have powers of h higher than two.

Most methods for the numerical solution of differential equations proceed in steps and have a local truncation error that depends on the stepsize: the shorter the stepsize, the lower the error. Usually the local truncation error can be expressed as a power series in increasing powers of h, as in (2.3.1), with a leading term Ah^n. Then the local truncation error can be approximated by Ah^n in the sense that

$$\lim_{h \to 0} \frac{\mathrm{TE}(h)}{h^n} = A. \tag{2.3.2}$$

The smaller the value of h, the better is the approximation. Much more to the point, the higher the value of n, the more rapidly does the local truncation error become small as h becomes small.

The number $n - 1$ is called the *order* of the method. For Euler's method $n = 2$, so the order of the method is one. In theory, the local truncation error can be made arbitrarily small with a sufficient reduction in the stepsize; but then the total number of steps needed to cover a given interval of x may be so large that round-off error will be appreciable. Up to a point, the higher the order of a method, the larger is the permissible stepsize for a given accuracy requirement. The principal method to be introduced later in this text has order five.

2.4 Numerical Confirmation of the Order of Euler's Method

It is very important that you acquire confidence in the order of whatever method you use, and that you be able to control the accuracy of your solutions through judicious handling of the stepsize. The method that we shall shortly learn makes clever use of the known order. Since analytical justification of the order can be very complicated, it can be helpful to confirm it numerically. The next project is to perform an experiment confirming the order of Euler's method.

To do this project, you will need to take several steps. Each step will start with the same initial conditions, but the stepsize will be varied. Thus, for

$$\frac{dy}{dx} = x + y; \quad y(0) = -0.5, \quad \text{stepsize } h, \tag{2.4.1}$$

the outcome of one step is

$$x_1 = h, \; y_1 = -0.5 - 0.5h. \tag{2.4.2}$$

The correct value at the end of this step is

$$y(x_1) = 0.5e^h - h - 1, \tag{2.4.3}$$

and the truncation error is

$$\mathrm{TE}(h) = y(x_1) - y_1. \tag{2.4.4}$$

In worrying about error, we are more concerned with its magnitude rather than with its sign; so consider

$$E(h) = |\mathrm{TE}(h)|. \tag{2.4.5}$$

We want to justify the approximation

$$E(h) \approx Ah^2 \tag{2.4.6}$$

for sufficiently small h. A standard procedure is to take logs (to any base) so that (2.4.6) becomes

$$\log E(h) \approx \log A + 2\log h. \tag{2.4.7}$$

Now if

$$X = \log h, \quad Y = \log E(h), \tag{2.4.8}$$

then

$$Y \approx \log A + 2X, \tag{2.4.9}$$

so that a graph of points X and Y as h varies should approximate a straight line having slope 2. To test this I generated the following figures (using logs to the base 10):

h	y_{Euler}	y_{correct}	$E(h)$	$X = \log h$	$Y = \log E(h)$
0.05	−0.525	−0.524364	0.000636	−1.301	−3.197
0.10	−0.550	−0.547415	0.002585	−1.000	−2.587
0.15	−0.575	−0.569083	0.005917	−0.824	−2.228
0.20	−0.600	−0.589299	0.010701	−0.699	−1.971
0.25	−0.625	−0.607987	0.017013	−0.602	−1.769
0.30	−0.650	−0.625071	0.024929	−0.523	−1.603
0.35	−0.675	−0.640466	0.034534	−0.456	−1.462
0.40	−0.700	−0.654088	0.045912	−0.398	−1.338
0.45	−0.725	−0.665884	0.059156	−0.347	−1.228
0.50	−0.750	−0.675639	0.074361	−0.301	−1.129

Figure 2.5 shows how the points appear in the X-Y plane, and how they lie convincingly close to a straight line having slope 2.

There are two ways in which you might run into trouble in this project. Notice that from (2.3.1) we have

$$A \approx \frac{1}{2}y''(x_0). \tag{2.4.10}$$

This might be small or even zero. The value of A (when it is not too small) can be found from the intercept of the line given by (2.4.9) with the X-axis. It can also be predicted analytically, since

$$y'' = \frac{d}{dx}y' = \frac{d}{dx}f(x,y) = \frac{\partial f}{\partial x} + \frac{\partial f}{\partial y}\frac{dy}{dx} = f_x + ff_y. \tag{2.4.11}$$

(Remember the chain rule?) Then

$$A = \frac{1}{2}y''(x_0) = \frac{1}{2}\left(f_x(x_0,y_0) + f(x_0,y_0)\,f_y(x_0,y_0)\right). \tag{2.4.12}$$

Calculate this value before you start your project. If it is zero, then, from (2.4.9), you may get a straight line having slope 3.

The other cause of trouble may be that you do not make h sufficiently small. In general, we have

$$\mathrm{TE}(h) = Ah^n + Bh^{n+1} + \cdots. \tag{2.4.13}$$

For the approximation (2.4.6) to be convincing, h must be small enough for the second and subsequent terms on the right of (2.4.13) to be small compared with the first. I suggest that you start with the same range of values for h that was used above. If you have trouble, try smaller values. (But don't make them so small that the difference in (2.4.4) is dominated by round-off error.)

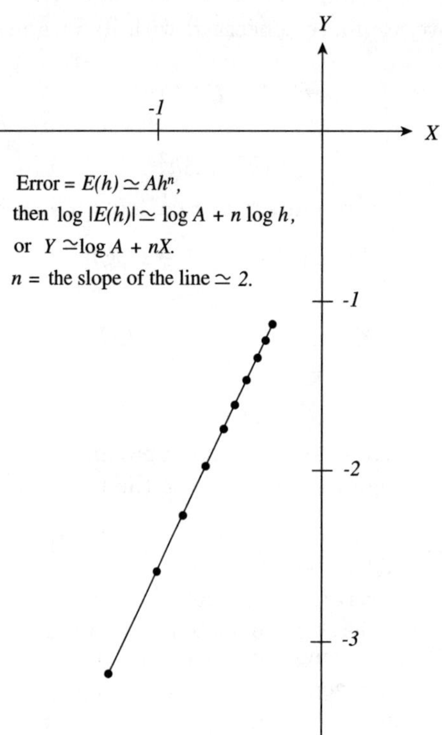

Figure 2.5: *Confirming the order of Euler's method.*

Chapter 3

One Approach to Solving a System of Ordinary Differential Equations

3.1 Generalities

Long courses are taught surveying different methods for the numerical solution of ordinary differential equations, but even they have little hope of being comprehensive. (I stress the word *ordinary*; even longer courses are needed for partial differential equations.) Among the treasury of methods there is none that is "best." The principal method that I have chosen for this text is excellent; it allows automatic control of the stepsize so that the local truncation error can be bounded. It is, I hope you will come to agree, simple to understand, to program and to control. But I do not wish to detract in any way from other approaches and other methods: I hope that you will have the luck to learn about them.

Let's start with the differential equation

$$\frac{dy}{dx} = f(x, y); \; y(x_0) = y_0. \tag{3.1.1}$$

We shall take for granted all that stuff about a unique solution existing in the regions in which we are working. If this solution is $y = y(x)$, then it satisfies the identity

$$\frac{dy(x)}{dx} = f\left(x, y(x)\right), \tag{3.1.2}$$

and then we can write

$$y(x) = y_0 + \int_{x_0}^{x} f\left(x, y(x)\right) dx. \tag{3.1.3}$$

If we are interested in the value of the solution when $x = x_1 = x_0 + h$, then

$$y(x_0 + h) = y_0 + \int_{x_0}^{x_0+h} f\left(x, y(x)\right) dx. \tag{3.1.4}$$

On the face of it, equation (3.1.4) is unhelpful, since evaluation of the right-hand side presupposes knowledge of $y(x)$; if we knew $y(x)$ we would not be bothering with this way to find $y(x_0 + h)$. However progress can be made if some method of approximation is applied to the evaluation of the integral.

Figure 3.1(a) shows the value of the definite integral $\int_{x_0}^{x_0+h} F(x)dx$ as an area between the x-axis and the curve $y = F(x)$. Figure 3.1(b) illustrates the approximation using the *rectangular rule*:

$$\int_{x_0}^{x_0+h} F(x)dx \approx hF(x_0). \qquad \text{Error}: \frac{1}{2}h^2F'(x_R). \tag{3.1.5}$$

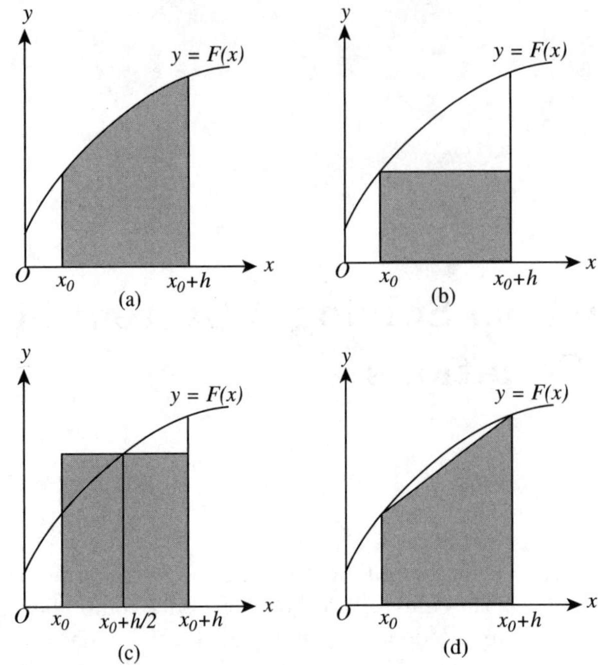

Figure 3.1: *The integral* $\int_{x_0}^{x_0+h} F(x)dx$ *and three methods of approximation.*

In the expression for the error of the approximation, x_R is some point between x_0 and $x_0 + h$. If this approximation is applied to (3.1.4), then we have

$$y(x_0 + h) \approx y_1 = y_0 + hf(x_0, y_0), \tag{3.1.6}$$

since $F(x) = f(x, y(x))$. We are back with Euler's method. Forget it!

Figure 3.1(c) illustrates the *midpoint rule*:

$$\int_{x_0}^{x_0+h} F(x)dx \approx hF\left(x_0 + \frac{1}{2}h\right). \qquad \text{Error}: \frac{1}{24}h^3F''(x_M). \tag{3.1.7}$$

x_M lies between x_0 and $x_0 + h$. This leads to the approximation

$$y(x_0 + h) \approx y_0 + hf\left(x_0 + \frac{1}{2}h,\, y(x_0 + \frac{1}{2}h)\right). \tag{3.1.8}$$

In order to deal with the term $y(x_0 + \frac{1}{2}h)$ recall the Taylor series

$$y(x_0 + k) = y(x_0) + ky'(x_0) + \frac{1}{2}k^2y''(x_0) + \frac{1}{6}k^3y'''(x_0) + \cdots. \tag{3.1.9}$$

(You will be seeing quite a bit of this in this chapter!) So

$$y\left(x_0 + \tfrac{1}{2}h\right) = y(x_0) + \tfrac{1}{2}hy'(x_0) + \cdots.$$

In making the midpoint approximation we have already thrown out terms involving powers of h greater than the second; continuing to throw out such terms, we find

$$y(x_0 + h) \approx y_1 = y_0 + hf\left(x_0 + \frac{1}{2}h,\, y(x_0) + \frac{1}{2}hf(x_0, y_0)\right), \tag{3.1.10}$$

where we have used the relation $y'(x_0) = f(x_0, y_0)$. (3.1.10) provides one step using the *modified Euler's method.*

Finally, we apply the *trapezoidal rule*, illustrated in figure 3.1(d):

$$\int_{x_0}^{x_0+h} F(x)dx \approx \frac{1}{2}h\big(F(x_0) + F(x_0+h)\big). \qquad \text{Error}: \frac{1}{12}h^3F''(x_T). \tag{3.1.11}$$

x_T lies between x_0 and $x_0 + h$. Substituting into (3.1.4) and using (3.1.9) as before, we find

$$\begin{aligned} y(x_0+h) &\approx y_0 + \frac{1}{2}h\left[f(x_0,y_0) + f\left(x_0+h,\, y(x_0+h)\right)\right] \\ &= y_0 + \frac{1}{2}h\left[f(x_0,y_0) + f\left(x_0+h,\, y(x_0) + hy'(x_0) + \cdots\right)\right] \\ &\approx y_0 + \frac{1}{2}h\left[f(x_0,y_0) + f\left(x_0+h,\, y_0 + hf(x_0,y_0)\right)\right] \\ &= y_1. \end{aligned} \tag{3.1.12}$$

This provides one step in the *improved Euler's method.*

(3.1.10) and (3.1.12) (and, indeed Euler's method also) are examples of *Runge-Kutta* methods. It can be shown, that if Simpson's rule is applied to the quadrature in (3.1.4) then the following set of formulas results.

Let

$$\left.\begin{aligned} f_0 &= f(x_0,y_0), \\ f_1 &= f\left(x_0 + \tfrac{1}{2}h,\, y_0 + \tfrac{1}{2}hf_0\right), \\ f_2 &= f\left(x_0 + \tfrac{1}{2}h,\, y_0 + \tfrac{1}{2}hf_1\right), \\ f_3 &= f\left(x_0 + h,\, y_0 + hf_2\right); \end{aligned}\right] \tag{3.1.13}$$

then

$$y(x_0+h) \approx y_1 = y_0 + \frac{1}{6}h(f_0 + 2f_1 + 2f_2 + f_3). \tag{3.1.14}$$

This is probably the best known Runge-Kutta method. I do not recommend its use in this text because of problems with stepsize control, but it is very easy to program. If you are in a hurry for results and have no available program, then it may be a good method to consider. It is a fourth-order method.

All the methods looked at so far have been *single-step* methods; these are methods where each step is like a separate initial value problem. There is also a large group of *multistep* methods in which the history of the solution preceding the current step is used. For instance, we might make use of the value of f at the current point and at, say, six preceding points; then we might fit a polynomial in h through these points; this polynomial would provide the integrand in (3.1.4). This procedure would make what is called a *prediction* of the value of y at the end of the step. Once that predicted value is known, it can be incorporated into the polynomial, and this new polynomial can be used in the integral to find a *correction.* These methods employ fewer function evaluations than do Runge-Kutta methods of the same order. (The function evaluations may be the most costly part of running the program.) Also multistep methods can be designed to a high order. They are especially efficient in programs where the stepsize need not be changed. But they can be tricky to set up, and they require some experience to control. Before a multistep method can begin, a set of values of y must already be known; these are usually provided by Runge-Kutta integration. So I do not recommend multistep methods at this stage.

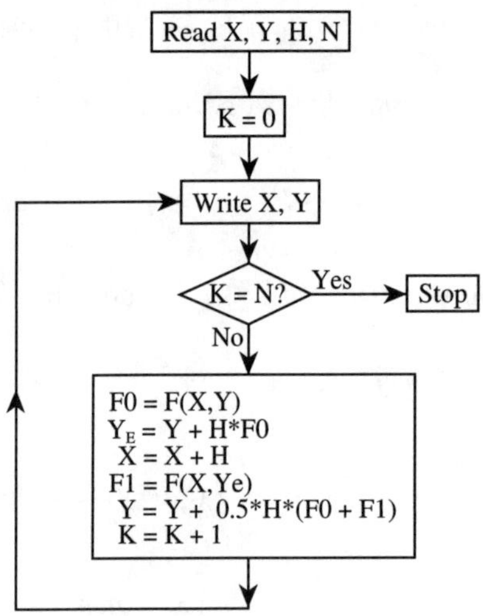

Figure 3.2: *Computation using the Improved Euler's Method.*

3.2 A Look at the Improved Euler's Method

The expression for y_1 in (3.1.12) can be better interpreted if it is organized as a sequence of calculations. For instance

$$\left.\begin{aligned} f_0 &= f(x_0, y_0), \\ y_E &= y_0 + hf_0, \\ x_1 &= x_0 + h, \\ f_1 &= f(x_1, y_E), \\ y_1 &= y_0 + \tfrac{1}{2}h\,(f_0 + f_1)\,. \end{aligned}\right] \tag{3.2.1}$$

If you already have a program for running Euler's method, then just two more lines will transform it to the improved method. Compare the flowchart in figure 3.2 with that given for Euler's method.

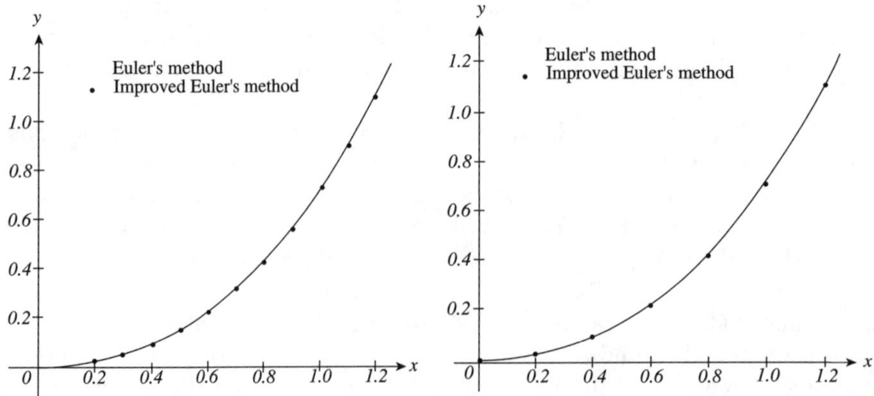

Figure 3.3: *Left: Comparison of the use of Euler's method and the improved Euler's method.* $y' = x + y$. *The stepsize is* $h = 0.1$. *Right: Same as the figure to the left but with stepsize* $h = 0.2$.

This is a second order method. You can confirm this numerically by repeating the project for verifying the order of Euler's method; you should generate a straight line having slope 3. A theoretical justification will be given in the following section.

A numerical comparison between Euler's and the improved Euler's methods is shown in the following Table 3.1. A better way to compare the methods is to see what happens when the stepsize is changed. This is illustrated in figure 3.3. The difference in accuracy is striking. Of more importance is the fact that when the stepsize in increased, the improved method is less drastically affected: a consequence of the higher order.

The improved method is easy to program, especially on a hand calculator; it is a useful tool to have available.

Table 3.1.

Comparison of the Euler's and Improved Euler's Methods.

	Approximations			Errors	
x	Euler	Improved Euler	y_{correct}	Euler	Improved Euler
0.0	−0.500000	−0.500000	−0.500000	0.000000	0.000000
0.1	−0.550000	−0.547500	−0.547415	0.002585	0.000085
0.2	−0.595000	−0.589488	−0.589299	0.005701	0.000189
0.3	−0.634500	−0.625384	−0.625071	0.009429	0.000313
0.4	−0.667950	−0.654549	−0.654088	0.013862	0.000461
0.5	−0.694745	−0.676277	−0.675639	0.019106	0.000637
0.6	−0.714220	−0.689786	−0.688941	0.025279	0.000845
0.7	−0.725641	−0.694213	−0.693124	0.032517	0.001090
0.8	−0.728206	−0.688606	−0.687230	0.040976	0.001376
0.9	−0.721026	−0.671909	−0.670198	0.050828	0.001711
1.0	−0.703129	−0.642960	−0.640859	0.062269	0.002100

3.3 Runge-Kutta Formulas

The general explicit Runge-Kutta step can be written as follows. For

$$\frac{dy}{dx} = f(x,y); \;\; y(x_0) = y_0 \tag{3.3.1}$$

and stepsize h, let

$$\left.\begin{aligned} f_0 &= f(x_0, y_0), \\ f_1 &= f(x_0 + \alpha_1 h,\; y_0 + h\beta_{1,0} f_0), \\ f_2 &= f\left(x_0 + \alpha_2 h,\; y_0 + h[\beta_{2,0} f_0 + \beta_{2,1} f_1]\right), \\ &\;\;\vdots \\ f_k &= f\left(x_0 + \alpha_k h,\; y_0 + h[\beta_{k,0} f_0 + \beta_{k,1} f_1 + \cdots + \beta_{k,k-1} f_{k-1}]\right). \end{aligned}\right] \tag{3.3.2}$$

Then

$$y(x_0 + h) \approx y_1 = y_0 + h(c_0 f_0 + c_1 f_1 + \cdots + c_k f_k). \tag{3.3.3}$$

Numerical values of the coefficients are provided as a part of whatever method is used. To illustrate how they might be determined, let's look at the case $k = 2$:

$$\left.\begin{aligned} f_0 &= f(x_0,\, y_0), \\ f_1 &= f(x_0 + \alpha h,\; y_0 + h\beta f_0), \\ y(x_0 + h) \approx y_1 &= y_0 + h(c_0 f_0 + c_1 f_1). \end{aligned}\right] \tag{3.3.4}$$

The α's, β's and c's are constants. We need to find them so that the local truncation error, $y(x_0 + h) - y_1$, is as small as possible. (Well, we don't need to, because heroes of a very special kind have done it for us. But just relax and watch it happen!) Reducing the local truncation error is equivalent to making the order of the method as high as possible; so it is necessary to expand $y(x_0 + h) - y_1$ in powers of the stepsize h. For a start,

$$y(x_0 + h) = y(x_0) + hy'(x_0) + \frac{1}{2}h^2y''(x_0) + \frac{1}{6}h^3y'''(x_0) + \cdots. \tag{3.3.5}$$

Now

$$y(x_0) = y_0, \text{ and } y'(x_0) = f(x_0, y_0) = f_0.$$

Further

$$y'' = \frac{d}{dx}(y') = \frac{d}{dx}f(x,y) = \frac{\partial f}{\partial x} + \frac{\partial f}{\partial y}\frac{dy}{dx} = f_x + ff_y,$$

and

$$\begin{aligned} y''' &= \frac{d}{dx}(y'') = \frac{\partial y''}{\partial x} + \frac{\partial y''}{\partial y}\frac{dy}{dx} \\ &= \frac{\partial(f_x + ff_y)}{\partial x} + \frac{\partial(f_x + ff_y)}{\partial y}f \\ &= f_{xx} + f_xf_y + 2ff_{xy} + ff_y^2 + f^2f_{yy}. \end{aligned}$$

Then

$$\begin{aligned} y(x_0 + h) &= y_0 + hf_0 + \frac{1}{2}h^2[f_x + ff_y]_0 \\ &\quad + \frac{1}{6}h^2[f_{xx} + f_xf_y + 2ff_{xy} + ff_y^2 + f^2f_{yy}]_0 + \cdots. \end{aligned} \tag{3.3.6}$$

$f(x, y)$ and all its derivatives are evaluated at the point (x_0, y_0).

Next we take note of the start of a Taylor series expansion of a function of two variables:

$$\begin{aligned} f(x + a, y + b) &= f(x,y) + af_x(x,y) + bf_y(x,y) \\ &\quad + \frac{1}{2}\left(a^2f_{xx}(x,y) + 2abf_{xy}(x,y) + b^2f_{yy}(x,y)\right) + \cdots. \end{aligned}$$

Then with a replaced by αh and b replaced by $h\beta f_0$, we have

$$\begin{aligned} y_1 &= y_0 + hc_0f_0 + hc_1f_1 \\ &= y_0 + hc_0f_0 + hc_1f(x_0 + \alpha h,\ y_0 + h\beta f_0) \\ &= y_0 + hc_0f_0 + hc_1\Big[f(x_0,y_0) + \alpha hf_x(x_0,y_0) + h\beta f_0f_y(x_0,y_0) \\ &\quad + \frac{1}{2}(\alpha h)^2f_{xx}(x_0,y_0) + (\alpha h)(h\beta f_0)f_{xy}(x_0,y_0) + \frac{1}{2}(h\beta f_0)^2f_{yy}(x_0,y_0)\Big] + \cdots \\ &= y_0 + hc_0f_0 + hc_1f_0 + h^2c_1(\alpha f_x + \beta ff_y)_0 \\ &\quad + h^3c_1\left(\frac{1}{2}\alpha^2f_{xx} + \alpha\beta ff_{xy} + \frac{1}{2}\beta^2f^2f_{yy}\right)_0 + \cdots. \end{aligned} \tag{3.3.7}$$

Combining (3.3.6) and (3.3.7), we find that

$$\begin{aligned} y(x_0+h)-y_1 &= hf[1-c_0-c_1] \\ &\quad +h^2\left[f_x\left(\frac{1}{2}-c_1\alpha\right)+ff_y\left(\frac{1}{2}-c_1\beta\right)\right] \\ &\quad +h^3\left[f_{xx}\left(\frac{1}{6}-\frac{1}{2}c_1\alpha^2\right)+ff_{xy}\left(\frac{1}{3}-c_1\alpha\beta\right)\right. \\ &\quad \left.+f^2f_{yy}\left(\frac{1}{6}-\frac{1}{2}c_1\beta^2\right)+\frac{1}{6}f_xf_y+\frac{1}{6}ff_y^2\right] \\ &\quad +\text{ terms with higher powers of } h. \end{aligned} \tag{3.3.8}$$

The order of the method can be made equal to two if the terms in h and h^2 are zero for any $f(x,y)$. This will be the case provided that

$$\left.\begin{aligned} 1-c_0-c_1 &= 0, \\ \tfrac{1}{2}-c_1\alpha &= 0, \\ \tfrac{1}{2}-c_1\beta &= 0. \end{aligned}\right] \tag{3.3.9}$$

These are called *equations of condition.* In this case they can be solved with one degree of freedom, and this freedom can be used with various strategies to try to minimize the h^3 term. Taking advantage of (3.3.9), this term can be written as

$$h^3\left(f_{xx}\left(\frac{1}{6}-\frac{1}{4}\alpha\right)+ff_{xy}\left(\frac{1}{3}-\frac{1}{2}\alpha\right)+f^2f_{yy}\left(\frac{1}{6}-\frac{1}{4}\alpha\right)+\frac{1}{6}f_xf_y+\frac{1}{6}ff_y^2\right). \tag{3.3.10}$$

All terms, as in (3.3.8), are evaluated at (x_0, y_0). This is the principal term in the local truncation error of the method. It confirms that the order is two. Notice that the modified and improved Euler's methods are special cases, with (3.3.9) solved in different ways. If (3.3.10) is written as Ah^3, then notice the complexity of the formula for A when compared with a similar formula for Euler's method. This complexity increases exponentially as the order of the method is increased.

3.4 Stepsize Control — Some Tactics to Avoid

The remainder term (3.3.10) is unwieldy, and such terms for higher order Runge-Kutta methods are even more involved; so they cannot, in any practical way, be made the basis for estimation of local truncation error or for stepsize control. We shall see in a moment how these formulas can be used implicitly; but first I want to warn you against an approach that has often been used in the past in Runge-Kutta calculations and should never be used again. This approach involves shifting tactics between halving and doubling the interval.

Let us suppose that you are using the algorithm (3.1.14) and have just completed a step with stepsize h. Was h too large? Have you just accumulated a ruinous truncation error? One way to try to deal with this alarm is to go back to the start of the step just taken and take *two* steps, each with stepsize $h/2$. If the difference between the end results exceeds some preset tolerance, then your alarm was justified: throw out h and use $h/2$ as the stepsize. BUT IS THIS REDUCED STEPSIZE TOO LARGE? Calm down. If it will make you feel better, you can halve the interval again and repeat the test. But remember that if you continue doing this, then the difference between the end results could arise from round-off error, and after that you will continue to halve the interval indefinitely, or at least until the men in white coats take you away.

Suppose, on the other hand, that you passed the halving test and feel confident that the stepsize h was all right. Now you start to worry that you are doing too much work and taking too many steps. That is, is your stepsize too small? Well, you have just found that the one step using h was all right. So take another step, also using h. If this is also all right, then go back to the start of the first step and take a step with stepsize $2h$. Then compare the end results. If the difference is small enough, then the larger stepsize can be used. Or would you like to try doubling it again?

Consider a model that involves travelling from the Earth to the Moon. Close to the Earth the acceleration is large and small stepsizes are needed. Between the Earth and Moon the acceleration is relatively low and the stepsize can be greatly increased; but, close to the Moon, the stepsize must be diminished again. The technique of halving and doubling would be time-consuming and extravagant, since the main expense of the calculation is likely to be evaluating the functions on the right-hand sides of the equations. It will also probably become unstable. So would you.

3.5 Fehlberg's RKF4(5) Method

In the 1960s E.Fehlberg published Runge-Kutta methods with order ranging from 2 to 9, in which an operator chooses an upper bound for the local truncation error. At the end of each step the program checks to see whether the truncation error satisfied this bound, and repeats the step, if necessary, with a reduced stepsize; if a step is satisfactorily taken, a new stepsize is predicted for the following step. In essence, Fehlberg runs two Runge-Kutta methods with different orders, in tandem. The first results in an estimate y_1 of $y(x_0+h)$. The second and more accurate method uses the same evaluated functions as the first, and at most two more, to give a better estimate, $\hat{y}_1$. The difference $|\hat{y}_1 - y_1|$ results in an estimate of the local truncation error of y_1. In Fehlberg's notation, the method written as RK4(5) uses calculations of fourth and fifth orders.

Here is a summary of his work:

1. RK1(2), with 2 function evaluations for y_1 and 3 for $\hat{y}_1$.
2. RK2(3), with 3 function evaluations for y_1 and 4 for $\hat{y}_1$.
3. RK3(4), with 4 function evaluations for y_1 and 5 for $\hat{y}_1$.
4. RK4(5), with 5 function evaluations for y_1 and 6 for $\hat{y}_1$.
5. RK5(6), with 6 function evaluations for y_1 and 8 for $\hat{y}_1$.
6. RK6(7), with 8 function evaluations for y_1 and 10 for $\hat{y}_1$.
7. RK7(8), with 11 function evaluations for y_1 and 13 for $\hat{y}_1$.
8. RK8(9), with 15 function evaluations for y_1 and 17 for $\hat{y}_1$.

These are to be found in NASA Technical Reports R287(1968) and R315(1969). They make interesting reading. There is no need to follow every detail in order to appreciate Fehlberg's genius.

We shall use the RK4(5) method. This is probably the most popular one, but if you master it, then the others will be simple to program and use. The main cause of errors in writing the programs is in entering values for the coefficients — this is harder than you may think! The numerical values for this method are given, in Fehlberg's notation, in Table 3.2.

For

$$\frac{dy}{dx} = f(x,y); \; y(x_0) = y_0 \tag{3.5.1}$$

and stepsize h, the detailed formulas for one step are as follows:

Table 3.2

κ	α_κ	$\beta_{\kappa\lambda}$ $\lambda=0$	1	2	3	4	c_κ	$\hat{c}_\kappa$
0	0						$\frac{1}{9}$	$\frac{47}{450}$
1	$\frac{2}{9}$	$\frac{2}{9}$					0	0
2	$\frac{1}{3}$	$\frac{1}{12}$	$\frac{1}{4}$				$\frac{9}{20}$	$\frac{12}{25}$
3	$\frac{3}{4}$	$\frac{69}{128}$	$-\frac{243}{128}$	$\frac{135}{64}$			$\frac{16}{45}$	$\frac{32}{225}$
4	1	$-\frac{17}{12}$	$\frac{27}{4}$	$-\frac{27}{5}$	$\frac{16}{15}$		$\frac{1}{12}$	$\frac{1}{30}$
5	$\frac{5}{6}$	$\frac{65}{432}$	$-\frac{5}{16}$	$\frac{13}{16}$	$\frac{4}{27}$	$\frac{5}{144}$		$\frac{6}{25}$

$$\left.\begin{aligned}
f_0 &= f(x_0\, y_0), \\
f_1 &= f(x_0+\alpha_1 h,\ y_0+h\beta_{1,0}f_0), \\
f_2 &= f\left(x_0+\alpha_2 h,\ y_0+h[\beta_{2,0}f_0+\beta_{2,1}f_1]\right), \\
f_3 &= f\left(x_0+\alpha_3 h,\ y_0+h[\beta_{3,0}f_0+\beta_{3,1}f_1+\beta_{3,2}f_2]\right), \\
f_4 &= f\left(x_0+\alpha_4 h,\ y_0+h[\beta_{4,0}f_0+\beta_{4,1}f_1+\beta_{4,2}f_2+\beta_{4,3}f_3]\right), \\
f_5 &= f\left(x_0+\alpha_5 h,\ y_0+h[\beta_{5,0}f_0+\beta_{5,1}f_1+\beta_{5,2}f_2+\beta_{5,3}f_3+\beta_{5,4}f_4]\right), \\
y_1 &= y_0+h(c_0f_0+c_1f_1+c_2f_2+c_3f_3+c_4f_4), \\
\hat{y}_1 &= y_0+h(\hat{c}_0f_0+\hat{c}_1f_1+\hat{c}_2f_2+\hat{c}_3f_3+\hat{c}_4f_4+\hat{c}_5f_5).
\end{aligned}\right] \tag{3.5.2}$$

Fehlberg states (and we believe him) that y_1 is of fourth-order accuracy, so that the local truncation error

$$y(x_0+h)-y_1 = Ah^5+Bh^6+\cdots. \tag{3.5.3}$$

Also $\hat{y}_1$ is of fifth-order accuracy, so

$$y(x_0+h)-\hat{y}_1 = Ch^6+\cdots. \tag{3.5.4}$$

Then (for positive h)

$$|\hat{y}_1-y_1| = |A|h^5+|B-C|h^6+\cdots. \tag{3.5.5}$$

Now the dominant term in the series for the local truncation error of y_1 is Ah^5; so

$|\hat{y}_1-y_1|$ is an estimate of the local truncation error of y_1.

To use this estimate we introduce a quantity that will be called `Tol`; this is the greatest tolerable local truncation error of an integration step. It is a number to be provided by the operator. The object of the method is to ensure that $|y(x_0+h)-y_1| <$ `Tol` (so the error of $\hat{y}_1$ will be smaller still).

Once a step has been taken, $|\hat{y}_1-y_1|$ is calculated, and then compared with `Tol`.

- If $|\hat{y}_1-y_1| >$ `Tol`, then we have taken a bad step; the step must be repeated, using a smaller stepsize.
- If $|\hat{y}_1-y_1| <$ `Tol`, then we have taken a good step, and we are ready for the next one, using, perhaps, a larger stepsize.

In either event, we need to find a new stepsize.

Let this new stepsize be h_1. If we were to be really foolhardy in making h_1 as large as possible, we might set

$$|A|h_1^5 = \texttt{Tol}. \tag{3.5.6}$$

That is, we are estimating that the local truncation error of y_1 in the following step will be equal to Tol. But from the step just taken, we have

$$|A|h^5 = |\hat{y}_1 - y_1|. \tag{3.5.7}$$

(I have used the "=" symbol in place of the "≈" symbol, but we shall allow for this in a moment.) Eliminating $|A|$ between (3.5.6) and (3.5.7) and solving for h_1, we find

$$h_1 = h\left(\frac{\texttt{Tol}}{|\hat{y}_1 - y_1|}\right)^{1/5}. \tag{3.5.8}$$

This formula will diminish the stepsize if a bad step has been taken and can increase it after a good step. Its disadvantage is that the assumptions made are somewhat risky; allowance can be made by multiplying the right-hand side of (3.5.8) by some number less than one; I call this the "chicken factor" since its value depends on how nervous you are about the assumptions. I have found the value 0.9 to be satisfactory. In this case the expression for the next stepsize becomes

$$h_1 = 0.9h\left(\frac{\texttt{Tol}}{|\hat{y}_1 - y_1|}\right)^{1/5}. \tag{3.5.9}$$

This is the version used in this text.

Testing a step by comparing $|\hat{y}_1 - y_1|$ with Tol is imposing an absolute value on the error. Another approach is to use a relative value. Suppose that you run two projects; in the first, a swinging pendulum, all the dependent variables have absolute values less then 10; in the second, the motion of a satellite, the numbers may be as high as 10^5. Using the absolute approach, the first project might have $\texttt{Tol} = 10^{-6}$ and the second $\texttt{Tol} = 10^{-1}$. The relative error would involve the magnitude of the variables multiplied by some small number, and that number might be the same in each case. The accuracy should, anyway, be set case by case; so using the absolute approach need not lead to any difficulty. We shall continue to use it here.

3.6 The Implementation of RKF4(5). One Equation

One notational change will be made before the implementation of the method is discussed. This has historical roots since the original programming language used was Fortran, which did not allow zero subscripts. Since this is still the case with many versions, the subscripts used in the preceding section and in Table 3.2 will all be increased by one. The amended table is shown in Table 3.3.

At the end of a successful step, $x_0 + h$ and $\hat{y}_1$ will be stored and used as starting values for the next step. As the difference $\hat{y}_1 - y_1$ is needed for testing a step and finding the new stepsize, y_1, is never needed. In place of y_1 we shall calculate

$$TE = \hat{y}_1 - y_1 = h\left(CT(1)F(1) + \cdots + CT(6)F(6)\right). \tag{3.6.1}$$

The coefficients $CT(L) = CH(L) - C(L)$ are shown in Table 3.3. The coefficients $C(L)$ are shown in the table, but will not be used.

Table 3.3

K	$A(K)$	B(K,L)					$C(K)$	$CH(K)$	$CT(K)$
		$L=1$	2	3	4	5			
1	0						$\frac{1}{9}$	$\frac{47}{450}$	$-\frac{1}{150}$
2	$\frac{2}{9}$	$\frac{2}{9}$					0	0	0
3	$\frac{1}{3}$	$\frac{1}{12}$	$\frac{1}{4}$				$\frac{9}{20}$	$\frac{12}{25}$	$\frac{3}{100}$
4	$\frac{3}{4}$	$\frac{69}{128}$	$-\frac{243}{128}$	$\frac{135}{64}$			$\frac{16}{45}$	$\frac{32}{225}$	$-\frac{16}{75}$
5	1	$-\frac{17}{12}$	$\frac{27}{4}$	$-\frac{27}{5}$	$\frac{16}{15}$		$\frac{1}{12}$	$\frac{1}{30}$	$-\frac{1}{20}$
6	$\frac{5}{6}$	$\frac{65}{432}$	$-\frac{5}{16}$	$\frac{13}{16}$	$\frac{4}{27}$	$\frac{5}{144}$		$\frac{6}{25}$	$\frac{6}{25}$

We shall change the notation to make it more oriented toward arrays. Replace x_0 and y_0 by X and Y, respectively. $\hat{y}_1$ will be written as $Y1$.

For $\dfrac{dY}{dX} = F(X,Y)$, we are to find Y_1 to approximate $Y(X+H)$.

$$\left.\begin{aligned}
F(1) &= F[X, Y], \\
F(2) &= F[X + A(2)*H,\ Y + H*B(2,1)*F(1)], \\
F(3) &= F[X + A(3)*H,\ Y + H*(B(3,1)*F(1) + B(3,2)*F(2))], \\
F(4) &= F[X + A(4)*H,\ Y + H*(B(4,1)*F(1) + B(4,2)*F(2) + \\
&\quad B(4,3)*F(3))], \\
F(5) &= F[X + A(5)*H,\ Y + H*(B(5,1)*F(1) + B(5,2)*F(2) + \\
&\quad B(5,3)*F(3) + B(5,4)*F(4))], \\
F(6) &= F[X + A(6)*H,\ Y + H*(B(6,1)*F(1) + B(6,2)*F(2) + \\
&\quad B(6,3)*F(3) + B(6,4)*F(4) + B(6,5)*F(5))], \\
Y1 &= Y + H*(CH(1)*F(1) + CH(2)*F(2) + CH(3)*F(3) + \\
&\quad CH(4)*F(4) + CH(5)*F(5) + CH(6)*F(6)), \\
TE &= H*(CT(1)*F(1) + CT(2)*F(2) + CT(3)*F(3) + \\
&\quad CT(4)*F(4) + CT(5)*F(5) + CT(6)*F(6)).
\end{aligned}\right] \tag{3.6.2}$$

At the end of the step, a new stepsize, $H1$, is calculated using

$$H1 = 0.9*H*(\mathtt{Tol}/|TE|)^{1/5}. \tag{3.6.3}$$

If $TE > \mathtt{Tol}$, then $H1$ is used in a repetition of the step. Otherwise, it will be used for the following step.

Figure 3.4 shows these operations organized in a flowchart. The initial conditions have been stored with the names $XTemp$ and $YTemp$; this enables the symbols X and Y to be used freely in the calculations. Note that the symbol H is used in the calculation of the new stepsize; then it is necessary to store the value of the stepsize that has just been used: this is called $HOld$. If the step was a good one, the value of X at the end of this step is $XTemp + HOld$, and H will be used for the following step.

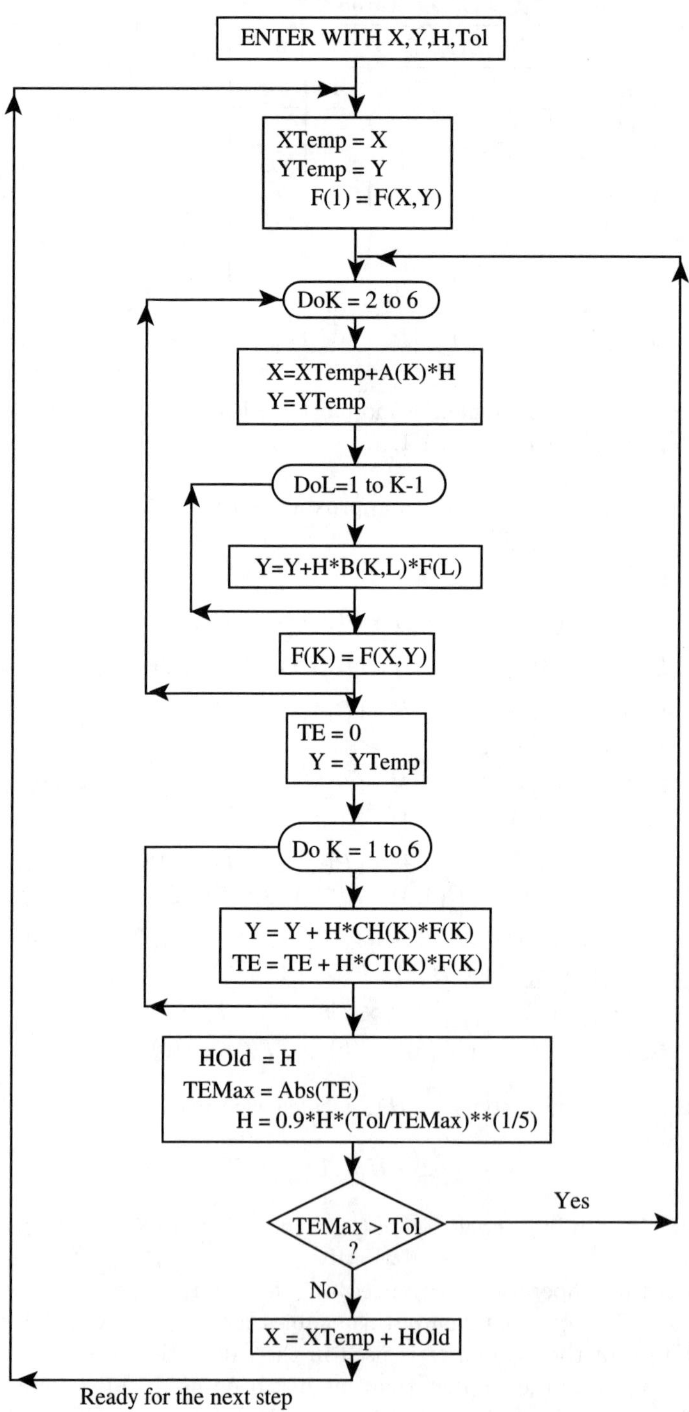

Figure 3.4: *Flowchart for a single differential equation:* $Y' = F(X, Y)$.

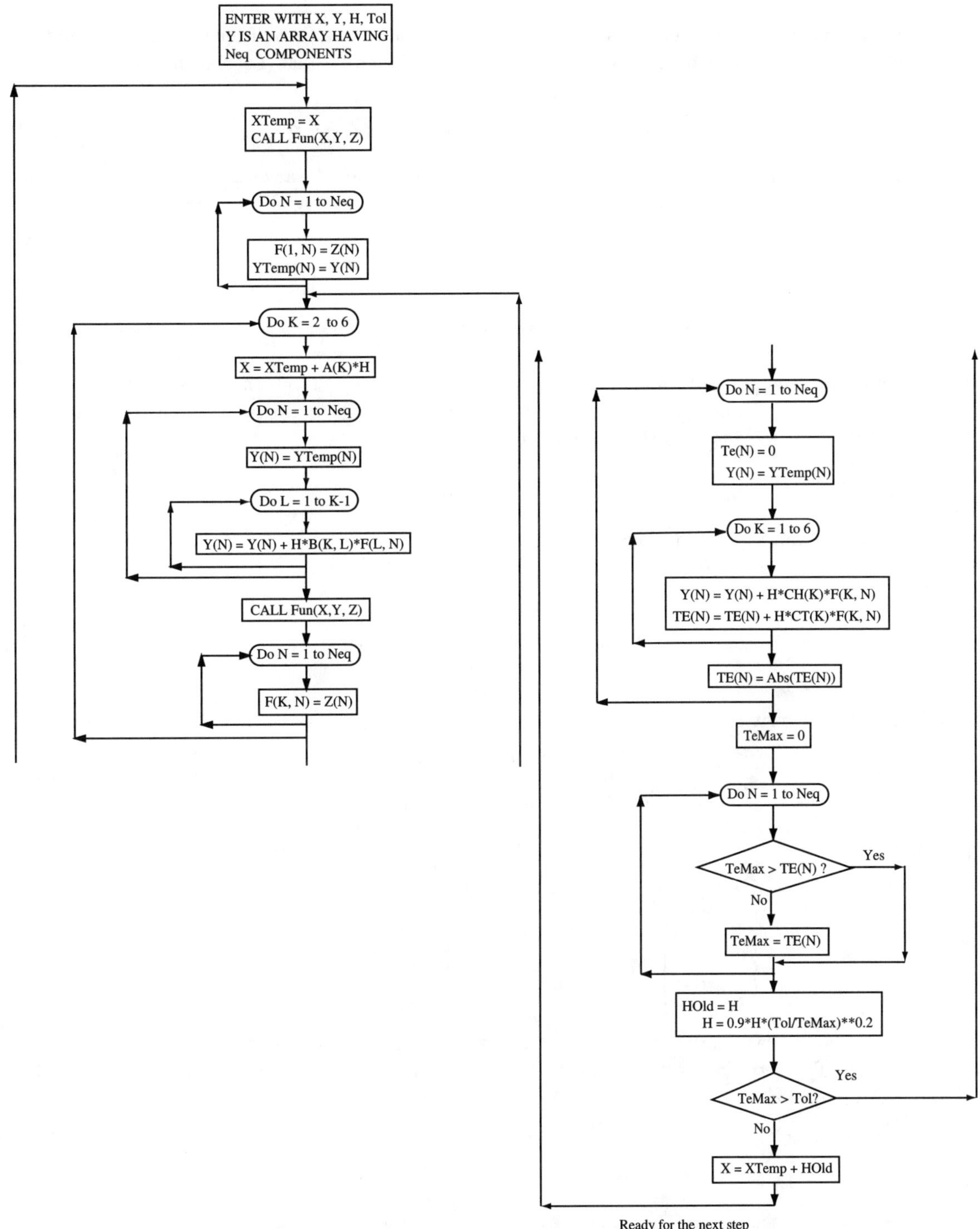

Figure 3.5: *Flowchart for a system of differential equations.*

3.7 The Implementation of RKF4(5). A System of Equations

Virtually no model of interest can be represented by just one first-order differential equation, so any useful program must be capable of solving a system of equations. Let us consider the general system

$$\frac{dy_i}{dx} = f_i(x, y_1, y_2, \cdots, y_n), \quad i = 1, 2, \cdots, n \tag{3.7.1}$$

with n dependent variables, but of course still just one independent variable, x.

For example, the predator-prey model of Volterra is described by the equations

$$\left.\begin{aligned} \frac{dx}{dt} &= ax - bxy, \\ \frac{dy}{dt} &= -cy + dxy. \end{aligned}\right] \tag{3.7.2}$$

Here x and y are the populations of the prey and predators, respectively, and t is the time. a, b, c and d are constants. To put this into the standard form that will be necessary if the program is to be used, make the changes in notation indicated by

$$x \to y_1, \; y \to y_2, \; t \to x.$$

Then in the new notation, equations (3.7.2) become

$$\left.\begin{aligned} \frac{dy_1}{dx} &= ay_1 - by_1y_2, \\ \frac{dy_2}{dx} &= -cy_2 + dy_1y_2, \end{aligned}\right] \tag{3.7.3}$$

which can also be written as

$$\frac{d}{dx}\begin{bmatrix} y_1 \\ y_2 \end{bmatrix} = \begin{bmatrix} ay_1 - by_1y_2 \\ -cy_2 + dy_1y_2 \end{bmatrix}, \tag{3.7.4}$$

or simply

$$\frac{dy}{dx} = f(x, y), \tag{3.7.5}$$

where

$$y = \begin{bmatrix} y_1 \\ y_2 \end{bmatrix} \text{ and } f(x, y) = \begin{bmatrix} ay_1 - by_1y_2 \\ -cy_2 + dy_1y_2 \end{bmatrix}. \tag{3.7.6}$$

The predator-prey model starts out as a system of first-order differential equations. Some models, particularly those associated with dynamics, start out with second-order equations. The Van der Pol equation is

$$\frac{d^2y}{dt^2} + a(y^2 - 1)\frac{dy}{dt} + y = 0. \tag{3.7.7}$$

Let

$$y_1 = y, \; y_2 = \frac{dy}{dt}, \quad x = t. \tag{3.7.8}$$

Then

$$\left.\begin{aligned} \frac{dy_1}{dx} &= y_2, \\ \frac{dy_2}{dx} &= -a(y_1^2 - 1)y_2 - y_1, \end{aligned}\right] \tag{3.7.9}$$

or

$$\frac{d}{dx}\begin{bmatrix} y_1 \\ y_2 \end{bmatrix} = \begin{bmatrix} y_2 \\ -a(y_1^2 - 1)y_2 - y_1 \end{bmatrix}. \tag{3.7.10}$$

You are likely to be confused initially by the changes of notation from that of a model to that of the program. If in doubt, write down every detail of the change. Try putting the old and new notations on different sheets of paper, with a complete reformulation of the model in the new notation, including a physical interpretation of each variable. For instance, in (3.7.10), y_1 is a displacement, y_2 a velocity, and x the time.

Figure 3.5 shows a flowchart for a system of equations. The number of equations is `Neq`, and the principal change from figure 3.4 is the inclusion of many loops: "`Do N = 1 to Neq`." It is assumed that the right-hand sides of the differential equations are found in a subroutine called `Fun(X,Y,Z)` that receives as input the independent variable `X` and the array of dependent variables `Y`, and produces as output the right-hand sides in the array `Z`. For instance, for (3.7.6), the subroutine might contain the lines:

```
Z(1) = A*Y(1) - B*Y(1)*Y(2)
Z(2) = - C*Y(2) + D*Y(1)*Y(2)
```

Note that `A, B, C` and `D` would be constants with previously assigned values. The array of six functions that was needed when solving a single differential equation must now become a double array, `F(K,N)`, where `K` takes the values 1 to 6, and `N`, the values 1 to `Neq`. For any step, each of the `Neq` equations will have its own local truncation error, `TE(N)`. The largest of these, in absolute value, is `TeMax`; it is this that is used to calculate a new stepsize and to test the validity of a step.

The heart of the program is a subroutine (or procedure) called `STEP` that takes as input these values: `X, Y, H`, the suggested stepsize, and `Tol`, the greatest tolerable local truncation error. Its output consists of values of `X` and `Y` at the end of a successful step and the recommended stepsize for the next step. This subroutine might include a listing of the constants of the method; or these might be put in a separate subroutine to be called once at the start of the program. It would contain the following lines:

```
A(2) = 2./9.
A(3) = 1./3.
A(4) = 3./4.
A(5) = 1.
A(6) = 5./6.

B(2,1) = 2./9.
B(3,1) = 1./12.
B(3,2) = 1./4.
B(4,1) = 69./128.
B(4,2) = - 243./128.
B(4,3) = 135./64.
B(5,1) = - 17./12.
B(5,2) = 27./4.
B(5,3) = - 27./5.
B(5,4) = 16./15.
B(6,1) = 65./432.
B(6,2) = - 5./16.
B(6,3) = 13./16.
B(6,4) = 4./27.
B(6,5) = 5./144.

CH(1) = 47./450.
```

```
CH(2) = 0.
CH(3) = 12./25.
CH(4) = 32./225.
CH(5) = 1./30.
CH(6) = 6./25.

CT(1) = - 1./150.
CT(2) = 0.
CT(3) = 3./100.
CT(4) = - 16./75.
CT(5) = - 1./20.
CT(6) = 6./25.
```

The subroutine `Step` might contain the following code:

```
XTemp = X
Call Fun(X,Y,Z)
Do N = 1, Neq
    F(1,N) = Z(N)
    YTemp(N) = Y(N)
End Do

Do While (TeMax.gt.Tol)
    Do K = 2,6
      X = XTemp + A(K)*H
      Do N = 1,Neq
        Y(N) = YTemp(N)
        Do L = 1,K-1
          Y(N) = Y(N) + H*B(K,L)*F(L,N)
        End Do
      End Do
      Call Fun(X,Y,Z)
      Do N = 1,Neq
        F(K,N) = Z(N)
      End Do
    End Do
    Do N = 1,Neq
      Y(N) = YTemp(N)
      TE(N) = 0
      Do K = 1,6
        Y(N) = Y(N) + H*CH(K)*F(K,N)
        TE(N) = TE(N) + H*CT(K)*F(K,N)
      End Do
      TE(N) = Abs(TE(N))
    End Do
    TeMax = 0
    Do N = 1,Neq
      If (TeMax.lt.TE(N)) TeMax = TE(N)
    End Do
    If(TeMax.eq.0) Then TeMax = Tol/10**5
    HOld = H
    H = 0.9*H*(Tol/TeMax)**0.2
```

```
End DO
X = XTemp + HOld
Return
End
```

If the stepsize is very small, or the solutions are nearly linear, the elements `TE(N)` may be computed to be zero, so that the final value of `TeMax` is zero. Since we cannot allow a division by zero in the computation of the next stepsize, the line

```
        TeMax = Tol/10.**5
```

has been added. This allows the stepsize to be increased by a factor of ten.

3.8 Projects for Debugging, Testing and Understanding the Program

This section is divided into five projects. They have two purposes.

The principal purpose is to understand how the program works so that you can trust it and control it. Even if you know that the code is correct, it is still worthwhile to run these exercises so that the program will become your own program and not someone else's black box. In fact the algorithm is so short and elegant that it is ridiculous to put it into the context of a "black box."

Secondly, if you have coded the method yourself, you will need to debug it, anyway. *Be patient.* Test only one facet of the program at a time. For instance, the first three projects involve taking *just one step.* If the program does not work satisfactorily for one step, it certainly will not work for more. You need to test the program using an equation for which you know the answer; so you should continue to use your first-order differential equation selected earlier. Set `Neq = 1` and write a subroutine, or procedure `Fun(X,Y,Z)`. For instance, in Fortran, for the differential equation

$$\frac{dy}{dx} = x + y, \tag{3.8.1}$$

the notation would be changed to

$$\frac{\mathtt{dY(1)}}{\mathtt{dX}} = \mathtt{X} + \mathtt{Y(1)},$$

and a suitable subroutine might be

```
Subroutine Fun(X,Y,Z)
Double Precision X, Y(10), Z(10)
    Z(1) = X + Y(1)
Return
End
```

(The dimensions allow for later use of up to ten equations; you can adapt this to suit yourself.) Similarly, in Pascal, we might first include at the start of the program the declaration:

```
Type
 Vector = Array[1..10] of Real;
```

Then use the code

```
Procedure Fun(X: Real; Y: Vector; Var Z: Vector)
Begin;
    Z[1] = X + Y[1];
End;
```

In C,

```
Const int NEQ = 1
```

Then

```
Void Fun (double Z[NEQ+1], double Y[NEQ+1],double X)
{
    Z[1] = X + Y[1]
}
```

And so on. You will need a line to calculate the correct solution. For equation (3.8.1) the general solution is

$$y = Ce^x - x - 1. \tag{3.8.2}$$

So you might code

```
    YCorrect = Constant*Exp(X) - X - 1
```

(For double precision in Fortran, use `dExp(x)`.) You will probably want to enter a variety of initial conditions. If $y(x_0) = y_0$, then from (3.8.2)

$$C = e^{-x_0}(y_0 + x_0 + 1). \tag{3.8.3}$$

If the initial conditions have just been read in as `X` and `Y(1)` then

```
    Constant = Exp(-X)*(Y(1) + X + 1)
```

(Be careful. It is humiliating to apply a wrong check to a correct program!) To structure your main program, you might have a subroutine `Initialize` to read in the numerical values of the Fehlberg coefficients, then a subroutine `Data` to enable the operator to enter starting conditions and parameters such as the stepsize, then the principal subroutine `Step`, and then a subroutine `Print` for writing out the results of the step. This will be referred to below.

For each project, we ask a question.

1. *After just one step, are we in the right ballpark?*

   Take one step only, so that the principal loop in `Step` should be deactivated; the parameter `Tol` is not needed, nor is the calculation of a new stepsize. Avoid initial conditions that involve a large initial value of the slope, dy/dx. I suggest that you use the stepsize `H = 0.1`; then, since we are using a fifth-order method, the error of `Y(1)` at the end of the step should be 10^{-6} or less. A value of 10^{-5} might indicate a poor choice of initial conditions, or it might warn you of a bug. A value of 10^{-4} would almost certainly indicate a bug: double-check the numerical values of the parameters. Print out the initial conditions

   ```
   X, Y(1)
   ```

   and the results at the end of the step

   ```
   HOld, X, Y(1), YCorrect, Error,
   ```

   where `Error = |YCorrect - Y(1)|`. Note that `HOld` was the stepsize used to make the step that you are recording. If the error is a lot less than 10^{-6} (say, 10^{-9}), then things are still healthy. (If the error is zero, something is wrong; you may have calculated the value of `Constant` after taking the step, instead of immediately after reading in the initial conditions.)

2. *Does TE say what it should?*

   The most significant instruction in the entire program is the one that calculates the new stepsize; for this to work, it is essential that in (3.5.2) the local truncation error of y_1 be well approximated by a term of the form Ah^5, so that `TeMax` is well approximated by the same term. Further, since we are using $\hat{y}_1$ for successive steps, the program is of *fifth-order* overall, with local truncation error approximated by Bh^6. The object of this project is to test these assertions experimentally.

   Again, we take just one step, but it will be repeated several times using different values of the stepsize (but the same initial conditions). We are repeating, in principle, the project of section 2.4. I suggest that you use the values

   ```
   H = 0.01, 0.02, 0.03, ..., 0,09, 0.10,
   ```

   but you may get more convincing results with different values. Remember that the formula for the truncation error is of the form

   $$\mathtt{AH}^5 + \mathtt{BH}^6 + \cdots,$$

   so `H` should be small enough for every term but the first to be negligible. On the other hand, if `H` is too small, then round-off errors can become important and the results will not be significant. Some experiment may be needed.

   For each value of `H` that you use, make a table of the following:

   ```
   H, X, Y(1), YCorrect, Error, TeMax, log(H), log(TeMax), Log(Error)
   ```

   (Note that, as coded, `TeMax` and `Error` should always be positive.) A plot of `log(TeMax)` against `log(H)` should resemble (over a suitable range of `H`) a straight line with slope 5. If this is not the case, check the coefficients used in the computation of the `TE(N)`. A plot of `log(Error)` against `log(H)` should resemble a straight line with slope 6. This confirms that the program is running a fifth-order method.

   The tables that you construct are worth careful inspection in that they will help you to understand how the errors behave as the stepsize is varied, and to build experience and confidence for the time when you do not know the errors but must trust the program to control them.

3. *Does the procedure for changing the stepsize work efficiently?*

   Step by step, the program is continually changing the stepsize. Is this done efficiently? To start the program, in the first place, a value for the stepsize must be entered; this might be much larger or much smaller than the optimal size for the project. Does this matter?

   To get insight into these matters, it is instructive to run some experiments in which the stepsizes will be changed, and to write them out as they change. In the subroutine `Step` include, in the appropriate syntax, (**for this project only**) three lines to add to the code:

   ```
       Write TeMax                             (a)
       Write H                                 (b)
       HOld = H
       H = 0.9*H*(Tol/TeMax)**0.2              (c)
   End DO                                      (d)
   Write H                                     (e)
   X = XTemp + HOld
   Return
   End
   ```

(The labels on the right are for later reference; they are not part of the code.) Let's see some results. For $y' = x + y$ with $y(0) = 0$, `Tol` $= 10^{-6}$ and initial stepsize `H` $= 1$, the following output was produced. This includes a summary of the successful step, as printed in the main program. (Numbers have been rounded.)

```
    1.04167E-03
    1.00000E+00
    1.04857E-06
    2.24232E-01
    5.98580E-07
    1.99903E-01
    1.99360E-01

 Stepsize  =  1.99903E-01
        X  =  1.99903E-01
        Y  =  2.13813E-02
 YCorrect  =  2.13813E-02
    Error  =  2.47534E-08
```

Let's interpret these numbers. We start with `TeMax = 1.04167E-03`, written in (a), which is larger than `Tol`, so the stepsize, `H = 1`, written in (b) is a bad one. The loop fails to end in (d), but is repeated using the new stepsize that was computed in (c). This produces `Temax = 1.04857E-06` which is still larger than `Tol`, so that the stepsize that was used, `H = 0.24232E-01` is, again, a bad stepsize. The loop is repeated once more, this time producing `TeMax = 5.98580E-07`, which is acceptable, so that the stepsize that was used to generate it, `H = 1.99903E-01` was a good one. But one further stepsize was computed in (c), and the value of this is written in (e). This is the stepsize that would be used if a further step is to be taken; so this might be called the "next stepsize." Finally, in the summary of the step from the main program, the "good stepsize" is repeated. Note, also, that the error of the step (which is the error of Fehlberg's $\hat{y}_1$) is well within acceptable bounds. So the output might be labelled as follows:

```
    1.04167E-03               TeMax too big
    1.00000E+00               Bad stepsize
    1.04857E-06               TeMax too big
    2.24232E-01               Bad stepsize
    5.98580E-07               TeMax OK
    1.99903E-01               Good stepsize
    1.99360E-01               Next stepsize

 Stepsize  =  1.99903E-01  Good stepsize
        X  =  1.99903E-01
        Y  =  2.13813E-02
 YCorrect  =  2.13813E-02
    Error  =  2.47534E-08
```

Let's repeat the experiment, but this time entering `H=10` as the initial stepsize.

```
    8.33333E+02               TeMax too big
    1.00000E+01               Bad stepsize
    1.36703E-07               TeMax OK
    1.47934E-01               Good stepsize
    1.98228E-01               Next stepsize
```

```
Stepsize  =  1.47934E-01  Good stepsize
       X  =  1.47934E-01
       Y  =  1.15030E-02
YCorrect  =  1.15030E-02
   Error  =  3.95330E-09
```

Division, in (c), by the large initial value of `TeMax`, led at once to an acceptable stepsize.

Now repeat the experiment with `H=100` as the initial stepsize.

```
1.02083E+09                 TeMax too big
1.00000E+02                 Bad stepsize
1.15108E-08                 TeMax OK
8.96296E-02                 Good stepsize
1.97003E-01                 Next stepsize
```

```
Stepsize  =  8.96296E-02  Good stepsize
       X  =  8.96296E-02
       Y  =  4.13948E-03
YCorrect  =  4.13948E-03
   Error  =  1.89343E-10
```

The initial value of `TeMax` is even larger, and the successful stepsize a lot smaller, but notice that the "next" stepsize is quite reasonable.

Now suppose that the starting stepsize is much too small. Let's try `H` = 10^{-4}.

```
2.12312E-23                 TeMax OK
1.00000E-04                 Good stepsize
1.94468                     Next stepsize
```

```
Stepsize  =  1.00000E-04  Good stepsize
       X  =  1.00000E-04
       Y  =  5.00015E-09
YCorrect  =  5.00015E-09
   Error  =  4.16006E-20
```

Obviously, the tiny stepsize is "good," but notice that, once more, in the "next" stepsize the program has returned to an efficient value.

Running this project with your own equation, and with different starting initial stepsizes is enjoyable. The experience should give a lot of confidence in the ability of the program to change the stepsize efficiently. I recommend that you write in the labelling by hand; it helps you to see where in the program, and under what circumstances, the various quantities were written. Once you have completed the project, be sure to remove the three "write" statements from `Step`.

4. *Does the program work over an extended interval?*

   At last we can take more than one step! We shall look at three different tactics that might be used to decide when to stop the running of the program.

   - **Take a specified number of steps.** Let's make it ten steps. Repetition of steps will be controlled from the main program. This might be structured as follows:

`Call Initialize`	(Enters numerical values of the Fehlberg coefficients)
`Call Data`	(Prompts for initial conditions, starting stepsize, `Tol`, etc.)
`Call Step`	(Takes a step. "Next" stepsize included in the output)
`Call Output`	(Prints a summary of results from the step)

The final two instructions must be repeated ten times. This might be achieved as follows:

```
Count = 0
Do While (Count .lt.  10)
  Count = Count + 1
  Call Step
  Call Output
End Do
```

Choose initial conditions so that the solution (for the appropriate range of `x`) is curvy, but without the slope becoming too steep. A direction field diagram is helpful when making a choice.

After each step, print out the same quantities that were shown in the first of these projects.

Follow the stepsize as it is changed from step to step. You may see a pattern; for instance, if the curvature of the solution is increasing, the stepsize may become smaller. Also follow the errors as the calculation progresses.

The program controls the *local* truncation error. The *global* or *accumulated* truncation error is a different matter; this is likely to increase, for two main reasons. First, separate local errors are being added. More importantly, the differential equation may magnify a small initial error into a much larger one as `x` increases.

As an example, suppose that you are solving

$$\frac{dy}{dx} = x + y, \quad \text{so} \quad y = Ce^x - x - 1.$$

Set initial conditions $x_0 = 0$, $y_0 = 0$ so that $C = 1$. We take a step with stepsize $h = 0.1$. At the end of the step, the correct value of y is 0.0051709. For the purpose of discussion, assume that the local truncation error of this step is 0.01; so that at the end of the computed step we have $x_1 = 0.1$, $y_1 = 0.0151709$. We are no longer on the solution having initial conditions with which we started. If we treat x_1 and y_1 as new initial conditions, we find $C = 1.009048$. Now suppose that there are no further errors, and we reach $x = 2$. Using $C = 1$ would give $y = 4.389056$; but $C = 1.009048$ gives $y = 4.455912$ so that the truncation error has been multiplied by a factor of ten. Of course, in reaching $x = 2$ in practice, there will have been many more truncation errors, similarly magnified. This makes the very important point that whatever method you use, you may still be at the mercy of the differential equations that you are solving. The behavior of the equations as `x` increases, and the accuracy you hope to achieve by the end of a calculation will be important factors in the choice of a value for `Tol`. Before you start a calculation, you should know something about the character of the solution.

- Stop once `x` has exceeded some specified value. Let's call this value `xEnd`. Choose a value that might be used in practice, one with at most one place of decimals, say, and one that will not involve taking more than around ten steps. For instance,

```
Do While (x .lt.  xEnd)
  Call Step
  Call Output
End Do
```

- Stop when `x = xEnd`. This can be approached in two ways. You might go past `xEnd` and then go back, using the negative stepsize `h = xEnd - x`, so that the code might be

```
Do While (x .lt.  xEnd)
  Call Step
  Call Output
End Do
h = xEnd - x
Call Step
Call Output
```

Since the stepsize that led to `x` exceeding `xEnd` was a good one and `h = xEnd - x` is smaller in magnitude, the final stepsize is virtually guaranteed to be good also. Another approach is to stop the main loop at the stage when another step would exceed `xEnd`:

```
Do While (x + h .lt.  xEnd)
  Call Step
  Call Output
End Do
```

Now take a step with positive stepsize `h = xEnd - x`; this may need to be repeated if it turns out not to be good:

```
Do While (Abs(x - xEnd) .gt.  Eps)
  h = xEnd - x
  Call Step
  Call Output
End Do
```

The quantity `Eps` should be a small positive number, just larger than the roundoff error to be expected in the floating point variables `x` and `xEnd`. Bear in mind that, because of roundoff error, the quantity `Abs(x - xEnd)` may *never* be zero; so it is wrong to try to stop when it is equal to zero. In fact, you should never use a logical "=" with floating point numbers.

5. *Does the program work for more than one equation?*

   Here we shall use two equations, so set `Neq = 2`.

   The model to be used is the harmonic oscillator,

$$\frac{d^2x}{dt^2} + x = 0. \tag{3.8.4}$$

   The general solution is

$$\left.\begin{aligned} x &= c_1 \cos t + c_2 \sin t, \\ \frac{dx}{dt} &= -c_1 \sin t + c_2 \cos t. \end{aligned}\right] \tag{3.8.5}$$

   If we have initial conditions

$$t = 0,\ x = 1,\ \frac{dx}{dt} = 0, \tag{3.8.6}$$

   then

$$x = \cos t,\quad \frac{dx}{dt} = -\sin t. \tag{3.8.7}$$

In order to run this model with our program, it will be necessary to change the one second-order differential equation into a system of two first-order differential equations. This is an operation that you will need to follow many times, especially when dealing with dynamical systems, where the application of Newton's second law automatically generates second-order differential equations. Here we have a dynamical system, and we must recognize that it follows *two* dependent variables, displacement and velocity, or x and $v = \frac{dx}{dt}$. Then we can write (3.8.4) as

$$\left.\begin{aligned} \frac{dx}{dt} &= v, \\ \frac{dv}{dt} &= -x. \end{aligned}\right] \tag{3.8.8}$$

For any model you will need to change the notation so that it conforms to the notation used in the code of the program. The dependent variables go into the array `y` and the independent variable is denoted by `x`. The transformation here might be described in the following table:

Model	Program	Explanation
Dependent variables:		
x	`y(1)`	Displacement
$v = \frac{dx}{dt}$	`y(2)`	Velocity
Independent variable:		
t	`x`	Time

The differential equations in the notation of the program are

$$\left.\begin{aligned} \frac{d\texttt{Y(1)}}{d\texttt{x}} &= \texttt{Y(2)}, \\ \frac{d\texttt{Y(2)}}{d\texttt{x}} &= -\texttt{Y(1)}. \end{aligned}\right] \tag{3.8.9}$$

These are entered into the subroutine `Fun(X,Y,Z)` through the lines:

```
z(1) = y(2)
z(2) = - y(1)
```

Initial conditions are, from (3.8.6),

$$\texttt{x} = 0,\ \texttt{y(1)} = 1,\ \texttt{y(2)} = 0.$$

The correct solutions for `y(1)` and `y(2)` are

$$\texttt{y1Correct} = \texttt{Cos(x)},\ \texttt{y2Correct} = -\texttt{Sin(x)}.$$

To run the project, set `Neq = 2`, modify `Fun`, enter the initial conditions (remembering to include `y(2)`); you might put `Tol` = 10^{-6} and the initial stepsize equal to 0.1. After calling `Step`, calculate the errors in `y(1)` and `y(2)` as

$$\texttt{Error1} = \texttt{Abs(Cos(x)} - \texttt{y(1))},\ \texttt{Error2} = \texttt{Abs(}-\texttt{Sin(x)} - \texttt{y(2))}.$$

You might end at `x = xEnd = 1`. After each step, show values of

`Stepsize, x, y(1), y(2), Error1, Error2.`

The errors should remain small: 10^{-7} or less.

3.9 Running the Program

The most important parameter to be chosen before the program is run is `Tol`. This should be chosen with regard to the order of magnitude of the variables. For instance, in following the motion of a simple pendulum with length 1 meter, `Tol` $= 10^{-6}$ might be appropriate; but for the motion of an artificial satellite, with distances of the order of 10^4 km, you might consider `Tol` $= 10^{-2}$. But bear in mind that over an extended computation the accumulated truncation error is almost certain to increase. Sometimes a moderate value of `Tol` can be used for a preliminary run; if this seems to be interesting, then a smaller value can be substituted for greater accuracy.

A factor that may influence the choice of `Tol` is graphics. The numerical accuracy might be satisfactory, but the stepsizes might then be so large that a graph (employing straight line segments) would be jerky, leading to the need for smaller `Tol`. Similarly, if the results are used for animation, stepsizes, and therefore `Tol`, must be small enough for smoothness.

If the animation is to be shown while the computations are taking place, then it will be distorted in time. The faster the actual motion, the smaller the stepsize, and the slower the computation. For instance, when calculating an orbit from the Earth to the Moon, the animation will appear slow close to either body, but fast in between; actually, the reverse is the case. This can be frustrating; but the more interesting physics is taking place at the close encounters.

It is essential to start a calculation with a value for the stepsize. (Otherwise it will default to zero — and remain at zero.) Enter a reasonable value according to the circumstances of the model. After the first step the stepsize is controlled by the program, using your value of `Tol`.

For many purposes, output with values of `x` following the changing stepsize is adequate. For some purposes, you might want to see output only for `x` at regular intervals. This might be done for storing data for use in realistic animation; it is also necessary for some types of Poincaré maps. Suppose that you want to see output at intervals `Interval` of `x`. You might follow this procedure. For input:

`x, y` for the starting conditions,
`Tol`, the greatest tolerable local truncation error,
`StepSize`, the starting stepsize,
`FinalTime`, the final value of `x`,

and as output:

`x,y` the conditions at regular intervals of `x`,

The code might include the following lines ("`x`" has been replaced by "`Time`"):

```
Do While (Time < FinalTime)
  NextTime = Time + Interval
  Do While (Time + StepSize) < NextTime
    Call Step(...)
  End Do
  SaveStepSize = StepSize
  Do While Abs(Time - NextTime) > Eps
    StepSize = NextTime - Time
    Call Step(...)
```

```
    End Do
    StepSize = SaveStepSize
    Print output
  End Do
```

Eps should be a small number, a bit larger than the roundoff error to be expected. If the second loop executes more than once, the stepsize may be drastically reduced; this is why the value of the stepsize before this loop is stored, and then restored after the loop.

Chapter 4

Introduction to Modeling

4.1 Generalities

No two projects are the same, and no two humans are the same. So insisting on rules that should be followed by humans when carrying out projects is not possible. What I am attempting to do here is to outline some recommendations that can lead to added enjoyment and profit, and, in the long run, save time. This last property is especially important for students if running the project is a scheduled assignment. It is easy to develop a mental block when computing. "I have some computer code; what do I do with it?" Or, if I am lucky, "I have some output; what can I say about it?" You can become lonely very fast when computing. The most basic rules are:

- Never try to outstare a computer; it will win every time. If you are not making progress in ten minutes, log off.
- If you cannot trace a bug in ten minutes, quit. Fresh eyes (yours or those of a friend) may later spot the trouble very quickly.
- When possible, work in a team. Educationally, this greatly enhances learning, is more fun and can save a lot of time. I urge all instructors to encourage team work. We need to talk with each other more.
- Interpret all results in terms of the actions of your model, not the output of a computer.
- Even if you will not write a report on what you have done and discovered, **think** in terms of communicating your work to others.

Those are general comments; here are some that are more specific:

- Try to understand the basic model before you write computer code. Even if you cannot completely follow a derivation, try to develop a feeling for what the model is **like** and what it may **do**. (Even if you are wrong, this will help you get started.)
- Try to understand the definitions and interpretations of all variables. These will fall into three categories:

  Independent variable. This is the variable with respect to which all derivatives on the left-hand sides of the differential equations are taken. In most cases this will be the time, and it will progress in a positive, or increasing, sense. But be careful: a negative sense is also possible. For instance, in the model for helium burning in a star, the independent variable might be the helium content, which is diminishing.

Dependent variables. These are the variables that appear in the numerators of the derivatives on the left-hand sides of the (first-order) differential equations. Take care when a system of second-order equations is to be reduced to those of first-order. It is the dependent and independent variables that are specified in the *initial conditions.*

Parameters. These are quantities that provide the physical specifications of the model. Ordinarily, you will give these numerical values, and then experiment with changes of the initial conditions. Change the values of the parameters with care, and always with physical interpretation.

- In most models it is important to be careful about units. For instance, in the model for the motion of Skylab, the unit of length is the kilometer. If you would like to input the satellite's radius in meters, include code to convert to kilometers as soon as the data have been entered. Also remember that, internally, **all** angles must be in radians. If you want the angles in your input and output to be in degrees, then you must calculate the conversions.

- Try to do some debugging by running the program for conditions where you know the character of the solution. For instance, in the trip to the Moon, you might run a case when the mass of the Moon (a parameter) is zero, when you should observe elliptic orbits that return to the starting point. Also look for possible nonsense in your output. I frequently get the sign of the potential energy wrong, with the result that gravity acts up instead of down; this can be detected easily, provided you are on the lookout for the possibility. If a model is complicated (like that for the heartbeat) build it up gradually, debugging as you go. Remember that there is nothing "stupid" about making programming errors: it is perfectly normal. Assume that you are making them, and look for them.

- Investigating any model should involve a dialog with the computer. Don't generate output aimlessly. Ask a question. Use the output to answer the question and to suggest further questions. Keep the conversation going; if it stops, log off!

- Two important quantities for you to specify are the accuracy needed (probably the maximum allowable local truncation error) and the length of the run. Don't require too great an accuracy at the start. Don't automatically require a definite number of decimals: the accuracy that you need will depend on the units used. If you are generating real-time animation, then you need to strike a balance between the speed of the animation and the smoothness of the graphics. Specifying, in advance, the length of a run can be difficult and will probably require experimentation. In a predator-prey model you may be looking for cycles; run the program long enough to detect the cycles but not so long that you see many repetitions. Units are important. In the model for Skylab, the unit of time is the second, and many thousands of seconds may be needed. In the trip to the Moon, only one or two units of the model's time may be needed. Be prepared to experiment.

- When debugging, you may need to print generous output. When running the program, decide carefully what output you need, and with what accuracy it should be displayed. If possible, examine it on the screen before deciding whether to print it. Even if you are using the output to generate graphics, it is a good idea to print some of the numbers, but don't be excessive. In his text, R.M.May [69] comments unkindly that some computing operations would benefit from the inclusion of an on-line incinerator. (Was he thinking of you?)

You may be playing with models for your private amusement; but you may need to present a project in writing, possibly for academic credit. In the latter case, it is essential to remember that a presentation is a communication, and that the readers will start from **their** preconceptions, **not yours**. In a presentation:

- Define all variables. Give symbols and meanings. Include symbols used in the computer program.
- Define the model, being careful to itemize all assumptions that have been made. Do not assume that the reader will have any degree of familiarity with the model.
- Make clear the purposes of your investigations.
- Interpret all output and conclusions. Figures are great; but they must be fully labeled and verbally described and interpreted.
- Include a listing of your program and some output. This will enable the work to be used at a later time. (It is very likely that you will want to refer to it.)
- Be critical of yourself. I often suggest showing work to a non-scientific roommate; he or she should understand what you have done. Don't hesitate to criticize others — particularly the presentations in this book. If you feel that I have not done an adequate job in presenting some project, then that is your cue for doing a better job. Remember, that if you do not learn how to present your projects well, then you will spend your life working for people with degrees in liberal arts from ■■■■■■ ■■■■ University.

4.2 A Model for Discussion: Richardson's "Arms Race" 

For illustrative purposes, I have chosen a simple model for which analytical solutions can be found. None of these solutions will be used, however, since we need to prepare for situations where they are not available. Rather, the aim is to see how qualitative properties can be derived from a preliminary survey of a problem. The numerical work can then follow along the lines suggested by these properties. Asking the computer questions helps to avoid aimless output.

The model presented is due to L.F.Richardson [83]. Discussions appear in several texts, in particular in those by Rapoport [81] and Braun [17]. Remember always that what we shall be looking at is "just" a model. That is, any conclusions drawn depend on the assumptions made, and these assumptions are bound to be oversimplified. Even so, you may find some conclusions interesting, suggestive, and even worrisome. They can lead to further questions to be asked, and often to generalizations of the model.

Richardson writes:

> Why are so many nations reluctantly but steadily increasing their armaments as if they were mechanically compelled to do so? Because, I say, they follow their traditions which are fixtures and their instincts which are mechanical; and because they have not yet made a sufficiently strenuous intellectual and moral effort to control the situation. The process described by the ensuing equations is not thought of as inevitable. It is what would occur if instinct and tradition are allowed to act uncontrolled.

Two countries are involved; these are called Jedesland and Andersland. Richardson quotes from a speech made by the defense minister of Jedesland:

> The intentions of our country are entirely pacific. We have given ample evidence of this in the treaties which we have recently concluded with our neighbors. Yet when we consider the state of unrest of the world at large and the menaces by which we are surrounded, we should be failing in our duty as a government if we did not take adequate steps to increase the defenses of our beloved land.

Hence an arms race.

To set up the model we need variables: dependent and independent. The independent variable is the time t; the unit of time need not be specified since, as you will see, there is some overall vagueness in the model. The dependent variables, which are not so easy to quantify, will represent the expenditures $x(t)$ and $y(t)$ on armaments of Jedesland and Andersland, respectively; these could also be interpreted in terms of actual armaments, military training, or some kind of "war potential." Now consider the factors that would cause x and y to change. For a start, let's return to that awful minister of defense of Jedesland; one of his concerns is the war preparedness of Andersland, or y, and the larger y becomes, the more he would like to arm his own country, Jedesland. His plan is to increase x according to

$$\frac{dx}{dt} = ay$$

for some positive constant a. Of course, the minister of defense of Andersland has similar ideals, and would like to have

$$\frac{dy}{dt} = bx$$

for positive b. If these equations described the model, we would be in real trouble. Differentiate the first equation, and use the second

$$\frac{d^2x}{dt^2} = a\frac{dy}{dt} = abx,$$

the solution of which involves exponentially growing armaments — and war!

To the rescue comes the finance minister of Jedesland. The larger x becomes, the less happy he is about the expense, so he introduces a curb, $-mx$, to its rate of growth, leading to

$$\frac{dx}{dt} = ay - mx,$$

with a corresponding equation for Andersland,

$$\frac{dy}{dt} = bx - ny.$$

m and n are positive constants. To complete the model Richardson introduces the concept of a state of "grievance" (or plain bloody-mindedness) of each country against the other, so that we have, eventually,

$$\frac{dx}{dt} = ay - mx + g, \tag{4.2.1}$$

and

$$\frac{dy}{dt} = bx - ny + h. \tag{4.2.2}$$

These are the equations of the model. Note that x and y must be nonnegative.

There are alternative interpretations of the terms of the equations. For example, the incentive to arm could depend on the imbalance of armaments so that $ay - mx = a\,(y - mx/a)$ would have a representing a rate of arming, with m/a a parameter describing the desired balance. ($m/a = 1$ would stand for parity.) Or the "grievance" terms might include covert activity, or even ceremonial expenses such as presidential guards or military bands. Or they could be negative, indicating goodwill rather than grievance. Further, the parameters might change with time; an election or change of administration or some international incident could change g or h abruptly. The consequences of a coup, with the assassination of a finance minister, might be serious. All these possibilities, and more, should be remembered when playing with the model and making interpretations.

The two equations can be solved completely, but we shall not do this here. But note that the solutions will involve exponential terms (although not, in this instance, trigonometric terms — do you see why?) A term e^{pt} with positive p will increase without bound and would lead to war! It would be satisfactory if p were negative, for then things might settle down for large values of the time t; we might even disarm.

A basic question to ask of this model is

"Is there an equilibrium?"

By "equilibrium" we mean a state of affairs in which everything remains constant. So the question can be rephrased as

"Is there a solution where nothing changes?"

Using the concepts of calculus, this can be rephrased as

"Is there a solution for which $\frac{dx}{dt}$ and $\frac{dy}{dt}$ are both zero?"

Now we can go further, using (4.2.1) and (4.2.2), and say

"Are there positive values of x and y for which

$$0 = ay - mx + g \quad \text{and} \quad 0 = bx - ny + h?"$$

In the x-y plane, this condition sets the equilibrium at the intersection of two lines L_1 and L_2:

$$\left.\begin{array}{ll} L_1: & 0 = ay - mx + g, \\ L_2: & 0 = bx - ny + h. \end{array}\right] \tag{4.2.3}$$

Provided that $D = nm - ab \neq 0$, these equations have the unique solution

$$x_e = (ah + ng)/D, \quad y_e = (bg + mh)/D. \tag{4.2.4}$$

Provided, further, that x_e and y_e are both positive, we have an equilibrium.

A second very important question to ask is

"If there is an equilibrium, is it stable?"

That is, if we start close to an equilibrium, will we forever remain close (stability), or will we drift further away (instability)? Discussion of stability is often not at all easy, and advanced theoretical mathematics can be involved; but the use of the computer can be very helpful.

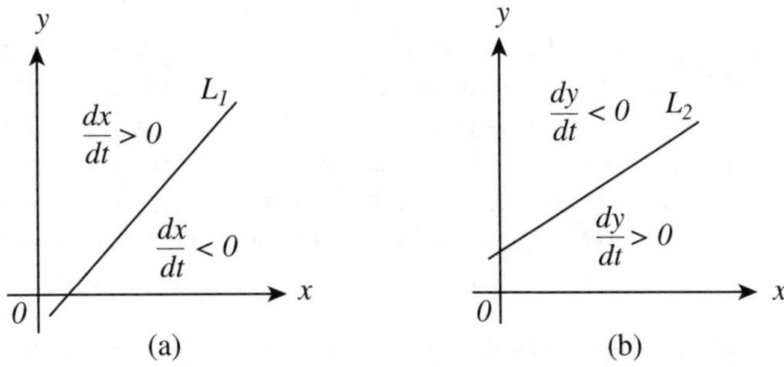

Figure 4.1: *The x-y phase-plane with lines L_1 and L_2.*

In discussing solutions of equations (4.2.1) and (4.2.2), you might assume that it would be best to show tables or diagrams of x and y as functions of the time. This might be so, but often it is more helpful to look at a "phase-plane" diagram in which one dependent variable is plotted against

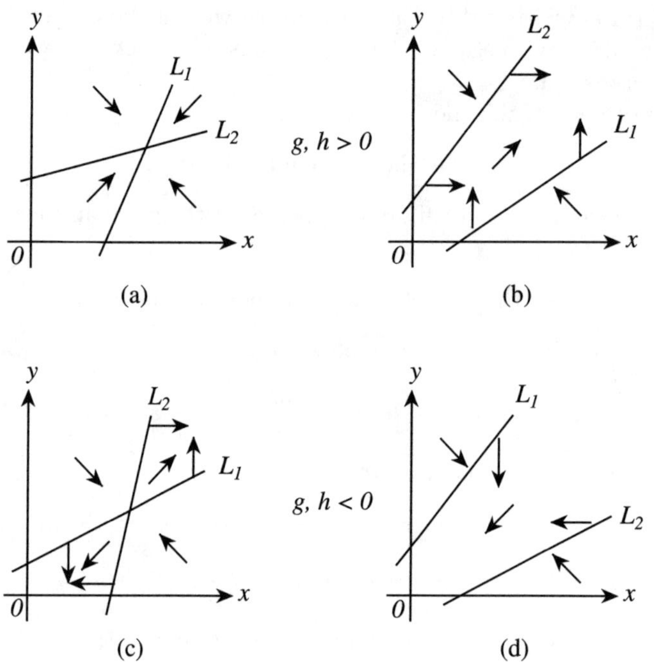

Figure 4.2: *The flow of solutions in the phase-plane.*

the other. Here this is the x-y plane. The straight lines L_1 and L_2 from equation (4.2.3) intersect at the equilibrium. Further, each of these lines divides the plane into regions where a derivative is positive or negative, as shown in figure 4.1

Figures 4.2(a) and (b) show situations for which g and h are both positive; in (a) there is an equilibrium; in (b) there is not. From the properties shown in figure 4.1, a few arrows have been sketched showing the directions of the "flow" of the solutions. These suggest a stable equilibrium in figure 4.2(a) and war in 4.2(b).

Next consider cases where g and h are both negative, so that there is a background of "goodwill." The two principal possibilities are shown in figures 4.2(c) and (d), where, again, some arrows have been sketched to show the flow of the solutions. In (d), where there is no equilibrium, we have total disarmament. The equilibrium of (c) is unstable: if we start close to it, we can end up with either disarmament or war.

Finally, equations (4.2.1) and (4.2.2) have been solved numerically, and solutions have been plotted in figure 4.3. In this case it is reassuring to see that the earlier qualitative predictions are confirmed. The lines L_1 and L_2 have been included for clarity. Note that, because of the overall vagueness of the model, the numerical values of the initial set of parameters do not mean very much; but **changes** in these values can be interpreted and linked with changes in the behavior of the model.

The following "assignments" are suggestions that are intended to show some ways in which a project can be discussed and expanded. See if you can think of some more.

1. Draw figures and discuss and interpret cases when g and h have opposite signs.

2. Discuss the cases when g and h are both zero.

3. Discuss all cases when the lines L_1 and L_2 are parallel.

4. Find numerical solutions and plot them for assignments 1 to 3.

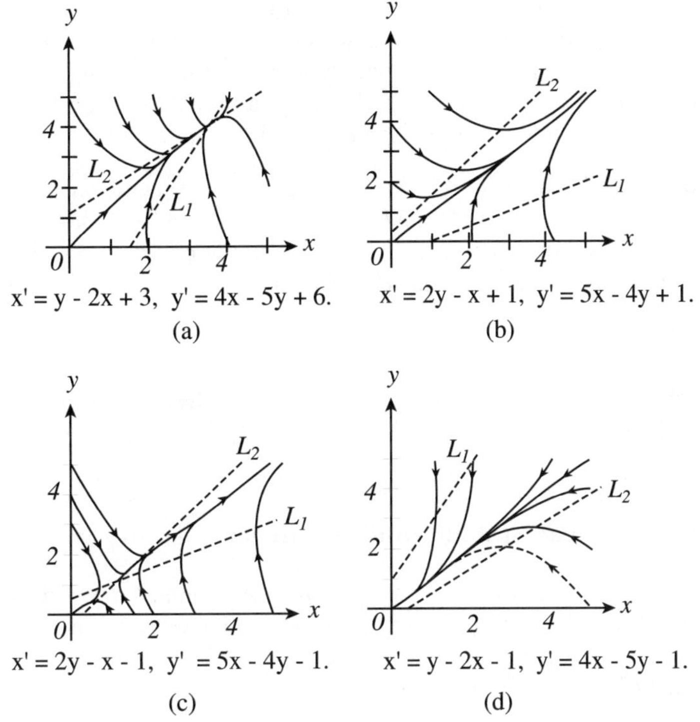

Figure 4.3: *Solutions calculated numerically.*

5. For several cases, plot x and y as functions of the time. What special information did you acquire?

6. Make a summary of *all* possible cases in terms of the properties of the parameters. See if you can then interpret these cases using physical interpretations of the parameters.

7. Solve the two equations of the model analytically. Confirm details of solutions and properties already found.

8. Divide one of the equations of the model into the other to eliminate the variable t and find an equation of the form $dy/dx = f(x, y)$. Look into the literature and see if you can find ways to solve this equation. Construct some direction field diagrams for the equation, and compare them with the sketches shown in this section.

9. Look up the discussions in the texts by Rapoport [81] and Braun[17], and see how the model has been applied in real cases.

10. Formulate the model for three countries, and discuss some special cases. Can you relate your model to actual nations today?

11. Suppose that x and y are separated into $x = x_1 + x_2$ and $y = y_1 + y_2$, where x_1 and y_1 stand for conventional weaponry and x_2 and y_2 for nuclear weaponry. Set up a model for this situation.

12. Instead of war, reformulate the model to describe the behavior of two neighbors who compete against each other for "status," buying cars, stereos, expensive vacations — and even computers.

13. Suppose the finance ministers become really tough, and the disincentive terms $-mx$ and $-ny$ become $-mx^2$ and $-ny^2$. The model is now nonlinear and much more complicated. But you can still discuss it in a qualitative way exactly as we did in the simple case. Look for possible equilibria and investigate their stability. When you think that you have a good feel for the system, perform some numerical integrations and fill in some details.

14. Consider parameters $m = n = g = h = b = 1$, but with a varying subject to periodic political pressure in such a way that $a = 1 + \sin t$. Notice that if a were suddenly to become constant, then the result could be disarmament or war, depending on when the change happened. Find out what can happen with this varying $a(t)$. Consider periodic variations in some other terms. (One at a time is best.)

15. Suppose that as arms expenditures mount, negotiations take place with intensity proportional to the product xy so that the term pxy is subtracted from each of the right-hand sides of equations (4.2.1) and (4.2.2). Discuss this case. Could it avert a war that would otherwise take place?

4.3 Linear Systems, Linear Stability and Nonlinear Stability

This project is intended to provide some essential background for the discussion and interpretation of *stability*, which will occur in many of the projects ahead. In many cases (although not all), solutions close to a position of equilibrium resemble those that occur in a linear system, so we shall start with a discussion of linear systems with two variables.

Consider the system

$$\frac{dx}{dt} = ax + by, \quad \frac{dy}{dt} = cx + dy. \tag{4.3.1}$$

If we differentiate the first equation, and then eliminate y and dy/dt, we find that

$$\frac{d^2x}{dt^2} - (a + d)\frac{dx}{dt} + (ad - bc)x = 0. \tag{4.3.2}$$

Now if we let $x = e^{rt}$ for constant r, we find that r must be a root of the *characteristic equation*

$$r^2 - (a + d)r + (ad - bc) = 0. \tag{4.3.3}$$

The origin, $(0, 0)$ is the equilibrium of the system (4.3.1), and the character of the motion near to the origin depends on the nature of the roots of (4.3.3). The main possibilities are illustrated by actual computations plotted in figure 4.4.

In figure 4.4(a) the equations are

$$\frac{dx}{dt} = 2x + y, \quad \frac{dy}{dt} = x + 2y, \quad \text{with} \quad r = 1, 3. \tag{4.3.4}$$

Each solution in the figure has a different initial condition. Since both roots for r are real and positive, all motion is away from the equilibrium. We have an *unstable node.*

In figure 4.4(b) the equations are

$$\frac{dx}{dt} = -4x + y, \quad \frac{dy}{dt} = x - 2y, \quad \text{with} \quad r = -3 \pm \sqrt{2}. \tag{4.3.5}$$

Both roots are real and negative, and all motion approaches the equilibrium. We have a *stable node.*

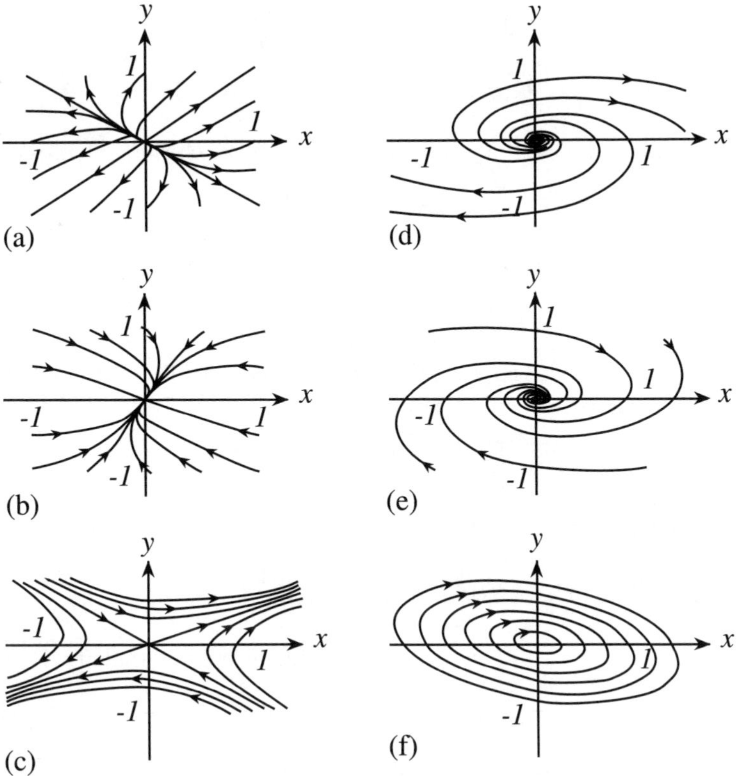

Figure 4.4: *Possible motion close to a linear equilibrium.*

In figure 4.4(c) the equations are

$$\frac{dx}{dt} = x + 4y, \quad \frac{dy}{dt} = 2x - y, \quad \text{with} \quad r = 3, -3. \tag{4.3.6}$$

Both roots are real, but one is positive and one, negative. We then have a *saddle point* which is *unstable*.

In figure 4.4(d) the equations are

$$\frac{dx}{dt} = x + 4y, \quad \frac{dy}{dt} = -2x + y, \quad \text{with} \quad r = 1 \pm i\sqrt{8}. \tag{4.3.7}$$

The roots are complex, with positive real part, and we have *unstable spirals*.

In figure 4.4(e) the equations are

$$\frac{dx}{dt} = -x + 4y, \quad \frac{dy}{dt} = -2x - y, \quad \text{with} \quad r = -1 \pm i\sqrt{8}. \tag{4.3.8}$$

The roots are complex, with negative real part, and we have *stable spirals*.

Finally, in figure 4.4(f) the equations are

$$\frac{dx}{dt} = x + 4y, \quad \frac{dy}{dt} = -2x - y, \quad \text{with} \quad r = \pm i\sqrt{7}. \tag{4.3.9}$$

The roots are purely imaginary, and all solutions are ellipses with centers at the equilibrium. In this case the equilibrium is called a *center* and is *stable*.

In cases 4.4(b) and (e) the stability is called *asymptotic*.

Next, consider two nonlinear equations

$$\frac{dX}{dt} = F(X,Y), \quad \frac{dY}{dt} = G(X,Y). \tag{4.3.10}$$

Suppose that there is an equilibrium at the point $X = A$, $Y = B$; then we must have

$$F(A,B) = G(A,B) = 0. \tag{4.3.11}$$

To investigate what happens *close* to this equilibrium, let

$$X = A + x, \quad Y = B + y, \tag{4.3.12}$$

where x and y are considered small enough, during the investigation, for their squares and products to be neglected. Next, substitute (4.3.12) into (4.3.10), and expand each right-hand side in a Taylor series in powers of x and y. For instance,

$$\begin{aligned}\frac{d}{dt}(A+x) &= F(A+x, B+y) \\ &= F(A,B) + F_X(A,B)x + F_Y(A,B)y + \frac{1}{2}\left(F_{XX}x^2 + 2F_{XY}xy + F_{YY}y^2\right) + \cdots.\end{aligned}$$

The leading term is zero, by (4.3.11). Neglecting nonlinear terms, we are left with the system (4.3.1), where

$$a = F_X(A,B), \; b = F_Y(A,B), \; c = G_X(A,B), \; d = G_Y(A,B). \tag{4.3.13}$$

It turns out that the stability characteristics of the nonlinear system and the linearized system are the same, with the possible exception of case 4.4(f), where the linear system has a center. You will see these characteristics repeatedly when following solutions that pass close to equilibria.

Equilibria of systems having more than two equations can be investigated in the same way, although clearly the geometrical classification is no longer simple.

Here are some assignments to help you gain experience with these ideas:

1. Choosing your own numerical values, confirm the qualitative details of the six cases presented in figure 4.4.

2. If $ad - bc = 0$, there is a *line of equilibria* through the origin. Verify this, and calculate some solutions.

3. What happens when the characteristic equation (4.3.3) has equal roots?

4. Here is an example where a nonlinear system has an unstable equilibrium at a point where the linearized equations predict stability.

$$\left.\begin{aligned}\frac{dX}{dt} &= Y + \alpha X(X^2+Y^2)^{1/2}, \\ \frac{dY}{dt} &= -X + \alpha Y(X^2+Y^2)^{1/2}, \; \alpha > 0.\end{aligned}\right] \tag{4.3.14}$$

The origin is an equilibrium, and, close to it, the linearized equations are

$$\frac{dx}{dt} = y, \quad \frac{dy}{dt} = -x,$$

which describe a center that is stable. To see that the origin is actually an unstable equilibrium, let

$$R^2 = X^2 + Y^2,$$

so that

$$R\frac{dR}{dt} = X\frac{dX}{dt} + Y\frac{dY}{dt} = \alpha R^3.$$

Then

$$\frac{dR}{dt} = \alpha R^2,$$

so that for α positive, every solution recedes away from the origin, regardless of how close to the origin it may start. Have a look at some actual solutions. (Note that for α negative, the origin is asymptotically stable.)

5. The following system is an example of the predator-prey model of Volterra.

$$\left.\begin{aligned} \frac{dx}{dt} &= x - xy, \\ \frac{dy}{dt} &= -y + xy. \end{aligned}\right] \tag{4.3.15}$$

Show that there are equilibria at $(0, 0)$ and $(1, 1)$. Investigate their stability using a linear analysis, and then by calculating solutions.

6. Into the system (4.3.15) introduce the (apparently) small change

$$\left.\begin{aligned} \frac{dx}{dt} &= x - 0.1x^2 - xy, \\ \frac{dy}{dt} &= -y + xy. \end{aligned}\right] \tag{4.3.16}$$

There is now an additional equilibrium. Repeat the procedures of the preceding assignment.

7. Investigate the linear and nonlinear stability of the origin (in 4-space) of the system:

$$\left.\begin{aligned} \frac{dx_1}{dt} &= -y_1 + x_2 y_1 + x_1 y_2, \\ \frac{dx_2}{dt} &= 2y_2 + x_1 y_1, \\ \frac{dy_1}{dt} &= x_1 + x_1 x_2 - y_1 y_2, \\ \frac{dy_2}{dt} &= -2x_2 + \frac{1}{2}\left(x_1^2 + y_1^2\right). \end{aligned}\right] \tag{4.3.17}$$

Chapter 5

An Introduction to Chaotic Systems

5.1 Introduction

The idea that dynamical systems might behave in what we now call a "chaotic" manner was introduced by Henri Poincaré [77] a century ago. With amazing genius and vision he described many properties of chaotic systems and invented methods by which they might be investigated. Later C.L.Siegel showed that among dynamical systems chaotic behavior should be the norm rather than the exception. Systematic investigation of such systems became possible with the use of the computer. A pioneering paper in this area was published by Hénon and Heiles [53] in 1964, where Poincaré's method was carried out numerically. Initially, the notion of chaos was not easily accepted. Thirty years ago I presented some work on the subject at a meeting; at the end of the talk several members of the audience kindly explained to me why I had to be wrong. But in the past twenty years the subject has suddenly spread to many areas of the mathematical, physical and biological sciences; chaotic behavior is now recognized as normal, not strange.

What is chaos? There is no perfect definition. A key *quality* of a chaotic system is unpredictability. We may be unable to forecast what the system will do next. If we set it in action in two slightly different ways, then we may observe wildly divergent behavior. Yet, in the midst of chaos there may be, as you will see, some remarkably simple structure. If you are approaching chaos for the first time, I recommend that you think of it as something to be discovered, experienced and enjoyed. The computer is the perfect tool for doing this.

Many of the models in this book can display chaotic behavior; the purpose of this chapter is to provide sufficient background and techniques so that you can recognize and play with these models for what they are. To become literate in the area, you should consult some of the books mentioned in this chapter. These, in turn, will suggest further references. There are many readable and enjoyable books available. There are also many ways in which a novice with a computer can derive and confirm results that not long ago would have been almost unthinkable.

The chapter is divided into four parts. The first deals with chaotic dynamical systems of the type considered by Poincaré. Examples of these in this text include several pendulum models such as the double pendulum, or the spring pendulum. Most problems in orbital dynamics are chaotic, and can respond to the type of treatment described in this section.

The equations for the type of system considered by Poincaré are not representative of equations for most physical models; they do not allow, for instance, for frictional, or dissipative forces. In 1963 E.N.Lorenz [66] presented an investigation of three nonlinear coupled differential equations. These equations, now known as the "Lorenz equations," showed chaotic behavior that could be investigated using a new range of numerical and mathematical methods (many invented by Lorenz). Many physical systems can be modeled by equations of this type, such as the model for the dynamo with chaotic reversal of a magnetic field. The second section deals with properties of the Lorenz equations and some of the methods for exploring them.

Many physical systems include terms that vary periodically. A population model may have cyclical variation in the birthrate, or a model for the spread of disease may have cyclical change in the degree of infectiousness of the disease. One of the most basic physical models is that of the simple pendulum; when this moves subject to a periodic forcing term, then its motion can become chaotic. The third section is concerned with this topic. The methods described can be used in several projects, such as the chaotic toppling of Hyperion, one of the satellites of Saturn.

Hénon and Heiles [53] showed that a system of difference equations could exhibit chaotic properties very similar to those of dynamical systems. The advantage of difference equations over differential equations is that numerical results can be found very easily and very fast. The final section of this chapter is concerned with chaotic difference equations. These are a lot of fun in their own right.

5.2 Chaos in Dynamical Systems 

In courses on mechanics, we deal initially with models such as the motion of a projectile with no resistance, or a simple pendulum with oscillations of small amplitude. These problems can easily be solved completely, by formula. Many more problems are known that can be solved completely, but with some difficulty. A classic text by Whittaker [107] devotes separate chapters to the "solvable problems" of dynamics. But most models cannot be completely solved. An example is the problem of describing the motion of the Moon, as it is attracted by the Earth and the Sun. This was first attempted by Newton, and then by many other mathematicians. It is an example of what has come to be called a "chaotic" dynamical system. Such systems are difficult, not because we are not yet smart enough to solve them, but because, from their nature, they defy complete solution.

One hundred years ago, Henri Poincaré [77] realized that dynamical systems could exhibit what we now call chaotic behavior. He described some properties of these systems, and also devised methods to discuss them. Later it was proved that, in a general sense, "most" dynamical systems are chaotic. With the advent of the computer, it was found that Poincaré's method provided a simple and practical way to investigate models and to predict their theoretical properties. We shall use this method, called the method of *Poincaré maps*, in this section.

One of the earliest papers to apply the use of computers to this method was published by Hénon and Heiles [53] in 1964. This considers a dynamical system that has the advantage of simplicity, but the disadvantage that it cannot be readily interpreted in terms of a system or machine "doing something." (The system arose, in the first place, in connection with the dynamics of a rotating galaxy of stars.) We shall use this model in order to introduce several concepts involved in playing with dynamical systems, and to describe and implement the method of Poincaré maps.

First, let's look at a system of equations that can be completely solved:

$$\frac{d^2x}{dt^2} = -x, \tag{5.2.1}$$

$$\frac{d^2y}{dt^2} = -y. \tag{5.2.2}$$

Since we have two uncoupled harmonic oscillators, the solution is easy. Suppose we multiply the equation (5.2.1) by $\dfrac{dx}{dt}$ and equation (5.2.2) by $\dfrac{dy}{dt}$ and add; then we obtain

$$\frac{d^2x}{dt^2}\frac{dx}{dt} + \frac{d^2y}{dt^2}\frac{dy}{dt} = -x\frac{dx}{dt} - y\frac{dy}{dt}$$

from which we find, on integration,

$$\frac{1}{2}\left(\left(\frac{dx}{dt}\right)^2 + \left(\frac{dy}{dt}\right)^2\right) = -\frac{1}{2}\left(x^2 + y^2\right) + A. \tag{5.2.3}$$

A is an arbitrary constant of integration. Similarly, if we multiply the equation (5.2.1) by y and equation (5.2.2) by x and subtract, then we obtain, on integration

$$\frac{dx}{dt}y - \frac{dy}{dt}x = B. \tag{5.2.4}$$

The expressions

$$\frac{1}{2}\left(\left(\frac{dx}{dt}\right)^2 + \left(\frac{dy}{dt}\right)^2\right) + \frac{1}{2}\left(x^2 + y^2\right) \quad \text{and} \quad \frac{dx}{dt}y - \frac{dy}{dt}x$$

are called *integrals* of the system. These are expressions that will not vary along any solution. The system just discussed is said to have *two degrees of freedom.* If two independent integrals can be found for such a system, then it will be non-chaotic. The solution of a non-chaotic system having two degrees of freedom may be expected (although not invariably) to involve two separate frequencies of oscillation. A system with two degrees of freedom that has at least one integral of the type (5.2.3) is called *conservative.*

Now let's turn to the system investigated by Hénon and Heiles:

$$\left.\begin{aligned} \frac{d^2x}{dt^2} &= -x - 2xy, \\ \frac{d^2y}{dt^2} &= -y - x^2 + y^2. \end{aligned}\right] \tag{5.2.5}$$

Multiplying the first of (5.2.5) by $\frac{dx}{dt}$ and the second of (5.2.5) by $\frac{dy}{dt}$ and adding, we obtain, in the same way as before,

$$\frac{1}{2}\left(\left(\frac{dx}{dt}\right)^2 + \left(\frac{dy}{dt}\right)^2 + x^2 + y^2\right) + x^2y - \frac{1}{3}y^3 = h, \tag{5.2.6}$$

a constant. No other integral can be found.

Such a system can be investigated using numerical integration. The notation can be changed to

$$y_1 = x,\ y_2 = \frac{dx}{dt},\ y_3 = y,\ y_4 = \frac{dy}{dt}. \tag{5.2.7}$$

Then the system (5.2.5) can be written as

$$\left.\begin{aligned} \frac{dy_1}{dt} &= y_2, \\ \frac{dy_2}{dt} &= -y_1 - 2y_1y_3, \\ \frac{dy_3}{dt} &= y_4, \\ \frac{dy_4}{dt} &= -y_3 - y_1^2 + y_3^2. \end{aligned}\right] \tag{5.2.8}$$

We have four dependent variables. Obviously, we cannot visualize them all as they change. Poincaré suggested the following method that can be used in any conservative dynamical system having two degrees of freedom.

Suppose that we specify a numerical value for the quantity h in equation (5.2.6), and stick to that value for a set of computer runs. We can then choose any three from y_1, y_2, y_3, and y_4 and calculate the fourth using equation (5.2.6). Let's pick y_1, y_3, and y_4. (In calculating y_2 from (5.2.6),

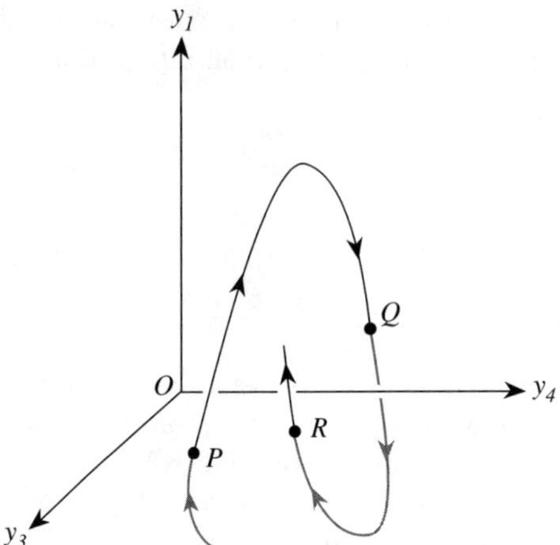

Figure 5.1: *Points where the solution crosses the plane* $y_1 = 0$.

choose the positive square root.) Now we follow a solution in the three-dimensional space of these three coordinates. Poincaré further proposed that a surface be defined in this space, and that points be recorded where the solution crosses this surface. The properties of this set of points can provide a lot of information about the dynamical system.

Let's be more specific. Suppose the surface is the plane $y_1 = 0$; then we are looking at crossing points in the y_3-y_4 plane. Let a solution cross this plane at the point P, where y_1 is increasing, or $y_1' = y_2 > 0$. The next crossing is at Q, where $y_1' = y_2 < 0$. The next crossing, at which y_1 is increasing, is at R. See figure 5.1.

R is said to be the Poincaré map of P.

Clearly, we will have a continuing sequence of points as R is mapped into T, and so on.

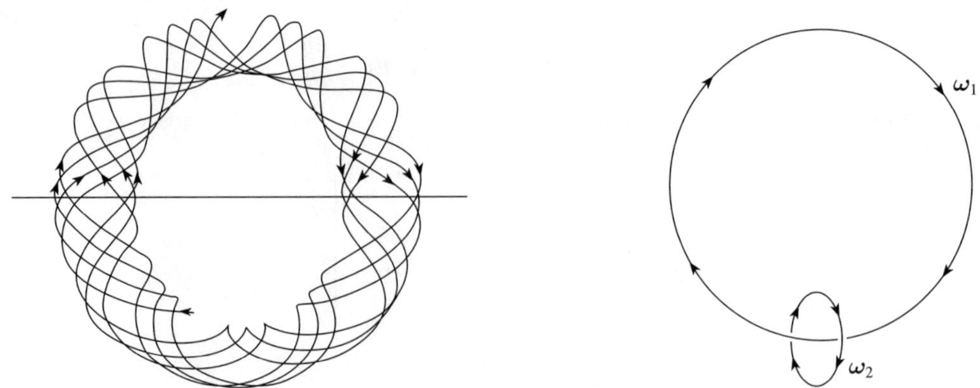

Figure 5.2: *A path winding around a torus.*

To interpret what might happen, let's first consider non-chaotic motion. If the solution is subject to two frequencies, ω_1 and ω_2, then expressions for y_1, y_3 and y_4 will contain sines and cosines of $\omega_1 t$, $\omega_2 t$ and multiples of these; so these expressions will define parametric equations to a surface, and this surface will cross the plane $y_1 = 0$ in a curve. We would not expect this curve to cross itself since conditions at a crossing point would violate the requirement of uniqueness. This simplest surface is

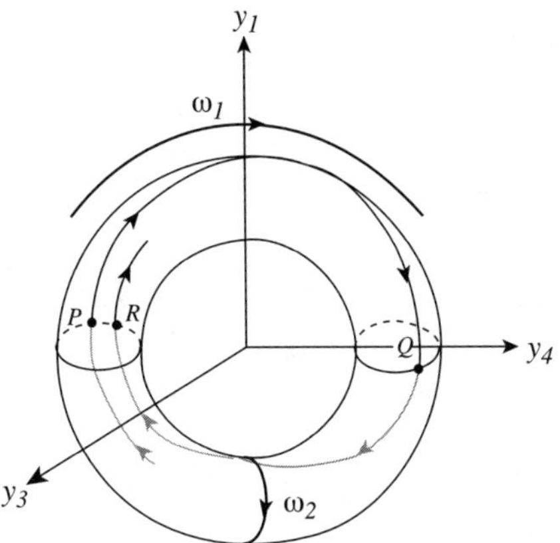

Figure 5.3: *Successive crossings when the solution lies on a torus.*

a torus. Figure 5.2 shows a path winding around a torus. Note the role of the two frequencies.

Figure 5.3 illustrates the mapping shown in figure 5.1, but now with the solution in the space of y_1, y_3 and y_4 lying on a torus.

The two modes in which the winding can take place are described as the angular rates ω_1 and ω_2, as shown in the figure. All crossing points of the plane $y_1 = 0$ will lie on the two closed curves that are sections of the torus. These are called *invariant curves* since every point on a curve is mapped onto another point on the same curve. The curves are said to be mapped onto themselves. It is possible that, starting from a point P, the mapped points eventually end up again at P. This will happen if the angular rates, ω_1 and ω_2, are rationally related. Then we will have a *periodic* solution. Otherwise, we have a *quasi-periodic* solution.

A feature of most chaotic systems is that they can exhibit non-chaotic behavior; but, as a parameter is changed, this disintegrates, and chaos takes over. The dynamical system describing the Sun and the planets is chaotic; but, fortunately, the configuration that exists today behaves in a non-chaotic way. (But it has been shown that the motion of some asteroids is chaotic, and so is the rotation of Hyperion, a satellite of Saturn.)

In our case the parameter to be changed is h, in equation (5.2.6). If h is small enough, then the mapped points in the y_1-plane all appear to lie on closed curves, indicating non-chaotic motion. As h is increased, these curves start to break up, and chaos takes over.

The range of values of h that can be used is limited. In the notation of (5.2.7), and setting $y_1 = 0$, write equation (5.2.6) as

$$y_2^2 = 2h - y_4^2 - y_3^2 + \frac{2}{3}y_3^3. \tag{5.2.9}$$

Since the right-hand side must be nonnegative, we have the inequality

$$2h \geq y_4^2 + y_3^2 - \frac{2}{3}y_3^3. \tag{5.2.10}$$

The largest possible value of y_4 will occur when $y_3 = 0$, so $y_4 \leq \sqrt{2h}$, and h must be positive. The largest value of y_3 will occur when $y_4 = 0$. Then we must have

$$6h \geq 3y_3^2 - 2y_3^3. \tag{5.2.11}$$

At a limit for the inequality, $6h = 3y_3^2 - 2y_3^3$. Now the function on the right has a local minimum value, 0, at $y_3 = 0$ and a local maximum, 1, at $y_3 = 1$. So if $0 < h < 1/6$, the equations

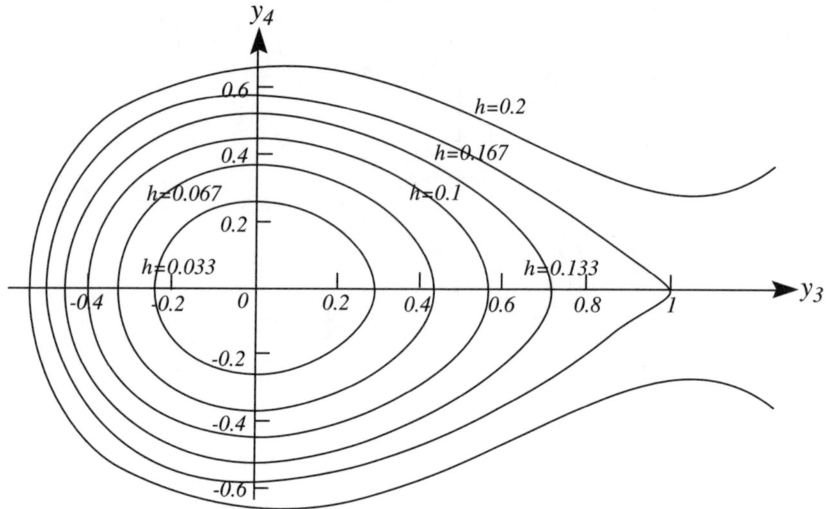

Figure 5.4: *Boundaries for permitted regions for various values of h.*

will have three solutions, and there will be an interval containing the origin where the inequality (5.2.11) will hold. In this case, there will be a closed region in the $y_3 - y_4$ plane in which all the mappings must lie. Some boundaries are shown in figure 5.4. If $h > 1/6$ then the mappings are not confined to a closed region. (An integral that results in restricted regions in which solutions may appear is called an *isolating integral.*)

Now for some technical details needed for the calculations. We start off by choosing a value for h between 0 and 1/6. Then we need to enter initial values for y_1, y_3 and y_4, where, since it is reasonable to start at a crossing point, we take $y_1 = 0$. Using these, y_2 is calculated using (5.2.9). Since this involves taking a square root, precautions are needed. For instance, a procedure `Data` might go as follows:

```
y(1) = 0
Repeat
    Enter values for y(3) and y(4)
    Test = 2*h - y(3)*y(3) - y(4)*y(4) + 2*y(3)*y(3)*y(3)/3
    If Test > 0 Then y(2) = Sqrt(Test)
Until Test > 0
Y1Sign = 1
```

Let the variable `Y1Sign` take values `Y1Sign = 1` if $y_1 > 0$ and `Y1Sign = -1` if $y_1 < 0$. It has been initialized to be $+1$ above since the initial rate of change of y_1 is positive.

The calculation proceeds with successive integration steps. Immediately after each step, find the product `y[1]*Y1Sign`. If this is negative, then you have just crossed the plane $y_1 = 0$, and you must find the value of x such that $y_1 = 0$. So in the main program we might have the lines:

```
Step(...)
If y(1)*Y1Sign < 0 Then FindPoincareCrossing
```

This is most simply coded using Newton's method. Recall that to solve the equation

$$f(x) = 0$$

using Newton's method, we generate the sequence

$$x_{n+1} = x_n - \frac{f(x_n)}{f'(x_n)}, \quad x = 0, 1, 2...,$$

where x_0 is the initial estimate. With x as the independent variable in the integration, the quantity $x_{n+1} - x_n$ is the stepsize. While running Newton's method, this must replace the stepsize calculated by the integration algorithm by one calculated by Newton's method. In our case, $f(x) =$ `y(1)` and $f'(x) =$ `y(2)`. So the stepsize for an iteration is `-y(1)/y(2)`. The iteration continues until $|y_1|$ is sufficiently small. (Just how small, is your decision.) It is a good idea to include a counter, so that no more than, say, 5 iterations are attempted. If Newton's method fails, then ignore the particular crossing and go on to the next. So the procedure `FindPoincareCrossing` might contain the lines:

```
SaveStepSize = StepSize
Count = 0
Repeat
    Count = Count + 1
    StepSize :  - y(1)/y(2)
    Step(...)
Until (Abs(y(1)) < Eps) Or (Count = 5)
If Count < 5 Then store (y(3), y(4))
End
StepSize = SaveStepSize
Y1Sign=-Y1Sign
```

(`Eps` is a small number of your choice; something of the order of `0.0001` will probably suffice. Newton's method will end up with a very small and perhaps negative stepsize; so the stepsize used **before** using the method should be saved for use after the method is finished.) Mapped points `(y(3), y(4))` might be plotted immediately, or stored in a file for later processing.

We should mention also a method suggested by Hénon. This is ingenious, and slightly faster if very many crossing points are to be found, but involves a lot more coding than the method just suggested. The idea is to change the system of equations so that the coordinate that is to be driven to zero is made into the independent variable. If we want $y_1 = 0$, then the system is solved, as before, until y_1 changes sign. Then the following system of equations is run:

$$\left.\begin{aligned} \frac{dt}{dy_1} &= \frac{1}{y_2}, \\ \frac{dy_2}{dy_1} &= -\frac{y_1 + 2y_1y_3}{y_2}, \\ \frac{dy_3}{dy_1} &= \frac{y_4}{y_2}, \\ \frac{dy_4}{dy_1} &= -\frac{y_3 + y_1^2 - y_3^2}{y_2}. \end{aligned}\right] \tag{5.2.12}$$

The suggested stepsize for the step to find the location where $y_1 = 0$ is the negative of the value of y_1 just after its sign has changed. This will almost certainly be a "good" stepsize (but allowance must be made for the possibility that it is not), so we can expect that only one step will be needed to reach the crossing point, as opposed to two or three when Newton's method is used.

The time for any particular run will depend entirely on the nature of the output. Sometimes the nature of the solution will be obvious very quickly, and at other times you will need to follow very many points. Figures 5.5 and 5.6 show Poincaré maps for two different values of h. The axes are y

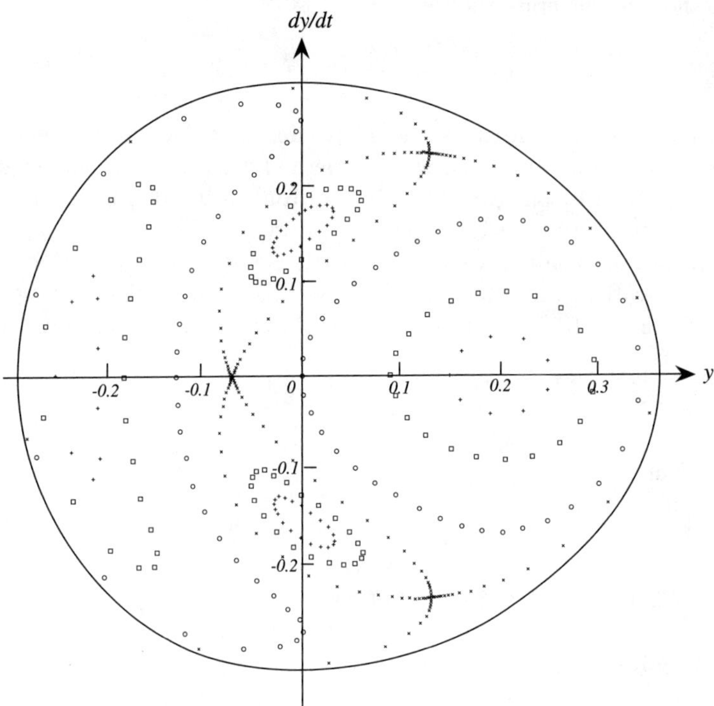

Figure 5.5: *Poincaré maps for* $h = 0.05$.

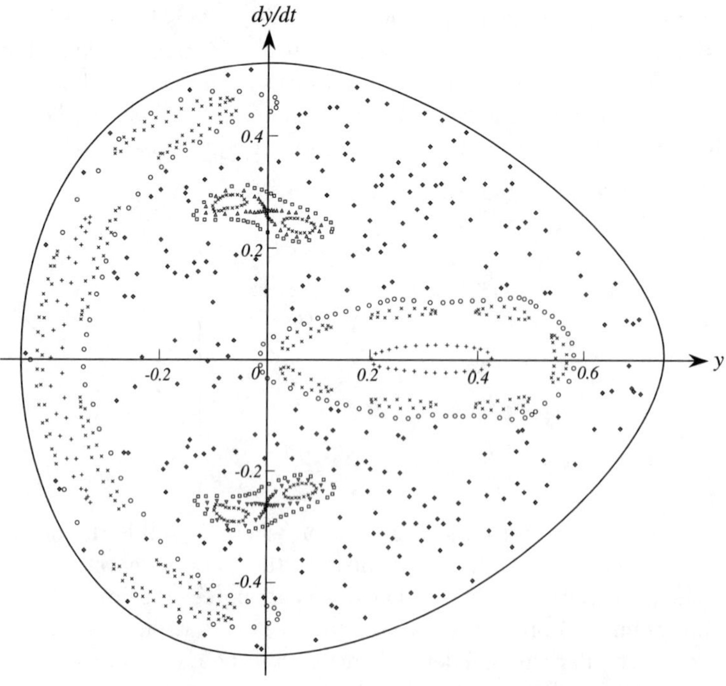

Figure 5.6: *Poincaré maps for* $h = 0.14$.

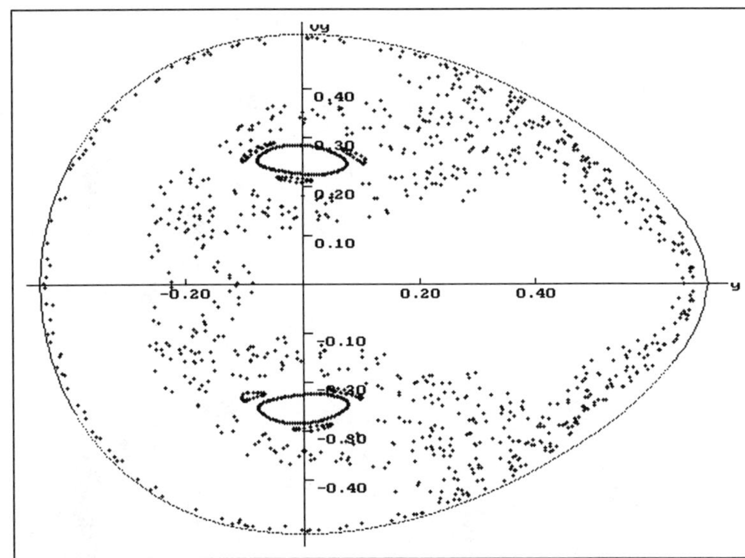

Figure 5.7: *Poincaré maps for $h = 0.13$. Points for three sets of initial conditions are shown. (a) $y = 0$, $dy/dt = 0.225$ leads to points on two invariant curves, (b) $y = 0$, $dy/dt = 0.215$ leads to three "islands" around the invariant curves of case (a). (c) $y = 0$, $dy/dt = 0.180$ leads to chaos.*

and dy/dt, or, in the notation used above, y_3 and y_4. For $h = 0.05$ no sign of chaos is visible. Six different starting conditions were used, and the organization of the invariant curves is clear. With $h = 0.14$, much of this organization has been destroyed. Six different starting conditions were used to generate the points showing some surviving structure; just one further start was used to generate the remaining, chaotic points. There is a nice example of a bifurcation in the structure along the y_4 axis.

Figure 5.7 has $h = 0.13$. Points for three sets of initial conditions are shown. (a) $y = 0$, $dy/dt = 0.225$ leads to points on two invariant curves, which are sections of a torus in the y-dy/dt-x space. (b) $y = 0$, $dy/dt = 0.215$ leads to three "islands" around the invariant curves of case (a). (c) $y = 0$, $dy/dt = 0.180$ leads to chaos. Figure 5.8, parts (a), (b) and (c), shows projections of the three-dimensional motion in the y-dy/dt-x space. Each projection is viewed from the same angle. In 5.8(a) the structure of the torus is clearly seen. In 5.8(b) a "tube" winds three times around the torus of part (a). 5.8(c) lacks any structure and is clearly chaotic.

Let's summarize Poincaré's method.

1. We have a system of four equations

$$y_i' = f_i(y_1, y_2, y_3, y_4), \quad i = 1, 2, 3, 4. \tag{5.2.13}$$

2. These equations have the integral

$$F(y_1, y_2, y_3, y_4) = h. \tag{5.2.14}$$

3. Select three variables out of y_1, y_2, y_3, y_4. For instance, y_1, y_3 and y_4.
4. Define a plane in the space of those three variables. For instance, $y_1 = 0$.
5. Select a numerical value for the parameter h.
6. Select initial conditions for the three chosen variables. (Pick this initial point to lie in the selected plane: so here, initially $y_1 = 0$.) Solve equation (5.2.14) for the fourth.

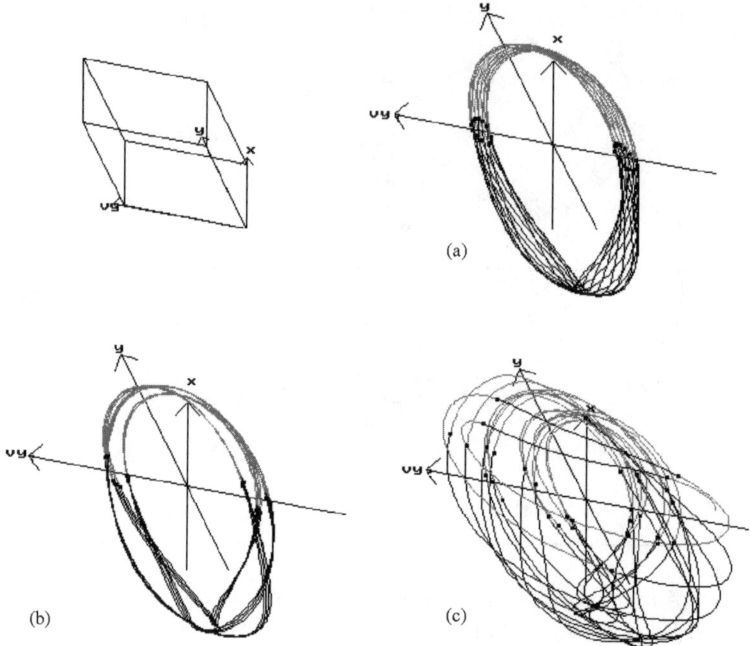

Figure 5.8: *Motion is followed as a curve in the three-dimensional space y-dy/dt-x; successive Poincaré maps are given by points where this curve crosses the $y = 0$ plane. Projections of this three-dimensional curve are shown for each of the three cases of figure 5.7. Each projection is viewed from the same angle, illustrated by the appearance of the parallelepiped, with origin at the lower right. In (a) the structure of the torus is clearly seen. In (b) a "tube" winds three times around the torus of part (a); (c) lacks any structure and is clearly chaotic.*

7. Integrate the equations, finding all points where the solution crosses the selected plane. These will fall into two categories, depending on the direction of the crossing. Record and plot the points.
8. Go back to step 6, changing initial conditions until you have a satisfactory picture describing the behavior of the system for the particular value of h.
9. Go back to step 5 and change h.

Project: Calculate Poincaré maps.

This project is open-ended in that you should follow the passage to chaos using several different values of h. In addition to looking at the complete region of possible motion, as shown in the figures, you will find it interesting to select smaller regions, and to look for more detail.

5.3 The Lorenz Equations 

The Lorenz equations are

$$\left.\begin{aligned} \frac{dx}{dt} &= -\sigma x + \sigma y, \\ \frac{dy}{dt} &= -xz + rx - y, \\ \frac{dz}{dt} &= xy - bz. \end{aligned}\right] \tag{5.3.1}$$

Historically, they arose from a representation of a layer in the Earth's atmosphere, heated from below by the ground that has absorbed sunlight, and cooled from above, as it loses heat into space. σ, r, and b are positive parameters. These innocent-looking equations were first investigated by E.N.Lorenz [66] in 1963; he found that they could pack a considerable chaotic punch. Today there is an enormous realm of research associated with them. Similar systems of three or more nonlinear equations are common; several appear later in this text. So you should be prepared for some quite peculiar phenomena.

Among references to these equations, I can recommend especially those of C.Sparrow [91] and S.H.Strogatz [93]. The former deals entirely with the Lorenz equations. The latter is an introductory textbook dealing with many aspects of chaotic systems; it is full of ideas, illustrations and exercises for investigating such systems. (These references describe an alternative model for the equations involving a waterwheel rotating in a vertical plane with leaky cups attached to the rim, and water falling from above. If you are practically inclined, you may wish to see whether using such an apparatus can rival computation.)

First, some general properties of the equations. Suppose that we have a volume, $V(0)$, in the x-y-z space. Suppose that a set of initial conditions, at time $t = 0$, consists of all points in $V(0)$. At a later time, t, the points will again fill a volume $V(t)$. It can be shown (see [93], p. 312) that

$$V(t) = V(0)e^{-(\sigma+1+b)t}. \tag{5.3.2}$$

So a large volume of initial conditions will shrink to a set with zero volume. This does not mean that they all converge at a point; what mostly happens is that the final sets form beautiful filigree patterns in space. Playing with these is a rewarding exercise in itself.

Given values of σ, b and r, we can expect that all solutions will end up with the same final set: this is an *attractor*. This produces the wonderful result that, in general, the method of integration need not be tremendously accurate for the final attractor to be found. In some work the initial *transient* motion should be ignored. How long may this last? You must be the judge.

To solve for equilibria, or "fixed points," we have

$$\left.\begin{array}{rcl} 0 &=& -\sigma x + \sigma y, \\ 0 &=& -xz + rx - y, \\ 0 &=& xy - bz. \end{array}\right] \tag{5.3.3}$$

Then

$$\left.\begin{array}{rrcl} & y &=& x, \\ \text{so} & 0 &=& x(r-1-z), \\ \text{and} & x^2 &=& bz. \end{array}\right] \tag{5.3.4}$$

So the origin is an equilibrium. Otherwise, provided that $r > 1$, we have two equilibria at points labeled C^+ and C^-, where

$$x = \pm\sqrt{b(r-1)},\ y = \pm\sqrt{b(r-1)},\ z = r-1. \tag{5.3.5}$$

For $r < 1$ the origin is a stable equilibrium, and all solutions end up there: not very exciting. For $r > 1$ the origin becomes unstable. At first, C^+ and C^- are stable and if $(\sigma - b - 1) < 0$, they remain stable. Otherwise they are stable in the range

$$1 < r < \frac{\sigma(\sigma + b + 3)}{(\sigma - b - 1)} = r_H. \tag{5.3.6}$$

For higher r all equilibria are unstable.

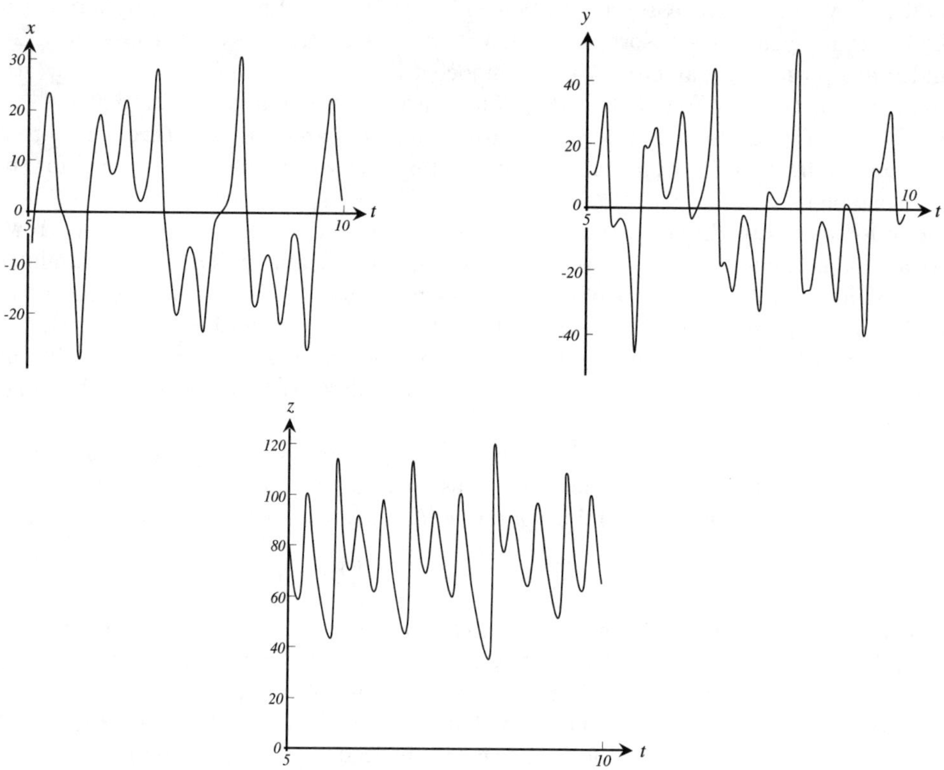

Figure 5.9: *Plots of coordinates versus the time.* $\sigma = 10$, $b = 8/3$ *and* $r = 80$, *for* $5 \leq t \leq 10$.

Lorenz chose the numerical values $\sigma = 10$ and $b = 8/3$. Then $r_H = 470/19 \approx 24.74$. His initial experiments used $r = 28$; since then an immense volume of work has been done keeping the same values for σ and b, but varying r. I suggest that you do the same. A survey of some results will follow. Many of these were found numerically, and all can be confirmed using numerical experiments. These are presented here in an oversimplified way to facilitate experimentation.

In playing with the model, you can plot the three coordinates as functions of the time, or you can view projections of the three-dimensional motion in the coordinate planes by plotting y versus x, z versus y or z versus x. It is also interesting to view the motion from an arbitrary direction to get better ideas about the shapes of the filigree patterns. These shapes can also be explored by plotting points of intersection with various planes. Figures 5.9 and 5.10 show various ways of graphing a single solution. Some other methods of investigation will be mentioned as the survey proceeds.

1. $0 < r < 1$. All solutions end up at the origin.

2. $1 < r < r_H \approx 24.74$. C^+ and C^- are stable. Three categories of motion may occur; these depend on two further values of r, $r_1 = 13.926$ and $r_2 = 24.06$.

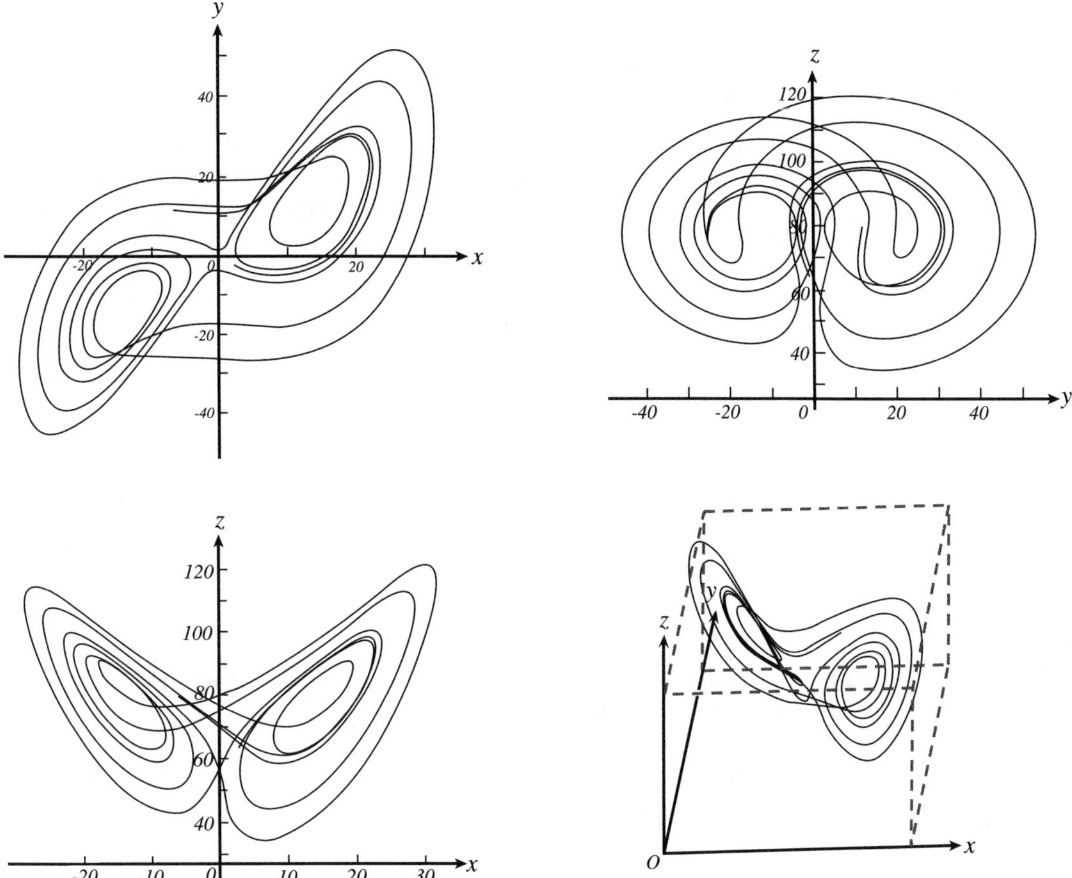

Figure 5.10: *Projections of the same solution as that of the preceding figure.*

- $1 < r < r_1$. Solutions end up at C^+ or C^-. There are two distinct regions such that initial conditions in one will end at C^+ and those in the other will end at C^-.
- $r_1 < r < r_2$. Solutions will still end up (eventually) at C^+ or C^-. But the two regions just mentioned have "fuzzy" borders such that solutions starting in the fuzzy regions may end up at either point. Further, the motion that takes place before the final descent into C^+ or C^- becomes longer and more complicated; in the limit, as r_2 is approached, it may last forever.
- $r_2 < r < r_H$. **Two** distinct types of motion may occur. Solutions may (a) end up at C^+ or C^- or (b) may approach an attractor involving many loops. This wandering, which is chaotic, is often followed in projection into one of the coordinate planes; it typically consists of a random number of oscillations around one of $C^\pm$ followed by a random number of loops around the other, and so on. Eventually, the solution approaches a set of points called a *strange attractor*.

3. $r > 313$. The attractor is a stable symmetric periodic orbit.

4. $r_H < r < 313$. For most r in this interval the motion is chaotic. But there are many (perhaps an infinite number) of "windows" in which non-chaotic solutions can be traced. Some of the widest of these are:

- $99.9 < r < 100.8$
- $145 < r < 166$
- $214 < r < 313$

Within these windows we see a sequence of stable periodic attractors. Moving from larger to smaller r, there is an evolution of *period-doubling*. A periodic orbit *bifurcates*, or divides into two new orbits, each, initially, having double the period of the original. This doubling occurs in a cascade that ends in chaos. This will be discussed further in a project to be described shortly.

To run the model requires a change in notation. Let

$$y_1 = x, \; y_2 = y, \; y_3 = z. \tag{5.3.7}$$

Then

$$\left.\begin{aligned} \frac{dy_1}{dt} &= -\sigma y_1 + \sigma y_2, \\ \frac{dy_2}{dt} &= -y_1 y_3 + r y_1 - y_2, \\ \frac{dy_3}{dt} &= y_1 y_2 - b y_3. \end{aligned}\right] \tag{5.3.8}$$

In code, y_i becomes `y(i)`. If the right-hand sides of the equations are entered into the array `z(i)` then a subroutine for finding them would contain the lines such as:

```
z(1) = - LS*y(1) + LS*y(2)
z(2) = - y(1)*y(3) + LR*y(1) - y(2)
z(3) = y(1)*y(2) - LB*y(3)
```

The usual reason for stopping an integration is that the time exceeds some prescribed maximum value. In preliminary exploration, this can be quite small. For $0 < t < 20$, for instance, you can acquire quite a lot of information. If you want to avoid transient terms, you will need to experiment. Sometimes they can disappear almost at once and sometimes they seem to take forever!

The following projects are suggestions for playing with the equations in order to get a feel for a chaotic system and some of the ways in which it can be investigated. As you try them, I am sure that you will get ideas of your own. Consult the literature for further ideas.

1. **Browse while varying r.**

   Keep $b = 8/3$ and $\sigma = 10$ fixed, and vary r. See if you can confirm the properties listed above. Explore the period-doubling windows, looking at what happens at the boundaries of these. See if you can find some more. Try to make up your own classification of the types of attractors.

   If you get fed up with varying r only, try reducing the value of b. Sparrow [91] describes different sorts of behavior when $b = 0.25$.

2. **Test sensitivity to initial conditions.**

   A quality of chaotic systems is that two solutions having almost the same initial conditions will initially separate exponentially. Let's state this more carefully. Let two solutions be given by $(x_1(t), y_1(t), z_1(t))$ and $(x_2(t), y_2(t), z_2(t))$ and let the distance between them, at time t, be

   $$\delta(t) = \sqrt{(x_1(t) - x_2(t))^2 + (y_1(t) - y_2(t))^2 + (z_1(t) - z_2(t))^2}. \tag{5.3.9}$$

   Initially,

   $$\delta(t) \sim \delta(0)e^{\lambda t}, \tag{5.3.10}$$

where the number λ is called a "*Liapunov exponent.*" This approximation will break down when $\delta(t)$ approaches the size of the attractor. Taking logs, (5.3.10) can be written as

$$\log \delta(t) \sim \log \delta(0) + \lambda t, \tag{5.3.11}$$

so if $\log \delta(t)$ is graphed as a function of t, it should wiggle around a straight line with slope λ.

To test this, choose a small number for $\delta(0)$ that is larger than the round-off error of your computations. If you are working with double precision, you might choose $\delta(0) = 10^{-12}$. Integrate a solution until you are sure that you are on the attractor, stopping at the point to be called $(x_1(0), y_1(0), z_1(0))$; let $x_2(0) = x_1(0) + \delta(0)$, $y_2(0) = y_1(0)$ and $z_2(0) = z_1(0)$. Now integrate the two solutions together, and record t and $\log \delta(t)$. Graph these, and estimate λ. Repeat this with different starting conditions and different values of the parameters.

This quality means that long-term prediction in a chaotic system is impossible. (Lorenz suggested that this partly explains why weather is hard to predict!) Test this in the following way. With $\delta(0) = 10^{-6}$, find out how long it will be until $\delta(t) > 10^{-3}$; call this time t_1. Now find similar times, with $\delta(0) = 10^{-7},\ 10^{-8},\ \cdots,\ 10^{-12}$. These times will increase, but by less than you probably expected.

Note that this sensitivity does not hurt any experiment for finding an attractor, because (x_1, y_1, z_1) and (x_2, y_2, z_2) will both lie on this attractor.

3. **The region $r_1 < r < r_H$.**

This project can take a lot of time and a lot of computation, but shows some beautiful results. The details can be varied, but the results should all be similar.

Keep $\sigma = 10$ and $b = 8/3$. Pick a value for r and find coordinates of $C^{\pm}$, say $(\pm x_C, \pm y_C)$. Choose a rectangle in this plane that includes both equilibria. (You will see presently that results will have symmetry about the origin, so only half of the rectangle need be involved in the computation.) Define a grid of points in the rectangle; for display on a computer screen, these points might correspond to pixels, or alternate pixels. (I warned you that you could expect a lot of computing!).

For each point in the grid, calculate a solution with initial conditions given by the x and y coordinates of the point, and with $z = r - 1$ (putting z in the right ballpark, from the start). Now compute the solution until (a) you end close to C^+, (b) you end close to C^-, or (c) you lose patience and stop. Depending on (a), (b) or (c), you color the starting point one of three different colors, say yellow, blue and black. You will have to decide on what distance is "close enough" to $C^{\pm}$ and after what time you quit without approaching close to either. We know that for $r_1 < r < r_2$, all solutions **eventually** end up at an equilibrium, but that the wandering time increases as r_2 is approached.

For $r = r_1$ you should see two symmetrical regions bearing the colors yellow and blue. As r increases from r_1 a "channel" grows between the two regions, and, at points inside this channel, a solution may end up at either of $C^{\pm}$. You should see wonderful patterns of colors within this region. The yellow and blue regions are "basins of attraction" for C^+ and C^-. This is a "fractal" pattern. If you now choose a smaller rectangle inside this region, and repeat the computation, you should see similar patterns.

If you have the patience to work in the interval $r_2 < r < r_H$ then the third color will correspond to solutions that end at the attractor, and not at one of $C^{\pm}$.

4. **Calculate plane sections of attractors.**

The structure of an attractor is hard to visualize from planar projections. Instead of seeing the full projection onto, say, the x-y plane, it can be helpful to see sections where the attractor is intersecting a sequence of planes parallel to the x-y plane. Successive points of crossing are called "return maps."

First, run an integration to find extreme values of z; these will be on either side of the value $r-1$, which is the z-coordinate of $C^{\pm}$. Choose a value c in the interval of possible values. In the calculation, carry a variable `zSign` which is equal to $+1$ if $z > c$ and -1 if $z < c$. Initialize `zSign` when the initial conditions for the run are entered. After each integration step, test to see if the product `(y(3)-c)*zSign` has become negative. If so, then you have just crossed the plane $z - c = 0$, and you must find the crossing point. The recommended method is to solve $z(t) - c = 0$ for t, by iteration, using Newton's method. If t_i and t_{i+1} are successive iterates, then

$$t_{i+1} = t_i - \frac{z(t_i) - c}{\dot{z}(t_i)} = t_i - \frac{z(t_i) - c}{x(t_i)y(t_i) - bz(t_i)}. \tag{5.3.12}$$

The stepsize for each iteration is $t_{i+1} - t_i$.

So the main program might contain the lines:

```
Step(...)
  If (y(3)-c)*zSign < 0 Then FindCrossing
```

The subroutine `FindCrossing` might contain code such as:

```
SaveStepSize = StepSize
Count = 0
Repeat
    Count = Count + 1
    StepSize = - (y(3) - c)/(y(1)*y(2) - LB*y(3))
    Step(...)
Until (Abs(y(3) - c) < Eps) Or (Count = 5)
If Count < 5 Then save values of y(1), y(2)
StepSize = SaveStepSize
zSign = - zSign
```

Points to bear in mind here are: (a) Save the good stepsize used before the iteration; Newton's method will end with a small and possibly negative stepsize. (b) Newton's method may not converge; if this happens, avoid an infinite loop by iterating only a few times. The number 5 was chosen arbitrarily. (c) The quantity `Eps` is up to your discretion; nothing is to be gained by making it too small. `0.0001` may be sufficient.

5. **Follow the evolution with changing r using return maps for any plane.**

This is not so much fun as seeing complete pictures with changing r, but is more economical. The best plane to use is probably $z = r - 1$ since this contains the equilibria $c^{\pm}$.

6. **Construct "Lorenz maps."**

A graph of z as a function of t is likely to have many wiggles around $z = r - 1$. They do not appear at first to be especially informative. Lorenz had the idea of finding successive maximum values: call these $z_1, z_2, \cdots, z_n, z_{n+1}, \cdots$. He then drew a Cartesian graph using points having coordinates (z_n, z_{n+1}). For instance, suppose that successive values of z_n are

$$30.1,\ 29.5,\ 31.2,\ 32.6,$$

then points in the graph would be

$$(30.1, 29.5),\ (29.5, 31.2),\ (31.2, 32.6).$$

(These numbers are hypothetical.) Amazingly, these points seem to fall on a curve, so that Lorenz found order out of chaos. If the curve is defined by a function f, then each z_n predicts the following z_{n+1}. I.e., $z_{n+1} = f(z_n)$.

Constructing a Lorenz map requires finding values of z when $\dot{z} = 0$ and $\ddot{z} < 0$. (In your computations you might find maxima and minima, and see how they combine.) Now

$$\left.\begin{aligned} \dot{z} &= xy - bz, \\ \ddot{z} &= \dot{x}y + x\dot{y} - b\dot{z} = \sigma(y-x)y + x(rx - y - xz) - b(xy - bz). \end{aligned}\right] \tag{5.3.13}$$

Solving $\dot{z}(t) = 0$ for t by Newton's method will involve iterations

$$t_{i+1} = t_i - \frac{\dot{z}_i}{\ddot{z}_i} = t_i - \frac{x_i y_i - bz_i}{\sigma(y_i - x_i)y_i + x_i(rx_i - y_i - x_i z_i) - b(x_i y_i - bz_i)}. \tag{5.3.14}$$

Here x_i stands for $x(t_i)$, etc.

For computation, let us have a variable `zDotSign` that is equal to $+1$ or -1 depending on whether $\dot{z}$ is positive or negative. It must be initialized when the initial conditions are entered, using $\dot{z} = xy - bz$. After each integration step, check whether `(y(1)*y(2)-b*y(3))*zDotSign` is negative; if it is, then find the point where $\dot{z} = 0$. The main program might contain the lines

```
Step(...)
If (y(1)*y(2)-b*y(3))*zDotSign < 0 Then FindCriticalPoint
```

The subroutine `FindCriticalPoint` might use the subroutine `Fun` that has as output the right-hand sides of the three differential equations, putting them into `z(1), z(2), z(3)`. It might contain code such as:

```
Call Fun
If z(1)*y(2) + y(1)*z(2) - LB*z(3) < 0 Then
Begin
    SaveStepSize = StepSize
    Count = 0
    Repeat
        Count = Count + 1
        Call Fun
        StepSize = - z(3)/(z(1)*y(2) + y(1)*z(2) - LB*z(3))
        Step(...)
    Until (Abs(y(1)*y(2)-LB*y(3)) < Eps) Or (Count = 5)
    If Count < 5 Then save value of y(3)
    StepSize = SaveStepSize
End
zDotSign = - zDotSign
```

If you want minima as well as maxima, then omit the first logical `If`, which allows only $\dot{z} < 0$.

7. **Follow bifurcations in a period-doubling window.**

Figure 5.11 shows a schematic version of a cascade of splitting, or bifurcation, of periodic attractors as the parameter r is diminished. Generating an actual diagram can be tricky; the

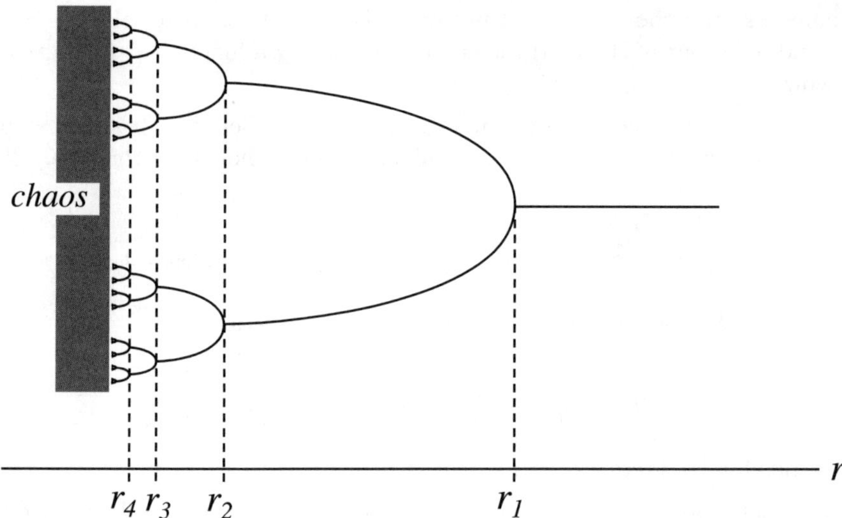

Figure 5.11: *Schematic diagram showing bifurcations of periodic attractors.*

principal object of this project will be to try to pinpoint the values of r where bifurcation takes place.

Figure 5.12 shows periodic attractors with two bifurcations as r is changed. These curves look attractive, but it can be hard to detect the actual points of bifurcation. A better method is to use a Lorenz map or the intersection of the attractor with a plane such as $z = r - 1$, so that only isolated points are recorded. It is essential that the initial transient motion is excluded. Select a window. Start with r at the right of the window, before the first bifurcation has taken place. (The Lorenz map might record several points for this attractor — two, for figure 5.12.) Now reduce r until a splitting occurs. Through experiment, try to approximate the value of r, where this takes place — call it r_1. Now continue reducing r to locate the next bifurcation, at r_2, and so on.

It is easy to write "and so on," but hard to carry out because the distance between successive bifurcations shrinks rapidly. The sequence $\{r_n\}$ approaches a limit, after which chaos takes over. The limit is approached geometrically, such that the ratio

$$\frac{r_n - r_{n-1}}{r_{n+1} - r_n}$$

approaches a limit. What is amazing is that the value of the limit, which was discovered by M.J.Feigenbaum in 1975, and is equal to

$$\lim_{n \to \infty} \frac{r_n - r_{n-1}}{r_{n+1} - r_n} = 4.669... \tag{5.3.15}$$

is the same in all period-doubling routes to chaos. (It has been observed in situations as widely ranging as experiments with chemical reaction, lasers and chicken hearts.) This is *Feigenbaum's constant*, a newly found universal constant of nature.

See if you can confirm the order of magnitude for your values of r_n. Note that you can use (5.3.14) to help look for r_{n+1} when you have already found r_n and r_{n-1}.

The bifurcation diagram that you generate need not be confined to the period-doubling windows. Outside these windows you will see chaos; but this can evolve in interesting ways as r changes, and offers a lot of scope for experiment.

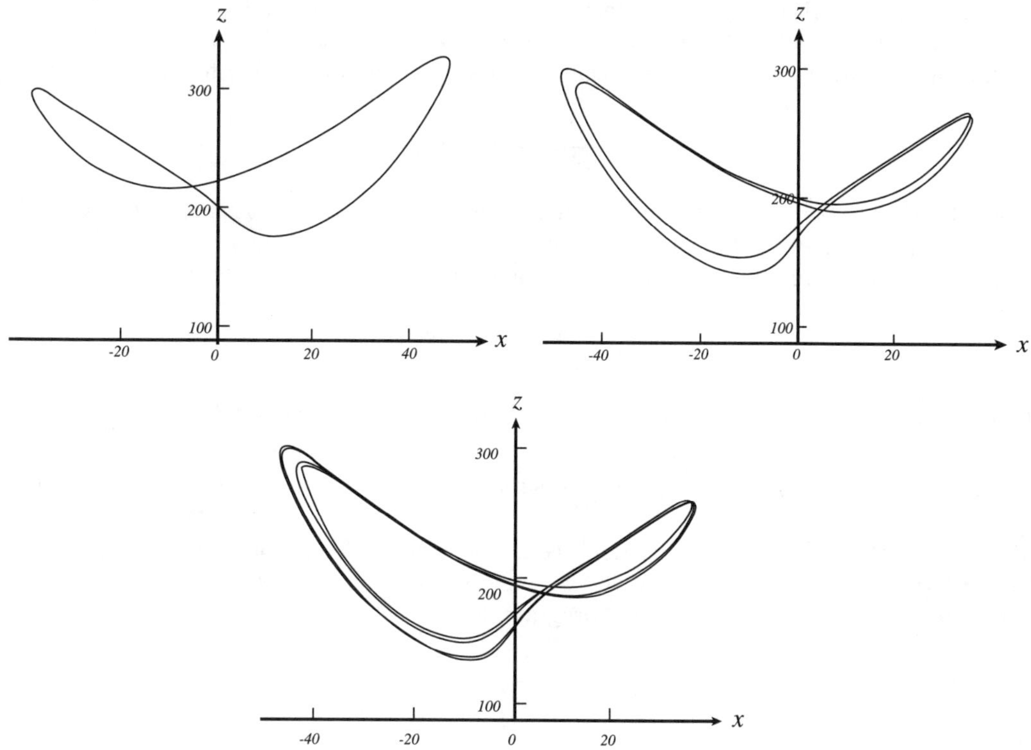

Figure 5.12: *Periodic attractors.* $\sigma = 10$ *and* $b = 8/3$. *Values of* r *are: single, 250; double, 220; quadruple, 217.*

It is worth mentioning another popular system, the Rössler attractor

$$\left.\begin{aligned} \frac{dx}{dt} &= -(y+z), \\ \frac{dy}{dt} &= x + ay, \\ \frac{dz}{dt} &= b + z(x-c). \end{aligned}\right] \tag{5.3.16}$$

Having only one nonlinear term, this looks even more innocent than the Lorenz system. This chaotic system has just one basic loop. To play with it, it is best to fix two parameters and vary the third. Again, ignore the start of the solution if you want to see the attractor. If you let $a = b = 0.2$ and increase c gradually from $c = 2.4$, then you will at first observe period-doubling. By the time you reach $c = 5.7$, the motion is chaotic, with the spatial structure resembling a Möbius band. Then it develops a "funnel" as c increases further.

5.4 A Periodically Forced Pendulum 

Many physical systems are subject to periodic forcing terms. For instance, models for the spread of disease can realistically involve infectiousness that varies periodically. These systems can exhibit chaotic behavior. A model that is often discussed is the simple pendulum that moves subject to a periodic forcing term.

A simple pendulum is discussed in detail in project (12.1). It consists of a light, inextensible rigid rod of length L, with a mass m attached at one end; the other end is connected to a fixed pivot. The pendulum moves subject to a constant downward gravitational force. If the pendulum makes the angle θ with the downward vertical, then the differential equation for its motion is

$$mL\frac{d^2\theta}{dt^2} = -mg\sin\theta, \tag{5.4.1}$$

where g is the acceleration due to gravity. To this, we shall add friction that is proportional to $d\theta/dt$, and a periodic *forcing term*, $f(t)$. This might be physically envisaged if the mass m is a bar magnet perpendicular to the pendulum, and an alternating current flows through the point of suspension. The new equation is

$$mL\frac{d^2\theta}{dt^2} = -mg\sin\theta - F\frac{d\theta}{dt} + f(t). \tag{5.4.2}$$

If $f(t)$ has frequency ω, then, with appropriate scaling, this equation can be written as

$$\frac{d^2\theta}{dt^2} + k\frac{d\theta}{dt} + \sin\theta = c\cos(\omega t). \tag{5.4.3}$$

Intuitively, since the model includes friction, we might expect all solutions eventually to lock into the forcing term, and become periodic with the same period. We shall see.

First, to transform (5.4.3) for use in a program, let

$$y_1 = \theta, \quad y_2 = \frac{d\theta}{dt}. \tag{5.4.4}$$

Then (5.4.3) can be written as the system

$$\left.\begin{aligned} \frac{dy_1}{dt} &= y_2, \\ \frac{dy_2}{dt} &= -ky_2 - \sin y_1 + c\cos(\omega t). \end{aligned}\right] \tag{5.4.5}$$

Then a subroutine for calculating the right-hand sides of these equations and putting them into the array `z(i)` might contain the lines:

```
z(1) = y(2)
z(2) = - k*y(2) - sin(y(1)) + c*cos(omega*t)
```

This system can be investigated in various ways.

1. Watch the motion in animation.

   There are plenty of ways to investigate and measure chaos. But it is best actually to see it.

   For entertainment, put the friction term k equal to zero.

   More realistically, $k \neq 0$. Then expect some introductory *transient* motion; this may look chaotic, and it is, in the sense that it is very sensitive to initial conditions. With the transient motion over, you may see periodic motion. This may be locked into the period of the forcing term, $2\pi/\omega$, or it may have period equal to a multiple of this. These longer period motions can be particularly entertaining, since they include combinations of oscillations and complete revolutions. Alternatively, the motion may remain forever chaotic.

2. **Investigate sensitivity to initial conditions.**

   One way to do this is to plot θ as a function of the time for various values of the parameters and the initial conditions. In many cases, you will observe nothing of particular interest. But

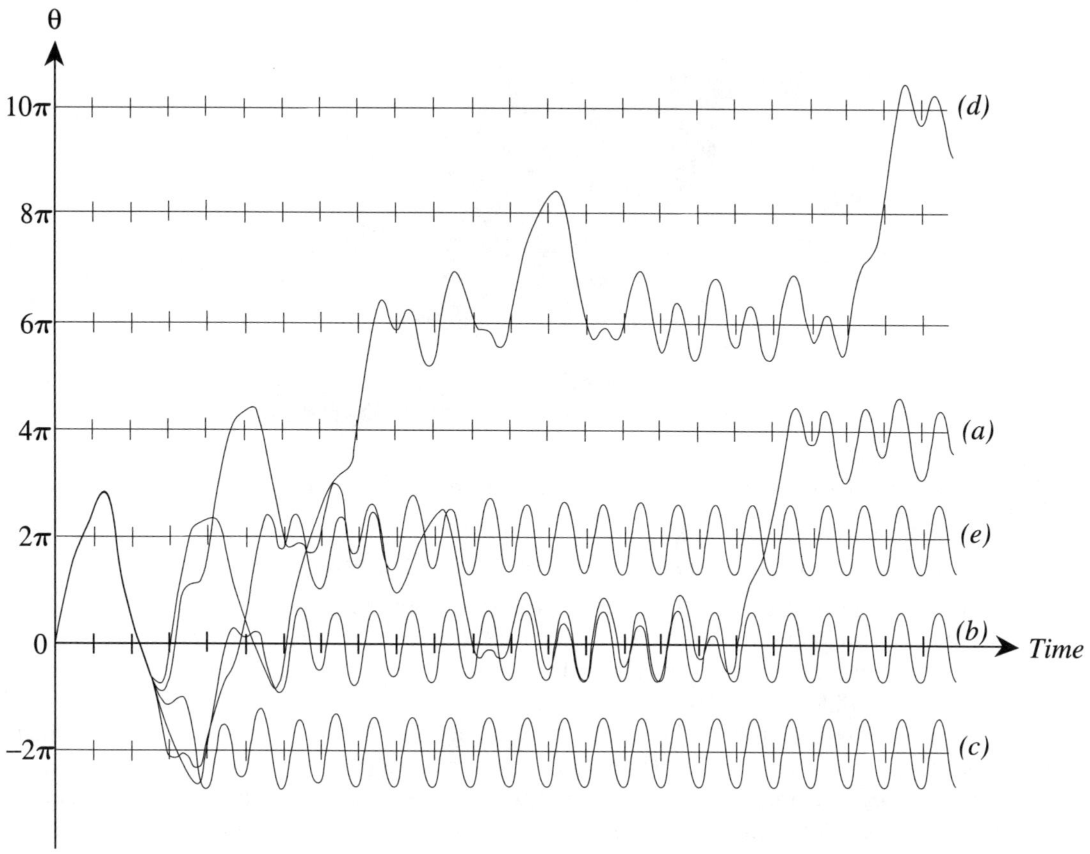

Figure 5.13: *Solutions with* $k = 0.1$, $\omega = 1$, $c = 1$, $\theta(0) = 0$. *Values for* $\dot{\theta}(0)$ *are: (a) 1.797; (b) 1.798; (c) 1.799; (d) 1.8; (e) 1.801.*

there are regions in the space of parameters where important properties of the model can be seen. For instance, take $k = 0.1$, $c = 1$ and $\omega = 1$, with initial conditions $\theta(0) = 0$. Now experiment with values of $\dot{\theta}$ in the vicinity of 1.8. See figure 5.13. The pendulum will circulate a number of times before settling into periodic motion; the circulation may be clockwise or counterclockwise, or a combination of both. Or the pendulum will never seem to become periodic. Further, very small changes in the initial conditions can lead to completely different qualities in the motion. This sensitivity to initial conditions is a key quality of chaotic motion. It means that numerical solutions cannot be individually trusted, since small errors, whether due to truncation or rounding, can alter the quality of a solution. So you may not be able to replicate results from another source unless you also replicate the computing methods.

Look for other values of the parameters and starting conditions showing similar sensitivity.

The motion might involve θ increasing or decreasing without limit; in this case, you might plot its derivative $\dot{\theta}$, or simply $\sin\theta$, as a function of the time.

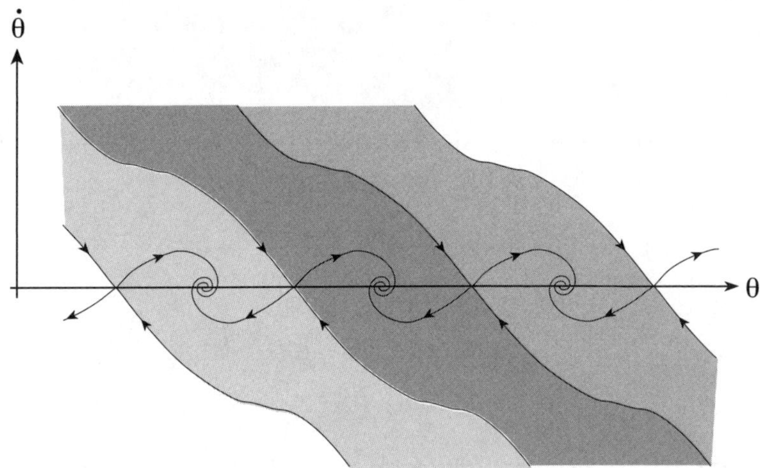

Figure 5.14: *"Basins of attraction" for equilibria for an unforced damped pendulum.*

3. **Relate initial conditions systematically to types of motion.**

In the preceding project the method is to experiment at random and have fun. The approach to be taken here is to consider initial conditions $\theta(0)$, $\dot{\theta}(0)$ from a grid of points in a rectangle on the $\theta(0)$-$\dot{\theta}(0)$ plane. For selected values of the parameters k, c and ω, the system is integrated repeatedly using different initial conditions taken from the grid. After a certain number of cycles of the forcing term (30, perhaps) the motion may have become periodic after n complete revolutions, or it may be chaotic. (It might later eventually become periodic; but you must draw the line somewhere.) In a chart of the $\theta(0)$-$\dot{\theta}(0)$ plane, a point is colored, depending on the value of n, or is not colored at all if the motion has not become periodic.

Warning! This project can take up a lot of time; try to manage it so that it is the computer's time, not yours, that is involved. If the colors are appearing on your computer screen, don't look at them, or you may be hypnotized for hours.

First, look at the model when there is no forcing term, or $c = 0$, but include a resisting term, so that $k > 0$. This is illustrated in figure 5.14. Then we have a phase-plane diagram showing possible motion. The diagram should include a big enough range in θ to show motion that has several complete revolutions before spiralling around the equilibrium. Suppose we label an equilibrium $\theta = 2n\pi$, for integer n, as E_n, so that n complete revolutions are made before the pendulum starts its final spiralling. It is easy to tell from the diagram which set of initial conditions will lead to a given E_n. One such set is shaded for E_2; this set is called the *basin of attraction* of E_2. When $c \neq 0$, the boundaries between the basins of attraction first become fuzzy and then very complicated. In a first exploration you can, at least, be sure of getting some good pictures. See figure 5.15.

Now for practical details of this project. Start with some limited region, preferably one that would include parts of two basins and their common boundary. Initially, don't include too many grid points; you can always repeat a computation with denser grids if things appear to be interesting. The numerical integrations will be nested in a double loop. Each integration must be carried out for a specified number of periods, $P = 2\pi/\omega$, of the forcing term; this is what takes up most of the time. Thirty periods seems to be an accepted value, but you can make up your own mind. Then, as soon as the time exceeds $30(2\pi/\omega)$, an integration over just one more cycle is needed. Let the period P be divided into m equal parts, $\Delta t = P/m$. If this final cycle starts at t_0 then we need values of $\theta(t_0 + \Delta t)$, $\theta(t_0 + 2\Delta t)$, $\theta(t_0 + 3\Delta t)$, ... $\theta(t_0 + m\Delta t)$. Let these be added and divided by m, to give a number A. If we are on a periodic orbit with period P, then A should be close to $2n\pi$, corresponding to the equilibrium E_n. Find $A/(2\pi)$; if it is sufficiently close to an integer, then we have our periodic orbit, we have n, and we color the starting point with the appropriate color.

We shall look at another way to tackle this project, but first we need to play with some other ways to follow solutions.

4. **Calculate Lyapunov exponents.**

   Refer to the second project in the preceding section for details.

5. **Plot solutions in the phase-plane.**

   For these plots, with θ and $\dot{\theta}$ on the horizontal and vertical axes, the transient motion looks chaotic although the final motion may be periodic; so it is best to start plotting only after a certain number of cycles of the forcing term. I shall refer to 30 cycles, but you must decide for yourself. I shall consider parameters $k = 0.5$ and $\omega = 2/3$, varying c, the amplitude of the forcing term, to produce an evolution of chaotic and non-chaotic motion. These parameters were used by Gwinn and Westervelt [49] in systematic investigation; they are also used in a text by Baker and Gollub [7].

   For now, start with initial conditions $\theta(0) = 0$, $\dot{\theta}(0) = 0$. First, consider the interval $0 < c \leq 1$. The motion becomes periodic. The "attractors" are closed curves, symmetrical about the axes. As c increases, the size of the attractors increases. Not much chaos here.

   Still starting at $\theta(0) = 0$, $\dot{\theta}(0) = 0$, take values $c = 1.01$, 1.02, ..., 1.06. You should see a departure of the symmetry about the $\dot{\theta}$, or vertical axis. Now try $c = 1.07$; you should see a periodic solution having **twice** the period of the forcing term.

   (In phase-plane plots there is a periodicity, period 2π, along the horizontal axis. Ultimately, you will have to plan your plots in a range $-n\pi \leq \theta \leq n\pi$, so that a solution moving off the right-hand side reappears on the left. You must decide how best to present your results.)

   Now try $c = 1.08$. (If possible, enjoy this in animation.) Next, $c = 1.09$; how do you interpret that? Chaos? Maybe. Next, $c = 1.10$, 1.11, 1.12, 1.13, 1.14; You will see some fancy periodic motion; plot θ versus the time, and observe that the period is three times that of the forcing term. $c = 1.15$: chaos, without a doubt!

   I suggest that you continue a systematic increase in c. For some highlights, try $c = 1.3$; chaos is over, for the time being; the periodic motion includes a complete revolution, and a wiggle. Increase c further to $c = 1.4$, and the wiggle is more pronounced. With $c = 1.44$, a period-doubling has occurred. With $c = 1.47$, there is a further doubling. $c = 1.5$: back to chaos.

6. **Plot "Poincaré" maps.**

   A phase-plane diagram for the case $c = 1.15$ mentioned above is fascinating if you can see it constructed in real time, because at times the chaotic motion seems to be attempting to become periodic; but once the diagram is finished it just resembles something that the cat has played with. To simplify this, suppose that a light, synchronized with the forcing term, flashes on very briefly, so that we see a *stroboscopic* view of the motion. This has come to be called a *Poincaré map* or a *Poincaré section*, although it was not what Poincaré had in mind, and does not carry Poincaré's geometrical interpretations. A periodic solution, as with $c = 1.4$, will appear as a single dot. For $c = 1.44$, and a doubling, we see two dots. With a further doubling at $c = 1.47$, there are four dots. These may seem boring, but they make identification of the types of motion easy. For chaotic motion, points form a complicated *fractal* set. If you choose a small area and expand it, you will always see the same sort of structure.

Computing these points requires the sampling of the integration at regular intervals of time. This can be done in several ways: here are some ideas. Initially, to avoid transient motion, the integration must run until the time is equal to n times the period of the forcing term; this will be called:

```
Interval = n*Period
```

Then, for the initial running,

```
Repeat
    Step(...)
Until Time + StepSize > Interval
SaveStepSize = StepSize
Repeat
    StepSize = Interval - Time
    Step(...)
Until Abs(Interval - Time) < Eps
StepSize= SaveStepSize
```

(Note that the second `Repeat ... Until` is necessary in case the initial stepsize, `(Interval - Time)`, turns out to be too great. The quantity `Eps` is a small number, at your discretion. I choose a number such as 0.001.) Assume, for the moment, that we shall sample the solution at the start of each cycle of the forcing term. Then the points might be generated as follows:

```
Repeat
    Time = 0
    Repeat
        Step(...)
    Until Time + StepSize > Period
    SaveStepSize = StepSize
    Repeat
        StepSize = Period - Time
        Step(...)
    Until Abs(Period - Time) < Eps
    StepSize = SaveStepSize
    Plot or store y(1) and y(2)
Until you have enough points
```

First, take the case $k = 0.5$, $\omega = 2/3$, $c = 1.5$, $\theta(0) = 0$, $\dot{\theta}(0) = 0$. Then the period is $P = 2\pi/\omega$. Plot points in the intervals $\pi \leq \theta \leq \pi$ and $-1 \leq \dot{\theta} < 3$. This means that a value of θ outside this interval must be diminished or increased by an appropriate multiple of 2π.

Pick a small rectangle that contains some interesting region of the figure you have just found. Plot the points in this region, on a much larger scale. (You may have to go back and calculate a lot more points in order to fill out this region satisfactorily.) In theory, you can go on picking smaller regions forever, but I leave this up to you.

If you sample the solution at different phases of the forcing cycle, you will see substantially different diagrams, although the basic principle is the same. Let m be an integer, not too large. Generate a sequence of maps, sampling at times equal to multiples of the period, P, plus jP/m, $j = 1, ..., m-1$. The only adjustment that you need make is to define

```
Interval = n*Period + j*Period/m
```

7. **Back to basins of attraction.**

With the technology for constructing Poincaré maps, we can return to the third project, running it in a different way.

If a solution experiences some complete revolutions, but eventually settles down to regular oscillations, then the successive Poincaré points will eventually appear fixed, although earlier points may appear to be chaotic. Suppose we choose initial conditions θ_0, $\dot{\theta}_0$ and that successive Poincaré points are $\theta_{0,n}$, $\dot{\theta}_{0,n}$. Each time a new map is found, calculate the difference

$$\Delta_n = |\theta_{0,n+1} - \theta_{0,n}| + |\dot{\theta}_{0,n+1} - \dot{\theta}_{0,n}|.$$

If this becomes less than some small quantity, δ, (0.1 will probably suffice), then we can (fairly) safely assume that the oscillations have settled down. Depending on the final value of $\theta_{0,n}$, we can count the net number of revolutions that have taken place. For instance if $-\pi < \theta_{0,n+1} < \pi$, then the final oscillations are around $\theta = 0$. If Δ_n has not become small after a given number of revolutions, say 30, then we can assume that things will never settle down.

Now choose your grid of points. Each point provides initial conditions for a solution. For each solution, calculate successive points of a Poincaré map. After the calculation of each of these points, calculate Δ_n. If this is small enough, find an integer k, such that $(2k-1)\pi < \theta_{0,n+1} < (2k+1)\pi$. Color your initial point according to the value of k. If n exceeds some number, such as 30, don't color the point (or color it black).

Figures 5.15(a) to (f) show results using $k = 0.1$, $\omega = 1$, and c given successive values 0.0, 0.2, 0.4, 0.6, 0.8 and 1.0. $c = 0$ corresponds to the unforced pendulum, so figure 5.15(a) is similar to figure 5.14. As c increases, the effects of chaos become more apparent.

8. **Still more on basins of attraction.**

We continue to use $k = 0.5$ and $\omega = 2/3$ in order to quote numerical values; but the ideas involved here are much more general. As c increases just above 1.0, a bifurcation occurs; but if you only use $\theta(0) = 0$, and $\dot{\theta}(0) = 0$, you will not notice it. To see the effect, try $c = 1.06$ and the two sets of initial conditions $\theta(0) = 0,\ \dot{\theta}(0) = 0$ and $\theta(0) = 0,\ \dot{\theta}(0) = 1$. Neglecting, as usual, the transient terms, you will see two distinct periodic solutions in the phase-plane.

Similarly, as c increases from around 1.25, and a chaotic phase ends, there is another doubling, caused by different initial conditions. Try $c = 1.4$ with initial conditions $\theta(0) = 0,\ \dot{\theta}(0) = 0$ and $\theta(0) = 0,\ \dot{\theta}(0) = 2$.

In each case it can be interesting to find out which initial conditions lead to the first solution and which lead to the second; consequently, finding basins of attraction for the two solutions. The method of the preceding section can be used here. First find the points for the Poincaré maps of the two solutions. Choose a grid of points for initial conditions. For each integration, test every point of the Poincaré map to see whether it is sufficiently close to one of the two solutions; if neither has been approached after a specified time, give up.

9. **Plot a bifurcation diagram.**

Another long one! But you get a lot of information. The aim is to illustrate a history of the types of solution throughout a given range of c. The method is very simple. Choose a set of values of c in the given interval. For each value of c find 20 to 30 points in the Poincaré maps of possible solutions, and plot values of $\dot{\theta}$ in a graph with horizontal and vertical axes c and $\dot{\theta}$, respectively.

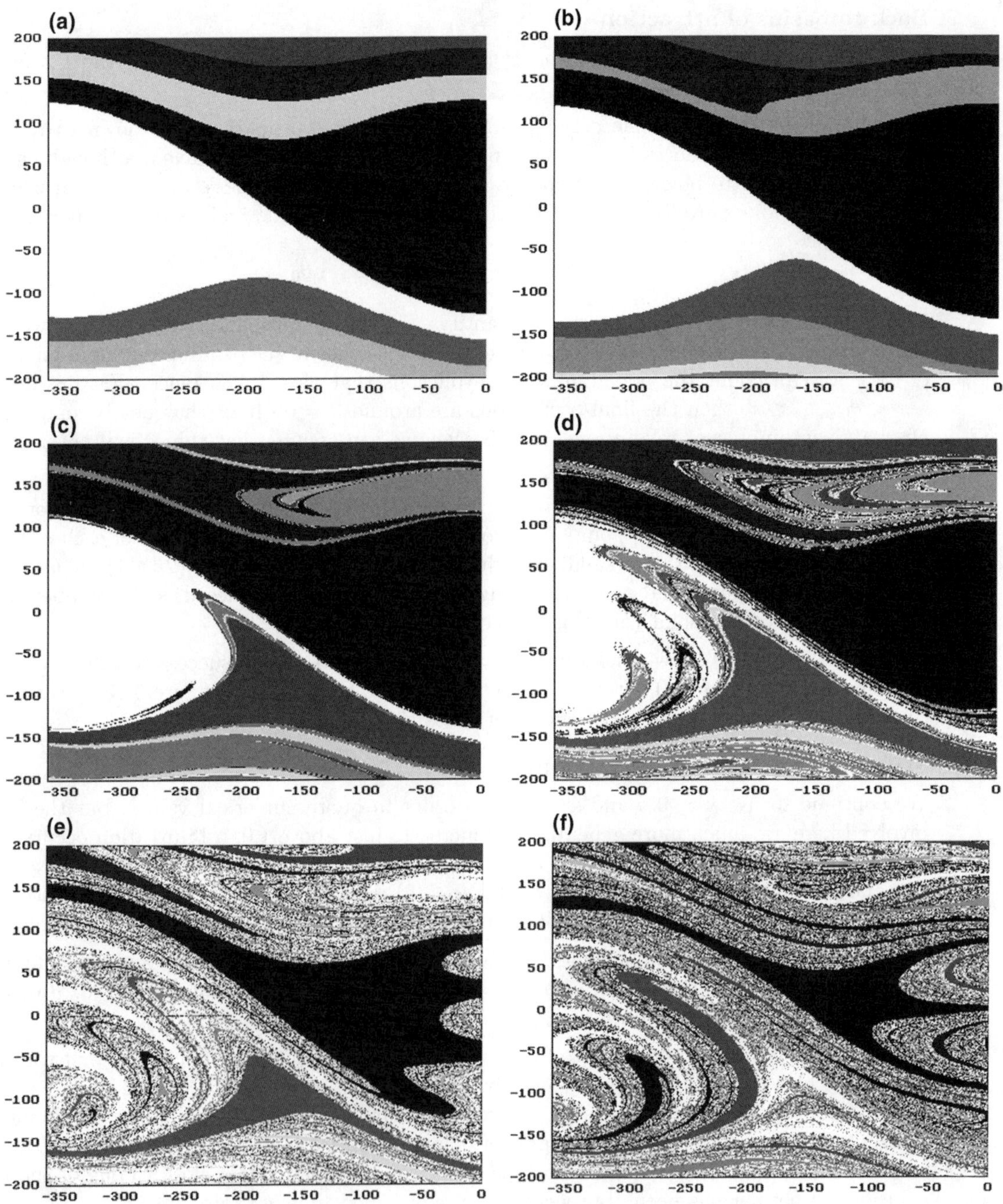

Figure 5.15: *If you look at figure 5.13 you see examples of solutions with different initial conditions eventually taking up regular oscillations, but only after several complete revolutions. In these figures we have taken $k = 0.1$ and $\omega = 1$ and have varied the value of c; for $c = 0$ there is no forcing term. As c increases, the likelihood of chaos also increases. Each point in one of these diagrams corresponds to initial conditions of a solution. The color (or shade) given to that point depends on the net number of revolutions taken before the solution settles down to regular oscillations. (If it fails to settle down after 30 periods of the forcing term, the point is not colored.) c is given successive values 0.0, 0.2, 0.4, 0.6, 0.8 and 1.0. In (a) $c = 0$; this corresponds to the unforced pendulum, and so is similar to figure 5.14. As c increases, the effects of chaos become more apparent.*

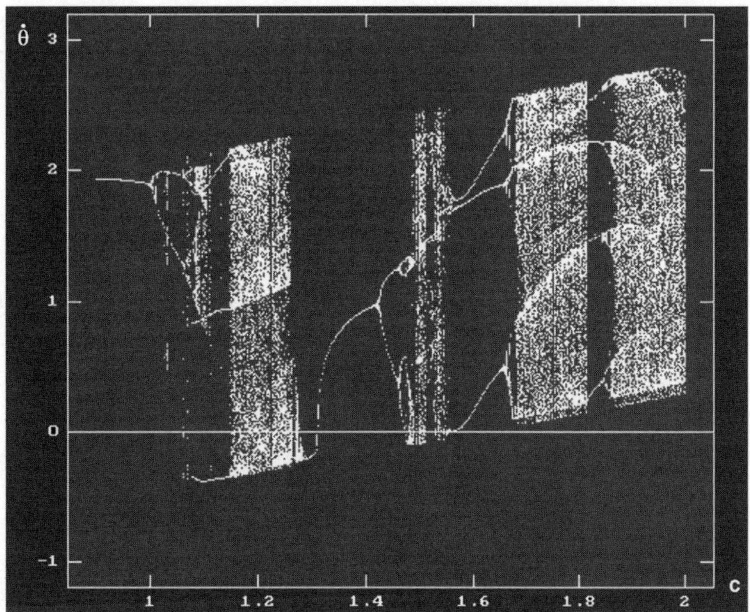

Figure 5.16: *A bifurcation diagram with $k = 0.5$ and $\omega = 2/3$. c takes values from 0.9 to 2. For each value of c, solutions were computed. Until the time exceeds 20 periods of the forcing term, the solution was not used; this reduces the chance of transient terms affecting the diagram. Subsequently, values of the angular rate $\dot{\theta}$ were found and plotted at times kP, where $P = 2\pi/\omega$ is the period of the forcing term and k is an integer. A regular oscillation results in one point. When a line of single points splits into two, it is called a bifurcation. Successive bifurcations lead to chaos.*

For each value of c, it is necessary to make several runs with different initial conditions, so that there will be at least one starting value in a basin of attraction for any possible periodic solution. This slows things down, but is essential. With the numerical values of the preceding section, I made a calculation for $0.95 \leq c \leq 1.5$; for each value of c, I made three runs with initial conditions $\theta(0) = 0$, and $\dot{\theta}(0) = 0,\ 1,\ 2$. You need to guard against transient terms messing up the diagram; they do not matter much when the motion is chaotic anyway, but they can obliterate the finer points in bifurcations. So discard the first 20 or 30 Poincaré points and then start to plot. The diagram that you generate will be similar in appearance to figure 5.20, but the evolution will be to the right. Figure 5.16 shows a bifurcation diagram for $k = 0.5$ and $\omega = 2/3$. c takes values from 0.9 to 2.

5.5 Chaos in Difference Equations 

5.5.1 Introduction

Difference equations can be powerful tools in modeling. They are easy to comprehend, requiring few of the concepts of calculus. Although trying to solve them analytically can be a bit of a bother (if not impossible), their solutions are extremely easy and fast to compute. They can also be chaotic.

An example of a difference equation is

$$S_{n+1} = S_n + rS_n,\ n = 0, 1, 2, \cdots. \tag{5.5.1}$$

Here S_n might represent the amount of money in a savings account after n years, where interest is compounded annually at the rate r (or $100r$ percent) and where the initial deposit was S_0. Nothing chaotic here. Fortunately. But consider another friendly looking difference equation

$$x_{n+1} = x_n^2 + c,\ n = 0, 1, \cdots. \tag{5.5.2}$$

Suppose $c = -2$. The following table shows successive values of x_n for three nearby values of x_0.

n	x_n		
0	0.4990	0.5000	0.5010
1	−0.7519	−1.7500	−1.7490
2	1.0660	1.0625	1.0590
3	−0.8636	−0.8711	−0.8785
4	−1.2541	−1.2412	−1.2282
5	−0.4272	−0.4594	−0.4915
6	−1.8175	−1.7889	−1.7584
7	1.3032	1.2002	1.0919
8	−0.3015	−0.5594	−0.8077
9	−1.9091	−1.6870	−1.3477
10	1.6447	0.8461	−0.1838
11	0.7052	−1.2841	−1.9662
12	−1.5027	−0.3511	1.8661
13	0.2581	−1.8767	1.4822

Two qualities of chaos appear. Firstly, there is no apparent trend from one value of P_n to the next. Secondly, a small initial difference in P_0 leads rapidly to greater differences, until there is nothing in the sequences to indicate that they started as close neighbors.

The sequence (5.5.2) is said to be generated by the function

$$f(x) = x^2 + c. \tag{5.5.3}$$

It is called the *quadratic map.* If you don't know any mathematicians, you will be surprised to hear that they call this a *dynamical system.* Further, the sequence of successive values of x_n is called an *orbit.* In fact, when properties of chaos are involved, there is a lot in common with dynamical systems defined in this way by mathematicians, and with dynamical systems as interpreted by almost everyone else; and this is particularly the case in the transition from order to chaos. An orbit from the Earth to the Moon is generated by a chaotic dynamical system (called the restricted problem of three bodies), but you will have to work long and hard to reveal properties of the chaos. On the other hand, you can be enjoying a system like the quadratic map in five minutes and developing some insight into its chaotic properties in ten.

The quadratic map is one of many simple examples of difference equations that can show chaotic behavior. Here are some others:

- The *logistic map*: $P_{n+1} = cP_n(1-P_n)$ models a population with growth rate proportional to the population and to some quantity, such as the available space, or food supply. (Some authors refer to **this** one as the "quadratic map.") A weakness in the interpretation of this model is that if the food supply is all taken, then the species dies out (in spite of the fact that the available food is being eaten by somebody). If the logistic differential equation, $P' = cP(1-P)$, is expressed as a difference equation, then it becomes $P_{n+1} = P_n + cP_n(1 - P_n)$. It is this difference equation that is the counterpart of logistic growth in calculus. But it still can be chaotic!

- The *doubling function*:

$$D(x) = \begin{cases} 2x, & 0 \le x \le 1/2, \\ 2x - 1, & 1/2 \le x < 1 \end{cases} \tag{5.5.4}$$

  generates a much discussed chaotic system.

- The *tent map* is defined by

$$T_c(x) = \begin{cases} cx, & 0 \le x \le \frac{1}{2}, \\ c - cx, & \frac{1}{2} < x \le 1. \end{cases} \tag{5.5.5}$$

  See if you can account for its name!

- $x_{n+1} = 2\cos x_n$ and $x_{n+1} = \cos 2x_n$ produce chaotic sequences.

In this section we shall see a brief survey of a few properties of chaotic difference equations. For an excellent introduction, with full but by no means advanced mathematics, you can do no better than to read the text by R.L.Devaney [34].

5.5.2 Projects

These projects refer specifically to the quadratic map. But they can be applied to any map of the form $x_{n+1} = f(x_n)$ with chaotic properties, such as those listed above. A programmable graphing calculator is an excellent tool for experimenting with these maps. If you use computer graphics, be prepared to slow the operation down. Compared with differential equations, you will be surprised how fast computations go with difference equations: that is one of their advantages.

1. Confirm the numbers given in the table at the start of this section. The starting values, x_0, are called *seeds*. Experiment with different seeds.

2. Instead of looking at numerical values, graph the x_n on a vertical scale with n horizontal. On a computer screen, it is best to advance horizontally one pixel each time n is incremented. A nice touch is to sound a short note with pitch depending on the value of x_0. Hearing chaos can be as impressive as seeing it.

3. Take a seed that shows chaos when $c = -2$. Keep the seed fixed, but gradually start to increase c, up to $c = -1$. Record what you find out.

4. In the preceding experiment you should see some non-chaotic behavior. When this occurs, vary the seed, and investigate to what extent the behavior is changed.

5. For a value of c showing chaotic behavior, such as $c = -2$, run the mapping simultaneously with two seeds, $x_{1,0}$ and $x_{2,0}$, very close to each other. Let $\Delta_n = x_{1n} - x_{2n}$. Initially, you might have $\Delta_0 = 10^{-10}$. Calculate Δ_n until it is of the order of 1. The absolute value of Δ_n can be expected to grow exponentially, so

$$\Delta_n \approx \Delta_{n0} e^{n\lambda}, \text{ or } \ln \Delta_n \approx \ln \Delta_{n0} + n\lambda.$$

   This means that the logarithm of Δ_n will, approximately, grow linearly, with n, with slope λ: called the *Lyapunov exponent.* Find this. Does its value depend on the seeds that are used?

   Now change c. Does λ change also?

6. For the quadratic map $x_{n+1} = f(x_n) = x_n^2 + c$. Pick a value of c, $c = -2$, perhaps. Graph $y_1 = x$ and $y_2 = f(x)$. Where do the curves meet? Interpret this, and call these points x_a and x_b. Now graph $y_3 = f(f(x))$, $y_4 = f(f(f(x)))$ and more. x_a and x_b should lie on all of these curves, so if either was used as a seed, successively mapped points would not vary. These are called *fixed points* and are analogous to equilibrium solutions for differential equations.

   Now graph y_1 and y_3. Call their intersection points x_a, x_b, x_c and x_d. Interpret these. Confirm that they also lie on the graph of y_5.

7. Make a graph with vertical and horizontal coordinates (x_{n+1}, x_n). For instance, using entries in the first column of the table, the first few points would be

$$(0.4990,\ -0.7519),\ (-0.7519,\ 1.0660),\ (1.0660,\ -0.8636),\ \text{etc.}$$

The points appear to lie on a simple curve. Their locations on this curve may seem chaotic, but there is nothing chaotic about the curve.

How is this curve affected when the seed is changed? How is it affected when c is changed?

5.5.3 Chaos in Difference Equations is not Funny

It is all very well for mathematicians to have fun (and generate breathtakingly beautiful art); but for many people difference equations are serious. In most methods for the numerical solution of differential equations, a step taken is an iteration in a system of difference equations. Newton's method for solving $g(x) = 0$ uses the sequence generated by

$$x_{n+1} = x_n - \frac{g(x_n)}{g'(x_n)}. \tag{5.5.6}$$

Lose faith in difference equations, and you are liable to wake up screaming.

The aim of this section is to view difference equations, and possible chaos, in the context of computation.

To fuel the fires of doubt further, I shall give two examples involving the solution of differential equations.

To solve the differential equation $y' = f(x, y)$, with stepsize h, *Nyström's formula* uses the approximation

$$\begin{aligned} y_{n+2} &= y_n + 2hy'_{n+1} \\ &= y_n + 2hf(x_{n+1}, y_{n+1}). \end{aligned} \tag{5.5.7}$$

This is an example of a *multistep* method. It can be justified with recourse to the midpoint rule for quadrature. If this is applied to

$$y' = Ay, \tag{5.5.8}$$

for constant A, then the difference equation

$$y_{n+2} = y_n + 2hAy_{n+1} \tag{5.5.9}$$

results. The solution of equation (5.5.9) can be written as

$$y_n = c_1 r_1^n + c_2 r_2^n, \tag{5.5.10}$$

where

$$\left.\begin{aligned} r_1 &= Ah + (1 + A^2h^2)^{1/2}, \\ r_2 &= Ah - (1 + A^2h^2)^{1/2}, \end{aligned}\right] \tag{5.5.11}$$

and c_1 and c_2 are constants that depend on the initial values y_0 and y_1. It can be shown by an appropriate limit process that the first term on the right of equation (5.5.10) approaches the solution that we want, as h is made smaller. Let's look at the second term. Suppose that A is negative. Then r_2 is negative, and smaller than -1. c_2 may be small, but it will not be zero, so with increasing n, the second term will alternate in sign, while increasing without bound. This second term is an example of a *parasitic solution* that results not from the differential equation to be solved, but from the method of solving it. The result is not chaotic, but is unstable.

For a second example, consider the system

$$\left.\begin{array}{rcl} y_1' &=& y_2, \\ y_2' &=& -100y_2, \\ y_1(0) &=& 1.01,\ y_2(0) = -1, \end{array}\right] \tag{5.5.12}$$

which has solution $y_1 = 1 + 0.01e^{-100t}$, $y_2 = -e^{-100t}$. Solve this system using a Runge-Kutta method with **fixed** stepsize. (For example, I omitted the two lines in the RKF4-5 code that change the stepsize.) With $h = 0.01,\ 0.02,\ 0.03$, results were all right. $h = 0.04$ was all right, but worrying. For $h = 0.05$ or greater, the results are complete garbage, and appear to be chaotic.

Things need not really be this bad! Plenty of multistep methods have good stability characteristics. Restore the stepsize control to RKF4-5, and the results for the fixed stepsizes will be a bad memory. The system (5.5.12) is an example of a *stiff* system, which may call for very small stepsize, although the solution itself is not too eventful. Special methods exist for taming such systems.

Why might we need to generate a sequence like

$$x_{n+1} = f(x_n),\ n = 0, 1, 2, ...? \tag{5.5.13}$$

One reason may be that we need to solve the equation $x = f(x)$, and can only do it by approximation. We would first have to know that a solution existed; call this $x = a$ so that $a = f(a)$. a is known as a *fixed point* of (5.5.13). To be useful, a sequence generated by (5.5.13) must converge towards a. Suppose we let

$$x_n = a + \epsilon_n$$

so that ϵ_n is the error in x_n. We assume that $f(x)$ is differentiable near a. Then, using the mean value theorem,

$$a + \epsilon_{n+1} = f(a + \epsilon_n) = f(a) + \epsilon_n f'(a_n),$$

where a_n is a number between a and $(a + \epsilon_n)$. So

$$\frac{\epsilon_{n+1}}{\epsilon_n} = f'(a_n). \tag{5.5.14}$$

It is clear that if the sequence is to converge to the fixed point a, then $|f'(x)| < 1$ for x lying in some interval containing a.

A sequence of iterations can be illustrated graphically. A fixed point of $x = f(x)$ is an intersection between the graphs of the two curves $f(x)$ and x. Notice that if $f'(a) > 0$, then the pattern is that of a staircase, but for $f'(a) < 0$, we have a spider's web. Figures 5.17 and 5.18 illustrate converging and diverging sequences. In each case, there is a fixed point; the first is called *attracting*, and the second, *repelling.*

Consider the quadratic map with $c = 0$, i.e., $x_{n+1} = x_n^2$. There is an attracting fixed point at $x = 0$ and a repelling fixed point at $x = 1$. The repelling fixed point cannot be found by this iteration. If it is important for you to calculate it, then you could apply Newton's method to the equation

$$g(x) = x^2 - x = 0.$$

Newton's method requires the iteration

$$x_{n+1} = x_n - \frac{g(x_n)}{g'(x_n)} = x_n - \frac{x_n^2 - x_n}{2x_n - 1} = \frac{x_n^2}{2x_n - 1}. \tag{5.5.15}$$

This has stable fixed points at $x = 0$ and $x = 1$. Using the test for stability of a fixed point of Newton's method,

$$x_{n+1} = f(x_n) = x_n - \frac{g(x_n)}{g'(x_n)},$$

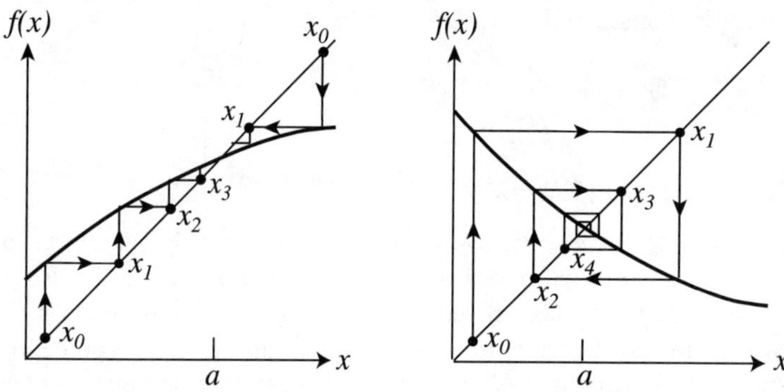

Figure 5.17: *Iterations toward an attracting fixed point.*

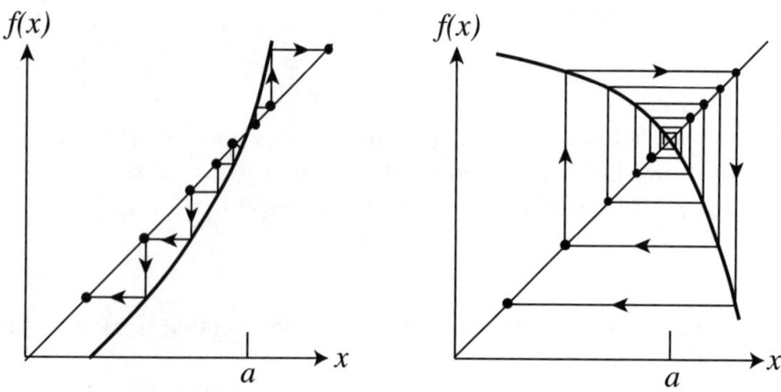

Figure 5.18: *Iterations away from a repelling fixed point.*

we find that $f'(a) = 0$ for a fixed point $x = a$, provided that $g'(a) \neq 0$. (Of course, if you try to apply Newton's method when $g'(a) = 0$, you deserve all the trouble you get.) Causes of trouble with Newton's method are best illustrated with a figure that shows the geometrical interpretation of the method. Examples of possible trouble are illustrated in figure 5.19. This shows one iteration using Newton's method. Different values of x_0 could make it impossible to converge on the fixed point, $x = a$. Find regions within which a starting estimate would lead to $x = a$. The overriding principle with this method, and with the results obtained in the section by calculus, is that they are **local**. They only apply if the calculations start sufficiently close to an attracting fixed point.

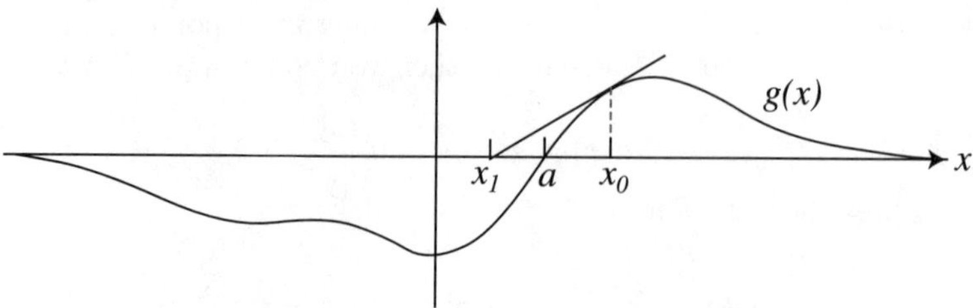

Figure 5.19: *An iteration using Newton's method.*

5.5.4 Projects

1. Confirm the results for the example using Nyström's method over a given range of x. (I find that this is most easily done using a hand calculator.) Take $A = -1$, so that the correct solution is $y = e^{-x}$. Start with $y_0 = 1$ and $y_1 = e^{-0.1}$ rounded to four decimal places; then the error is of the order of $0.4 \cdot 10^{-5}$. Note that the parasitic term is then approximately $0.4 \cdot 10^{-5} \cdot (-1.1)^n$. Confirm that by the time you reach $x = 4$, the results are meaningless, with the parasitic term greater than the correct solution. Explain this. Now repeat, using stepsizes $h = 0.05$ and $h = 0.2$. What do you find?

2. Select an integration method using fixed stepsize. The simplest method may be to use one with variable stepsize but, temporarily, to suppress the instructions for the variation. Or you might use the well-known fourth-order method:

$$\begin{aligned}
f_0 &= f(x_0, y_0), \\
f_1 &= f\left(x_0 + \frac{1}{2}h,\ y_0 + \frac{1}{2}hf_0\right), \\
f_2 &= f\left(x_0 + \frac{1}{2}h,\ y_0 + \frac{1}{2}hf_1\right), \\
f_3 &= f\left(x_0 + h,\ y_0 + hf_2\right); \\
y_1 &= y_0 + \frac{1}{6}h(f_0 + 2f_1 + 2f_2 + f_3).
\end{aligned}$$

   Run the system (5.5.12), using the stepsizes suggested, and confirm the results. Then run the system using a method with variable stepsize and note the difference.

3. One can play forever with a difference equation of the type $x_{n+1} = f(x_n)$. A hand calculator is a good tool; it helps if you also have graphics, and you can have extra pleasure by using sound. The pitch of a note can depend on the value of x_n; to be more adventurous, the duration of the note can be proportional to x_{n-1}. (But be warned that this sort of program may lose you some friends.)

4. A computer program that will draw the webs is especially useful. There are, of course, endless generating functions to be used; for a specific project, I suggest that you try

$$x_{n+1} = cx_n - x_n^3.$$

   For $c > 0$, there are three fixed points. Start first with $0 < c < 1$ and investigate the nature of these points. If the seed x_0 is above some critical value, the process will diverge. Can you find this value and explain it? What happens when $c = 1$? Next consider $1 < c \leq 2$. Then, for $2 < c \leq 3$, start with $c = 1.1$ and gradually increase it. You should see limit cycles and then chaos.

5. Let's see if we can make Newton's method look bad. Consider

$$x^3 - x^2 - 1 = 0,$$

   which, in Newton's method, gives the difference equation

$$x_{n+1} = x_n - \frac{x_n^3 - x_n^2 - 1}{3x_n^2 - 2x_n}.$$

First, plot the function $y = x^3 - x^2 - 1$ and confirm that there is one real root. Find this root and find an interval around it so that any value of x_0 in this interval will lead to convergence using Newton's method. This means that anyone with intelligence can use Newton's method correctly to find the solution. We shall step outside this interval, assuming that we cannot be unintelligent provided we are having fun. There is clearly an interval, roughly $0 < x < 0.7$, where a value of x_n will lead to x_{n+1} further away from the solution; so if we land in this interval during iteration, then something interesting may happen.

First confirm that if $x_0 = 0.26236655$ then x_5 takes (to this degree of accuracy) the same value; so we have a cycle that will never approach the solution. This demonstrates that not all x_0 will lead to the solution. Next decide on some number, N, such that if the iteration has not converged for $n = N$, you can feel confident in asserting that it will not converge. (You may or may not be correct; but if unlimited iterations are allowed, then, eventually, round-off errors may put you onto an x_n that will lead to convergence.) For instance, try $N = 20$. Now look for regions that do not lead to convergence. One way to investigate this is to generate (on the computer) a diagram where the horizontal axis shows values of x_0, and the vertical axis shows values of x_1, x_2,..., x_N. There will be a horizontal line showing the value of the solution, but it will contain many gaps.

5.5.5 The Quadratic Map

The iteration

$$x_{n+1} = x_n^2 + c, \; n = 0, 1, 2, ... \tag{5.5.16}$$

will have a fixed point at $x = a$ if $a = a^2 + c$. This quadratic equation has solutions

$$a_1 = \frac{1}{2}\left(1 + \sqrt{1-4c}\right), \; a_2 = \frac{1}{2}\left(1 - \sqrt{1-4c}\right). \tag{5.5.17}$$

If $c > 1/4$, then there is no fixed point, and it is easy to see, by construction, that all sequences are unbounded. The sequence is generated by $f(x) = x^2 + c$, so $f'(x) = 2x$. If $c < 1/4$, then $f'(a_1) > 1$ so that a_1 is repelling. If $-3/4 < c < 1/4$, then $-1/2 < a_2 < 0$ so $|f'(a_2)| < 1$, and a_2 is attracting. You should confirm this by hand calculation. (But show that the starting value x_0 must lie between a_1 and a_2 for a_2 to be reached.) For $c < -3/4$ neither point is attracting. What happens then?

A clue lies in the study of the Lorenz equations, where we saw the phenomenon of *period-doubling* as part of the route to chaos. Suppose that, instead of asking for $x_{n+1} = x_n$, as we did above, we ask for $x_{n+2} = x_n$. Then

$$x_n = x_{n+2} = x_{n+1}^2 + c = \left(x_n^2 + c\right)^2 + c,$$

so x_n is a solution of $x = (x^2 + c)^2 + c$, or

$$0 = x^4 + 2x^2c - x + c + c^2 = (x^2 - x + c)(x^2 + x + c + 1).$$

The solutions include a_1 and a_2 from (5.5.17) and

$$a_3 = \frac{1}{2}\left(-1 + \sqrt{-4c-3}\right), \; a_4 = \frac{1}{2}\left(-1 - \sqrt{-4c-3}\right). \tag{5.5.18}$$

This provides an attracting "2-cycle" solution for $-5/4 < c < -3/4$; for $c < -5/4$ the 2-cycle becomes repelling, and splits once more. The process continues until the solutions become chaotic. There is a sequence of numbers, $c_0, c_1, c_2, ...$ at which the splitting occurs. The sequence

$$f_0 = \frac{c_0 - c_1}{c_1 - c_2}, \; f_1 = \frac{c_1 - c_2}{c_2 - c_3}, \; f_2 = \frac{c_2 - c_3}{c_3 - c_4}, ..., \tag{5.5.19}$$

approaches a limit 4.669..., known as *Feigenbaum's constant.*

As with the forced pendulum and the Lorenz equations, a bifurcation diagram is useful in demonstrating the changes in the solutions as c decreases. See figure 5.20. A nice thing about chaotic difference equations is that the generation of a bifurcation diagram is very quick. Another approach is to plot successive points (x_{n+1}, x_n) in a "phase-diagram." For cyclic motion, there will be a few points repeated over again. For chaotic motion, there is a surprising degree of organization, with all but the first few points lying on an *attractor.* An element of chaos remains, however, in that the points seem to wander at random about the attractor.

5.5.6 Projects

1. Show, by constructing a web diagram, that if $C > 1/4$, then the iteration diverges for any starting point.

2. What happens when $c = 1/4$?

3. Verify by calculation that if $-3/4 < c < 1/4$, a_1 is a repelling and a_2 is an attracting fixed point.

   Demonstrate graphically that if the seed x_0 lies in between a_2 and a_1, then x_n will always converge to a_2.

   What happens when $c = -3/4$?

4. Demonstrate that if $c < -3/4$, then both a_1 and a_2 are repelling. For $5/4 < c < -3/4$ demonstrate the appearance of the stable 2-cycle.

5. Try $c = -1.3$. Look for the second bifurcation. Next try $c = -1.4$. What do you see? Now try $c = -1.5$.

6. Now try $c = -2.1$. There **are** starting values that do not result in divergence. See if you can find one!

7. The projects so far are best discussed by using web diagrams. In this project we want to find, as accurately as possible, the values of c for which each phase of period-doubling starts. For this you should plot x_n as a function of n. Before any doubling (but after transient effects have disappeared) you will see a single horizontal line of points. Gradually decrease c; it will be fairly clear when the line starts to double. Make a note of this value of c; call it c_0. Continue to decrease c, but more gradually, to look for the next doubling value, c_1, and so on. The interval between successive c_i diminishes rapidly, so you will have to give up eventually, but try to find enough values to estimate Feigenbaum's constant.

8. This project is concerned with construction of a bifurcation diagram, and will need a computer program. An example of the diagram to be generated is shown in figure 5.20. The basic logic is simple. There is an outer loop that changes the value of c. In the inner loop, choose a seed, such as $x_0 = 0$, then iterate the map `NIt` times, `For N = 1 To NIt`; when `N` is greater than some number, `nCrit` (less than `NIt`), assume that all transient terms have passed, and print a point with coordinates (c, x). Suppose that you are to see the diagram for values of c between cMin and `cMax`, and that you are to plot for 500 values of c; the number 500 would represent the number of screen pixels (measured horizontally) that you are to use. Then consider code such as this:

```
Delc = (cMax - cMin)/500
c = cMax
Do Nc = 0 To 500
```

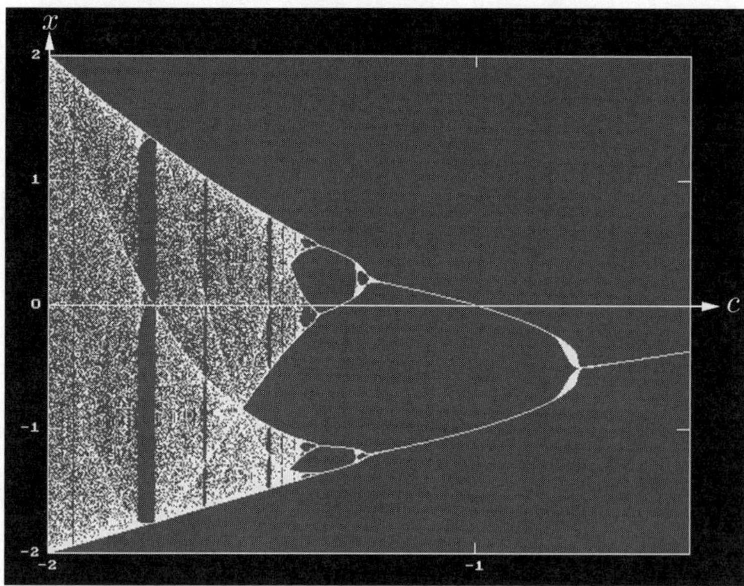

Figure 5.20: *A bifurcation diagram for the quadratic map.*

```
Begin
    X = 0
    Do N = 1 TO NIt
    Begin
        X = X*X - c
        If N ≥ NCrit Then plot (c, X)
    End
    c = c - Delc
End
```

Start with c varying between 0.25 and –2.

In the bifurcation diagram you will see clearly the period-doubling as it takes place, and as it lies on the route to chaos.

9. Choose a small rectangle in the figure just found that contains the start of a bifurcation with a chaotic ending. Plot the bifurcation diagram inside this region. Qualitatively, you should see a figure that is very similar to the larger one. Now choose a similar small rectangle in the new figure, and again plot the bifurcation diagram. In theory, this can go on forever! (Ultimately this will break down in practice. To delay this, increase `NCrit` and `NIt`.)

10. In the original bifurcation diagram there are "windows" in which chaos temporarily ceases. Magnify some of these and explore their properties.

5.5.7 Second-Order Difference Equations

There are parallels to be drawn between the forced pendulum and first-order difference equations such as the quadratic map. Let us return to the true Poincaré map, based on a conservative dynamical system with two degrees of freedom. It turns out that very similar maps can be generated by systems of second-order difference equations. Pioneers in this respect are again Hénon and Heiles.

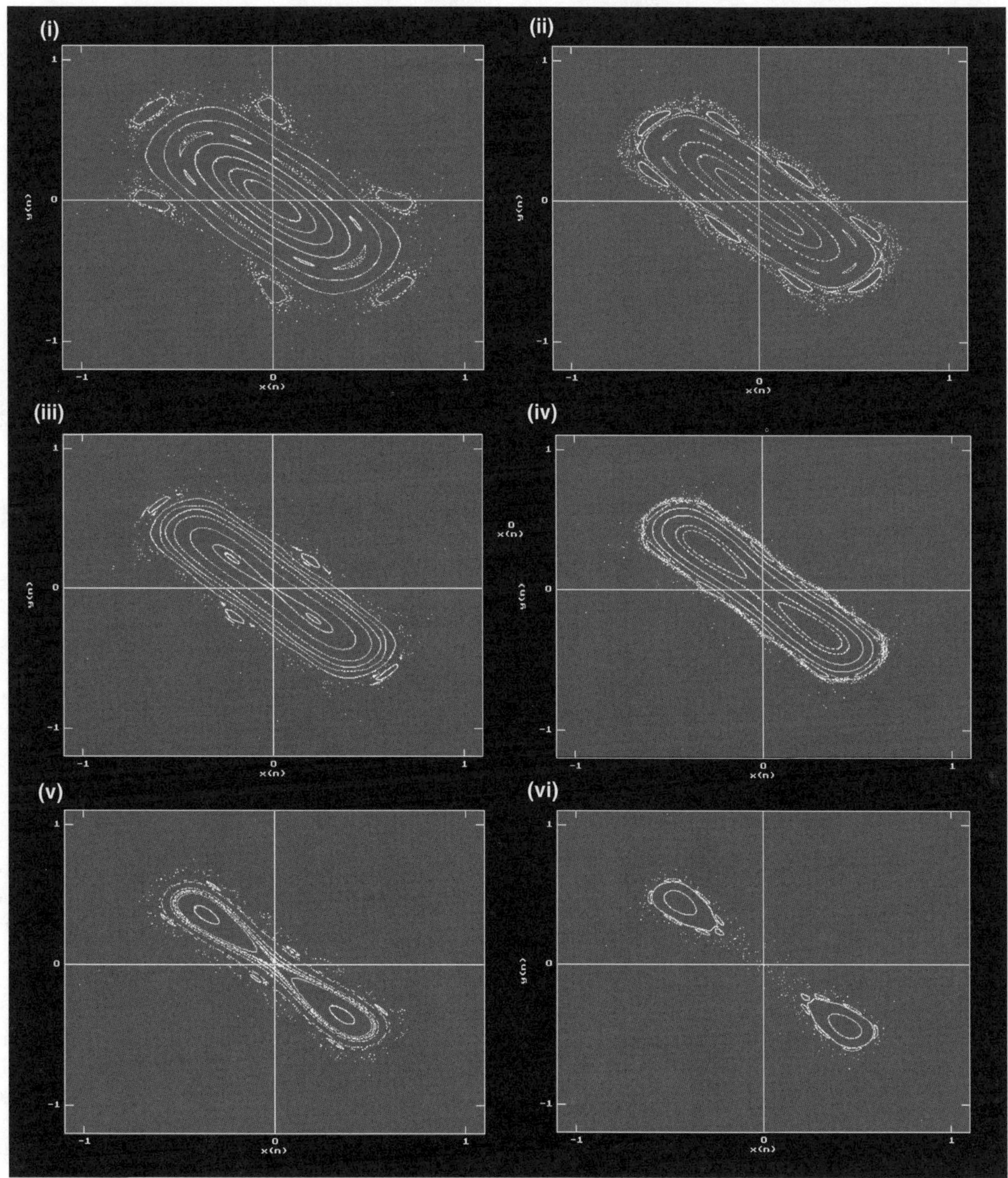

Figure 5.21: *Mappings for (5.5.20). Values for the parameters a are: (i)* $a = 1.6$, *(ii)* $a = 2.0$, *(iii)* $a = 2.1$, *(iv)* $a = 2.2$, *(v)* $a = 2.3$, *(vi)* $a = 2.5$. *Note the shrinking of the non-chaotic region and the temporary survival of "islands" among the chaos. Also note the bifurcation at the origin where closed curves about the origin are replaced by a figure eight.*

In their paper [53], in addition to the dynamical system, they also considered the difference equations

$$\left.\begin{aligned} x_{n+1} &= x_n + a(y_n - y_n^3), \\ y_{n+1} &= y_n - a(x_{n+1} - x_{n+1}^3). \end{aligned}\right] \tag{5.5.20}$$

For a given value of a, different starting conditions, (x_0, y_0), result in sets of points similar to those found for the dynamical system (but very much faster). As the parameter a is increased, so is the chaos. Figures 5.21(i) to (vi) show results with $a = 1.6$, 2.0, 2.1, 2.2, 2.3 and 2.5. Note the bifurcation at the origin.

Another system often quoted is Hénon's *quadratic map* [52],

$$\left.\begin{aligned} x_{n+1} &= x_n \cos\alpha - y_n \sin\alpha + x_n^2 \sin\alpha, \\ y_{n+1} &= x_n \sin\alpha + y_n \cos\alpha - x_n^2 \cos\alpha. \end{aligned}\right] \tag{5.5.21}$$

You might also read a paper by Hénon [54] and another by Curry [28] on the simple looking system

$$\left.\begin{aligned} x_{n+1} &= y_n + 1 - ax_n^2, \\ y_{n+1} &= bx_n, \end{aligned}\right] \tag{5.5.22}$$

where the authors discuss *strange attractors*.

A different sort of chaotic picture can be generated by Newton's method for a system of two equations. Suppose that we want to find solutions of

$$f(x, y) = 0, \text{ and } g(x, y) = 0. \tag{5.5.23}$$

Starting with some estimate (x_0, y_0), we find Δx_0 and Δy_0 from

$$\left.\begin{aligned} f_x(x_0, y_0)\Delta x + f_y(x_0, y_0)\Delta y = -f(x_0, y_0), \\ g_x(x_0, y_0)\Delta x + g_y(x_0, y_0)\Delta y = -g(x_0, y_0). \end{aligned}\right] \tag{5.5.24}$$

Then the improved estimate by Newton's method is

$$x_1 = x_0 + \Delta x_0, \; y_1 = y_0 + \Delta y_0. \tag{5.5.25}$$

The process continues, as usual, until the adjustments become sufficiently small. The initial estimate can be important, because there are likely to be several solutions, only one of which is wanted; the qualities of Newton's method, such as quadratic convergence, are local, and only appear when "sufficiently" close to the solution.

Suppose equations (5.5.23) have several solutions. For a given starting value (x_0, y_0) which of these solutions will be found? Each solution will have an associated region around it in which all points can be used as starting values; this region will be part of the *basin of attraction* for that solution. But we might expect boundaries to exist separating the basins of different solutions. If $f(x, y)$ and $g(x, y)$ are sufficiently simple functions, the boundaries will consist of lines; otherwise they break up into fractal patterns. One of the projects is concerned with coloring the basins of attraction of different solutions. You may be surprised at the variety and beauty of the pictures that you generate. If you pick a small region, where the patterns look interesting, and repeat within that region (blown-up), you will see a repetition of the chaos. Continually reducing the size of the region will result in similar repetitions.

Figures 5.22 and 5.23 were generated using the system

$$\left.\begin{aligned} x^2 + xy^3 = 9, \\ 3x^2y - y^3 = 4. \end{aligned}\right] \tag{5.5.26}$$

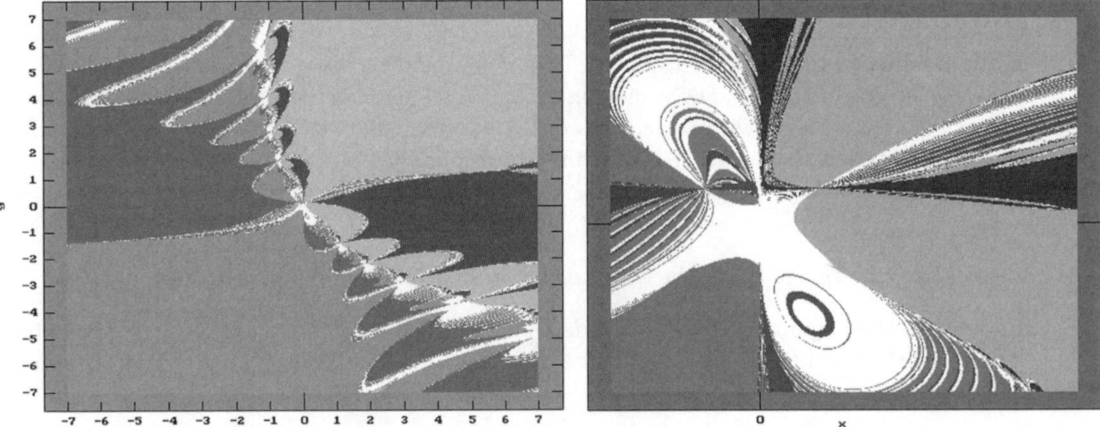

Figure 5.22: *Each point in the figures is used as a starting point in the solution of equations (5.5.26) using Newton's method. The point is shaded depending on which of the four solutions is reached. The smaller region shown in (b) shows similar patterns of chaos, and this will continue indefinitely for smaller and smaller regions. This is a "fractal" property. For the smaller region* $-0.2932 < x < 0.6018$ *and* $-0.5026 < y < 0.7841$.

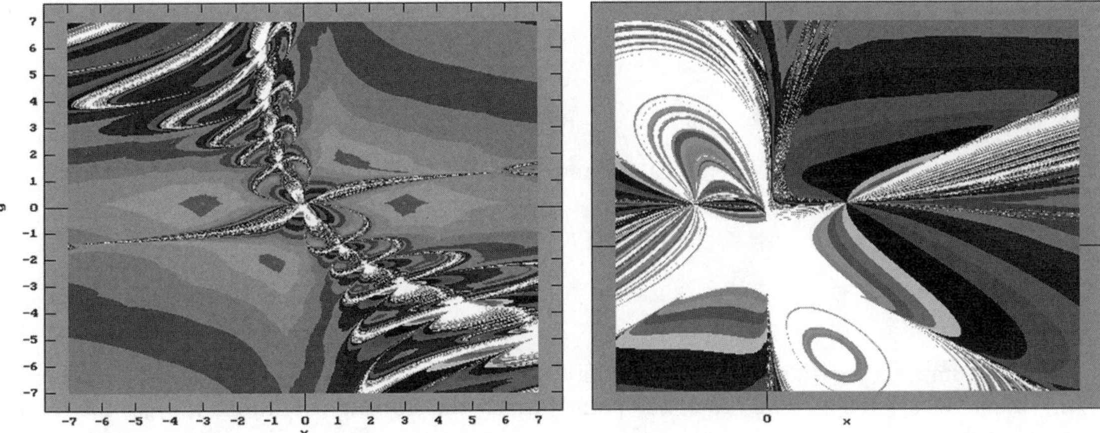

Figure 5.23: *Each point is shaded depending on the number of iterations needed for convergence — regardless of the final root to which the sequence converges. For the smaller region* $-0.3858 < x < 0.8178$, *and* $-0.7037 < y < 0.8645$.

This has four solutions; approximately, (1.34, 1.75), (−3.00, 0.15), (3.00, 0.15) and (−0.90, −2.09). Each point in the diagram defines starting conditions for the iteration. In figure 5.22 the color of a point depends on which of the four solutions is reached after 20 iterations or less. (If there is no convergence, the point is colored black.) Figure 5.22(b) contains a small region from 5.22(a); smaller and smaller regions will continue to show similar patterns. Another way to color points ignores the final point of convergence, but counts the number of iterations needed for convergence to any of the four points. The color depends on that number. This is shown in figures 5.23(a) and (b).

In the literature on Newton's method and chaos, you may find an emphasis given to the "complex Newton's method;" i.e., if $z = x + iy$, then solve the complex equation $f(z) = 0$. But just about any two equations (5.5.23) can be used.

5.5.8 Projects

1. Experiment with the mapping (5.5.20). Take $a = 1$, and try a set of starting points beginning close to the origin and gradually moving away. You should see a neat set of closed invariant curves. Now increase a with increments of 0.1. Watch the pattern disintegrate. You will see the same patterns that were produced in section one by Poincaré maps, but now the points are produced quickly and easily. Isolate small regions, and blow up the pattern to see more detail.

2. Repeat the experiment using the quadratic map (5.5.21). Try different angles, α.

3. Investigate the mapping (5.5.22). Take $b = 0.3$ and look into values of a: 1.4 (investigated in detail by Hénon), 1.0721, 1.0752, 1.0768, and 1.08 (considered by Curry). Then experiment with your own.

4. For playing with Newton's method for a system of two equations you can pick just about any two, provided that they involve more than quadratic terms. Here we shall look at a system generated by the complex equation

$$z^3 - 1 = 0, \text{ where } z = x + iy.$$

This has solutions $z = 1, -0.5, \pm\sqrt{3}/2i$. The corresponding equations for x and y are

$$\left.\begin{aligned} f(x,y) &= x^3 - 3xy^2 - 1 = 0, \\ g(x,y) &= 3x^2y - y^3 = 0. \end{aligned}\right] \tag{5.5.27}$$

So

$$f_x = 3x^2 - 3y^2,\ f_y = -6xy,\ g_x = 6xy, \text{ and } g_y = 3x^2 - 3y^2.$$

For given x and y, the corrections Δx and Δy are calculated from

$$\left.\begin{aligned} \Delta x &= (-f \cdot g_y + g \cdot f_y)/\Delta, \\ \Delta y &= (-g \cdot f_x + f \cdot g_x)/\Delta, \\ \text{where} \quad \Delta &= f_x \cdot g_y - g_x \cdot f_y. \end{aligned}\right] \tag{5.5.28}$$

The computer screen must be divided into a grid of points, and Newton's method run for each point, where the coordinates of the point furnish the starting conditions (x_0, y_0) for the run. Decide on a number N, say 20, so that if more than that number of iterations is made without convergence, then the method is declared to diverge.

There are two ways to run this project.

- Calculate all solutions of the equations. If an iteration approaches a solution within some limit, say 0.1, then declare the iteration to have converged to that solution, and color the starting points accordingly. If the iteration diverges, then color the point black.
- Declare the process to have converged if two successive points fall within a given distance (such as 0.1) of each other. Then color the starting point according to the number of iterations, for convergence, or black for divergence.

Figures 5.24(a) and (b) show results for these two methods.

A more interesting system is generated by $(z^2-1)(z^2+c) = 0$, with $z = x+iy$. Figures 5.25(a) and (b) show results for the case $c = 0$.

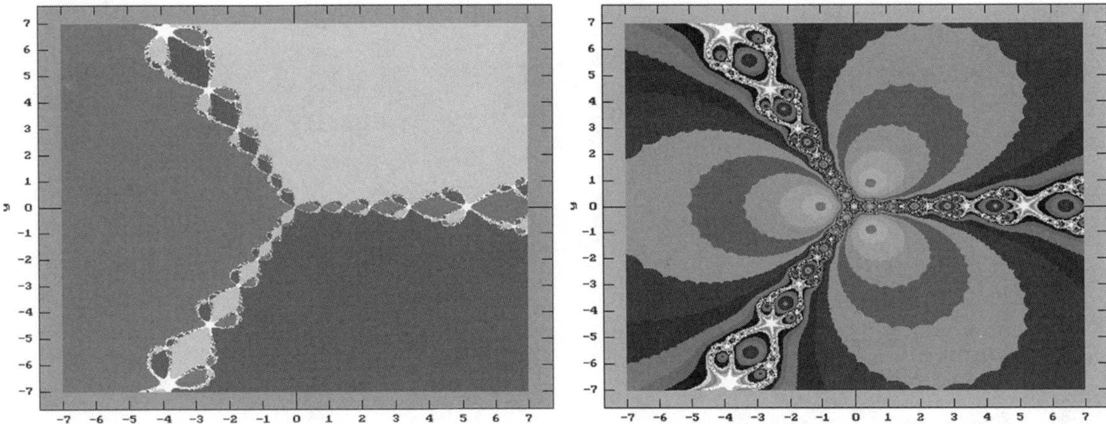

Figure 5.24: *Some results for this project. Each point in the figures is used as a starting point in the iteration. In* (a) *the point is colored depending on which of the three solutions is reached. In* (b) *the point is colored depending on the number of iterations needed to converge to any of the three points.*

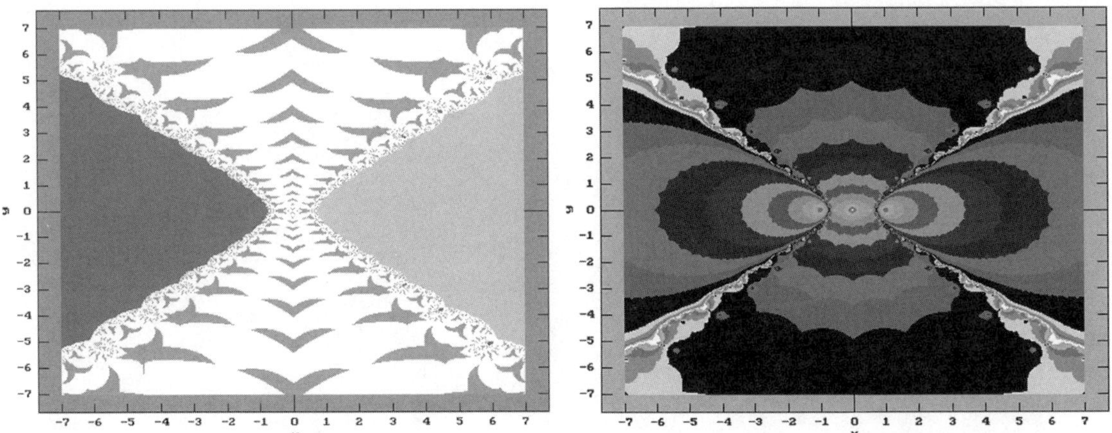

Figure 5.25: *This is similar to figure 5.24. But the system that is solved is* $(z^2 - 1)(z^2 + c) = 0$, *with* $z = x + iy$ *and with* $c = 0$.

Chapter 6

Population Growth and Ecology

6.1 The Predator-Prey Model of Volterra 

In the predator-prey model of Volterra, we are concerned with just two species: the predators can survive only if they can consume their prey, whereas the prey population is limited only by the predation. Presentations of this model include many pairs: birds and worms, wolves and deer, sharks and tuna, to name a few. I have found that my students prefer foxes and rabbits, so I shall refer to these. After all, who identifies with a worm?

With t standing for the time, let $x(t)$ represent the prey population and $y(t)$, the predator population. These variables can be scaled: one unit of x, for instance, might represent a thousand or a million actual individuals. Life will be easier if you deal with moderate numbers for x and y.

First, assume that you are a rabbit, and that there are no foxes. You are surrounded by other soft, furry, like-minded rabbits. What happens?

$$\frac{dx}{dt} = ax.$$

This is the law of *Malthusian* population growth. Next you should imagine yourself to be a fox, with no rabbits yet in the model. What happens? (Remember, there are no chickens either.)

$$\frac{dy}{dt} = -by.$$

You die.

Next, both species are allowed to mingle with one another. The number of contacts between rabbits and foxes is taken to be proportional to the product, xy, of their populations. Then the rabbit population is depleted at the rate $-cxy$, where the parameter c depends on the foxes' hunting ability (or is inversely proportional to the rabbits' ability to hide). The fox population increases at the rate dxy, where d depends on the nutritional value of the rabbits to the foxes. The model is, therefore,

$$\left.\begin{aligned} \frac{dx}{dt} &= ax - cxy, \\ \frac{dy}{dt} &= -by + dxy. \end{aligned}\right] \qquad (6.1.1)$$

These equations constitute Volterra's justly famous model. It was developed in the 1920s by an Italian mathematician, Vito Volterra. (It was also found independently by Lotka, and is often referred to as the Lotka-Volterra model.)

If one equation is divided into the other, then the time t disappears, and we have a separable equation in x and y that can be solved; but the result is in a form that gives no immediate information about the nature of the solutions. (Try it!) To follow changes with the time, numerical integration is needed. However if you have software for constructing direction field diagrams, for a differential equation $dy/dx = f(x, y)$, then it is worth using to give a good idea of the flow of the solutions in the x-y or (prey)-(predator) plane. This same comment applies to many other models in this chapter.

If possible, it is a good idea to start some dialog with a model before starting to compute. A computation should respond to a question, and the information gained from it should suggest further questions. You should start with some ideas about what you can expect, partly because in the first few runs you should be verifying that the program is working as it should. In this, and many other models, there may be equilibrium solutions around which you can build. So let's start by asking

"Are there any equilibrium solutions?"

This is equivalent to the question

"Are there solutions where nothing changes?"

Or, in mathematical jargon,

$$\text{“Are there solutions where } \frac{dx}{dt} = 0 \text{ and } \frac{dy}{dt} = 0\text{?”}$$

Or, finally,

$$\text{“Are there solutions where } 0 = ax - cxy \text{ and } 0 = -by + dxy\text{?”}$$

One solution is $x = y = 0$, but this is obvious and boring. The other is

$$x_e = \frac{b}{d},\ y_e = \frac{a}{c}. \tag{6.1.2}$$

So the answer is "Yes."

The next question is

"Is the equilibrium solution stable?"

"Stability" can be tricky to define mathematically. But the concept is clear. If a solution starting close to the equilibrium drifts continually further away, the equilibrium is unstable; but if the solution remains close, then the equilibrium is stable. To address this question, we move to the computer.

What values should we give to the parameters a, b, c, and d? In one sense, it does not matter. The model has been set up quite generally, so that specific numerical values have little meaning; however, **changes** in these values can be interpreted: an increase in c, for instance, shows what happens if the foxes become more efficient at hunting.

Personally, I start by setting all four parameters equal to one, and getting on with the computation. The equilibrium in this case is at $x_e = 1$, $y_e = 1$. Don't set initial conditions **at** the equilibrium. You know what happens, anyway. Also, if you use a program with stepsize control, you may get a division by zero. I recommend that you first choose your parameters, then locate the equilibrium, and then start with initial conditions close to the equilibrium. Move further away gradually. In this model, look for *cycles*, i.e., periodic solutions. It is these that make the model potentially useful.

Probably the most satisfactory way to exhibit results is to plot the solutions in the x-y plane. This shows the cycles, but does not tell you how rapidly different stages depend on the time. So some additional plots of $x(t)$ and $y(t)$ can be helpful. Some solutions are plotted in the x-y plane in figure 6.1. Times histories are shown in figure 6.2.

There are two essential features of the model:

- All solutions are cycles. So you must integrate for long enough to confirm this.
- Neither species dies out. But if you choose initial conditions too far away from the equilibrium, you will see large cycles where one and then the other population becomes very small. It is easy to think that they have all died.

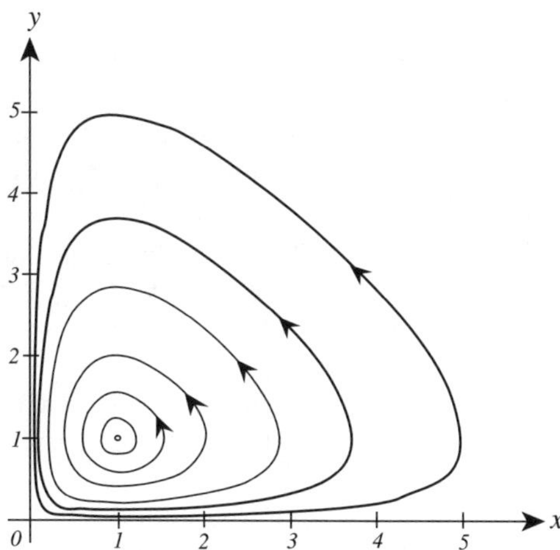

Figure 6.1: *Solutions plotted in the "predator-prey" plane.*

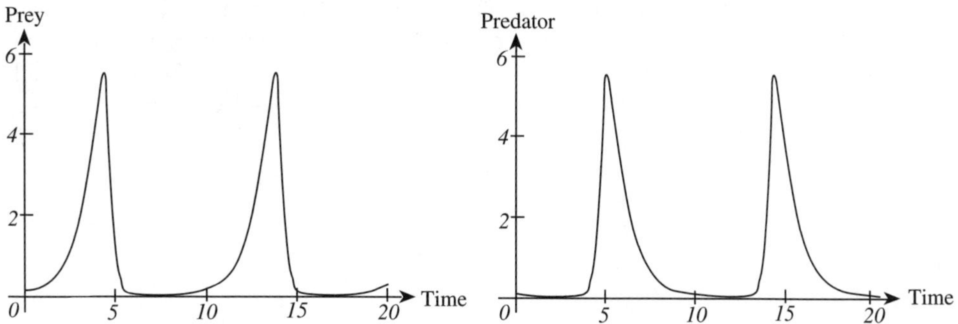

Figure 6.2: *Populations plotted against the time.*

So the equilibrium (x_e, y_e) is stable. Note that the other equilibrium, (0,0), is unstable.

Now consider the following situation. In the spring, a population of pests starts to grow in an orchard according to the formula $dx/dt = ax$, where x represents the pest population. The growth is to be controlled by introducing a given number of a predator species. Once they have been introduced, cyclic variation will commence. Choosing the number of predators to introduce, and deciding when to introduce them, is equivalent to picking initial conditions. The best control would result in the smallest cycles; if too many predators were introduced, then there could be very wide population variations that would not be what the owner of the orchard had in mind.

The equations of this model have been applied to a variety of situations. You will see an application to economics in section 8.5. Another application is in a mathematical model for the sleep cycle [72].

6.2 Volterra's Model with Periodic Birthrate 

All four parameters are positive constants. One way to generalize the model is to allow some of them to vary. For instance, the reproduction of the prey might be seasonal, so that

$$a = a_0 + a_1 \cos pt, \quad a_1 < a_0. \tag{6.2.1}$$

This introduces a forcing term. The resulting system is chaotic; it might be investigated using some of the techniques suggested for the forced pendulum. A few possibilities are illustrated here. We shall take $a_0 = 1$ and $p = 1$.

Figure 6.3 shows two time plots, each with starting conditions $x = 1,\ y = 2$. The first, (a), has $a_0 = 0.2$; this indicates a rather long cycle. The second has $a_0 = 0.4$ and is irregular and chaotic.

Figure 6.4(a) shows a phase-plane plot in the prey-predator plane for the case of figure 6.3(a). It shows a completed cycle. It is also confusing. A better approach when considering chaotic effects in this plane is to plot points at regular periods of the forcing term, generating a "Poincarè map." This is shown in figure 6.4(b), where things appear to be more orderly.

Figure 6.5 shows a variety of Poincarè maps for the case $a_0 = 0.2$, but with many different initial conditions. Close to the old equilibrium at (1,1), things look non-chaotic. Moving away, islands develop and eventually chaos takes over.

The advantage of using the method of Poincarè maps is demonstrated in figure 6.6. 6.6(a) shows a chaotic set of points from one set of initial conditions, (2,3). A time plot for the same conditions is indecisive.

6.3 The Predator-Prey Model with Fishing

The word "fishing" is used here because the first discussion was about the populations of tuna and shark in the Mediterranean Sea between the years 1914 and 1923. During World War 1, the intensity of the fishing diminished; after the war, with increased fishing, the tuna population increased on average. A good discussion of this can be found in Braun [17]. The model can be applied to any situation in which both species are hunted or harvested equally. Equations (6.1.1) are modified to

$$\left.\begin{aligned}\frac{dx}{dt} &= ax - cxy - fx,\\ \frac{dy}{dt} &= -by + dxy - fy.\end{aligned}\right] \tag{6.3.1}$$

The coefficient f depends on the fishing "effort."

The introduction of the fishing terms does not change the basic mathematics of the predator-prey model. But the equilibrium is shifted to the point

$$x_e = \frac{b+f}{d},\quad y_e = \frac{a-f}{c}. \tag{6.3.2}$$

This leads to the surprising result that, on average, fishing reduces the predator population and increases the prey population. If $f > a$, then the predators die out.

Another application of fishing is to pest control in an orchard. Suppose there are two kinds of insect present, the prey (pests) and the predators (good guys). The owner introduced the predators to control the pests, but he becomes impatient, and decides to try to reduce the pest population by spraying the orchard with insecticide, which is equally deadly to either species. What happens?

Start working on this project with $f = 0$. Calculate several cycles. Then introduce small f; use the same initial conditions as before, and compare results. Then increase f further until $f = a$, or exceeds it.

The fishing effort might vary with time. You might try

$$f = f_0 + f_1 \cos pt,\quad f_1 < f_0. \tag{6.3.3}$$

Also try some of the techniques suggested in the preceding project.

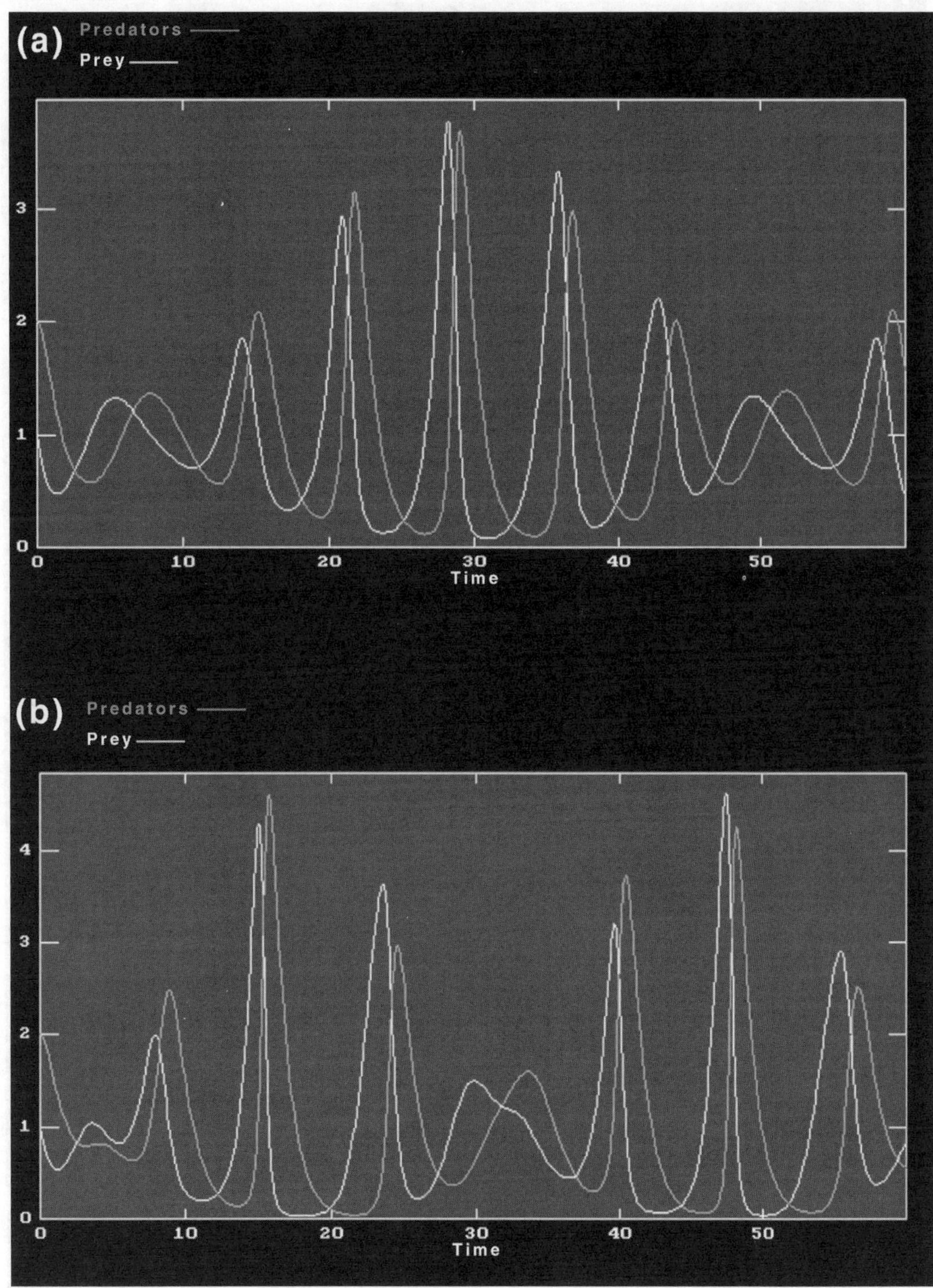

Figure 6.3: *Time plots for the predator and prey populations with initial conditions* $x = 1,\ y = 2$. *For (a) the birthrate of the prey is* $a = 1 + 0.2 \sin t$, *and for (b), the birthrate is* $a = 1 + 0.4 \sin t$. *The first case is periodic; the second is chaotic.*

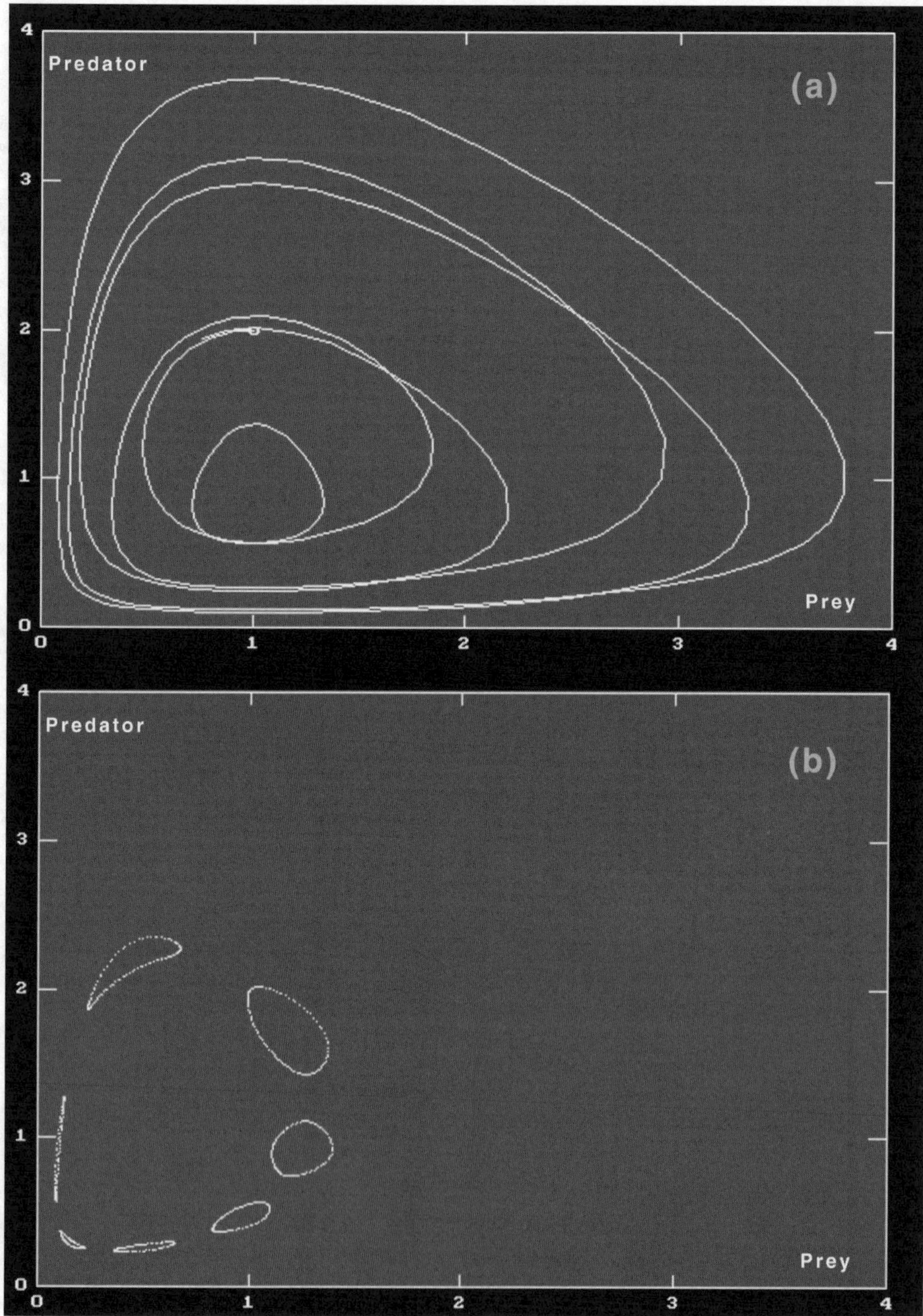

Figure 6.4: *Plots in the predator-prey plane. (a) corresponds to the solution shown in part (a) of figure 6.3; a complete cycle is shown. (b) shows points on the solution plotted in (a) at regular intervals of the time; i.e., $t = P, 2P, 3P, \ldots$ where P is the period of the forcing term in the birthrate. This is the method of Poincarè maps.*

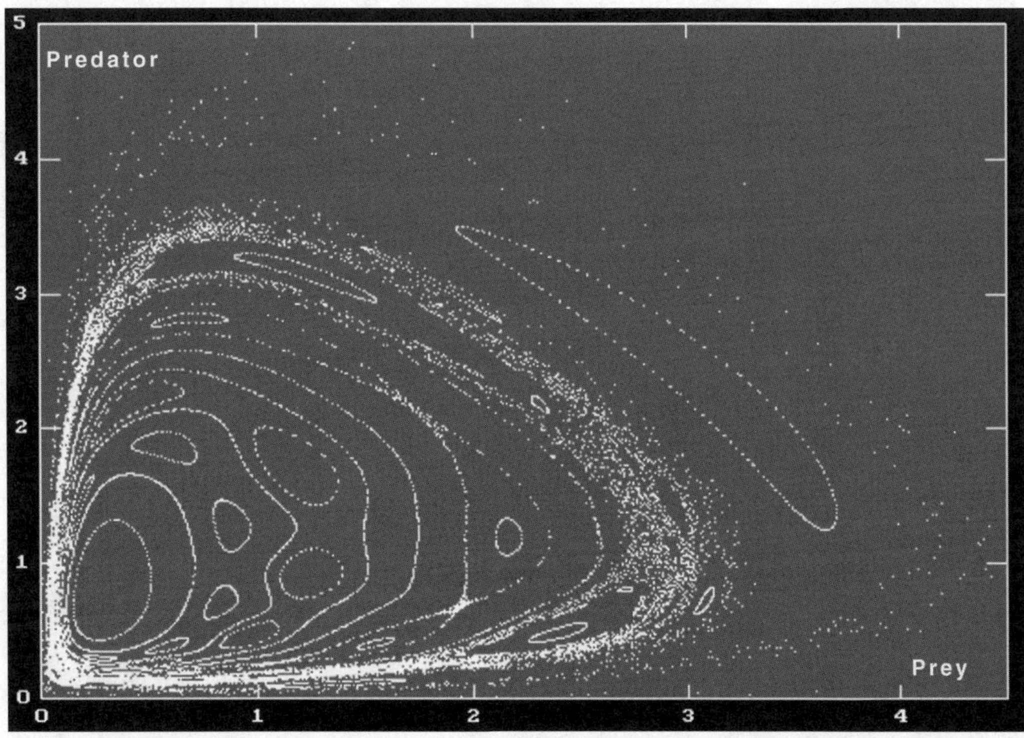

Figure 6.5: *This is a generalization of figure 6.4(b). Many different initial conditions have been used. Around the point (1,1) the solutions appear to be non-chaotic. But moving away, islands form and then chaos takes over. This demonstrates the strength of the method for comparing different starting conditions and seeing the onset of chaos in one figure.*

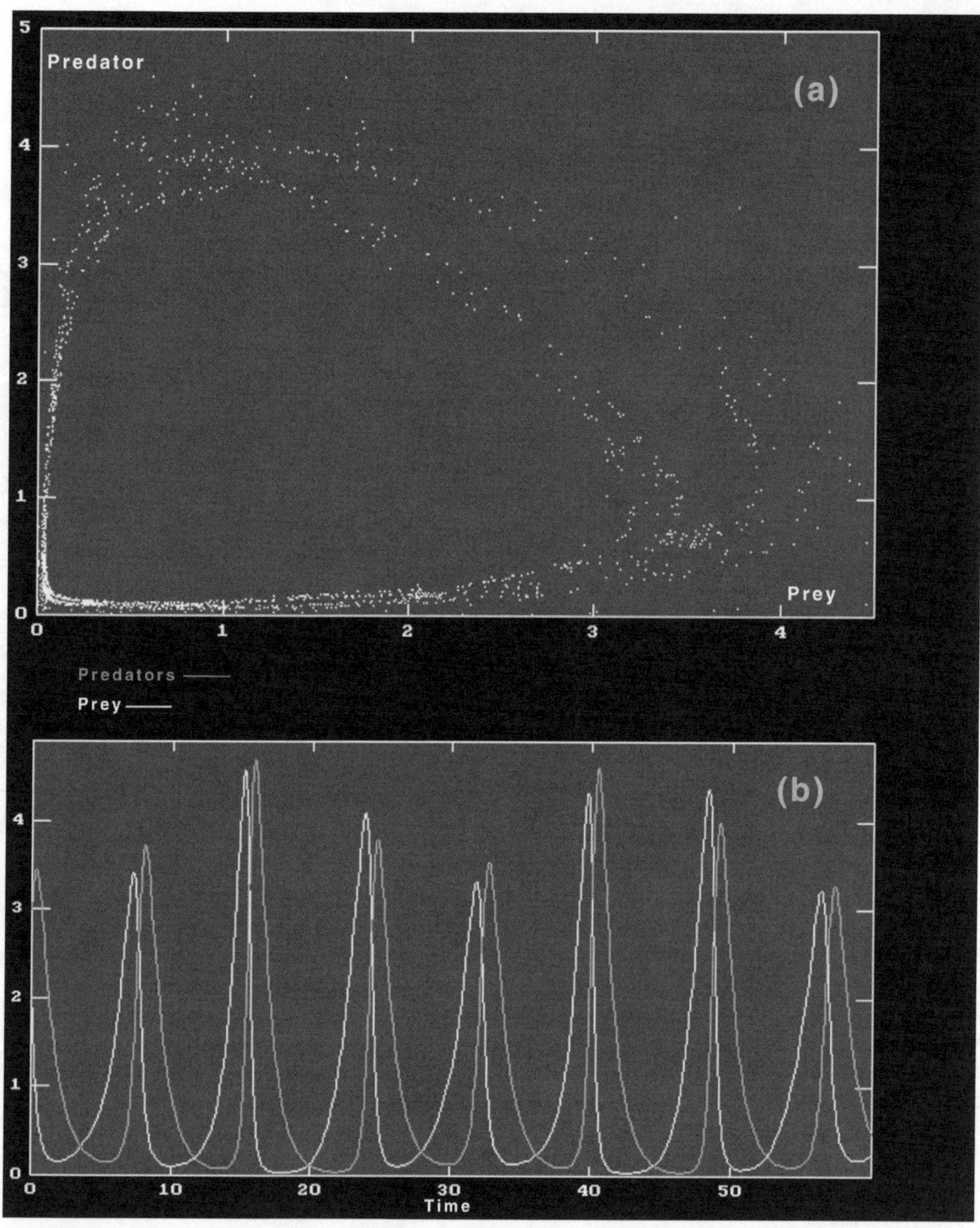

Figure 6.6: *Part (a) shows chaotic points generated from one initial condition; these points appear also in figure 6.5. Part (b) shows the start of a time plot for the same conditions; it is not immediately clear that the solution is chaotic. Again, the superiority of the method of Poincarè maps is demonstrated.*

6.4 The Predator-Prey Model with Logistic Growth for the Prey 

Because of limited resources, the Malthusian model for population growth becomes invalid for large populations. For given space and food supply, there is likely to be a maximum population that an environment can sustain. Suppose this is M. The model for *logistic growth* is

$$\frac{dx}{dt} = kx(M - x). \tag{6.4.1}$$

k is positive. If $x < M$, then $dx/dt > 0$ so the population increases; but if $x > M$, it will decrease. This equation can be written as

$$\frac{dx}{dt} = ax - ex^2, \tag{6.4.2}$$

where $M = a/e$, $k = e$. So logistic growth for the prey can be introduced into the predator-prey model with the system

$$\left.\begin{aligned} \frac{dx}{dt} &= ax - ex^2 - cxy, \\ \frac{dy}{dt} &= -by + dxy. \end{aligned}\right] \tag{6.4.3}$$

Equilibria are at $(0, 0)$, $(a/e, 0)$ and $(b/d, (ad - eb)/(cd))$. Start with $e = 0$; then introduce small e. What happens? You will find that the cycles have been destroyed, so that the "improvement" we have made has actually made things worse.

6.5 The Predator-Prey Model with Logistic Growth for Both Species 

Let's see if we can improve on the preceding model if we introduce logistic growth for the predators. Their "maximum" population will depend on the food supply, so it will be proportional to x. One model for this is due to P.H.Leslie [65]. The new equations are

$$\left.\begin{aligned} \frac{dx}{dt} &= ax - ex^2 - cxy, \\ \frac{dy}{dt} &= y\left(b - \frac{dy}{x}\right). \end{aligned}\right] \tag{6.5.1}$$

$dy/dt = 0$ if $y = bx/d$. Also if x becomes too small, $dy/dt < 0$, which is an essential part of the model.

Confirm that this model has a non-trivial equilibrium. Have things improved?

6.6 An Alternative Law for Predation 

A weakness in the models up to this point lies in the assumption that whenever a fox meets a rabbit, he will eat it. But imagine: a fox has just eaten a rabbit; he is full and contented, and wants to go home to sleep it off. (Suppose you have finished a Thanksgiving meal, and you ate the entire turkey.) On the way home he meets another rabbit; will he eat it? The fact is that if the rabbit population was extremely high, so that a fox could pick one up at any time, then the predation rate would be proportional to the number of foxes. A predation rate that allows for this is due to Holling [55]. It is proportional to

$$\frac{xy}{1 + px}.$$

For small x we have the rate already considered; but as x increases, we approach a rate proportional to y.

Let's try

$$\left.\begin{aligned}\frac{dx}{dt} &= ax - \frac{cxy}{1+px},\\ \frac{dy}{dt} &= -by + \frac{dxy}{1+px}.\end{aligned}\right] \qquad (6.6.1)$$

Confirm that there is a nontrivial equilibrium if $p < d/b$. Start playing with the model with $p = 0$. Then introduce small p. Any good?

6.7 A Predator-Prey Model Due to R.M.May: Limit Cycles

So far, attempts to improve on Volterra's model have only destroyed its greatest asset: cycles. We are already seeing a bewildering variety of possibilities. An excellent survey of possible forms for laws of predation and population growth is given by R.M.May [69][1]. May neatly describes the possibilities as components of a "build-a-model" toy. (This text, which is extremely rewarding to read, also has illustrations showing the introduction of random processes, and systems with time delay.) One particular model has been chosen here from those constructed by May. It assembles some of the toys we have already played with:

$$\left.\begin{aligned}\frac{dx}{dt} &= ax - bx^2 - \frac{cxy}{x+d},\\ \frac{dy}{dt} &= ey\left(1 - f\frac{y}{x}\right).\end{aligned}\right] \qquad (6.7.1)$$

This can be simplified, and the number of effective parameters reduced, if we let

$$\xi = x/d,\ \eta = fy/d,\ \tau = at. \qquad (6.7.2)$$

Then the system can be written as

$$\left.\begin{aligned}\frac{d\xi}{d\tau} &= \xi - (bd/a)\xi^2 - (c/af)\frac{\xi\eta}{1+\xi},\\ \frac{d\eta}{d\tau} &= (e/a)\eta\left(1 - \frac{\eta}{\xi}\right).\end{aligned}\right] \qquad (6.7.3)$$

A special case considered by May, and illustrated in figure 6.7, has the numerical values

$$(bd/a) = 0.1,\ (c/af) = 1,\ (e/a) = 1/6. \qquad (6.7.4)$$

This case has an equilibrium at $\xi = \eta = \frac{1}{2}(-1 + \sqrt{41})$, which is unstable. But solutions starting nearby do not depart from it indefinitely, and they all approach what is called a *limit cycle.* In fact, solutions starting from outside the limit cycle also approach it; so, for obvious reasons, it is called a *stable* limit cycle. A solution on the limit cycle stays there forever. So, after all these "improvements," we once again have a model that might be useful!

This is the first time in these projects that we have met a limit cycle, but it will not be the last. Limit cycles are an important feature of many nonlinear systems. There is a mathematical background for limit cycles based on the "Poincaré-Bendixson theorem" which you can look up in many references. Its application to predator-prey problems, due to Kolmogorov, is described by May. The theorem gives sufficient conditions for a system to have a stable equilibrium or a stable limit cycle.

This model is rich in its possibilities. For the project, start with the numerical values given in (6.7.4) and confirm the details of the figure and the properties of the limit cycle. According to May, the limit cycle is more likely if

[1]From Robert M. May, *Stability and Complexity in Model Ecosystems.* Copyright ©1973 by Princeton University Press. Model 4.5, p 84, and excerpt p. 90, adapted by permission of Princeton University Press.

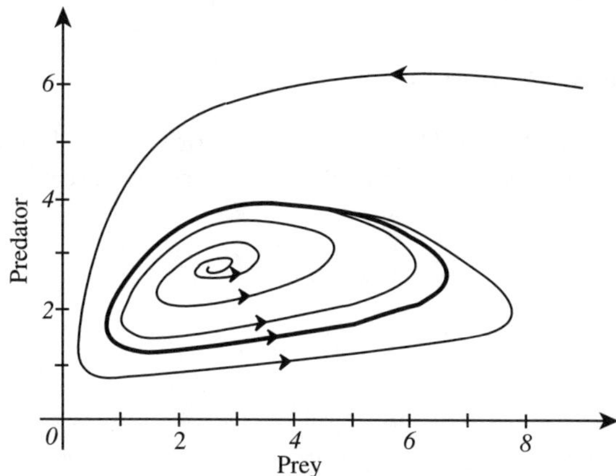

Figure 6.7: *Regions in the Q-R plane where there are one or three equilibria.*

1. (a/e) is large, i.e., the prey reproduce more vigorously than the predators, or
2. (a/b) is large, i.e., the influence of the environment on the maximum prey population is weak.

So try reducing these quantities, and see if you can follow the system to one with a stable equilibrium. Or see what can happen if these quantities are increased. Or just sit back and play.

6.8 The Predator-Prey Model with Internal Competition 

If both predator and prey are competing for resources in the environment, the equations for the model might be written as

$$\left.\begin{aligned} \frac{dx}{dt} &= ax - cxy - ex^2, \\ \frac{dy}{dt} &= -by + dxy - fy^2. \end{aligned}\right] \tag{6.8.1}$$

For equilibria, we have $(0,0)$, $(a/e, 0)$ and possibly the intersection of the two lines

$$L_1 : \ a - cy - ex = 0, \quad L_2 : \ -b + dx - fy = 0. \tag{6.8.2}$$

For numerical work, start from results with e and f equal to zero. Then introduce small values. It can be shown that if $be - ad$ is positive, then the predators will die out. See if you can justify this mathematically, but make a numerical confirmation. You might set all parameters expect e equal to one, but vary e to be less than, equal to, and then greater than one.

6.9 Cooperation Between Two Species

Different species do not have to eat one another; the reverse process is "cooperation," producing food, for instance, that enhances the growth of both. For this case, equations (6.8.1) might be modified to give

$$\left.\begin{aligned} \frac{dx}{dt} &= ax + cxy - ex^2, \\ \frac{dy}{dt} &= by + dxy - fy^2. \end{aligned}\right] \tag{6.9.1}$$

If $c = d$, the cooperation is symmetrical between the species.

Look for equilibrium solutions and investigate stability in the usual qualitative ways. Then investigate the system numerically.

6.10 Competition Between Two Species

This model is due to G.F.Gause [46]. There is no predation, but two species are competing against each other for limited resources. In contrast with the preceding model, the equations are

$$\left.\begin{aligned} \frac{dx}{dt} &= ax - cxy - ex^2, \\ \frac{dy}{dt} &= by - dxy - fy^2. \end{aligned}\right] \tag{6.10.1}$$

There are several equilibria: find them all. If one exists for which neither x nor y is zero, then it will be at the point of intersection of the two lines

$$L_1 : \; a - cy - ex = 0, \quad L_2 : \; b - dx - fy = 0. \tag{6.10.2}$$

To be of practical use, the point of intersection must have positive x and y. To help your discussion, construct the cases shown in figure 6.8, and draw in arrows showing the flow of the solutions in different regions.

Don't forget the option of dividing one equation of (6.10.1) into the other, thereby eliminating t, and then constructing a direction field diagram for the resulting equation in x and y.

Now calculate solutions to make numerical verification of the cases that you have discussed.

If there is an equilibrium with both x and y positive, then it can be shown that this is stable if $cd - ef$ is positive. Try to confirm this analytically and then numerically. What happens if $cd - ef = 0$?

6.11 The Predator-Prey Model with Child Care

Suppose the prey population x is divided into x_1 children and x_2 adults, so that $x = x_1 + x_2$. The children are protected from the predators; x_1 is increased by birth at the rate ax_2. It is decreased by natural death (or maybe being eaten by the adults) at the rate a_1x_1, and by growing up into adulthood at the rate a_2x_1. Then

$$\frac{dx_1}{dt} = ax_2 - a_1x_1 - a_2x_1. \tag{6.11.1}$$

The adults' numbers are increased by the kids growing up at the rate a_2x_1, and are decreased by natural death at the rate a_3x_2 and predation at the rate cx_2y, y being the predator population. So

$$\frac{dx_2}{dt} = a_2x_1 - a_3x_2 - cx_2y. \tag{6.11.2}$$

For the predators

$$\frac{dy}{dt} = -by + dx_2y. \tag{6.11.3}$$

The system is now of third-order, so is not so easy to discuss. It should be explored gradually. If $y = 0$, we can follow the population of the prey when left to itself. This follows a linear system with equilibrium at $x_1 = x_2 = 0$. If this were stable, the population would die out even without predation. Look for parameters such that the prey population will always increase without predation. Now introduce predation. For $y \neq 0$ there is a nontrivial equilibrium. Find it.

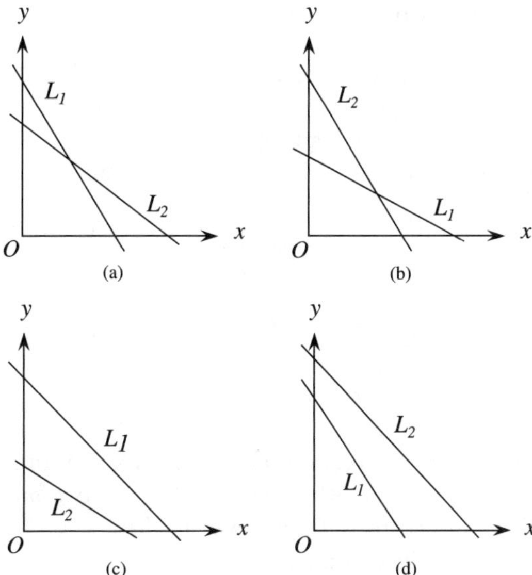

Figure 6.8: *(a) Stability. Coexistence. (b) Instability. Only one survives. (c) x always survives. (d) y always survives.*

You might take $a = 2$, $a_1 = a_2 = a_3 = 0.5$, and $b = c = d = 1$. (Or, better, make up your own values.) Confirm that, without predation, the prey population increases without limit. Find the equilibrium when predation is included, and investigate its stability by calculating solutions starting close to the equilibrium. Try plotting the three variables as functions of t, and also $x = x_1 + x_2$ and y. Can you observe cyclical behavior? Investigate other changes, putting a physical interpretation on any change that you make with the parameters.

6.12 Predator-Prey Models with More than Two Species

A third species having population z can be introduced into Volterra's model in many ways. For instance, it might prey on both of the others, but be preyed upon by neither. We would than have the system of equations

$$\left.\begin{aligned}\frac{dx}{dt} &= ax - cxy - exz,\\ \frac{dy}{dt} &= -by + dxy - fyz,\\ \frac{dz}{dt} &= -gz + hxz + iyz.\end{aligned}\right] \qquad (6.12.1)$$

We could start this model with no z and a state of equilibrium between x and y. Now introduce small values of e and f and see what happens. See if you can find values for the parameters such that there is a nontrivial equilibrium (i.e., one for which no population is zero). Then investigate its equilibrium numerically.

Alternatively, the third species might prey on one of the first two but cooperate with the other. Look for variations and make up possible interpretations.

The system of three equations, and the systems that follow in the next two projects, bear some similarity to the *Lorenz equations* discussed in section (5.3). Be on the lookout for any of their chaotic properties.

6.13 Carnivores, Vegetarians and Plants

A model described by Braun [17] concerns three species on the island of Komodo in Malaysia: we have giant carnivorous reptiles, vegetarian mammals, and plants. Let the populations of these be given respectively by x, y, and z. The reptiles eat the mammals, the mammals eat the plants, and the plants compete among themselves. The resulting system is

$$\left.\begin{aligned} \frac{dx}{dt} &= -ax + bxy, \\ \frac{dy}{dt} &= -cy - dxy + eyz, \\ \frac{dz}{dt} &= fz - gz^2 - hyz. \end{aligned}\right] \tag{6.13.1}$$

As usual, choose simple values for the parameters, and look for and investigate the stability of equilibria. If one species dies out, can the others survive? If the two animal species were to fertilize the plants with their droppings and corpses, then the terms $+ix+jy$ should be included on the right of the equation for $\dot{z}$. What effect will this have?

6.14 Violets, Ants and Rodents

This model involving three species, some predation and some cooperation was proposed by R.E.Heithaus, D.C.Culver and A.J.Beattie [51]. An account can be found in an article by W.M.Post, et al. [78]. The species for the model are violets, ants, and rodents. Violets produce seeds, with density x. Some of the seeds are taken by ants, which have density y. The ants use the seed covering for food, but leave the remainder, which is still an intact seed, in their refuse piles, which are good sites for germination. The seeds are also destroyed by rodents, which have density z. The model has the following equations

$$\left.\begin{aligned} \frac{dx}{dt} &= ax - ex^2 + bxy - gxz, \\ \frac{dy}{dt} &= cy - fy^2 + dxy, \\ \frac{dz}{dt} &= -hz + ixz. \end{aligned}\right] \tag{6.14.1}$$

Without the rodents, we have the model for cooperation between two species (6.9.1), so start with a relatively small value of g. Again, find nontrivial equilibria and investigate their stability numerically. See if you can vary a parameter to switch from stability to instability, or the reverse.

Incidentally, *mutualism* is another word you will see for cooperation that results in mutual benefit.

6.15 A Model for the Population Growth of a Parasite

In this model a species of parasite has population $P(t)$. The food supply is $F(t)$. The birthrate of the parasites is proportional to the square of their population, and to the food supply per capita. Then

$$\frac{dP}{dt} = aP^2\left(\frac{F}{P}\right) - bP = aPF - bP, \tag{6.15.1}$$

where bP is the death rate.

The food supply grows at the constant rate, c, dies at the rate dF and is consumed by the parasites at the rate eP. So

$$\frac{dF}{dt} = c - dF - eP. \tag{6.15.2}$$

Show that there is an equilibrium if $F = b/a$ and $P = (ac - db)/ae$. Clearly, if the species are to survive, $ac > db$. Choose parameters so that this is the case. Then start with initial conditions close to the equilibrium, and gradually move further away. What do you find?

6.16 A Model for Cannibalism

I am indebted to my colleague Dr. John Bishir[2] for this model and for the details to be described. Cannibalism is common in many species. It may be explicit, as a source of food or as a means of population control. Or it may be implicit: members of the same species compete for limited resources, and the young have to accept what is left over when the adults have satisfied themselves; or in a forest young trees suffer from a shortage of resources and light because of the presence of older trees.

For this model a species is divided into four stages: eggs, larvae, pupae, and adults. An individual may eat members of the same or a lower stage; so, for instance, a larva may eat other larvae or eggs, but not pupae or adults. Eggs are laid only by adults; also eggs do not eat other eggs. In the first three stages depletion may be caused by natural death, by being eaten by members of the same or a higher stage, or by growing into the next stage.

Let the members of the respective stages have populations p_1, p_2, p_3 and p_4. Then the following equations result:

$$\left.\begin{aligned}
\frac{dp_1}{dt} &= \beta p_4 - \gamma_1 p_1 - \delta_1 p_1 - p_1(\eta_{12}p_2 + \eta_{13}p_3 + \eta_{14}p_4), \\
\frac{dp_2}{dt} &= \gamma_1 p_1 - \gamma_2 p_2 - \delta_2 p_2 - p_2(\eta_{22}p_2 + \eta_{23}p_3 + \eta_{24}p_4), \\
\frac{dp_3}{dt} &= \gamma_2 p_2 - \gamma_3 p_3 - \delta_3 p_3 - p_3(\eta_{33}p_3 + \eta_{34}p_4), \\
\frac{dp_4}{dt} &= \gamma_3 p_3 - \delta_4 p_4 - \eta_{44}p_4^2.
\end{aligned}\right] \tag{6.16.1}$$

The logic for the notation is that β denotes birth, γ denotes growing up, δ denotes natural death, and η denotes being eaten.

The following theoretical results have been derived for the model by Bishir. Let

$$\left.\begin{aligned}
B &= \beta\gamma_1\gamma_2\gamma_3, \\
D &= (\gamma_1 + \delta_1)(\gamma_2 + \delta_2)(\gamma_3 + \delta_3)\delta_4.
\end{aligned}\right] \tag{6.16.2}$$

1. In the absence of cannibalism, i.e., with $\eta_{ij} = 0$, there is a population explosion if $B > D$. If $B \leq D$ and at least one of the η_{ij} is nonzero, then there is extinction in the sense that $\lim_{t\to\infty} P_i = 0, \ i = 1, 2, 3, 4$.

2. The $p_i(t)$ remain bounded if any class eats itself or an adjacent class.

3. The origin is stable provided $B < D$, or $B = D$ and at least one of the η_{ij} is nonzero. The origin is unstable if $B > D$.

4. If $B > D$ and at least one η_{ij} is nonzero, then there is one additional, nontrivial equilibrium. For cannibalism with up to four classes, this equilibrium is stable.

[2]Dr. John Bishir is a Professor of Mathematics at North Carolina State University.

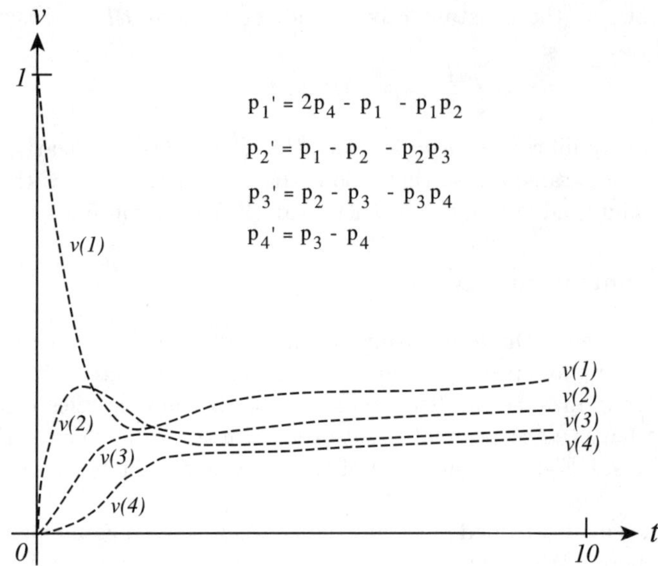

Figure 6.9: *Initial values:* $p_1 = 1,\ p_2 = p_3 = p_4 = 0.$

This information should enable you to get a start in choosing some simple parameters and following the model. Certainly, to begin with, set most of the parameters equal to zero. Some solutions are plotted in figure 6.9.

6.17 Population Growth in a Changing Environment

For a single species, consider the logistic equation

$$\frac{dx}{dt} = ax\left(1 - \frac{x}{K(t)}\right). \tag{6.17.1}$$

According to the equation, the maximum population that the environment can support varies with the time. This is an example of Bernoulli's equation, which can be solved by formula; but unless $K(t)$ is a very obliging function, the integral in the solution would have to be evaluated numerically. So you might as well solve (6.17.1) numerically, in the first place.

For the project, try cases with $K(t)$ steadily increasing or decreasing, or varying periodically. There might, for instance, be an annual variation in the environment; try $K(t) = 2 - \cos pt$. Notice that x will follow the periodic fluctuations of K, but with maxima displaced from the maxima of K. Does x settle down to a regular pattern? Does this pattern depend on the initial conditions?

Similar adjustments can be made to earlier models, so that what were constant parameters become periodic variables. The resulting forced systems may then have chaotic properties that can be investigated using some of the techniques suggested for the forced pendulum.

6.18 A Model for Lake Pollution

This model comes from an example given by J.L.Casti [22][3]. Three components are involved in the model. x is the total biomass of all algal species; y is the soluble phosphate concentration

[3]Permission to quote the model and to use some numerical data was given by the International Institute for Applied Systems Analysis (IIASA), Austria.

forming the principal nutrient; z is the concentration of Anabaena, one of the phytoplankton genera (the plankton vegetation and part of the algae).

x satisfies a generalized logistic equation; as x increases, its growth rate decreases. However, whereas in the usual logistic equation the reduction in the growth rate with respect to increasing x is linear in x, here the reduction with respect to x is taken to be quadratic in x, so that the growth rate at higher densities is more limited than in the conventional logistic equation. The linear part of the growth rate is proportional to the concentration y of the nutrient. The death rate of x is proportional to z: algal die-offs are observed to be preceded by an accumulation of Anabaena on the surface. So

$$\frac{dx}{dt} = -c_1 x^3 + c_2 xy - c_3 z. \tag{6.18.1}$$

For the phosphates,

$$\frac{dy}{dt} = -c_4 x(y - a_0), \tag{6.18.2}$$

where a_0 is the equilibrium concentration. For Anabaena, the growth rate is proportional to the product yx of the amount of food y, and the population z. Because of competition among the algae, the death rate is proportional to the product of z and x. So

$$\frac{dz}{dt} = c_5 yz - c_6 xz. \tag{6.18.3}$$

These are the three equations of the model.

For an experimental comparison with observation, the following numerical values were used:

$$\begin{aligned} c_1 &= 3.10(\mu\text{gChl/ml})^{-2}(\text{time})^{-1}, & c_2 &= 0.60(\mu\text{gP/ml})^{-1}(\text{time})^{-1}, \\ c_3 &= 0.05(\text{time})^{-1}, & c_4 &= 1.00(\mu\text{gChl/ml})^{-1}(\text{time})^{-1}, \\ c_5 &= 1.35(\mu\text{gP/ml})^{-1}(\text{time})^{-1}, & c_6 &= 1.95(\mu\text{gChl/ml})^{-1}(\text{time})^{-1}, \\ a_0 &= 0. \end{aligned}$$

The initial conditions were $t = 0$; $x_0 = 0.11$, $y_0 = 1.28$, $z_0 = 0.02$. One unit of time in the equations is 1.75 days.

Run the model for these values. Vary the initial conditions, and see how these can affect the results. The system is capable of *catastrophic* behavior; that is, it is possible that small changes in parameters can lead to large changes in the outcome. Try to generate a catastrophe! There are three nonlinear equations. Is this system chaotic?

6.19 A Model in Ecology: The Spruce Budworm versus the Balsam Fir

This example is taken from a paper by D.Ludwig, D.D.Jones and C.S.Holling [67][4] The account given here cannot do justice to the original presentation, which is masterly. Read it if you possibly can.

There are three dependent variables in the model: B represents the budworm density; S represents the total surface area in a stand of trees; and E represents the "health" or "energy reserves" of the trees. Of these, B is the most rapid variable. The time t is the independent variable.

The equations will be developed gradually. For a start, B satisfies a logistic equation with added predation

$$\frac{dB}{dt} = r_B B\left(1 - \frac{B}{K_B}\right) - g(B). \tag{6.19.1}$$

[4] D.Ludwig, D.D.Jones and C.S.Holling, "Qualitative Analysis of Insect Outbreak Systems: The Spruce Budworm and Forest," *Journal of Animal Ecology* **47**: (1978), 315-332. Numerical data reproduced with permission.

r_B is a constant. K_B is the "carrying capacity" of the trees, which depends on the amount of foliage available. Predation is due to birds, and it saturates at high densities of prey, so that $g(B)$ tends to a finite limit as B becomes large. In addition, there is a decrease in the effectiveness of the predation for small B, since the worms become hard to find. In the model

$$g(B) = \beta \frac{B^2}{\alpha^2 + B^2} \tag{6.19.2}$$

for constant β; α will depend on S.

Suppose for a moment that B is the only dependent variable in (6.19.1); on a short time scale, this is approximately the case. Equilibria are found by setting $\dot{B} = 0$. If the parameters

$$\mu = B/\alpha, \;\; R = \alpha r_B/\beta, \;\; Q = K_B/\alpha \tag{6.19.3}$$

are introduced, then the condition for equilibrium can be written as

$$R\left(1 - \frac{\mu}{Q}\right) = \frac{\mu}{1+\mu^2}. \tag{6.19.4}$$

In scaled variables, the left-hand side is the per capita growth rate, and the right-hand side is the per capita death rate.

The roots of (6.19.4) number at least one and at most three; they are given by the intersections of the graphs of the functions on the left and right of (6.19.4), plotted separately. The situation is shown in figure 6.10 for the case of three roots (and hence, three equilibria). (The figure shows the nature of the geometry. The curve is distorted in order to clarify the discussion.) The three equilibria are labelled μ_-, μ_c and μ_+; $B = \alpha\mu$, for constant α, so we can also refer to them as B_-, B_c and B_+. As the slow variables R and Q change, the straight line in the figure moves, and the equilibria can disappear or appear in pairs. We shall see in a moment that when there are three equilibria, the two outer ones, B_- and B_+ are stable, while B_c is unstable. If there is only one equilibrium, it is stable. Suppose that there are three equilibria with B temporarily at B_-, and that with R and Q changing, B_- and B_c disappear together, then B will move quickly to the remaining equilibrium, B_+, and there will be an abrupt jump up in the budworm population. In the same way, if B was at B_+, and B_c and B_+ disappear together, then B will move to B_-, and there will be an abrupt jump down in the budworm population. This kind of behavior can be categorized in *catastrophe theory*, and the particular behavior we are seeing here is called a *cusp catastrophe*.

In figure 6.11 there is a sketch of the Q-R plane showing the regions corresponding to one or three roots of equation (6.19.4). When working with the full equations, it is helpful to know the situation here, so accurate plotting of the figure should be a part of this project. The critical boundaries occur when the cubic equation

$$\mu^3 - Q\mu^2 + \mu\left(1 + \frac{Q}{R}\right) - Q = 0 \tag{6.19.5}$$

has two identical roots. The repeated root must be shared with the derivative curve

$$3\mu^2 - 2Q\mu + 1 + \frac{Q}{R} = 0. \tag{6.19.6}$$

Solving (6.19.5) and (6.19.6) for Q and R, we find

$$Q = \frac{2\mu^3}{\mu^2 - 1}, \quad R = \frac{2\mu^3}{(\mu^2+1)^2}. \tag{6.19.7}$$

These are parametric equations for the curve dividing the regions of one or three equilibria. Figure 6.11 also shows how a jump will occur when a boundary is crossed, passing from three equilibria to one.

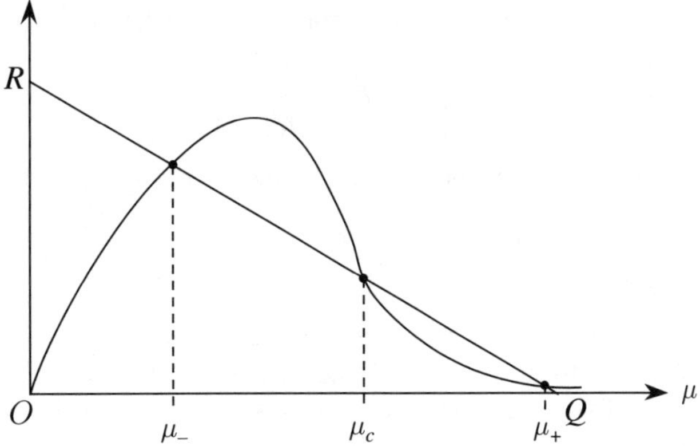

Figure 6.10: *Positions of equilibrium as the intersections of two curves.*

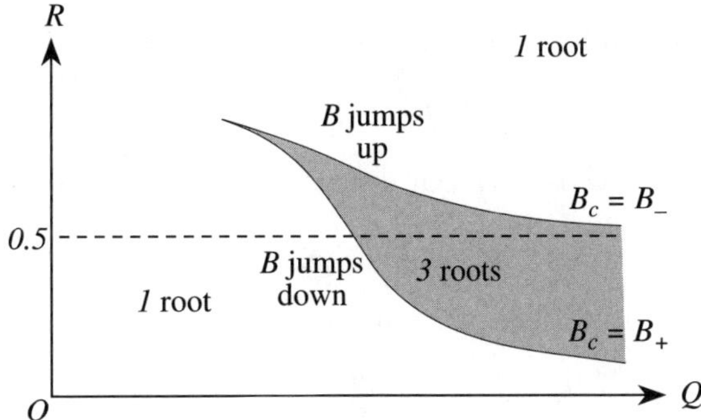

Figure 6.11: *Regions in the Q-R plane where there are one or three equilibria.*

Before adding to the model, I suggest that you get experience with these properties of equation (6.19.1). Using (6.19.3), we can write

$$\frac{d\mu}{dt} = \frac{\beta}{\alpha}\left[R\mu\left(1 - \frac{\mu}{Q}\right) - \frac{\mu^2}{1+\mu^2}\right]. \tag{6.19.8}$$

Set $\alpha/\beta = 1$. Now select a value (greater than one) for a double root, μ_1. If the three roots are then μ_1, μ_1 and μ_2, then an alternative to (6.19.5) is

$$(\mu - \mu_1)(\mu - \mu_1)(\mu - \mu_2) = 0,$$

so $\mu_1\mu_1\mu_2 = Q$ or, from (6.19.7),

$$\mu_2 = \frac{2\mu_1}{\mu_1^2 - 1}. \tag{6.19.9}$$

Find Q and R corresponding to μ_1. Locate the position on the cusp of figure 6.11. Using the figure, change the value of R by just a little so that there will be three equilibria, and run equation (6.19.8). First, choose initial conditions close to each equilibrium in turn, and verify the nature of their stability. When you run the model with initial conditions close to the stable equilibrium that will later disappear, the solution should approach and stay at this equilibrium. Now change R so that there will be only one equilibrium. Keep the same starting conditions. Run the equation again, and see the solution jump to the other remaining equilibrium. The demonstration can be made more dramatic if R is automatically, slowly changed while the integration is taking place.

We are now ready to develop the equations for the slow variables. S is to satisfy the logistic equation

$$\frac{dS}{dt} = r_S S\left(1 - \frac{S}{K_S}\frac{K_E}{E}\right), \tag{6.19.10}$$

which allows the maximum size of S to depend on E, the energy reserve. Finally, E is to satisfy the equation

$$\frac{dE}{dt} = r_E E\left(1 - \frac{E}{K_E}\right) - P\frac{B}{S}, \tag{6.19.11}$$

which allows for logistic growth and also for "predation" by the budworms. The latter is called a *stress term* and is proportional to the number of budworms per branch, or B/S. The new parameters are constants, with the possible exception of P, which will be discussed in a moment.

A model for the slow variables is provided by equations (6.19.10) and (6.19.11) if it is assumed that in this time scale, B is constant. See if you can confirm that for small enough B there are two equilibria, one stable and one unstable; but if B becomes too large, there is no equilibrium and the forest dies out.

Now return to equations (6.19.1) and (6.19.2) for the budworms. Put

$$K_B = K_1 S, \tag{6.19.12}$$

where K_1 is a parameter (not a constant) that depends on the "carrying capacity" of larvae per unit of branch area. In the same way, let

$$\alpha = \alpha_1 S, \tag{6.19.13}$$

for constant α_1. Using these in (6.19.3), we find that

$$Q = K_1/\alpha_1, \quad R = (\alpha_1 r_B/\beta)S. \tag{6.19.14}$$

Now we can begin to see the effect of changes in the slow variables; here it is S that is important. If we start with a young forest, with sufficiently small S (so R is very small), then we will have, from (6.19.4), just one equilibrium, B_-, which will be stable. As the forest grows, and S and R increase, two more equilibria, B_c and B_+, may appear, but the one occupied will still be B_-. But if S increases further, B_c and B_- will disappear. Now the model will jump up to B_+, and the dynamics of the forest will change. If this higher value is too high for the "submodel" defined by just the slow variables (i.e., equations (6.19.10) and (6.19.11)) to have an equilibrium, then the forest will die out.

One adjustment will be made in reaching the final model. Set

$$K_B = K_2 S\frac{E^2}{T_E^2 + E^2}, \quad P = P_1\frac{E^2}{I_E^2 + E^2}. \tag{6.19.15}$$

It seems reasonable that these terms should be reduced for small E. T_E and I_E are parameters controlling this reduction. Now the complete model is:

$$\left.\begin{aligned}
\frac{dB}{dt} &= r_B B\left(1 - \frac{B}{K_2 S}\cdot\frac{T_E^2 + E^2}{E^2}\right) - \beta\frac{B^2}{\alpha_1^2 S^2 + B^2}, \\
\frac{dS}{dt} &= r_S S\left(1 - \frac{S}{E}\cdot\frac{K_E}{K_S}\right), \\
\frac{dE}{dt} &= r_E E\left(1 - \frac{E}{K_E}\right) - P_1\frac{B}{S}\cdot\frac{E^2}{I_E^2 + E^2}.
\end{aligned}\right] \tag{6.19.16}$$

The paper [61] (which I hope you are arranging to read) includes a set of numerical values based on observation. These are given below, and will help you get started in performing numerical experiments with the model. Vary individual experiments, and see if you can bring about some catastrophes. Incidentally, a theoretical discussion of this model is given by Casti [22]. You may find this discussion helpful. Take $T_E = I_E = 0$.

Variable	Meaning	Value
r_B	intrinsic budworm growth rate	1.52 $(\text{year})^{-1}$
K_2	maximum budworm density	355 larvae/branch
β	maximum budworm predation	43,200 larvae/acre/year
α_1	$\frac{1}{2}$ maximum density for predation	1.11 larvae/branch
r_S	intrinsic branch growth rate	0.095 $(\text{year})^{-1}$
K_S	maximum branch density	25,440 branches/acre
K_E	maximum E level	1.0
r_E	intrinsic E growth rate	0.92
P_1	consumption rate of E	0.00195
R	$\alpha_1 r_B S/\beta$	$0.994(S/K_S)$
Q	K_2/α_1	302

I hope that you will agree that this beautiful model is a fitting climax to the projects in this chapter.

Chapter 7

Sickness and Health

7.1 A Model for the Spread of Disease 

An infectious disease is spreading among a population of N individuals; all changes in the disease will be assumed to be continuous. In this model we shall neglect the incubation period of the disease (or assume it to be zero). Someone who is cured will have immunity. The population contains the following groups:

- I, *infective.* Those who have got it.
- S, *susceptible.* Those who are in danger of getting it.
- R, *removed.* Those who have died, those who are isolated for treatment, and those who have recovered and are immune.

If these symbols refer to actual numbers, then

$$N = I + S + R. \tag{7.1.1}$$

In practice, the units can be scaled; $S = 1$, for instance, might represent one thousand, or one million, actual individuals. Note that in (7.1.1) we are assuming that there is no change in the overall population; there are no births.

We assume that the rate at which the disease spreads depends on the number of contacts between infected and susceptible individuals, so is proportional to the product SI. We also assume that the rate of removal is proportional to I. Then, with the time t as the independent variable, the equations for the model are

$$\left.\begin{aligned} \frac{dS}{dt} &= -aSI, \\ \frac{dI}{dt} &= -bI + aSI, \\ \frac{dR}{dt} &= bI. \end{aligned}\right] \tag{7.1.2}$$

Only the first two equations need to be worried about, since, once they are solved, R can be found from (7.1.1).

If the first equation is divided by the second, the time is eliminated, and we have the separable equation

$$\frac{dS}{dI} = \frac{aSI}{bI - aSI} = \frac{aS}{b - aS} \tag{7.1.3}$$

which has the solution

$$I = I_0 - (S - S_0) + \frac{b}{a} \ln\left(\frac{S}{S_0}\right). \tag{7.1.4}$$

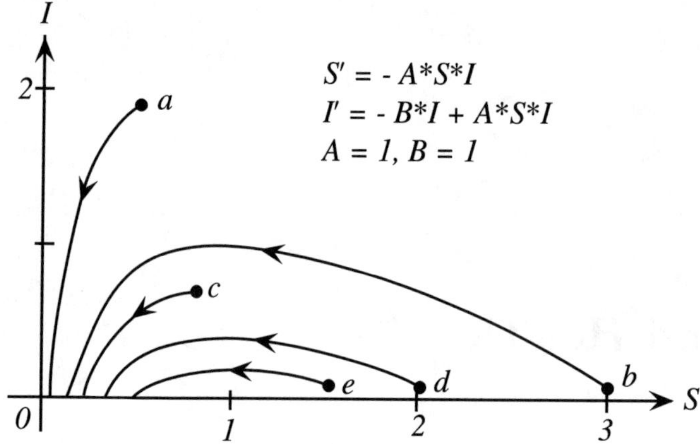

Figure 7.1: *Relations between numbers of infectives and susceptibles.*

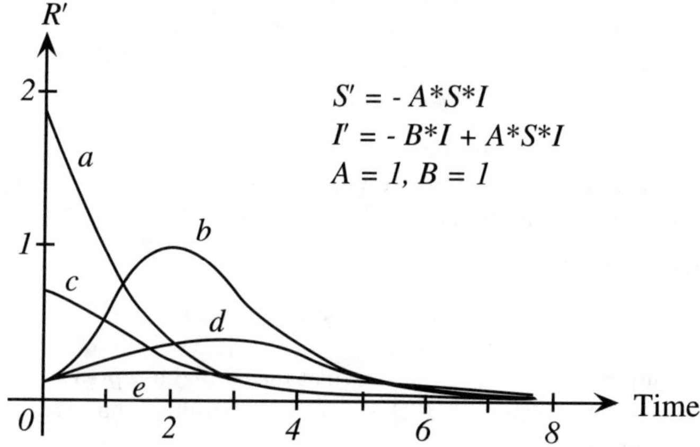

Figure 7.2: *Rate of removal as a function of the time..*

Here I_0 and S_0 are initial conditions. I has a maximum value for $S = b/a$. So if S_0 is less than b/a, the disease will immediately start to die out; but if S_0 is greater than b/a, I will initially increase, and we have an "epidemic." Notice that when the disease has died out, and $I = 0$, S is positive, so there are always some survivors. Some solutions in the S-I plane are shown in figure 7.1.

If the progress of the disease is to be followed as a function of the time, then equations (7.1.2) must be integrated. For displaying results, graph $I(t)$ and $S(t)$ as functions of the time, as well as I as a function of S in the I-S plane. A quantity of interest is the rate dR/dt at which infectives are removed. This rate might be the most visible sign of the disease so far as records are concerned; it might also be proportional to the death rate. Curves for $dR/dt = R'$ are plotted in figure 7.2 with the same initial conditions as the cases plotted in figure 7.1.

Notice that with the unit of time free, we can set $a = 1$. Also the "interesting" values of the parameters will depend on whether actual population figures are used, or, if they are scaled, how they are scaled. To be practical, start with a small number of infectives. Consider how things might change if the disease became more infectious (a increases) or the diagnosis more effective (b increases). You might get some information on a disease, such as measles, and see if you can model its spread in an actual community.

Discussion of these equations and many generalizations can be found in many texts. A good one is by N.T.J.Bailey [6]. See also the text by Braun [17].

7.2 Possible Effects of Vaccination

Vaccination reduces the number of susceptibles, which means that we shall be modifying the first equation of (7.1.2). If the number vaccinated at any time is V, we need a model for dV/dt. Accordingly, consider:

1. $dV/dt = cS$ for constant c. Then
$$\frac{dS}{dt} = -aSI - cS. \tag{7.2.1}$$

2. $dV/dt = cSI^k$, for constant c and k. Then
$$\frac{dS}{dt} = -aSI - cSI^k. \tag{7.2.2}$$

In particular, consider $k = 1$ or 2. Since I is proportional to the removal rate, it is natural that the rate of vaccination should increase as the number of reported cases increases. The higher the value of k, the greater the effect of the epidemic on the nervousness of the susceptibles, or the enterprise of the department of health.

For this project you might include the equation for dV/dt in the system, since it is interesting to see how many get vaccinated. Start with results from the preceding project, where there is no vaccination. Then, with the same starting conditions, introduce vaccination, and follow its effects. Vary c and k.

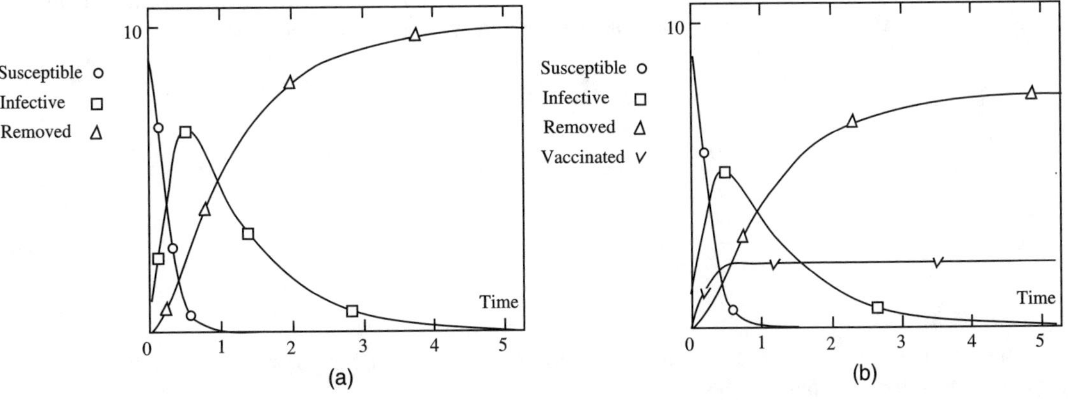

Figure 7.3: *Part (a) illustrates the course of the disease with no vaccination. In part (b) there is vaccination at the rate $V = S$. Compare the rates at which the disease dies out.*

Figure 7.3 shows a comparison between no vaccination, (a), and vaccination, (b). In each case, numerical values for the parameters are: Infection rate, $a = 1$; Cure rate, $b = 1$. Initial conditions are: Time, $t = 0$; Susceptibles, $S = 9$; Infectives, $I = 1$; Removed, $R = 0$. For case (a) there is no vaccination; for (b), the vaccination rate is $V = cSI^k$ with $c = 1$ and $k = 0$. Compare the rates at which the disease dies out.

7.3 Possible Effects of Migration

The first two equations of (7.1.2) can be modified to allow for changing populations if

$$\left.\begin{aligned}\frac{dS}{dt} &= -aSI - f(t),\\ \frac{dI}{dt} &= -bI + aSI - g(t).\end{aligned}\right] \tag{7.3.1}$$

The functions $f(t)$ and $g(t)$ would be negative in the case of an increase in the population.

Changes in the population might be abrupt, as in the case of students arriving at or leaving a community that includes a college, tourists arriving at the start of a holiday season, or the navy coming to town. Or the changes might be continuous, reflecting gradual changes in a population. For your project, start once more with project 7.1. But at some early time, abruptly increase S. (Suppose that a lot of healthy students arrive in the community.) What happens? Or have a situation with low infection, and abruptly increase both S and I. (A not very healthy group of tourists has just arrived.) You can also reverse the cases to consider what happens when the students or the tourists leave.

You might introduce a continuous immigration or emigration, perhaps at a constant rate, or a rate proportional to the total population. For emigration, assume that everyone alive is equally likely to leave. So you will need to decide on what proportion of those removed are still alive. Suppose that a portion αR survive. Then the three groups will lose numbers in the proportions

$$S/(S+I+\alpha R),\ I/(S+I+\alpha R),\ \alpha R/(S+I+\alpha R).$$

7.4 The Spread of Disease in a Population with Birth and Death Included in the Model: 1

To start, we shall assume that the birthrate is proportional to the total population, and that deaths are natural (i.e., not due to the disease). Then we have the model

$$\left.\begin{aligned}\frac{dS}{dt} &= b(S+I+R) - d_1S - aSI,\\ \frac{dI}{dt} &= aSI - d_2I - cI,\\ \frac{dR}{dt} &= cI - d_3R,\\ N &= S+I+R.\end{aligned}\right] \tag{7.4.1}$$

Note that N, the number denoting the total population is no longer constant. The quantities d_i are the parameters for the death rates.

Again, you might start with a result from project 7.1, and then introduce small parameters for birth and death. The parameters d_i could be different; for instance, if the infectives are more likely to die, d_2 might be larger than the others.

Notice that this model *can* have an equilibrium that is nontrivial. (Set the derivatives equal to zero. Solve the second equation for S, and then the first and third for I and R. This is easier to do after selecting numerical values.) Choose suitable numerical values, find the equilibrium and then investigate its stability.

For a modification of the system, you might use the formula

$$b_1S + b_2I + b_3R \tag{7.4.2}$$

for the birthrate. For a disease that causes sterility, both b_2 and b_3 would be zero (and, unless you choose the other parameters with care, you have lost the equilibrium).

7.5 The Spread of Disease in a Population with Birth and Death Included in the Model: 2

The newly born members of the population in the preceding model were somewhat precocious. We shall modify the model to allow for the fact that kids don't reproduce. Let

$$S = S_K + S_A, \tag{7.5.1}$$

where the right-hand side is the sum of the kids and adults, respectively. The new model can be written as

$$\left.\begin{aligned}
\frac{dS_K}{dt} &= b(S_A + I + R) - gS_K - d_{1K}S_K - a_K S_K I,\\
\frac{dS_A}{dt} &= gS_K - d_{1A}S_A - a_A S_A I,\\
\frac{dI}{dt} &= a_K S_K I + a_A S_A I - d_2 I - cI,\\
\frac{dR}{dt} &= cI - d_3 R,\\
N &= S_K + S_A + I + R.
\end{aligned}\right] \tag{7.5.2}$$

Here the kids grow up into adulthood at the rate gS_K, die at the rate $d_{1K}S_K$ and become infected at the rate $a_K S_K I$. The adults and kids can have different death and infection rates.

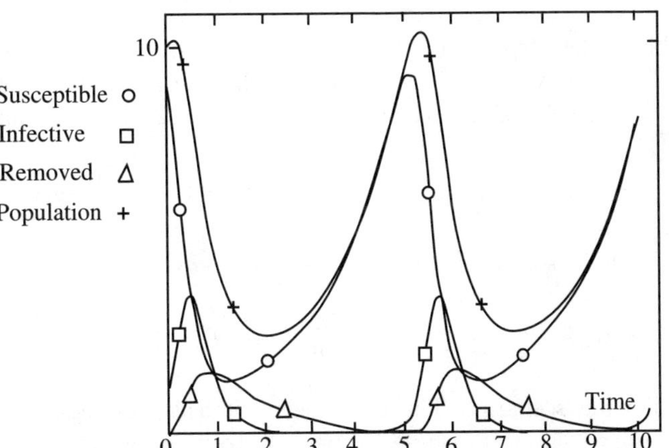

Figure 7.4: *Periodic fluctuations in the progress of a disease. The infection rate is constant at $a = 1$. For the susceptibles, the birth and death rates are $b_1 = 3,\ d_1 = 2.4$. For the infectives, $b_2 = 0,\ d_2 = 3$, and for those removed (cured) the numbers are $b_3 = 0,\ d_3 = 1$. Initially, $t = 0,\ S = 9,\ I = 1$.*

The price to pay for trying to be more realistic is a fourth differential equation to solve. If you have run the preceding project, then compare results by graphing $S = S_K + S_A$ as a function of the time. Start with $d_{1K} = d_{1A}$ and $a_K = a_A$. Then make these different.

In playing with numbers it is not easy to avoid the population either dying out or "exploding." Figure 7.4 shows cycles; this is more realistic behavior, although in this instance the wild fluctuations in the total population would make living in the community difficult! The parameters used in this figure are: $a = 1,\ b_1 = 3,\ b_2 = b_3 = 0,\ d_1 = 2.4,\ d_2 = 3,\ d_3 = 1$. Initial conditions were $S = 9,\ I = 1$. Another way to follow the cycles is to plot curves in the S-I plane. Some of these are shown in figure 7.5 where 6 sets of initial conditions have been used. We see that the wildness of the fluctuations depends on the starting conditions. If the disease progresses from a point where I is very small, then the fluctuations, and resulting severity, are large.

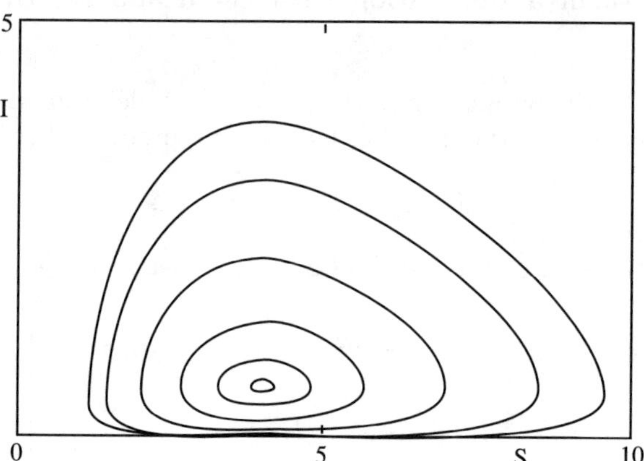

Figure 7.5: *The parameters are those of figure 7.4; now only the variables S and I are followed, with points plotted in the S-I plane. Different starting conditions all lead to periodic behavior.*

What happens if we now include a periodic infection rate for a? We get chaos. This will be illustrated in a later section.

7.6 Cross-Infection Between Two Species

We shall use the model of project 7.1, but now there are two different species involved. Let these have numbers N_1 and N_2 and let S_i, I_i and R_i be the numbers of susceptible, infected and removed members, respectively, of the ith species, with $i = 1, 2$. Then we have the equations

$$\left.\begin{aligned} \frac{dS_1}{dt} &= -a_1 S_1 (I_1 + I_2), & \frac{dS_2}{dt} &= -a_2 S_2 (I_1 + I_2), \\ \frac{dI_1}{dt} &= -b_1 I_1 + a_1 S_1 (I_1 + I_2), & \frac{dI_2}{dt} &= -b_2 I_2 + a_2 S_2 (I_1 + I_2), \\ \frac{dR_1}{dt} &= b_1 I_1, & \frac{dR_2}{dt} &= b_2 I_2. \end{aligned}\right] \tag{7.6.1}$$

Consider the following scenario. The first species consists of regular inhabitants of a resort. They have high immunity to a local disease (something to do with the water, perhaps). The second species consists of tourists with low immunity, so $a_2 > a_1$. If they are all treated by the same doctors, we can assume $b_2 = b_1$. Assume that, initially, no tourist is infected. What happens? Alternatively, the tourists might bring a new brand of flu into an otherwise healthy community.

Think up some other applications.

In one version of cross-infection, the disease cannot be transmitted between members of the same species. Then

$$\left.\begin{aligned} \frac{dS_1}{dt} &= -a_1 S_1 I_2, & \frac{dS_2}{dt} &= -a_2 S_2 I_1, \\ \frac{dI_1}{dt} &= -b_1 I_1 + a_1 S_1 I_2, & \frac{dI_2}{dt} &= -b_2 I_2 + a_2 S_2 I_1, \\ \frac{dR_1}{dt} &= b_1 I_1, & \frac{dR_2}{dt} &= b_2 I_2. \end{aligned}\right] \tag{7.6.2}$$

Make up some stories for this model and experiment with it.

7.7 The Spread of Disease with Incubation Included

This model is similar to 7.1, except that we are adding another category E to allow for the incubation of the disease. This is the number in the population that has been exposed to the disease, but which is not yet infectious. The equations are now

$$\left.\begin{aligned} \frac{dS}{dt} &= -aSI, \\ \frac{dE}{dt} &= aSI - cE, \\ \frac{dI}{dt} &= cE - bI, \\ \frac{dR}{dt} &= bI. \end{aligned}\right] \tag{7.7.1}$$

First, run project 7.1. Next, keep the same initial conditions, but put $E = 0$ initially. Start with a value of c that is larger than the other parameters, maybe quite a bit larger; then the effects of incubation should be relatively small. Compare the sum $E + I$ for this project with I for 7.1. Then diminish c so that incubation becomes more important.

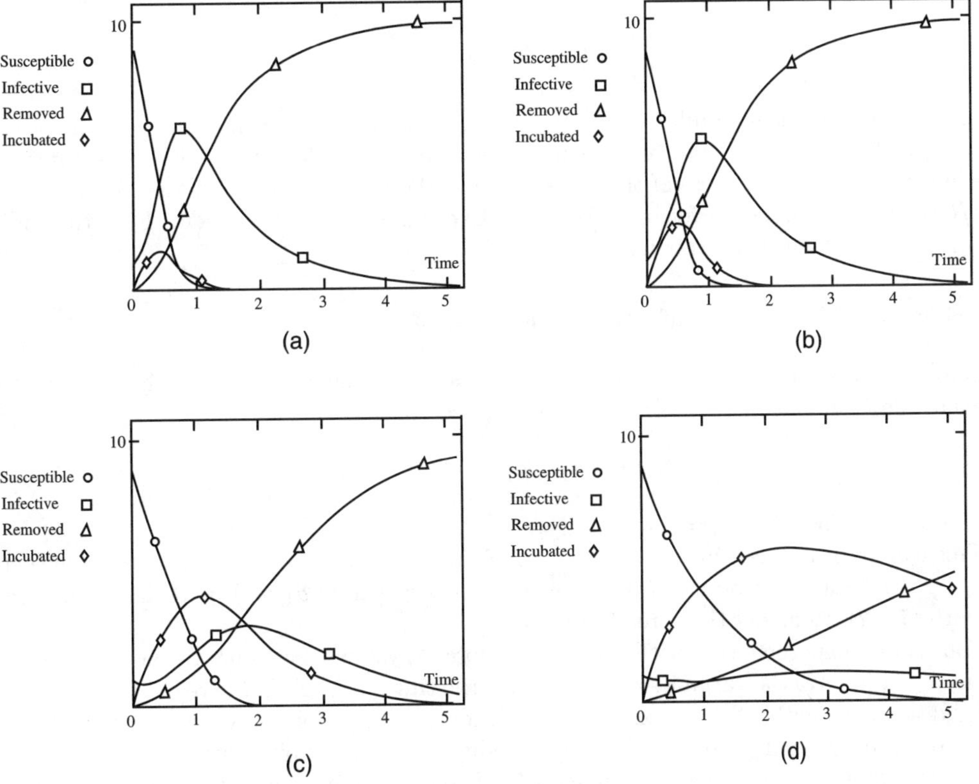

Figure 7.6: *Effects of varying the incubation coefficient, c. In (a), c = 10, and the figure resembles figure 7.3(a), where there is no incubation. The coefficient c represents the rate at which those incubated (infected but not infectious) become infectious, so as c is diminished, incubation becomes more significant. This can be seen as c takes the values 5 in (b), 1 in (c) and 0.2 in (d).*

Figures 7.6(a) to (d) illustrate this. Figure 7.6(a), with $c = 10$ shows very little change from figure 7.3(a), where there is no incubation. For figures 7.6(b), (c) and (d), we have, respectively,

$c = 5$, 1 and 0.2. It is clear that greater incubation slows down the progress of the disease, although the eventual outcome may be the same. But slower progress gives time for more precautionary measures. In figure 7.7, $c = 1$, as in figure 7.6(c), but vaccination at the rate $V = SI$ has been included; because of the slower progress, more people are vaccinated, compared with the case of no incubation.

The inclusion of incubation can be made in the other projects also, if you don't object to the extra equation. In particular, allowing for birth and death leads to a model that has an equilibrium and might be useful in reality. One such model is

$$\left.\begin{aligned} \frac{dS}{dt} &= d(1-S) - aSI, \\ \frac{dE}{dt} &= aSI - (d+c)E, \\ \frac{dI}{dt} &= cE - (d+b)I, \\ \frac{dR}{dt} &= bI - dR. \end{aligned}\right] \tag{7.7.2}$$

If $N = S + E + I + R$ then

$$\frac{dN}{dt} = d(1-N), \text{ so } N = 1 + Ce^{-dt}. \tag{7.7.3}$$

This model approaches an equilibrium with $N = 1$, so, clearly, the initial conditions must be scaled accordingly. The interpretations of the parameters are: $1/d$ is the average life expectancy, a is the coefficient for the infectiousness of the disease, $1/c$ is the average latency period for the incubation, and $1/b$ is the average period for infectiousness. Experiment with this model. Find the equilibrium positions, and confirm their stability.

7.8 Seasonal Changes in Infectiousness

Some diseases have seasonal variations, such as those that are worse in the winter. Then the coefficient a for the infectiousness might be expressed as

$$a = a_0 + a_1 \sin pt, \; a_0 \geq a_1. \tag{7.8.1}$$

For an annual variation, $2\pi/p = 1$ year.

This can be introduced into any of the models considered so far in this chapter. Once you have results for constant a, introduce (7.8.1), varying the parameters a_1 and p. It has been successfully used with (7.7.2), to model the spread of measles.

You will be experimenting with periodically forced systems that may be chaotic. Chaos might be observed in plots of the variables as functions of the time, or in plots where one dependent variable is plotted against another. As a_1 increases, look for period-doubling, which occurs at the start of passage to chaos. If your system is chaotic, consider constructing bifurcation diagrams.

Figure 7.8 is to be compared to figure 7.5. The only difference is that the parameter for the infection rate is now $a = 1 + 0.2\sin(t)$, and that the method of Poincaré maps has been used. Solutions were generated for a variety of initial conditions, and points were plotted in the S-I plane at times $t = 0, 2\pi, 4\pi, \ldots$.

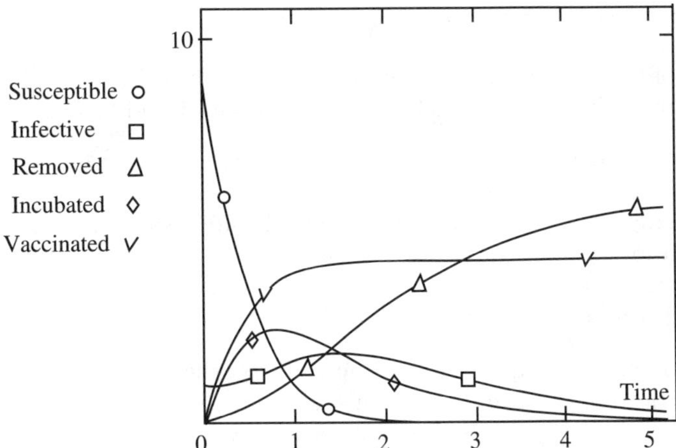

Figure 7.7: *With incubation included, the rate at which the disease spreads is slowed down, so a measure such as vaccination becomes more effective. In this figure the parameters for figure 7.6(c) have been used, with the addition of vaccination at the rate $V = S$. Compared with figure 7.3(b), where there is vaccination but no incubation, more people are vaccinated.*

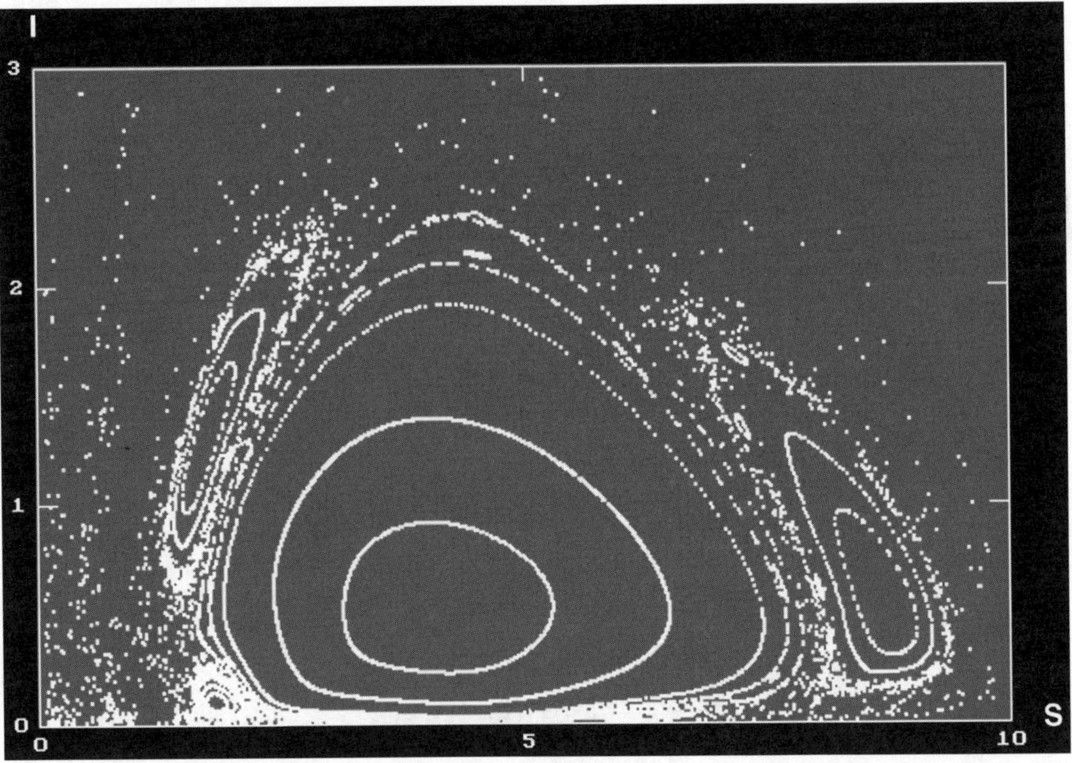

Figure 7.8: *Chaotic behavior in the spread of a disease. The infection rate a is periodic, with $a = 1 + 0.2\sin(t)$. Birth and death are included in the model, with the parameters the same as those used in figures 7.4 and 7.5 (with the exception of the infection rate). The method of Poincaré maps is used; points are plotted at times $t = 0, 2\pi, 4\pi, \ldots$.*

7.9 The Epidemiology of Malaria

A description of this model can be found in the text by N.T.J.Bailey[6]. There are two species, humans and mosquitos, denoted by variables with subscripts 1 and 2. Let

n_i be the total population at any time t,
y_i be the number of infected individuals,
f_i be the proportion of infected individuals who are also infectious,
g_i be the recovery rate,
m_i be the birthrate,
k_i be the death rate, where $i = 1, 2$.

Let the rate at which mosquitos bite people be b_2; then in time dt, y_2 infected mosquitos make $b_2 f_2 y_2 dt$ infectious bites. The numbers of susceptible humans is $n_1 - y_1$, so the proportion of susceptible humans is $(n_1 - y_1)/n_1$. So the number of new infections during the time dt is

$$\frac{b_2 f_2 y_2 (n_1 - y_1) dt}{n_1}.$$

So, taking into account the recovery and death rates,

$$\frac{dy_1}{dt} = \frac{b_2 f_2 y_2 (n_1 - y_1)}{n_1} - (g_1 + k_1) y_1. \tag{7.9.1}$$

Also, in time dt, $n_2 - y_2$ susceptible mosquitos make $b_2(n_2 - y_2)$ bites. The proportion of humans bitten that is infectious is $f_1 y_1 / n_1$. So

$$\frac{dy_2}{dt} = \frac{b_2 f_1 y_1 (n_2 - y_2)}{n_1} - (g_2 + k_2) y_2. \tag{7.9.2}$$

It is assumed that all newborn babies are uninfected, but are immediately susceptible.

For simplification, suppose that the birth and death rates are the same, i.e., $m_i = k_i$. Suppose also that for humans k_1 is much smaller than g_1, while the opposite is true for mosquitos. Let

$$Y_1 = y_1/n_1, \; Y_2 = y_2/n_2, \; n = n_2/n_1, \tag{7.9.3}$$

where n is constant, under our hypotheses. Then

$$\left.\begin{aligned} \frac{dY_1}{dt} &= b_2 f_2 n Y_2 (1 - Y_1) - (g_1 + k_1) Y_1, \\ \frac{dY_2}{dt} &= b_2 f_1 Y_1 (1 - Y_2) - (g_2 + k_2) Y_2. \end{aligned}\right] \tag{7.9.4}$$

The simplified equations are

$$\left.\begin{aligned} \frac{dY_1}{dt} &= b_2 f_2 Y_2 n (1 - Y_1) - g_1 Y_1, \\ \frac{dY_2}{dt} &= b_2 f_1 Y_1 (1 - Y_2) - m_2 Y_2. \end{aligned}\right] \tag{7.9.5}$$

Confirm that there are two equilibria. (Set the derivatives to zero; divide each equation by the product $Y_1 Y_2$, then solve the linear equations for $1/Y_1$ and $1/Y_2$.) The one at the origin will not be called "trivial" for this project, because it is just the equilibrium that we would like to see occur. A theoretical result is that the equilibrium at the origin is stable provided that

$$P = \frac{n b_2^2 f_1 f_2}{g_1 m_2} < 1. \tag{7.9.6}$$

Can you confirm this numerically?

For your project, start by choosing simple values for the parameters so that the origin is stable. Can you find the other equilibrium? You may find it helpful to plot solutions in the $Y_1 - Y_2$ plane. Now increase b_2 (or another parameter, such as n) so that P becomes larger than one; the change should be made gradually, with the case $P = 1$ included. What happens when the origin becomes unstable? Investigate the *hypothesis* that the solutions starting close to the origin move toward the other equilibrium, which is stable.

The simplifying assumptions just made can be dispensed with at the cost of two further equations. Suppose the populations n_1 and n_2 vary logistically. Then we can write

$$\left.\begin{aligned}\frac{dn_1}{dt} &= m_1n_1(P_1 - n_1) - k_1y_1,\\ \frac{dn_2}{dt} &= m_2n_2(P_2 - n_2) - k_2y_2,\end{aligned}\right] \tag{7.9.7}$$

where deaths due to malaria have been included. P_1 and P_2 are the maximum sustainable populations of humans and mosquitos. If we let $y_3 = n_1$ and $y_4 = n_2$, the complete system of equations can be written

$$\left.\begin{aligned}\frac{dy_1}{dt} &= \frac{b_2f_2y_2(y_3 - y_1)}{y_3} - (g_1 + k_1)y_1,\\ \frac{dy_2}{dt} &= \frac{b_2f_1y_1(y_4 - y_2)}{y_3} - (g_2 + k_2)y_2,\\ \frac{dy_3}{dt} &= m_1y_3(P_1 - y_3) - k_1y_1,\\ \frac{dy_4}{dt} &= m_2y_4(P_2 - y_4) - k_2y_2.\end{aligned}\right] \tag{7.9.8}$$

Finally, experiment with periodic variation of infectiousness by allowing b_2 to vary periodically.

7.10 The Spread of Gonorrhea

An excellent discussion of this model and some of its variations is given in the text by Braun [17]. There you will find, with more detail than you may wish, a discussion of the parameters and their dependence on the personal preferences of the groups involved. Gonorrhea has a short incubation period of 3 to 7 days, which will be neglected in this model. The disease does not confer immunity: immediately after recovery, an individual is as susceptible as ever — assuming of course that he or she hasn't learned any better.

The two species in this model are males and females. Suppose that there are in a community, at time t,

$m(t)$ active and promiscuous males, of which $x(t)$ are infected, and
$f(t)$ active and promiscuous females, of which $y(t)$ are infected.

We assume that male infectives are cured at the rate a_1x, and females, at the rate a_2y. a_1 is larger than a_2 since the male symptoms develop rapidly and are painful; females can be asymptomatic and so are infectious for much longer periods of time. We assume that the rate of increase of x is proportional to the product of y, the number of infected females, and $(m - x)$, the number of uninfected males, with a similar property for y. Then we have the following model (which includes only heterosexual contacts):

$$\left.\begin{aligned}\frac{dx}{dt} &= -a_1x + b_1y(m - x),\\ \frac{dy}{dt} &= -a_2y + b_2x(f - y).\end{aligned}\right] \tag{7.10.1}$$

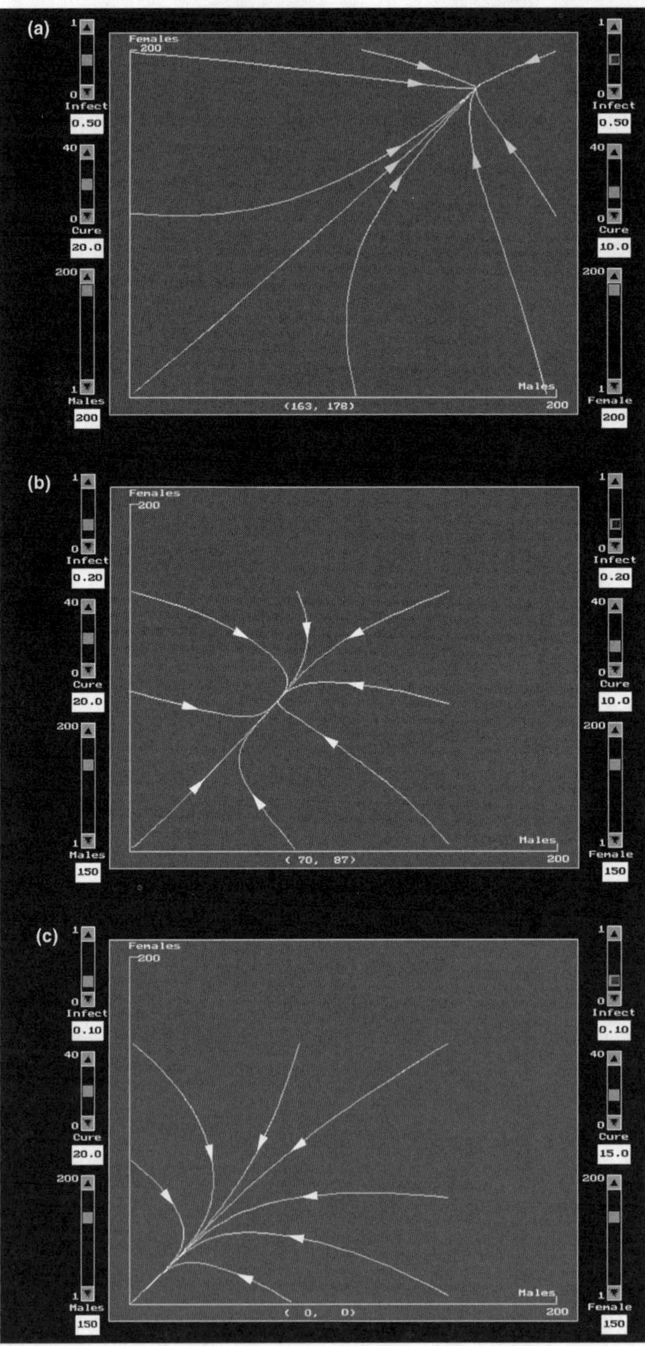

Figure 7.9: *Each figure shows the progress of the disease, starting from different initial points. In (a) and (b) there are two equilibria, the origin being unstable. A critical quantity for the existence of an equilibrium other than the origin is $b_1b_2mf - a_1a_2$, which must be positive. Comparison of (a) with (b) shows relatively few promiscuous members of either sex in (b); also greater precautions have reduced the infection rate. In (c) the infection rates are reduced further, and the female cure rate has increased; now the disease dies out completely.*

Start discussion of the system holding m and f constant. The origin is always an equilibrium. To look for another, set the derivatives to zero, divide each equation by xy, and solve the resulting linear equations for $X = 1/x$ and $Y = 1/y$. Confirm that the equilibrium is at

$$x_e = \frac{b_1 b_2 m f - a_1 a_2}{b_1 b_2 f + a_1 b_2}, \quad y_e = \frac{b_1 b_2 m f - a_1 a_2}{b_1 b_2 m + a_2 b_1}. \tag{7.10.2}$$

This will only exist if $b_1 b_2 m f - a_1 a_2 > 0$.

Investigate the stability of the two equilibria. Change parameters so that the second equilibrium disappears. What happens? Include an interpretation of the changing parameters in your discussion. For instance, a change in b_1 and b_2 could be interpreted in terms of an increase (or decrease) in precautions taken.

Figures 7.9(a), (b) and (c) illustrate effects of changing parameters. Numerical values are shown at the side. In 7.9(a), with total populations of each sex at 200, the equilibrium is at $x_e = 163$, $y_e = 178$. In 7.9(b), 50 of each sex have seen the light so that only 150 are active; also the infection parameters have gone from 0.5 to 0.2. The new equilibrium is at $x_e = 70$, $y_e = 87$. Finally, in 7.9(c), where still more precautions are taken and the female cure rate has increased, the equilbrium does not exist, and the disease dies out.

Next, look at models where m and f are changing, due to changes in population, changes in precautions taken, or perhaps a change in morality. Consider gradual changes, of the type $m = m_0 + m_1 t$, $f = f_0 + f_1 t$, where a switch in the properties of the equilibria might be included. Or consider abrupt changes, like those discussed in project 7.3. Compare this model with the preceding one.

At the cost of a third equation, you might introduce a third "species," bisexual males.

7.11 A Model for the Initial Spread of the HIV Virus

The HIV virus that eventually leads to the *acquired immune deficiency syndrome* or *AIDS*, is spread mainly through sexual contact and the transfer of blood through transfusions or the sharing of needles by drug users. In some, though not all, communities around the world, the principal initial sufferers were male homosexuals. There is no cure, and, if there was an original group involved, the disease has spread far beyond it.

First, we shall consider just the spread of the HIV virus through sexual contact, where the initial group is homosexual. Suppose that at time t there are in a group of individuals p_1 homosexual males, of which $x_1(t)$ are infected, p_2 bisexual males, of which $x_2(t)$ are infected, q heterosexual females, of which $y(t)$ are infected and r heterosexual males, of which $z(t)$ are infected. Assuming that the rate of infection is proportional to the number of contacts, the following system results:

$$\left.\begin{aligned}
\frac{dx_1}{dt} &= a_1 x_1(p_1 - x_1) + a_2 x_2(p_1 - x_1),\\
\frac{dx_2}{dt} &= b_1 x_1(p_2 - x_2) + b_2 x_2(p_2 - x_2) + b_3 y(p_2 - x_2),\\
\frac{dy}{dt} &= c_1 x_2(q - y) + c_2 z(q - y),\\
\frac{dz}{dt} &= d_1 y(r - z).
\end{aligned}\right] \tag{7.11.1}$$

Only the relative sizes of the parameters are important (since the time can be scaled). You would expect the largest to be a_1, since the highest density of contacts is in the first group. Next might be a_2 and b_1, which can be taken to be equal. For a start, you might take $a_1 = 10$, $a_2 = b_1 = 5$, and the remaining parameters equal to one. The populations should be scaled; try $p_1 = p_2 = 5$ and

$q = r = 100$. Initially, try $x_1 = 0.01$ and $x_2 = y = z = 0$. Find out how the virus will spread in the four groups.

The effects of blood transfusion might be modeled by adding terms

$$+e(p_1 - x_1),\ +e(p_2 - x_2),\ +e(q - y),\ +e(r - z),$$

where e is small, to the four equations. The effects of removal can be included by subtracting terms $r_1 x_1$, $r_2 x_2$, $r_2 y$, and $r_4 z$ from the equations.

Experiment with these effects. Note that the only equilibria in the system (7.11.1) occur when nobody has the virus — or everyone has it.

7.12 A Model for Weight Change

This model is based on the article, "A Linear Diet Model," by Arthur C. Segal [89]. We shall make the model nonlinear.

Your weight is W_0 lb, and you wish that it were less. You might take two steps to deal with the situation: eat less and exercise more. We shall set up a model to investigate how weight change might be influenced by diet and exercise.

The unit of time is the day. You eat C calories per day. You also burn up some calories through taking exercise; the amount is assumed to be proportional to the product of your weight and the amount and nature of the exercise. We shall assume that EW calories are burnt per day, where W is your weight and E represents calories per unit weight. This depends on your metabolism as well as the amount of exercise; it is usually between 14 to 20 calories per pound.

If C and EW are not equal, then there will be a change of weight that will be proportional to their difference. So

$$\frac{dW}{dt} = k(C - EW). \tag{7.12.1}$$

t is the time. Taking one pound to be the equivalent of 3,500 calories, we have $k = 1/3500$ pound/calorie.

This is Segal's model. He assumes that, during the period of dieting, C and E remain constant. Then

$$W = \frac{C}{E} + \left(W_0 - \frac{C}{E}\right) e^{-kEt}. \tag{7.12.2}$$

W approaches the ratio C/E, but it does so asymptotically. If we take $W_0 = 180$ lb, $E = 20$ cal/lb, then the *half-life* of the process is 121 days. This means that 20 lb are lost in the first 121 days, but then 10 lb are lost in the following 121 days and only 5 lb in the next 121 days. Very discouraging. But this seems to be a genuine feature of weight change, and may be a big factor in so many decisions to give it up. (It is of interest that the half-life of this exponential process depends on E but not on C; this underlines the role of exercise in any effective program of weight loss.)

The principal drawback in this model is that C and E are held constant. In fact, each one of W, C and E is likely to depend on the other two. The model ought to include "feed-back," if that phrase is acceptable in this context. If you exercise more, you are likely to eat more. The incentive to eat less and exercise more is likely to increase if the difference between what you weigh and what you want to weigh increases. This is a situation that calls for your own imagination. I suggest adding the following two equations to equation (7.12.1)

$$\frac{dC}{dt} = a(E - E_0) - b(W - W_1), \tag{7.12.3}$$

$$\frac{dE}{dt} = c(W - W_1) - d(E - E_1). \tag{7.12.4}$$

Here W_1 might be the weight that you want. E_0 might represent some minimal level (operating the TV) and E_1 a value where the exercise becomes too unpleasant or too time-consuming. The coefficients will depend on psychological factors that only you can determine.

In planning your lifestyle, the following approximate numbers may help:

Activity	Heat rate Cal/hr/lb
Watching television	0.5
Attending class	1
Walking	1.5
Jogging	4
Running	7

7.13 Zeeman's Model for the Heartbeat

This model will take some effort to understand, and care in programming. If you can be patient in building it up gradually, you will be amply rewarded. The model was motivated by the concept of catastrophes; it appeared in an article by E.C.Zeeman [110]. The model is also described and discussed in a text by D.S.Jones and B.D.Sleeman [61].

The heart has a relaxed equilibrium called *diastole*. From this state, a heartbeat is triggered by a pacemaker; this starts off an electrochemical wave which first causes a slow contraction of the muscles to push blood into the ventricles, and then a rapid contraction to pump the blood down the arteries. The fully contracted state is called *systole*. This is followed by a relaxation back to diastole, and the cycle is repeated.

There are two dependent variables in the model: x refers to muscle fiber length, and b refers to the electrochemical activity. The values for diastole will be x_0, b_0, and those for systole will be x_1, b_1. As we shall see, each of these states is an equilibrium of the model. The main parameter will be T, which refers to the overall tension of the system.

We first consider half of the model — the part that follows the progress from diastole to systole, producing the pumping action. The equations for this are

$$\left.\begin{aligned} \epsilon\frac{dx}{dt} &= -(x^3 - Tx + b), \\ \frac{db}{dt} &= x - x_1, \end{aligned}\right] \tag{7.13.1}$$

where ϵ is a small parameter that depends on the time scale. For numerical experiments, it will probably be sufficient to take $\epsilon = 0.1$. In order that the systole state should be an equilibrium, we need

$$x_1^3 - Tx_1 + b_1 = 0. \tag{7.13.2}$$

In the b-x phase-plane, the cubic curve

$$x^3 - Tx + b = 0 \tag{7.13.3}$$

is important, because it divides the plane into regions of different types. The flow in each of these regions can be found qualitatively by looking at the signs of the derivatives, and also by constructing direction field diagrams for the equation

$$\frac{dx}{db} = -\frac{x^3 - Tx + b}{\epsilon(x - x_1)},$$

found by dividing the second equation of (7.13.1) into the first.

The tension T is critical. The case $T = 0$ is illustrated in figure 7.10. First, the cubic (7.13.3) is drawn in; this is the solid curve. Then a value is chosen for x_1 (this will be negative) and the corresponding value for b_1 is found from (7.13.2). These values are the coordinates of S, the position of systole. Now solutions are calculated, using (7.13.1) and a variety of initial conditions. These solutions appear as dashed loci in the figure. Notice that the cubic curve seems to form an "attractor" for these solutions, which appear to approach it and then flow close to it toward the equilibrium S.

In figures 7.11 and 7.12, T has the values 1 and 3, respectively. The cubic now forms an S-shape, with the inner part of the S acting as a "repeller." To start your project, confirm the details of these figures and construct further, similar figures. The diastole position, D, will be somewhere on the cubic curve in the second quadrant. Its precise position in these figures is arbitrary, but you can see that a solution starting from this position exhibits the initial slow contraction and then the rapid pumping in reaching S. In the case $T = 0$, the action from diastole to systole is slow at all times, so that in this relaxed state there is no rapid pumping. In figure 7.12, where the tension has increased to 3, the systole equilibrium can be reached only after b has first reached a value much larger than b_1. Since this may not be possible, the conditions are set for a heart attack, where pumping cannot take place.

Once you have developed the confidence to follow the progress from diastole to systole, you must learn how to complete the cycle. This turns out to be simple: if x_0 replaces x_1 in (7.13.1), with x_0 positive, that is all we need. There is no mathematical change, and so no new properties to be learned. The physical difference is that only relaxation is taking place; there is no great pumping effort required.

The two parts of the cycle can be combined into one system of equations as follows. (This form can be found in the discussion given by Jones and Sleeman.) Consider the system

$$\left.\begin{aligned} \epsilon\frac{dx}{dt} &= -(x^3 - Tx + b), \\ \frac{db}{dt} &= (x - x_0) + u(x_0 - x_1), \end{aligned}\right] \qquad (7.13.4)$$

where u is the control for the pacemaker. When $u = 1$, the cycle starts from diastole; when systole is reached, u must switch to $u = 0$, and the cycle returns to diastole.

For practical use in a program, you want the change in u to be triggered when the point (b, x) is *close* to an equilibrium; otherwise, the integration program will just approach the equilibrium asymptotically, and the cycle will not progress. Recalling that the coordinates for diastole are (b_0, x_0) and those for systole are (b_1, x_1), I suggest that you use the conditions

$$\left.\begin{aligned} u &= 1 \text{ if } (b - b_0)^2 + (x - x_0)^2 < \delta, \\ u &= 0 \text{ if } (b - b_1)^2 + (x - x_1)^2 < \delta, \end{aligned}\right] \qquad (7.13.5)$$

where δ is a small number for you to choose.

A complete diastole-systole cycle is illustrated in figure 7.13. See if you can replicate this. Experiment first by changing initial conditions. You will find that whatever your initial conditions (within reason), the cycle is rapidly approached; so we have another example of a *limit cycle*.

For the simplest mathematics, choose x_0 and x_1, then T; it is then simple to find b_0 and b_1 using the fact that the equilibria must lie on the cubic curve (7.13.3). If you start with b_0 and b_1, then use an iteration such as Newton's method to solve for x_0 and x_1. Start with $T = 0$, and increase T gradually, keeping track of b_1.

If T is increased to a point where

$$T^{3/2} > \frac{3\sqrt{3}}{2} b_1, \qquad (7.13.6)$$

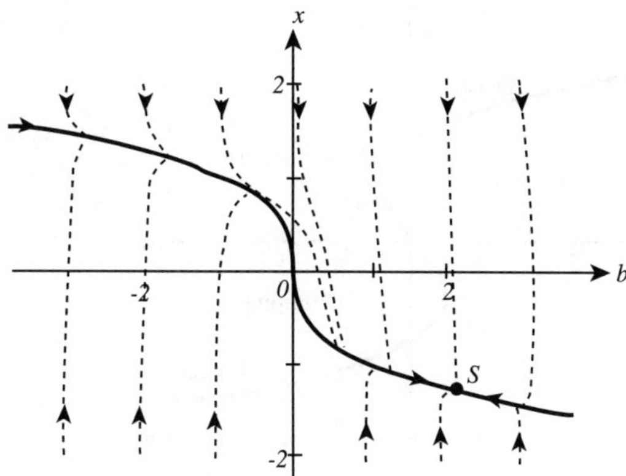

Figure 7.10: *$T = 0$, $x_1 = -1.3$, $b_1 = 2.2$. S is the systole equilibrium. The solid curve is the "attractor."*

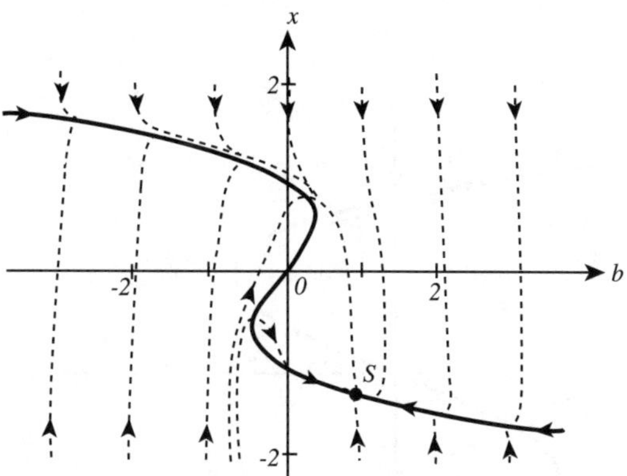

Figure 7.11: $T = 1$, $x_1 = -1.3$, $b_1 = 0.9$.

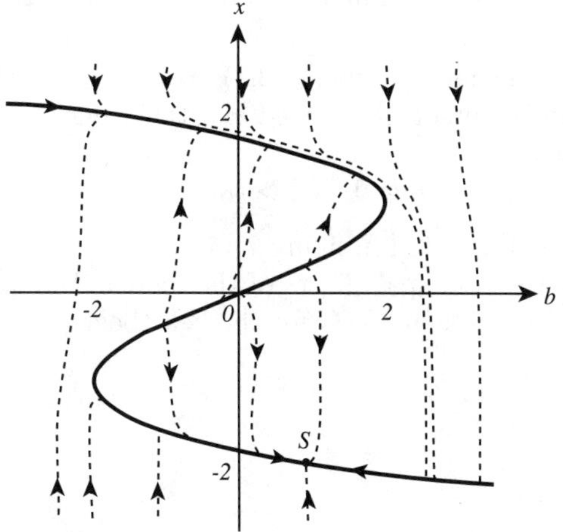

Figure 7.12: $T = 3$, $x_1 = -1.75$, $b_1 = 1$.

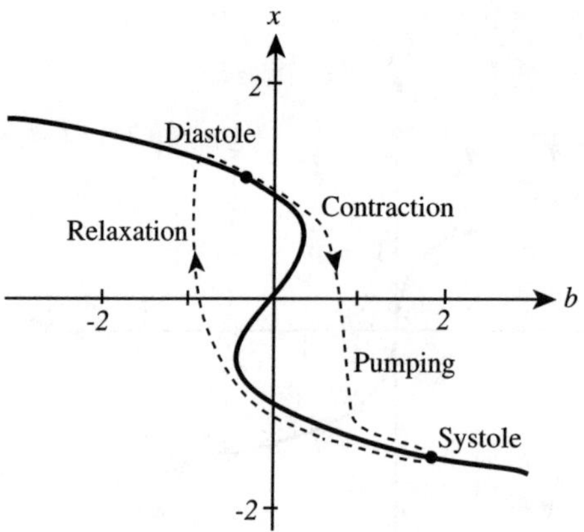

Figure 7.13: *A complete cycle. The separation of the solution near systole has been exaggerated. Parameters are:* $T = 1,\ x_0 = 1.1, b_0 = -0.231,\ x_1 = -1.5,\ b_1 = 1.875$.

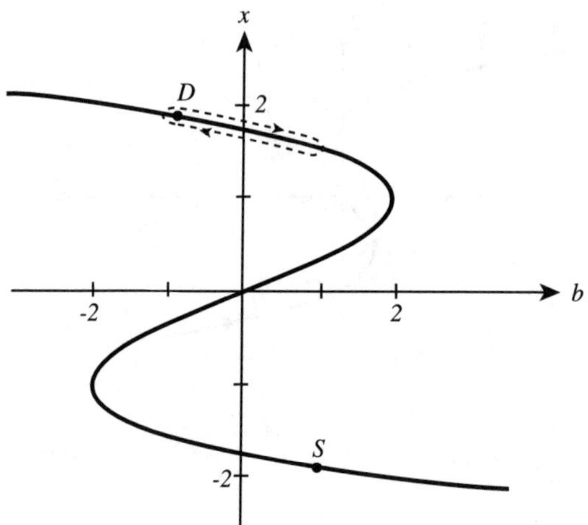

Figure 7.14: *Representation of limited action associated with a heart attack.*

then the systole falls underneath the cubic curve (7.13.3), as in figure 7.12. Then the effort needed for the pumping exceeds b_1, systole cannot be reached and there may be a heart attack. To model this, you must add the condition

$$u = 0,\ \text{if}\ b > b_0 \tag{7.13.7}$$

to (7.13.5). A run where $b > b_1$ is illustrated in figure 7.14.

Plots in the b-x plane show the principal effects of the model. But you should show some of b with respect to the time. This represents an EKG for the heartbeat.

Chapter 8

Competition and Economics

8.1 Lanchester's Combat Models

F.W.Lanchester [64] published these models in 1916. They are discussed in the text by M.Braun [17], where it is shown how they can be applied to the battle of Iwo Jima. To appreciate this model you must be prepared to be imaginative and inventive.

Forces numbering $x(t)$ and $y(t)$ are fighting each other. As usual, t denotes the time. The numbers change for three reasons:

1. *The operational loss rate.* This refers to noncombat casualties such as disease, accident, and desertion. Lanchester assumes that the rate of loss is proportional to the total number x or y. The assumption seems to be rather simplistic; you might try to generalize it, putting in an actual disease, for instance. The linear law is assumed below.

2. *The combat loss rate.* This can be of two kinds. If the x-force is *conventional* and out in the open, with every member within "killing range" of the y-force, then the rate of loss is taken to be proportional to y; the coefficient of proportionality, a, is called the "combat effectiveness coefficient" of the y-force. If x represents a *guerilla* force, invisible to y, and occupying a definite region, then the rate of loss will be proportional to xy.

3. *The reinforcement rate.* This will be a function of the time and is controlled by you, the operator.

We consider three combinations:

1. Two conventional armies:

$$\left.\begin{aligned}\frac{dx}{dt} &= -ay - ex + f(t),\\ \frac{dy}{dt} &= -bx - fy + g(t).\end{aligned}\right] \tag{8.1.1}$$

2. The x-force is a guerilla force and the y-force is conventional:

$$\left.\begin{aligned}\frac{dx}{dt} &= -cxy - ex + f(t),\\ \frac{dy}{dt} &= -bx - fy + g(t).\end{aligned}\right] \tag{8.1.2}$$

3. Both are guerilla forces:

$$\left.\begin{aligned}\frac{dx}{dt} &= -cxy - ex + f(t),\\ \frac{dy}{dt} &= -dxy - fy + g(t).\end{aligned}\right] \tag{8.1.3}$$

First, show that for the first of these cases, if there are no reinforcements and the operational loss rates are zero, then x will win provided that

$$bx_0^2 > ay_0^2, \tag{8.1.4}$$

where x_0 and y_0 are initial values. Then the critical value for the x-force is proportional to the combat effectiveness and to the square of the initial value of the y-force; it illustrates Lanchester's "square law" for conventional combat. For any solution, $bx^2 - ay^2 = C$, a constant. Is this law modified if e and f are not zero?

Experiment with these models. For instance, can you get the guerillas to win in the second case? Can you reach a stalemate (nontrivial equilibrium)? Think about modifications; desertions might be made to the opposing side; include a disease that temporarily incapacitates those infected. This is a project where, whether the output is printed or graphical, you need some written comments to go along with it.

8.2 Production and Exchange

This model[1] is due to A.Rapoport and can be found in his book *Fights, Games and Debates* [81]. This is a wonderful book, full of models involving contention; it should be on your reading list.

A "society" consists of two men; each produces goods, and they exchange part of their produce. Let the men be X and Y and their goods be quantified by x and y, respectively. Suppose that each gives away to the other the same fraction of goods that he produces. That is, if this fraction is q, then he keeps the fraction $p = 1 - q$. To account for *why* a man would produce or exchange goods, the concept of *utility* is introduced. Maybe *satisfaction* would be a better term. We assume that this notion can be quantified, and we call the satisfaction for the two men S_x and S_y.

The first assumption is that work is unsatisfying. (If you wish to include the work ethic in your model, then that is a generalization that you can make later.) So there is *negative* satisfaction proportional to the work done, leading to contributions $-rx$ to S_x and $-ry$ to S_y, r being a constant. Positive satisfaction is derived from ownership. Here we assume as a basic law "equal increases in satisfaction arise from equal ratios of goods owned." Think of "goods" as a stimulus and "satisfaction" as a sensation. Then this law, which is followed in our perception of light or sound, is known as *Fechner's law.* Here it is applied to satisfaction, or even happiness: if we are twice as happy with \$10 as with \$1, then to be three times as happy requires \$100, and four times as happy requires \$1,000, and so on. (Doubling your happiness if you are a millionaire is tough!) On the basis of this assumption we find that satisfaction depends on the logarithm of the goods owned. (In the same way, in astronomy, the "magnitude" of a star depends on the logarithm of its luminosity.) Rapoport assumes that

$$\left.\begin{aligned} S_x &= \log(1 + px + qy) - rx, \\ S_y &= \log(1 + qx + py) - ry. \end{aligned}\right] \tag{8.2.1}$$

Now assume that a man will increase his production only if he will increase his satisfaction. Then dx/dt will be proportional to the partial derivative of S_x with respect to x, with a similar rule for dy/dt. The model is then described by

$$\left.\begin{aligned} \frac{dx}{dt} &= c\left(\frac{p}{px + qy + 1} - r\right), \\ \frac{dy}{dt} &= c\left(\frac{p}{qx + py + 1} - r\right). \end{aligned}\right] \tag{8.2.2}$$

[1] Adapted with permission from A.Rapoport, *Fights, Games and Debates.*

We can choose the unit of time so that $c = 1$.

For your project, first establish that there is a nontrivial equilibrium with x and y positive, provided that p is greater than r; note that this can be interpreted as the intersection of two lines in the x-y phase-plane. Try an analysis, looking at the flow given by dy/dx to investigate the stability of the equilibrium. Also, dividing the second equation of (8.2.2) by the first, obtain a differential equation for dy/dx and plot direction fields. Confirm your conclusions through numerical experiments. If one of the variables becomes zero, then the corresponding man has reached a stage when he is producing nothing for himself, but is absorbing resources from the rest of society. That is, the man is a *parasite*. Do your experiments provide clues about when this parasitism might occur? What happens when $p = r$ or when p is less than r? How sensitive is the model to small changes in p and r?

In the model, as described, there is a symmetry between the two men, sharing, for instance, the same value of r. You might consider the effects when this symmetry is removed.

Can you generalize the model to apply to three men?

8.3 The Economics of Fishing: One Species of Fish 

The dependent variables for this model are $x(t)$, which refers to the population of a stock of fish, and $E(t)$, the effort put into catching them. t is the time. If, in the absence of fishing, the population of fish would follow a logistic law, and if the rate at which fish are caught is proportional to the product Ex, then

$$\frac{dx}{dt} = ax - bx^2 - Ex. \tag{8.3.1}$$

Let c be the cost per unit effort, and p be the price per unit catch. Then the profit per unit catch is $Epx - Ec$. We assume that the effort will increase if the profit increases, so that

$$\frac{dE}{dt} = kE(px - c), \tag{8.3.2}$$

where k is a constant of proportionality. These are the equations of the model.

First, assume that all the parameters are constant. The origin is an equilibrium, but not one that we want. When is there another equilibrium? What is its stability? Perform a sequence of computations with parameters changing so that you can observe a transition from a situation with a stable equilibrium to one in which the stock dies out.

Suppose next that c is periodic: you would expect to see an annual effect, due to the seasons. Try

$$c = c_0 + c_1 \sin pt, \;\; c_1 < c_0. \tag{8.3.3}$$

You might start with conditions at equilibrium of $c_1 = 0$. Then introduce a small c_1. What happens? Now increase c_1. Alternatively, experiment with abrupt changes in c. Can the model exhibit chaos?

Again, suppose the model is running happily, with all parameters constant, when suddenly the demand goes up, and p is increased. What happens?

8.4 The Economics of Fishing: Two Species of Fish

First, consider Volterra's predator-prey model with fishing. Think in terms of tuna and shark, with populations x and y, respectively. Equal effort goes into catching both, but tuna sells for p per unit catch and shark, for q; q will be considerably less than p. The equations become

$$\left.\begin{aligned}\frac{dx}{dt} &= ax - cxy - Ex,\\ \frac{dy}{dt} &= -by + dxy - Ey,\\ \frac{dE}{dt} &= kE(px + qy - c).\end{aligned}\right] \tag{8.4.1}$$

We saw that, on average, the prey population increased with moderate fishing, and the predator population decreased. Choose simple values for a, b, c, and d (such as one) and repeat the sort of analysis made in the preceding project.

Any of the models involving two species might be used here, including ones with cooperation. Look in particular at May's model, which can have limit cycles.

The model consists of three nonlinear equations. Is it chaotic?

8.5 Goodwin's Growth Cycle

This model, published in 1967, is described by its author, R.M.Goodwin [47][2], as "starkly schematized and hence quite unrealistic." On the other hand, it is characterized by G.Gandolfo [45], as "a step toward more realistic interpretations of cycles and growth." J.M.Blatt [13] provides another complimentary discussion. Anyway, it is a neat model.

We start with definitions of the quantities involved. Keep track of them carefully.

n is the labor supply. It is assumed to grow according to $n = n_0e^{\beta t}$, where n_0 and β are constants.

t is the time.

l is the number of people actually employed.

q is the output.

$a = q/l$ is the labor productivity. Steady technological progress is assumed, so that the labor productivity will increase in time; this increase is modeled by $a = a_0e^{\alpha t}$, where a_0 and α are constants.

w is the wage rate. Then the workers' share of the product is w/a, and the capitalists' share is $1 - w/a$.

k is the capital; its rate of increase is the rate of investment. In the model all profits are saved and invested, so

$$\frac{dk}{dt} = q\left(1 - \frac{w}{a}\right). \tag{8.5.1}$$

$\sigma = k/q$ is the capital-output ratio; this is assumed here to be constant.

The profit rate is $\dfrac{1}{k}\dfrac{dk}{dt}$; and so

$$\frac{1}{k}\frac{dk}{dt} = \frac{1}{q}\frac{dq}{dt} = \frac{1}{\sigma}\left(1 - \frac{w}{a}\right). \tag{8.5.2}$$

[2]R.M.Goodwin, "A Growth Cycle," in G.H.Feinstein, *Socialism, Capitalism, and Economic Growth.* New York: Cambridge University Press. With permission of the publisher.

Also, since $l = q/a$,

$$\frac{1}{l}\frac{dl}{dt} = \frac{1}{q}\frac{dq}{dt} - \frac{1}{a}\frac{da}{dt} = \frac{1}{\sigma}\left(1 - \frac{w}{a}\right) - \alpha. \tag{8.5.3}$$

Let ν be the proportion of the labor force that is employed. Then $\nu = l/n$, and

$$\frac{1}{\nu}\frac{d\nu}{dt} = \frac{1}{\sigma}(1-u) - (\alpha+\beta), \tag{8.5.4}$$

where

$$u = \frac{w}{a}, \tag{8.5.5}$$

the workers' share of the product.

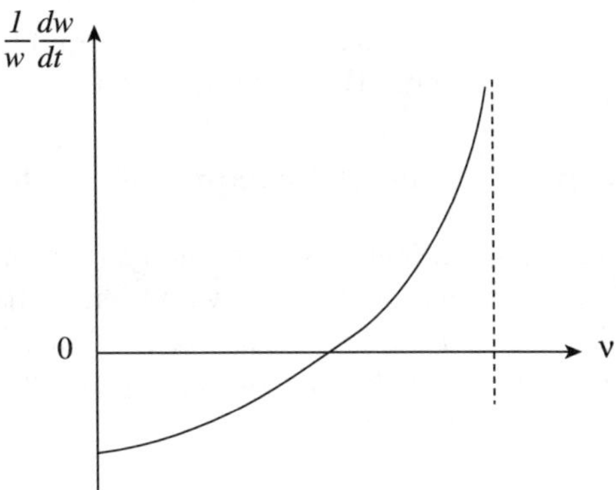

Figure 8.1:

It is assumed that the real wage rate rises in the neighborhood of full employment; then $\dot{w}/w$ is an increasing function of ν. This relationship is shown schematically in figure 8.1; Goodwin approximates this by the linear relation

$$\frac{1}{w}\frac{dw}{dt} = f(\nu) = -\gamma + \rho\nu. \tag{8.5.6}$$

Now

$$\frac{1}{u}\frac{du}{dt} = \frac{1}{w}\frac{dw}{dt} - \alpha. \tag{8.5.7}$$

So, with (8.5.6), we end up with the following equations for the model

$$\left.\begin{aligned} \frac{d\nu}{dt} &= \left(\frac{1}{\sigma} - (\alpha+\beta) - \frac{u}{\sigma}\right)\nu. \\ \frac{du}{dt} &= \left(-(\alpha+\gamma) + \rho\nu\right)u. \end{aligned}\right] \tag{8.5.8}$$

These are mathematically equivalent to the equations of Volterra's predator-prey model, and we are familiar with the possible cyclical motion around the equilibrium. Such motion, then, can correspond to business cycles. The equilibrium is at

$$\nu_e = \frac{\alpha+\gamma}{\rho}, \quad u_e = 1 - \sigma(\alpha+\beta). \tag{8.5.9}$$

So ν_e, the equilibrium value of the proportion of the labor force that is actually employed, depends critically on the approximation (8.5.6) to the curve of figure 8.1. In running the model, make sure that your interpretations all deal with basic properties of the parameters, using their definitions. A detailed description of the model in terms of the economics of what happens at various stages of a cycle is given by Goodwin, and his article is recommended.

Now here is the project. The cyclical nature of the model depends critically on the linear approximation (8.5.6). Construct a nonlinear function

$$\frac{1}{w}\frac{dw}{dt} = f(\nu) \tag{8.5.10}$$

which follows the curve better. Get the concavity right, and give it a vertical asymptote at $\nu = 1$. One possibility is

$$f(\nu) = \frac{A}{(1-\nu)^2} - B, \; A < B. \tag{8.5.11}$$

Then use (8.5.7) in place of the second equation of (8.5.8). The equilibrium should continue to exist, but what will be the effect of motion around the equilibrium? Can the cycles still exist?

8.6 A One-sector, Two-capital Model of Economic Growth

This model is due to C.Caton and K.Shell [23].[3] Its interpretation is not easy, and I recommend that you refer to the original article when interpreting your computations.

An output Y is produced by labor L and two kinds of machine, K_1 and K_2. The variables are expressed per unit of labor. Investment in the machines is k_1 and k_2, respectively, and the output per unit labor is given in the model by

$$y = y(k_1, k_2) = k_1^{\alpha_1} k_2^{\alpha_2} \tag{8.6.1}$$

for constant α_1 and α_2. The rent charged per machine for K_i is

$$r_i = \frac{\partial y}{\partial k_i} = \frac{\alpha_i}{k_i} y, \; i = 1, 2. \tag{8.6.2}$$

It is assumed that all rentals are saved and all wages are consumed. Then at any instant, savings and gross investment per head are each equal to

$$z = (\alpha_1 + \alpha_2) y. \tag{8.6.3}$$

The demand for consumption per head is

$$y - z = (1 - \alpha_1 - \alpha_2) y. \tag{8.6.4}$$

We must have the inequalities

$$\alpha_1 > 0, \; \alpha_2 > 0, \; 1 - \alpha_1 - \alpha_2 > 0. \tag{8.6.5}$$

Next, let z_1 and z_2 be the gross investments in the machines, where it is assumed that

$$z_1^2 + z_2^2 = z^2. \tag{8.6.6}$$

Let μ be the rate of depreciation of the machines. Let the growth in the labor force be given by

$$\frac{dL}{dt} = nL, \tag{8.6.7}$$

[3] With permission for C.Caton and K.Shell, " An Exercise in the Theory of Heterogeneous Capital Accumulation," *Review of Economic Studies*, **38** (1970), 13-21.

for constant n. Then if $\lambda = \mu + n$,

$$\left.\begin{aligned} \frac{dk_1}{dt} &= z_1 - \lambda k_1, \\ \frac{dk_2}{dt} &= z_2 - \lambda k_2. \end{aligned}\right] \tag{8.6.8}$$

Now let

$$z_1 = p_1 z, \; z_2 = p_2 z. \tag{8.6.9}$$

From (8.6.6) we have

$$p_1^2 + p_2^2 = 1. \tag{8.6.10}$$

But p_1 and p_2 are proportional to the prices of the machines. Hence, allowing the prices to change, the consumption rates of return for the two types of machine are

$$\frac{1}{p_1}\frac{dp_1}{dt} + \frac{r_1}{p_1} \quad \text{and} \quad \frac{1}{p_2}\frac{dp_2}{dt} + \frac{r_2}{p_2}.$$

These are set equal to each other, so that the wealth holders will not concentrate on one rather than the other.

Next, let

$$p = \frac{p_2}{p_1}, \;\; \text{so} \;\; p_1 = (1+p^2)^{-1/2}, \;\; \text{and} \;\; p_2 = p(1+p^2)^{-1/2}. \tag{8.6.11}$$

Then

$$\left.\begin{aligned} \frac{dk_1}{dt} &= (\alpha_1 + \alpha_2) y (1+p^2)^{-1/2} - \lambda k_1, \\ \frac{dk_2}{dt} &= p(\alpha_1 + \alpha_2) y (1+p^2)^{-1/2} - \lambda k_2, \end{aligned}\right] \tag{8.6.12}$$

where y is given by (8.6.1).

Putting in the equality

$$\frac{1}{p_1}\frac{dp_1}{dt} + \frac{r_1}{p_1} = \frac{1}{p_2}\frac{dp_2}{dt} + \frac{r_2}{p_2}$$

and using the expressions (8.6.2) for r_1 and r_2, we find that

$$\frac{dp}{dt} = y(1+p^2)^{1/2}\left(p\frac{\alpha_1}{k_1} - \frac{\alpha_2}{k_2}\right). \tag{8.6.13}$$

The three equations (8.6.12) and (8.6.13) constitute the model.

In the model there is an equilibrium corresponding to “balanced growth.” In their paper, Caton and Shell consider solutions in the k-p plane, where $k = k_1/k_2$. The equilibrium turns out to be a saddle point and is therefore unstable. Do some numerical experiments to confirm this result, and find the nature of the solutions in the k-p plane. What is the effect of playing with the values of α_1 and α_2?

Chapter 9

Sports

9.1 The Dynamics of a Spinning Ball

In this, and the following few projects, we shall look at some of the factors that affect the motion of projectiles in sport. Of necessity, the treatment given here will be superficial. But you will see that a lot can be learned about the physics of sport at this elementary level. Also you may be able to run experiments, and be a star athlete more easily, perhaps, at the computer than outdoors.

The interest of scientists in sport goes back at least as far as Newton. Although it is an area that is sadly neglected in education, there are some excellent books and articles on almost every sport; these have been written by people who love sports and who love science, and want to share their experience with their readers. You will be well rewarded by following up the references provided in this chapter. Books recommended especially include those by Brancazio [16], Daish [29], Hart and Croft [50], Townend [98] and Watts and Bahill [105]. There is a wonderful selection of papers in "The Physics of Sports," edited by C.Frohlich [40]. For additional reading, I guarantee that you can spend many happy hours scanning papers in the *American Journal of Physics.*

In most sports involving balls, the spinning of the ball plays a decisive role. Spinning balls move subject to three forces:

- **Gravity** is assumed to produce a constant downward acceleration, $\vec{g}$.

- **Drag** is a force opposite to the velocity of the ball relative to the air. If this velocity is $\vec{v}_{\text{rel}}$ then the drag force is

$$\vec{D} = -\frac{1}{2} C_D \rho A v_{\text{rel}} \vec{v}_{\text{rel}} . \tag{9.1.1}$$

  ρ is the density of the air; in this formula, it is expressed in terms of *mass* per unit volume. A is the cross-sectional area of the ball. v_{rel} is the magnitude of $\vec{v}_{\text{rel}}$. C_D, a non-dimensional number, is the *drag coefficient.* This is discussed below. The factor 1/2 appears through tradition. Note that, if C_D is constant, then equation (9.1.1) gives a resistance that is proportional to the *square* of the relative speed.

- **Lift**, in the present context, where we are following the motion of a sphere, is caused by the spinning of the ball. If $\vec{\omega}$ is the angular velocity of the ball about its center, then the lift force is

$$\vec{L} = \frac{1}{2} C_L^* \rho A \vec{\omega} \times \vec{v}_{\text{rel}} . \tag{9.1.2}$$

  Another version of this uses the more conventionally defined *lift coefficient*, C_L

$$\vec{L} = \frac{1}{2} C_L \rho A v_{\text{rel}}^2 \hat{\omega} \times \hat{v}_{\text{rel}} . \tag{9.1.3}$$

$\hat{\omega}$ and $\hat{v}_{\text{rel}}$ are unit vectors. C_L is dimensionless, whereas C_L^* has the dimension of a length.

The Drag Coefficient

C_D can vary in complicated ways that depend on velocity, dimensions, the viscosity of the medium through which the ball is moving, and the roughness of the ball. The first three of these are incorporated into a non-dimensional quantity called the *Reynolds number*

$$Re = \rho V L/\nu, \tag{9.1.4}$$

where $V = v_{\text{rel}}$, the speed relative to the resisting medium, L is a typical length scale (such as the diameter) and ν is the viscosity of the medium through which the ball is moving.

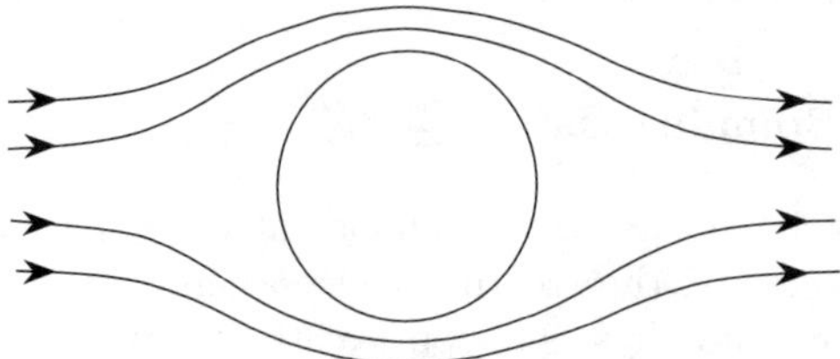

Figure 9.1: *Flow of air around a non-spinning ball.*

Figure 9.1 illustrates a non-spinning ball passing slowly through air. The figure shows the motion of the air relative to the ball; so the ball is, in fact, moving to the **left** (as is the case in similar figures below). The lines, showing paths of air particles, are called streamlines. In this instance, the flow is smooth and is called *laminar.* In this situation the drag is proportional to the speed, so C_D must be inversely proportional to the speed. There is a thin layer close to the surface of the ball called the *boundary layer.* As the speed v_{rel} increases, the boundary layer separates to the rear of the ball, as in figure 9.2, leaving a wake in which the air moves in eddies. The figure shows the *angle of separation,* α. Kinetic energy is absorbed by the eddying motion, and this is taken from the kinetic energy of the moving ball. So the wake creates a drag which increases as α increases.

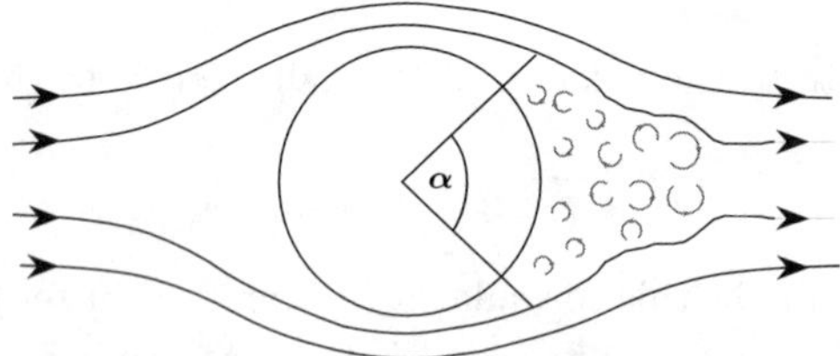

Figure 9.2: *Separation of the boundary layer. α is the separation angle.*

As the speed increases further, the motion in the wake becomes turbulent, and there is mixing between the material in the wake and the stream of air outside. This lowers the pressure in the boundary layer, and the separation points move back toward each other, lowering the drag. This jump in the value of C_D occurs when $Re \sim 1.4 \times 10^5$. For instance, De Mestre [33], p. 137, gives

$$C_D = 0.45, \text{ for } Re < 1.4 \times 10^5, \quad \text{and} \quad C_D = 0.20, \text{ for } Re > 1.4 \times 10^5. \tag{9.1.5}$$

Taking $\rho = 1.23$ kg m^{-3} and $\nu = 1.5 \times 10^{-5}$ m^{2}s^{-1}, and $V = 40$ ms^{-1}, he calculates $Re = 1.9 \times 10^5$ for a baseball. Figures are comparable for other balls used in sports. In fact there is a range of values for R_e where C_D is changing; its behavior in this transition region is not well known. This means that, during flight, the drag can change. The change can be from the order of 0.5 to 0.2. This has been suggested as the reason for sudden changes toward the end of a baseball pitch, but the idea has not been generally accepted; the pitched baseball slows down very little during its half-second trajectory. However, there is nothing to stop you from including an abruptly changing C_D in your model. The transition occurs for lower speeds if there is an increase in the roughness of the surface of the ball. This is the reason for the dimples on a golf ball; the range of a driven dimpled ball is around twice that of a smooth ball.

For some detailed numerical data for baseball, see an article by R.K.Adair [1].

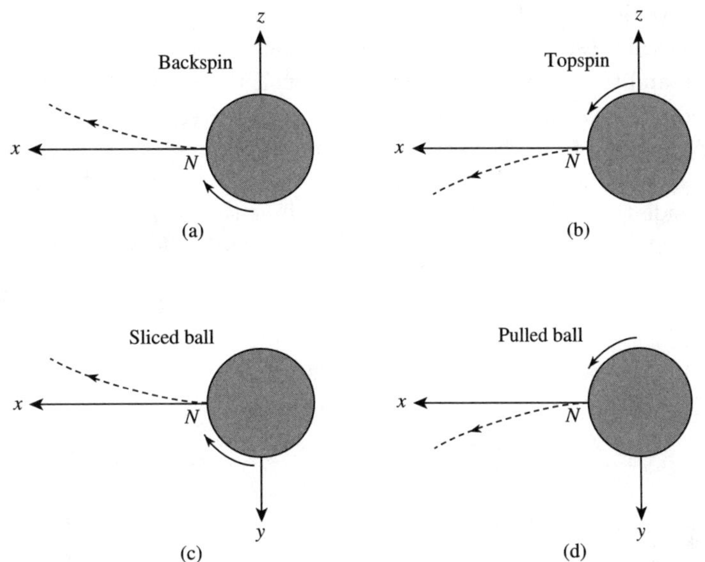

Figure 9.3: *The deflection of a spinning ball. The ball is moving to the left.*

The Magnus Effect

There is a wonderful paper by J.J.Thomson [96] based on a lecture given to non-specialists, in which many demonstrations were included. Although specifically addressing golf, his remarks have much more general application. Having remarked that the behavior of a non-spinning ball is regular but uninteresting, he continues:

> But a golf ball when it leaves the club is only in rare cases devoid of spin, and it is spin which gives the interest, variety and vivacity to the flight of the ball. It is spin which accounts for the behavior of a sliced or pulled ball, it is spin which makes the ball soar or "douk," or execute those wild flourishes which give the impression that the ball is endowed with an artistic temperament, and performs these eccentricities as an acrobat might throw in an extra somersault or two for the fun of the thing. This view, however, gives an entirely wrong impression of the temperament of a golf ball, which is, in reality, the most prosaic of things, knowing while in the air only one rule of conduct, which it obeys with unintelligent conscientiousness, that of always following its nose. This rule is the key to the behavior of all balls while in the air, whether they are golf balls, baseballs, cricket balls or tennis balls.

By the "nose" of a ball, Thomson meant that point of the ball that was furthest in front. It is the point N in figure 9.3, where the ball is moving to the left, in the direction of the x-axis; the z-axis points vertically upward, and the y-axis points toward you, the reader. In figures 9.3(a) and

(b) the motion is seen from the side. In figure 9.3(a), the ball is rotating clockwise, and the nose is moving forward and upward; so as the ball tries to follow its nose, it will rise and move in the curve illustrated by the dashed line. This is the case of *backspin* or *bottom-spin*, typical of the drive of a golf ball. In figure 9.3(b), we see *topspin*, with the rotation counterclockwise, and the deflection downward; this can be used in a serve in tennis, making the ball fall more quickly than it otherwise would, and so tending to prevent it going out of court. In figures 9.3(c) and (d) the spin is about the vertical, and the ball is observed from above. For figure 9.3(c) the rotation is clockwise, and the ball moves off toward the right, as with a sliced golf ball; in figure 9.3(d), the rotation is reversed, as with a pulled golf ball. If the ball were to spin around the x-axis, then its nose would always move forward, and there would be no deflection.

We can summarize these observations with the rule that the deflection is perpendicular to the direction of motion and to the axis of the spin. In fact, if the forward velocity is $\vec{v}$ and the angular velocity is $\vec{\omega}$, the direction of deflection is the same as the direction of $\vec{\omega} \times \vec{v}$.

The first explanation of this behavior was given by Newton, who suggested that tennis balls curve because the side of the ball that moves most rapidly, relative to the air, feels more resistance than the opposite side that moves more slowly. The first thorough investigation was made around 1850 by G.Magnus, and the behavior is known as the *Magnus effect.*

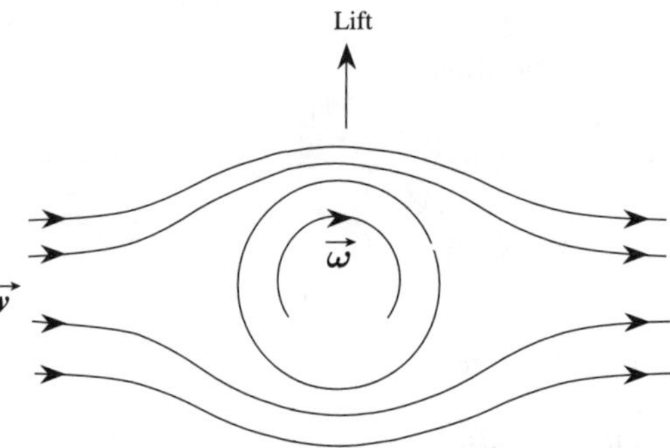

Figure 9.4: *Flow of air around a slowly moving spinning ball.*

We shall discuss the Magnus effect sufficiently, I hope, to make it appear plausible. Figure 9.1 shows the pattern of airflow relative to a non-spinning ball. Now consider how the figure is modified if the ball is spinning. Assume, first, that the spin axis is perpendicular to the velocity vector. For a slowly moving ball, the streamlines are shown in figure 9.4. Air is dragged more rapidly over the top than under the bottom; so, by Bernoulli's law, the pressure is less on top, and there is a net upward force.

The modification for a rapidly moving ball is shown in figure 9.5. (Note, again, that the arrows show the velocity of the flow relative to the ball; so the actual velocity of the ball is in the opposite direction.) The spin is clockwise. The flow lines near the top are dragged along by the spin and have a separation point well to the rear. In contrast, the spin opposes the flow at the bottom, resulting in an early separation point. So the wake is deflected down, leading to an upward lift force. For a counter-clockwise spin, the "lift" force would be downward.

The word "lift" is a convenient term, but, as we have seen, the force just described does not have to be vertically upward. But it must be perpendicular to the angular velocity $\vec{\omega}$ and the velocity $\vec{v}$. Note that if these two vectors were parallel, then there would be no lift force. What matters is the component of $\vec{\omega}$ that is perpendicular to $\vec{v}$. This is why we need the cross-product $\vec{\omega} \times \vec{v}_{\rm rel}$ in equation (9.1.2).

In sports (with the exception of table tennis) the balls used are "rough." The rules for smooth balls are different; in particular, if the rotation rate is slow enough, the curve is **opposite** that

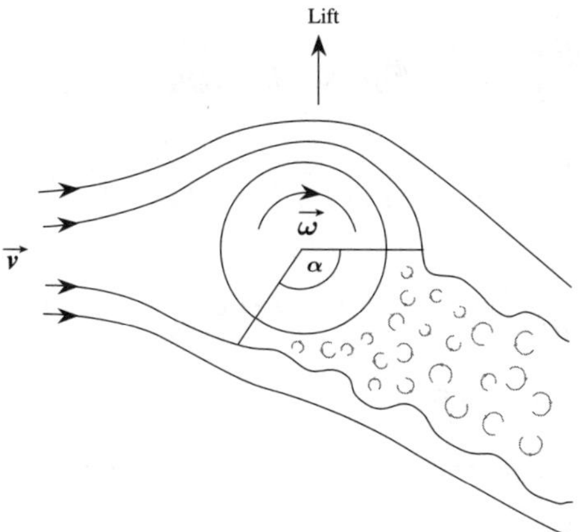

Figure 9.5: *Flow of air around a rapidly moving spinning ball.*

predicted by the Magnus rules. Consider the two sides of the ball moving fastest and slowest relative to the air; that moving slowest will feel laminar flow with a large separation angle; that moving fastest will feel turbulent flow with a small separation angle, so the ball curves away from its nose. A common parameter to use when discussing the lift coefficient is the ratio of the speed $u = r\omega$ of the surface of the ball due to rotation (r is the radius of the ball), to v, the speed of the center of the ball through the air. For the smooth ball, the inverse Magnus effect occurs if u/v is less than approximately 0.4.

There is one instance where the smoothness of a ball is exploited. A cricket ball has a seam of raised stitches around a circumference, separating two hemispheres; when the ball is new, these hemispheres are smooth and shiny. If the ball is bowled *without* spin such that the surface facing the air has one half rough, because of the seam, and the other half smooth, then the ball will curve in the direction of the rough side. After some use, the shine wears off, and this particular method of curving (called "seam bowling") cannot be used.

Equations of motion

The x- and y-axes will be taken to be horizontal, with the z-axis pointing vertically upward. We shall assume that there is no wind. The equations of motion are

$$\left.\begin{aligned} \frac{d\vec{r}}{dt} &= \vec{v}, \\ \frac{d\vec{v}}{dt} &= \vec{g} - k_D v\, \vec{v} + k_L\, \vec{\omega} \times \vec{v}\, . \end{aligned}\right] \tag{9.1.6}$$

Here

$$k_D = \frac{C_D \rho A}{2m} \quad \text{and} \quad k_L = \frac{C_L^* \rho A}{2m}. \tag{9.1.7}$$

Note that k_D and k_L have dimensions the inverse of length.

Let $\vec{r}$, $\vec{v}$ and $\vec{\omega}$ have components $\langle x,\, y,\, z\rangle$, $\langle v_x,\, v_y,\, v_z\rangle$, $\langle \omega_x,\, \omega_y,\, \omega_z\rangle$. Then the system of equations can be written as

$$\left.\begin{aligned}
\frac{d^2x}{dt^2} &= -k_D v v_x + k_L(\omega_y v_z - \omega_z v_y), \\
\frac{d^2y}{dt^2} &= -k_D v v_y + k_L(\omega_z v_x - \omega_x v_z), \\
\frac{d^2z}{dt^2} &= -k_D v v_z + k_L(\omega_x v_y - \omega_y v_x) - g,
\end{aligned}\right] \tag{9.1.8}$$

where $v = \sqrt{v_x^2 + v_y^2 + v_z^2}$. For a program, let

$$y_1 = x,\ y_2 = v_x,\ y_3 = y,\ y_4 = v_y,\ y_5 = z,\ y_6 = v_z.$$

Then

$$\left.\begin{aligned}
v &= \sqrt{y_2^2 + y_4^2 + y_6^2} \\
\frac{dy_1}{dt} &= y_2, \\
\frac{dy_2}{dt} &= -k_D v y_2 + k_L(\omega_y y_6 - \omega_z y_4), \\
\frac{dy_3}{dt} &= y_4, \\
\frac{dy_4}{dt} &= -k_D v y_4 + k_L(\omega_z y_2 - \omega_x y_6), \\
\frac{dy_5}{dt} &= y_6, \\
\frac{dy_6}{dt} &= -k_D v y_6 + k_L(\omega_x y_4 - \omega_y y_2) - g.
\end{aligned}\right] \tag{9.1.9}$$

9.1.1 Projects

The most satisfying course is probably to go at once to the main projects. But there are a number of ways to play with the equations just given that will provide insight and experience.

1. For a start, ignore spin, and just play with the drag force in two dimensions, x and z. At this stage, there is no need to be particular about the units or numbers used. Calculate and plot a solution with $k_D = 0$; you can do this by formula. Now introduce gradually increasing values for k_D, plotting each solution to see the effects on the shape of the trajectory and the range.

2. Next, keep the initial speed constant, but for increasing values of k_D find initial angles (between the velocity and the x-axis) that maximize the range.

3. Experiment with changing values of k_D during flight. For instance, you might take $k_D = 0.02$ for $v > 100$ and $k_D = 0.01$ for $v < 100$.

4. Introduce a wind, with velocity $\vec{v}_w$, so that $\vec{v}_{\text{rel}} = \vec{v} - \vec{v}_w$ is used in the expression for the drag force. Start with $\vec{v}_w$ in the x-z plane, and find the effects if it is helping or opposing the motion. How might the starting angle be changed to maximize the range? Now add the third dimension, y. Plot projections of the paths in the x-y, y-z and x-z planes. Note particularly the effects if C_D is increased. This might be like comparing playing tennis or badminton on a windy day.

5. Now introduce spin. First, just use the component ω_z. Plot the curves; in the x-y plane, to show the curving and in the y-z plane to show how the flight of the ball would appear to someone at the receiving end. Start with $k_D = 0.001$ and increase it gradually.

6. Repeat the preceding project, but now only consider ω_y; note that $\omega_y > 0$ will give topspin. For a run of experiments keep k_L fixed, but vary ω_y, observing the effect on the path. Look at the path projected in the x-z plane.

7. Introduce wind. In particular look for modifications in the effects already seen, when the wind is parallel to the x-axis and behind or in front of the thrower.

8. If k_L becomes too big, then strange things will happen, not yet observed in any sports arena. Loops will appear. See what you can find! Increasing k_L can be interpreted in terms of a bigger rate of spin; but the same effect can be produced by increasing the surface area of the ball and decreasing its mass. Get a large light inflated rubber ball; strike it at one side to produce spin, and see if you can produce looping trajectories.

9.2 A Model for a Baseball Pitch

We shall use equations (9.1.8) or (9.1.9). The origin of coordinates is at the pitcher's mound, with the x-axis pointing toward home plate and the y-axis toward first base. We assume that there is no wind.

Units are feet, seconds and pounds. Some of the numbers are very uncertain; but bear in mind that, while modeling at the computer, you can make up your own rules.

Baseball diameter:	$D = 2.9$ in $= 0.242$ ft.
Baseball weight:	$w = 5.1$ oz $= 0.319$ lb.
An exceptional spin rate is:	$\omega = 2000$ rpm $= 209$ rad/s.
Typical spin rates are: Fastball:	1600 rpm $=$ 167 rad/s.
Slider:	1700 rpm $=$ 178 rad/s.
Curve ball:	1900 rpm $=$ 199 rad/s.
Initial speeds are: Fastball:	85 to 95 mph or 125 to 140 ft/s.
Slider:	75 to 85 mph or 110 to 125 ft/s.
Curve ball:	70 to 80 mph or 103 to 107 ft/s.

The atmospheric density, ρ, in the formulas is in terms of mass per unit volume. So if we take the value 0.075 lb/ft^3, we would have $\rho = 0.0023$ slugs/ft^3. Remember that the mass m, occurring in the equations, is w/g.

For C_D it is usual to use values of 0.5 to 0.2.

Based on experimental data involving golf balls and base balls, described by Bearman and Harvey [9], Watts and Bahill [105] suggest a formula for the magnitude of the lift force as

$$F_L = \frac{1}{2}\rho A R \omega v, \tag{9.2.1}$$

where R is the radius of the ball. v refers to the velocity of the ball relative to the air. Then, in the notation of equations (9.1.2) and (9.1.3), we have

$$F_L = \frac{1}{2}\rho A R \omega v = \frac{1}{2}C_L^* \rho A \omega v = \frac{1}{2}C_L \rho A v^2. \tag{9.2.2}$$

Then $C_L^* = R$, the radius, a very convenient approximation, that we shall use in most calculations in this chapter.

Then, using $C_D = 0.4$, we find numerical values are $k_D = 0.0021$ and $k_L = 0.00063$.

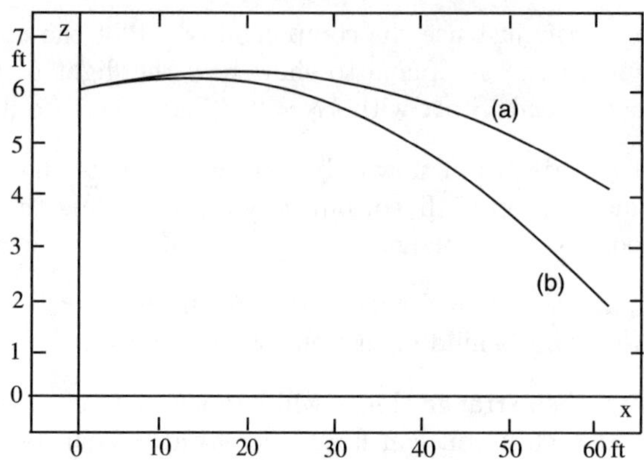

Figure 9.6: *In this figure the origin is at the pitcher's mound and the x-axis points toward home plate. In (a) the ball is pitched with no spin from a height of 6 ft with initial velocity components $v_x = 125$, $v_y = 0$, $v_z = 5$ft/sec, so the motion takes place in a vertical plane. (b) is similar, except that there is a topspin, $\omega_y = 200$rad/sec. This produces a downward force.*

In running the model, I suggest that you start with neither spin nor drag (when you can check results using pencil and paper). For initial conditions, x should be zero, y should be zero, or close to zero, depending on whether you want to be a left or right-handed pitcher, and z is the height of the pitch.

Next, introduce drag, and measure its effect. Next, introduce backspin ($\omega_y < 0$) and confirm the lift. (Also try topspin, and see what may happen.) Next, experiment with spins of all kinds, and record the deflections. Finally, introduce small initial values for the y- and z-components of velocity. It is often said that the curving happens toward the end of the pitch. Looking at a projection of the trajectory in the $x - y$ plane, see if you agree. You should see a curve that resembles part of a parabola, since the lateral force due to the spinning is nearly constant.

The pitched ball travels 60 ft to the batter; so a computation should stop when $x > 60$ or $y_1 > 60$, or `y(1) > 60`. (It should also stop if z becomes negative; bouncing is not allowed!) The duration of the pitch is around half a second, so make sure that you will compute enough points in this short time span. Also bear in mind that a legal pitch must pass through the "strike zone," which is a small area, roughly, $x = 60$, $-1 < y < 1$ and z between the batter's knees and head.

Figure 9.6 illustrates the effect of topspin on the flight of the ball. In 9.6(a) the starting conditions are: height 6 ft; velocity components $v_x = 125$, $v_y = 0$, $v_z = 5$ft/sec and no spin. For 9.6(b) the conditions are the same but now there is a topspin with $\omega_y = 200$rad/sec. The "lift" force is downward, and the ball drops, relative to 9.6(a), by a further two feet.

Figure 9.7 shows two cases of three-dimensional motion. For 9.7(a) the only spin is $\omega_z = 200$rad/sec, so the ball moves toward the pitcher's left. Initial velocity components are $v_x = 125$, $v_y = 0$, $v_z = 5$ft/sec. In 9.7(b) the only change is that initially $v_y = -5$ft/sec to compensate for the leftward drift."

9.3 Pitching a Knuckle Ball

A non-spinning baseball experiences a small lateral force that depends on its orientation. If the seams on the ball were to appear symmetrical, as seen by the batter, the force would be zero, so if the ball is rotating slowly, the lateral force will vary sinusoidally, with period equal to one quarter the period of spin. This can cause the ball to change its direction of curving during flight; a characteristic of the knuckle ball.

Watts and Sawyer [106] give the formula $2.16 \times 10^{-5}v^2$ lb for the maximum value of this force,

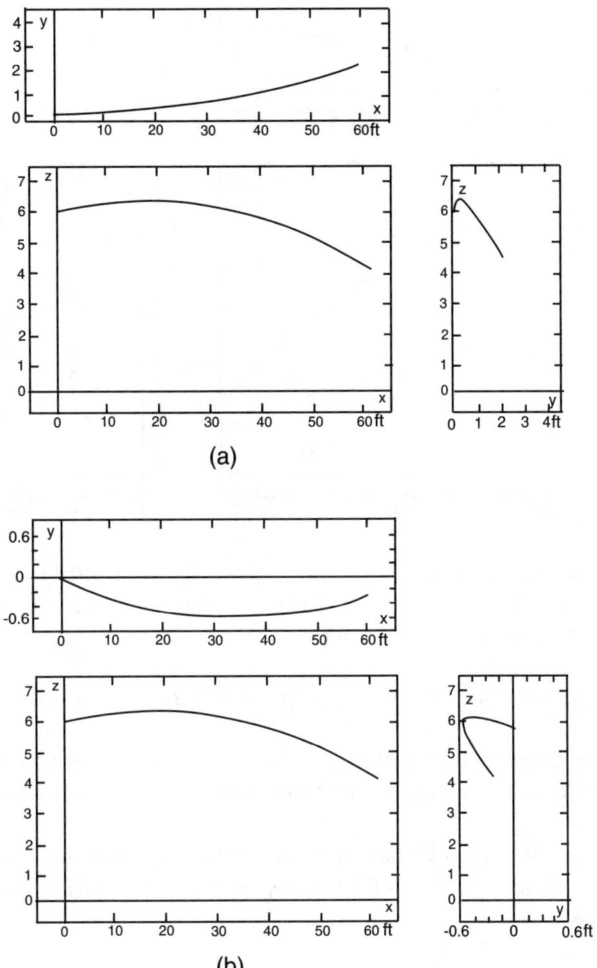

Figure 9.7: *These figures show three projections of the flight of the ball, seen from above, from the left and from the view of the catcher. In (a) the starting conditions are those of figure 9.6(a) with the addition of a spin about the vertical axis, $\omega_z = 200$rad/sec. This leads to a force action toward the left of the pitcher. In (b) an additional velocity component $v_y = 5$ft/sec is added to compensate for the leftward drift of (a).*

where v is the speed. So we shall use

$$F_{\text{lat}} = 2.16 \times 10^{-5} v^2 \sin(4pt + q) \tag{9.3.1}$$

for the force as the ball rotates, with period $2\pi/p$. The equations for the model are

$$\left.\begin{aligned} \frac{d^2x}{dt^2} &= -k_D v v_x, \\ \frac{d^2y}{dt^2} &= -k_D v v_y + F_{\text{lat}}/m, \\ \frac{d^2z}{dt^2} &= -k_D v v_z - g. \end{aligned}\right] \tag{9.3.2}$$

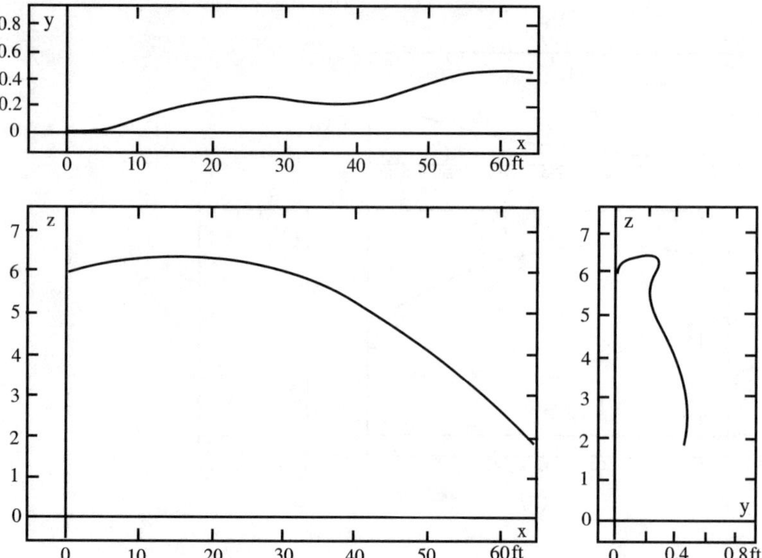

Figure 9.8: *The flight of a knuckleball seen from the top, from the side and by the catcher. Starting conditions were: height of the pitch, 6 ft, spin, $p = 4$ rad/sec, initial deflection, $q = 1.5$ rad. Initial velocity components, $v_x = 100$. $v_y = 0$, $v_z = 5$ ft/sec.*

Here the reference system and notation are those of project 9.2. m is the mass of the ball and $k_D = C_D \rho A/(2m)$.

Pitching speeds should be between 60 to 70 mph. If the rotation rate is too rapid, the changing curve will have no time to build up, so allow at most one revolution in the half-second flight of the ball.

Figure 9.8 shows the flight of a knuckleball with the following starting conditions: height of the pitch, 6 ft, spin, $p = 4$ rad/sec, initial deflection, $q = 1.5$ rad. Initial velocity components, $v_x = 100$. $v_y = 0$, $v_z = 5$ ft/sec.

9.4 The Flight of a Flyball

A good background for this section is given in a paper by R.G.Watts and S.Baroni [104], where they discuss the collisions of baseballs with bats, and the resulting trajectories of the spinning balls. This model has the same equations as the model for a baseball pitch. At the start, it will be best to consider only motion in the x-z plane, with only backspin or topspin. The difference is in the initial conditions. The launch angle can be as high as 45°, the initial speed might be 120 mph, and the backspin might be 7,000 rpm, depending on how the ball is hit. Of course, at a computer, you are free from practical limitations.

I suggest that you keep the initial speed and launch angle constant, while varying the spin rate. Look for the maximum range. Then try varying the first two parameters.

The terminal speed of a baseball is about 140 ft/sec. To hit a home run, the starting speed must be substantially greater than this. For different initial angles of elevation, find suitable starting conditions for home runs.

A softball experiences forty percent more drag than a baseball, so the shape of its path is different. See the following project (9.5) for more details. Compare the two flights. Find conditions for home runs, and compare them with those for baseball.

Finally, introduce a wind, to find out how important this might be. See the project on golf, (9.6), for more detail.

You might also experiment with changes in the drag coefficient, as suggested by De Mestre [33]. As the speed v diminishes, the drag coefficient increases, but the v^2 factor makes the overall effect of drag become much smaller. See section 9.1 for details.

9.5 Pitching a Softball

A softball weighs 0.32 lb, and has a diameter of 3.82 in. The ratio area divided by weight is 0.25 ft^2/lb, or 1.7 times the same ratio for a baseball. So the parameters for drag and lift are greater for a softball than for a baseball. But the pitches are quite different. The softball pitch (here we consider only the *slow* pitch) is delivered underhand, starting from below the waist, travels in an arc with maximum height between 6 and 12 ft, covering a distance of 42 to 45 ft. The total trajectory may take around one second. Pitchers use spin; this is intended to contribute to mis-hits, but some also claim that it affects the trajectory. (Certainly, batters can become highly confused over the pitcher's tactics.) Investigating this claim is the object of this project.

The equations for the model are the same as those for the baseball pitch

$$\left.\begin{aligned} \frac{d^2x}{dt^2} &= -k_D v v_x + k_L(\omega_y v_z - \omega_z v_y), \\ \frac{d^2y}{dt^2} &= -k_D v v_y + k_L(\omega_z v_x - \omega_x v_z), \\ \frac{d^2z}{dt^2} &= -k_D v v_z + k_L(\omega_x v_y - \omega_y v_x) - g, \end{aligned}\right] \tag{9.5.1}$$

where $v = \sqrt{v_x^2 + v_y^2 + v_z^2}$. Taking $C_D = 0.4$, we have $k_D = 0.0037$ and $k_L = 0.0029$.

It is simplest to consider motion only in the x-z plane, using only ω_y. First, find sample trajectories neglecting drag and lift, using

$$x = v_0 \cos\alpha t,\ y = H + v_0 \sin\alpha t - \frac{1}{2}gt^2,$$

where H is the height of the start of the pitch, v_0 is the initial speed and α is the angle the initial velocity makes with the horizontal. Select a pitch and record its trajectory and especially the point of landing. Next, introduce drag. Measure its effect, and then modify v_0 so that the pitch lands at the landing point selected earlier. Finally, introduce lift. Again, modify v_0 so that the landing point is the same. The final two trajectories may look very similar, but the times at which the ball is at specified points will differ. Compare trajectories with and without lift; it could be the relative timing that confuses the batter.

9.6 Driving a Golf Ball

The basic model here is similar to that for the baseball pitch. The x-axis is in the direction of the (intended) drive, with the z-axis vertically upward. Ideally, the spin of the ball will be a backspin, parallel to the y-axis. But slicing and hooking, resulting from sidespin, are not unknown in golf, so we shall use

$$\vec{\omega} = \omega_y \hat{\jmath} + \omega_z \hat{k} = \omega(\hat{\jmath}\cos\alpha + \hat{k}\sin\alpha). \tag{9.6.1}$$

So $\alpha = 0$ would correspond to backspin only. $\alpha = \pi/2$ would correspond to sidespin only; nobody is perfect. We shall also introduce a wind with velocity

$$\vec{v}_w = v_{wx}\hat{\imath} + v_{wy}\hat{\jmath} + v_{wz}\hat{k}. \tag{9.6.2}$$

Then the velocity of the ball relative to the wind is

$$\vec{v}_{rel} = \vec{v} - \vec{v}_w = v_{rx}\hat{\imath} + v_{ry}\hat{\jmath} + v_{rz}\hat{k}. \tag{9.6.3}$$

It is $\vec{v}_r$ that must be used in the calculation of drag and lift. Then the equations of the model are

$$\left.\begin{aligned} \frac{d^2x}{dt^2} &= -k_D v_{rel} v_{rx} + k_L(\omega_y v_{rz} - \omega_z v_{ry}), \\ \frac{d^2y}{dt^2} &= -k_D v_{rel} v_{ry} + k_L(\omega_z v_{rx}), \\ \frac{d^2z}{dt^2} &= -k_D v_{rel} v_{rz} + k_L(-\omega_y v_{rx}) - g, \end{aligned}\right] \tag{9.6.4}$$

where $v_{rel} = \sqrt{v_{rx}^2 + v_{ry}^2 + v_{rz}^2}$. As before,

$$k_D = \frac{C_D \rho A}{2m} \quad \text{and} \quad k_L = \frac{C_L^* \rho A}{2m}. \tag{9.6.5}$$

The weight of a golf ball is 1.62 oz. The diameter can be 1.632 (British) or 1.692 (American) in. Take your pick. The drag and lift coefficients vary in complicated ways; for our purposes, we shall take them to be constant. (For more detail see the paper by Bearman and Harvey [9].) Accordingly, we shall assume

$$C_D = 0.4, \qquad C_L^* = R = 0.846/12 = 0.0706. \tag{9.6.6}$$

(This assumes an American ball.) With atmospheric density 0.075 lb per ft^3, and bearing in mind that ρ in the equations refers to *mass* per unit volume, we find

$$k_D = 0.00578 C_D = 0.00231, \quad \text{and} \quad k_L = 0.00578 C_L^* = 0.00041. \tag{9.6.7}$$

An initial speed for a drive can be taken to be between 150 to 250 ft/sec. Spin rates of several thousand rpm can be assumed. (To convert from revolutions per minute to radians per second, multiply by $\pi/30$.) A launch angle of around 10° would be reasonable.

To experiment with the model, start with no drag or lift forces. Then introduce drag. Next, introduce backspin, gradually increasing the magnitude of ω. You might even take this to impossibly high values. What happens if you introduce topspin? The calculations so far are in two dimensions. Move into three, with a nonzero value for ω_z. Finally, do some driving on a windy day, and investigate possible changes you might try to make to produce a straight drive.

Figures 9.9(a) and (b) show comparisons between trajectories of golf balls with (i) no drag or lift, (ii) drag but no lift, and (iii) both drag and lift. The drives start with velocity 200 ft/sec at an angle of 10° with the horizontal. Drag and lift coefficients are those given in the text. In figure 9.9(a) the backspin is an angular velocity component $\omega_y = -300$ rad/sec leading to a lift force that is vertically upward. For (i) the trajectory is a parabola. (ii) shows how drag drastically reduces the range, while (iii) shows the dramatic effect of lift. In figure 9.9(b) the backspin is $\omega_y = -400$ rad/sec, and the range is increased. Notice that for case (iii) the initial rising path of the ball is nearly linear, showing that the lift and gravitational forces are nearly balanced.

Figure 9.10(a) shows projections of the path in three dimensions of a mis-driven, pulled ball: $\omega_y = -300$, $\omega_z = 100$ rad/sec. Finally, in figure 9.10(b) we have a situation where the lift force has increased by a factor of ten. Perhaps the driven ball has cross-section ten times that of a golf ball, or the computer operator made a keying error, or maybe he wanted to have fun. At all events, we are seeing motion not observed, so far, on any links. It certainly did not improve the range!

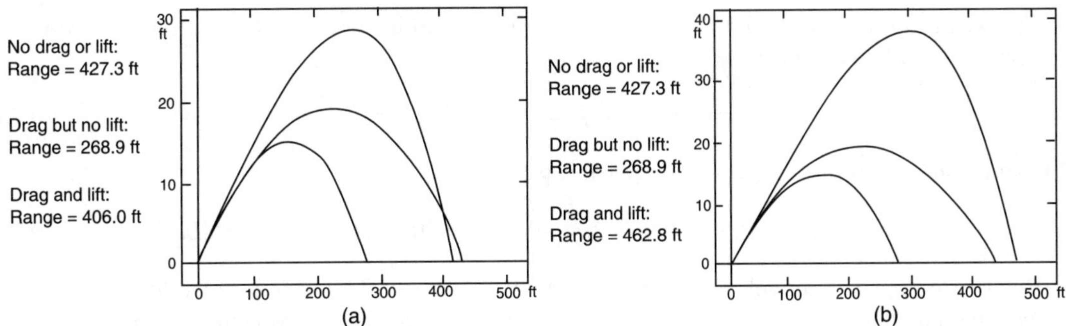

Figure 9.9: *Two comparisons between trajectories with (i) no drag or lift, (ii) drag but no lift, and (iii) both drag and lift. The drives start with velocity 200ft/sec at an angle of* 10° *with the horizontal. In (a) the backspin is* $\omega_y = -300$ *rad/sec,and in (b) it is* $\omega_y = -400$*rad/sec.*

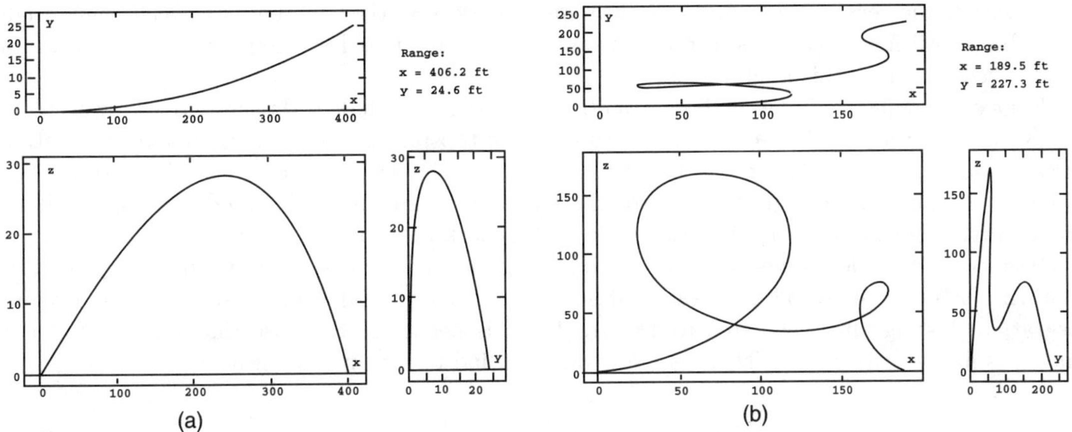

Figure 9.10: *(a) shows a pulled drive;* $\omega_y = -300$, $\omega_z = 100$. *Conditions for (b) are the same as those for (a) with the exception that the lift coefficient has been increased from* $k_L = 0.00041$ *to* $k_L = 0.0041$. *Motion such as this has not been observed, so far, on any links!*

9.7 Serving in Tennis

We shall be serving on a windless day. The serve will be launched parallel to the x-axis. With the z-axis pointing vertically upward, the only spin considered will be topspin, parallel to the y-axis. The model may easily be made more complicated, following the pattern of that for the drive in golf. But I think that you will find the model set out here to be sufficiently intriguing.

The equations for the model are

$$\left.\begin{aligned} \frac{d^2x}{dt^2} &= -k_D v v_x + k_L \omega_y v_z, \\ \frac{d^2z}{dt^2} &= -k_D v v_z - k_L \omega_y v_x - g, \end{aligned}\right] \tag{9.7.1}$$

where $v = \sqrt{v_x^2 + v_z^2}$. As before,

$$k_D = \frac{C_D \rho A}{2m} \quad \text{and} \quad k_L = \frac{C_L^* \rho A}{2m}. \tag{9.7.2}$$

The weight of a tennis ball is 0.13 lb. The diameter 2.56 inches. We shall assume the drag and lift coefficients to be constant:

$$C_D = 0.4, \qquad C_L^* = R = 1.28/12 = 0.107. \tag{9.7.3}$$

With atmospheric density 0.075 pounds per ft^3, we find

$$k_D = 0.01031 C_D = 0.00412, \quad \text{and} \quad k_L = 0.01031 C_L^* = 0.00110. \tag{9.7.4}$$

Before running the model, let's consider some geometry. The server must hit the ball over the net; this has height 3 ft, and is distant 39 ft. The ball must land within the opposite service line, distant 60 ft. Initially, it is helpful to do some hand calculations, in which drag and spin are neglected. Assume that the ball is hit from a height of 8 ft. First, find the initial speed for a serve that just clears the net. Second, find the minimum speed for a serve that just reaches the service line. There are two possible angles for this serve; which would be better? Next, for increasing values of the initial speed, find the initial angles of the serve at which the ball just clears the net, and is just within the service line. As the initial speed increases, the difference between these angles diminishes, until for a really fast serve of around 160 ft/sec, it is less then 0.5°. Can you find an initial speed for which this angle is zero?

Neglecting spin, modify the above results when drag is included. Is there any improvement? Finally, keeping the initial speed fixed, introduce some topspin ($\omega_y > 0$). This should substantially increase the difference between the two angles, making the serve more practicable. How about backspin? In each case, find paths that would land at the same place, with no drag or spin, with no spin, and with both drag and spin. Along the paths, mark positions at regular intervals of time.

Bounces can be deceptive, because of spin. To model the bounce, it is first necessary to determine when it takes place. That is, we must solve the equation $z(t) = 0$. To do this, run a regular integration, testing after each step to see whether z is negative. Suppose that the value of t for which z is first negative is t_0. Then use Newton's method to set up the iteration

$$t_{n+1} = t_n - z(t_n) \bigg/ \left(\frac{dz}{dt}\right)\bigg|_{t=t_n}, n = 0, 1, 2, \ldots. \tag{9.7.5}$$

$t_{n+1} - t_n$ is the stepsize. If you make the usual change in notation

$$y_1 = x, \ y_2 = \frac{dx}{dt}, \ y_3 = z, \ y_4 = \frac{dz}{dt}, \tag{9.7.6}$$

then this stepsize becomes $-y_3/y_4$. So as soon as z has turned negative, call a procedure that should include lines such as:

```
Repeat
    StepSize = - y(3)/y(4)
    Step(...)
Until Abs(y(3)) < Eps
```

Eps is some small number at your discretion.

First, neglect the effects of spin. When the ball hits the court its velocity will have components $y(2)$ forward and $-y(4)$ down. Due to these components, after the bounce it will have a velocity with components $y(2)$ forward and $-ey(4)$ up, where e is the *coefficient of restitution* of the tennis ball. This quantity varies according to the speed. For low speeds, around 15 mph, it is 0.7; but for a speed of 55 mph it is 0.5. The latter number would be preferable here. (But if you want to model a lob made with spin, the larger number might be appropriate.) Now consider **only** the effect of spin. The instant before hitting the court, the point at the bottom of the ball is travelling relative to the

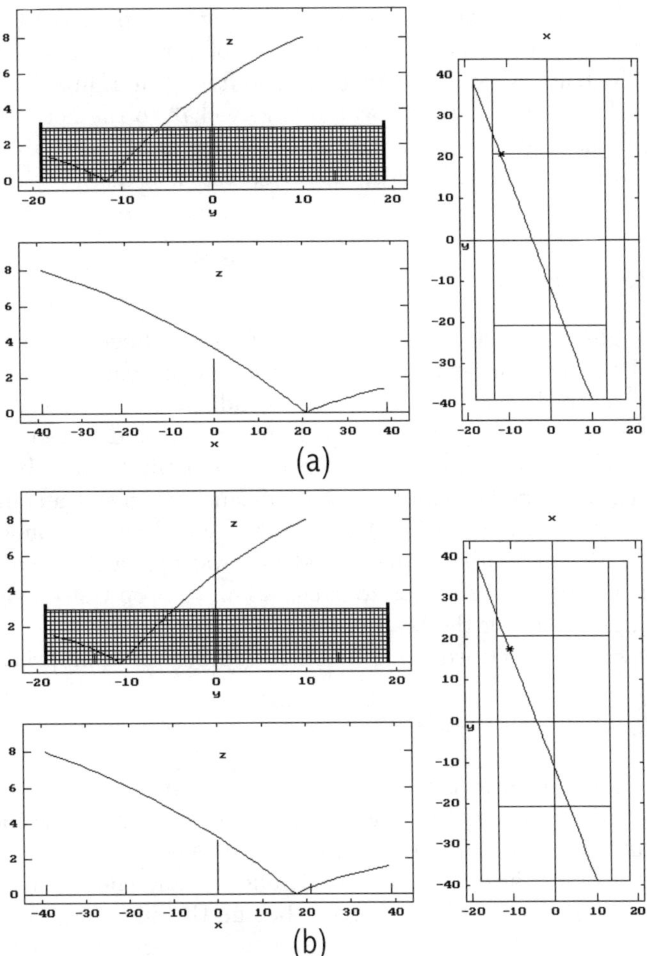

Figure 9.11: *Two serves. The first just clears the net and the second just lands in court. The initial conditions are the same for each serve, with the exception of the angle that the initial velocity makes with the horizontal; in (a) it is −4.7°, and in (b), −4.1°. There is no drag or spin. But if topspin is added to the starting conditions, the margin of error nearly doubles to about one degree.*

court at the speed $-\omega_y R$, where R is the radius of the ball. Immediately after the bounce, the ball will move forward at the speed $c\omega_y R$, where c lies between 0 and 1. c will depend on the nature of the contact between the ball and the surface of the court. If there is no slippage between the ball and the ground, during the point of contact, then $c = 1$. Combining these effects, the velocity immediately after the bounce will have components

$$v_{x0} = y_2 + c\omega_y R \text{ forward and } v_{z0} = -ey_4 \text{ up.} \tag{9.7.7}$$

These numbers will now serve to provide initial conditions for the bounce. The bounce itself can be modeled by neglecting drag and spin. Then the maximum height of the bounce is $v_{z0}^2/(2g)$, which is reached after time v_{z0}/g, and travelling the horizontal distance $v_{x0}v_{z0}/g$. Find the effects of spinning on both the serve and the subsequent bounce.

If you want to play in three dimensions, then use the equations from section 9.5, and the more general model for the bounce from section 9.9.

The narrow margin of error for a fast serve is illustrated in figures 9.11(a) and (b). The origin is at the center of the net. The serves start from the point $x = -39$, $y = 10$, $z = 8$ ft. Drag and lift are neglected. The ball is served at a speed of 150 ft/sec, in a direction making $-20°$ with the x-axis. In figure 9.11(a) the ball is served at the angle $-4.7°$ to the horizontal, and just clears the net. In figure 9.11(b) the angle is $-4.1°$, and the ball lands barely in court. The margin of error is $0.6°$. If topspin $\omega_y = 50$ rad/sec is included in the serve, then the margin of error is increased to about one degree.

9.8 Kicking a Ball in Soccer

A soccer ball weighs 0.94 lb, and has a diameter of 8.75 in. Speeds as high as 60 mph (88 ft/sec) can occur. The model is the same as that for the drive of a golf ball. A drag coefficient $C_D = 0.2$ is recommended, with the coefficient $C_L^* = 8.75/12$, the radius.

A ball kicked for maximum range is dropped onto a foot and kicked essentially without spin. The range is highly influenced by drag. (You can include a wind, too.) In the case of a corner or free kick, or for a long pass, the ball can be kicked off-center to give it a spin ω_z that will make the ball swerve to the right or left. For a free kick, the ball could curve around the line of defenders; for a corner kick it could curve around the defenders toward the goal, where it could be kicked or headed in. Another possible use of spin is to cause a ball to drop fast enough to go under the bar of the goal after being kicked over the head of the goalkeeper.

All these effects can be described using this model. Look for appropriate initial conditions.

9.9 Bowling a Cricket Ball

In the center of a cricket field is the *pitch*, an area 12 ft wide and 66 ft in length, as shown in figure 9.12. Centered at each end is a *wicket*, a fragile structure that the *bowler* would like to demolish and the *batsman* hopes to defend. The bowler *bowls* the cricket ball using an overarm action, with the bowling arm held straight. (A significant difference from the baseball pitch.) At the time of delivery, the bowler must have one foot behind the line containing the wicket. The point "D" in figure 9.12 might mark the actual position of the bowler's hand at the point of delivery. D can be on either side of the wicket. The batsman, B, (right-handed in figure 9.12) stands just behind a line 4 ft in front of the wicket, slightly to one side of the wicket, ready to defend the wicket by hitting the ball with his *bat*. Depending on how and where the ball is hit, *runs* can be scored; the object is, of course, to score as many as possible.

The objective of the bowler is to deceive (and sometimes intimidate) the batsman into missing the ball (so that his wicket may be demolished), or mis-hitting it so that it will be caught on the fly; then the batsman will be *out*, and can no longer contribute to the score of his side. This is, to put it mildly, an inadequate presentation of the game of cricket, but will be enough for this project, which is concerned with the wiles of the bowler.

The principal difference between the pitch of a baseball and the delivery of a cricket ball is that, almost invariably, the latter bounces. Because of spin imparted to the ball, the bounce is unlikely to be straight; so that the bowler can make use of the motion of the ball through the air, and of the nature of the bounce to confuse the batsman. So our model will have separate components for these two phenomena.

The equations for the flight of the cricket ball will be the same as those for a baseball. The origin is on the ground at the center of the wicket at the bowler's end. The x-axis will be parallel to the wickets, pointing toward the batsman. The z-axis will point vertically upward. See figure 9.13. The velocity components are v_x, v_y, and v_z, and the components of the spin are ω_x, ω_y and ω_z.

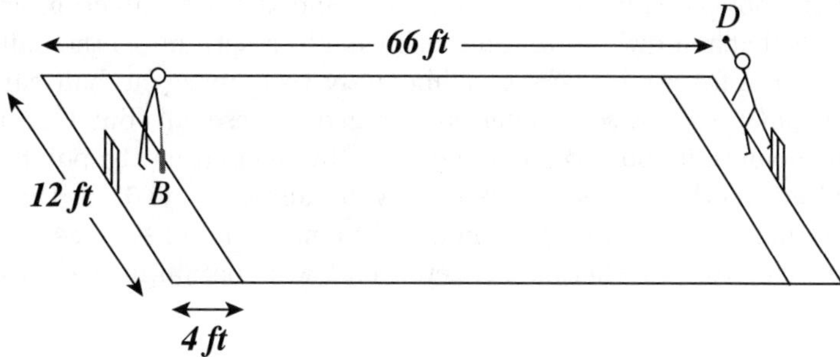

Figure 9.12: *A cricket pitch.*

Then

$$\left.\begin{aligned}\frac{d^2x}{dt^2} &= -k_D v v_x + k_L(\omega_y v_z - \omega_z v_y),\\ \frac{d^2y}{dt^2} &= -k_D v v_y + k_L(\omega_z v_x - \omega_x v_z),\\ \frac{d^2z}{dt^2} &= -k_D v v_z + k_L(\omega_x v_y - \omega_y v_x) - g,\end{aligned}\right] \tag{9.9.1}$$

where $v = \sqrt{v_x^2 + v_y^2 + v_z^2}$. Also

$$k_D = \frac{C_D \rho A}{2m} \quad \text{and} \quad k_L = \frac{C_L^* \rho A}{2m}. \tag{9.9.2}$$

The radius of a cricket ball is 0.116 ft, and its weight is 0.344 lb. So we have $\rho A/2m = 0.00461$, where $\rho = 0.075$ lb/ft^2. Try $C_D = 0.4$ and, as with the model of the baseball, take $C_L^* = 0.116$, the radius. The ball may be delivered from either side of the wicket; a starting position of $x = 1$, $y = 2$, $z = 7$ would not be unreasonable. Speeds do not rival the top speeds of baseball, but fast bowlers can achieve speeds in excess of 100 ft/sec. But speed, as such, may not be the main factor where deception is concerned: it is spin that matters here. Up to 20 revolutions per second, or 377 radians per second should be tried. (But if you want to be a super bowler and exceed such values, why not?)

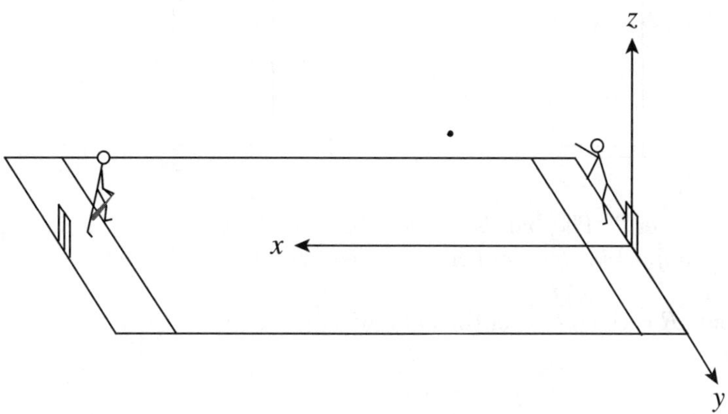

Figure 9.13: *Reference system.*

The position of the bounce is important. Too late, and the new direction will not have much effect; too early, and the batsman will have too much time to react, unless the ball is very fast. One less endearing habit of the fastest bowlers is deliberately to bounce the ball early so that it flies at the head of the batsman — not something encouraged in baseball, but OK, in moderation, in cricket! Wherever the bounce, its position must be found by calculating the point where $z = 0$. This is best done by Newton's method. Assume that $z=$ `y(5)` and $v_z =$ `y(6)` in the code. During the integration of the first flight, the sign of `y(5)` must be monitored. As soon as it becomes negative, a procedure must be called to find when it was zero. This will contain lines equivalent to:

```
Repeat
    StepSize = - y(5)/y(6)
    Step(...)
Until Abs(y(5)) < Eps
```

`Eps` is some small number at your discretion.

The velocity after the bounce will have two components, one due to the velocity before the bounce and one due to the spin of the ball. A velocity

$$\vec{v}_1 = \langle v_x,\ v_y,\ v_z \rangle$$

just before the bounce will result in a velocity

$$\vec{v}_2 = \langle v_x,\ v_y,\ -e \cdot v_z \rangle.$$

just after the bounce, where e is the *coefficient of restitution.* For a cricket ball, $e \approx 0.32$. Just before the bounce, the point on the ball that will make contact with the ground will have velocity

$$\vec{v}_1 + \vec{\omega} \times (-R\hat{k})$$

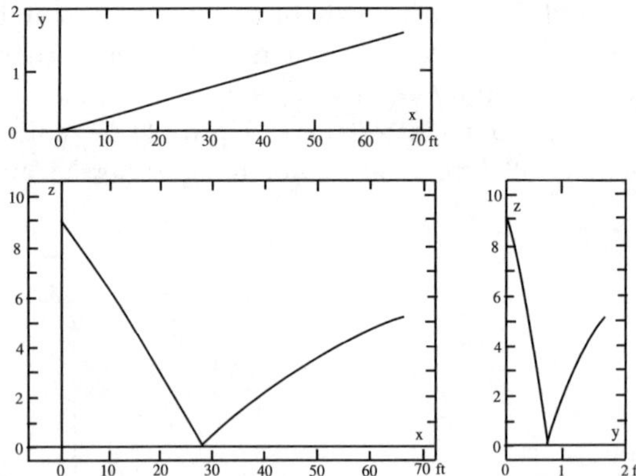

Figure 9.14: *A "bouncer." The ball is bowled fast and bounces early, aimed, preferably, at the batsman's head. The important factors here are speed and intimidation.*

relative to the ground. R is the radius of the ball. After the bounce, the part of the velocity resulting from the spin will be

$$-c\,\vec{\omega} \times (-R\hat{k}) = cR(\omega_y \hat{\imath} - \omega_x \hat{\jmath}),$$

where $0 \le c \le 1$. c depends on the amount of slipping relative to the ground. On a hard, dry pitch c may be close to zero; but if the pitch is moist, the grip of the ball will increase. If the pitch is wet,

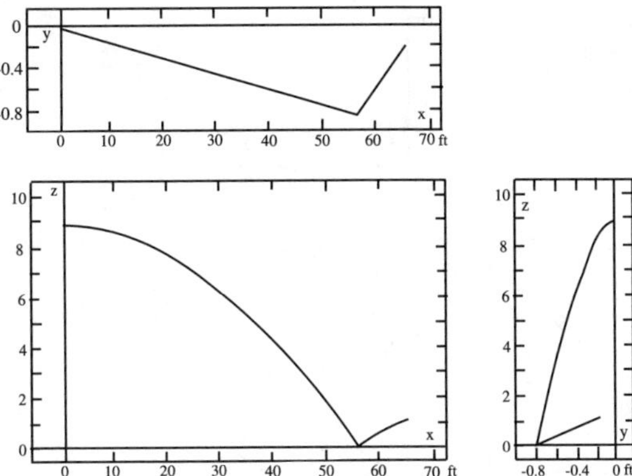

Figure 9.15: *A slower ball with spin parallel to the x-axis. The purpose of the spin is to cause an unexpected deviation at the bounce.*

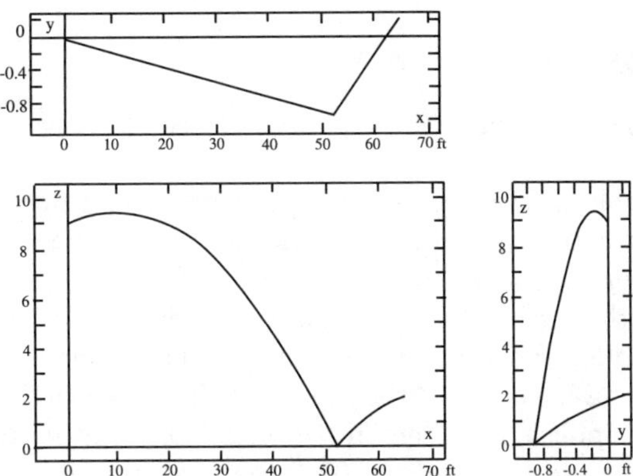

Figure 9.16: *An even slower ball. Deception rather than speed is the factor here.*

then it may be classified as *sticky*, when, not only is c close to one, but the ball will penetrate the mud, so that the resulting bounce has a random component: no fun for the batsman. The value of c will also depend on the condition of the seam of the ball, (more on this in the following section), since the point of contact is, optimally, a point on the seam. In summary, the velocity after the bounce is

$$\vec{v} = (v_x + cR\omega_y)\hat{\imath} + (v_y - cR\omega_x)\hat{\jmath} - ev_z\hat{k}, \tag{9.9.3}$$

where v_x, v_y, and v_z refer to the velocity components just before the bounce.

The spin imparted to the ball is usually nearly parallel to the x-axis, so that the ball breaks as much as possible to the right or left. But you can experiment at will. You will discover a remarkable variety. If you have never seen cricket played, you may become interested in seeing the real thing!

Figure 9.14 shows a "bouncer," that is, a fast ball that bounces early and is intended to intimidate the batsman, if not to hurt him. The three projections view the trajectory from the top, from the side and as seen by the batsman. Initial components of velocity are $v_x = 120$, $v_y = 3$, $v_z = -35$ft/sec. The coefficient of restitution for the bounce was taken to be 0.5.

Figure 9.15 shows a slower ball, starting with velocity $v_x = 80$, $v_y = -1$, $v_z = 0$ft/sec and spin $\omega_x = -50$rad/sec. The purpose of the spin is to move the ball in an unexpected deviation at the bounce. Figure 9.16 shows an even slower ball, starting with velocity $v_x = 60$, $v_y = -1$, $v_z = 5$ft/sec. Deception rather than speed is the important factor here.

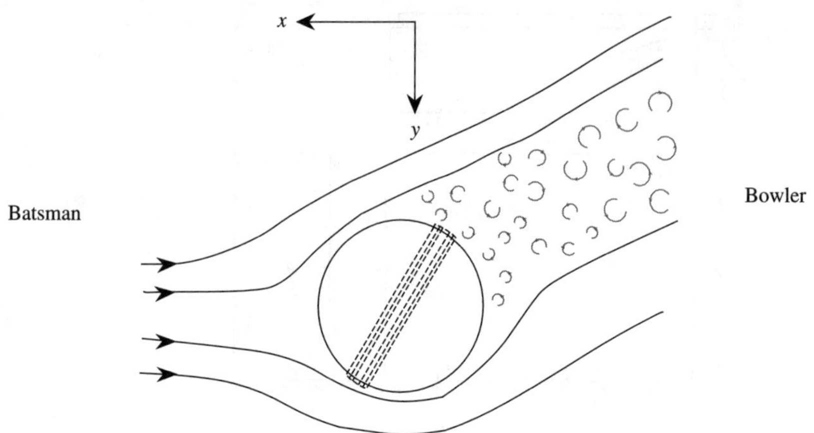

Figure 9.17: *Flow of air around a cricket ball. The ball, which is not spinning, is seen from above.*

9.10 The Swing of a Cricket Ball

A good reference for this section is given by Mehta [71]. See also discussions by DeMestre [33] and Townend [98].

Spin plays an important role in cricket, not least because a ball delivered by a bowler to a batsman usually bounces. The nature of the bounce will depend on the spin of the ball. But the "swing" of a cricket ball does not depend on spin, but on the construction and condition of the ball.

A cricket ball is a sphere; the surface is made from two hemispherical pieces of leather, joined by six rows of raised stitches, called the *seam*. When new, the ball is highly polished and the seam is prominent. A new ball may be introduced, the old one being discarded, several times during a match. The raised seam and the polish are essential factors in contributing to the swing of the ball.

If the ball were smooth, then for a speed of 100 ft/sec, the separation points would be close together near the front. Now suppose that the orientation of the ball, as seen from above, is that of figure 9.17. The upper part in the figure is the right-hand side, as seen by the bowler. The hemisphere on the right is polished, so the separation point on that hemisphere will remain close to the front. But the boundary layer on the left can become turbulent because of the seam; the separation point moves to the left, and the wake becomes inclined as shown. So there will be a force from the higher pressure on the right to the lower pressure on the left, and the ball will swing to the left. This force can be increased if the hemisphere on the left is deliberately roughened. (Yes, this is permitted, according to the rules. The other hemisphere is kept as polished as possible.)

In flight the orientation of the seam should not change, but some spin is usually given perpendicular to the seam to help stability. The lateral force depends on the orientation of the seam, and the velocity, as well as the condition of the ball. It is not surprising that, out of a great deal of experimental data, there is a considerable scatter in estimates of this force. For instance, different balls may have different characteristics. On one point there is agreement: the lateral force increases with speed up to a critical speed of about 98 ft/sec (30 m/sec), and then diminishes sharply at higher speeds; so if the ball is bowled too fast, there is no swing.

The late curve in a baseball has a parallel with a late swing in cricket. There are two schools of thought here. If there is a constant lateral force, the projected motion in the x-y plane is parabolic, with most of the curving at the end. Alternatively, suppose that the ball is bowled with initial speed just greater than the critical speed, so initially there is no swing; if the reduction in speed is enough, the lateral force will start to act during the flight, and swinging will commence. Experiments with either point of view can be performed in this project.

Let the lateral force be F_L and let $F_L/mg = L$. This is a function of the speed, v. With the x-axis parallel to the line between the wickets, and the z-axis pointing vertically upward, the equations for the model are

$$\left.\begin{aligned} \frac{d^2x}{dt^2} &= -k_D v v_x, \\ \frac{d^2y}{dt^2} &= -k_D v v_y + L, \\ \frac{d^2z}{dt^2} &= -k_D v v_z - g, \end{aligned}\right] \tag{9.10.1}$$

where $v = \sqrt{v_x^2 + v_y^2 + v_z^2}$.

$k_D = C_D \rho A/2m$. The radius of a cricket ball is 0.116 ft, and its weight is 0.344 lb. Then $\rho A/2m = 0.00461$. Take $C_D = 0.4$. As mentioned, there is a lot of variation in empirical expressions for L. I suggest

$$L = \left[\begin{array}{ll} 0.0058v - 0.2, & 50 \le v \le 100, \\ 0, & v > 100. \end{array}\right. \tag{9.10.2}$$

The elbow of the bowler must not be bent, so an initial height of around 7 ft would be realistic. The length of the pitch (wicket to wicket) is 66 ft. But the distance between the batsman and the point where the ball is released is nearer 60 ft. However, the ball will probably be bounced before it reaches the batsman, so you have plenty of scope for experiment.

Figure 9.18 shows the trajectory of a swinging cricket ball. Initially, the velocity has components $v_x = 100,\ v_y = -4.5,\ v_z = -5$ ft/sec. The formula for the lateral force uses the factor 0.4 given above, to model the maximum effect that might be experienced.

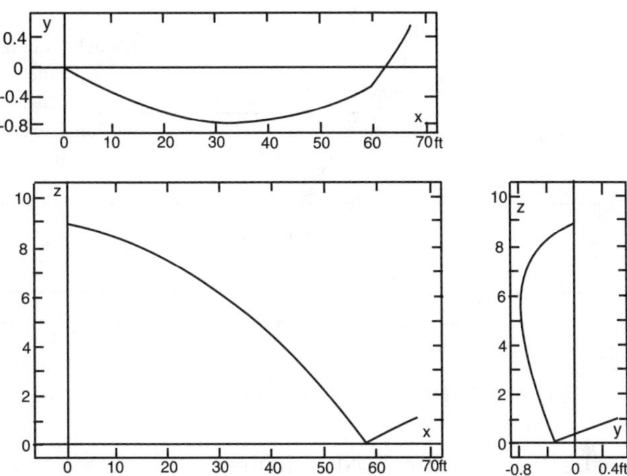

Figure 9.18: *The trajectory of a "swinging" cricket ball. The initial velocity has components* $v_x = 100,\ v_y = -4.5,\ v_z = -5$ *ft/sec.*

9.11 Shuttlecock Trajectories in Badminton

One measure of the drag force on a projectile is the *terminal speed*, or, not so accurately, *terminal velocity*. If a body is falling vertically downward then the differential equation for its speed, v, can be written as

$$m\frac{dv}{dt} = -kv^2 + mg, \tag{9.11.1}$$

where we assume resistance proportional to the square of the velocity. If v is constant, then its derivative is zero, and the speed is v_t where

$$v_t = \sqrt{mg/k}. \tag{9.11.2}$$

This is the terminal speed, and it is approached asymptotically as the time is increased.

The table shows some typical values of terminal speeds for projectiles used in sport:

Projectile	v_t, ft/sec
16 lb shot	480
Baseball	140
Golf ball	130
Tennis ball	100
Soccer ball	80
Basketball	65
Ping-pong ball	22.8
Shuttlecock	22.3

The final two figures, obtained experimentally, are given by Peastrel, Lynch and Armenti [76]. They are remarkable, in comparison with the others, in that v_t is relatively low. For most shots, the initial speed is much greater than v_t, so drag plays an important role in the trajectories. This is particularly the case in badminton, where the distances travelled are much greater than those for table tennis.

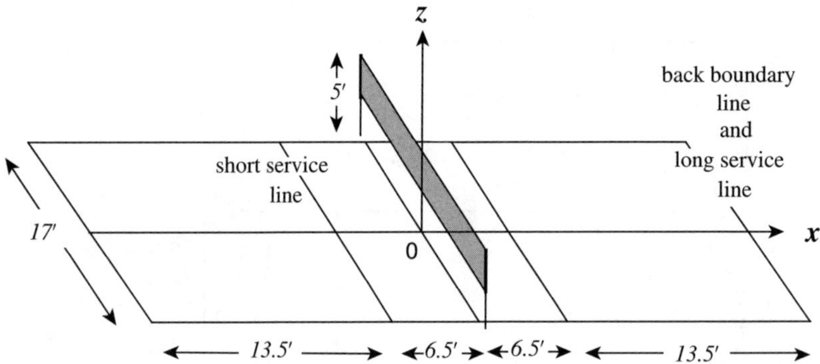

Figure 9.19: *The singles court in badminton.*

The badminton singles court is illustrated in figure 9.19. It measures 17 by 44 ft (the doubles court being 3 ft wider) and the top of the net is 5 ft above the surface of the court. For a start, we shall play indoors, so that there will be no wind, and any trajectory will take place in a vertical plane. Let the origin be at the center of the court, with the x-axis pointing down the court and the z-axis pointing vertically upward. The ceiling will be taken to be 30 ft in height, so this is the maximum allowable height. The equations for the motion are

$$\left.\begin{aligned}\frac{d^2x}{dt^2} &= -k_D v v_x,\\ \frac{d^2z}{dt^2} &= -k_D v v_z - g,\end{aligned}\right] \tag{9.11.3}$$

where

$$v_x = \frac{dx}{dt}, \quad v_z = \frac{dz}{dt} \text{ and } v = \sqrt{v_x^2 + v_z^2}.$$

$k_D = 0.0643\ \text{ft}^{-1}$, for consistency with the terminal speed.

The assumption has been made that the coefficient k_D is constant. A trajectory will start with the base of the shuttlecock following, since it is the base that is struck. During flight, this is reversed by a torque that acts as the curvature of the path becomes pronounced. This reversal is very quick. The areas of the shuttle as viewed from the front or side are nearly the same, so this flipping of the shuttlecock should not affect the trajectory. However, when the feathers are leading, they will be splayed out, to some extent; indeed, the shuttlecock sometimes becomes reversed, like an umbrella in a stiff wind. So the model underestimates the drag in the early stages of a trajectory, especially for shots like the smash. Data on this matter would be welcome. In the meantime, assume constant k_D.

There is an infinite variety of shots. They should land in court (if not struck in return by an opponent) and should not hit the ceiling. Here is a classification of the principal shots:

1. Services must be made from the area between the long and short service lines, and must land inside the similar area on the other side of the net. At the instant of service, the shuttlecock must be below the server's waist. The **high deep service** originates from about 4 ft behind the short service line and should land as close as possible to the back boundary line. The **low short service** just clears the net, and lands just beyond the short service line.

2. Overhead shots may originate from near the back of the court. The **overhead clear** should land near the back on the other side. The **overhead drop** should land as close as possible to the net. The **smash** is hit as hard as possible, just clearing the net.

3. Underhand shots may be made close to the net. They include the **underhand clear**, which lands as close to the back of the court as possible, and the **underhand lob**, which lands as close to the net as possible.

4. A **drive** might originate near shoulder height and be hit nearly horizontally; it is aimed toward the back of the court.

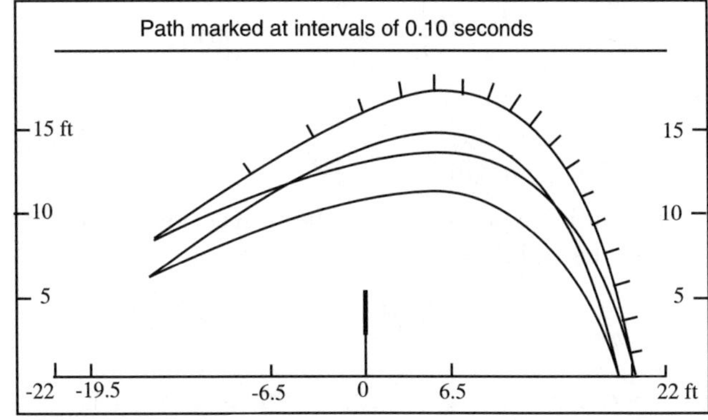

Figure 9.20: *Four serves, all with the initial speed 100 ft/sec. Initial heights are 6 ft and 8 ft and initial angles of the velocity to the horizontal are* $20°$ *and* $30°$.

At the start of a trajectory, speeds can vary from around the terminal speed for a drop shot to up to ten times that amount for a smash. The deceleration can be impressive, so any presentation of computer output should show the times along the trajectories. Initial speeds and launching angles will need to be found by experiment. Needless to say, there are endless other trajectories that may be used in the heat of the game.

Now let us step outside and play with the wind blowing. The motion is now three-dimensional, so we include the y-axis across the court. Let the wind have velocity

$$\vec{v}_w = v_{wx}\hat{\imath} + v_{wy}\hat{\jmath} + v_{wz}\hat{k}. \tag{9.11.4}$$

Then the velocity of the ball relative to the wind is

$$\vec{v}_r = \vec{v} - \vec{v}_w = v_{rx}\hat{\imath} + v_{ry}\hat{\jmath} + v_{rz}\hat{k}. \tag{9.11.5}$$

It is $\vec{v}_r$ that must be used in the calculation of drag. The new equations are

$$\left.\begin{aligned} \frac{d^2x}{dt^2} &= -k_D v_r v_{rx}, \\ \frac{d^2y}{dt^2} &= -k_D v_r v_{ry}, \\ \frac{d^2z}{dt^2} &= -k_D v_r v_{rz} - g. \end{aligned}\right] \tag{9.11.6}$$

Run some experiments and find out why tournament badminton is played indoors.

Figure 9.20 shows four serves. All start 15 ft from the net, and have initial speed 100 ft/sec. Initial heights are 6 ft and 8 ft and initial angles of the velocity to the horizontal are 20° and 30°. Notice the shapes of the paths, with rapid deceleration and nearly vertical descent. Also notice that, in spite of the changing starting conditions, the final location of landing varies very little.

9.12 Table Tennis

The terminal speed of a table tennis ball, as given by Peastrel, Lynch and Armenti [76] is $v_t = 22.8$ft/sec. This was found by laboratory experiment, and, although somewhat lower than that quoted elsewhere, will be used in this section. It is simple to introduce another value.

If the acceleration due to drag is $k_D v^2$, for speed v, then

$$k_D = \frac{\rho A C_D}{2m} = \frac{g}{v_t^2} = 0.0616. \tag{9.12.1}$$

Then if $C_D = 0.4$,

$$\frac{\rho A}{2m} = \frac{g}{C_D v_t^2} = 0.154. \tag{9.12.2}$$

The acceleration due to lift will be expressed using the conventional, non-dimensional lift coefficient C_L, so that the acceleration due to lift is

$$\frac{\rho A}{2m} C_L v^2 \hat{\omega} \times \hat{v}. \tag{9.12.3}$$

Then if the acceleration is written as $k_L\, \vec{\omega} \times \vec{v}$, as in the other models,

$$k_L = \frac{\rho A}{2m} C_L \frac{v}{\omega}. \tag{9.12.4}$$

Because the table tennis ball is smooth, the approximation used in other models cannot be applied. C_L is a complicated function of the quantity $R\omega/v$, where R is the radius of the ball; $R = 0.72$ in. For small values of $R\omega/v$ the "lift" turns out to be negative. This function is described by Davies [32]; he discusses the phenomenon of negative lift. A clear graphical representation of C_L is given in a paper by R.D.Mehta [71]. I have approximated it as shown in the following table:

$x = R\omega/v$	C_L
$0 < x < 0.251$	$-0.40x + 0.79x^2$
$0.251 < x < 0.435$	$0.128 - 1.416x + 2.821x^2$
$0.435 < x < 0.625$	$-0.386 + 1.222x - 0.528x^2$

Davies does not give data for $R\omega/v > 0.625$, which is unfortunate, since values greater than one can occur in table tennis. I recommend using the final expression to extrapolate values of C_L for $R\omega/v$ as large as is needed.

The table tennis table is 5 ft wide and 9 ft long; the height of the net is 6 in. If the origin is at the center of the table, with the y-axis along the net and the z-axis pointing vertically upward, then the equations for the model are

$$\left.\begin{aligned}\frac{d^2x}{dt^2} &= -k_D v v_x + k_L(\omega_y v_z - \omega_z v_y),\\ \frac{d^2y}{dt^2} &= -k_D v v_y + k_L(\omega_z v_x - \omega_x v_z),\\ \frac{d^2z}{dt^2} &= -k_D v v_z + k_L(\omega_x v_y - \omega_y v_x) - g,\end{aligned}\right] \tag{9.12.5}$$

k_L being given by equation (9.12.4).

Since volleying is not allowed in table tennis, at least two trajectories must be calculated for any stroke: before and after a bounce. For a service, two bounces and three trajectories will be involved.

After any step in the calculation of a trajectory, the sign of z must be checked; after it becomes negative, the point for which $z = 0$ must be found. For the bounce, I suggest the same model that was used for the cricket ball. The coefficient of restitution, e, for the table tennis ball depends on the speed of the bounce. For $v = 20$ ft/sec, $e = 0.8$ and for $v = 80$ft/sec, $e = 0.7$. You might combine these in a linear relation, or compromise by using an intermediate value. In the absence of a realistic model to describe the possible sliding during a bounce, I suggest that you assume that bounce is instantaneous, with the frictional forces doing no work. Let the linear and angular velocities just before the bounce be

$$\vec{v}_1 = \langle v_x,\ v_y,\ v_z\rangle \text{ and } \vec{\omega} = \langle \omega_x,\ \omega_y,\ \omega_z\rangle.$$

The linear velocity after the bounce will be

$$\begin{aligned}\vec{v}_2 &= \langle v_x,\ v_y,\ -e\cdot v_z\rangle - c\,\vec{\omega}\times(-R\hat{k})\\ &= \langle v_x,\ v_y,\ -e\cdot v_z\rangle + cR\langle \omega_y,\ -\omega_x,\ 0\rangle.\end{aligned} \tag{9.12.6}$$

c, lying between 0 and 1, depends on the amount of slipping relative to the table. If in doubt, set it equal to 1. The angular velocity will be unaltered by the bounce.

9.13 Shooting in Basketball

Brancazio [15][1] has written a very readable and comprehensive paper containing a mathematical analysis of shooting at basketball. I am grateful to the author for permission to use some of his material in the discussion that follows. He advises that if you follow his recommendations, then you may become a better player. Most of the analysis is concerned with the ball passing cleanly through the hoop without bouncing, and with the effects of drag ignored. Then the details of the trajectory can all be worked using formulas. He reports the results of calculations that include drag, and points

[1] Abstracted, with permission, from "Physics of Basketball" P.J.Brancazio, *American Journal of Physics*, **49** (1981) 356–365. Copyright 1981, American Association of Physics Teachers.

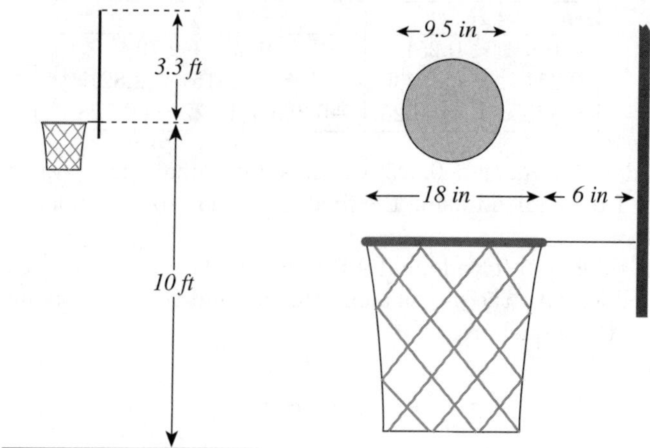

Figure 9.21: *Dimensions and heights of hoop, backboard and ball.*

out that the range can be affected by as much as one foot. So drag will be included in the model to be described here.

The model is in two dimensions, in a vertical plane perpendicular to the backboard. The origin is at the player's feet, with then z-axis pointing upward; the x-axis points toward the basket. Then the equations of motions are

$$\left.\begin{aligned} v &= \sqrt{v_x^2 + v_z^2}, \\ \frac{dx}{dt} &= v_x, \\ \frac{dv_x}{dt} &= -k_D v v_x, \\ \frac{dz}{dt} &= v_z, \\ \frac{dv_z}{dt} &= -k_D v v_z - g. \end{aligned}\right] \tag{9.13.1}$$

Here

$$k_D = \frac{C_D \rho A}{2m}. \tag{9.13.2}$$

C_D, the drag coefficient can be taken to be 0.5. With the diameter of the ball taken to be 9.5 in or 0.79 ft, the cross-sectional area is $A = 0.49\text{ft}^2$. Taking the weight of the ball to be 21 oz, its mass is $m = (21/16)/32 = 0.041$ slugs. With atmospheric density $\rho = 2.38 \cdot 10^{-3}$ slugs ft^{-3}, we have $k_D = 0.0071$ ft^{-1}. If possible read the paper by Brancazio.

Note the dimensions shown in figure 9.21. First, only consider shots that pass cleanly through the hoop. The diameter of the ball is 0.79ft and that of the hoop is 1.5ft. A ball falling vertically could pass through the hoop if its center was 0.35ft from the center of the hoop. But this margin diminishes as the angle between the vertical and the velocity of the ball increases; if this angle is equal to arccos(0.79/1.5), or approximately 58°, then the ball cannot pass directly through the basket, although it might still bounce into it. So scoring may not be easy, even on the computer. Decide on an initial height and a distance from the basket; you might start with the free-throw distance of 13.5ft.

A calculation should be run until $y_3 = z = 10$, the height of the hoop, and $y_4 = dz/dt < 0$, so that the ball is descending. You might have a variable `zSign` that takes the value +1 when $z > 10$

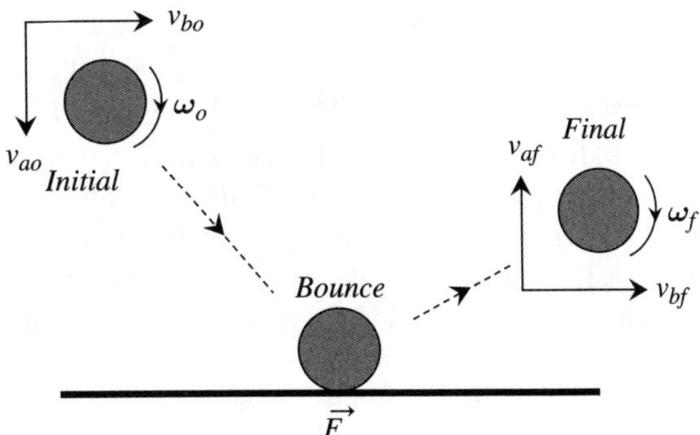

Figure 9.22: *Notation for velocity changes in a bounce.*

and -1 when $z < 10$. It could be initialized to $+1$. After each step, test to see whether the hoop has been passed by the descending ball. For instance,

```
Step
If (zSign*y(3) < 0) and (y(4) < 0) then FindHoop
```

The procedure FindHoop should use Newton's method to find the time (or the value of x) at which $z - 10 = 0$. The stepsize for an iteration would be

```
StepSize = - (y(3)-10)/y(4)
```

Provided that the distance between the center of the ball and the center of the hoop is less than 0.35ft, the shot is good.

Address the following questions. Here v_0 is the initial speed and θ_0 is the angle between the initial velocity and the horizontal.

- Choose a value for v_0 large enough for the basket to be reached. There will be two possible trajectories that will reach the basket, but it may not be possible to score with the lower one. Find intervals for θ_0 for shots that will score. Now vary v_0 and look for a value that will lead to the largest margin of error in θ_0.
- Choose θ_0 and find the possible interval (if it exists) for v_0. Vary θ_0 and look for a value that leads to the greatest possible margin of error for v_0.
- How are these margins affected if the initial height is changed?
- How are these margins affected if the initial distance is changed?
- Can you summarize your results so that you could advise someone (maybe yourself) how to improve performance?

The ball may bounce on the backboard or the rim; when this happens, spin is likely to be an important factor. We shall assume that (so far as the ball is concerned) the bounce takes place on a flat surface. In the notation of figure 9.22, the component of the velocity perpendicular to the surface is v_{ao} toward the surface just before the bounce, and v_{af} away from the surface just after. Then

$$v_{af} = C_r v_{ao}, \tag{9.13.3}$$

where C_r is the coefficient of restitution. For a basketball this is approximately equal to 0.75 on a hard surface; it may be less for the backboard.

The component of velocity parallel to the surface and the angular velocity of the ball are linked through the mechanism of the bounce. We shall follow the discussion given by Brancazio. Before the bounce, we have the values v_{bo} and ω_o; after the bounce, the respective values are v_{bf} and ω_f. During the bounce, when the ball is in contact with the surface, it experiences a horizontal force $\vec{F}$ for a time Δt. There is no slipping. m is the mass of the ball, and R is its radius. The moment of inertia of the ball about a diameter would be $I_1 = 2mR^2/5$ if the ball were homogeneous or $I_2 = 2mR^2/3$ if the ball were a thin shell. Brancazio adopts the homogeneous model, although the other seems to be more realistic; you can decide for yourself. The equations for linear momentum and angular momentum about the center of the ball are

$$\left.\begin{aligned} F\Delta t &= m(v_{bf} - v_{bo}), \\ R(F\Delta t) &= I(\omega_o - \omega_f), \end{aligned}\right] \tag{9.13.4}$$

where the clockwise ω, as shown in figure 9.22, is taken to be positive. Eliminating the product $F\Delta t$, and dividing by m, we have

$$v_{bf} - v_{bo} = \frac{2}{5}R(\omega_o - \omega_f), \tag{9.13.5}$$

for the homogeneous ball or

$$v_{bf} - v_{bo} = \frac{2}{3}R(\omega_o - \omega_f), \tag{9.13.6}$$

for the shell. Finally, if there is no slipping, we must have

$$v_{bf} = R\omega_f. \tag{9.13.7}$$

Then

$$v_{bf} = \frac{1}{7}(5v_{bo} + 2R\omega_0), \tag{9.13.8}$$

for the homogeneous ball or

$$v_{bf} = \frac{1}{5}(3v_{bo} + 2R\omega_0), \tag{9.13.9}$$

for the shell. There is an overall loss of energy due to the work done by the force $\vec{F}$. Considering only the contribution to the energy from v_{bo} and the spin, Brancazio shows that the energy loss is

$$\frac{m}{7}(v_{bo} - R\omega_0)^2.$$

(For the shell model, the factor 1/7 is replaced by 1/5.) This means that more energy is lost if ω_0 is negative, or if the ball has backspin; needless to say, it is backspin that is used in practice.

To test the effects of this spin, I suggest that you aim for the backboard. Spin is unlikely to affect the trajectory (although you might experiment with this), so the model described by equations (9.13.1) need not be changed. Start with no spin, and see if the bounces end in the basket. Then introduce spin, and follow the consequences.

The backboard is 6 in behind the rim or 15 in behind the center of the hoop. If it is Dft from the player, you must find the instant when $x = D$. This can be done using Newton's method in a way very like that used to find when $z = 10$. The notation for the velocities just before and after the bounce is shown in figure 9.23. Just before, we have

$$v_{ao} = \frac{dx}{dt} = y_2, \text{ and } v_{bo} = -\frac{dz}{dt} = -y_4. \tag{9.13.10}$$

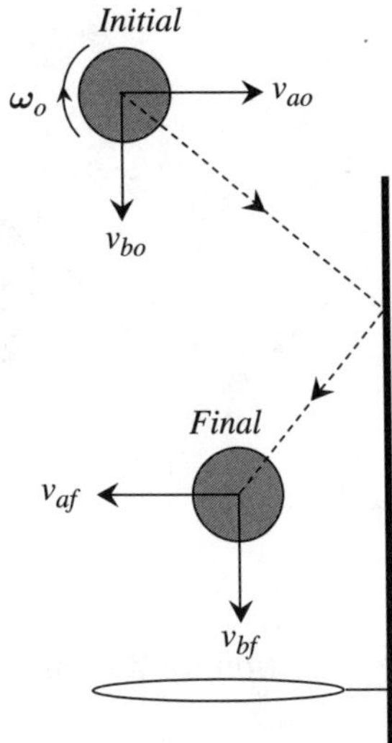

Figure 9.23: *Notation for a bounce off the backboard.*

v_{af} and v_{bf} are found from (9.13.3) and (9.13.8) or (9.13.9). Then the components of velocity immediately after the bounce are

$$\frac{dx}{dt} = y_2 = -v_{af}, \text{ and } \frac{dz}{dt} = y_4 = -v_{bf}. \tag{9.13.11}$$

The angular velocity after the bounce is not needed, unless you are planning a second bounce: probably more trouble to compute than it is worth. You can then use formulas for the remainder of the calculation; if the bounce occurs Hft above the rim, then the ball will descend that distance in time

$$t = \frac{1}{g}\left(-v_{bf} + \sqrt{v_{bf}^2 + 2gH}\right).$$

During this time, the ball travels to the left the distance

$$\Delta x = \frac{v_{af}}{g}\left(-v_{bf} + \sqrt{v_{bf}^2 + 2gH}\right). \tag{9.13.12}$$

Provided this is less than about 14.4in, the bounce should score.

Start with no spin. Then introduce backspin, gradually increasing its magnitude. What is the effect of using topspin?

Bouncing off the rim requires more work (on the computer). First, you must find the configuration at the start of the bounce. We assume that the part of the rim that is struck is that closest to the player, in the vertical plane in which all motion is being followed in this project. If this point has coordinates (x_r, z_r), then x_r depends on the initial distance of the player from the basket and $z_r = 10$. Let $\Delta x = x_r - x$ and $\Delta z = z_r - z$; the rim is struck when

$$\Delta x^2 + \Delta z^2 = R^2,$$

R being the radius of the ball, 4.75in. After each integration step, find the sign of $\Delta x^2 + \Delta z^2 - R^2$; if it is negative, you must find the time at which it is zero, i.e.,

```
Step
If Sqr(Xr - y(1)) + Sqr(Zr - y(3)) - R*R < 0 then FindBounce
```

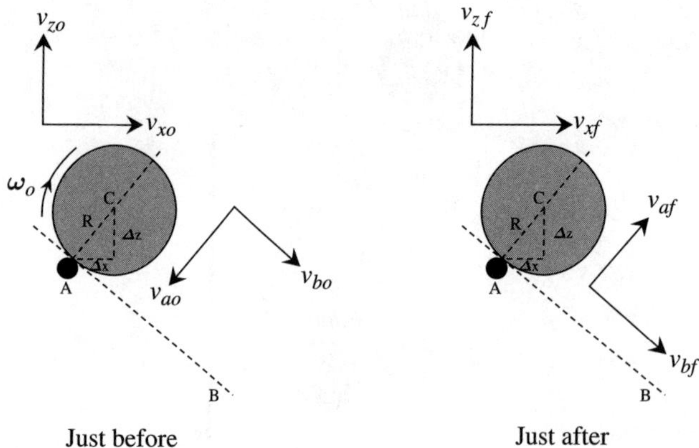

Figure 9.24: *Notation for a bounce off the rim.*

The procedure `FindBounce` should use Newton's method; the stepsize for an iteration would be

```
StepSize = - (Sqr(Xr - y(1)) + Sqr(Zr - y(3)) - R*R)/
             (2*(Xr - y(1))*(-y(2)) + 2*(Zr - y(3))*(-y(4)))
```

The notation for the bounce is shown in figure 9.24. A is the point of contact with the rim and C is the center of the ball. We assume that the bounce will take place as if it were on a plane AB, perpendicular to AC and to the plane of motion. Note that the unit vector parallel to $\overrightarrow{\text{AC}}$ has components

$$\left\langle \frac{\Delta x}{R}, \frac{\Delta z}{R} \right\rangle.$$

That parallel to $\overrightarrow{\text{AB}}$ has components

$$\left\langle \frac{\Delta z}{R}, -\frac{\Delta x}{R} \right\rangle.$$

If the velocity components *just* before the bounce are v_{xo} and v_{zo} then the corresponding bounce components are given by

$$\left. \begin{aligned} v_{ao} &= \frac{\Delta x}{R} v_{xo} + \frac{\Delta z}{R} v_{zo}, \\ v_{b0} &= \frac{\Delta z}{R} v_{xo} - \frac{\Delta x}{R} v_{zo}. \end{aligned} \right] \tag{9.13.13}$$

The velocity components v_{af} and v_{bf} *just* after the bounce are found as before. Then the components in the x-z system are

$$\left. \begin{aligned} v_{xf} &= \frac{\Delta x}{R} v_{af} + \frac{\Delta z}{R} v_{bf}, \\ v_{zf} &= \frac{\Delta z}{R} v_{af} - \frac{\Delta x}{R} v_{bf}. \end{aligned} \right] \tag{9.13.14}$$

Let τ be the time after the bounce, and let the values of Δx and Δz at the instant of the bounce now be written as Δx_0 and Δz_0. Then

$$\Delta x = \Delta x_0 + \tau v_{xf}, \text{ and } \Delta z = \Delta z_0 + \tau v_{zf} - \frac{1}{2} g \tau^2. \tag{9.13.15}$$

Find (positive) τ such that $\Delta z = 0$. The corresponding value of Δx will tell you if the bounce resulted in a score.

9.14 A Badly Kicked Football

Ideally, a well kicked (or thrown) football travels so that its longest axis remains parallel to the velocity; the motion is stable and drag is minimized. The cross-sectional area in this case is 232 cm^2. Seen sideways, this area is 381 cm^2. So if the ball is toppling, then the drag can increase substantially, and the range of the kick will be affected. The purpose of this project is to investigate this effect.

The motion of a toppling football is discussed by Brancazio [14]. In the absence of a torque, the ball will precess about a fixed direction, so that its longest axis makes a fixed angle with that direction. The direction of the axis of precession, and the angle and angular rate of precession, will depend on the initial spin and the moments of inertia of the ball. With origin at the center of the ball, let axes u, v, w point along the principal axes of the ball, with w pointing along the largest axis. Let the moments of inertia about the principal axes be I_u, I_v and I_w, where $I_u = I_v = I_{uv}$. Numerically, $I_{uv} = 0.00321$kg m^2 and $I_w = 0.00194$ kg m^2. The lengths of the semiaxes are $a = b = 8.6$ cm and $c = 14.1$ cm. Let the initial components of spin about these axes be ω_{u0}, ω_{v0} and ω_{w0}. The angular rate of precession is

$$\omega_p = \omega_{w0}\left[\left(\frac{I_w}{I_{uv}}\right)^2 + \frac{\omega_{u0}^2 + \omega_{vo}^2}{\omega_{w0}^2}\right]^{1/2}. \tag{9.14.1}$$

If θ is the angle between the w-axis and the axis of precession, then

$$\cos\theta = \left[1 + \left(\frac{I_{uv}}{I_w}\right)^2 \frac{(\omega_{u0}^2 + \omega_{vo}^2)}{\omega_{w0}^2}\right]^{1/2}. \tag{9.14.2}$$

For our purposes, it may be easier to assume values for ω_p and θ, rather than starting with the spin components.

We shall use the same Cartesian reference system as that used in the other sports projects, with the origin at the starting point, the x-axis pointing forward, and the z-axis pointing vertically upward. Let the unit vector $\hat{\zeta} = \langle l_3,\ m_3,\ n_3\rangle$ be parallel to the axis of precession. Let $\hat{\xi} = \langle l_1,\ m_1,\ n_1\rangle$ and $\hat{\eta} = \langle l_2,\ m_2,\ n_2\rangle$ complete a right-handed reference system. Then we might have

$$\left.\begin{array}{lllll} \hat{\xi} & = & \langle l_1,\ m_1,\ n_1\rangle & = & \hat{k}\times\hat{\zeta} & = & \langle -m_3,\ l_3,\ 0\rangle/\sqrt{l_3^2+m_3^2}, \\ \hat{\eta} & = & \langle l_2,\ m_2,\ n_2\rangle & = & \hat{\zeta}\times\hat{\xi} & = & \langle -n_3 l_3,\ -n_3 m_3,\ l_3^2+m_3^2\rangle/\sqrt{l_3^2+m_3^2}, \\ \hat{\zeta} & = & \langle l_3,\ m_3,\ n_3\rangle. & & & & \end{array}\right] \tag{9.14.3}$$

Let

$$\phi = \phi_0 + \omega_p t. \tag{9.14.4}$$

Then after time t the long axis of the ball will point in the direction

$$\hat{w} = \hat{\xi}\sin\theta\cos\phi + \hat{\eta}\sin\theta\sin\phi + \hat{\zeta}\cos\theta, \tag{9.14.5}$$

and this can be expressed in x-,y-, z- system using equations (9.14.3).

Now let the angle between $\hat{w}$ and the velocity $\vec{v}$ be α. Then

$$\cos\alpha = \hat{w}\cdot\vec{v}\,/\|\,\vec{v}\,\|. \tag{9.14.6}$$

For simplicity, we shall assume that the ball is a spheroid. As viewed parallel to the velocity, the ball will appear to be an ellipse with semiaxes

$$a \text{ and } \left(\frac{\sin^2\alpha}{a^2} + \frac{\cos^2\alpha}{b^2}\right)^{-1/2}.$$

So the area to be used in the terms for the drag is

$$A = \pi a \left(\frac{\sin^2 \alpha}{a^2} + \frac{\cos^2 \alpha}{b^2} \right)^{-1/2} . \tag{9.14.7}$$

Finally, we are ready for the differential equations for the trajectory

$$\left. \begin{aligned} \frac{d^2x}{dt^2} &= -k_D v v_x, \\ \frac{d^2y}{dt^2} &= -k_D v v_y, \\ \frac{d^2z}{dt^2} &= -k_D v v_z - g, \end{aligned} \right] \tag{9.14.8}$$

where $v = \sqrt{v_x^2 + v_y^2 + v_z^2}$. $k_D = 0.59A$, where A, given by equation (9.14.7) is in m^2.

A good kick might have initial speed 25 m/sec. To get an idea of the role of drag, first find a trajectory with no drag. Then introduce constant (minimum) drag using the same initial conditions. Vary the starting angle. Then introduce toppling, starting with slow values. Experiment with different direction for the precession axis, $\hat{\zeta}$.

9.15 The Path of a Discus

This project is based on a paper by Frohlich [42].[2] I am grateful to the author for his permission to use some of his material in the discussion that follows. A discus is thrown with a sufficiently large spin, perpendicular to its plane, so that the spin vector remains constant and its attitude does not change. It moves in a vertical plane subject to the forces of gravity, drag and lift. A wind, blowing horizontally in the same plane, with velocity independent of altitude, is included in the model.

Let the x- and z-axes be horizontal and vertical, respectively, in the plane of motion, with the z-axis pointing upward. Let the velocity of the discus be $\vec{v}_d$. If the velocity of the wind is $\vec{v}_w$, as shown in figure 9.25, then the velocity of the discus relative to the air is

$$\vec{v}_r = \vec{v}_d - \vec{v}_w . \tag{9.15.1}$$

If A and m are the cross-sectional area and mass of the discus, and ρ is the atmospheric density, the drag and lift forces are

$$\vec{F}_{\text{drag}} = \frac{1}{2} C_D \rho A v_r^2, \qquad \vec{F}_{\text{lift}} = \frac{1}{2} C_L \rho A v_r^2. \tag{9.15.2}$$

C_D and C_L depend on the angle between the plane of the discus and the velocity, ψ, called the *angle of attack.* So this angle must be calculated as the equations are solved.

The equations of motion are

$$\left. \begin{aligned} \frac{d^2x}{dt^2} &= -\frac{\rho A v_r^2}{2m} \left(C_D \cos\beta + C_L \sin\beta \right), \\ \frac{d^2z}{dt^2} &= -\frac{\rho A v_r^2}{2m} \left(C_D \sin\beta - C_L \cos\beta \right) - g. \end{aligned} \right] \tag{9.15.3}$$

Here β is the angle between $\vec{v}_r$ and the horizontal, so that

$$\cos\beta = (\dot{x} - v_w)/v_r, \text{ and } \sin\beta = \dot{z}/v_r, \text{ where } v_r = \| \vec{v}_r \|. \tag{9.15.4}$$

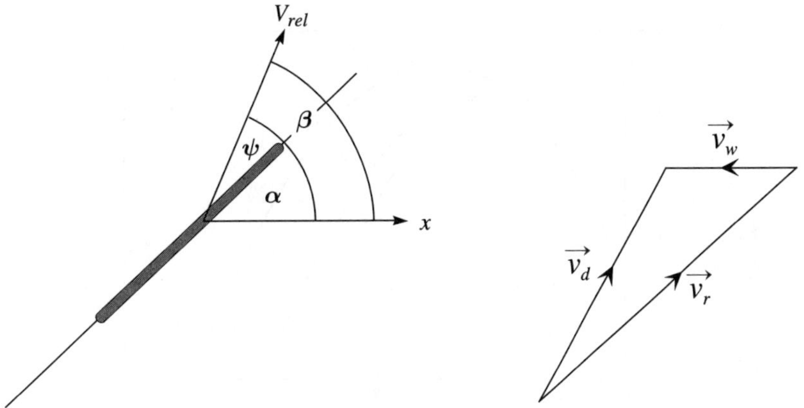

Figure 9.25: *The geometry of a discus in flight.*

g is the acceleration due to gravity. Letting

$$y_1 = x,\ y_2 = \dot{x},\ y_3 = z,\ y_4 = \dot{z}, \tag{9.15.5}$$

we have the system

$$\left.\begin{aligned} \frac{dy_1}{dt} &= y_2, \\ \frac{dy_2}{dt} &= -\frac{\rho A v_r}{2m}\left(C_D(y_2 - v_w) + C_L y_4\right), \\ \frac{dy_3}{dt} &= y_4, \\ \frac{dy_4}{dt} &= -\frac{\rho A v_r}{2m}\left(C_D y_4 - C_L(y_2 - v_w)\right) - g, \\ v_r &= \sqrt{(y_2 - v_w)^2 + y_4^2}, \\ \psi &= \left|\arctan\left(y_4/(y_2 - v_w)\right) - \alpha\right|. \end{aligned}\right] \tag{9.15.6}$$

Frolich tabulates the following values of C_D and C_L, as functions of the angle of attack, ψ, and suggests linear interpolation in any interval:

ψ	C_D	ψ	C_L
0°	0.06	0°	0.00
5°	0.06	28°	0.875
30°	0.54	35°	0.60
70°	1.00	70°	0.35
90°	1.07	90°	0.00

For instance, suppose that you want to find C_L for $\psi = 60°$. In the interval $35° \le \psi \le 70°$, C_L can be represented by the linear equation

$$C_L = 0.60 + \frac{0.35 - 0.60}{70 - 35}(\psi - 35).$$

Substituting $\psi = 60$ gives $C_L = 0.42$.

[2]Abstracted, with permission, from "Aerodynamic Effects on Discus Flights," C. Frohlich. *American Journal of Physics*, **49** (1981) 1125–1132. Copyright 1981, American Association of Physics Teachers.

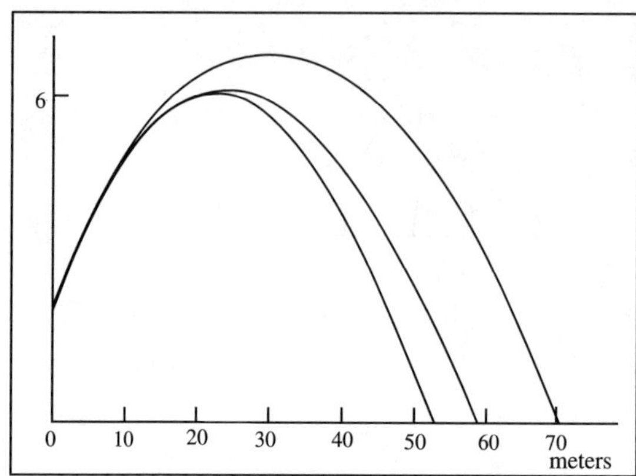

Figure 9.26: *Three trajectories, all starting with the same conditions. The opposing wind speeds are 0, 10 and 20 m/sec; the corresponding ranges are 53.2, 59.2 and 69.6 m. This confirms that when a discus is thrown into a wind, the range increases.*

Numerical values for the men's discus are: mass = 2.0 kg, and diameter = 0.221 m. So the cross-sectional area is $A = 0.038$ m^2. Frolich advises that the value of α should be less than the initial value of β by about 5-10°. A good starting speed is 25 m/sec. The atmospheric density at sea level is $\rho = 1.29$ kg/m^3.

First, I suggest that you run the model without a wind. Experiment with different starting values of β to find the maximum range for a given initial speed. (The record is 71 m). A feature of this model (and of reality) is that if the discus is thrown into a moderate wind, the range is increased. Confirm this, and investigate the range of wind speeds for which it applies. Suppose that the discus is being thrown with a following wind. What tactics might be used to maximize the range?

It is doubtful whether the model and the drag and lift coefficients can apply to the frisbee (mass 0.087 kg, diameter 0.227 m), but that need not prevent you from trying it anyway.

Figure 9.26 shows three trajectories. Each starts at a height of 2 m, with velocity 25 m/sec making the angle 20° with the horizontal. The only difference is the speed of the wind, which is blowing from right to left, opposing the motion of the discus. The three wind speeds are 0, 10 and 20 m/sec; the corresponding ranges are 53.2, 59.2 and 69.6 m. This confirms that when a discus is thrown into a wind, the range increases.

9.16 The Motion of a Javelin

The motion of a javelin has stimulated a lot of research, due to the aerodynamical problems involved. Discussions of the general problem in three dimensions and with the wind blowing are to be found in papers by Hubbard and Rust, [58] and [59]. These are complicated by an elaborate dependence of drag and lift on the geometry of the motion. The project described here follows the motion of a non-spinning javelin moving in a vertical plane, unaffected by wind. The model follows the motion of the center of mass, and the pitching of the javelin. It uses parameters for drag and lift given by Best and Bartlett, [11], that are also used in an excellent discussion by Hart and Croft [50], these last two authors also include BASIC code for a program to follow the motion in animation.

The geometry of the javelin and the forces acting on it are illustrated in figure 9.27. The javelin makes an angle θ with the horizontal x-axis. The center of gravity is at G, and the velocity $\vec{V}$ of the center of gravity makes an angle ϕ with the x-axis. $\vec{V}$ also makes an angle α with the javelin. α is called the *angle of attack*. The drag force is antiparallel to $\vec{V}$, and the lift force is perpendicular

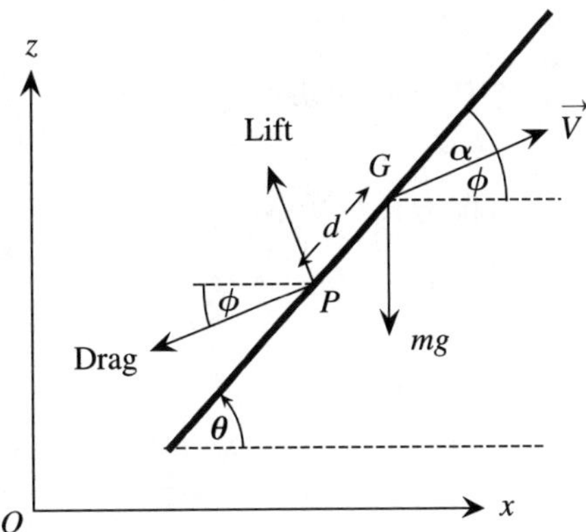

Figure 9.27: *The geometry of the javelin flight.*

to $\vec{V}$. These two latter forces are considered to act at a point P, called the *center of pressure*, which is a fixed distance, d, from C. The javelin has mass m; its moment of inertia about G is I.

The magnitudes of the drag and lift forces are given, respectively, by

$$D = \frac{1}{2} C_D A \rho V^2 = K_D V^2, \qquad L = \frac{1}{2} C_L A \rho V^2 = K_L V^2. \tag{9.16.1}$$

Formulas for K_D and K_L, which have dimension m^{-1}, are given based on experimental data. In terms of the angle of attack, α, they are

$$K_D = 0.00024\, e^{5.157\alpha}, \qquad K_L = 0.0127\, \alpha^{1.34}. \tag{9.16.2}$$

Note: α is expressed in radians.

With the z-axis pointing vertically upward, the equations of motion are

$$\left.\begin{aligned} m\frac{d^2x}{dt^2} &= -K_D V^2 \cos\phi - K_L V^2 \sin\phi, \\ m\frac{d^2z}{dt^2} &= -K_D V^2 \sin\phi + K_L V^2 \cos\phi - mg, \\ I\frac{d^2\theta}{dt^2} &= d(-K_D V^2 \sin\alpha - K_L V^2 \cos\alpha). \end{aligned}\right] \tag{9.16.3}$$

We have $\phi = \arctan(\dot{z}/\dot{x})$ and $\alpha = |\theta - \phi|$.

For computation, set

$$y_1 = x, \; y_2 = \dot{x}. \; y_3 = z, \; y_4 = \dot{z}, \; y_5 = \theta, \; y_6 = \dot{\theta}. \tag{9.16.4}$$

Then

$$\left.\begin{aligned}
V &= \sqrt{y_2^2 + y_4^2},\\
\phi &= \arctan(y_4/y_2),\\
\alpha &= |y_5 - \phi|,\\
K_D &= 0.00024\, e^{5.157\alpha},\\
K_L &= 0.0127\, \alpha^{1.34},\\
\frac{dy_1}{dt} &= y_2,\\
\frac{dy_2}{dt} &= -(K_D V^2 \cos\phi + K_L V^2 \sin\phi)/m,\\
\frac{dy_3}{dt} &= y_4,\\
\frac{dy_4}{dt} &= -(K_D\, V^2 \sin\phi - K_L\, V^2 \cos\phi)/m - g,\\
\frac{dy_5}{dt} &= y_6,\\
\frac{dy_6}{dt} &= d(-K_D\, V^2 \sin\alpha - K_L\, V^2 \cos\alpha)/I.
\end{aligned}\right] \tag{9.16.5}$$

Suggested numerical values are: $m = 0.80625$ kg, $d = 0.255$ m, $I = 0.42$ kg m^2. Initially, set $t = 0$ and $x = 0$. Choose a reasonable value for v. Plausible initial speeds are in the vicinity of 20–30 m/sec. Initially, θ and ϕ should be equal. (If you enter degrees, remember to change them at once to radians in the calculation.) If the initial speed is V_0, then initial values of the velocity components are $\dot{x} = V_0 \cos\theta$, $\dot{y} = V_0 \sin\theta$. Start with $\dot{\theta} = 0$. See if you can find the optimal launch angle. Then repeat with nonzero initial $\dot{\theta}$.

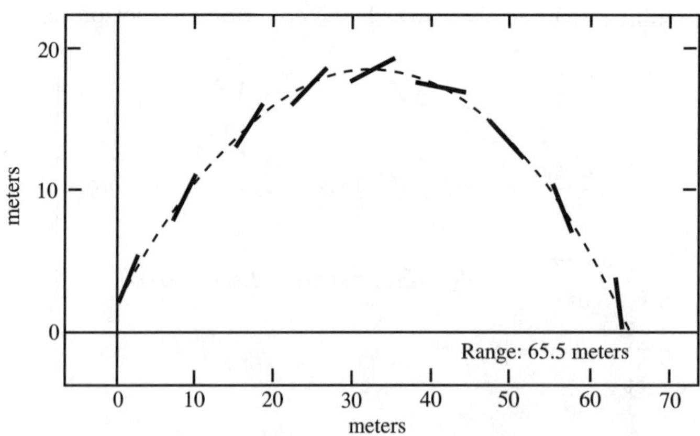

Figure 9.28: *A trajectory of a javelin. The length of the javelin has been exaggerated by a factor of three.*

Figure 9.28 shows a trajectory. The curve is the location of the center of mass, and the javelin (with length exaggerated by a factor of 3) is shown every half second. Numerical values of parameters are taken from the text. The javelin is thrown from a height of 2 m at a speed of 24 m/sec, and elevation angle 45°. The initial angular rate of rotation about its center is zero.

9.17 A Model for the Ski Jump

This model is based on a paper by Ward-Smith and Clements [103]. They divide the operation into the phases: in-run, take-off, free flight, landing and out-run. We shall be following the in-run, when the skier is gaining speed for the jump, and the free flight, when the skier is airborne.

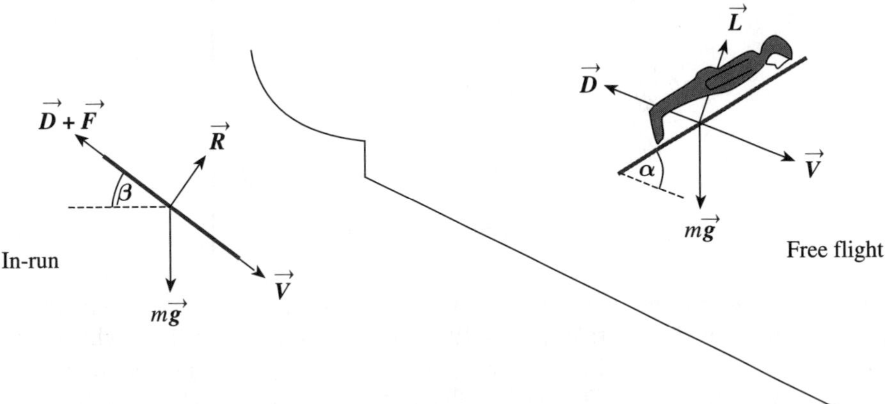

Figure 9.29: *A ski jump, and the forces acting on the skier.*

Figure 9.29 shows a formal model for the course and the forces acting on the skier when airborne, to the right, and during the in-run, to the left. The motion will take place in a vertical plane, with the x-axis horizontal, in the direction of the motion, and the z-axis vertically upward. The origin will be at the point of take-off.

During the in-run, let the velocity $\vec{v}$ make an angle β with the horizontal, as shown. The forces on the skier are the weight, $-mg$, vertically downward, the drag force, $\vec{D}$, opposite to $\vec{v}$, with magnitude $D = \frac{1}{2}\rho v^2 A_D$, a force perpendicular to the slope, $\vec{R}$, with magnitude $R = v^2/r$, where r is the radius of curvature, and a friction force, $\vec{F}$, opposite to $\vec{v}$, with magnitude $F = \mu R$. μ is the coefficient of friction between the skis and the snow. The differential equations are

$$\left.\begin{aligned} \frac{dx}{dt} &= v_x, \\ \frac{dz}{dt} &= v_z, \\ m\frac{dv_x}{dt} &= -\frac{v_x}{v}(D+F) - \frac{v_z}{v}R, \\ m\frac{dv_z}{dt} &= -\frac{v_z}{v}(D+F) + \frac{v_x}{v}R - mg, \\ v &= \sqrt{v_x^2 + v_z^2}. \end{aligned}\right] \tag{9.17.1}$$

If the shape of the slope is defined by $z = f(x)$, then the radius of curvature is found from

$$r = \left(1 + (f'(x))^2\right)^{3/2} / |f''(x)|. \tag{9.17.2}$$

Numerical values will be considered shortly.

During the free flight, the skier is aligned parallel to the skis, making a constant angle, α, with the velocity. α is the *angle of attack*. The forces are weight, drag, as before, and lift, $\vec{L}$, perpendicular to $\vec{D}$, with magnitude $\frac{1}{2}\rho v^2 A_L$. The equations of motion are

$$\left.\begin{aligned}\frac{dx}{dt} &= v_x,\\ \frac{dz}{dt} &= v_z,\\ m\frac{dv_x}{dt} &= -\frac{1}{2}\rho v\left(v_x A_D + v_z A_L\right),\\ m\frac{dv_z}{dt} &= -\frac{1}{2}\rho v\left(v_z A_D - v_x A_L\right) - mg,\\ v &= \sqrt{v_x^2 + v_z^2}.\end{aligned}\right] \tag{9.17.3}$$

For numerical values, assume $g = 9.81\ \mathrm{m/sec}^2$. The atmospheric density depends on altitude and temperature, but, if in doubt, take $\rho = 1.19\ \mathrm{kg/m}^3$. In the paper from which this model is taken, the authors use $m = 75$ kg. In the in-run, $A_D = 0.2\ \mathrm{m}^2$ (this depends on the shape of the skier at the time). Also, $\mu = 0.05$. During free flight, the angle of attack is taken to be $\alpha = 45°$, with $A_D = 1.25$ and $A_L = 0.31$. The paper includes a chart showing the variation of these quantities with α.

In order to run the model, you will have to design your own ski run. For simplicity, I suggest that you make the in-run curve to be part of a circle, so that the radius of curvature is constant. But the initiative is yours.

At the instant of take-off, the skier may add to the vertical component of velocity by pressing down onto the ground. In your experiments, you might see what effect this will have on the length of the trajectory.

9.18 Running 💻💻💻

A popular model to represent running was produced by Furusawa *et al.* in 1927 [43], based on the use of Newton's second law of motion. Two forces on the runner were assumed: a driving force proportional to the runner's weight and a resisting force emanating from within the runner's body. This latter force was given the form mv/a, where m is the mass of the runner, v is the speed and a is a constant. Then if x is the distance covered, and t is the time, application of Newton's second law produces

$$m\frac{d^2x}{dt^2} = bmg - \frac{mv}{a}. \tag{9.18.1}$$

Here g is the acceleration due to gravity and b is a second constant. This equation can be solved by formula; several authors have applied it to times from sprinting events and calculated numerical values for a and b. A term for air resistance, proportional to v^2, has also been included. A beauty of this model is that it can be used as a class project in calculus. However it relies on empirical assumptions that have no physical basis; also it produces the incorrect property that, as the time increases, the speed approaches a limit (like the limiting speed of a falling object).

The model to be used here is due to Ward-Smith [102]. He uses considerations of energy and power. For a detailed discussion, you should read his paper, and also consult the text *Biomechanics and Energetics of Muscular Exercise* by Margaria [68].

The fundamental equation expresses that the chemical energy released by the runner is equal to the mechanical energy of running plus the energy converted into heat. Denoting these energies by C, W and H, we have

$$C = H + W. \tag{9.18.2}$$

Differentiating this, we have

$$\frac{dC}{dt} = \frac{dH}{dt} + \frac{dW}{dt}, \tag{9.18.3}$$

which can be written as

$$P_C = P_H + P_W, \tag{9.18.4}$$

where $P_C = dC/dt$, $P_H = dH/dt$ and $P_W = dW/dt$. The symbol P stands for "power."

Consider first P_W. It has two components, the rate of increase of kinetic energy, and the rate of working against atmospheric drag. The kinetic energy is

$$\frac{1}{2}mv^2, \quad \text{so its rate of increase is} \quad mv\frac{dv}{dt}.$$

The drag force has magnitude

$$D = \frac{1}{2}C_D S\rho v^2.$$

S is the frontal cross-section area of the runner. We assume that there is no wind. (In the presence of a wind, then v_{rel}, the speed relative to the wind, would have to be used.) Then the rate of working against this force is

$$Dv = \frac{1}{2}C_D S\rho v^3.$$

So

$$P_W = mv\frac{dv}{dt} + \frac{1}{2}C_D S\rho v^3. \tag{9.18.5}$$

It has been found empirically that

$$P_H = Av \tag{9.18.6}$$

for constant A.

P_C has two components. The *aerobic* power, involving oxygen, increases exponentially to a maximum value R, and is given by

$$P_{\text{aer}} = R\left(1 - e^{-\lambda t}\right). \tag{9.18.7}$$

The time t is measured from the start of the race. According to Margaria [68] the half-life of the process is around 30 sec; this would make $\lambda = \ln 2/30 \approx 0.023\,\text{sec}^{-1}$. The *anaerobic* power diminishes exponentially from a maximum value P_{max}, and is represented by

$$P_{\text{an}} = P_{\text{max}}e^{-\lambda t}. \tag{9.18.8}$$

Note that the same half-life is assumed in each case. Then

$$P_C = R\left(1 - e^{-\lambda t}\right) + P_{\text{max}}e^{-\lambda t} = \lambda S_0 e^{-\lambda t} + R, \text{ where } S_0 = \frac{P_{\text{max}} - R}{\lambda}. \tag{9.18.9}$$

The equation for the model can now be written from (9.18.4) as

$$\lambda S_0 e^{-\lambda t} + R = Av + mv\frac{dv}{dt} + \frac{1}{2}C_D S\rho v^3. \tag{9.18.10}$$

Dividing through by m, we have

$$\lambda S_0^* e^{-\lambda t} + R^* = A^* v + v\frac{dv}{dt} + K^* v^3, \tag{9.18.11}$$

where

$$S_0^* = \frac{S_0}{m}, \ R^* = \frac{R}{m}, \ A^* = \frac{A}{m} \text{ and } K^* = \frac{\rho S C_D}{2m}. \tag{9.18.12}$$

This is the model derived by Ward-Smith [102].

For numerical values Ward-Smith uses

$$A^* = 3.9\,\mathrm{J\,m^{-1}\,kg^{-1}}. \tag{9.18.13}$$

The drag coefficient C_D varies with speed as well as with the individual runner. The range $C_D = 0.8 - 0.9$ is acceptable. The area S is typically 0.4 to 0.5 m^2.

Ward-Smith takes the product $SC_D = 0.385\,\mathrm{m}^2$. Then with $\rho = 1.22\,\mathrm{kg\,m^{-3}}$,

$$K^* = \frac{0.235}{mg}\,\mathrm{m}^{-1}, \tag{9.18.14}$$

where mg is the runner's weight in kg. Then, using data from Olympic events from 100 to 10,000 m, he derives the values

$$S_0^* = 900\,\mathrm{J\,kg^{-1}},\ R^* = 23.5\,\mathrm{J\,s^{-1}\,kg^{-1}},\ \lambda = 0.03\,\mathrm{s}^{-1}. \tag{9.18.15}$$

Equation (9.18.11) must be expressed as two first-order equations, using

$$y_1 = x,\ y_2 = v = \frac{dx}{dt}. \tag{9.18.16}$$

Then

$$\left.\begin{aligned} \frac{dy_1}{dt} &= y_2, \\ \frac{dy_2}{dt} &= \frac{1}{y_2}\left(\lambda S_0^* e^{-\lambda t} + R^* - A^* y_2 - K^* y_2^3\right). \end{aligned}\right] \tag{9.18.17}$$

There is a problem when starting from rest, since the second equation has a singularity for $v = y_2 = 0$. Ward-Smith deals with this in the following way. Consider the motion when $0 \le t \le \Delta t$, where Δt is small. During this time (9.18.11) can be approximated by

$$vdv = (\lambda S_0^* + R^*)dt, \tag{9.18.18}$$

which can be integrated to give

$$v = \sqrt{2(\lambda S_0^* + R^*)}(\Delta t)^{1/2}. \tag{9.18.19}$$

At time Δt the runner will have covered the distance

$$\Delta x = \frac{2}{3}\sqrt{2(\lambda S_0^* + R^*)}(\Delta t)^{3/2}. \tag{9.18.20}$$

Once this step has been taken, the equations can be solved in the usual way. Some experiment may be needed to find a suitable Δt; make sure that your choice does not influence the subsequent calculations.

If possible, read the paper by Ward-Smith [102]. First run some races using the maneuvers derived by him. Next, making physical interpretations, change some of the basic parameters, such as $P_{\max}$ or R or λ. What happens if the two exponential processes have different half-lives? Not everyone is an Olympic athlete; how about finding parameters that account for your own performance?

Now include a wind in the model; how does this affect times? For a shorter race, the wind would be constant relative to the runner; for a longer one, it would vary around a circuit, sometimes helping, sometimes hindering. Do these effects cancel each other?

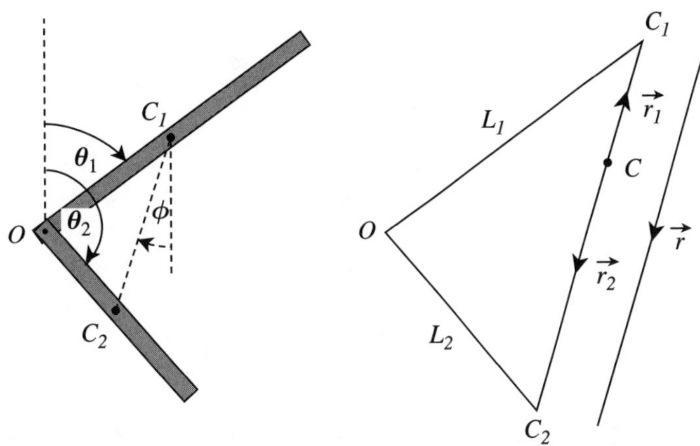

Figure 9.30: *The geometry of a "hinged diver.".*

9.19 Diving

We shall be concerned with the dynamical effects when a diver changes bodily configuration during the dive. (The methods can also be applied to stunts performed on a trampoline.) The model is that considered by Frohlich [41] and [40].[3] I am grateful to the author for permission to use some of his material in the discussion that follows. During the change the diver is modeled by two rigid bodies hinged together. For instance, the arms might move, when the hinge would be at the shoulders; in a jackknife change, the hinge would be at the waist.

In figure 9.30 the hinge is at O. One section, with mass M_1, makes the angle θ_1 with the upward vertical, as shown; its center of mass is at C_1 and the length $OC_1 = L_1$. The second section, with mass M_2, makes the angle θ_2 with the vertical, and has its center of mass at C_2, where $OC_2 = L_2$. The line C_1C_2 makes the angle ϕ with the vertical. The center of mass of the entire body is at C, which will lie on C_1C_2. $\overrightarrow{CC_1} = \vec{r}_1$ and $\overrightarrow{CC_2} = \vec{r}_2$. The moments of inertia of the bodies about axes perpendicular to the plane OC_1C_2, through their respective centers of mass, are I_1 and I_2.

All motion takes place in a fixed vertical plane. The angular momentum of the system remains constant, and is perpendicular to this plane. It has magnitude

$$H = I_1\dot{\theta}_1 + M_1\| \vec{r}_1 \times \dot{\vec{r}}_1\| + I_2\dot{\theta}_2 + M_2\| \vec{r}_2 \times \dot{\vec{r}}_2\|. \tag{9.19.1}$$

Now $\| \vec{r}_1 \times \dot{\vec{r}}_1\| = r_1^2\dot{\phi}$ and $\| \vec{r}_2 \times \dot{\vec{r}}_2\| = r_2^2\dot{\phi}$. Also, if $\vec{r} = \vec{r}_2 - \vec{r}_1$, so that r is the distance between C_1 and C_2, then

$$r_1 = \frac{M_2}{M_1 + M_2} r, \text{ and } r_2 = \frac{M_1}{M_1 + M_2} r. \tag{9.19.2}$$

So

$$\begin{aligned} H &= I_1\dot{\theta}_1 + M_1 r_1^2\dot{\phi} + I_2\dot{\theta}_2 + M_2 r_2^2\dot{\phi} \\ &= I_1\dot{\theta}_1 + I_2\dot{\theta}_2 + M^* r^2\dot{\phi}, \end{aligned} \tag{9.19.3}$$

where M^* is the reduced mass

$$M^* = \frac{M_1 M_2}{M_1 + M_2}. \tag{9.19.4}$$

[3] Abstracted, with permission, from "Do Springboard Divers Violate Angular Momentum Conservation," C. Frohlich. *American Journal of Physics*, **47** (1979) 583–592. Copyright 1979, American Association of Physics Teachers.

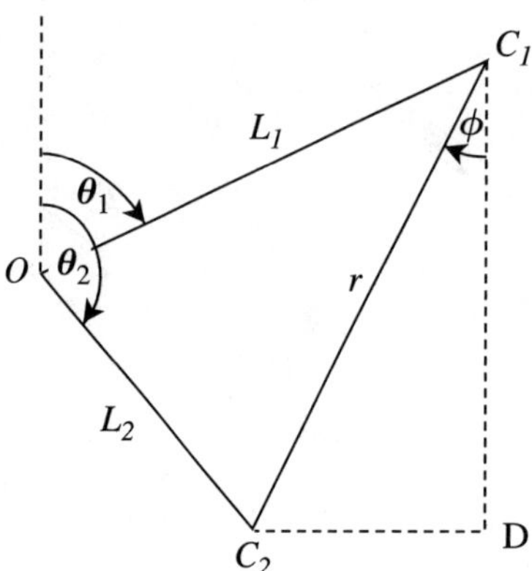

Figure 9.31: $C_1D = L_1 \cos\theta_1 - L_2 \cos\theta_2$, $C_2D = L_1 \sin\theta_1 - L_2 \sin\theta_2$.

To eliminate ϕ, see the right-angled triangle C_1C_2D in figure 9.31, where

$$C_1C_2 = r, \; C_1D = L_1 \cos\theta_1 - L_2 \cos\theta_2, \text{ and } C_2D = L_1 \sin\theta_1 - L_2 \sin\theta_2.$$

Then

$$\tan\phi = \frac{C_2D}{C_1D} = \frac{L_1 \sin\theta_1 - L_2 \sin\theta_2}{L_1 \cos\theta_1 - L_2 \cos\theta_2}. \tag{9.19.5}$$

The derivative of $\tan\phi$ with respect to the time is

$$\sec^2\phi\,\dot{\phi} = \frac{r^2}{C_1D^2}\dot{\phi},$$

so, differentiating (9.19.5), using the quotient rule, we can write

$$\begin{aligned} \frac{r^2}{C_1D^2}\dot{\phi} &= -\Big((-L_1\dot{\theta}_1 \sin\theta_1 + L_2\dot{\theta}_2 \sin\theta_2)(L_1 \sin\theta_1 - L_2 \sin\theta_2) \\ &\quad - (L_1\dot{\theta}_1 \cos\theta_1 - L_2\dot{\theta}_2 \cos\theta_2)(L_1 \cos\theta_1 - L_2 \cos\theta_2)\Big) /C_1D^2. \end{aligned}$$

Simplifying,

$$r^2\dot{\phi} = \left(L_1^2 - L_1L_2\cos(\theta_2 - \theta_1)\right)\dot{\theta}_1 + \left(L_2^2 - L_1L_2\cos(\theta_2 - \theta_1)\right)\dot{\theta}_2. \tag{9.19.6}$$

Substituting into (9.19.3), we have

$$H = [I_1 + M^*L_1\left((L_1 - L_2\cos(\theta_2 - \theta_1)\right))]\dot{\theta}_1 + [I_2 + M^*L_2\left((L_2 - L_1\cos(\theta_2 - \theta_1)\right))]\dot{\theta}_2. \tag{9.19.7}$$

Now let the hinge angle $\theta_2 - \theta_1 = \psi$. Then (9.19.7) can be written in terms of θ_1 (or θ_2) and ψ. ψ will be a known function of the time, so by solving (9.19.7) the changes in θ_1 and θ_2 can be calculated.

To run the project, first decide where on the body the hinge will be. Then derive numbers for the masses and moments of inertia. Then pick starting and ending values for ψ, and the time for the change. Choose a value for the total angular momentum, and a starting value for θ_1; then solve the equation for θ_1 for the duration of the change.

To help design the project, here are some rough figures for percentage masses of parts of a typical body: head, 7%, trunk, 43%, arms (each), 6%, thighs (each), 12%, lower legs and feet (each), 7%. The head can be modeled by a sphere and the remaining parts, by cylinders. The moment of inertia of a sphere of radius a and mass M about its center of mass is $\frac{1}{5}Ma^2$. The moment of inertia of a homogeneous cylinder of length $2b$ and mass M about its center of mass, and about a perpendicular axis through the center of mass, is $\frac{1}{3}Mb^2$. The moment of inertia of a body about any axis is equal to its moment of inertia about a parallel axis through the center of mass, plus the product of the mass of the body and the square of the distance between the axes.

9.20 The Pole Vault

The combination of pole and athlete in the pole vault forms a remarkable machine for transforming horizontal into vertical motion. Since considerable artistry is involved in the motion of the athlete's body at every stage of the vault, the models considered here will fall well short of reality. But they will allow you to experiment with some of the principal parameters.

We shall look at three models here. The first is totally unrealistic, since it uses a spring for the pole. It uses the model of the spring pendulum, project (13.11), with which you may already be familiar; it possesses the principal dynamical feature of the pole vault, and may be easier to set up than the more realistic models. In fact the pole is a flexible rod, an "elastica," with properties investigated by Euler. The relation between its bending and the applied thrust is complicated. We shall look at a model in which the vaulter is a passive mass at the end of the pole, and finally one in which he or she is a variable pendulum swinging from the end. In all cases, the models are chaotic! For realism, allowance should be made for changes in the positions where the pole is grasped and additional torques applied by the athlete. These are discussed in articles by Hubbard [57] and Griner [48].

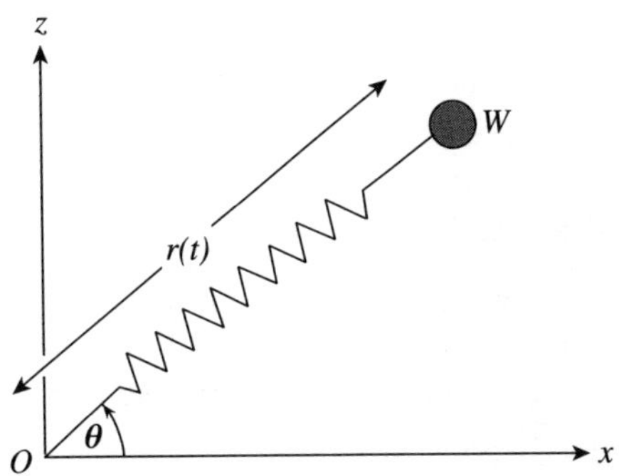

Figure 9.32: *A weight W on a compressed spring, pivoted at the origin.*

9.20.1 An Application of the Spring Pendulum

Once again, let me stress that I am not attempting to model the bending of a pole. The model of project (13.11) is modified as shown in figure 9.32, with the displacement angle measured from the horizontal x-axis. The origin is at the point at which the "pole" pivots on the ground, actually, six to eight inches below ground level. The length of the spring is r and the uncompressed length is r_0. The vaulter has weight W and the spring constant is k. Then, adapting equation (13.11.1),

$$\left.\begin{aligned} \frac{d^2r}{dt^2} &= \left(\frac{d\theta}{dt}\right)^2 - g\sin\theta - \frac{kg}{W}(r - r_0), \\ \frac{d^2\theta}{dt^2} &= -\frac{2}{r}\frac{dr}{dt}\frac{d\theta}{dt} - \frac{g}{r}\cos\theta. \end{aligned}\right] \tag{9.20.1}$$

g is the acceleration due to gravity.

First, consider possible values for k. If $\theta \equiv 0$ then motion is along the x-axis. Initially $t = 0$, and $x(0) = 15$ ft, the length of a pole. Suppose $\dot{x}(0) = -28$ ft/sec. Then if

$$\omega = \sqrt{\frac{kg}{W}}, \tag{9.20.2}$$

$$x(t) = 15 - \frac{28}{\omega}\sin\omega t, \text{ and } \dot{x}(t) = -28\cos\omega t. \tag{9.20.3}$$

Suppose the minimum length of the spring is 7 ft. Then $\omega = 4\text{sec}^{-1}$. For $W = 160$ lb, $k = 80$ lb/ft. In general, initially $\theta(0) = 0$; if the initial upward speed is 10 ft/sec, then $\dot{\theta}(0) = 10/15\ \text{sec}^{-1}$.

We are not allowed to let the length exceed $r_0 = 15$ or θ to exceed $\pi/2$. Release might take place at the earlier of these cases, or earlier still — you decide. After release, find the quantities x_1, $\dot{x}_1$, z_1 and $\dot{z}_1$. If we measure time τ from the instant of release, then

$$x = x_1 + \tau\dot{x}_1, \text{ and } y = y_1 + \tau\dot{y}_1 - \frac{1}{2}g\tau^2. \tag{9.20.4}$$

There are four principal quantities to play with. You might fix W and then experiment with different values of k and the initial conditions. Experiment with one at a time: for instance, if W, $\dot{r}(0)$ and $\dot{\theta}(0)$ are fixed, find the best value for k.

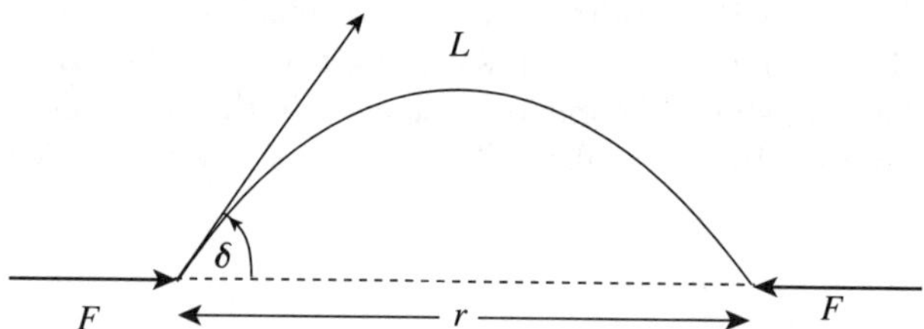

Figure 9.33: *A bent elastica of length L under loads F.*

9.20.2 Properties of the Elastica

Before making further progress we must summarize some properties of the elastica. Figure 9.33 illustrates a bent elastica with length L under end loads F; the distance between the ends is r. The figure is parameterized by the angle δ between the tangent to the curve at one end and the line joining the ends. Further, let

$$\mu = \sin\frac{\delta}{2}. \tag{9.20.5}$$

The formulas involve the complete elliptic integrals of the first and second kind

$$\left.\begin{aligned} K(\mu) &= \int_0^{\pi/2} \left(1 - \mu^2\sin^2 u\right)^{-1/2} du, \\ E(\mu) &= \int_0^{\pi/2} \left(1 - \mu^2\sin^2 u\right)^{+1/2} du. \end{aligned}\right] \tag{9.20.6}$$

Then

$$\frac{r}{L} = 2\frac{E(\mu)}{K(\mu)} - 1 \tag{9.20.7}$$

and

$$F = \frac{4B}{L^2}K^2(\mu). \tag{9.20.8}$$

B is the *stiffness* of the rod.

Notice that when μ approaches zero then the force F approaches $4B(\pi/2L)^2$. This is the minimum force to cause buckling. It is discussed in project (13.5), where the force is given as $EI(\pi/2L)^2$; E is *Young's modulus* and I is the moment of inertia of the column about its axis.

What we shall need for computation is some way, given r, to find F. If high accuracy is required, then this is not a trivial problem. However, in the context of the range of bending that is likely and the approximate nature of the models, the following approximations are suggested:

$$\mu^2 \approx 1 - \left(2\frac{E(\mu)}{K(\mu)} - 1\right) = \frac{L-r}{L}. \tag{9.20.9}$$

So for given r the amount of bending can be estimated, and excessive bending avoided. Also

$$K^2 - \left(\frac{\pi}{2}\right)^2 \approx (1.3) \cdot \left(\frac{L-r}{L}\right).$$

So

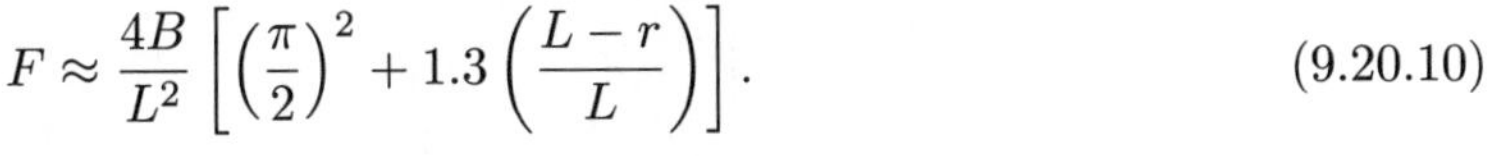

$$F \approx \frac{4B}{L^2}\left[\left(\frac{\pi}{2}\right)^2 + 1.3\left(\frac{L-r}{L}\right)\right]. \tag{9.20.10}$$

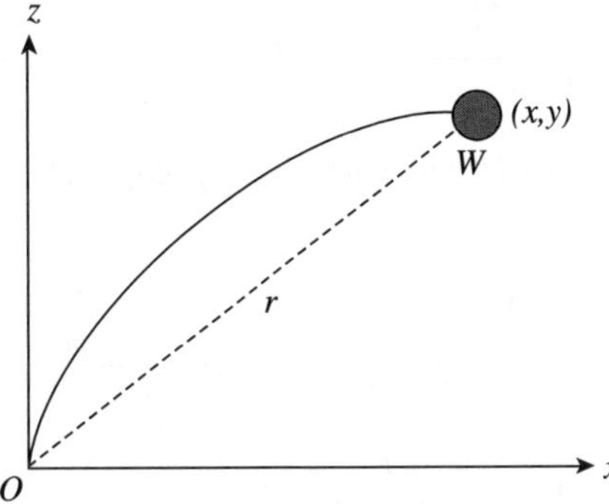

Figure 9.34: *Pole pivoted at the origin with a weight W attached to its free end.*

9.20.3 A Weight Fixed at One End of the Elastica

Here the vaulter is a passive mass at the end of the pole. See figure 9.34. If his coordinates are (x, z), then

$$\left.\begin{aligned} r &= \sqrt{x^2+z^2}, \\ F &= \frac{4B}{L^2}\left[\left(\frac{\pi}{2}\right)^2 + 1.3\left(\frac{L-r}{L}\right)\right], \\ \frac{d^2x}{dt^2} &= \frac{g}{W}\frac{x}{r}F, \\ \frac{d^2z}{dt^2} &= \frac{g}{W}\frac{z}{r}F - g. \end{aligned}\right] \tag{9.20.11}$$

You can expect a very different start, compared with that for the spring; the stiffness of the pole results in a considerable initial deceleration. You will find results very sensitive to the input numbers. Consider values of B around 4750 lb.ft^2.

9.20.4 A Vaulter Suspended from One End of the Elastica

In this model, due to Walker and Kirmser [101], the vaulter is represented by a compound pendulum swinging from the free end of the pole, which forms a pivot at P. See figure 9.35. The center of mass of the vaulter is at C, with coordinates (x, z), distant ρ from P, and his moment of inertia about an axis through C and perpendicular to the x-z plane is I. But he (or she) can vary r and I in ways that are planned before the jump. So $r(t)$ and $I(t)$ become input functions.

Let CP make the angle ϕ with the x-axis, as shown. Then the rate of change of the angular momentum $I\dot{\phi}$ is equal to the moment of the forces about C. Hence, since the coordinates of P are $(x + \rho\cos\phi, z + \rho\sin\phi)$,

$$I\frac{d^2\theta}{dt^2} + \frac{dI}{dt}\frac{d\theta}{dt} = F\frac{z+\rho\sin\phi}{r}\rho\cos\phi - F\frac{x+\rho\cos\phi}{r}\rho\sin\phi. \tag{9.20.12}$$

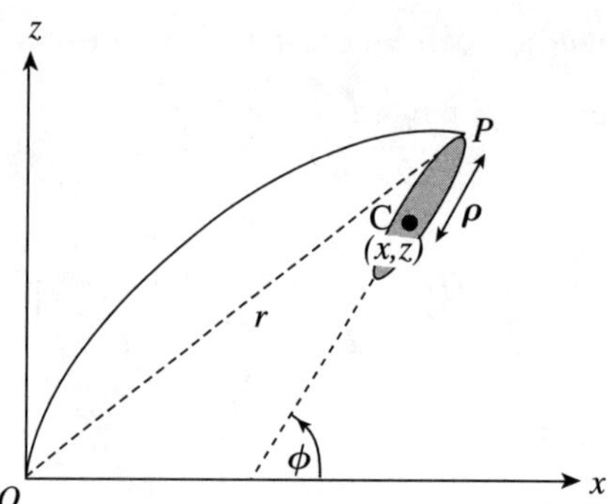

Figure 9.35: *C, distant ρ from P, the end of the pole, is the center of mass of the vaulter.*

The complete set of equations for the model is now

$$\left.\begin{aligned}
r &= \sqrt{x^2 + z^2 + \rho^2 + 2x\rho\cos\phi + 2z\rho\sin\phi}, \\
F &= \frac{4B}{L^2}\left[\left(\frac{\pi}{2}\right)^2 + 1.3\left(\frac{L-r}{L}\right)\right], \\
\frac{d^2x}{dt^2} &= \frac{g}{W}\frac{x+\rho\cos\phi}{r}F, \\
\frac{d^2z}{dt^2} &= \frac{g}{W}\frac{z+\rho\sin\phi}{r}F - g \\
I\frac{d^2\theta}{dt^2} &= -\frac{dI}{dt}\frac{d\theta}{dt} + F\frac{z+\rho\sin\phi}{r}\rho\cos\phi - F\frac{x+\rho\cos\phi}{r}\rho\sin\phi.
\end{aligned}\right] \tag{9.20.13}$$

These equations must be written as six first-order equations in the usual way.

The functions $\rho(t)$ and $I(t)$ initially represent the vaulter vertically at full stretch. They are then diminished to optimize the swing of the "pendulum," and finally increased again to full stretch. The tactics used are important, so you may want to develop a table and use interpolation in the program. To help get started, here are some functions that are plausible:

$$\rho(t) = \left[\begin{array}{ll} 4 - 3\cos\left(\dfrac{t-0.4}{0.4}\dfrac{\pi}{2}\right), & 0 \le t \le 0.8, \\ 3.5, & t > 0.8. \end{array}\right. \tag{9.20.14}$$

$$I(t) = \left[\begin{array}{ll} 12 - 4.6\cos\left(\dfrac{t-0.3}{0.3}\dfrac{\pi}{2}\right), & 0 \le t \le 0.6, \\ 12, & t > 0.6. \end{array}\right. \tag{9.20.15}$$

Chapter 10

Travel and Recreation

10.1 The Dynamics of Flight

The model described here was proposed by Patrick W. Canupp, who was my student at the time. It is reproduced here with his permission.

We shall investigate two-dimensional flight, involving change in altitude but not in direction. First, consider steady-state flight, where there is no change in speed or altitude. The plane is subject to four forces, as shown in figure 10.1. Horizontally, they are the thrust, T, and the drag, D. Vertically, they are the lift, L, and the weight, W.

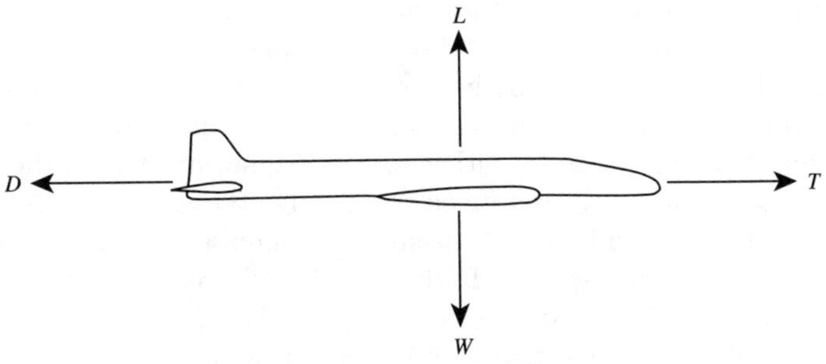

Figure 10.1: *The forces acting on a plane in flight.*

In a steady state, these forces must balance, so that

$$T = D, \quad (10.1.1)$$

$$L = W. \quad (10.1.2)$$

For a jet, the engines produce thrust that is chiefly a function of altitude, due to the varying amount of oxygen in the atmosphere. We shall consider only altitudes below 36,000 ft; then

$$T = T_{SL}\sigma^{0.7}, \quad (10.1.3)$$

where σ is the ratio of the atmospheric density at the flight altitude to that at sea level, and T_{SL} is the full-throttle thrust at sea level. For an altitude, h, measured in ft, the density ratio is given by

$$\sigma = e^{-h/30,500}. \quad (10.1.4)$$

The thrust in equation (10.1.3) will vary little with airspeed, and can be assumed to be constant at a given altitude and throttle setting.

The drag on a jet varies according to the equation

$$D = \frac{1}{2}\rho_{SL}\sigma V^2 SC_{D0} + \frac{2KW^2}{\rho_{SL}\sigma V^2 S}, \tag{10.1.5}$$

where ρ_{SL} is the atmospheric density at sea level, measured in slugs per ft^3, $2.3769 \cdot 10^{-3}$ lb s^2/ft^4,
V is the flight speed relative to the air, in ft/sec,
S is the wing area, in ft^2,
C_{D0} is the zero-lift drag coefficient,
K is the lift-induced drag coefficient,
and W is the weight of the aircraft, in lb.

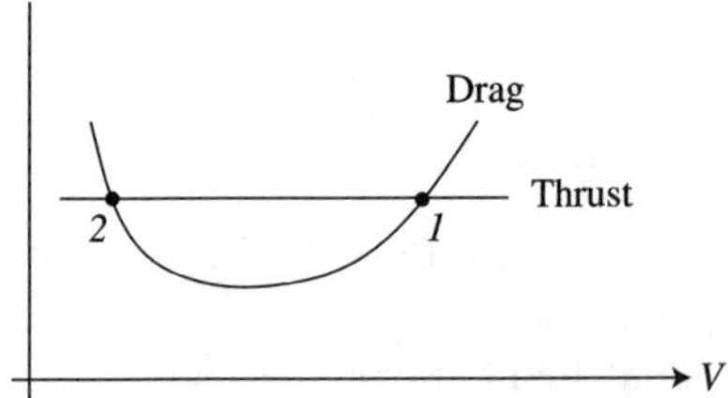

Figure 10.2: *Comparison of drag and thrust at a given altitude.*

If, for a given altitude, we plot the thrust and drag curves against flight speed, we have the curves shown in figure 10.2. This tells us that there are two speeds at which equation (10.1.1) will be satisfied; they can be interpreted as equilibria. Are they stable?

Consider case 1. Let the speed be V_1. If the speed is increased, then there is an increase in drag, with no change in thrust, so the aircraft is slowed down. If the speed is decreased, the drag will decrease, and the aircraft will speed up. In either case, a displacement from the equilibrium will be followed by restoration, so the speed V_1 is termed "statically stable."

Now consider case 2. Let the speed be V_2. If the speed is increased, then the drag will decrease, resulting in continuing increase of the speed. If the speed is decreased, the drag will increase, resulting in continuing decrease of the speed. The speed V_2 is termed "statically unstable."

Now consider equation (10.1.2). The expression for the lifting force on an aircraft is

$$L = \frac{1}{2}\rho_{SL}\sigma SC_L V^2. \tag{10.1.6}$$

C_L, the lift coefficient, will depend on many factors, including Mach number and altitude; but here it will be assumed to be constant for a given aircraft and given initial conditions. One physical interpretation of this assumption is to let the pilot vary the angle of attack to achieve a constant lift coefficient. For given values of the lift coefficient and altitude there exists a unique speed for which the plane will neither descend nor ascend. Any variation in speed or altitude will result in a change in the conditions for steady-state level flight in the vertical plane.

In this model we shall assume that C_{D0}, K, C_L, S and T_{SL} are constant. The weight decrease of the plane as fuel is consumed will also be neglected, so W will be constant. Then, with the x-axis horizontal, in the direction of motion, and the y-axis pointing vertically upward, the dynamical equations follow from Newton's second law as

$$m\frac{d^2x}{dt^2} = T - D, \tag{10.1.7}$$

$$m\frac{d^2y}{dt^2} = L - W. \tag{10.1.8}$$

Substituting equations (10.1.3) and (10.1.5) into (10.1.7) and equation (10.1.6) into (10.1.8), and letting $m = W/g$, we obtain

$$\frac{d^2x}{dt^2} = \frac{gT_{SL}\sigma^{0.7}}{W} - \frac{g\rho_{SL}\sigma V^2 SC_{D0}}{2W} - \frac{2gKW}{\rho_{SL}\sigma V^2 S}, \tag{10.1.9}$$

$$\frac{d^2y}{dt^2} = \frac{g\rho_{SL}\sigma SC_L V^2}{2W} - g. \tag{10.1.10}$$

These are the equations of the model. To run the model, first specify numerical values of the parameters. Then choose initial conditions for a starting speed, dx/dt, with $x = 0$, and starting altitude, y, with dy/dt the initial speed of climbing. Then allow the computer to follow the subsequent flight history.

It is convenient to group the constant terms as

$$A = \frac{T_{SL}}{W}g \qquad B = \frac{g\rho_{SL}SC_{D0}}{2W} \qquad C = \frac{2gKW}{\rho_{SL}S} \qquad E = \frac{g\rho_{SL}S}{2W}$$

Now let $y_1 = x,\ y_2 = \dfrac{dx}{dt},\ y_3 = y,\ y_4 = \dfrac{dy}{dt}$.

The equations are

$$\left.\begin{aligned} \frac{dy_1}{dt} &= y_2, \\ \frac{dy_2}{dt} &= A\sigma^{0.7} - B\sigma V^2 - \frac{C}{\sigma V^2}, \\ \frac{dy_3}{dt} &= y_4, \\ \frac{dy_4}{dt} &= EC_L\sigma V^2 - 32.2, \end{aligned}\right] \tag{10.1.11}$$

where $V^2 = y_2^2 + y_4^2$ and $\sigma = e^{-y_3/30500}$, for $y_3 < 36000$.

The following represent possible values for the parameters for a medium range jet: $W = 140,000$ lb, $S = 2,333$ ft^2, $T_{SL} = 37,800$ lb, $C_{D0} = 0.018$, $K = 0.048$.

These give: $A = 8.694$, $B = 1.1479 \cdot 10^{-5}$, $C = 7.8042 \cdot 10^4$, $E = 6.377 \cdot 10^{-4}$.

Verify that for an altitude of 20,000 ft, the stable and unstable speeds from (10.1.5) are 950 and 170 ft/sec, respectively. Now consider equation (10.1.9) with level flight and confirm the stability and instability of these speeds, by starting with initial speeds close to them.

Next, for chosen initial altitude and speed, find the value of C_L needed for level flight, by setting the right-hand side of (10.1.10) equal to zero. Thereafter, keep it constant, at this value.

Finally, follow flight in two dimensions. Start with level flight ($y_4 = 0$). Don't start too far away from the stable speed.

10.2 The Motion of a Hovercraft

A hovercraft is a vehicle that moves just above the surface of the ground or water, supported on a cushion of air supplied by pumps on the craft that are directed downward. The model for this project is taken from the text by R.H.Cannon [21].[1]

The model is illustrated in figure 10.3. The craft moves through the action of jets directed horizontally. At first, only one jet will be included. Let the craft be a rectangle with mass m, and center of mass C which has coordinates (x, y) with respect to a fixed horizontal reference system. Let the edge which contains the jet make an angle θ with the x-axis. The dependent variables of

[1] R.H.Cannon, Jr., *Dynamics of Physical Systems.* New York: McGraw-Hill Book Company, 1967. With permission from McGraw-Hill Book Company.

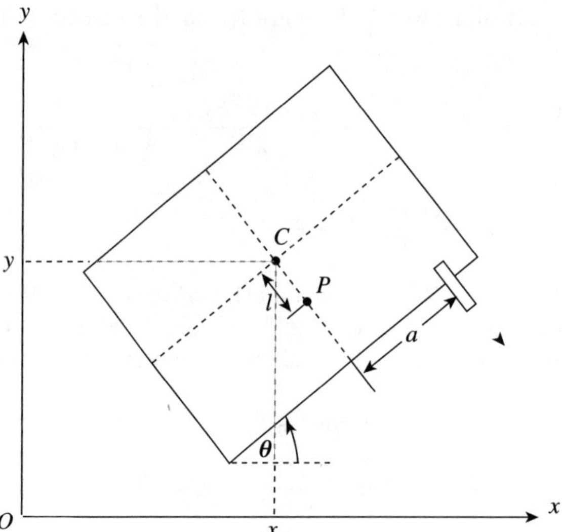

Figure 10.3: *Adapted from R.H.Cannon, Jr., Dynamics of Physical Systems. New York: McGraw-Hill Book Company, 1967.*

the model are x, y and θ. Suppose that, apart from the force of the jet, which has magnitude f, the craft experiences friction with the ground, which can be considered to be concentrated at a point P. P is off-center due to nonsymmetry, and is distant l from C, as shown in the figure. The frictional force is taken to be proportional to the velocity of P with respect to the ground. The coordinates of P are

$$(x + l\sin\theta,\ y - l\cos\theta),$$

so the velocity of P has components

$$\vec{v}_P = \left(\frac{dx}{dt} + l\frac{d\theta}{dt}\cos\theta\right)\hat{x} + \left(\frac{dy}{dt} + l\frac{d\theta}{dt}\sin\theta\right)\hat{y}. \tag{10.2.1}$$

Then the frictional force can be written as $-b\,\vec{v}_P$. The x and y components of the force due to the jet are $f\sin\theta\,\hat{x}$ and $-f\cos\theta\,\hat{y}$; so the differential equations for x and y are

$$\left.\begin{aligned} m\frac{d^2x}{dt^2} &= -b\left(\frac{dx}{dt} + l\frac{d\theta}{dt}\cos\theta\right) + f\sin\theta, \\ m\frac{d^2y}{dt^2} &= -b\left(\frac{dy}{dt} + l\frac{d\theta}{dt}\sin\theta\right) - f\cos\theta. \end{aligned}\right] \tag{10.2.2}$$

Now let I be the moment of inertia of the craft about a vertical axis through C. Then, taking moments about C, we have

$$\begin{aligned} I\frac{d^2\theta}{dt^2} &= af - (l\cos\theta)b\left(\frac{dx}{dt} + l\frac{d\theta}{dt}\cos\theta\right) - (l\sin\theta)b\left(\frac{dy}{dt} + l\frac{d\theta}{dt}\sin\theta\right) \\ &= af - bl\left(\frac{dx}{dt}\cos\theta + \frac{dy}{dt}\sin\theta\right) - bl^2\frac{d\theta}{dt}. \end{aligned} \tag{10.2.3}$$

(10.2.2) and (10.2.3) are the equations of the model.

These equations must be written as six first-order equations. So let

$$y_1 = x,\ y_2 = \frac{dx}{dt},\ y_3 = y,\ y_4 = \frac{dy}{dt},\ y_5 = \theta,\ y_6 = \frac{d\theta}{dt}. \tag{10.2.4}$$

Then

$$\left.\begin{aligned}
\frac{dy_1}{dt} &= y_2,\\
\frac{dy_2}{dt} &= -\frac{b}{m}(y_2 + ly_6\cos y_5) + \frac{f}{m}\sin y_5,\\
\frac{dy_3}{dt} &= y_4,\\
\frac{dy_4}{dt} &= -\frac{b}{m}(y_4 + ly_6\sin y_5) - \frac{f}{m}\cos y_5,\\
\frac{dy_5}{dt} &= y_6,\\
\frac{dy_6}{dt} &= \frac{af}{I} - \frac{bl}{I}(y_2\cos y_5 + y_4\sin y_5) - \frac{bl^2}{I}y_6.
\end{aligned}\right] \tag{10.2.5}$$

For initial conditions, you might as well set all the variables equal to zero. As for the parameters, you can design your own craft. However Cannon suggests the following:

$$\frac{b}{m} = 1\ \text{sec}^{-1},\quad \frac{bl^2}{I} = 2\ \text{sec}^{-1},\quad \frac{f}{bl} = 0.5\ \text{sec}^{-1},\quad a = 1.51.$$

Try these, but also vary the quantities to suit yourself. With just the single jet, plot the path of C. Finally, include more jets in your model.

10.3 Pitching and Rolling at Sea

The model comes from a paper by A.H.Nayfeh, D.T.Mook, and L.R.Marshal [74].[2] If you are not a good sailor, skip this project. Even if you are, you are still lucky that we are only looking at pitching and rolling. The full motion of a ship at sea has six degrees of freedom; these are associated with the motions of pitch, roll, yaw, sway, surge and heave. (I warned you.)

When the ship is at rest, let the x-axis point from stern to prow, and the y-axis from port to starboard; so the x-y plane is horizontal. The angle of pitching is measured as a rotation of θ about the y-axis, and that of rolling as a rotation of ϕ about the x-axis. In the model these angles are considered to be small. To build the equations for the model start with the uncoupled equations

$$\left.\begin{aligned}
\frac{d^2\theta}{dt^2} + c_1\frac{d\theta}{dt} + \omega_1^2\theta &= M_1\cos(\Omega t + \tau_1),\\
\frac{d^2\phi}{dt^2} + c_2\frac{d\phi}{dt} + \omega_2^2\phi &= M_2\cos(\Omega t + \tau_2).
\end{aligned}\right] \tag{10.3.1}$$

These represent harmonic oscillators with natural frequencies ω_1 for pitching, and ω_2 for rolling. Resisting terms proportional to the angular rates of change are added; the coefficients c_1 and c_2 can be interpreted in terms of the ship's stabilizers. If the sea is calm, then the terms on the right will be zero. But suppose that the ship is in a "regular" sea with waves given by the frequency Ω; then the forcing terms must be included. (The quantities τ_1 and τ_2 are phase terms.) Each equation is

[2] A.H.Nayfeh, D.T.Mook, and L.R.Marshal, "Nonlinear coupling of pitch and roll modes in ship motions," *Journal of Hydronautics* 7: (1973), 145–152. Copyright ©American Institute of Aeronautics and Astronautics and reprinted with permission.

linear and is discussed in any introductory course on differential equations. Note that if Ω is close to either of the natural frequencies, then there is going to be trouble due to near resonance.

In practice, the energy associated with pitching and rolling can be exchanged between one mode and the other. So the equations must be coupled. The coupling terms used in the cited paper [74] modify (10.3.1) to become

$$\left.\begin{aligned}\frac{d^2\theta}{dt^2}+c_1\frac{d\theta}{dt}+\omega_1^2\theta &= M_1\cos(\Omega t+\tau_1)+k_1\phi^2,\\ \frac{d^2\phi}{dt^2}+c_2\frac{d\phi}{dt}+\omega_2^2\phi &= M_2\cos(\Omega t+\tau_2)+k_2\theta\phi.\end{aligned}\right] \tag{10.3.2}$$

This coupling is especially strong when the pitch frequency is approximately twice the roll frequency. This quality first arose as the result of observation; it received theoretical explanation in the paper [74]. The authors used theoretical perturbation methods to solve the differential equations, with numerical methods employed to verify the results; we shall have to confine ourselves to the latter exercise.

Let $\omega_1 = 1$. Then consider values of ω_2 close to 0.5. The difference $(\omega_2 - 0.5)$ can be one of the parameters of the model to be varied. It is remarked in [74] that provided Ω is not close to one of ω_1, ω_2, $\omega_1/4$, or $3\omega_1/4$, then the linear approximation of the model is adequate. So if you want to cause trouble and excite the nonlinear coupling, choose Ω near to one of these values.

The constants k_1 and k_2 can be eliminated from the equations by letting

$$\overline{\theta} = k_2\theta, \quad \overline{\phi} = (k_1k_2)^{1/2}\phi.$$

Then if

$$\overline{M}_1 = k_2M_1, \quad \overline{M}_2 = (k_1k_2)^{1/2}M_2,$$

it follows that the equations with the barred quantities are the same as the original equations, (10.3.2), but without k_1 and k_2. Therefore, in working numerically with (10.3.2), it is all right to set $k_1 = k_2 = 1$. Also you might let $\tau_1 = \tau_2 = 0$.

Start the project off with $M_1 = M_2 = 0$ and low resistance, $c_1 = c_2 = 0.001$, for instance. Give yourself a little initial rolling, say, and see what happens; you will experience some interchange of energy between the rolling and pitching motions. Try this with ω_2 close to and far from the critical value of 0.5.

Now introduce a "regular" sea. Since you will be looking for resonance effects, where a small stimulus can produce a large result, M_1 and M_2 need not be large. For fixed ω_2 take different values of Ω, so that at least one of the critical values mentioned is spanned. You should observe a phenomenon known as *saturation*. Start with pitching alone; the pitching will increase until the pitching mode becomes saturated, and then additional energy entering the system is fed into the rolling mode.

With the companionship of a computer we can endure conditions which we would rather not experience at sea. To enjoy this, model you can design your boat in such a manner that no sane ship builder would ever contemplate, and subject it to conditions unthinkable even for your worst enemy. So here goes! Figures 10.4(a) to (d) show change in the pitch and roll angles as functions of the time. Parameters were chosen as follows: the natural frequencies, $\omega_1 = 1, \omega_2 = 0.5$; the frequency of the waves, $\Omega = 0.5$; the resisting, or stabilizing terms, $c_1 = 0.0001, c_2 = 0.001$; the terms linking pitching and rolling, $k_1 = 1, k_2 = 1$, as indicated above. Then the amplitudes of the forcing terms were $\overline{M}_1 = 0.001, \overline{M}_2 = 0.002$. All starting conditions were zero with the exception of the initial angular velocity of the pitching. In figure 10.4(a) the initial value was $\dot{\theta}_0 = 5°$ per unit time. The interchange of energy between pitching and rolling is clear; the amplitudes remain bounded. In figure 10.4(b), $\dot{\theta}_0 = 10°$ per unit time; we observe in figure 10.4(c), $\dot{\theta}_0 = 14.6°$ per unit time; now things appear to be irregular, and maybe chaotic. Finally, in figure 10.4(d), there is a small increase to $\dot{\theta}_0 = 15°$ per unit time. Get another boat!

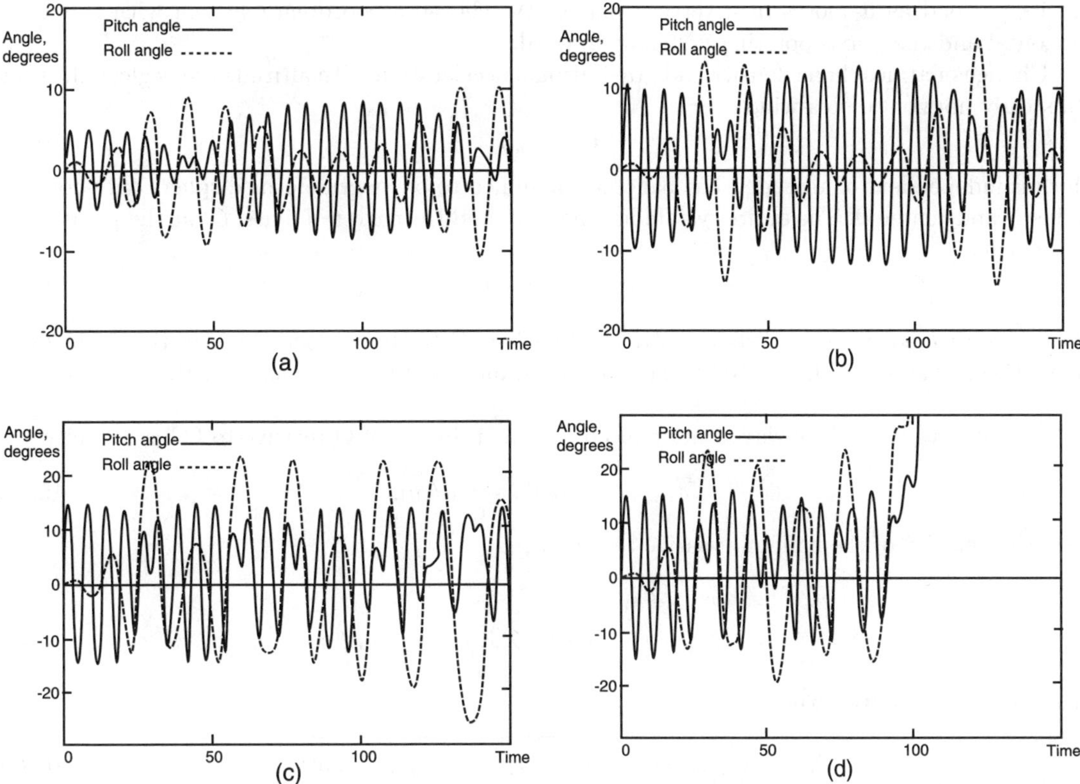

Figure 10.4: *Each figure shows plots of the pitch and roll angles as functions of the time. Initially, these angles are zero, as is the rate of change of the roll angle. The initial pitch angular velocity is: (a) $\dot{\theta}_0 = 5$, (b) $\dot{\theta}_0 = 10$, $\dot{\theta}_0 = 14.6$, and (d) $\dot{\theta}_0 = 15$; each in degrees per unit time. In (a) and (b) we see the interchange of energy between pitching and rolling; things become uncomfortably chaotic in (c), and fatal in (d).*

Since it is the amplitude of the oscillations that may make you unhappy in a rough sea, a good way to investigate the system is by the method of variation of parameters. Let

$$\left.\begin{aligned} \theta &= A_1\cos(\omega_1 t - \delta_1), & \frac{d\theta}{dt} &= -A_1\omega_1\sin(\omega_1 t - \delta_1), \\ \text{and}\qquad \phi &= A_2\cos(\omega_2 t - \delta_2), & \frac{d\phi}{dt} &= -A_2\omega_2\sin(\omega_2 t - \delta_2). \end{aligned}\right] \tag{10.3.3}$$

Let A_1, A_2, δ_1, and δ_2 become variables. Express equations (10.3.2) as four first-order differential equations, and substitute the expressions (10.3.3) into them. Solve the resulting equations for the four derivatives of A_1, A_2, δ_1, and δ_2. This will give you, directly, differential equations for the amplitudes.

10.4 The Motion of a Balloon and its Payload

I am grateful to the author for his permission to use some of his material in the discussion that follows. In this model, which is due to R.A.Bachman [5],[3] we shall follow the motion of a balloon

[3] Abstracted, with permission, from "Idealized Dynamics of Balloon Flight," R.A. Bachman. *American Journal of Physics*, **52** (1984) 309–312. Copyright ©1984, American Association of Physics Teachers.

and its payload as it moves in a vertical plane. We choose a coordinate system with the x-axis horizontal and the y-axis pointing vertically upward.

Change of atmospheric density and gravitational acceleration with altitude are neglected. There is a steady horizontal crosswind,

$$\vec{v}_w = v_w \hat{x}, \tag{10.4.1}$$

which is independent of altitude. The balloon is assumed to be an undeformed sphere with constant radius R and center O. The entire system has mass m, and the center of mass, C, at the point (x, y), has velocity

$$\vec{v}_{cm} = v_x \hat{x} + v_y \hat{y}. \tag{10.4.2}$$

$\overrightarrow{CO} = \vec{L}$, with L equal to the distance CO. The line from O to the payload P makes the angle θ with the vertical, as shown in figure 10.5. The moment of inertia of the system about the center of mass is I.

$\dot{\theta}$ is positive for a clockwise rotation of OP, so the rotation of O relative to C has velocity

$$\vec{v}_{rot} = L\dot{\theta}(\cos\theta\,\hat{x} - \sin\theta\,\hat{y}). \tag{10.4.3}$$

Then the velocity of the balloon, relative to the air, is

$$\begin{aligned}\vec{v}_{rel} &= \vec{v}_w - (\vec{v}_{cm} + \vec{v}_{rot}) \\ &= (v_w - v_x - L\dot{\theta}\cos\theta)\hat{x} + (-v_y + L\dot{\theta}\sin\theta)\hat{y}.\end{aligned} \tag{10.4.4}$$

$\vec{v}_{rel}$ has magnitude v_{rel} where

$$v_{rel} = \sqrt{(v_w - v_x - L\dot{\theta}\cos\theta)^2 + (-v_y + L\dot{\theta}\sin\theta)^2}. \tag{10.4.5}$$

We consider three forces on the system: drag, gravity and buoyancy. The drag force is proportional to the square of v_{rel} and will take the form

$$\begin{aligned}\vec{F}_D &= \frac{1}{2} C_D \pi R^2 \rho v_{rel} \vec{v}_{rel} \\ &= k v_{rel} \vec{v}_{rel},\end{aligned} \tag{10.4.6}$$

where ρ is the atmospheric density. The point of action of the drag force is the center of the balloon.

The force due to gravity is

$$\vec{F}_g = -mg\hat{y}. \tag{10.4.7}$$

By Archimedes' principle, the buoyant force is equal to the weight of the displaced air. So

$$\vec{F}_b = \frac{4}{3}\pi R^3 \rho g \hat{y}, \tag{10.4.8}$$

acting through the center of the balloon, O.

To find the variation of θ, we need the torque about the center of mass

$$\vec{\tau} = \vec{L} \times \vec{F}_b + \vec{L} \times \vec{F}_D. \tag{10.4.9}$$

If $\hat{z} = \hat{x} \times \hat{y}$, then

$$\vec{L} \times \vec{F}_b = L \| \vec{F}_b \| \sin\theta\,\hat{z} = \frac{4}{3}\pi R^3 L \rho g \sin\theta\,\hat{z}.$$

Also

$$\begin{aligned}\vec{L} \times \vec{F}_D &= \Big(L\sin\theta\, k v_{rel}(-v_y + L\dot{\theta}\sin\theta) - L\cos\theta\, k v_{rel}(v_w - v_x - L\dot{\theta}\cos\theta)\Big)\,\hat{z} \\ &= kLv_{rel}\Big(L\dot{\theta} - v_y\sin\theta + (v_w - v_x)\cos\theta\Big)\,\hat{z}.\end{aligned}$$

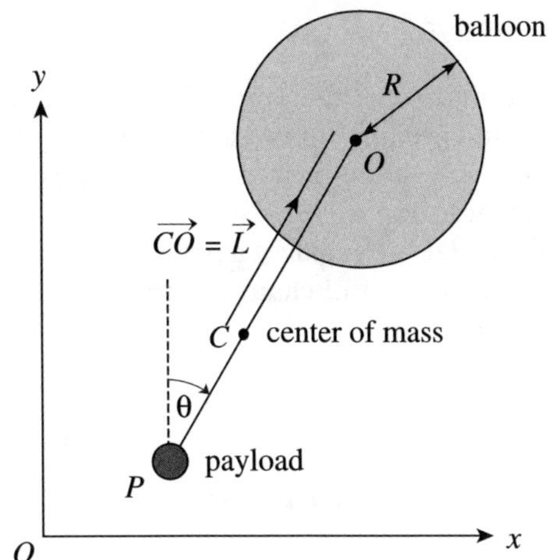

Figure 10.5: *A balloon and its payload.*

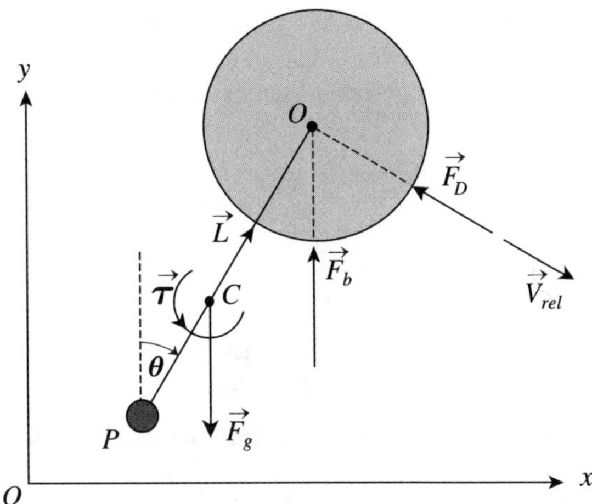

Figure 10.6: *The forces on the balloon.*

With the definition of θ, and the sense in which it is increasing, we have

$$\vec{\tau} = I\dot{\vec{\omega}} = -I\ddot{\theta}\hat{z}. \tag{10.4.10}$$

We can now summarize the equations for the model

$$\left.\begin{aligned} m\frac{dv_x}{dt} &= k(v_w - v_x - L\frac{d\theta}{dt}\cos\theta)v_{rel}, \\ m\frac{dv_y}{dt} &= k(-v_y + L\frac{d\theta}{dt}\sin\theta)v_{rel} + \frac{4}{3}\pi R^3\rho g - mg, \\ I\frac{d^2\theta}{dt^2} &= -\frac{4}{3}\pi R^3 L\rho g\sin\theta - kLv_{rel}\left(L\frac{d\theta}{dt} - v_y\sin\theta + (v_w - v_x)\cos\theta\right). \end{aligned}\right] \tag{10.4.11}$$

In running this model it is wise to start with an equilibrium for which $\dot{\theta} = 0$. Then move carefully away from the equilibrium. There are many parameters that can be varied; you could, for instance, let the cross-wind be a function of the time.

10.5 Jogging with a Companion

Two joggers are running around a circular track. Either one may like or dislike the other and this may influence their tactics in speeding up or slowing down. We shall look at several possible models; none is very satisfactory, so you are invited to make up your own.

Let O be the center of the track, and let A be some reference point on the track. If the runners are at points P_1 and P_2, let OP_1 and OP_2 make angles θ_1 and θ_2 respectively with OA. We shall only treat running speeds in terms of rates of change of these angles.

The equations for the first model are

$$\left.\begin{aligned}\frac{d\theta_1}{dt} &= \omega_1 + k_1 \sin(\theta_2 - \theta_1),\\ \frac{d\theta_2}{dt} &= \omega_2 + k_2 \sin(\theta_1 - \theta_2).\end{aligned}\right] \tag{10.5.1}$$

Here ω_1 and ω_2 are the angular rates that the joggers would adopt if they were alone. k_1 and k_2 are parameters that depend on how strongly the joggers feel about one another: positive for attraction and negative for repulsion. Finally, it is assumed that the greatest incentive to deviate from ω_1 and ω_2 occurs when the joggers are 90° apart, with the incentive zero if they are together or separated by 180°.

Let $\phi = \theta_1 - \theta_2$. Then, subtracting the second equation of (10.5.1) from the first, we have

$$\frac{d\phi}{dt} = \omega_1 - \omega_2 - (k_1 + k_2)\sin\phi. \tag{10.5.2}$$

There are equilibria if

$$|(\omega_1 - \omega_2)/(k_1 + k_2)| < 1, \tag{10.5.3}$$

when it is at

$$\sin\phi_e = \frac{\omega_1 - \omega_2}{k_1 + k_2}. \tag{10.5.4}$$

If there is no equilibrium, the joggers will continue to lap one another, although moving at varying rates, since $\dot{\phi}$ will always be positive or negative. If (10.5.3) is satisfied, then there will be two equilibria; you should verify that one is stable and the other, unstable, and that solutions approach the stable equilibrium asymptotically. This produces the odd result that (unless $\omega_1 = \omega_2$), however much the joggers may like one another, they do not run together, although they eventually run at the same speed.

For maximum enjoyment, you should follow the progress of the separate angles θ_1 and θ_2. Fix one parameter, say $\omega_1 = 1$, and vary the other three. There can be some entertaining scenarios when the k_i have opposite signs: the first jogger may like the second, but the second cannot stand the first. See if you can make one jogger change direction in order to avoid the other!

A drawback of the preceding model is that there really should be an equilibrium when $\theta_1 - \theta_2 = 0$, or, with sufficient ill-will, when $\theta_1 - \theta_2 = \pi$; or, if there is no equilibrium, then small oscillations around these states should be possible. Also the circumstances will provide the urge for a jogger to change speed, that is, to accelerate or decelerate. In addition, in a realistic model, the joggers should be able to start from rest. Let the normal rates of jogging be ω_{n1} and ω_{n2}, and the maximum rates, ω_{m1} and ω_{m2}. Consider the following

$$\left.\begin{aligned}\frac{d^2\theta_1}{dt^2} &= p_1\left(\omega_{n1} - \frac{d\theta_1}{dt}\right) + k_1\sin(\theta_2 - \theta_1)\left(\omega_{m1} - \frac{d\theta_1}{dt}\right),\\ \frac{d^2\theta_2}{dt^2} &= p_2\left(\omega_{n2} - \frac{d\theta_2}{dt}\right) + k_2\sin(\theta_1 - \theta_2)\left(\omega_{m2} - \frac{d\theta_2}{dt}\right).\end{aligned}\right] \tag{10.5.5}$$

Experiment with this model and see if it can be more true to life. If you introduce hostility, so that a jogger may reverse direction, then the absolute values of the derivatives should be used in the right-hand sides.

Finally, see if you can produce a better model for the variation of attraction with $\theta_1 - \theta_2$. For instance, instead of $\sin(\theta_1 - \theta_2)$, you might try

$$\sin(\theta_1 - \theta_2)\cos^2\left((\theta_1 - \theta_2)/2\right).$$

This emphasizes the interval $0 < |\theta_1 - \theta_2| < \pi/2$ over $\pi/2 < |\theta_1 - \theta_2| < \pi$. Or how about

$$\left.\begin{aligned} \frac{d^2\theta_1}{dt^2} &= p_1\left(\omega_{n1} - \frac{d\theta_1}{dt}\right) + k_1\psi(\theta_2 - \theta_1)\left(\omega_{m1} - \frac{d\theta_1}{dt}\right), \\ \frac{d^2\theta_2}{dt^2} &= p_2\left(\omega_{n2} - \frac{d\theta_2}{dt}\right) + k_2\psi(\theta_1 - \theta_2)\left(\omega_{m2} - \frac{d\theta_2}{dt}\right), \end{aligned}\right] \tag{10.5.6}$$

where

$$\psi(x) = \begin{cases} 1, & \text{if } \sin(x) > 0, \\ -1 & \text{if } \sin(x) < 0, \\ 0 & \text{if } \sin(x) = 0. \end{cases} \tag{10.5.7}$$

Experiment for yourself.

10.6 A Bunjy Jump

The first bunjy jump is reputed to have occurred in 1986 when a New Zealander attached one end of a length of elastic to himself and the other end to the Eiffel tower, in Paris, and jumped. Since then, the activity has become quite popular, especially in New Zealand, where recreation, spiced with a little risk, is very popular. (As a notice stated at one recreational center: "Too much is not enough!") Typically the participant pays out quite a lot of money, has one end of the bunjy attached to his or her ankles, jumps or dives off a bridge and oscillates a few times before being lowered to the river bank, or hauled up with a rope. There is sometimes the option of being dunked in the river at the end of the initial descent. Typically, the height of the bridge may be 120 ft above the water, but much greater drops can be arranged for those who don't mind falling off a helicopter.

For the model, take the origin at the initial jumping point, and let the z-axis point vertically downward. We assume that air resistance is proportional to the square of the speed. Depending on the construction of the bunjy, there may be separate links rubbing against each other as it expands and contracts; if the resulting friction is modeled as dry friction, then the resisting force will be d, a constant.

If the unstretched length of the bunjy is L, then we assume that when it is stretched, the restoring force is proportional to $z - L$. The differential equation of motion can be written as

$$\frac{W}{g}\frac{d^2z}{dt^2} = W - f_r\left(r\left(\frac{dz}{dt}\right)^2 + d\right) - f_k k(z - L). \tag{10.6.1}$$

Here W is the weight of the jumper, k is the "spring" constant for the bunjy, and r is a constant for the resistance. f_r is a factor that is equal to $+1$ when $dz/dt > 0$ and -1 when $dz/dt < 0$. f_k is a factor that is equal to 0 when $z < L$ and 1 when $z > L$.

(10.6.1) can be written as

$$\frac{d^2z}{dt^2} = g - f_r\left(R\left(\frac{dz}{dt}\right)^2 + D\right) - f_k K(z - L). \tag{10.6.2}$$

If we let

$$y_1 = z, \text{ and } y_2 = \frac{dz}{dt},$$

then

$$\left.\begin{aligned} \frac{dy_1}{dt} &= y_2, \\ \frac{dy_2}{dt} &= -g - f_r(Ry_2^2 + D) - f_k K(y_1 - L), \end{aligned}\right] \tag{10.6.3}$$

where

$$f_r = \begin{bmatrix} +1, & y_2 > 0, \\ -1, & y_2 < 0, \end{bmatrix} \quad f_k = \begin{bmatrix} 0, & y_1 < L, \\ 1, & y_1 > L. \end{bmatrix} \tag{10.6.4}$$

Now design your bunjy. I suggest that you start with numerical values for L, K, R and D. Try $R = 0.005$, which is on the high side, and experiment with values of D. If the unstretched length of the bunjy is $L = 30$ft, find a value of K so that the greatest value of z is equal to an assigned value (just above the water).

Now assume that the values of R and K refer to a specific weight, say 150lb. The next candidate for the jump weighs 160lb. Then for him, the values of R and K are changed by the factor 150/160. If you use $L = 30$, he is going to get wet (and you need to modify the model to include drag through water); find a new value of L so that he stops just short of the water. Repeat this for a lighter weight. The drag coefficient k will be uncertain; find out what happens (especially to the depth of the lowest point) when it is diminished or increased.

For a detailed project, suppose that you have been hired as a consultant to design the bunjy for a specific location. Draw up specifications and include instructions for choosing suitable values of L for different weights. Allow for variation in the drag coefficient.

10.7 A Model for the Motion of a Yo-yo

Whenever I try to play with a yo-yo it descends to its lowest point and stays there; but I can do better on the computer.

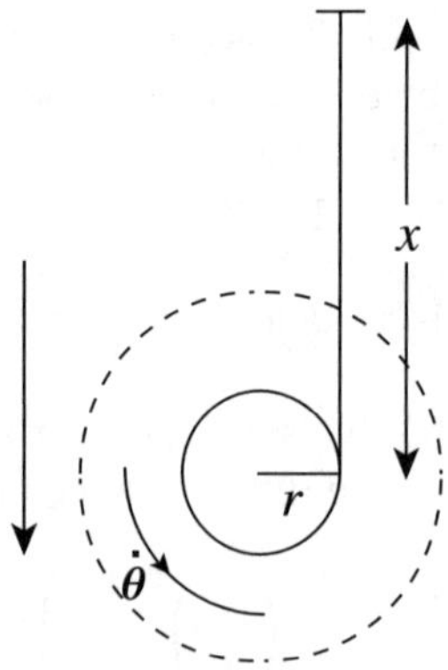

Figure 10.7: *A descending yo-yo.*

When a yo-yo descends, its angular velocity increases. The kinetic energy of this rotation comes at the expense of the energy of descent, so that after release, the yo-yo may first accelerate and then slow down. When fully unwound, the yo-yo can rotate freely, or *sleep*, with the end of the string looped around a central cylindrical peg. It is then that the operator can perform tricks such as "walking the dog," so the greater the speed of rotation at the lowest point, the better. To start the ascent, friction is re-established between the string and peg.

As the yo-yo descends, the string unwinds, and the radius of the combination "peg and string" decreases. Suppose that the outer radius of the combination, when the string is fully wound, is r_1 and the radius of the peg itself is r_0. Let the radius be r when a length s is wound around the peg. Then if the yo-yo has turned through the angle θ since starting to unwind,

$$r = r_1 - \alpha\theta \tag{10.7.1}$$

for constant α. This will depend in part on the thickness of the string; it can be found by specifying r_0, r_1, and the total length, l, of the string. Now

$$ds = -r d\theta, \text{ so } \frac{ds}{d\theta} = -r = -r_1 + \alpha\theta. \tag{10.7.2}$$

When $s = l$, $r = r_1$ and $\theta = 0$. When $s = 0$, $r = r_0$, let $\theta = T$. Integrating equation (10.7.2),

$$s = -r_1\theta + \frac{1}{2}\alpha\theta^2 + c = -r_1\theta + \frac{1}{2}\alpha\theta^2 + l,$$

so

$$0 = -r_1 T + \frac{1}{2}\alpha T^2 + l. \tag{10.7.3}$$

From equation (10.7.1), $r_0 = r_1 - \alpha T$. Multiplying equation (10.7.3) by α,

$$\begin{aligned} 0 &= r_1(\alpha T) + \frac{1}{2}(\alpha T)^2 + \alpha l \\ &= -r_1(r_1 - r_0) + \frac{1}{2}(r_1 - r_0)^2 + \alpha l \\ &= -\frac{1}{2}\left(r_1^2 - r_0^2\right) + \alpha l, \end{aligned}$$

so

$$\alpha = \frac{1}{2l}\left(r_1^2 - r_0^2\right). \tag{10.7.4}$$

We shall assume that the yo-yo descends vertically from a point that remains fixed, and that the angle between the string and the vertical can be neglected. We shall also assume that the string is non-elastic, and that its mass can be neglected. If the yo-yo has descended a distance x and rotated through an angle θ then

$$dx = r d\theta, \text{ or } \frac{d\theta}{dt} = \frac{1}{r}\frac{dx}{dt}. \tag{10.7.5}$$

Let the mass of the yo-yo be M and the moment of inertia about the central peg be I. Then the Lagrangian is

$$\begin{aligned} L &= \frac{1}{2}M\dot{x}^2 + \frac{1}{2}I\dot{\theta}^2 + Mgx \\ &= \frac{1}{2}\dot{x}^2\left(M + I/r^2\right) + Mgx. \end{aligned} \tag{10.7.6}$$

Using

$$\frac{dr}{dt} = -\alpha\frac{d\theta}{dt} = -\frac{\alpha}{r}\frac{dx}{dt} \text{ and } \frac{dr}{dx} = \frac{dr}{d\theta}\frac{d\theta}{dx} = -\frac{\alpha}{r},$$

we find the equation of motion to be

$$\frac{d^2x}{dt^2}\left(M + \frac{I}{r^2}\right) + \frac{\alpha I}{r^4}\left(\frac{dx}{dt}\right)^2 = Mg. \tag{10.7.7}$$

This must be solved simultaneously with the second equation of (10.7.5). Let

$$y_1 = \theta,\ y_2 = x,\ y_3 = \dot{x}. \tag{10.7.8}$$

Then the system of equations to be solved is

$$\left.\begin{aligned} r &= r_1 - \alpha y_1, \\ \frac{dy_1}{dt} &= \frac{1}{r} y_3, \\ \frac{dy_2}{dt} &= y_3, \\ \frac{dy_3}{dt} &= \left(g - \frac{\alpha I/M}{r^4} y_3^2\right) \Big/ \left(1 + \frac{I/M}{r^2}\right). \end{aligned}\right] \tag{10.7.9}$$

The parameters, r_0, r_1, l and I/M depend on how you choose to design your yo-yo. If the radius of the yo-yo is R, then the ratio I/M could be as small as $R^2/5$ or as large as R^2; the largest value would refer to a model with most of the mass in metal rings around the outer circumference. You might examine actual yo-yos, or use your imagination.

For initial conditions, the time $t = 0$, $\theta = 0$ and $x = 0$. Experiment with different starting values of $\dot{x}(0) = \dot{x}_0$. The descent ceases when $x = l$. To start the ascent, reverse the sign of $\dot{x}$ and then continue the integration. An effective way to present results is to graph x, $\dot{x}$ and $\dot{\theta}$ as functions of the time. This shows the dramatic change in $\dot{x}$ during the descent.

The conservation of energy is given by

$$\frac{1}{2}\dot{x}^2 \left(M + I/r^2\right) - Mgx = E = \frac{1}{2}\dot{x}_0^2 \left(M + I/r_1^2\right), \tag{10.7.10}$$

where E has been evaluated for a descent. This provides information on the variation of $\dot{x}$, and so $\dot{\theta}$ as x changes; but to follow the time variation, you need to solve the differential equations.

This model allows plenty of scope for experiment. It can be generalized; for instance, non-vertical motion could be introduced by defining the angle between the string and the downward vertical to be ϕ, and the length of the string to be ρ. Then the Lagrangian becomes

$$L = \frac{1}{2}M(\dot{\rho}^2 + \rho^2\dot{\phi}^2) + \frac{1}{2}I(\dot{\theta} \pm \dot{\phi})^2 + Mg\rho\cos\phi, \tag{10.7.11}$$

where the sign of the $\pm$ depends on whether the rotation of the yo-yo is clockwise or counterclockwise. Since $\dot{\theta}$ is likely to be much larger numerically than $\dot{\phi}$, the term $\pm\dot{\phi}$ can probably be neglected.

Another variation is to retain vertical motion, but have the hand move up or down in some predetermined way.

10.8 Chaos in the Amusement Park

The title for this project is taken from a paper by R.L.Kautz and B.M.Huggard [62].[4] I am grateful to the authors for their permission to use some of their material in the discussion that follows. The Tilt-a-whirl consists of seven identical circular platforms rotating about a central axis; and passing over a sinusoidal curve. Each platform rotates about its center, and holds a chair which is off-center. One such platform is illustrated in figure 10.8. The rotation around the central axis is driven at a constant angular rate. The rotation of each platform about its center is free, and is chaotic.

[4]Abstracted, with permission, from "Chaos at the Amusement Park: Dynamics of the Tilt-a-Whirl," R.L. Kautz & B.M. Huggard. *American Journal of Physics*, **62** (1994) 59–66. Copyright ©1994, American Association of Physics Teachers.

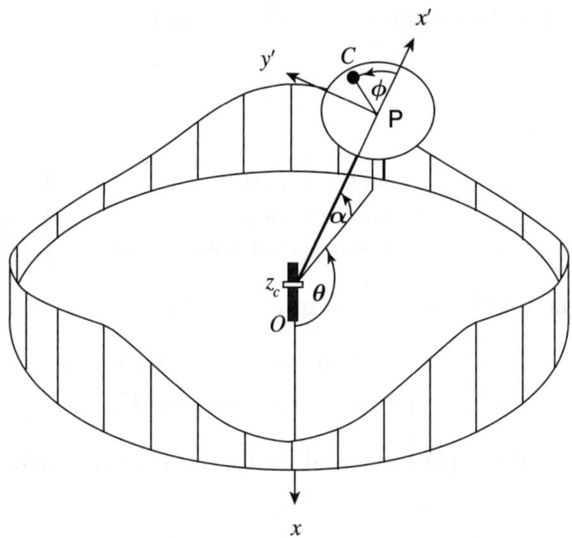

Figure 10.8: *One platform of a Tilt-a-Whirl.*

We shall follow the motion of one platform. The rod attached to the platform, which has center P, joins the central axis at z_c above the origin, O; the x-y plane is horizontal, with the z axis pointing upward. The angle between the rod OP and the x-y plane is α, and the projection of OP in the x-y plane makes the angle θ with the x-axis. On the platform there are local coordinates, x' and y', with the x' axis parallel to OP, as shown. The y' axis is parallel to the curve over which the platform is riding, and makes the angle β with the horizontal, as shown in figure 10.9. The chair is at C. The lengths of OP and PC are r_1 and r_2, respectively.

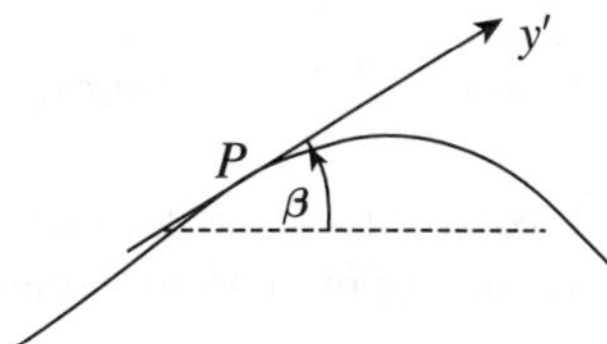

Figure 10.9: *The vertical motion of a platform.*

The angles α and β are sufficiently small (around 10° at most) for their squares or products to be ignored. So the cosine of any one will be taken to equal one. This means that, so far as x- and y- coordinates are concerned, the angles can be neglected. The curve on which the platform rides is given by

$$\alpha = \alpha_0 - \alpha_1 \cos 3\theta, \tag{10.8.1}$$

where α_0 and α_1 are also small. The coordinates of P are

$$\left.\begin{array}{rcccl} x_p &=& r_1 \cos\alpha \cos\theta &=& r_1 \cos\theta, \\ y_p &=& r_1 \cos\alpha \sin\theta &=& r_1 \sin\theta, \\ z_p &=& z_c + r_1 \sin\alpha &=& z_c + r_1 \alpha. \end{array}\right] \tag{10.8.2}$$

Maintaining these approximations,

$$\beta = \tan\beta = \frac{1}{r_1}\frac{dz_p}{d\theta} = 3\alpha_1 \sin 3\theta. \tag{10.8.3}$$

If ω is the rate of rotation of the platform about the z-axis, then

$$\theta = \omega t. \tag{10.8.4}$$

The coordinates of C are

$$\left.\begin{aligned} x &= r_1\cos\theta + r_2\cos(\theta+\phi), \\ y &= r_1\sin\theta + r_2\sin(\theta+\phi), \\ z &= z_c + r_1\alpha + r_2(\alpha\cos\phi + \beta\sin\phi). \end{aligned}\right] \tag{10.8.5}$$

Here PC makes the angle ϕ with Px', as shown in figure 10.8. Then we have the derivatives

$$\begin{aligned} \dot{x} &= -r_1\omega\sin\theta - r_2(\omega+\dot{\phi})\sin(\theta+\phi), \\ \dot{y} &= r_1\omega\cos\theta + r_2(\omega+\dot{\phi})\cos(\theta+\phi). \end{aligned}$$

We shall neglect the mass of the platform, and let the mass of the chair and its occupants be m. Then the Lagrangian is

$$\begin{aligned} L &= \frac{1}{2}m(\dot{x}^2+\dot{y}^2+\dot{z}^2) - mgz \\ &= \frac{1}{2}m\left(r_1^2\omega^2 + r_2^2(\omega+\dot{\phi})^2 + 2r_1r_2\omega(\omega+\dot{\phi})\cos\phi\right) \\ &\quad -mg\left(z_c + r_1\alpha + r_2(\alpha\cos\phi+\beta\sin\phi)\right). \end{aligned} \tag{10.8.6}$$

Note that $\dot{z}^2$ does not contribute to the kinetic energy. The differential equation of motion is

$$mr_2^2\frac{d^2\phi}{dt^2} + mr_1r_2\omega^2\sin\phi = mgr_2(\alpha\sin\phi - \beta\cos\phi). \tag{10.8.7}$$

Finally, a resisting term proportional to $\dot{\phi}$ is added, so that the equation for the model becomes

$$mr_2^2\frac{d^2\phi}{dt^2} + k\frac{d\phi}{dt} + mr_1r_2\omega^2\sin\phi = mgr_2(\alpha\sin\phi - \beta\cos\phi). \tag{10.8.8}$$

This is to be used in conjunction with equations (10.8.1), (10.8.3) and (10.8.4).

Kautz and Huggard suggest the following numerical values:

$$r_1 = 4.3 \text{ m},\ r_2 = 0.8 \text{ m},\ \alpha_0 = 0.036 \text{ rad.},\ \alpha_1 = 0.058 \text{ rad.},\ \omega/2\pi = 6.5 \text{ rpm}.$$

The parameter k/m is to be varied in experiments. You are free to use these, or other values, provided that the angles remain small, and you observe safety regulations. Any of the techniques used for investigating chaotic forced systems can be applied.

10.9 Playing Ball in a Space Station

In future space stations the effects of gravity will be simulated by rotating the station. Let the angular velocity of rotation be ω about the z_1-axis. With the origin at a point on the axis of rotation, and the x_1 and y_1 axes rotating with the spacecraft, the equations of motion of a freely moving object are

$$\left.\begin{aligned} \frac{d^2x_1}{dt^2} &= 2\omega\frac{dy_1}{dt} + \omega^2x_1, \\ \frac{d^2y_1}{dt^2} &= -2\omega\frac{dx_1}{dt} + \omega^2y_1, \\ \frac{d^2z_1}{dt^2} &= 0. \end{aligned}\right] \tag{10.9.1}$$

The terms on the right are the Coriolis and centrifugal accelerations. Now let the radius of the station be R. Set the new origin at the point $x_1 = -R$ with axes $x_2,\ y_2,\ z_2$ parallel to the old axes. Then, since, $x_2 = x_1 + R$,

$$\left.\begin{aligned} \frac{d^2x_2}{dt^2} &= 2\omega\frac{dy_2}{dt} + \omega^2 x_2 - \omega^2 R, \\ \frac{d^2y_2}{dt^2} &= -2\omega\frac{dx_2}{dt} + \omega^2 y_2, \\ \frac{d^2z_2}{dt^2} &= 0. \end{aligned}\right] \tag{10.9.2}$$

The term $-\omega^2 R$ is equal to the simulated gravitational acceleration at the origin.

In the models for sports, we kept to the convention that the x-axis pointed forward (from the pitcher to the batter, for instance) and the z-axis pointed upward. We shall use the same convention here, so that those models can be more easily adapted. Two cases will be considered:

1. The y-axis is parallel to the axis of rotation. Then the notation of (10.9.2) is changed so that $z_2 = y,\ x_2 = z,\ y_2 = x$. Then

$$\left.\begin{aligned} \frac{d^2x}{dt^2} &= -2\omega\frac{dz}{dt} + \omega^2 x, \\ \frac{d^2y}{dt^2} &= 0, \\ \frac{d^2z}{dt^2} &= 2\omega\frac{dx}{dt} + \omega^2 z - \omega^2 R. \end{aligned}\right] \tag{10.9.3}$$

2. The x-axis is parallel to the axis of rotation. Let's modify (10.9.2) so that the origin is on the y_1-axis, with new coordinates $x_3,\ y_3,\ z_3$. Then

$$\left.\begin{aligned} \frac{d^2x_3}{dt^2} &= 2\omega\frac{dy_3}{dt} + \omega^2 x_3, \\ \frac{d^2y_3}{dt^2} &= -2\omega\frac{dx_3}{dt} + \omega^2 y_3 - \omega^2 R, \\ \frac{d^2z_3}{dt^2} &= 0. \end{aligned}\right] \tag{10.9.4}$$

Now let $z_3 = x\ x_3 = y,\ y_3 = z$. Then

$$\left.\begin{aligned} \frac{d^2x}{dt^2} &= 0, \\ \frac{d^2y}{dt^2} &= 2\omega\frac{dz}{dt} + \omega^2 y, \\ \frac{d^2z}{dt^2} &= -2\omega\frac{dy}{dt} + \omega^2 z - \omega^2 R. \end{aligned}\right] \tag{10.9.5}$$

Let us assume that $\omega^2 R = g$, the terrestrial value of the acceleration due to gravity at sea level; so that if you pick a value for R, ω is determined. Also assume that the density of the air in the space station has the corresponding sea level value. Now choose a ball game.

You might start by playing catch, tossing a baseball from one astronaut to another, neglecting air resistance. Then the equations (10.9.3) or (10.9.5) can be used without modification. (Note that an astronaut space-walking outside the station would see the ball moving in a straight line.) Now start throwing the ball harder, including air resistance. Finally, model a baseball pitch. For this the equations (10.9.5) would be modified as

$$\left.\begin{aligned}
\frac{dx}{dt} &= v_x, \\
\frac{dv_x}{dt} &= -k_D v v_x + k_L(\omega_y v_z - \omega_z v_y), \\
\frac{dy}{dt} &= v_y, \\
\frac{dv_y}{dt} &= 2\omega v_z + \omega^2 y - k_D v v_y + k_L(\omega_z v_x - \omega_x v_z), \\
\frac{dz}{dt} &= v_z, \\
\frac{dv_z}{dt} &= -2\omega v_y + \omega^2 z - \omega^2 R - k_D v v_z + k_L(\omega_x v_y - \omega_y v_x), \\
v &= \sqrt{v_x^2 + v_y^2 + v_z^2}.
\end{aligned}\right] \tag{10.9.6}$$

See section 9.1 on the motion of a spinning ball for further details. The Coriolis terms will add considerable interest to the trajectories.

It may be too ambitious to include golf as a sport in the next generation of spacecraft, but you might want to plan ahead. Court games such as tennis and badminton may be feasible; in fact the arts of badminton may need to be redefined. Note that as a trajectory rises, the simulated gravitational acceleration diminishes. If you want to play a sport as you would on Earth, keep shots low and fast. Anyone for table tennis?

10.10 Fireworks

A firework is a wonderful illustration of a system of differential equations run simultaneously with different initial conditions. Let $\vec{r}$ be displacement, and

$$\vec{v} = \frac{d\vec{r}}{dt}, \quad v = \| \vec{v} \|, \quad \hat{v} = \frac{\vec{v}}{v},$$

so $\hat{v}$ is the unit vector parallel to $\vec{v}$. Let resistance be proportional to v^α. The model for the motion of a single particle is

$$\begin{aligned}
\frac{d^2\vec{r}}{dt^2} &= -kv^\alpha \hat{v} + \vec{g} \\
&= -kv^{\alpha-1}\vec{v} + \vec{g}.
\end{aligned} \tag{10.10.1}$$

Note that for $\alpha = 0$, or 1, the equations can be solved by formula.

We shall look at two fireworks here. In the first, particles are expelled from a single point with the same speed in random directions. If there is no resistance, then it is easy to show that the particles always lie on the surface of an expanding sphere; with a bit of work, it can be shown that the same is true when resistance is proportional to the first power of v. But these cases are not realistic since the initial expansion is too slow relative to the later motion. To produce the initial burst that is actually observed, we need $\alpha = 2$, at least. It is interesting that as α increases, the particles continue to lie on an expanding sphere. This is a speculation based on numerical experiment; I am not aware of any theoretical justification.

For the second firework, we shall look at particles projected simultaneously from the rim of a spinning wheel. If the axis of the wheel is horizontal, so that the wheel is spinning in a vertical plane, then it appears that the particles always lie on a circle.

First, consider the practical implementation of equations (10.10.1) for the first firework. Let the z-axis point vertically upward, and let

$$y_1 = x,\ y_2 = \frac{dx}{dt},\ y_3 = y,\ y_4 = \frac{dy}{dt},\ y_5 = z, \text{ and } y_6 = \frac{dz}{dt}. \tag{10.10.2}$$

Then

$$\left.\begin{aligned} v &= \sqrt{y_2^2 + y_4^2 + y_6^2}, \\ \frac{dy_1}{dt} &= y_2, \\ \frac{dy_2}{dt} &= -kv^{\alpha-1}y_2, \\ \frac{dy_3}{dt} &= y_4, \\ \frac{dy_4}{dt} &= -kv^{\alpha-1}y_4, \\ \frac{dy_5}{dt} &= y_6, \\ \frac{dy_6}{dt} &= -kv^{\alpha-1}y_6 - g. \end{aligned}\right] \tag{10.10.3}$$

Choose the origin to be the initial point. Pick values for k and the initial speed. Start with $\alpha = 2$; experiment with different values later. The initial directions might be chosen at random, or they might conform to some regular pattern. More will be said about this later.

Suppose that you are working with `Fn` particles; their coordinates might be stored in a double array, `Fw(n, i)`, where `n` and `i` take the values `1` to `Fn` and `1` to `6`, respectively. For an integration step, there is an outer loop with `n` taken from `1` to `Fn`, and an inner loop for `y(i) = Fw(n, i)`, with `i` taken from `1` to `6`. Each particle will have to be advanced through the same time interval, `DelT`. I find it convenient to initialize the time to be zero at the start of each step. You might use a procedure such as this:

```
Procedure AdvanceByDelT
        Time = 0
        StepSize = DelT
        Do While Time < DelT
            Step(...)
        End Do
        Do while Abs(DelT - Time) > Eps
            StepSize = DelT - Time
            Step(...)
        End Do
```

`Eps` is a small number of your choice. Usually I want to use the coordinates for animation, when `DelT` is small — probably no larger than the stepsize that would be chosen by the integration method. In this case the first loop can be omitted. Then for one complete step:

```
    Do n = 1, Fn
        Do i = 1, 6
```

```
        y(i) = Fw(n, i)
    End Do
    AdvanceByDelT
    Do i = 1, 6
        Fw(n, i) = y(i)
    End Do
End Do
```

To investigate whether the particles lie on a sphere, note that there is symmetry about the z-axis, so a particle shot vertically upward will remain at the top of the sphere, A, and one shot vertically downward will remain at the bottom, B. The point C midway between A and B is at the center, and the radius of the sphere is one half of the distance AB. If the values `n = 1, 2` refer to these particles, then C will have coordinates `(0, 0, Cz) = (0, 0, (Fw(1, 5) + Fw(2,5))/2)`, and the radius is `Radius = (Fw(1, 5) - Fw(2,5))/2`. Then we should have

```
    Radius*Radius =
Fw(n, 1)*Fw(n, 1) + Fw(n, 3)*Fw(n, 3) + (Fw(n, 5) - Cz)* (Fw(n, 5) - Cz)
```

within the accuracy of the computation.

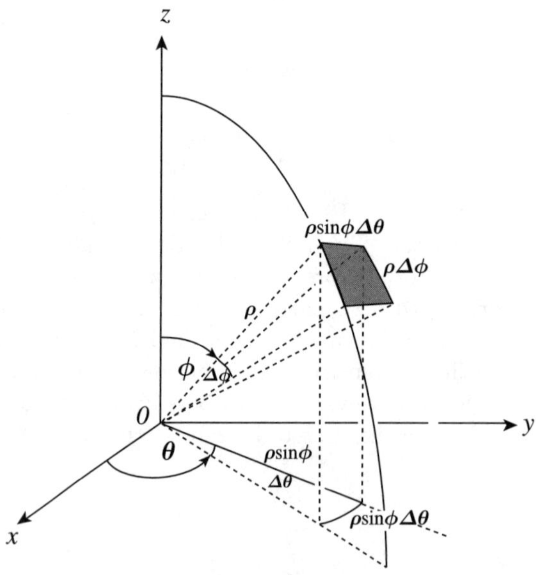

Figure 10.10: *Surface area on a sphere.*

Fireworks look great when shown in animation. For realism, the initial directions of the velocities should be chosen at random. We shall use spherical polar coordinates, (ρ, θ, ϕ), as shown in figure 10.10. If the initial speed is v_0, then the components are

$$\left.\begin{aligned} y_2 &= v_0 \cos\theta \sin\phi, \\ y_4 &= v_0 \sin\theta \sin\phi, \\ y_6 &= v_0 \cos\phi. \end{aligned}\right] \tag{10.10.4}$$

The area of a small section bounded by θ, $\theta + \Delta\theta$, and ϕ, $\phi + \Delta\phi$ is $\rho^2 \sin\phi\Delta\theta\Delta\phi$. ($\rho$ is the radius of the sphere.) For a random distribution of directions, θ can lie anywhere between 0 and 2π with equal probability. But if ϕ were to lie anywhere between 0 and π, with equal probability, there would be a concentration near $\phi = 0$ and $\phi = \pi$. In fact, it is $\sin\phi$ that must lie anywhere between 1 and -1, with equal probability. Suppose that the code Random produces a number randomly selected between 0 and 1, giving a different value each time it is used. Positions and velocities might be found as follows:

```
Do n = 1, Fn
    Theta = 2*Pi*Random
    SinPhi = Random
    f(n, 1) = 0
    f(n, 3) = 0
    f(n, 5) = 0
    f(n, 2) = v0*Cos(Theta)*SinPhi
    f(n, 4) = v0*Sin(Theta)*SinPhi
    f(n, 6) = v0*Sqrt(1 - SinPhi*SinPhi)
    If Random > 0.5 Then y(6) = - y(6)
End Do
```

The final line in the loop is necessary to ensure that positive and negative values of the z-component are equally likely.

For viewing on a screen, the three-dimensional figure must be projected into two dimensions. Here we shall discuss an *orthogonal* projection, as the firework would be seen from a great distance. A unit vector $\hat{e} = \langle e_x,\, e_y,\, e_z\rangle$ points toward the eye of the viewer. The set of axes $Oxyz$ has been defined. The screen coordinates will be given by OXY, with the Y-axis vertical. We shall assume that the z-axis is projected into the Y-axis; this means that $e_z \neq 1$. A point P has coordinates (x, y, z); we want to find the corresponding number pair (X, Y).

Let

$$\overrightarrow{\mathrm{OP}} = \vec{r} = x\hat{\imath} + y\hat{\jmath} + z\hat{k} \quad \text{and} \quad \hat{e} = e_x\hat{\imath} + e_y\hat{\jmath} + e_z\hat{k}.$$

$\hat{k}$ will have component $(\hat{k}\cdot\hat{e})\hat{e} = e_z\hat{e}$ **parallel** to $\hat{e}$, and will, therefore, have component

$$\hat{k} - e_z\hat{e}$$

perpendicular to $\hat{e}$. By assumption, this is parallel to the Y-axis. So the unit vector parallel to this axis is

$$\hat{Y} = (\hat{k} - e_z\hat{e})/\|\hat{k} - e_z\hat{e}\| = (\hat{k} - e_z\hat{e})/f, \text{ where } f = \sqrt{1 - e_z^2}. \tag{10.10.5}$$

Then the unit vector parallel to the X-axis will be

$$\hat{X} = \hat{Y} \times \hat{e} = (\hat{k} \times \hat{e})/f, \tag{10.10.6}$$

since $\hat{e} \times \hat{e} = 0$.

The X and Y coordinates will be

$$\left.\begin{aligned} X &= \vec{r}\cdot\hat{X} = (ye_x - xe_y)/f, \\ Y &= \vec{r}\cdot\hat{Y} = (z - e_z(xe_x + ye_y + ze_z))/f. \end{aligned}\right] \tag{10.10.7}$$

If we use spherical polar coordinates, with

$$\hat{e} = \cos\theta\sin\phi\hat{\imath} + \sin\theta\sin\phi\hat{\jmath} + \cos\phi\hat{k}, \tag{10.10.8}$$

then $f = \sin\phi$ and

$$\left.\begin{aligned} X &= y\cos\theta - x\sin\theta, \\ Y &= z\sin\phi - \cos\phi(x\cos\theta + y\sin\theta). \end{aligned}\right] \tag{10.10.9}$$

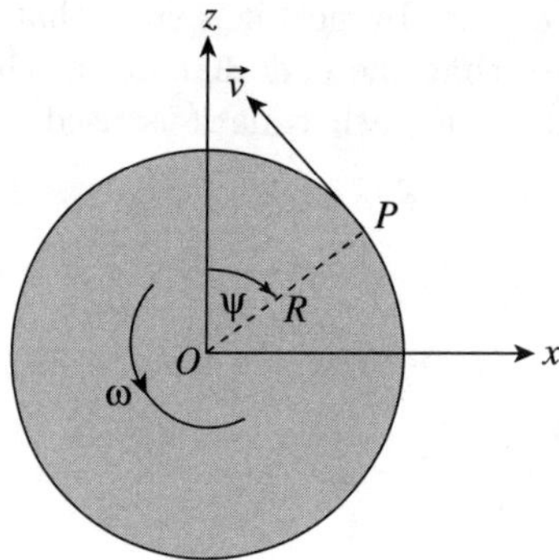

Figure 10.11: *A particle at P leaving a spinning wheel.*

(If the eye is distant D from the origin, then X and Y should be divided by the factor $g = 1 - \vec{r} \cdot \hat{e}/D$. Be careful if you use this projection, since matters can become very confused if the eye gets in among the particles!)

For the second firework, particles are projected from the rim of a spinning wheel. If it is spinning in a vertical plane, then only two-dimensional motion is involved. Let the wheel have center at O, radius R and angular velocity is ω. Let the motion take place in the $x - z$ plane, with the z-axis pointing vertically upward; then if P is a point on the rim, and OP make the angle ψ with the z-axis, the initial conditions are

$$x = R\sin\psi,\ z = R\cos\psi,\ \frac{dx}{dt} = -R\omega\cos\psi,\ \frac{dz}{dt} = R\omega\sin\psi. \tag{10.10.10}$$

See figure 10.11. For this model, the particles can be placed at equal intervals of ψ. It seems that, for any value of α, the particles lie on an expanding circle. See if you can confirm this.

Chapter 11

Space Travel and Astronomy

11.1 The Motion of Three Bodies

In this chapter we shall mainly be looking at projects involving the dynamics of objects moving in space. For a start, we shall review some of the dynamical principles involved in setting up the equations of motion of three bodies moving under their mutual gravitational attraction. If you are impatient over the details, by all means just skip to the equations of motion and their applications. For more details, see the text *Fundamentals of Celestial Mechanics*, Danby [30], and for astronomical applications, see *Astrophysical Simulations* by Danby, Kouzes and Whitney [31].

The use of the word "body" requires some explanation. Most astronomical bodies can be approximated by spheres, and can be considered to be built up in spherically symmetrical layers. At points outside such a body, the gravitational properties are the same as those of a point mass concentrated at the center of the sphere. So in applications, we shall substitute for the Earth, for instance, a point with the mass of the Earth, located at the center of the Earth. Here, the words "body" and "mass" will be interchangeable.

We shall be using Newton's *law of gravitation.* This can be stated as follows: A mass A attracts another mass B with a force that is proportional to the product of their masses, is inversely proportional to the square of the distance between them, and takes place in the line joining them.

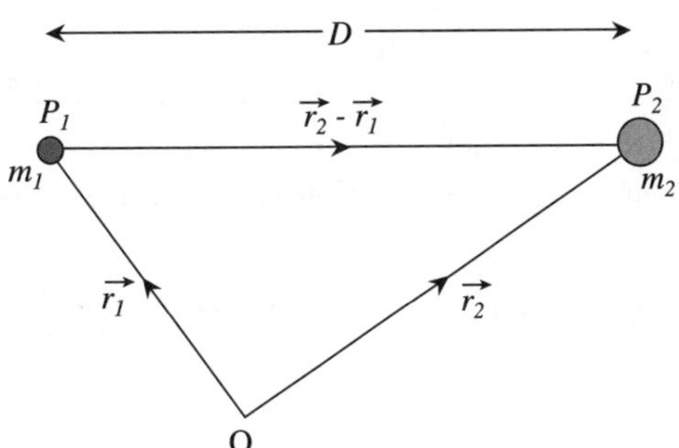

Figure 11.1: *The gravitational attraction of one body on another.*

To put this into symbolic form, suppose we have masses m_1 at P_1 and m_2 at P_2, with position vectors $\vec{r}_1$ and $\vec{r}_2$ with respect to an origin O. The vector $\overrightarrow{P_1P_2} = \vec{r}_2 - \vec{r}_1$. Let this have length $\| \vec{r}_2 - \vec{r}_1 \| = D$. Then the force exerted by m_2 on m_1 is

$$\vec{F} \quad = \quad Gm_1m_2\left(\frac{1}{D^2}\right)\left(\frac{\vec{r}_2 - \vec{r}_1}{D}\right)$$

$$= Gm_1m_2\frac{\vec{r}_2 - \vec{r}_1}{D^3}$$

$$= Gm_1m_2\frac{\vec{r}_2 - \vec{r}_1}{\| \vec{r}_2 - \vec{r}_1 \|^3}. \tag{11.1.1}$$

The term $(\vec{r}_2 - \vec{r}_1)/D$ is the unit vector in the direction of the gravitational force. The constant of proportionality, G, is the *constant of gravitation.*

The force $\vec{F}$ can be expressed differently, if we introduce the *potential*

$$V_{12} = -\frac{Gm_1m_2}{\| \vec{r}_2 - \vec{r}_1 \|}. \tag{11.1.2}$$

Suppose we have a coordinate system so that $\vec{r}_1 = \langle x_1, y_1, z_1\rangle$ and $\vec{r}_2 = \langle x_2, y_2, z_2\rangle$. Then

$$D = \| \vec{r}_2 - \vec{r}_1 \| = \sqrt{(x_2 - x_1)^2 + (y_2 - y_1)^2 + (z_2 - z_1)^2},$$

and

$$\frac{\partial V_{12}}{\partial x_1} = -Gm_1m_2\frac{x_2 - x_1}{D^3},$$

which is the negative of the x-component of $\vec{F}$ in equation (11.1.1). Then if the operator $\vec{\nabla}_1$ is defined by

$$\vec{\nabla}_1 = \hat{\imath}\frac{\partial}{\partial x_1} + \hat{\jmath}\frac{\partial}{\partial y_1} + \hat{k}\frac{\partial}{\partial z_1}, \tag{11.1.3}$$

we have

$$\vec{F} = -\vec{\nabla}_1 V_{12}. \tag{11.1.4}$$

Now let's apply this to find the equations of motion of three mutually attracting bodies, m_1, m_2 and m_3 with position vectors $\vec{r}_1$, $\vec{r}_2$ and $\vec{r}_3$, respectively, relative to the origin O. We shall apply Newton's laws of motion, and it is important to make certain that his *first* law is true before we consider using the second law. This is equivalent to stating that O is an origin of an *inertial reference system.* At this stage, we just assume that such a system exists. The equation of motion of m_1 is

$$m_1\frac{d^2\vec{r}_1}{dt^2} = Gm_1m_2\frac{\vec{r}_2 - \vec{r}_1}{\| \vec{r}_2 - \vec{r}_1 \|^3} + Gm_1m_3\frac{\vec{r}_3 - \vec{r}_1}{\| \vec{r}_3 - \vec{r}_1 \|^3}. \tag{11.1.5}$$

Then by symmetry, we find the equations of motion for m_2 and m_3 to be

$$m_2\frac{d^2\vec{r}_2}{dt^2} = Gm_2m_3\frac{\vec{r}_3 - \vec{r}_2}{\| \vec{r}_3 - \vec{r}_2 \|^3} + Gm_2m_1\frac{\vec{r}_1 - \vec{r}_2}{\| \vec{r}_1 - \vec{r}_2 \|^3}, \tag{11.1.6}$$

and

$$m_3\frac{d^2\vec{r}_3}{dt^2} = Gm_3m_1\frac{\vec{r}_1 - \vec{r}_3}{\| \vec{r}_1 - \vec{r}_3 \|^3} + Gm_3m_2\frac{\vec{r}_2 - \vec{r}_3}{\| \vec{r}_2 - \vec{r}_3 \|^3}. \tag{11.1.7}$$

If we add these last three equations, then all the terms on the right-hand sides cancel, and we are left with

$$m_1\frac{d^2\vec{r}_1}{dt^2} + m_2\frac{d^2\vec{r}_2}{dt^2} + m_3\frac{d^2\vec{r}_3}{dt^2} = 0,$$

which can be integrated to give

$$m_1\frac{d\vec{r}_1}{dt} + m_2\frac{d\vec{r}_2}{dt} + m_3\frac{d\vec{r}_3}{dt} = \vec{A} \tag{11.1.8}$$

and

$$m_1 \vec{r}_1 + m_2 \vec{r}_2 + m_3 \vec{r}_3 = \vec{A} t + \vec{B} \tag{11.1.9}$$

for constant vector $\vec{A}$ and $\vec{B}$. This means that the center of mass of the three bodies is not accelerated relative to the original inertial system; therefore, the center of mass is a valid inertial origin.

Equations (11.1.8) and (11.1.9) represent *integrals* of the dynamical system. It can be useful, when integrating the equations, to verify their accuracy; they can provide a check on the numerical accuracy of the integration. Two other integrals will be mentioned. If equations (11.1.5) to (11.1.7) are multiplied vectorially respectively by $\vec{r}_1 \times$, $\vec{r}_2 \times$ and $\vec{r}_3 \times$ and added, all terms on the right cancel, and we have

$$\vec{r_1} \times \frac{d^2 \vec{r}_1}{dt^2} + \vec{r_2} \times \frac{d^2 \vec{r}_2}{dt^2} + \vec{r_3} \times \frac{d^2 \vec{r}_3}{dt^2} = \vec{0},$$

from which we can derive

$$\vec{r_1} \times \frac{d \vec{r}_1}{dt} + \vec{r_2} \times \frac{d \vec{r}_2}{dt} + \vec{r_3} \times \frac{d \vec{r}_3}{dt} = \vec{c}, \tag{11.1.10}$$

for constant $\vec{c}$. This expresses the conservation of angular momentum of the system. Now define

$$V = V_{12} + V_{23} + V_{31}, \tag{11.1.11}$$

where equation (11.1.2), and two similar ones are used for V_{ij}, and

$$T = \frac{1}{2}\left(m_1 \left(\frac{d \vec{r}_1}{dt}\right)^2 + m_2 \left(\frac{d \vec{r}_2}{dt}\right)^2 + m_3 \left(\frac{d \vec{r}_3}{dt}\right)^2 \right). \tag{11.1.12}$$

If equations (11.1.5) to (11.1.7) are multiplied scalarly respectively by $\dot{\vec{r}}_1\cdot$, $\dot{\vec{r}}_2\cdot$ and $\dot{\vec{r}}_3\cdot$ and added, then the terms can be integrated with respect to the time, to give the equation equivalent to the conservation of energy,

$$T + V = h. \tag{11.1.13}$$

Equations (11.1.5) to (11.1.7) can be numerically integrated right away. It is a good idea to choose the center of mass as origin; this involves choosing initial conditions so that the constant vectors $\vec{A}$ and $\vec{B}$ in equations (11.1.8) and (11.1.9) are zero.

It is often convenient to move the origin to the center of one of the attracting bodies. For instance, for motion from the Earth to the Moon, the origin is at the Earth. For motion among the planets, the origin is at the Sun. We shall move the origin to m_1, using the notation of figure 11.2.

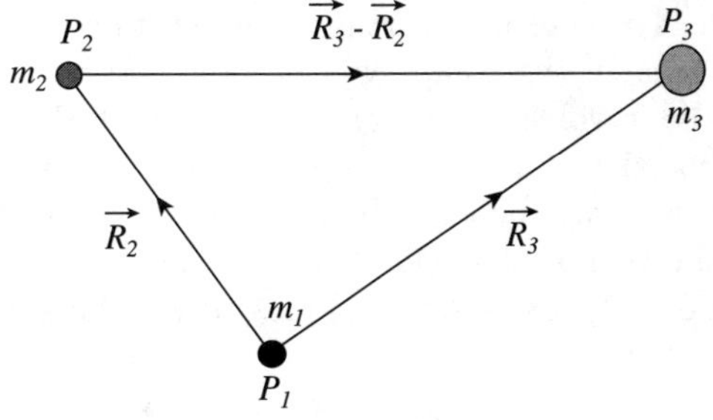

Figure 11.2: *The system is referred to the mass* m_1.

We shall find equations for the motion of m_2 at $\vec{R}_2 = \vec{r}_2 - \vec{r}_1$. Now equations (11.1.5) and (11.1.6) can be written as

$$\frac{d^2 \vec{r}_1}{dt^2} = Gm_2 \frac{\vec{r}_2 - \vec{r}_1}{\| \vec{r}_2 - \vec{r}_1 \|^3} + Gm_3 \frac{\vec{r}_3 - \vec{r}_1}{\| \vec{r}_3 - \vec{r}_1 \|^3} = m_2 G \frac{\vec{R}_2}{R_2^3} + m_3 G \frac{\vec{R}_3}{R_3^3},$$

and

$$\frac{d^2 \vec{r}_2}{dt^2} = Gm_3 \frac{\vec{r}_3 - \vec{r}_2}{\| \vec{r}_3 - \vec{r}_2 \|^3} + Gm_1 \frac{\vec{r}_1 - \vec{r}_2}{\| \vec{r}_1 - \vec{r}_2 \|^3} = Gm_3 \frac{\vec{R}_3 - \vec{R}_2}{\| \vec{R}_3 - \vec{R}_2 \|^3} - Gm_1 \frac{\vec{R}_2}{R_2^3}.$$

Subtracting the first from the second, we find

$$\frac{d^2 \vec{R}_2}{dt^2} = Gm_3 \left(\frac{\vec{R}_3 - \vec{R}_2}{\| \vec{R}_3 - \vec{R}_2 \|^3} - \frac{\vec{R}_3}{R_3^3} \right) - G(m_1 + m_2) \frac{\vec{R}_2}{R_2^3}. \tag{11.1.14}$$

Similarly,

$$\frac{d^2 \vec{R}_3}{dt^2} = Gm_2 \left(\frac{\vec{R}_2 - \vec{R}_3}{\| \vec{R}_2 - \vec{R}_3 \|^3} - \frac{\vec{R}_2}{R_2^3} \right) - G(m_1 + m_3) \frac{\vec{R}_3}{R_3^3}. \tag{11.1.15}$$

These equations are not intuitive. This is because we now have a non-inertial origin. One important result is found by setting $m_3 = 0$. Then we have the equation for the relative motion of two bodies

$$\frac{d^2 \vec{R}_2}{dt^2} + G(m_1 + m_2) \frac{\vec{R}_2}{R_2^3} = \vec{0}\ . \tag{11.1.16}$$

If m_3 is small, compared with the other masses, or if it is relatively at a much greater distance, then equation (11.1.14) can be interpreted as providing the *perturbation* of the two-body motion of m_2 about m_1 by the third body m_3.

In playing with these equations it is best, at first, to stay in two dimensions. It is absolutely essential to use an integration method that varies the stepsize. Close approaches are frequent. Since the gravitational attraction involves the inverse square of the mutual distance, singularities cannot be ruled out, in which case any method may crash. But stepsize reduction deals fairly well with most close approaches. This can be frustrating for purposes of animation since the integration slows down just when the actual motion speeds up, but it is here that the interesting physics is taking place. Here are some areas in which you might run experiments.

- One property of the motion of three bodies is that, if the masses are all of the same order of magnitude, then it is virtually impossible to find any solution where the mutual distances are of the same order. Try entering starting configurations; it is a safe bet to predict that one of the bodies will escape; the escape will be preceded by a close encounter with another body. If two of the bodies revolve around one another, with the third relatively far away, then permanent solutions can exist. This is observed in astronomy in triple star systems. You might experiment to see how far away the third body must be. In experiments of this kind, you will be concerned with qualitative results. Don't worry about units. I recommend that you set the gravitational constant $G = 1$. Use numerical magnitudes for masses, distances and speeds of the order of one unit.

- The Sun-Jupiter-Saturn system could be considered as an approximation, dynamically, of the solar system; as such it is certainly stable, i.e., it can remain in its present state indefinitely. But if the masses of the planets are increased, or if the sizes of their orbits are changed, will this remain the case?

To investigate this, we need some further astronomical background. This is provided by *Kepler's third law* of planetary motion. Johannes Kepler used observations of the planetary positions made by Tycho Brahe to deduce three laws describing the motion of the planets. The first states that the motion of a planet is an ellipse, with the Sun at one focus. The second describes the orbital speeds at different parts of the orbit. The third relates the size of an orbit to the period of revolution. One hundred years later, Newton formulated his law of gravitation to generalize these laws and to apply them to the motion of any two bodies, moving subject to equation (11.1.16). In particular, he reformulated Kepler's third law as follows:

> If two bodies with masses m_1 and m_2 revolve around one another in an elliptic orbit with semimajor axis a, then the period of revolution (i.e., the minimum time for a configuration to be repeated) is
>
> $$P = 2\pi\sqrt{\frac{a^3}{G(m_1+m_2)}}. \qquad (11.1.17)$$
>
> This is one of the most important formulas in astronomy, and is responsible for much of our knowledge of the masses of objects in the universe.

For work in the solar system it is customary to choose the unit of length to be the *astronomical unit.* This is the semimajor axis of the orbit of the Earth around the Sun (with a very slight modification that need not concern us). The unit of mass will be taken to be the mass of the Sun. Then the mass of the Earth is approximately $3 \cdot 10^{-6}$. Let us choose a unit of time so that the gravitational constant $G = 1$. Applying equation (11.1.17) to the Earth and Sun, and neglecting the mass of the Earth, we have

$$\text{One year } = 2\pi \text{ units of time.} \qquad (11.1.18)$$

So one unit of time is $365.25/2\pi$ days.

In these units, Jupiter has mass $9.5 \cdot 10^{-4}$; its orbit has semimajor axis 5.2 astronomical units. Equivalent figures for Saturn are $3 \cdot 10^{-4}$ and 9.5. For starting conditions, assume that the orbits are circular; then the initial speed is found by dividing the circumference of the orbit by its period. There is no point in running the program using these values, except to debug it, since the orbits will remain essentially unchanged. However, increasing the masses by at least a factor of 10, and changing the distances may lead to some interesting results. The periods of Jupiter and Saturn are 11.9 and 29.3 years. You might try reducing the radius of Saturn's orbit so that its period is, initially, twice that of Jupiter. This will introduce resonance, which can lead to strong perturbations.

- In the outer regions of the solar system there is a ring of comets, called the *Oort cloud* after the astronomer who first suggested its existence. Comets from this cloud sometimes enter the inner solar system in nearly parabolic orbits, many approaching the Sun within the orbit of the Earth, before again receding to the distance of the Oort cloud. (But see project (11.16) to investigate the possibility of a capture by Jupiter.) Most comets in the Oort cloud will have orbits that are roughly circular; how can these be perturbed so that they become nearly parabolic?

  One suggested mechanism is through perturbation by a star that is a companion to the Sun. The existence of such a star is pure hypothesis, but this has not prevented it from receiving the name "Nemesis." OK. The central body is the Sun. The second body is a comet, moving in a circular orbit with radius 100 astronomical units; its mass is so small that it cannot possibly affect the motion of the other two bodies. The third body is Nemesis; its mass and orbit are up to you. But modify the starting conditions so that it will move close to the comet. What can you find?

11.2 A Trip to the Moon

In this project, our principal object is to start from a circular "parking orbit" around the Earth and change to an orbit that will hit the Moon, or pass very close to it.

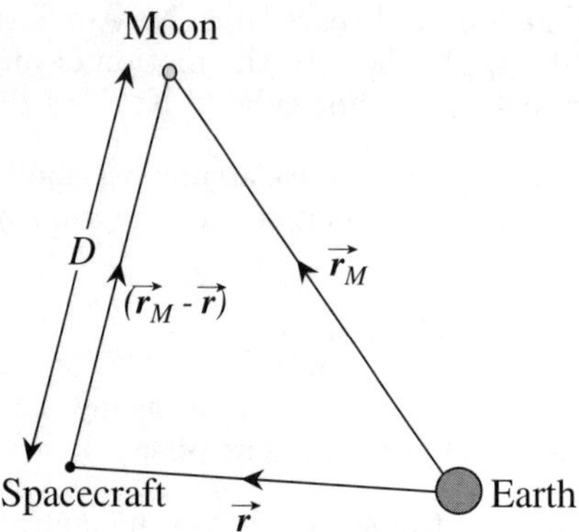

Figure 11.3: *Earth, Moon and spacecraft.*

The origin of coordinates will be at the center of the Earth. Let the vector from the Earth to the spacecraft be $\vec{r}$ and that from the Earth to the Moon be $\vec{r}_M$. Then the vector from the spacecraft to the Moon will be $(\vec{r}_M - \vec{r})$. See figure 11.3. Let the Earth and Moon have masses E and M, respectively, and let the gravitational constant be G. (Units will be discussed later.) The mass of the spacecraft is S, which will be included in the initial equation, but will later be neglected. The origin is non-inertial, so we use the form of equation (11.1.14) to derive the equation of motion

$$\frac{d^2\vec{r}}{dt^2} + G(E+S)\frac{\vec{r}}{\|\vec{r}\|^3} = GM\left[\frac{\vec{r}_M - \vec{r}}{\|\vec{r}_M - \vec{r}\|^3} - \frac{\vec{r}_M}{\|\vec{r}_M\|^3}\right]. \tag{11.2.1}$$

We shall work in two dimensions, and shall make the plausible assumption that the orbit of the Moon is a circle, with center at the origin. In order to keep the numbers reasonable, we shall introduce a special set of units for mass, length and time.

- The unit of mass will be the mass of the Earth. So $E = 1$; then $M = 1/81.3$.
- The unit of length will be the (constant) distance of the Moon from the Earth.
- The unit of time will be chosen so that the numerical value of the constant of gravitation $G = 1$.

To specify the unit of time, we use Kepler's third law of planetary motion (11.1.17). For the Earth-Moon system, the period P is a sidereal month, or 27.32 days; using equation (11.1.17) it is also 6.245 units in our new time. So one unit of this time is about 4.375 days. If we take the distance between the Earth and Moon to be 384,400 km, then we find that one unit of speed is equivalent to 1.017 km/sec.

The x- and y-axes can be oriented at will. Let us suppose that at time $t = 0$, when blast-off from the parking orbit takes place, the Moon is on the positive x-axis. Then at any time, the coordinates of the Moon will be

$$x_m = \cos nt, \ y_m = \sin nt, \ \text{where } n = 2\pi/P = (1+M)^{1/2}. \tag{11.2.2}$$

Let

$$\left.\begin{aligned} r^2 &= x^2 + y^2, \\ D^2 &= (x - x_M)^2 + (y - y_M)^2, \end{aligned}\right] \tag{11.2.3}$$

so that r is the distance of the spacecraft to the Earth, and D is its distance from the Moon. Then the vector equation (11.2.1) can be written as two scalar equations

$$\left.\begin{aligned} \frac{d^2x}{dt^2} &= -\frac{x}{r^3} + M\left(\frac{x_M - x}{D^3} - x_M\right), \\ \frac{d^2y}{dt^2} &= -\frac{y}{r^3} + M\left(\frac{y_M - y}{D^3} - y_M\right). \end{aligned}\right] \tag{11.2.4}$$

These are the equations of the model.

To set up a computer program, the first-step that you must take is to write these two second-order equations as a system of four first-order differential equations. I suggest that you define

$$y_1 = x,\ y_2 = \frac{dx}{dt},\ y_3 = y,\ y_4 = \frac{dy}{dt}. \tag{11.2.5}$$

The equations of the model can now be written as

$$\left.\begin{aligned} n &= (1+M)^{1/2},\ x_M = \cos nt,\ y_M = \sin nt, \\ r &= (y_1^2 + y_3^2)^{1/2}, \\ D &= \left((y_1 - x_M)^2 + (y_3 - y_m)^2\right)^{1/2}, \\ \frac{dy_1}{dt} &= y_2, \\ \frac{dy_2}{dt} &= -\frac{y_1}{r^3} + M\left(\frac{x_M - y_1}{D^3} - x_M\right), \\ \frac{dy_3}{dt} &= y_4, \\ \frac{dy_4}{dt} &= -\frac{y_3}{r^3} + M\left(\frac{y_M - y_3}{D^3} - y_M\right). \end{aligned}\right] \tag{11.2.6}$$

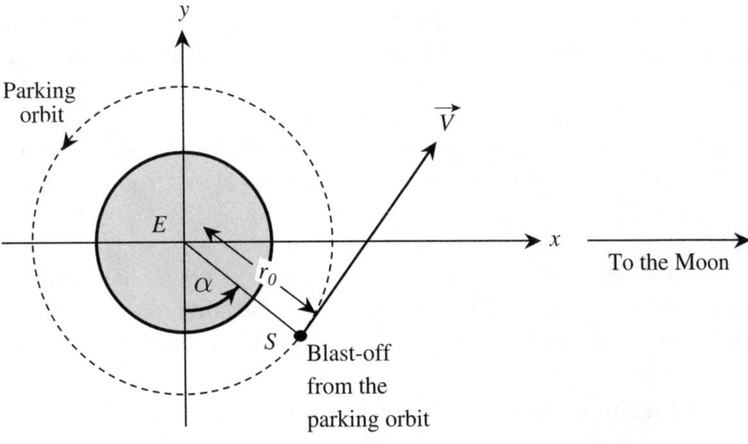

Figure 11.4: *Initial conditions for the trip.*

A possible configuration for the initial conditions is shown in figure 11.4. Let the radius of the parking orbit be r_0, the speed immediately after blast-off be V, and let the radius ES make the angle α with the negative y-axis, as shown. Then the initial conditions are

$$\left.\begin{array}{rclrclrcl} t & = & 0; & y_1 & = & r_0 \sin\alpha, & y_2 & = & V\cos\alpha, \\ & & & y_3 & = & -r_0\cos\alpha, & y_4 & = & V\sin\alpha. \end{array}\right] \tag{11.2.7}$$

The radius of the Earth is 0.0166 units. A reasonable parking orbit, with altitude 300 km, would have radius $r_0 = 0.0175$ units. The formula for the speed of escape at distance r_0 from a mass m is

$$V_{esc} = \sqrt{2mG/r_0}. \tag{11.2.8}$$

This is $\sqrt{2/r_0}$ in our units. For $r_0 = 0.0175$ this would give a speed of escape of 10.69. You should be able to use a slightly smaller value to reach the Moon, since, if you get close, the Moon's gravitational pull will help. The radius of the Moon in our units is 0.0045. If D becomes less than this, you have scored a hit. To help you start, I found that the numbers $r_0 = 0.0175$, $V = 10.7$ and $\alpha = -47°$ led to a direct hit. (Remember, if you use degrees for input, convert them **at once** into radians, for calculation.) Some people get frustrated when trying to hit the Moon, and make V *very* large; then the Moon hardly gets to move at all; be sporting, and give it a chance! Anyway, for reasons of fuel economy, you should keep V as low as practicable. If you have a value of V that enables you to reach the distance to the Moon, then playing with the parameter α should enable you to score a hit. Once you have done that, play with the value of V, and see how low you can make it. Note that a direct hit may only take about three days. As you run the program, keep track of the distance to the Moon. You might stop the program when the time exceeds one unit or the distance to the Moon is less than its radius.

Actually, there are two other maneuvers you might carry out. You might approach close to the Moon, circle around it, and then return to the Earth; this was the procedure for the first few flights to the Moon. If the spacecraft approaches *very* close to the Moon, then its orbit can pick up extra energy and leave the Earth-Moon system entirely. This is the "slingshot" effect. It has been used many times, to save fuel or to enable interplanetary spacecraft to pick up energy, and reach regions of the solar system that would be inaccessible by the use of chemical propellant.

Figures 11.5, 11.6 and 11.7 illustrate the three principal maneuvers. Each starts from a parking orbit with altitude 100 km, and with initial speed 10 km/sec. The only variable is the initial orientation angle, α. Corresponding points in the orbits of the spacecraft and Moon are joined every 12 hours.

Figure 11.5 has $\alpha = -39°$. Figure 11.5(a) follows the orbit up to a close approach with the Moon. The inset figure shows the expanded details of the approach; relative to the Moon, the spacecraft approaches from the left. Figure 11.5(b) follows the continuation of the orbit, back to the Earth.

Figure 11.6 has $\alpha = -41°$; the spacecraft hits the Moon.

Figure 11.7 has $\alpha = -43°$. Figure 11.7(a) follows the orbit up to a close approach to the Moon, and 11.7(b) shows the subsequent motion, with the orbit escaping from the Earth-Moon system, with a slingshot maneuver.

For output, print t, x, y, x_M, y_M and D. A diagram showing the paths of the spacecraft and Moon indicating corresponding positions for some given times, gives a good description of a project.

This is a complicated program so be careful with the debugging. You might try some runs with $M = 0$ in which case the orbits (with V less than V_{esc}) should all be closed ellipses. Bon voyage!

11.3 The Motion of a Space Station Around L_4 or L_5: 1

Two rigid spherical bodies move around one another in elliptic orbits according to Newton's laws of motion and gravitation. A third body of negligible mass (so that it cannot affect the motion of the other two bodies) can remain in "equilbrium" relative to the others in five different positions.

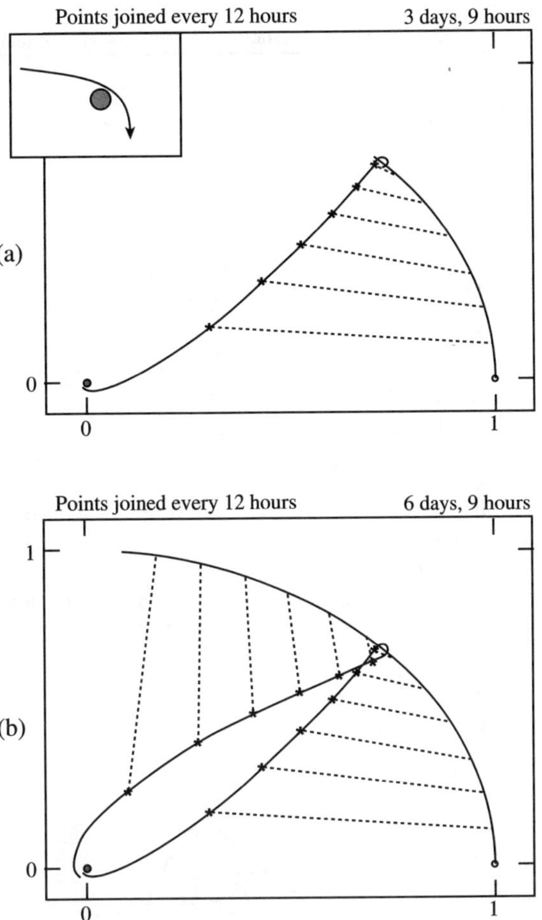

Figure 11.5: *An orbit passing close to the Moon and returning to the Earth. Corresponding positions of the Earth and Moon are joined every 12 hours.(a) shows the path up to the time of close approach. An expanded view of the close approach is shown in the inset.*

See figure 11.8. The first three positions (found by Euler) lie on the line joining the first two bodies. The final two lie in the plane of motion of these two bodies, and form equilateral triangles with them. The three collinear points are called L_1, L_2 and L_3; the two triangular ones are called L_4 and L_5. "L" stands for *Lagrange* who found L_4 and L_5.

These five equilibrium points have been considered as possible "parking" locations for spacecraft moving in the field (primarily) of the Earth and Moon; they have even been considered for permanent space stations. The collinear points are all unstable: a small displacement will in time lead to a larger drift away, and so on. But for the masses of the Earth and Moon, the triangular positions are stable. (These points are also stable in the Sun-Jupiter system; certain asteroids called the "Trojan asteroids" are clustered around each one.) The purpose of this project is to investigate, by numerical experiments, motion close to a triangular point. The orbits are rather attractive, with elaborate looping, and can venture some way away from the triangular point and still return. You might look into conditions for this return, or for escape.

We shall assume that the orbits of the first two bodies are circles; we then have the conventional form of the "restricted problem of three bodies." It is approximated by many physical systems. The origin of coordinates will be at the center of mass of the system, with the x- and y-axes in the plane of the circular motion. The axes are rotating so that the x-axis always contains the first two masses.

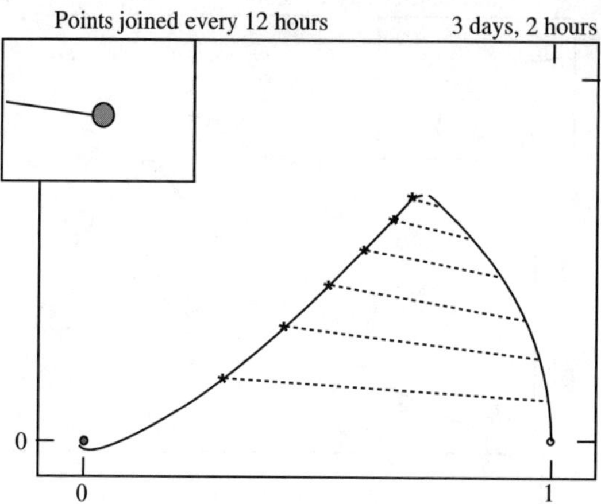

Figure 11.6: *An orbit hitting the Moon.*

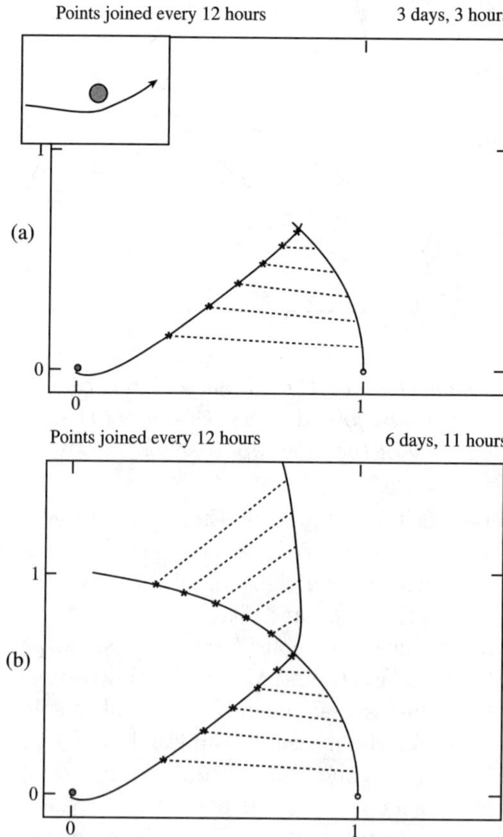

Figure 11.7: *An illustration of the slingshot effect. The spacecraft picks up kinetic energy relative to the Earth-Moon system, and escapes.*

Figure 11.8: *The five positions of equilibrium in the restricted problem of three bodies. They are shown relative to the rotating line joining the attracting masses, E and M.*

Since we are using a rotating reference system, *Coriolis* and *centrifugal* terms will appear in the equations.

To make the equations cleaner, we shall use a *canonical* set of units:

1. The unit of mass will be the sum of the masses of the two bodies. These bodies will be referred to as the Earth and the Moon, although such identification is not essential. Thus, if the separate masses are E and M, then $E + M = 1$. We define the number μ by
$$\mu = \frac{M}{E + M}, \tag{11.3.1}$$
where, traditionally, $\mu \leq 0.5$.
2. The unit of length is the constant distance between the two masses E and M.
3. The unit of time is chosen so that the time taken for E and M to complete one circular revolution is 2π units of time. This is equivalent to taking the constant of gravitation to be numerically equal to one. (Note the similarities with the units used in the project for the trip to the Moon.)

μ is the basic parameter of the restricted problem of three bodies. If we perform a linear analysis, we find that *linear* stability exists for L_4 and L_5 for
$$\mu < \mu_1 = \frac{1}{2}\left(1 - \frac{\sqrt{69}}{9}\right) \approx 0.03852. \tag{11.3.2}$$

This is a classical result. Quite recently, it has been shown that with nonlinear effects taken into account, the points are unstable for μ taking either of the values
$$\mu_2 = \frac{1}{2}\left(1 - \frac{\sqrt{611}}{15\sqrt{3}}\right) \approx 0.02429, \tag{11.3.3}$$
and
$$\mu_3 = \frac{1}{2}\left(1 - \frac{\sqrt{213}}{15}\right) \approx 0.01352. \tag{11.3.4}$$

For the case of the Earth and Moon, we can take $\mu = 0.01215$. For the Sun and Jupiter, $\mu = 0.00095$.

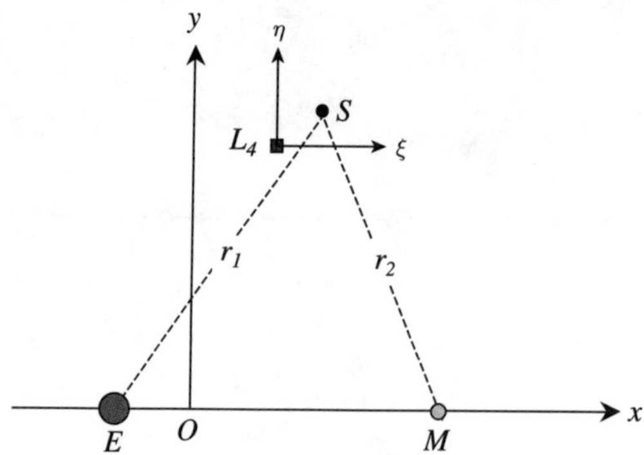

Figure 11.9: *The rotating reference system.*

In the notation of figure 11.9 the coordinates of E and M are $(-\mu, 0)$ and $(1-\mu, 0)$, respectively. So, if the respective distances of the spacecraft from E and M are r_1 and r_2, then

$$r_1^2 = (x+\mu)^2 + y^2, \text{ and } r_2^2 = (x-1+\mu)^2 + y^2. \tag{11.3.5}$$

The equations of motion are derived in the following section. They can be written as

$$\left.\begin{aligned} \frac{d^2x}{dt^2} - 2\frac{dy}{dt} - x &= -(1-\mu)\frac{x+\mu}{r_1^3} - \mu\frac{x-1+\mu}{r_2^3}, \\ \frac{d^2y}{dt^2} + 2\frac{dx}{dt} - y &= -(1-\mu)\frac{y}{r_1^3} - \mu\frac{y}{r_2^3}. \end{aligned}\right] \tag{11.3.6}$$

On the left we have first the conventional accelerations, then the Coriolis terms, and then the centrifugal terms.

Equations (11.3.6) must now be written as a system of four first-order differential equations. Let

$$y_1 = x,\ y_2 = \frac{dx}{dt},\ y_3 = y,\ y_4 = \frac{dy}{dt}. \tag{11.3.7}$$

Then

$$\left.\begin{aligned} r_1 &= \sqrt{(y_1+\mu)^2 + y_3^2},\ r_2 = \sqrt{(y_1-1+\mu)^2 + y_3^2}, \\ \frac{dy_1}{dt} &= y_2, \\ \frac{dy_2}{dt} &= 2y_4 + y_1 - (1-\mu)\frac{y_1+\mu}{r_1^3} - \mu\frac{y_1-1+\mu}{r_2^3}, \\ \frac{dy_3}{dt} &= y_4, \\ \frac{dy_4}{dt} &= -2y_2 + y_3 - (1-\mu)\frac{y_3}{r_1^3} - \mu\frac{y_3}{r_2^3}. \end{aligned}\right] \tag{11.3.8}$$

The coordinates of L_4 are $x = (1-2\mu)/2$, $y = \sqrt{3}/2$. The primary interest here is deviation away from L_4. Let this be given by coordinates (ξ, η) (so in this system the origin is at L_4); then I suggest that you enter initial values

$$x_0 = \frac{1}{2}(1-2\mu) + \xi_0,\ y_0 = \frac{\sqrt{3}}{2} + \eta_0,$$

where ξ_0 and η_0 are small (such as 0.001); initial values of the velocity components can be zero (or, again, very small numbers). At each integration step, display, or print out

$$\xi = y_1 - \frac{1}{2}(1 - 2\mu) \text{ and } \eta = y_3 - \frac{\sqrt{3}}{2}. \tag{11.3.9}$$

You will be looking for looping orbits that are constantly returning to the vicinity of L_4. If an orbit strays further than about 0.2 units of distance from L_4, it will probably escape, but part of the project is for you to test this. Orbits that do escape are fun to follow, but are outside the scope of this project.

I suggest that you start with a small value of μ, such as that for the Sun-Jupiter case. As μ is increased toward μ_1, the possible regions for orbits that return periodically close to L_4 will become smaller. See if you can find out what is special about μ_2 and μ_3. You may notice that there are two basic periods involved in the looping; for very small μ, one period is much longer than the other; as μ approaches μ_1, the periods approach equality. For $\mu = \mu_2$, one period is twice the other; for $\mu = \mu_3$, one period is three times the other. Try to confirm this, numerically.

Each of the figures 11.10 to 11.14 has the same starting conditions. Relative to L_4 the x-component is 0.0132; the y-component and the velocity components are all zero. The only parameter to be changed is μ, which takes the values $\mu = 0.01$, $\mu = 0.02$, $\mu = 0.03$, $\mu = \mu_2 = 0.02429$ and $\mu = \mu_3 = 0.01352$. According to linear theory, L_4 should be a stable equilibrium for all these values of μ so that orbits around L_4 should all resemble those of figures 11.10, 11.11 and 11.12. The true instability for μ_2 and μ_3 is shown clearly in figures 11.13 and 11.14.

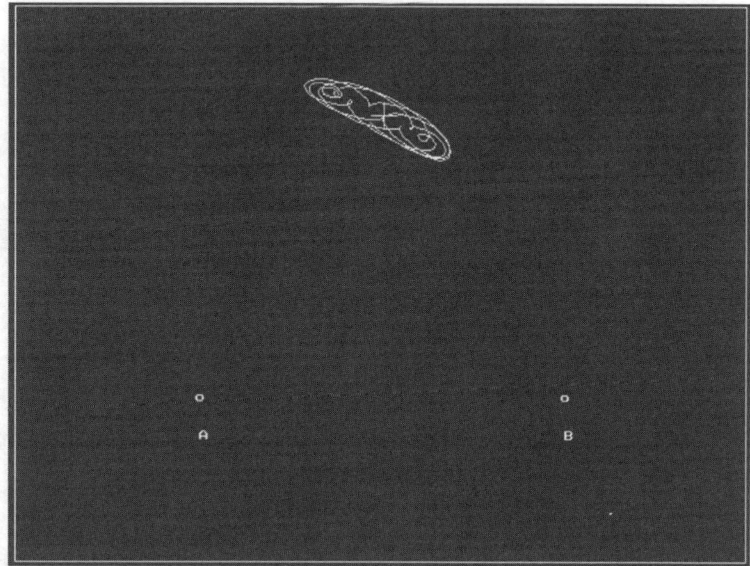

Figure 11.10: *For this and the next four figures, the starting conditions are the same. Relative to L_4 the x-component is 0.0132; the y-component and the velocity components are all zero. The only quantity changed is μ. For this figure, $\mu = 0.01$ and L_4 is stable, with orbits starting close to it, and remaining close. Note that the orbits in this and the following four figures are plotted in a rotating coordinate system in which the two attracting bodies are fixed.*

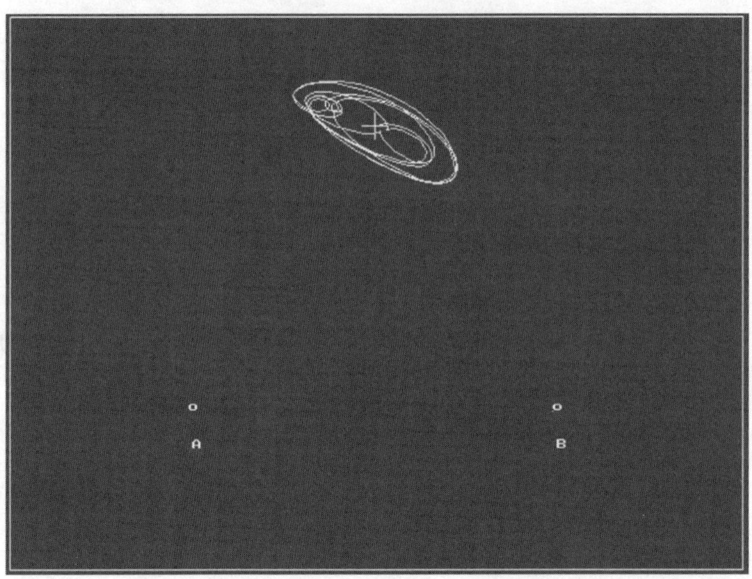

Figure 11.11: $\mu = 0.02$. *Again, we have stability.*

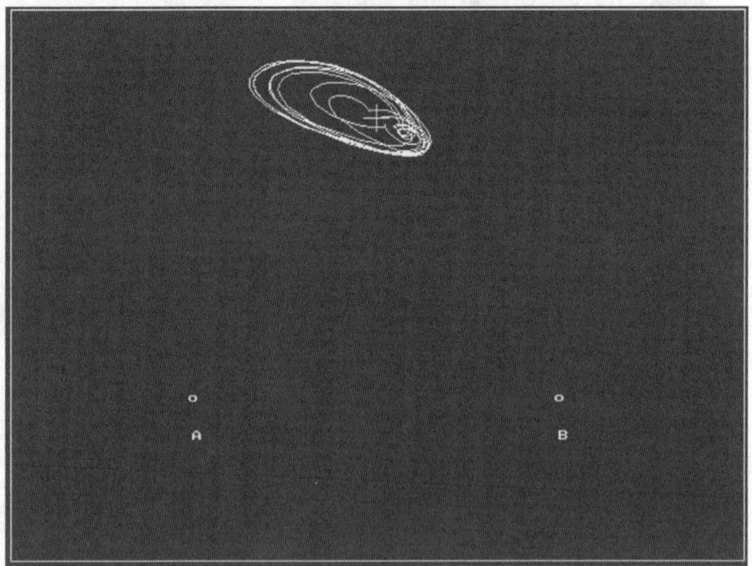

Figure 11.12: $\mu = 0.03$. *Again, we have stability.*

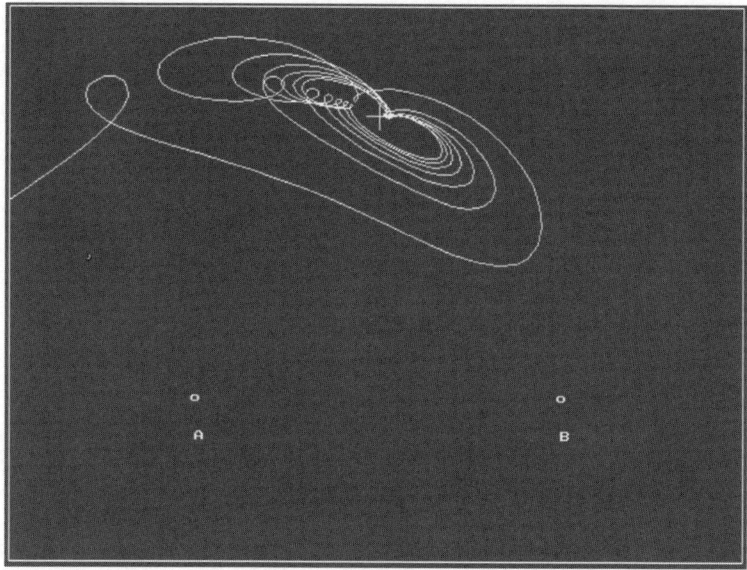

Figure 11.13: $\mu = \mu_2 = 0.02429$. *This value lies inside the range* $0 < \mu < \mu_1 = 0.03852$, *for which a linear analysis indicates that* L_4 *is stable. But for this value of* μ, L_4 *is actually unstable, as is demonstrated by this figure.*

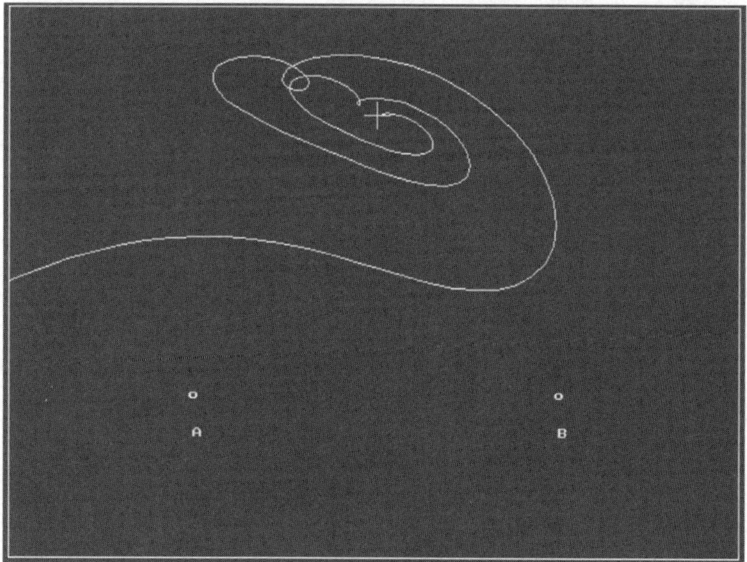

Figure 11.14: $\mu = \mu_3 = 0.01352$. *Again, this value lies inside the range* $0 < \mu < \mu_1 = 0.03852$. *But the figure shows that for this value of* μ, L_4 *is unstable.*

11.4 The Motion of a Space Station Around L_4 or L_5: 2

In this section, we shall view the restricted problem of three bodies as a chaotic dynamical system, and use Poincaré maps to explore motion near L_4 and L_5, as well as other types of chaotic and non-chaotic motion.

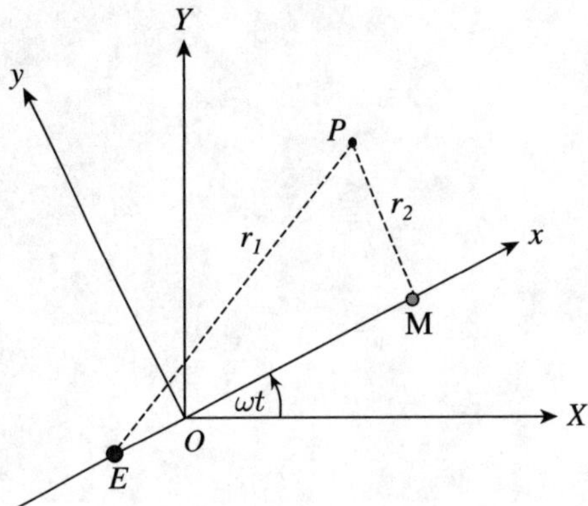

Figure 11.15: *A fixed and a rotating reference system.*

First, we shall derive the equations of motion. In figure 11.15 the axes XOY are fixed, and the axes xOy are rotating with constant angular velocity ω relative to XOY. The point P has coordinates (X, Y) or (x, y), where

$$X = x\cos\omega t - y\sin\omega t, \text{ and } Y = x\sin\omega t + y\cos\omega t.$$

Differentiating with respect to the time, we find

$$\dot{X}^2 + \dot{Y}^2 = (\dot{x} - \omega y)^2 + (\dot{y} + \omega x)^2.$$

Define the potential function

$$V = -\frac{1-\mu}{r_1} - \frac{\mu}{r_2}. \tag{11.4.1}$$

Then the Lagrangian for the system can be written as

$$L = \frac{1}{2}\left((\dot{x} - \omega y)^2 + (\dot{y} + \omega x)^2\right) - V. \tag{11.4.2}$$

The equations of motion are

$$\left.\begin{aligned} \frac{d^2x}{dt^2} - 2\omega\frac{dy}{dt} - \omega^2 x &= -\frac{\partial V}{\partial x}, \\ \frac{d^2y}{dt^2} + 2\omega\frac{dx}{dt} - \omega^2 y &= -\frac{\partial V}{\partial y}. \end{aligned}\right] \tag{11.4.3}$$

ω is shown explicitly so that the dimensions are clear. The terms $-2\omega\dot{y}$ and $2\omega\dot{x}$ are *Coriolis* terms, while $-\omega^2 x$ and $-\omega^2 y$ are *centrifugal* terms. In the remainder of this section, we set $\omega = 1$. Then equations (11.4.3) are the same as equations (11.3.6).

If the first equation of (11.4.3) is multiplied by $\dot{x}$ and the second by $\dot{y}$, and the two are added, then the resulting expression can be integrated with respect to the time to give the integral

$$\frac{1}{2}\left[\left(\frac{dx}{dt}\right)^2 + \left(\frac{dy}{dt}\right)^2\right] - \frac{1}{2}(x^2 + y^2) = -V + \text{constant}. \tag{11.4.4}$$

(This can also be derived using the property that L is conservative, so that

$$\dot{y}\frac{\partial L}{\partial \dot{y}} - L = \text{constant.})$$

Define

$$\Phi(x, y) = \frac{1}{2}(x^2 + y^2) - V + \frac{1}{2}\mu(1 - \mu). \tag{11.4.5}$$

Equation (11.4.4) can be written as

$$\left(\frac{dx}{dt}\right)^2 + \left(\frac{dy}{dt}\right)^2 = 2\Phi - C. \tag{11.4.6}$$

This is known as *Jacobi's integral.* The choice of Φ in equation (11.4.5) is made so that, independent of the value of μ, when the velocity is zero, C is equal to 3 at L_4 or L_5.

Now for the computation of Poincaré maps. I suggest that you plot values of

$$\xi = x - \frac{1}{2}(1 - 2\mu) \text{ and } \dot{\xi} = \dot{x}, \text{ when } \eta = y - \sqrt{3}/2 = 0.$$

Suppose that you have a variable **SignEta** which is equal to $+1$ if $\eta > 0$ and -1 if $\eta < 0$. We use the same notation that was used in the preceding project. After each integration step, test for a crossing of the plane $\eta = y - 0.866025$:

```
If SignEta*(y[3] - 0.866025) < 0 then FindCrossing
```

The procedure **FindCrossing** should use Newton's method to find the value of the time, when $\eta = 0$, or $y_3 - \sqrt{3}/2 = 0$; it should contain lines equivalent to:

```
Count = 0
SaveStepSize = StepSize
Repeat
    Count = Count + 1
    StepSize = - (y(3) - 0.866025)/y(4)
    Step(.....)
Until (Abs(y(3) - 0.866025) < Eps) Or (Count = 5)
If Count < 5 then store y(1), y(2)
StepSize = SaveStepSize
SignEta = - SignEta
```

Use a value of C equal to 3, or **very** close. If $C > 3$ then points in a region around L_4 will be excluded. For initial values you pick ξ and $\dot{\xi}$ with $\eta = 0$. Then $y_1 = \xi + \frac{1}{2}(1 - 2\mu)$, $y_3 = \dot{\xi}$ and $y_3 = \sqrt{3}/2$. Solve for y_4 using Jacobi's integral (11.4.6), picking the positive value. (You may have to persevere to find y_1 and y_2 to make $y_4^2 > 0$.) Pick a value of μ that ensures stability at L_4. Start with y_1 and y_2 very small, and gradually increase them to see the transition from stability to instability, as the size of the orbit around L_4 increases. Now vary μ, perhaps approaching one of the values that makes L_4 unstable. It is helpful, in some cases, to have a picture of the actual orbit, in the x-y plane, along with the Poincaré map, so this project combines well with the preceding one.

A different project in the restricted problem, involving Poincaré maps, is based on the system of asteroids. These mostly have orbits between the orbits of Jupiter and Mars; their dynamics is strongly influenced by Jupiter, while the mass of any asteroid is so small that it will not affect the motion of Jupiter. In particular, if the ratio of the period of an asteroid to the period of Jupiter is a rational number, such as 1/2, then the effect of Jupiter is particularly great. The orbit is said to be *commensurable* with that of Jupiter. For some commensurabilities, such as 1/2, there are gaps in the system of asteroids, called the *Kirkwood gaps.* But for the value 2/3 (where the asteroid revolves three times around the Sun while Jupiter revolves twice), there is a concentration of asteroids; these form a family known as the *Hilda group.* (It includes minor planet number 3415, named "Danby.") You might consider the problem with $\mu = 0.001$, which is close to the true value, or, if you are impatient for stronger effects (and who isn't?), increase it.

In inertial space, an asteroid, distant $x_0 + \mu$ from the Sun, could have a circular orbit about the Sun with orbital speed $\sqrt{(1-\mu)/(x_0+\mu)}$. Relative to the *rotating* system that we are working with, this speed would be $v_c = \sqrt{(1-\mu)/(x_0+\mu)} - x_0$. Now suppose we start an orbit on, and moving perpendicular to, the x-axis. The starting conditions would be: $x = x_0$, $y = 0$, $\dot{x} = 0$, $\dot{y} = v_c$. With these values, calculate C from equation (11.4.6). This will be your value of C for a selection of initial conditions. Find Poincaré maps for points for which $y = 0$. A circular (or a non-circular, but periodic) orbit around the Sun would result in one point, mapped onto itself: a *fixed point.* Orbits nearby should result in points lying on a curve surrounding the fixed point. Moving further away, you may find chaos developing, or some sort of complicated structure. Change x_0 (equivalent to changing C). See what can happen when the periods of the asteroid and Jupiter are close to being rationally related.

For a good introduction to the system of asteroids, see *Introduction of Asteroids* by C.J.Cunningham [26].

An interesting modification of this problem allows for radiation pressure from one or both of the attracting bodies; this would only be significant if the third body was a small particle; the two massive bodies might be stars. (11.4.1) is modified to

$$-\frac{\alpha(1-\mu)}{r_1} - \frac{\beta\mu}{r_2}, \tag{11.4.7}$$

for $0 < \alpha,\ \beta < 1$. You can confirm that if $\alpha^{1/3} + \beta^{1/3} < 1$ then the triangular points exist, with distances from the primaries $\rho_1 = \alpha^{1/3}$ and $\rho_2 = \beta^{1/3}$. (11.4.6) becomes

$$\frac{1}{2}\left[\left(\frac{dx}{dt}\right)^2 + \left(\frac{dy}{dt}\right)^2\right] = x^2 + y^2 + 2\frac{\alpha(1-\mu)}{r_1} + 2\frac{\beta\mu}{r_2} - C + \mu(1-\mu) + 3\left(1 - \alpha^{2/3}(1-\mu) - \beta^{2/3}\mu\right), \tag{11.4.8}$$

where C will be equal to 3 at the triangular points. The equations of motion are

$$\left.\begin{aligned} \frac{d^2x}{dt^2} - 2\frac{dy}{dt} - x &= -\alpha(1-\mu)\frac{x+\mu}{r_1^3} - \beta\mu\frac{x-1+\mu}{r_2^3}, \\ \frac{d^2y}{dt^2} + 2\frac{dx}{dt} - y &= -\alpha(1-\mu)\frac{y}{r_1^3} - \beta\mu\frac{y}{r_2^3}. \end{aligned}\right] \tag{11.4.9}$$

Suppose $\beta = 1$. Consider the dynamics with α gradually reduced — as though the Sun were getting hotter.

11.5 The Descent of Skylab

Skylab landed in little hot pieces on July 11, 1979. It had been hoped that the satellite would remain up in orbit long enough for the space shuttle to come to its rescue. But the launch of the first shuttle took place later than anticipated. Also there was a miscalculation of the effects of solar activity on the density of the Earth's upper atmosphere. (Plasma ejected from the Sun, particularly by flares, can temporarily increase the density when it interacts with the atmosphere.) Skylab experienced more atmospheric drag than had been anticipated, and down she came. The aim of this project is to model the last few revolutions before the final descent. The title is a convenience; "Skylab" can, of course, apply to any satellite, real or imagined.

For nearly all of her life, the principal force acting on Skylab was that due to the Earth's gravitational field. Our first approximation will be to assume that the Earth is a rigid sphere. But it was the Earth's atmosphere that caused the descent, so we must have a model to approximate its density. In fact, this density varies considerably and in complicated ways, according to time and place, due to such factors as day, night, tides — and solar activity; it would be much too difficult to introduce a *good* model here. For a start, we shall also assume that the atmosphere is non-rotating. Since the true atmosphere rotates once every 24 hours, and a revolution of Skylab around the Earth takes (took) about 90 minutes, this assumption is not too bad. We shall assume that the density depends on altitude, but not on latitude or longitude or time. We shall also assume that during the motion the cross-sectional area that Skylab presents to the atmosphere is constant. (In fact, this was deliberately changed during the final revolutions by reorientation, to try to regulate the landing area.)

The problem can now be formulated in two dimensions. There are two forces acting on Skylab, as illustrated in figure 11.16. The gravitational force is

$$\vec{F}_g = -GES\frac{\vec{r}}{r^3}, \tag{11.5.1}$$

where E and S are masses of the Earth and Skylab, and G is the constant of gravitation.

The drag force is assumed to be proportional to the atmospheric density, ρ, the cross-sectional area of the satellite, A, and the square of the speed, v, relative to the atmosphere. This is directed opposite to the velocity, $\vec{v}$, so the force can be written as

$$\vec{F}_d = \frac{C_D}{2}\rho A v^2\left(-\frac{\vec{v}}{v}\right) = -\frac{C_D}{2}\rho A v\,\vec{v}\,. \tag{11.5.2}$$

C_D, the constant of proportionality, is the *drag coefficient*, which is dimensionless. Typically, it has value of the order of one or two.

Combining these with Newton's second law of motion, we derive the differential equation

$$S\frac{d^2\vec{r}}{dt^2} = \vec{F}_g + \vec{F}_d = -GES\frac{\vec{r}}{r^3} - \frac{C_D}{2}\rho A v\,\vec{v}\,. \tag{11.5.3}$$

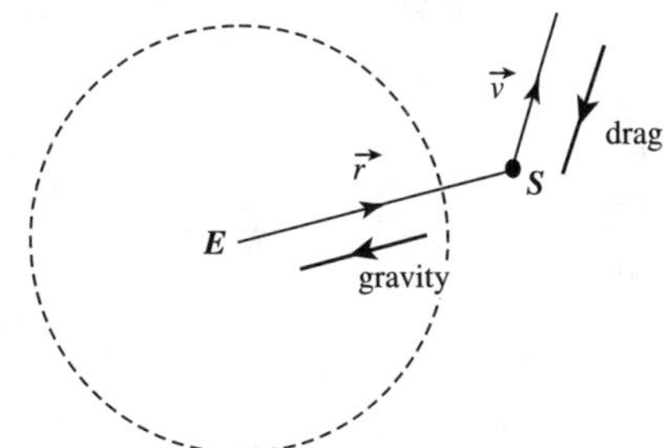

Figure 11.16: *E is at the center of the Earth. S is the position of Skylab.*

Dividing by S, we see that the effect of drag on the acceleration is proportional to the ratio A/S. Let

$$\mu_E = EG = 3.986 \times 10^{14}\text{m}^3\,\text{s}^{-2} = 3.986 \times 10^{5}\text{km}^3\,\text{s}^{-2}, \tag{11.5.4}$$

called the *geocentric gravitational constant*, and

$$D = C_D A/2S. \tag{11.5.5}$$

Then equation (11.5.3) can be written in component form as

$$\left.\begin{aligned} \frac{d^2x}{dt^2} &= -\mu_E\frac{x}{r^3} - D\rho v\frac{dx}{dt}, \\ \frac{d^2y}{dt^2} &= -\mu_E\frac{y}{r^3} - D\rho v\frac{dy}{dt}. \end{aligned}\right] \tag{11.5.6}$$

Here

$$r = \sqrt{x^2+y^2}, \text{ and } v = \sqrt{\left(\frac{dx}{dt}\right)^2 + \left(\frac{dy}{dt}\right)^2}.$$

The equatorial radius of the Earth is $r_E = 6,378$ km. Then the altitude of Skylab is *Alt*, where

$$Alt = r - r_E. \tag{11.5.7}$$

The density in the lower atmosphere can be approximated by

$$\begin{aligned} \rho &= 1.225\, e^{-0.1385\times Alt}\ \text{kg/m}^3 \\ &= 1.225\times 10^9 e^{-0.1385\times Alt}\ \text{kg/km}^3,\ 0 < Alt < 90. \end{aligned} \tag{11.5.8}$$

Note that *Alt* is measured in km. This exponential law gives a density that eventually falls off too sharply with altitude. Above 90 km, I suggest that you use

$$\begin{aligned} \rho &= 18.471\times 10^3(10.01\times Alt - 751.44)^{-4.411}\ \text{kg/m}^3 \\ &= 18.471\times 10^{12}(10.01\times Alt - 751.44)^{-4.411}\ \text{kg/km}^3,\ Alt > 90. \end{aligned} \tag{11.5.9}$$

Using this formula won't get you a contract with NASA, but it should be adequate. To do better would require interpolation from tables.

Next, we need to write equations (11.5.6) as a system of four first-order differential equations. Let

$$y_1 = x,\ y_2 = \frac{dx}{dt},\ y_3 = y,\ y_4 = \frac{dy}{dt}. \tag{11.5.10}$$

Then

$$\left.\begin{aligned} r &= \sqrt{y_1^2+y_3^2},\ v = \sqrt{y_2^2+y_4^2}, \\ \frac{dy_1}{dt} &= y_2, \\ \frac{dy_2}{dt} &= -\mu_E\frac{y_1}{r^3} - D\rho v y_2, \\ \frac{dy_3}{dt} &= y_4, \\ \frac{dy_4}{dt} &= -\mu_E\frac{y_3}{r^3} - D\rho v y_4. \end{aligned}\right] \tag{11.5.11}$$

Some plausible numbers for the parameters are

$$\begin{aligned} C_D &= 1, \\ S &= 77\times 10^3\ \text{kg}, \\ A &= 10\ \text{m}^2 = 10^{-5}\ \text{km}^2. \end{aligned}$$

The units for times and length are seconds and kilometers. Make sure that you use the appropriate values of ρ. One revolution around the Earth, in an orbit with altitude of 100 to 200 km, will have a period of about 90 minutes, or 5400 seconds; allow for this in setting maximum times for integrations. The maximum tolerable local truncation error need not be smaller than around 10^{-2}.

Skylab's death throes started when its closest approach to the surface of the Earth was around 130 km, and this figure was 100 km for the final few revolutions. The simplest way to choose initial conditions for an integration is to start on the x-axis, moving perpendicular to that axis. Then the two variables are the starting altitude and speed. Suppose that you pick the altitude to be 100 km; then initially, $x_0 = 6378 + 100 = 6478$. You will find the orbit is highly sensitive to the initial speed. With the numerical values suggested, 7.86 to 7.90 will result in just a few revolutions. A value less than 7.5 could result in the satellite dropping to Earth due to gravity, not drag. A value much greater than 7.9 could lead to so many revolutions before final descent, that the whole process becomes too boring. Be prepared for this kind of sensitivity.

In 1994 a set of spheres was launched from the space shuttle. These had precise dimensions and reflectivity and were to be used by ground-based radar to help calibrate their observations of space debris. The launching equipment was designed and built by undergraduates at North Carolina State University, and I had the privilege of taking part in the project. One of the requirements in the design process was that the spheres should remain in orbit for more than 30 but less than 100 days. The model was essentially the one used for this project, but computation over much longer periods of time was involved. The problem is this: for a diameter of 10in, find the weight of a sphere so that it will remain in orbit for, say, 50 days, if launched in a circular orbit at an altitude of 150km. (The three numbers can, of course, be varied.)

Figures 11.17(a) to (e) show successive revolutions before crashing. The scale of the altitude has been exaggerated by a factor of 50, and the dashed circle is at an altitude of 100 km. The orbit was started 6480 km from the center of the Earth (an altitude of 93 km) with velocity 7.89 km/sec perpendicular to the radius to the Earth's center. In discussing an orbit around the Earth, a point closest to the Earth is denoted by *perigee* and one furthest from the Earth by *apogee.* So this particular orbit started at perigee. Since the density of the atmosphere diminishes rapidly with increasing altitude, most of the drag takes place near perigee. At the end of the first revolution, shown in figure 11.17(a), the satellite reaches perigee, and loses energy due to drag; so in the second revolution, shown in figure 11.17(b), the orbit does not extend so far at apogee. Notice that while the apogee distance steadily decreases, the perigee distance remains nearly the same. This process continues until the orbit is close enough to a circle so that effective drag occurs all around; then the satellite descends rapidly. A good way to exhibit results is to plot the altitude as a function of the time. Such a plot is shown in figure 11.18.

If you want to plot the orbit as it goes *around* the Earth, then you must exaggerate the scale of the altitude. Here is one way to do this:

```
Radius = Sqrty(1)*y(1) + y(3)*y(3)
Altitude = Radius - EarthRadius
ScaledRadius = EarthRadius + Altitude*ScaleFactor
XScaled = ScaledRadius*(y(1)/Radius)
YScaled = ScaledRadius*(y(3)/Radius)
```

`ScaleFactor` is the factor for the exaggeration. Plot `XScaled` and `YScaled`.

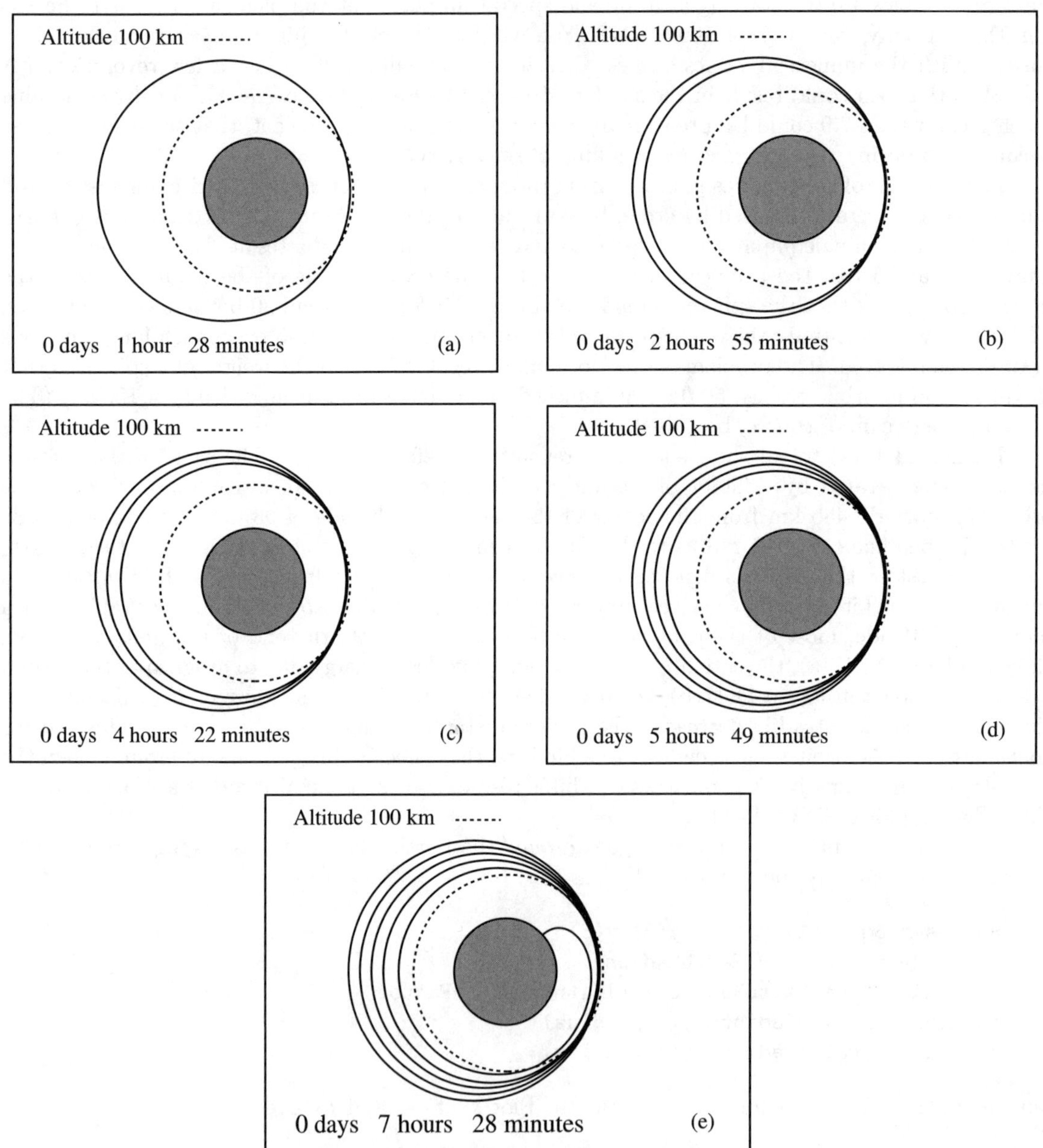

Figure 11.17: *Successive revolutions in the orbit of a satellite shortly before it crashes. Most of the drag takes place near perigee, a point in the orbit closest to the Earth. So each time the satellite passes through perigee it loses energy, and remains closer to the Earth in the following revolution. Eventually the orbit is nearly circular, drag is effective at all points, and the satellite descends rapidly.*

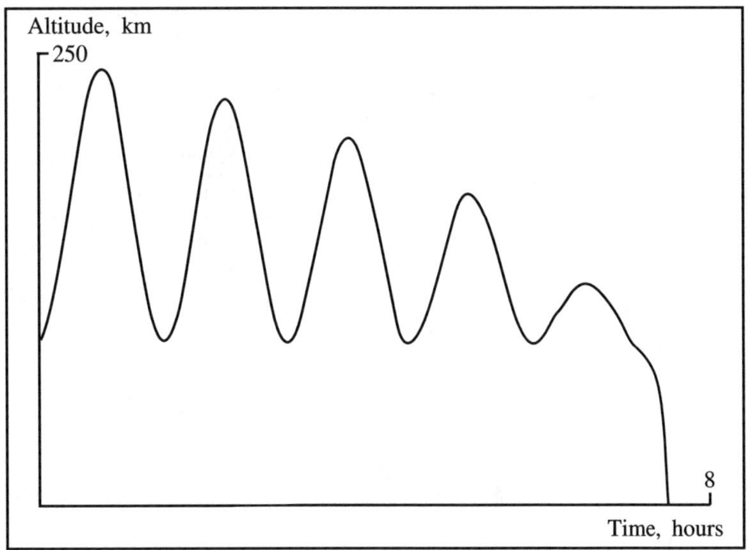

Figure 11.18: *Changes in altitude during a final descent. The orbit is the same as that shown in figure 11.18. Notice that while the apogee distance steadily decreases, the perigee distance remains nearly the same.*

11.6 The Range of an ICBM

The basic model for this project is the same as that for the descent of Skylab. The initial conditions occur at the time of "burnout," so that we shall not be concerned here with powered rocket flight. The quantities describing the initial conditions will be the altitude, initial speed, and the angle of elevation of the initial velocity vector. How, for instance, can this angle be varied in order to attain the maximum range?

I suggest that you use the geometry of figure 11.19. Suppose the y-axis points north, with the origin, E, at the center of the Earth. Take the latitude of the burnout point to be 45°. Let the initial altitude be A_0 km, and the initial speed be v_0 km/sec. The angle of elevation, α, is the angle between the initial velocity vector, $\vec{v}_0$, and the *local horizon.* This is a plane through the point of burnout, perpendicular to the line joining this point to the center of the Earth. Then the initial conditions are

$$\left.\begin{array}{rclrcl} t = 0; \quad y_1 & = & (r_E + A_0)\cos(\pi/4), & y_2 & = & -v_0\cos(\alpha+\pi/4), \\ y_3 & = & (r_E + A_0)\sin(\pi/4), & y_4 & = & v_0\sin(\alpha+\pi/4), \end{array}\right] \tag{11.6.1}$$

where r_E is the radius of the Earth.

The equations for the model are (11.5.10) and (11.5.11). In order to find the range, it will be necessary to locate the point of impact, and to do this, it will be necessary to find the point for which the altitude is zero (or, rather, less than some prescribed small number). This is best done using Newton's method. During the regular integration process, with the stepsize varied in the usual way, the altitude, *Alt*, is calculated at every step. As soon as *Alt* becomes negative, the regular process for finding the stepsize must stop, and Newton's method takes over.

We need to solve the equation $Alt(t) = 0$ for t. So we shall calculate a sequence $\{t_i\}$, $i = 0, 1, 2, ...$

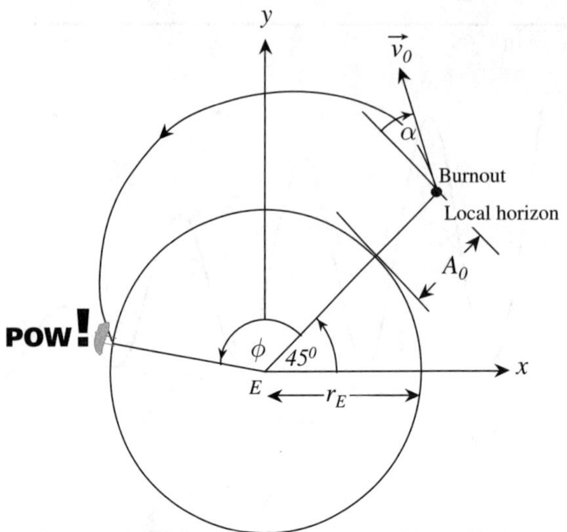

Figure 11.19: *Geometry at burnout for an ICBM.*

which converges to this solution. By Newton's method,

$$t_{i+1} = t_i - Alt(t_i) \Bigg/ \left(\frac{dAlt(t)}{dt} \right) \Bigg|_{t=t_i}, \tag{11.6.2}$$

where t_0 is the time at which the altitude first became negative. The quantity $t_{i+1} - t_i$ is the stepsize. Since

$$Alt = r - r_E, \text{ and } r = (x^2 + y^2)^{1/2} = (y_1^2 + y_3^2)^{1/2}$$

it follows that

$$\frac{dAlt}{dt} = \frac{dr}{dt} = \frac{1}{r}\left(y_1 \frac{dy_1}{dt} + y_3 \frac{dy_3}{dt} \right) = \frac{1}{r}(y_1 y_2 + y_3 y_4). \tag{11.6.3}$$

So the stepsize, while using Newton's method, is

$$\texttt{StepSize} = -\frac{Alt\sqrt{y_1^2 + y_3^2}}{y_1 y_2 + y_3 y_4}. \tag{11.6.4}$$

The first stepsize will be negative, and will be smaller in magnitude than the preceding one, so there should be no trouble with a too large local truncation error.

Let us assume that when the procedure `Step` is called, it returns, among other things, the altitude. (Otherwise, you will need to insert lines to calculate *Alt* immediately after each call to `Step`.) Then, after each call to `Step`, there should be a line like

```
If Alt < 0 then FindLanding
```

The procedure `FindLanding` should contain lines equivalent to:

```
Repeat
    StepSize = -Alt*Sqrt(y[1]^2 + y[3]^2)/(y[1]*y[2] + y[3]*y[4])
    Step(.....)
Until Abs(Alt) < Eps
```

Remember to use the **absolute** value of *Alt* in the test; `Eps` is a small quantity of your own choice.

To find the range, you might find the angle subtended at the center of the Earth between the initial and final positions. Suppose this angle is ϕ, then, using the formula for the scalar product of two vectors,

$$\cos\phi = (y_1 + y_3)/(r_E\sqrt{2}). \tag{11.6.5}$$

Then the range, over the surface of the Earth, is $r_E\phi$ (ϕ is in radians).

For a start, you might pick $A_0 = 10$ km and $V_0 = 8$ km/sec. Vary α to maximize the range. Then look for the effects of varying A_0 and V_0. Alternatively, pick a value of α, and find V_0 to maximize the range.

11.7 The Accuracy of an ICBM

The model for this project is the same as that used in the preceding one. But different questions are to be asked.

We have all heard about the great accuracy of ICBMs. There are reports that the error at impact (the error between what is predicted at launch and what actually takes place) can be just one or two meters. The question is: "What demands does such accuracy make on the precision of the conditions at burnout and on the model of the atmospheric density?"

To find some answers, I suggest that you do the following. Integrate one orbit in the preceding project, from burnout to impact, using enough accuracy to give errors of less than one meter, and taking care over the calculation of the point of impact. Then, change the burnout parameters by small amounts, one by one, and find out how sensitive the point of impact may be to these changes. In addition, note the changes in the time of flight, allowing for the rotation of the Earth; how will this affect the point of impact? Then introduce a factor $1 + a$, where a is small, into the formula for the atmospheric density; how important is this change? The drag coefficient, C_D, and the cross-sectional area, A, might also be varied.

11.8 Aero-Braking the Orbit of a Spacecraft

When a spacecraft approaches a planet, it will travel past it, moving in a hyperbolic orbit relative to the planet. If it is required that the craft be "captured" by the planet, then energy must be lost, so that the hyperbola becomes an ellipse. Usually, this is achieved by firing the rocket engines to produce a change in the velocity; but this is expensive, because the necessary fuel must be included in the payload for the original launch of the spacecraft. Another way to lose energy is to direct the orbit into the atmosphere of the planet, and let the drag forces do the work. A drawback is that the kinetic energy is transformed into heat: a lot of heat. (Ask any meteorite that has been unlucky enough to hit the Earth's atmosphere.) So there is danger of the spacecraft, and its contents, being fried. Accordingly, special shields are being designed, so that they can be deployed to increase the surface area (and hence the drag force) and, literally, to take the heat.

For the present, we shall ignore the heating and be concerned with dynamics. We shall use the Skylab model once again, but with different initial conditions, and different questions to be asked. The forces considered are gravitation and drag; lift will be included in a later project. Let's start the computation with initial conditions:

$$x = x_0,\ y = y_0,\ \dot{x} = -v_0,\ \dot{y} = 0,$$

where x_0 is much larger then y_0, so that the approach is almost along the x-axis. Suppose that $x_0 = 10^6$ km. Start off modestly, with $v_0 = 1$ km/sec. Pick a mass for your spacecraft, but keep the area, A, as a parameter that you can vary. For a given A, vary the starting value y_0 to find values such that the spacecraft will travel into the Earth's atmosphere, and, on emerging from it, be travelling in an elliptic orbit relative to the Earth. This requires that the quantity

$$E = \frac{1}{2}v^2 - \frac{\mu_e}{r} < 0. \tag{11.8.1}$$

Change A and see how the results are affected. Then increase v_0.

The first pass is the most important, since capture must occur then, or never. Later passes can then be used to "circularize" the orbit; so you might follow several revolutions, to see this happening.

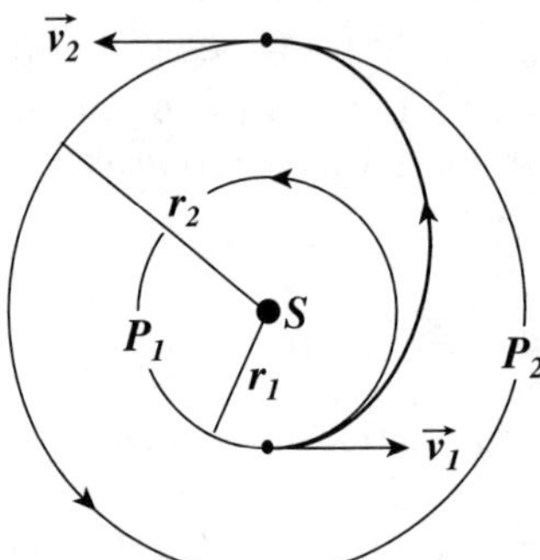

Figure 11.20: *A Hohmann transfer between two circular orbits.*

For realistic values of v_0, this project needs to be set in the context of interplanetary missions involving transfer from one planet to another. The simplest, and one of the best ways to do this is to use a *Hohmann transfer.* Suppose we want to transfer from a planet P_1 to another, P_2; they have coplanar, circular orbits with radii r_1 and r_2. If $r_1 < r_2$, then a Hohmann transfer would consist of half an elliptic orbit, having perihelion (the point closest to the Sun) on the orbit of P_1 and aphelion (the point furthest from the Sun) on the orbit of P_2. This is illustrated in figure 11.20. The following results will be quoted without derivation; derivations can be found in texts on celestial mechanics, such as Danby[30]. Note that in the design of this transfer, the gravitational effects of the two planets are ignored; only the Sun's gravitational field is used.

For a start, we shall use the unit of time to be the day; the unit of length to be the astronomical unit (AU) which is, essentially, the distance between the Earth and the Sun. One AU is equal to 1.496×10^8 km. The semimajor axis of the Hohmann ellipse is

$$a = \frac{1}{2}(r_1 + r_2). \tag{11.8.2}$$

The eccentricity of the ellipse is

$$e = \frac{r_2 - r_1}{r_2 + r_1}. \tag{11.8.3}$$

The time of transfer is

$$T = \frac{\pi a^{3/2}}{k}, \tag{11.8.4}$$

where $k = 0.017202$ is the *Gaussian gravitation constant.* The speeds at perihelion and aphelion are, respectively,

$$v_1 = k\left(\frac{1+e}{a(1-e)}\right)^{1/2}, \text{ and } v_2 = k\left(\frac{1-e}{a(1+e)}\right)^{1/2}. \tag{11.8.5}$$

Since the speeds in the circular orbits of the planets are $v_{c1} = kr_1^{-1/2}$ and $v_{c2} = kr_2^{-1/2}$, the differences in speeds at the beginning and end of the transfer are

$$\Delta v_1 = v_1 - v_{c1}, \text{ and } \Delta v_2 = v_{c2} - v_2. \tag{11.8.6}$$

It can be shown that for all possible elliptic transfer orbits from one planetary orbit to the other, the Hohmann transfer minimizes the sum $\Delta v_1 + \Delta v_2$. (Remember that the planetary forces have been neglected.)

Let us see some numbers for the case of the Earth ($r_1 = 1$) and Mars ($r_2 = 1.5237$). We find $a = 1.2618$ AU and $e = 0.2075$. The transfer time is 258.9 days. The speeds, as given above, are in AU/day. Since 1 AU/day = 1731.5 km/sec, these are easily converted to km/sec. Then with all speeds given in km/sec, $v_{c1} = 29.78$, $v_1 = 32.73$, so $\Delta v_1 = 2.95$. $v_{c2} = 24.13$, $v_2 = 21.48$, so $\Delta v_2 = 2.65$.

Suppose that you want to get captured by Mars. The equatorial radius is 3393 km. For the gravitational attraction, use $\mu_m = 0.4283 \times 10^5$ km^3/sec^2 in place of μ_e for the Earth. The density of the atmosphere is very variable. A reasonable formula is

$$\rho_{Mars} = 0.02439 e^{-0.118\,\mathrm{Alt}}\ \mathrm{kg/m}^3, \tag{11.8.7}$$

where Alt is the altitude measured in km.

Figure 11.21 illustrates the process of capture. The parameters used were as follows: Mass, 1 Earth mass. Radius, 6000 km. Atmospheric density at ground level, 1 kg/m^3. Scale height, 10 km. Mass of spacecraft, 10,000 kg. Cross-sectional area of spacecraft, 100 m^2. (Note that if the scale height is h, then the formula for the density is $\rho = \rho_0\, e^{-\mathrm{Alt}/h}$.) Starting conditions were: $x = 200,000$, $y = 14,830.2$ km, $v_x = 5.07895$, $v_y = 0$ km/sec. You can see from these numbers how sensitive the process is to the starting conditions!

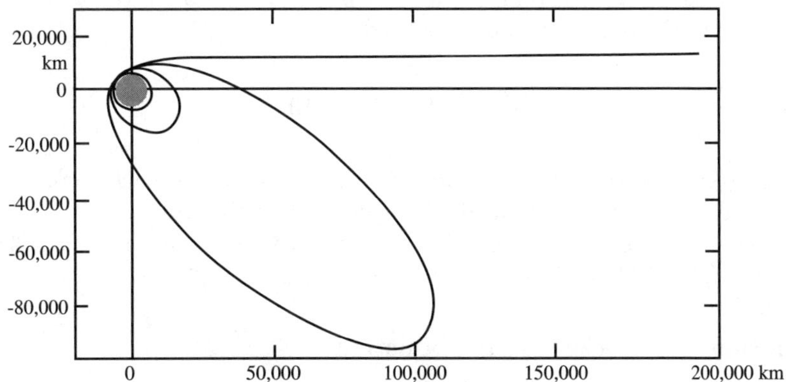

Figure 11.21: *Capture by aerobraking. The spacecraft approaches from the right in a hyperbolic orbit. It enters the atmosphere of the planet and revolves around it three times. The first atmospheric entry results in a new orbit which is elliptical, so that capture has taken place. The next two reduce the size of the ellipse.*

Heating of spacecraft is complicated. I shall summarize a simple treatment given by Ruppe [88], section 5.2.6, which provides some ideas about the order of magnitude involved. Ruppe starts by calculating that one kg of matter entering the Earth's atmosphere at parabolic speed carries enough kinetic energy to vaporize 20.7 kg of ice (initially at 0°C). This shows convincingly that only a small part of the energy dissipated in reentry can be absorbed by the spacecraft. The rate at which thermal energy flows onto the surface of the spacecraft is given by

$$\frac{dq}{dt} = \frac{1}{4} C_F \rho v^3, \tag{11.8.8}$$

where C_F, the skin friction coefficient, can be numerically approximated by

$$C_F = \frac{1}{300}. \tag{11.8.9}$$

It is convenient to express the atmospheric density ρ in terms of the value at sea level, $\rho_0 = 1.225$

kg m^{-3}, and the speed in units of the circular speed at zero altitude,

$$v_c = \sqrt{\frac{\mu_e}{R_e}} = \sqrt{\frac{3.986 \times 10^{14}}{6.378 \times 10^6}} = 7905 \text{ ms}^{-1}.$$

Then

$$\frac{dq}{dt} = \frac{1}{4}\frac{1}{300}\frac{\rho}{\rho_0}(0.1255)\left(\frac{v}{v_c}(7905)\right)^3 = 5.2 \times 10^7 \frac{\rho}{\rho_0}\left(\frac{v}{v_c}\right)^3. \tag{11.8.10}$$

In the worst-case scenario the spacecraft cools only by radiation. In this case the rate of cooling per unit area is given by Stefan's law,

$$\frac{dq_r}{dt} = \epsilon\sigma T^4, \tag{11.8.11}$$

where ϵ is the emissivity coefficient, T is the temperature in degrees Kelvin and $\sigma = 5.67 \times 10^{-8}$ Watt m^{-2}K^{-4}. Then, with $\epsilon = 0.9$,

$$\frac{dq_r}{dt} = 5.10 \times 10^{-11} T^4 \left[\frac{\text{kw}}{\text{m}^2}\right] = 5.10 \times 10^{-8} T^4. \tag{11.8.12}$$

Let us assume that, at a given temperature, T, we are in trouble if there is a net gain in heat. For $T = 700°$K, or 423°C, to avoid trouble, we need

$$\frac{\rho}{\rho_0}\left(\frac{v}{v_c}\right)^3 < 2.4 \times 10^{-5}. \tag{11.8.13}$$

So during the integration of the orbits, calculate the left-hand side at each step.

There are, of course, other ways to dissipate heat; but this calculation provides some clues about when to expect trouble. If you increase the critical temperature to $T = 1000°$K, or 723°C, the number on the right of (11.8.13) increases by the factor $(10/7)^3 \approx 4$.

11.9 The Motion of a Rocket. 1: Introduction

In this and the next few projects we shall be looking at some elementary facets of rocket propulsion. For further reading, there are several texts that include this or similar material with a lot more essential details. These include texts by Ball [8], Ruppe [88], Thomson [95], Vinh [100] and Wiesel [108].

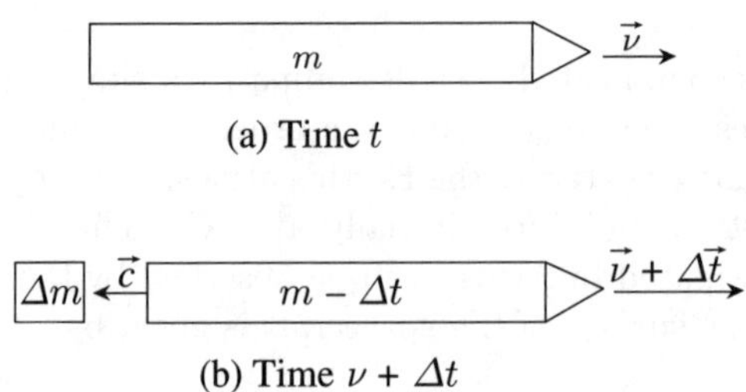

Figure 11.22: *The kinematics of a rocket at times t and $t + \Delta t$.*

We start by deriving a fundamental equation for the motion of a rocket. This was first given by the Russian scientist I.V. Meshchersky in 1897. A rocket has variable mass. In figure 11.22 part (a) shows a mass m moving with velocity $\vec{v}$, at time t. In part (b), a mass Δm has been expelled with velocity $\vec{c}$ *relative to the rocket* (so that it has velocity $\vec{v} + \vec{c}$ in inertial space); what is left of the rocket, with mass $m - \Delta m$ now has velocity $\vec{v} + \Delta\vec{v}$. The linear momentum of the system before the expulsion is

$$m\vec{v}.$$

After expulsion it is

$$(m - \Delta m)(\vec{v} + \Delta\vec{v}) + \Delta m(\vec{c} + \vec{v}).$$

By Newton's second law, the difference between these is $\vec{F}_{ext}\,\Delta t$ where $\vec{F}_{ext}$ is the external force acting on the system. So

$$(m - \Delta m)(\vec{v} + \Delta\vec{v}) + \Delta m(\vec{c} + \vec{v}) - m\vec{v} = \vec{F}_{ext}\,\Delta t. \tag{11.9.1}$$

Simplifying this, and neglecting the product $\Delta m \Delta\vec{v}$, we have

$$m\Delta\vec{v} + \vec{c}\,\Delta m = \vec{F}_{ext}\,\Delta t. \tag{11.9.2}$$

The quantity Δm is positive. It is usual to work with $\dot{m}$, the rate of change of the rocket's mass, which is negative. So

$$\Delta m = -\dot{m}\Delta t.$$

Then, dividing equation (11.9.2) by Δt and taking the limit as Δt goes to zero, we have

$$m\frac{d\vec{v}}{dt} - \vec{c}\,\dot{m} = \vec{F}_{ext}, \tag{11.9.3}$$

Meshchersky's equation.

This equation is easily solved if there are no external forces, and if the exhaust velocity, $\vec{c}$, is constant. Then it is separable, so that $dv = cdm/m$; so if $\vec{v}_0$ and m_0 represent initial values, and $\Delta\vec{v}$ is the velocity increment,

$$\Delta\vec{v} = \vec{v} - \vec{v}_0 = -\vec{c}\ln\left(\frac{m_0}{m}\right). \tag{11.9.4}$$

$\Delta\vec{v}$, or, colloquially, "delta-vee," is the *characteristic velocity.* It depends on the fuel expenditure and the exhaust velocity, but not on the time for the maneuver.

The *thrust* of the engine is

$$\vec{T} = \vec{c}\,\dot{m}. \tag{11.9.5}$$

Returning briefly to the time interval t to $t + \Delta t$, the *impulse* given to the rocket is $\vec{T}\,\Delta t = -\vec{c}\,\Delta m$. The weight of fuel used in this time is $-(\dot{m}\Delta t)g = g\Delta m$. The ratio of the scalar value of the impulse divided by the weight of fuel used (or the impulse per unit weight of the propellant) is called the *specific impulse,*

$$I_{sp} = \frac{c}{g} = \frac{T}{\dot{m}g} = \frac{T}{\dot{w}}. \tag{11.9.6}$$

This is also defined as the thrust of unit weight of propellant multiplied by the number of seconds required to burn it. Values of I_{sp} are in the range of 200 to 500 seconds, corresponding to exhaust speeds of about 2000 to 5000 m/sec.

Another thrust force, usually not as important as $\vec{c}\,\dot{m}$ in (11.9.5), needs to be included. The actual matter ejected from the rocket will be gas streaming out of a nozzle, with area A_e. Let the pressure in the nozzle be P_e and that of the ambient atmosphere be P_a. The difference between these pressures acting on the area A_e will create a force at the nozzle

$$(P_e - P_a)A_e$$

in the direction of the unit vector $\hat{n}$ pointing into the rocket. Then the total propulsive force is

$$-\vec{c}\,\dot{m} + (P_e - P_a)A_e\hat{n} = -\left(1 + \frac{(P_e - P_a)A_e}{\dot{m}c}\right)\vec{c}\,\dot{m} = -\vec{c}_e\,\dot{m}, \tag{11.9.7}$$

where $\vec{c}_e$ is the *effective exhaust velocity.* This will increase with increasing altitude. The *effective specific impulse* is

$$I_{sp,e} = \frac{c_e}{g}. \tag{11.9.8}$$

1. For a first project, I suggest that you investigate vertical motion. For this case, the equations can be solved by formula, for some applications; but numerical integration will be essential later, so you might as well start off numerically. Initially, ignore the contribution to the thrust due to the pressures at the nozzle. For the moment, assume a flat Earth. The model will be defined by the quantities

   m_0 initial mass in kg,
   m_{bo} final mass, at burnout,
   t_{bo} time, in seconds, from launch to burnout,
   I_{sp} specific impulse.

   Then

   $$c = I_{sp}g,\ \dot{m} = -\frac{m_0 - m_{bo}}{t_{bo}},\quad m = m_0\left(1 + \frac{\dot{m}}{m_0}t\right).$$

   g is the acceleration due to gravity. If the z-axis points vertically upward, the equations to be solved are

   $$\left.\begin{aligned}\frac{dz}{dt} &= v,\\ \frac{dv}{dt} &= -c\frac{\dot{m}}{m} - g.\end{aligned}\right] \tag{11.9.9}$$

   The numerical values are, of course, up to you. For a start, you might try

   $$m_0 = 5000\,\text{kg},\ m_{bo} = 1000\,\text{kg},\ t_{bo} = 60\,\text{sec},\ I_{sp} = 400\,\text{sec}.$$

   Start with $t = 0,\ z = 0,\ \dot{z} = 0$. Plot z and $\dot{z}$ as functions of the time. Next, keep the same $\dot{m}$, while letting $m_{bo} = 900$. What effect does this have on the altitude and speed at burnout? Decrease m_{bo} some more, and continue to discuss these changes.

2. The model given by equations (11.9.9) ignores atmospheric drag, and assumes constant gravitational acceleration. To investigate the justification for this, first modify the second equation to

   $$\frac{dv}{dt} = -c\frac{\dot{m}}{m} - g\frac{R_E^2}{(R_E + z)^2}, \tag{11.9.10}$$

   where $g = 9.81$ m/sec^2 and $R_E = 6.378 \cdot 10^6$ m is the radius of the Earth. Compare the results for this equation when the distance from the center of the Earth reaches 42,227 km, the value for a geosynchronous Earth orbit, with results when the acceleration is assumed constant. In particular, note the differences in the Δv's. For constant acceleration,

   $$\Delta v = v - v_0 = c\ln\left(\frac{m_0}{m}\right) - gt. \tag{11.9.11}$$

   So, with this approximation, the Δv's found by neglecting gravity must be reduced by gt where t is the time of burnout. For burnout time of one minute, this amounts to nearly 600 m/sec. This approximation is valid for a low Earth orbit, with altitude between 200 and 300 km. Investigate the time reduction when higher altitudes are involved.

3. To test for the effects of drag, try

$$\frac{dv}{dt} = -c\frac{\dot{m}}{m} - \frac{1}{2}C_D\frac{A\rho}{m}v^2 - g, \tag{11.9.12}$$

where C_D is the drag coefficient; appropriate values are of the order of 1 or 2. A is the cross-sectional area of the rocket; you pick that. ρ is the density of the Earth's atmosphere. An adequate formula is

$$\rho = 1.225e^{-0.1385z}\,\text{kg/m}^3, \quad z < 100\text{km}. \tag{11.9.13}$$

How much does atmospheric drag influence the height and speed at burnout?

4. Now consider the effects of the extra force due to the imbalance of pressure, $(P_e - P_a)$. Suppose that we have two numbers, the effective specific impulses at ground level, when $P_a = P_g$, and outside the atmosphere, when $P_a = 0$. Call these I_g and I_∞, respectively. Then the effective specific impulse at altitude z will be

$$I_{sp,e} = I_\infty - (I_\infty - I_g)\frac{P_z}{P_g} = I_\infty - (I_\infty - I_g)e^{-\alpha z}. \tag{11.9.14}$$

Try numbers such as $I_g = 400$ sec and $I_\infty = 420$ sec. Compare the use of the variable specific impulse and constant $I_{sp} = 400$ sec. Find out how much the maximum height of a vertical rocket is affected.

11.10 The Motion of a Rocket. 2: Multi-Stage Rockets

As before, we shall have to develop some definitions and concepts before the computations can begin. In most of the discussion in this section, external forces such as gravity and drag will be neglected.

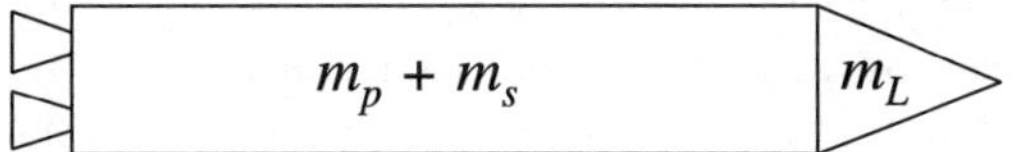

Figure 11.23: *A single-stage rocket.*

First, we need to introduce notation for the parts of a single-stage rocket. There are several masses to be considered:

- m_L is the *payload mass.* Ultimately, this is what really matters.
- m_p is the mass of the propellant.
- m_s is the *structural mass,* which includes rocket engines, controls and associated instruments.
- m_0 is the initial mass: $m_0 = m_p + m_s + m_L$. m_b is the mass at burnout: $m_b = m_s + m_L$, assuming that all the fuel has been used.

Associated with these masses, there are three important parameters:

$$R = \frac{m_0}{m_b} = \frac{m_0}{m_s + m_L} \tag{11.10.1}$$

is the *mass ratio.* Note that from equation (11.9.4) we have

$$\Delta v = c\ln R. \tag{11.10.2}$$

$$\lambda = \frac{m_L}{m_p + m_s} \tag{11.10.3}$$

is the *payload ratio.*

$$\epsilon = \frac{m_s}{m_p + m_s} \tag{11.10.4}$$

is the *structural ratio.*

In terms of these, we have

$$R = \frac{1+\lambda}{\epsilon+\lambda}. \tag{11.10.5}$$

Let's see what would be needed to give a payload of 1000 kg a Δv of 8 km/sec or 8,000 m/sec. Take $I_{sp} = 400$ sec, and $\epsilon = 0.1$.
From equation (11.9.6), the exhaust speed is $c = I_{sp}g = 400g = 3924$ m/s.
From equation (11.10.2), the mass ratio $R = e^{\Delta v/c} = 7.68$.
From equation (11.10.5), $\lambda = \dfrac{1-R\epsilon}{R-1} = 0.0347$.
From equation (11.10.3), $m_p + m_s = \dfrac{m_L}{\lambda} = 28800$ kg. Then $m_s = \epsilon(m_p + m_s) = 2880$ kg and $m_p = 25900$ kg.

Finally, $m_0 = m_p + m_s + m_L = 29800$ kg.

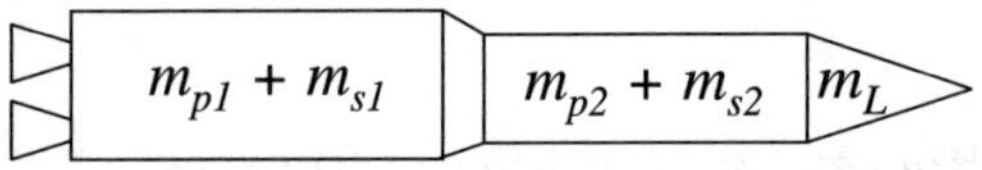

Figure 11.24: *A two-stage rocket.*

Next, let's consider a two-stage rocket. The engine for the first stage has masses m_{p1}, m_{s1}, and parameters c_1, λ_1, ϵ_1. The payload is m_{L1}, which consists of the masses of all remaining components. Then the starting mass for the first stage is $m_1 = m_{p1} + m_{s1} + m_{L1}$. At the completion of the first stage, m_{p1} has been burned off, and m_{s1} is jettisoned.

Let the engine for the second stage have masses m_{p2}, m_{s2}, and parameters c_2, λ_2, ϵ_2. It will have starting mass $m_2 = m_{L1} = m_{p2} + m_{s2} + m_{L2}$. If there are only two stages, then $m_{L2} = m_L$, the mass of the final payload.

For the first stage, the appropriate mass ratio is

$$R_1 = \frac{m_{p1} + m_{s1} + m_{p2} + m_{s2} + m_L}{m_{s1} + m_{p2} + m_{s2} + m_L} = \frac{m_{p1} + m_{s1} + m_{L1}}{m_{s1} + m_{L1}}. \tag{11.10.6}$$

For the second stage

$$R_2 = \frac{m_{p2} + m_{s2} + m_{L2}}{m_{s2} + m_{L2}} = \frac{m_{p2} + m_{s2} + m_L}{m_{s2} + m_L}. \tag{11.10.7}$$

Let's see some numbers. For both stages, take $I_{sp} = 400$ sec, so $c = 3924$ m/sec and $\epsilon = 0.1$. Let $\Delta v_1 = 6000$ m/sec and $\Delta v_2 = 2000$ m/sec. The values of λ will be derived. The final payload is to have mass $m_L = m_{L2} = 1000$ kg.

We work back from the second stage. Calculating as before, we find

$$R_2 = 1.665, \lambda_2 = 1.254, m_{p2} + m_{s2} = 798, m_{s2} = 800 \text{ kg}, m_{p2} = 720 \text{ kg},$$
$$m_2 = m_{L1} = 1800 \text{ kg}.$$

Next, for the first stage,

$$R_1 = 4.614, \lambda_1 = 0.149, m_{p1} + m_{s1} = 12070, m_{s1} = 1207 \text{ kg}, m_{p1} = 10860 \text{ kg},$$
$$m_1 = 12660 \text{ kg}.$$

Note the striking saving of fuel, when these results are compared with those for the single-stage rocket.

Two questions arise from this discussion. Could we have made a better choice of the values of Δv for the two stages? How much better off can we be if we use three stages?

The first of these will now be addressed.

Let us specify quantities c_1, c_2, ϵ_1, ϵ_2 for the first and second stages, a final payload, m_L kg and a total velocity increment Δv_T m/sec. Then

$$\Delta v_T = c_1 \ln R_1 + c_2 \ln R_2. \tag{11.10.8}$$

We want to find values of R_1 and R_2 to minimize the mass at launch, $m_1 = m_{p1} + m_{s1} + m_{L1}$, subject to the condition (11.10.8). First, verify the identity

$$\frac{(1-\epsilon)R}{1-\epsilon R} = \frac{m_p + m_s + m_L}{m_L}. \tag{11.10.9}$$

Then note that

$$\frac{m_{p1} + m_{s1} + m_{L1}}{m_{L1}} \cdot \frac{m_{p2} + m_{s2} + m_{L2}}{m_{L2}} = \frac{m_{p1} + m_{s1} + m_{L1}}{m_{L2}} = \frac{m_1}{m_L}. \tag{11.10.10}$$

Therefore

$$\frac{m_1}{m_L} = \frac{(1-\epsilon_1)R_1}{1-\epsilon_1 R_1} \cdot \frac{(1-\epsilon_2)R_2}{1-\epsilon_2 R_2},$$

so if we define

$$f(R_1, R_2) = \ln\left(\frac{m_1}{m_L}\right) \tag{11.10.11}$$

$$= \sum_{i=1}^{2} \left(\ln(1-\epsilon_i) + \ln R_i - \ln(1-\epsilon_i R_i)\right), \tag{11.10.12}$$

then we want to minimize $f(R_1, R_2)$ subject to the constraint

$$g(R_1, R_2) = \Delta v_T - \sum_{i=1}^{2} c_i \ln R_i = 0, \tag{11.10.13}$$

which is derived from equation (11.10.8).

Minimizing a function $f(x,y)$, subject to a constraint $g(x,y) = 0$, can be done using a *Lagrange multiplier*, μ. It is necessary to solve the equations

$$\left.\begin{aligned} \frac{\partial g}{\partial x} + \mu\frac{\partial g}{\partial x} &= 0, \\ \frac{\partial g}{\partial y} + \mu\frac{\partial g}{\partial y} &= 0, \\ g(x,y) &= 0. \end{aligned}\right] \tag{11.10.14}$$

For the current problem, the first two equations are

$$\frac{1}{R_i} + \frac{\epsilon_i}{1-\epsilon_i R_i} - \mu\frac{c_i}{R_i} = 0, \; i = 1, 2, \tag{11.10.15}$$

having solutions

$$R_i = \frac{\mu c_i - 1}{\mu c_i \epsilon_i}, \; i = 1, 2. \tag{11.10.16}$$

Substituting into the constraint equation (11.10.13), we have

$$h(\mu) = \Delta v_T - \sum_{i=1}^{2} c_i \ln\left(\frac{\mu c_i - 1}{\mu c_i \epsilon_i}\right) = 0. \tag{11.10.17}$$

Equation (11.10.17) must be solved for the multiplier μ. In the case $c_1 = c_2$, $\epsilon_1 = \epsilon_2$, this is easy; it is also simple to see that in this case $R_1 = R_2$, $\Delta v_1 = \Delta v_2 = \Delta v_T/2$. More generally, I recommend the use of the secant method. So I shall digress for a moment to describe this.

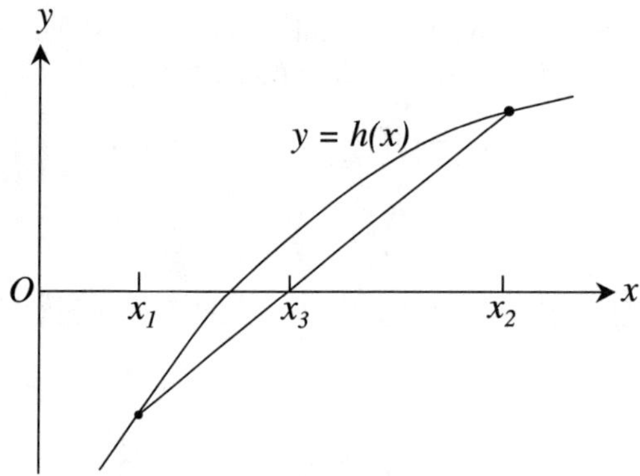

Figure 11.25: *Use of the secant method to make one iteration in solving* $h(x) = 0$.

To solve $h(x) = 0$ by the secant method involves the calculation of a sequence $\{x_n\}, n = 1, 2, 3, ...,$ that, if all goes well, will converge to a solution. Each iteration starts with two values of x; in figure 11.25 these are x_1 and x_2. The chord joining the points with coordinates $(x_1, h(x_1))$ and $(x_2, h(x_2))$ intersects the x-axis at the point x_3, where

$$x_3 = \frac{x_1 h(x_2) - x_2 h(x_1)}{h(x_2) - h(x_1)}. \tag{11.10.18}$$

x_1 is then discarded, and the same construction is made, using x_2 and x_3 to calculate x_4, and so on. (Note that the point x_3 need not lie between x_1 and x_2, as it is shown in figure 11.25.) The trick is to start off with two values of x that are close to the required solution. One technique is to conduct a search; start with a value for μ and an increment. Calculate $h(\mu)$ for successive values of μ until its sign changes. Then the values of μ just before and after the change are used to start the secant iterations. This requires careful monitoring, since, with a bad choice of the increment, the sign may not change. Another suggestion for the equation (11.10.17), $h(\mu) = 0$, is to use the value of μ found by setting $c_2 = c_1$ and $\epsilon_2 = \epsilon_1$ and then the value of μ found by setting $c_1 = c_2$ and $\epsilon_1 = \epsilon_2$. Once μ has been found, the R_i are known, and the masses can be calculated.

Continue with the example discussed above, with $c_1 = c_2 = 3924$ m/sec, and $\epsilon_1 = \epsilon_2 = 0.1$. $m_L = m_{L2} = 1000$ kg. From the second stage,

$$R_2 = 2.771, \lambda_2 = 0.408, m_{p2} + m_{s2} = 2451, m_{s2} = 245 \text{ kg}, m_{p2} = 2206 \text{ kg},$$
$$m_2 = m_{L1} = 3451 \text{ kg}.$$

Next, for the first stage,

$$R_1 = 2.771, \lambda_1 = 0.408, m_{p1} + m_{s1} = 8455, m_{s1} = 845 \text{ kg}, m_{p1} = 7611 \text{ kg},$$
$$m_1 = 11.910 \text{ kg},$$

a small reduction from the non-optimal value of 12580 kg calculated above.

An advantage of equations (11.10.15), (11.10.16) and (11.10.17) is that if the index i is allowed to range from 1 to 3, we immediately have the equations for the three-stage rocket; and we can continue, in principle, with any number of stages. Consider the three-stage rocket where all the $c_i = 3924$ and the $\epsilon_i = 0.1$. With $\Delta v_T = 8000$ m/sec, each $\Delta v_i = 8000/3$ m/sec, giving $R_i = 1.973$ and $\lambda_i = 0.8250$. With the final payload $m_L = m_{L3} = 1000$ kg, we have, for successive stages,

$$m_{p3} + m_{s3} = 1212 \text{ kg}, \; m_{s3} = 121 \text{ kg}, \; m_{p3} = 1091 \text{ kg}, \; m_3 = m_{L2} = 2212 \text{ kg}.$$
$$m_{p2} + m_{s2} = 2681 \text{ kg}, \; m_{s2} = 268 \text{ kg}, \; m_{p2} = 2417 \text{ kg}, \; m_2 = m_{L1} = 4893 \text{ kg}.$$
$$m_{p1} + m_{s1} = 5931 \text{ kg}, \; m_{s1} = 593 \text{ kg}, \; m_{p1} = 5338 \text{ kg}, \; m_1 = 10820 \text{ kg}.$$

Projects for this section are similar to those in the preceding one, but should now be addressed in the context of multi-stage rockets. The analysis just given ignores all forces other than thrust. If we want to finish a maneuver with a given Δv, then allowance must be made for the loss due to gravity. For a start, only consider maneuvers within a few 100 km from the surface of the Earth, when this reduction is gt, t being the burnout time.

From the expression $\lambda = (1 - R\epsilon)/(R - 1)$ it is clear that

$$R\epsilon < 1. \tag{11.10.19}$$

You can verify that if $R\epsilon = 1$, then the mass of the payload is zero. So for given ϵ and I_{sp}, there is a maximum Δv. For $\epsilon = 0.1$ and $I_{sp} = 400$ sec, you can verify that $\Delta v = 10,000$ m/sec is impossible to achieve in one stage. But this Δv can be achieved by a multi-stage rocket. Design such a rocket.

For a geosynchronous Earth orbit, the radius is 42,227 km, with orbital speed 3071 m/sec. Set up multi-stage rockets that are capable of reaching this altitude. For instance, design one so that the speed on attaining this altitude is zero. (In this case, a horizontal $\Delta v = 3,000$ m/sec would be needed to put the payload into circular orbit.)

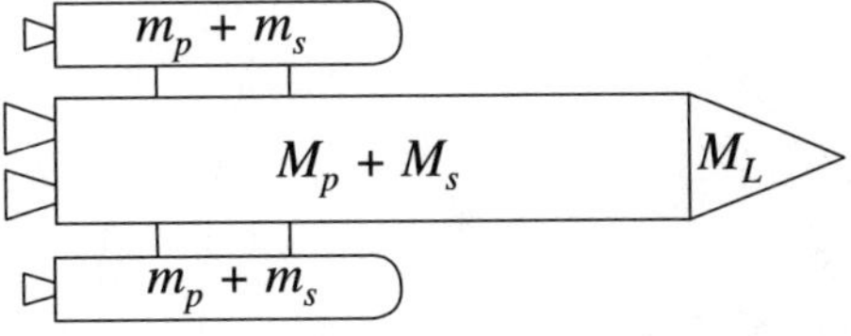

Figure 11.26: *Parallel staging of rockets.*

The launching of many spacecraft involves *parallel staging.* An example is shown in figure 11.26. The main engine has structural and propellant masses M_s and M_p and exhaust speed C. Two identical smaller booster rockets have similar parameters m_s, m_p and c. The payload has mass M_L. During the first stage of burning the boosters are completely burned, and the mass of fuel M_{p1} is burned from the main engine. The boosters are then discarded, and during the second stage the remaining fuel is burned.

The total thrust in the first stage is

$$T = 2\dot{m}c + \dot{M}C = (2\dot{m} + \dot{M})\overline{C}.$$

Then we have

$$\left.\begin{aligned} R_1 &= \frac{2m_p + 2m_s + M_p + M_s + M_L}{2m_s + M_s + (M_p - M_{p1}) + M_L}, \\ \epsilon_1 &= \frac{2m_s + M_s}{2m_s + 2m_p + M_s + M_{p1}}, \\ \overline{C} &= \frac{2\dot{m}c + \dot{M}C}{2\dot{m} + \dot{M}}, \\ \Delta v_1 &= \overline{C} \ln R_1. \end{aligned}\right] \tag{11.10.20}$$

For the second stage,

$$\left.\begin{aligned} R_2 &= \frac{M_s + (M_p - M_{p1}) + M_L}{M_s + M_L}, \\ \epsilon_2 &= \frac{M_s}{(M_p - M_{p1}) + M_s}, \\ \Delta v_2 &= C \ln R_2. \end{aligned}\right] \qquad (11.10.21)$$

With these definitions, the parallel-staged craft can be treated as if it were simply staged.

Construct such a vehicle. For a given total $\Delta v = \Delta v_1 + \Delta v_2$ see if you can adapt the theory to optimize the configuration.

11.11 The Motion of a Rocket. 3: Two-Dimensional Motion

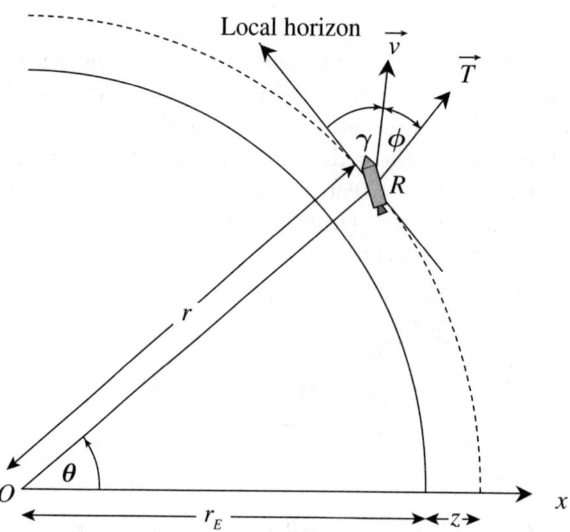

Figure 11.27: *Notation for the two-dimensional motion of a rocket.*

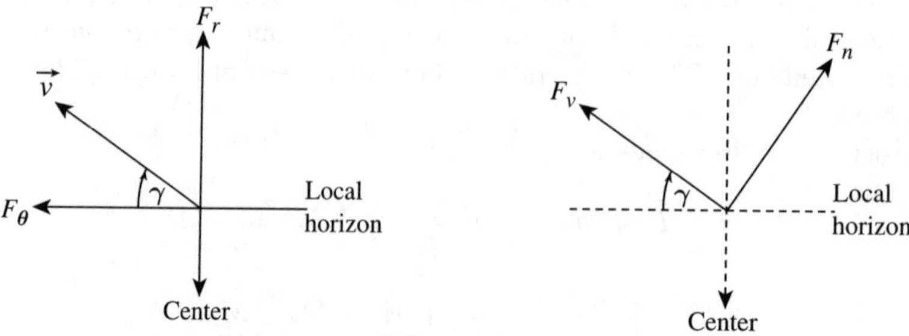

Figure 11.28: *Different force resolutions.*

We shall consider motion of a rocket with respect to a non-rotating Earth. The motion will take place in two dimensions, and the position of the rocket will be given by polar coordinates (r, θ) where the origin is at the center of the Earth, and θ is measured from a reference x-axis, as shown in figure 11.27. The altitude of the rocket is $z = r - r_E$, where r_E is the radius of the Earth. Let the orbital velocity, having magnitude v, make the angle γ with the local horizon. Let the thrust,

T, make the angle ϕ with the velocity. D is the drag force, and the acceleration due to gravity is k/r^2.

To derive the equations, first note that, since the radial and transverse components of the velocity are $\dot{r}$ and $r\dot{\theta}$, respectively, then

$$\dot{r} = v \sin\gamma \text{ and } r\dot{\theta} = v\cos\gamma. \tag{11.11.1}$$

If F_r and F_θ are the radial and transverse components of force, as shown in figure 11.28, then the equations of motion are

$$m(\ddot{r} - r\dot{\theta}^2) = F_r, \text{ and } m(r\ddot{\theta} + 2\dot{r}\dot{\theta}) = F_\theta. \tag{11.11.2}$$

For ease of interpretation we want to resolve the forces tangentially, or parallel to $\vec{v}$ and normally, with respective components F_v and F_n, as shown. Then

$$F_v = F_r \sin\gamma + F_\theta \cos\gamma \text{ and } F_n = F_r \cos\gamma - F_\theta \sin\gamma. \tag{11.11.3}$$

Now $v^2 = \dot{r}^2 + r^2\dot{\theta}^2$. So

$$\begin{aligned} v\dot{v} &= \dot{r}\ddot{r} + r\dot{r}\dot{\theta}^2 + r^2\dot{\theta}\ddot{\theta} \\ &= \dot{r}(F_r/m + r\dot{\theta}^2) + r\dot{r}\dot{\theta}^2 + r\dot{\theta}(F_\theta/m - 2\dot{r}\dot{\theta}). \end{aligned}$$

So

$$m\dot{v} = \frac{\dot{r}}{v}F_r + \frac{r\dot{\theta}}{v}F_\theta = F_v. \tag{11.11.4}$$

Differentiating equations (11.11.1),

$$\ddot{r} = \dot{v}\sin\gamma + v\dot{\gamma}\cos\gamma \text{ and } r\ddot{\theta} + \dot{r}\dot{\theta} = \dot{v}\cos\gamma - v\dot{\gamma}\sin\gamma.$$

Using equations (11.11.2),

$$F_r/m + r\dot{\theta}^2 = \dot{v}\sin\gamma + v\dot{\gamma}\cos\gamma \text{ and } F_\theta/m - \dot{r}\dot{\theta} = \dot{v}\cos\gamma - v\dot{\gamma}\sin\gamma.$$

Multiply the first by $\cos\gamma$ and the second by $-\sin\gamma$ and add, to eliminate $\dot{v}$. Then

$$(F_r/m)\cos\gamma - (F_\theta/m)\sin\gamma + r\dot{\theta}^2\cos\gamma + \dot{r}\dot{\theta}\sin\gamma = v\dot{\gamma}.$$

The terms $r\dot{\theta}^2\cos\gamma + \dot{r}\dot{\theta}\sin\gamma$ can be simplified as $(v^2/r)\cos\gamma$, with the help of equations (11.11.1). Finally,

$$F_n + m\frac{v^2}{r}\cos\gamma = mv\dot{\gamma}. \tag{11.11.5}$$

Here we have $F_v = T\cos\phi - D - mk\sin\gamma/r^2$ and $F_n = T\sin\phi - mk\cos\gamma/r^2$. So we can finally assemble the complete set of equations as

$$\left.\begin{aligned} \frac{dv}{dt} &= \frac{T\cos\phi}{m} - \frac{D}{m} - \frac{k\sin\gamma}{r^2}, \\ \frac{d\gamma}{dt} &= \frac{v\cos\gamma}{r} + \frac{T\sin\phi}{mv} - \frac{k\cos\gamma}{vr^2}, \\ \frac{dr}{dt} &= \frac{dz}{dt} = v\sin\gamma, \\ \frac{d\theta}{dt} &= \frac{v\cos\gamma}{r}, \\ T &= -\dot{m}c = -\dot{m}I_{sp}g_0, \\ m &= m_0 + \dot{m}t = m_0\left(1 - \frac{1}{I_{sp}}\frac{T}{m_0 g_0}t\right). \end{aligned}\right] \tag{11.11.6}$$

g_0 is the acceleration due to gravity at zero altitude. Equations (11.9.12) and (11.9.13) can be used to give D. But D can usually be neglected. (If in doubt, verify this!)

The simplest case is to let $\phi = 0$, so that the thrust is directed along the flight path. The resulting change in the direction of $\vec{v}$ is called a *gravity turn.*

In applying these equations, suppose that the first stage burning is finished, and that the rocket has been rotating so that it is no longer vertical. The second stage flight, following equations (11.11.1), will carry the payload into a nearly circular orbit. That is, burnout should occur when $\gamma \approx 0$ and when the speed is close to the circular speed, or $v \approx \sqrt{k/r}$. If the latter condition is hard to meet, then a small Δv might be applied in a third-stage burn to give the payload the correct circular speed.

There are a lot of parameters to be considered. In fact, for given starting conditions, you will feel pretty good if you can find *any* parameters that will lead to a satisfactory orbit. But persevere!

For example the following figures led to an orbit at burnout with altitudes at perigee and apogee of 215 km and 440 km:

$$\begin{aligned} m_p &= 10{,}000 \text{ kg} \\ m_s + m_L &= 160 \text{ kg} \\ I_{sp} &= 340 \text{ sec} \\ t_b &= 328 \text{ sec} \end{aligned}$$

Initial conditions

$$\begin{aligned} \text{Altitude} &= 10{,}000 \text{ m} \\ \text{Speed} &= 2{,}000 \text{ m/sec} \\ \gamma &= 41^\circ \end{aligned}$$

Another approach is to start with a low Earth orbit, and transfer to a circular geosynchronous orbit, with radius 42227 km. Or go to the Moon.

11.12 The Motion of a Rocket. 4: Low-Thrust Orbits

We have been discussing high-thrust rockets with chemical propellants and short burn intervals, and thrust to weight ratios of the order of one. In contrast, electrically powered rockets have very low thrust to weight ratios, and are powered essentially continuously; they may be capable of producing accelerations of only $10^{-5}g_0$ to $10^{-3}g_0$ where g_0 is the acceleration due to gravity on the surface of the Earth. The launching of a rocket requires high-thrust engines. But once you have reached a parking orbit, and if you are not in too much of a hurry, you might consider leisurely maneuvers using low thrust.

The ratio $\dot{m}/m_0$ is very small, and although there may be substantial mass loss over an entire mission, we shall neglect it here. (It can be introduced fairly easily, using the rocket equations.) So the acceleration due to thrust will be constant: call it ϵ km/sec^2. This thrust will be directed tangentially.

We shall start with orbits around the Earth. With origin at the center of the Earth, and with kilometers and seconds as units of length and time, the equation of motion of the rocket, with position vector $\vec{r}$ is

$$\frac{d^2\vec{r}}{dt^2} = -\mu_e \frac{\vec{r}}{r^3} + \epsilon\frac{\vec{v}}{v}, \tag{11.12.1}$$

where $\vec{v}$ is the velocity. μ_e, the *geocentric gravitational constant*, is given by

$$\mu_e = 3.986005 \times 10^5 \text{ km}^3/\text{sec}^2. \tag{11.12.2}$$

With $\epsilon > 0$, this assumes that the thrust is forward. You will need to reverse the thrust at times; then change the signs before ϵ.

One way to resolve equation (11.12.1) is to use the notation of figure 11.27 and equations (11.11.6). Then the equations can be written as

$$\left.\begin{aligned}\frac{dv}{dt} &= -\mu_e\frac{\sin\gamma}{r^2}+\epsilon,\\ \frac{d\gamma}{dt} &= -\mu_e\frac{\cos\gamma}{vr^2}+\frac{v\cos\gamma}{r},\\ \frac{dr}{dt} &= v\sin\gamma,\\ \frac{d\theta}{dt} &= \frac{v\cos\gamma}{r}.\end{aligned}\right] \tag{11.12.3}$$

Alternatively, you can use Cartesian coordinates

$$\left.\begin{aligned}r &= \sqrt{x^2+y^2},\\ v &= \sqrt{v_x^2+v_y^2},\\ \frac{dx}{dt} &= v_x,\\ \frac{dv_x}{dt} &= -\mu_e\frac{x}{r^3}+\epsilon\frac{v_x}{v},\\ \frac{dy}{dt} &= v_y,\\ \frac{dv_y}{dt} &= -\mu_e\frac{y}{r^3}+\epsilon\frac{v_y}{v}.\end{aligned}\right] \tag{11.12.4}$$

For a first project, consider the transfer between two circular orbits, from a smaller to a larger one. Note that the equatorial radius of the Earth is 6378 km. Choose a value for ϵ in the range $10^{-5}g_0$ to $10^{-3}g_0$ where $g_0 = 0.00981$ km/sec^2. You will need to start with forward thrust, resulting in an orbit that is spiralling outward. Then if you were to turn off the engine, you would not be moving at right angles to the radius, so you would not be moving in a circular orbit. Consequently, the thrust will have to be reversed before the required orbit is reached. Experiment with this. One way to get started is to use forward thrust until r has increased substantially; then reverse the thrust, and continue calculation until $\gamma = 0$, or, equivalently, $\dot{r} = 0$. If you become frustrated, consider changing the magnitude of ϵ when the thrust is reversed. See if you can go from a low Earth orbit to a synchronous orbit.

One problem to be faced is that of computer output. The spiralling is **slow** to get going. Watching graphics on a screen is no problem, assuming that you can keep your patience. If you are watching numerical output on a screen, it is best to use equations (11.12.3), since you can then keep track of r. Guard against excessive printout.

Once the spiralling gets going, it progresses rapidly. One use of low-thrust engines is to escape from the Earth. This is interpreted as having a speed relative to the Earth that exceeds the speed of escape, v_p; this is given by

$$v_p = \sqrt{2\mu_e/r}. \tag{11.12.5}$$

Starting with a circular orbit with altitude, say, 200 km, find the time taken for escape, the distance from the Earth, and the speed, for different values of the thrust ϵ.

Another project is to design an orbit from the Earth to Mars. Several simplifications are in order. Assume that the two planets move in circular orbits in the same plane. Then assume that the mission can be divided into three dynamical problems:

1. Escape from the Earth. The origin will be at the center of the Earth, and only the gravitational force of the Earth will be considered. The motion will start with a circular orbit of low altitude.

2. Motion between the orbits of the planets. The origin will be at the Sun, and only the solar attraction will be considered.

3. Capture by Mars. Now the origin is at the center of Mars, and only Martian attraction is considered. The motion should end in a circular orbit of low altitude.

To set the stage, we need some way to decide when each section begins or ends. Since we are making some fairly gross approximations, there is no precise solution. If we are close enough to the Earth, then it is best to use equations with the origin at the Earth, and perturbations by the Sun. As we move away from the Earth, there comes a stage where it is better to use equations with the origin at the Sun, and perturbations by the Earth. The border between these two states is usually defined by a sphere, centered at the Earth, called the *activity sphere.* If the masses of the Earth and Sun are m_e and m_s, and their mutual distance is D, then the radius of the activity sphere is

$$r_{act,e} = D\left(m_e/m_s\right)^{2/5}. \tag{11.12.6}$$

The distance from the Earth to the Sun is one *astronomical unit*, 1 AU, equal to 1.49598×10^8 km. Taking $m_e = 5.9742 \times 10^{24}$ kg and $m_s = 1.9981 \times 10^{30}$ kg, we find the radius of the activity sphere for the Earth to be

$$r_{act,e} = 0.006170 \text{ AU} \ = 923000 \text{ km}. \tag{11.12.7}$$

Mars has mass $m_m = 0.6419 \times 10^{24}$ kg and is distant 1.5237 AU from the Sun. So the radius of the activity sphere for Mars is

$$r_{act,m} = 0.003869 \text{ AU} \ = 579000 \text{ km}. \tag{11.12.8}$$

I suggest that you first escape from the Earth, following the integration until the distance from the Earth is equal to $r_{act,e}$. Note the velocity relative to the Earth, v_e; it will be in km/sec.

Next, run an escape from Mars, starting with the orbit that you want to be your final parking orbit. (Eventually, this orbit will be run in reverse, for the capture.) For Mars, the equatorial radius is 3393 km, and the martian equivalent of the geocentric gravitational constant is

$$\mu_m = 0.4283 \times 10^5 \text{ km}^3/\text{sec}^2. \tag{11.12.9}$$

Note the velocity relative to Mars, v_m.

For the motion between the planets, I recommend following the astronomical practice of using the AU for the unit of length, and the day as the unit of time. Then the equation of motion, with origin at the Sun, is

$$\frac{d^2\vec{r}}{dt^2} = -k^2\frac{\vec{r}}{r^3} + \epsilon\frac{\vec{v}}{v}, \tag{11.12.10}$$

where $k = 0.017202$ is called the *Gaussian gravitational constant.* Note that it is squared in equation (11.12.10).

First, convert v_e and v_m to AU/day; 1 km/sec = 0.0005774 AU/day. The Earth's orbital speed is 0.0172 AU/day. Add the converted v_e to this to find the starting speed with respect to the Sun; call this v_1. Assume that the starting velocity is perpendicular to the radius to the Sun. The orbital speed of Mars is 0.0139 AU/day. Subtract the converted v_m from this, to find the speed relative to the Sun, just before the final phase of capture by Mars. Call this speed v_2. Finally, the value of ϵ that you have been using must be converted to the new units. 9.81 m/sec^2 is equivalent to 0.490 AU/day^2.

Now comes the hard part. You must start with velocity v_1, perpendicular to the radius to the Sun, at one AU from the Sun. You must finish with velocity v_2, perpendicular to the radius to the Sun, at 1.5237 AU from the Sun. This is similar, in principle, to the transfer between circular orbits around the Earth; but you may find there are no winding spirals; the path will be direct. But negative thrust will need to be included.

Once you have completed this stage, you will need to place Mars, relative to the rocket, so that the final capture can take place. This may seem somewhat artificial; but it enables you to say where Mars would have been at the time of launch, and this enables you to specify when launch might be possible.

For ideas on this project, see a paper by E. Stuhlinger [94], "Flight Path of an Ion-Propelled Spaceship."

11.13 Reentering the Earth's Atmosphere

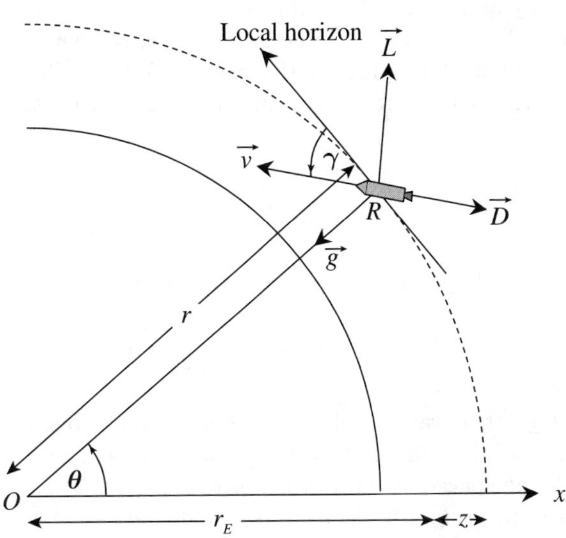

Figure 11.29: *Geometry for reentry.*

The equations for the reentry of a spacecraft into a planetary atmosphere differ from those for launch in that there is no thrust (except perhaps for final guidance to a landing site) and the forces of drag and maybe lift are dominant. In the notation of figure 11.29 equations (11.11.6) can be modified as

$$\left.\begin{aligned} \frac{dv}{dt} &= -\frac{D}{m} - \frac{k\sin\gamma}{r^2}, \\ v\frac{d\gamma}{dt} &= \frac{L}{m} + v^2\frac{\cos\gamma}{r} - \frac{k\cos\gamma}{r^2}, \\ \frac{dr}{dt} &= \frac{dz}{dt} = v\sin\gamma, \\ \frac{d\theta}{dt} &= \frac{v\cos\gamma}{r}, \end{aligned}\right] \tag{11.13.1}$$

where

$$\left.\begin{aligned} D &= \tfrac{1}{2}\rho A C_D v^2, \\ L &= \tfrac{1}{2}\rho A C_L v^2, \\ \rho &= \rho_0 e^{-\alpha z},\ z = r - r_E. \end{aligned}\right] \tag{11.13.2}$$

The drag and lift coefficients are complicated functions; however, in order to make progress in this project, we shall assume that they remain constant. We shall assume $C_D = 1$ and use C_L (more usually, it is C_L/C_D) as a parameter. I suggest that you concentrate on reentry into the Earth's atmosphere, when $\alpha = 0.1385$ km^{-1}. To include drag effects at altitudes higher than $z = 90$km, then consider using the formula (11.5.9). For the Earth, take $r_E = 6378$ km.

There are many scenarios that you might construct. Here are two. Start in a circular orbit around the Earth with radius r_0 km. Then the speed will be

$$v_c = \sqrt{\frac{\mu_E}{r_0}} = \sqrt{\frac{3.986 \times 10^5}{r_0}} \text{ km s}^{-1}. \tag{11.13.3}$$

(μ_E is the geocentric gravitational constant; to find the corresponding constant for another planet, multiply by the ratio M_P/M_E, where M_P and M_E are masses of the planet and the Earth, respectively.) Reduce the speed by an amount Δv; follow the subsequent motion. Start with $C_L = 0$; then increase the lift coefficient. Since there are three parameters, r_0, Δv and C_L, the investigation can become fairly elaborate. Look for "skipping" of the spacecraft when $C_L \neq 0$. In one maneuver, when rising from the initial dip, the spacecraft rotates through 180° so that the lift force is *downward*; try this.

Alternatively, use initial conditions

$$x = x_0, \ y = y_0, \ \dot{x} = -v_0, \ \dot{y} = 0, \tag{11.13.4}$$

such that the approach is in a hyperbolic orbit; this requires that

$$v_0^2 > \frac{2\mu_E}{r_0}, \text{ where } r_0 = \sqrt{x_0^2 + y_0^2}. \tag{11.13.5}$$

Pick values for v_0 and C_L; then vary y_0, keeping it positive. This should illustrate the *reentry corridor*. With y_0 too great, the spacecraft will not be captured, due to low drag or to skipping away. With y_0 too small, the spacecraft may crash or overheat.

Consider heating as in project 11.8. At each step, calculate

$$H = \frac{1}{1200}\frac{\rho}{\rho_0}\left(\frac{v}{v_c}\right)^3, \tag{11.13.6}$$

where $v_c = \sqrt{\mu_E/r}$ is the circular speed at zero altitude. If $H > 2.3 \times 10^{-5}$, then (considering only radiation cooling) the spacecraft may have an external temperature of $T = 700$°K or higher. You can select your own numerical value for when heating becomes critical.

11.14 De-spinning a Satellite 1: A Space Yo-yo

When a satellite is placed into orbit it may have a spin rate that is too large. A way to reduce this spin is to transfer angular momentum to masses that are initially wrapped around the satellite by light strings of equal length. When the masses are released, the strings unwind; when they are fully unwound, they are separated from the satellite. Initial, intermediate and final stages are shown in figure 11.30 in which two masses are used. The device is known as a "space yo-yo."

Figure 11.31 shows the yo-yo at an intermediate stage when the masses are still attached; only one mass is shown. The satellite has rotated through the angle θ relative to inertial space, shown by the x-axis. A is the point at which the mass was initially attached. B is the point of instantaneous separation of the string from the satellite. The angle between A and B is ϕ, so the length of the free string is $l = R\phi$ where R is the radius of the satellite. The mass m is at the end of the string at C.

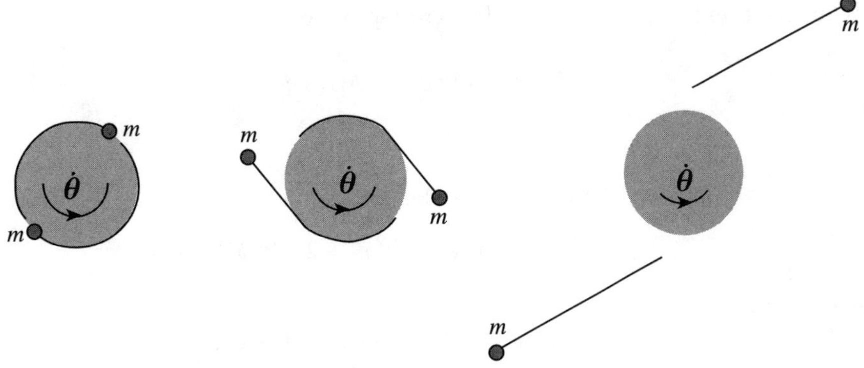

Figure 11.30: *Successive stages in de-spinning a satellite.*

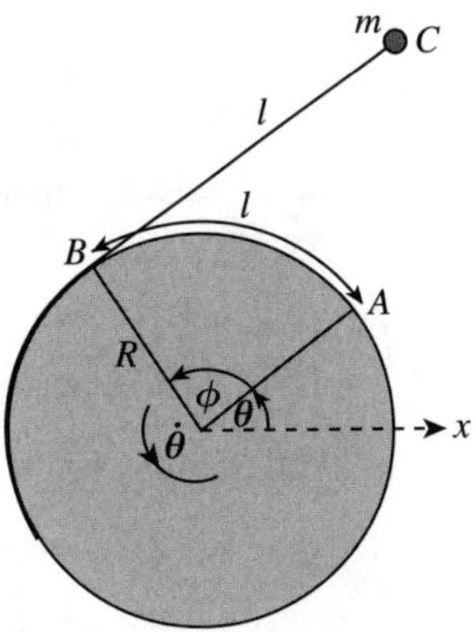

Figure 11.31: *Geometry of the space yo-yo.*

If $\psi = \theta + \phi$, the coordinates of C, with origin at the center of the satellite, are

$$\overrightarrow{\mathrm{OC}} = \langle R\cos\psi + l\sin\psi,\ R\sin\psi - l\cos\psi\rangle. \tag{11.14.1}$$

The components of its velocity are

$$\vec{V} = \langle -R\dot{\psi}\sin\psi + l\dot{\psi}\cos\psi + R\dot{\phi}\sin\psi,\ R\dot{\psi}\cos\psi + l\dot{\psi}\sin\psi - R\dot{\phi}\cos\psi\rangle. \tag{11.14.2}$$

Then

$$V^2 = R^2\dot{\theta}^2 + l^2\dot{\psi}^2. \tag{11.14.3}$$

As there are no dissipative forces, kinetic energy is conserved. If $\dot{\theta}_0$ is the initial angular velocity of the satellite, and I is the moment of inertia of the satellite about its axis of rotation, then, allowing for two masses,

$$\begin{aligned}\frac{1}{2}(I + 2mR^2)\dot{\theta}_0^2 &= \frac{1}{2}I\dot{\theta}^2 + m(R^2\dot{\theta}^2 + l^2\dot{\psi}^2)\\ &= \frac{1}{2}(I + 2mR^2)\dot{\theta}^2 + mR^2\phi^2(\dot{\theta} + \dot{\phi})^2.\end{aligned} \tag{11.14.4}$$

This can be written as

$$(I + 2mR^2)(\dot{\theta}_0^2 - \dot{\theta}^2) = 2mR^2\phi^2(\dot{\theta} + \dot{\phi})^2. \tag{11.14.5}$$

Angular momentum is also conserved. The cross-product

$$\overrightarrow{OC} \times \overrightarrow{V} = (R^2\dot{\theta} + l^2\dot{\psi})\hat{x} \times \hat{y}. \tag{11.14.6}$$

So

$$\begin{aligned} (I + 2mR^2)\dot{\theta}_0 &= I\dot{\theta} + 2m(R^2\dot{\theta} + l^2\dot{\psi}) \\ &= (I + 2mR^2)\dot{\theta} + 2mR^2\phi^2(\dot{\theta} + \dot{\phi}). \end{aligned} \tag{11.14.7}$$

This can be written as

$$(I + 2mR^2)(\dot{\theta}_0 - \dot{\theta}) = 2mR^2\phi^2(\dot{\theta} + \dot{\phi}). \tag{11.14.8}$$

Dividing equation (11.14.8) into (11.14.5), we have

$$(\dot{\theta}_0 + \dot{\theta}) = \dot{\theta} + \dot{\phi},$$

so

$$\dot{\phi} = \dot{\theta}_0. \tag{11.14.9}$$

So the free length, l, increases at a constant rate. Solving equations (11.14.8) and (11.14.5) for $\dot{\theta}^2$ and $\dot{\theta}$, and dividing the second into the first, we find

$$\dot{\theta} = \dot{\theta}_0 \left(\frac{I/(2m) + R^2 - l^2}{I/(2m) + R^2 + l^2} \right). \tag{11.14.10}$$

Then if the total length of a string is l_f, the final angular velocity of the satellite is

$$\dot{\theta}_f = \dot{\theta}_0 \left(\frac{I/(2m) + R^2 - l_f^2}{I/(2m) + R^2 + l_f^2} \right). \tag{11.14.11}$$

For a required value of $\dot{\theta}_f$ this enables l_f to be found. Note that if $\dot{\theta}_f = 0$, then l_f is independent of the initial angular velocity of the satellite.

That appears to solve the problem. So why have I included it here? In part, because it is a really cool mechanical system. Also it is interesting to trace out the paths of the points A, B and C from figure 11.31. Equation (11.14.10) can be solved numerically or analytically. Taking the second way, leads to

$$\theta = 2f \arctan \frac{t\dot{\theta}_0}{f} - t\dot{\theta}_0, \text{ where } f = \sqrt{I/(mR^2) + 1}. \tag{11.14.12}$$

So, for given t we can find θ and $\phi = t\dot{\theta}_0$ and $l = R\phi$.

There are some other questions that can be asked of this model. Suppose that everything was planned to de-spin a satellite, but the values of $\dot{\theta}_0$ or I turned out to be different from those planned. What will happen? What will happen if the total length of each string exceeds the length necessary for de-spinning down to $\dot{\theta} = 0$? What will happen if, on attaining the desired angular velocity, $\dot{\theta}_f$, the strings fail to separate, but remain forever attached to the satellite? Will we then have a real space yo-yo?

11.15 De-spinning a Satellite 2: The Stretch Yo-yo

The model for de-spinning just presented is sensitive to errors in the initial spin or the moment of inertia of the satellite. A better model was proposed by Cornille [25]; this was investigated analytically by Fedor [36]. The cord attaching the masses to the satellite is elastic, so that it stretches during unwinding. If the initial spin is greater than expected, then there will be more elongation of the cord, so more momentum will be transferred away from the satellite; the reverse is true if the initial spin is less than expected. So we have a neat adaptive control system. It also turns out that the model is relatively insensitive to small changes in the moment of inertia of the satellite about its spin axis. In the model the mass of the cords will be neglected. In practice, this has been found to be satisfactory if one third of the mass of a cord is added to the mass of the body at its end; so it will be assumed that m, the mass of that body, has been so adjusted.

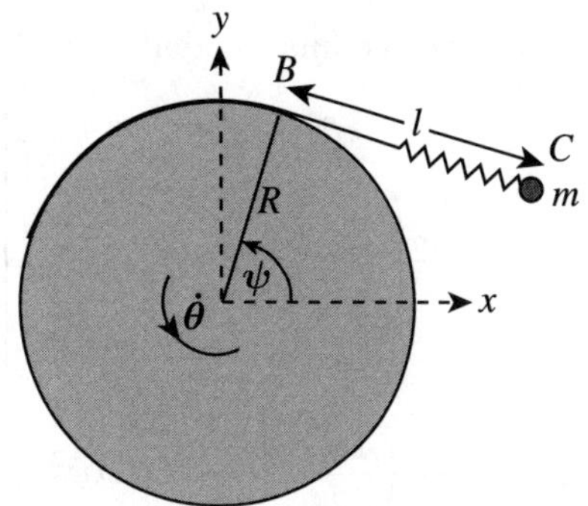

Figure 11.32: *Stretch yo-yo. Phase 1.*

There are two phases to the motion. In the first, illustrated in figure 11.32, the cord is unwinding, and is tangent to the satellite. Only one of the two masses is shown, since there will be symmetry between the masses. In the figure the x- and y- axes are fixed in inertial space. The point of separation, B, makes the angle ψ with the x-axis. The rate of rotation of the satellite is $\dot{\theta}$, and the radius of the satellite is R. Initially, $\theta = \psi = 0$. After the satellite has turned through the angle θ, B is separated from the initial separation point by the angle $\psi - \theta$. Then the length of the cord is

$$l = R(\psi - \theta) + \delta, \tag{11.15.1}$$

where δ is the amount by which the cord has stretched. Then

$$\dot{l} = R(\dot{\psi} - \dot{\theta}) + \dot{\delta}. \tag{11.15.2}$$

Now the coordinates of the mass are (x, y), where

$$x = R\cos\psi + l\sin\psi, \quad y = R\sin\psi - l\cos\psi. \tag{11.15.3}$$

Then their derivatives are

$$\left.\begin{aligned} \dot{x} &= -R\dot{\psi}\sin\psi + l\dot{\psi}\cos\psi + \dot{l}\sin\psi = -R\dot{\theta}\sin\psi + l\dot{\psi}\cos\psi + \dot{\delta}\sin\psi, \\ \dot{y} &= R\dot{\psi}\cos\psi + l\dot{\psi}\sin\psi - \dot{l}\cos\psi = R\dot{\theta}\cos\psi + l\dot{\psi}\sin\psi - \dot{\delta}\cos\psi, \end{aligned}\right] \tag{11.15.4}$$

where we have used (11.15.2). Then

$$\dot{x}^2 + \dot{y}^2 = R^2\dot{\theta}^2 + l^2\dot{\psi}^2 + \dot{\delta}^2 - 2R\dot{\theta}\dot{\delta}. \tag{11.15.5}$$

The potential energy for the stretching of one cord is

$$V = \frac{1}{2}k\delta^2, \tag{11.15.6}$$

where k is the spring constant. Then, if I is the moment of inertia of the satellite about its axis of rotation, the Lagrangian for the entire system, with both masses included, is

$$L = \frac{1}{2}I\dot{\theta}^2 + m(R^2\dot{\theta}^2 + l^2\dot{\psi}^2 + \dot{\delta}^2 - 2R\dot{\theta}\dot{\delta}) - k\delta^2. \tag{11.15.7}$$

It follows that Lagrange's equations are

$$\left.\begin{aligned} 2ml^2\ddot{\psi} + 4ml\dot{l}\dot{\psi} &= 2mlR\dot{\psi}^2, \\ I\ddot{\theta} + 2mR^2\ddot{\theta} - 2mR\ddot{\delta} &= -2mRl\dot{\psi}^2, \\ 2m\ddot{\delta} - 2mR\ddot{\theta} &= 2ml\dot{\psi}^2 - 2k\delta. \end{aligned}\right] \tag{11.15.8}$$

Solving for the second derivatives, we have the final model:

$$\left.\begin{aligned} l &= R(\psi - \theta) + \delta, \\ \ddot{\psi} &= -2\frac{\dot{l}}{l}\dot{\psi} + R\frac{\dot{\psi}^2}{l}, \\ \ddot{\theta} &= -\frac{2kR}{I}\delta, \\ \ddot{\delta} &= -k\left(\frac{2R^2}{I} + \frac{1}{m}\right)\delta + l\dot{\psi}^2. \end{aligned}\right] \tag{11.15.9}$$

Energy and angular momentum are conserved. This is expressed analytically by

$$\frac{1}{2}I\dot{\theta}^2 + m(R^2\dot{\theta}^2 + l^2\dot{\psi}^2 + \dot{\delta}^2 - 2R\dot{\theta}\dot{\delta}) + k\delta^2 = c_1 \tag{11.15.10}$$

for the energy and

$$I\dot{\theta} + 2m(R^2\dot{\theta} - R\dot{\delta} + l^2\dot{\psi}) = c_2 \tag{11.15.11}$$

for the angular momentum. If $\dot{\theta}_0$ is the initial value of the spin, then these may be expressed as

$$\left.\begin{aligned} (I + 2mR^2)(\dot{\theta}^2 - \dot{\theta}_0^2) &= -2m(l^2\dot{\psi}^2 + \dot{\delta}^2 - 2R\dot{\theta}\dot{\delta}) - 2k\delta^2, \\ (I + 2mR^2)(\dot{\theta} - \dot{\theta}_0) &= 2m(R\dot{\delta} - l^2\dot{\psi}). \end{aligned}\right] \tag{11.15.12}$$

Note that if $\delta = \dot{\delta} = 0$, then, dividing the second equation into the first, we have

$$\dot{\theta} + \dot{\theta}_0 = \dot{\psi}, \tag{11.15.13}$$

as in the preceding model.

Although we have not completed the model, phase one should be run independently. One problem is that the first differential equation of (11.15.9) causes difficulties at the initial step, since $l = 0$ appears in two denominators. This might be handled in one of two ways. You might assume that

$$l = l_0 + R(\psi - \theta) + \delta, \tag{11.15.14}$$

where l_0 is small. Or, for the first step, assume that the stretch δ is small enough so that the approximation (11.15.13) can be used. Then, for this step only, the first differential equation of (11.15.9) is ignored. After the first step, conditions should be numerically acceptable.

This is not a simple model to run, in part because of the number of parameters. Here is one way in which you might get started:

- Consider a homogeneous spherical satellite. Choose a radius, R.
- Choose a mass, M; then $I = 2MR^2/5$.
- Choose a value for m.

- Choose values for $\dot{\theta}_0$ and $\dot{\theta}_f$, the initial and final values of $\dot{\theta}$.
- Using the preceding model (with no stretch), find a value for the length of the cords. This will become l_0, the unstretched length of the cord.
- Now choose a value for the spring constant, k.
- Run the model just until the cord is unwound, using Newton's method to find the instant at which $l = R(\psi - \theta) + \delta = l_0$. Modify k to get a satisfactory stretch, of the order of l_0; also be prepared to modify l_0.

Once you have a satisfactory model, test to see how well the system compensates for errors in $\dot{\theta}_0$. Leaving everything else fixed, change $\dot{\theta}_0$ to see the effect on $\dot{\theta}_f$. Also investigate the sensitivity of the system to small changes in I. Compare the sensitivities that you find with those from the preceding model.

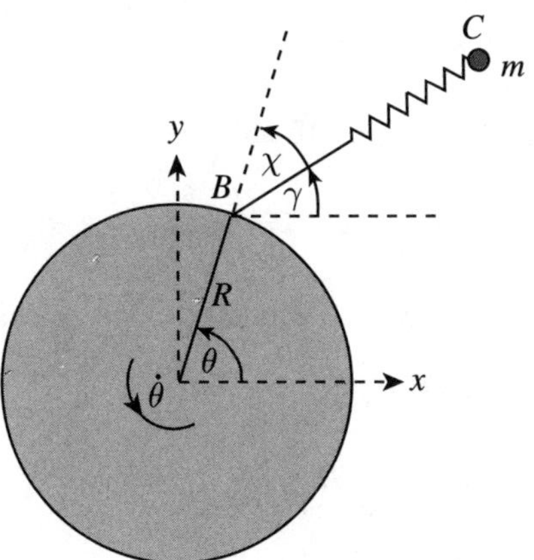

Figure 11.33: *Stretch yo-yo. Phase 2.*

In the second phase, shown in figure 11.33, the cord remains attached to the satellite at B, but rotates, relative to the satellite until it points in a radial direction. Then detachment takes place. The point of separation, B, is the point at which an end of the cord is fastened to the satellite; so with $\dot{\theta}$ as the angular velocity of the satellite, the radius to B can be taken to make the angle θ with the x-axis. Then if BC makes the angle γ with the x-axis, the angle

$$\chi = \theta - \gamma \tag{11.15.15}$$

starts at $\chi = \pi/2$ and ends at $\chi = 0$, when detachment takes place. The length of BC is

$$l = l_0 + \delta, \tag{11.15.16}$$

where l_0 is the unstretched length of the entire cord. The coordinates of C are

$$x = R\cos\theta + l\cos\gamma,\ \ y = R\sin\theta + l\sin\gamma.$$

Then

$$\dot{x} = -R\dot{\theta}\sin\theta - l\dot{\gamma}\sin\gamma + \dot{\delta}\cos\gamma,\ \ \dot{y} = R\dot{\theta}\cos\theta + l\dot{\gamma}\cos\gamma + \dot{\delta}\sin\gamma.$$

Then

$$\dot{x}^2 + \dot{y}^2 = R^2\dot{\theta}^2 + l^2\dot{\gamma}^2 + \dot{\delta}^2 + 2Rl\dot{\theta}\dot{\gamma}\cos\chi - 2R\dot{\theta}\dot{\delta}\sin\chi.$$

The Lagrangian for the complete system is, then,

$$L = \frac{1}{2}I\dot{\theta}^2 + m(R^2\dot{\theta}^2 + l^2\dot{\gamma}^2 + \dot{\delta}^2 + 2Rl\dot{\theta}\dot{\gamma}\cos\chi - 2R\dot{\theta}\dot{\delta}\sin\chi) - k\delta^2. \quad (11.15.17)$$

Lagrange's equations, after a little simplification, are

$$\left.\begin{aligned}\left(\frac{I}{m} + 2R^2\right)\ddot{\theta} + 2Rl\cos\chi\,\ddot{\gamma} - 2R\sin\chi\,\ddot{\delta} &= -4R\dot{\delta}\dot{\gamma}\cos\chi - 2Rl\dot{\gamma}^2\sin\chi,\\ 2Rl\cos\chi\,\ddot{\theta} + 2l^2\ddot{\gamma} &= -4l\dot{\delta}\dot{\gamma} + 2Rl\dot{\theta}^2\sin\chi,\\ -2R\sin\chi\,\ddot{\theta} + 2\ddot{\delta} &= 2R\dot{\theta}^2\cos\chi + 2l\dot{\gamma}^2 - \frac{2k}{m}\delta.\end{aligned}\right\} \quad (11.15.18)$$

Multiply the second of these by $(R/l)\cos\chi$ and the third by $-R\sin\chi$ and add. Then

$$2R^2\ddot{\theta} + 2Rl\cos\chi\,\ddot{\gamma} - 2R\sin\chi\,\ddot{\delta} = -4R\dot{\delta}\dot{\gamma}\cos\chi - 2Rl\dot{\gamma}^2\sin\chi + \frac{2kR}{m}\delta\sin\chi.$$

Subtracting this from the first equation of (11.15.18), we have

$$\frac{I}{m}\ddot{\theta} = -\frac{2kR}{m}\delta\sin\chi.$$

Then we can write equations for the individual second derivatives as

$$\left.\begin{aligned}\ddot{\theta} &= -\frac{2kR}{I}\delta\sin\chi,\\ \ddot{\gamma} &= -\frac{2}{l}\dot{\delta}\dot{\gamma} + \frac{R}{l}\dot{\theta}^2\sin\chi - \frac{R}{l}\ddot{\theta}\cos\chi,\\ \ddot{\delta} &= R\dot{\theta}^2\cos\chi + l\dot{\gamma}^2 - \frac{k}{m}\delta + R\ddot{\theta}\sin\chi.\end{aligned}\right\} \quad (11.15.19)$$

As a check, you might verify, by differentiation, that the angular momentum of the system,

$$M = I\dot{\theta} + 2m\left(R^2\dot{\theta} + l^2\dot{\gamma} + Rl(\dot{\theta} + \dot{\gamma})\cos\chi - R\dot{\delta}\sin\chi\right) \quad (11.15.20)$$

is constant.

Initial conditions are the final conditions of phase one, with $\gamma_0 = \theta_0 - \pi/2$. After each step, find the sign of $\chi = \theta - \gamma$. When it changes, use Newton's method to find the instant when it is zero. Design a system using both phases. Again, discuss the sensitivity of the system to errors in $\dot{\theta}_0$ and I. How important is it to include the second phase?

11.16 If You Were Jupiter, Could You Catch a Comet?

Comets are thought to be "stored" in a region of the solar system way outside the orbit of Pluto. The comets there constitute the *Oort cloud*, so called after the astronomer whose idea it was. At that distance, the comets are subject to perturbations from passing stars, and from time to time one of them enters the inner part of the solar system, travelling in a nearly parabolic orbit. In any year, several of these *parabolic comets* are usually discovered, and many people make a hobby of searching for them. Normally, a comet is named after the first person who spots it. After its close approach to the Sun, a parabolic comet will again recede to the Oort cloud; it may be several million years before it returns. In the solar system there are also many *periodic comets* moving in elliptic orbits having periods of a few years. Since a periodic comet is short-lived, by astronomical standards, there must be a mechanism for the renewal of their numbers. Over the years, there have been many suggestions, including the long-abandoned idea that comets are volcanic debris from Jupiter. For many periodic comets the aphelion distance (the greatest orbital distance from the Sun) is roughly equal to the distance of Jupiter from the Sun. It is thought that these periodic comets started off as parabolic comets, but by chance they passed so close to Jupiter that their orbits were radically perturbed into much smaller ellipses — a sort of reverse slingshot effect. (It is also possible for a perturbed orbit to become hyperbolic, so that the comet escapes altogether from the solar system.) The object of this project is to investigate numerically the phenomena of capture by Jupiter, or escape.

I suggest that you start by working in two dimensions, although you might ultimately want to consider three. In the model the Sun is at the origin of the x-y coordinate system, with Jupiter moving in a circular orbit around it. We shall use the *astronomical unit*, AU, as the unit of length. Roughly, this is the semimajor axis of the orbit of the Earth around the Sun; it sets the scale for many astronomical distances. The unit of mass will be the mass of the Sun; then the mass of Jupiter is $m_J = 0.001$. The unit of time will be chosen so that the constant of gravitation is numerically equal to one. With this unit of time, the period of one revolution of the Earth around the Sun is 2π units of time, by Kepler's third law. So one unit of our "project time" is $365.25/(2\pi)$ days. The mass of a comet is so small that the motion of Jupiter is quite unaffected by it. (Comets have been known to pass close to Jupiter's satellite without any observable effect on the orbits of the satellites. The cometary orbits were never the same again.)

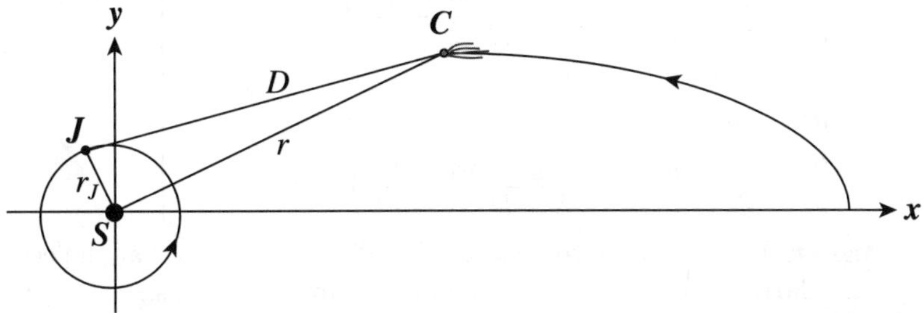

Figure 11.34: *The geometry of a Sun-Jupiter-Comet system.*

The geometry for the project is shown in figure 11.34. The Sun is at the origin, and the comet has coordinates (x, y). The distance of Jupiter from the Sun is $r_J = 5.21$ AU. The coordinates of Jupiter are (x_J, y_J). The time for a complete revolution of Jupiter around the Sun is, by Kepler's third law,

$$P_J = 2\pi r_J^{3/2}(1 + m_J)^{-1/2}. \tag{11.16.1}$$

Then if

$$n_J = \frac{2\pi}{P_J}, \tag{11.16.2}$$

it follows that

$$x_J = r_J \cos n_J(t - t_0), \; y_J = r_J \sin n_J(t - t_0), \tag{11.16.3}$$

where the value of t_0 depends on the initial position of Jupiter; it will be a parameter of the model. The period of Jupiter is 11.86 y, or 74.53 units of our time; so, if you use $r_J = 5.21$, then $0 < t_0 < 74.53$.

If r and D are the distances of the comet from the Sun and Jupiter, respectively, then

$$r = \sqrt{x^2 + y^2} \text{ and } D = \sqrt{(x - x_J)^2 + (y - y_J)^2}. \tag{11.16.4}$$

The differential equations for the motion of the comet are

$$\left.\begin{aligned}\frac{d^2x}{dt^2} &= -\frac{x}{r^3} + m_j\left(\frac{x_J - x}{D^3} - \frac{x_J}{r_J^3}\right),\\ \frac{d^2y}{dt^2} &= -\frac{y}{r^3} + m_j\left(\frac{y_J - y}{D^3} - \frac{y_J}{r_J^3}\right).\end{aligned}\right] \tag{11.16.5}$$

Next, we need to write equations (11.16.5) as a system of four first-order differential equations. Let

$$y_1 = x,\ y_2 = \frac{dx}{dt},\ y_3 = y,\ y_4 = \frac{dy}{dt}. \tag{11.16.6}$$

Then

$$\left.\begin{aligned}x_J &= r_J \cos n_J(t - t_0),\ y_J = r_J \sin n_J(t - t_0),\\ r &= \sqrt{y_1^2 + y_3^2},\\ D &= \sqrt{(y_1 - x_J)^2 + (y_3 - y_J)^2},\\ \frac{dy_1}{dt} &= y_2,\\ \frac{dy_2}{dt} &= -\frac{y_1}{r^3} + m_j\left(\frac{x_J - y_1}{D^3} - \frac{x_J}{r_J^3}\right),\\ \frac{dy_3}{dt} &= y_4,\\ \frac{dy_4}{dt} &= -\frac{y_3}{r^3} + m_j\left(\frac{y_J - y_3}{D^3} - \frac{y_J}{r_J^3}\right).\end{aligned}\right] \tag{11.16.7}$$

In running the program, I suggest that you choose initial conditions so that the comet is on the x-axis, moving perpendicularly to that axis. You should look for conditions so that, at the closest approach to the Sun, the comet is nearly distant r_J from the Sun; this will optimize conditions for a close encounter and a large perturbation. Now if an orbit has semimajor axis a and eccentricity e, then the distances at perihelion and aphelion are, respectively, $p = a(1 - e)$ and $q = a(1 + e)$. The speed, v, when distant r from the Sun, is given by the formula

$$v^2 = (1 + m_j)\left(\frac{2}{r} - \frac{1}{a}\right). \tag{11.16.8}$$

Then, with a little algebra, we can find the speed at aphelion to be

$$v_a = \left(\frac{2p(1 + m_J)}{q(p + q)}\right)^{1/2}. \tag{11.16.9}$$

If you start 100 AU from the Sun, then $q = 100$. If you want the perihelion distance (when Jupiter's attraction is neglected) to be 5.21 AU, then the speed at aphelion is 0.03149 in our units. The initial conditions would then be

$$t = 0;\ y_1 = 100,\ y_2 = 0,\ y_3 = 0,\ y_4 = 0.03149.$$

Now you need to play with the parameter t_0 so that the comet and Jupiter come close to one another. For instance, I found that with $t_0 = 45.8$, I saw a very satisfactory capture. If you choose the value of p in equation (11.16.9) to be less than r_J, then the two orbits are bound to cross, and possibilities for capture are increased.

Figures 11.35 and 11.36 show two possible orbits, the first with capture and the second with ejection. For each run, the mass of Jupiter was 0.001 solar masses, and the radius of its orbit was

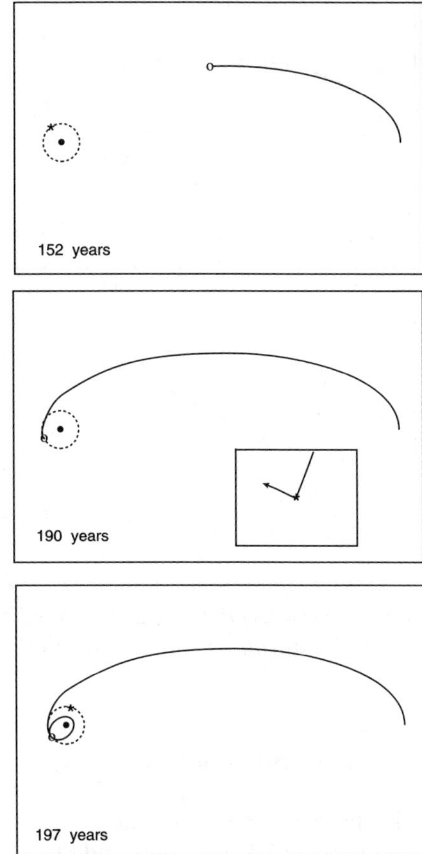

Figure 11.35: *Three stages in the orbit of a comet that is captured by Jupiter, resulting in the change from a long-period to a short-period comet.*

5.2 AU. The comet started at aphelion, on the x-axis, 100 AU from the Sun. The initial velocity was 0.03086 units, in the direction of the y-axis. For figure 11.35 the initial angle that the radius to Jupiter makes with the x-axis is 187°. (So the quantity $n_J(t - t_0)$ becomes $n_Jt - 187(\pi/180)$.) Figure 11.35(a) shows the start of the orbit, figure 11.35(b) shows the close approach with Jupiter, and figure 11.35(c) shows the resulting small elliptical orbit of a short-period comet. For figure 11.36 the starting angle for Jupiter is 186°. Figure 11.36(a) shows the close approach with Jupiter and figure 11.36(b) shows the orbit as the comet escapes from the solar system.

With the units chosen, the program may start off with relatively large stepsizes; you might make your initially suggested stepsize to be at least ten units. If you are writing a program to produce animated motion, then you will need to introduce an upper limit for the stepsize; otherwise the calculated points will be too far apart to produce a smooth-looking curve.

If the comet escapes from the solar system, it is usually fairly obvious; but if you are not sure, then calculate

$$E = \frac{1}{2}(y_2^2 + y_4^2) - \frac{1}{r} \tag{11.16.10}$$

when the encounter with Jupiter is over. This quantity is negative for an elliptic orbit, but positive for a hyperbolic orbit.

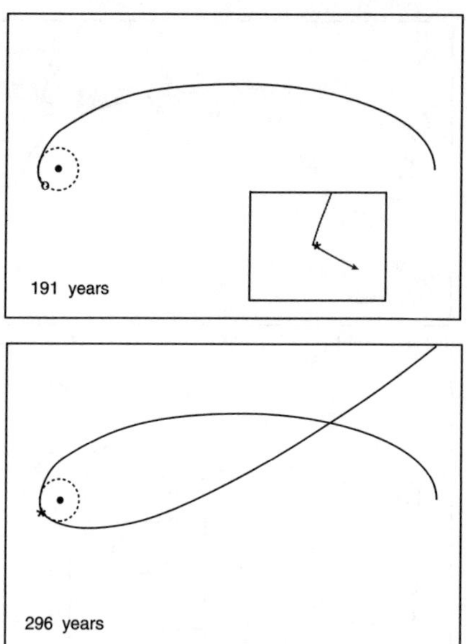

Figure 11.36: *Ejection from the solar system. All conditions are the same as those that produced the orbit in figure 11.36, except that the initial orientation of Jupiter with respect to the Sun has been changed by one degree.*

11.17 Using Jupiter to Boost the Orbit of a Spacecraft

The model here is dynamically the same as that of the preceding project. The only differences are that we are following a spacecraft instead of a comet, and the orbit starts at perihelion, within the orbit of Jupiter. The aim is to use the slingshot effect to get Jupiter to kick the spacecraft into an orbit of higher energy, so that an orbit that might otherwise only just reach Jupiter could go on, say, to Saturn. (Saturn might than do its share of kicking; but let's do one thing at a time.)

Let us start at perihelion on the x-axis, with $p = 1$ AU, the distance of the Earth from the Sun. (The gravitational attraction of the Earth will be neglected.) If aphelion is at the distance of Jupiter, then $q = 5.21$. From equations in the preceding section, especially (11.16.8), we can show that the speed at perihelion is

$$v_p = \left(\frac{2q(1+m_J)}{p(p+q)}\right)^{1/2}. \tag{11.17.1}$$

Initial conditions are

$$t = 0;\ y_1 = 1,\ y_2 = 0,\ y_3 = 0,\ y_4 = v_p.$$

Experiment with t_0 as before.

Be careful. Jupiter has equatorial radius 71398 km, or 4.77×10^{-4} AU. This is the radius of the visible planet, so it includes the atmosphere. If you get too close, in real life, then you may find yourself unexpectedly aerobraking, and spending the remainder of your short existence as an unwilling guest of Jupiter. Clearly, there is a limit to the maximum amount of boost that you can get. Investigate this.

11.18 A Grand Tour of the Solar System

We are taking the preceding project one stage further. The Voyager II spacecraft visited the major planets, gaining enough energy from each passage to reach the next planet, and eventually leaving the solar system. In this project you will plan your own tour.

I suggest that you start with the passage close to Jupiter, from the preceding project. This must provide enough energy for you to reach the orbit of Saturn. Then, deliberately place Saturn so that a close approach will occur, so that the spacecraft will reach the orbit of Uranus. And so on. This may seem very artificial; but it will tell you where the planets should be, relative to one another, so that the tour can take place. This is quite a rare configuration.

A table is provided, showing physical and orbital details of the planets. In addition to the grand tour, you might address such questions as: Can a close approach to Mars help in reaching Jupiter? Can a close approach to Venus help reach Mars?

Planet	Equatorial radius km	Mass 10^{24}kg	Mass solar masses $\times 10^{-6}$	Semimajor axis AU
Mercury	2439	0.330	0.1653	0.3871
Venus	6051	4.869	2.437	0.7233
Earth	6378	5.974	2.990	1.0000
Mars	3393	0.641	0.3213	1.5237
Jupiter	71400	1899	950.3	5.2102
Saturn	60000	568.5	284.5	9.5381
Uranus	25400	86.62	43.35	19.1833
Neptune	24764	102.78	51.44	30.0551
Pluto	1151	0.015	0.0075	39.5376

11.19 The Motion of the Perihelion of a Planetary Orbit under General Relativity: An Application of the Method of Variation of Parameters.

In this project we deal with the effects of non-Newtonian mechanics. The project is also designed to give an example of the method of variation of parameters applied (as, in practice, it usually is) to a nonlinear system.

If a planet of mass m revolves around the Sun, of mass M, then according to Newton's laws, the motion takes place in a fixed plane. Using polar coordinates (r, θ) in this plane, with origin at the Sun, and using formulas for the radial and transverse components of acceleration in these coordinates, it can be shown that these components must satisfy the differential equations

$$\left.\begin{aligned} \frac{d^2r}{dt^2} - r\left(\frac{d\theta}{dt}\right)^2 &= -\frac{\mu}{r^2}, \\ \frac{d}{dt}\left(r^2\frac{d\theta}{dt}\right) &= 0. \end{aligned}\right] \tag{11.19.1}$$

Here $\mu = G(M+m)$, where G is the constant of gravitation. It is assumed that the bodies are rigid spheres, moving subject only to their mutual gravitation.

From the second equation, we have

$$r^2\frac{d\theta}{dt} = h, \tag{11.19.2}$$

a constant relating to the conservation of angular momentum. (From this equation, it is possible to deduce Kepler's second law, that the line joining the planet to the Sun sweeps out equal areas in equal intervals of time.) Then the first equation can be written as

$$\frac{d^2r}{dt^2} - \frac{h^2}{r^3} = -\frac{\mu}{r^2}. \tag{11.19.3}$$

Next, we make the following transformation

$$\text{Let } r = u^{-1}.$$

Then

$$\frac{dr}{dt} = -u^{-2}\frac{du}{dt} = -u^{-2}\frac{du}{d\theta}\frac{d\theta}{dt} = -h\frac{du}{d\theta}.$$

Also

$$\frac{d^2r}{dt^2} = -h\frac{d}{d\theta}\left(\frac{du}{d\theta}\right)\frac{d\theta}{dt} = -h^2u^2\frac{d^2u}{d\theta^2}.$$

Then equation (11.19.3) can be written as

$$\frac{d^2u}{d\theta^2} + u = \frac{\mu}{h^2} = p. \qquad (11.19.4)$$

So the problem has been transformed into that of the harmonic oscillator.

The solution of equation (11.19.4) can be written

$$u = \frac{1}{r} = p\left(1 + e\cos(\theta - \omega)\right), \qquad (11.19.5)$$

the polar equation of an ellipse. The arbitrary constant e is the eccentricity of the ellipse (so that e lies between zero and one), and ω gives the orientation of the major axis of the orbit relative to the fixed axis from which θ is measured. (See figure 11.37.)

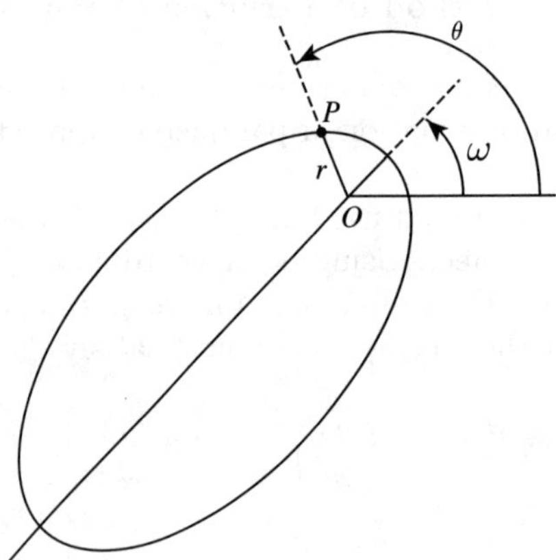

Figure 11.37: *The orientation of an elliptic orbit.*

Einstein showed that according to general relativity, equation (11.19.4) should be changed to

$$\frac{d^2u}{d\theta^2} + u = p + \epsilon u^2, \qquad (11.19.6)$$

where

$$\epsilon = 3\frac{\mu}{c^2}, \qquad (11.19.7)$$

c being the speed of light. It is this equation from which the model is derived.

Equation (11.19.6) can actually be solved using elliptic functions, but the resulting mathematical formulas give us no immediate information about the *nature* of the solution. It was through this equation that general relativity passed one of its most important tests. It had been known for nearly a hundred years that the orbit of Mercury showed a discrepancy between what was predicted on the basis of Newton's laws and what was actually observed. The major axis of the orbit was steadily *advancing* at the (unexplained) rate of 43 seconds of arc per century. Efforts to explain this included attempts to modify the inverse square law, and the hypothesis of an inter-Mercurial planet called Vulcan. But the discrepancy has apparently been explained by Einstein, by replacing Newton's laws with those of general relativity. (But there is still some controversy. Dicke has postulated a version of relativity that predicts a smaller motion for the major axis; he has suggested that the remaining discrepancy is caused by oblateness in the shape of the Sun.) The point in the orbit closest to the Sun is called *perihelion*; the forward motion of the major axis is usually expressed by the phrase *advance of perihelion.*

If perihelion is to advance, then the angle ω in figure 11.37 must increase. One way to discuss the problem is to continue to use the formula (11.19.5) as the solution, but now e and ω are treated as variables. This is the method of "variation of parameters," where constants in the solution to a simple problem become variables in the solution to a more complicated one. The method was first used, in principle, by Newton, and first formulated in the language of differential equations by Euler.

If equation (11.19.4) were written as two first-order differential equations using $v = du/d\theta$, then its solution could be written as

$$u = p(1 + e\cos f), \quad v = -pe\sin f, \tag{11.19.8}$$

where

$$f = \theta - \omega. \tag{11.19.9}$$

Now write equation (11.19.6) as

$$\frac{du}{d\theta} = v, \quad \frac{dv}{d\theta} = p - u + \epsilon u^2. \tag{11.19.10}$$

If we substitute into these equations the expressions (11.19.8), but treat e and ω as functions of θ, then we find that

$$\frac{de}{d\theta}\cos f + e\frac{d\omega}{d\theta}\sin f = 0,$$

and

$$-\frac{de}{d\theta}\sin f + e\frac{d\omega}{d\theta}\cos f = \epsilon p(1 + e\cos f)^2.$$

Then, solving for the derivatives, we find

$$\left.\begin{aligned} \frac{de}{d\theta} &= -\epsilon p\sin f\,(1 + e\cos f)^2, \\ \frac{d\omega}{d\theta} &= \epsilon p\cos f\,(1 + e\cos f)^2/e. \end{aligned}\right] \tag{11.19.11}$$

f is still defined by (11.19.9).

The integration of these equations provides a geometrical interpretation of how the shape and orientation of the orbit change with time. Apart from periodic fluctuations that balance out each revolution, there is a steady increase in ω, so that the ellipse is *precessing.* For the parameters of the orbit of Mercury, the effect is far too slow to show up in a numerical integration. Forget Mercury. There is a double-star system known as the "binary pulsar" PSR 1913 + 16 that has a period of about 8 hours and eccentricity 0.617; the rate of precession is about 4.2° per year! I suggest that you take $p = 1$, let $e = 0.5$ or greater, and try values of ϵ around 0.01. Experiment with different e and ϵ. A good way to exhibit results is in the phase-plane $(e\cos\omega)$-$(e\sin\omega)$.

Because θ changes much more rapidly than e or ω, one approach to equations (11.19.11) is to assume that the changes in e and ω over one revolution (i.e., one cycle of θ) can be ignored. Then the quantities e and ω as they appear on the *right-hand sides* are treated as constants. The equations are then said to be *averaged*, and these averaged equations are easily solved to give

$$\left.\begin{aligned}\bar{e} - e_0 &= \epsilon p \left(\cos f + e\cos^2 f + \tfrac{1}{3}\cos^3 f\right), \\ \bar{\omega} - \omega_0 &= \epsilon p e^{-1}\left(ef + (1+e^2)\sin f + e\sin f\cos f - \tfrac{1}{3}\sin^3 f\right).\end{aligned}\right] \tag{11.19.12}$$

The method of averaging is very popular. How good is it here?

11.20 The Poynting-Robertson Effect: or "How would you like to be a grain of dust in the Solar System?"

If you were born as a grain of dust at the same time as the solar system, then you would probably no longer be with us; but you might have had an interesting life! The important force in this section is radiation pressure as exerted by the Sun. The size of the grains must be large compared with the wavelength of the incident radiation, but still small enough to make the pressure significant in their dynamics.

At the distance of the Earth from the Sun (one *astronomical unit*, AU, or 1.496×10^{11} m) radiative energy from the Sun strikes an area of one square cm, normal to the Sun's rays, at the rate

$$S = 1.36 \times 10^6 \text{ ergs sec}^{-1}\text{ cm}^{-2}. \tag{11.20.1}$$

This is known as the *solar constant.* A spherical grain with cross-section A cm^2 will experience radiation pressure resulting in a force AS/c, where c is the speed of light. ($c \approx 3 \times 10^8$ m/sec.) If the grain were to be moved away from the Sun, the incident energy would be reduced, in proportion to the inverse square of its distance from the Sun. So if it is distant r AU from the Sun, the outward force due to radiation is AS/cr^2. This has the effect of diluting the gravitational attraction of the Sun, which is equal to MmG/r^2, where M and m are the masses of the Sun (2×10^{30} kg) and the grain. Then, if $\mu_0 = MG$, the equation of motion of the grain would be

$$\frac{d^2\vec{r}}{dt^2} = -\mu_0\frac{\hat{r}}{r^2} + \frac{AS}{mc}\frac{\hat{r}}{r^2} = -\left(\mu_0 - \frac{3S}{4R\rho c}\right)\frac{\hat{r}}{r^2}, \tag{11.20.2}$$

where the grain has radius R and density ρ. $\vec{r}$ is the position vector of the grain relative to the Sun; $\hat{r}$ is the unit vector parallel to $\vec{r}$.

If this were the whole story, there would be nothing left to say, since the orbit would be of constant size. That radiation pressure had an additional role was first suggested by J.H.Poynting [79] in 1903. In 1937 H.P.Robertson [86] derived the equations using relativity. The equations have been discussed in detail, and generalized by J.A.Burns et al. [20].

The key to this role is in the phenomenon of the aberration of starlight. This was first discovered by J.Bradley, a contemporary of Newton. Because light moves at a finite speed, a telescope does not point precisely at a star that is observed, but is displaced by a small angle from the direction of the incoming rays. Suppose that you are in a rainstorm with the rain falling vertically with speed v_1; you are moving forward with speed v_2. If you are holding an umbrella, you will not point it vertically upward, but, for best protection, will point forward in the direction of your motion. The angle will depend on the relative magnitudes of v_1 and v_2. Now imagine that you are a grain of dust, travelling with speed v in a circular orbit around the Sun. If you wish to protect yourself from the Sun's rays with a parasol, you will point it slightly forward; to a first approximation, the angle of tilt is v/c. (It is of interest that the first correct discussion of this aberration was given by Einstein, who derived a formula for this angle in powers of v/c.) Therefore there is a component of the radiation pressure resisting your forward motion. To find that component, multiply the radiation pressure by the sine of the angle of tilt, or v/c.

This deviation will not cause the plane of the orbit to change. Let's take polar coordinates, (r, θ) in the plane. The velocity has components

$$\text{radial}: \frac{dr}{dt}. \qquad \text{transverse}: r\frac{d\theta}{dt}.$$

The acceleration has components

$$\text{radial}: \frac{d^2r}{dt^2} - r\left(\frac{d\theta}{dt}\right)^2. \qquad \text{transverse}: \frac{1}{r}\frac{d}{dt}\left(r^2\frac{d\theta}{dt}\right).$$

Define

$$\alpha = \frac{3S}{4R\rho c^2} = \frac{3.6 \times 10^{-8}}{\rho R}, \tag{11.20.3}$$

where R and ρ are measured in cgs units, but otherwise the unit of length is the AU and the unit of time is the year. Then $\mu_0 = (2\pi)^2$. Resolving acceleration and force transversely, we find

$$\frac{1}{r}\frac{d}{dt}\left(r^2\frac{d\theta}{dt}\right) = -\frac{3S}{4R\rho c r^2}\frac{r\dot{\theta}}{c} = -\frac{\alpha}{r}\frac{d\theta}{dt}. \tag{11.20.4}$$

Next consider radial motion away from the Sun with speed $\dot{r}$. Because of this, the grain will absorb less radiative energy in unit time than it would if it were at rest, the dilution factor being $\dot{r}/c$. In addition, the radiation that it receives has already been diluted by the Doppler effect, also having the factor $\dot{r}/c$. Then the equation for motion in the radial direction becomes

$$\frac{d^2r}{dt^2} - r\left(\frac{d\theta}{dt}\right)^2 = -\frac{\mu}{r^2} - \frac{2\alpha}{r}\frac{dr}{dt}, \; \mu = \mu_0 - \alpha c. \tag{11.20.5}$$

Equations (11.20.4) and (11.20.5) are the equations of the model.

To get some idea of their effects, suppose that all motion is circular, with the change of radius very slow. Then, if the radius is a, from equation (11.20.5), $\dot{\theta} = \sqrt{\mu/a^3}$ and (11.20.4) can be written as

$$\frac{d}{dt}\sqrt{\mu a} = -\alpha\sqrt{\frac{\mu}{a^3}} \quad \text{or} \quad a\frac{da}{dt} = -2\alpha.$$

Suppose the motion starts at a_1 AU and ends at a_2 AU from the Sun, where $a_1 > a_2$. Then the time spent will be

$$T_{12} = \frac{a_1^2 - a_2^2}{4\alpha} = 7.0 \times 10^6 (a_1^2 - a_2^2) R\rho \text{ years}. \tag{11.20.6}$$

This shows that, in the lifetime of the solar system, the process is efficient in sweeping up grains. It also shows that if we use true-to-life figures, then the model, as it is, cannot be realistically used in a computer project. My suggestion is that you use the model, but with a greatly reduced value for the speed of light, c. Then start off with an elliptic orbit. If the perihelion distance is p and the aphelion distance is q, then if you start at perihelion, initial conditions would be

$$t = 0; \; r = p, \; \frac{dr}{dt} = 0, \; \theta = 0, \; \frac{d\theta}{dt} = \left(\frac{2q\mu}{p^3(p+q)}\right)^{1/2}. \tag{11.20.7}$$

Look for changes in the eccentricity, and semimajor axis of the orbit, as well as its orientation.

To program the model, first let

$$y_1 = r, \; y_2 = \frac{dr}{dt}, \; y_3 = \theta, \; y_4 = \frac{d\theta}{dt}. \tag{11.20.8}$$

Then

$$\left.\begin{aligned}\frac{dy_1}{dt} &= y_2,\\ \frac{dy_2}{dt} &= y_1y_4^2 - \frac{\mu}{y_1} - \frac{2\alpha y_2}{y_1^2},\\ \frac{dy_3}{dt} &= y_4,\\ \frac{dy_4}{dt} &= -2y_2y_4 - \frac{\alpha y_4}{y_1^2}.\end{aligned}\right] \tag{11.20.9}$$

Radiation pressure from the Sun can also play a role if the grain is in orbit around a planet. In this case, it is sufficient to assume that the radiation force has constant magnitude and is in a constant direction. If this direction is parallel to the x-axis, the equations for the model would be

$$\left.\begin{aligned}r &= \sqrt{x^2+y^2},\\ \frac{d^2x}{dt^2} &= -\mu_p\frac{x}{r^3} - \epsilon x,\\ \frac{d^2y}{dt^2} &= -\mu_p\frac{y}{r^3}..\end{aligned}\right] \tag{11.20.10}$$

I suggest that you start by setting $\mu_p = 1$, and $\epsilon = 0.01$ or thereabouts. Start with a circular orbit. You may be surprised at what you see.

11.21 Gravitational Interaction Between Two Galaxies

This is a beautiful project, but it requires more in the way of memory storage and running time than do most of the others, as well as more elaborate programming. It is also essential to have a satisfactory way in which to plot the results: a printout consisting of lists of numbers will not be satisfactory. The basic idea is due to A. and J. Toomre [97], who have published several papers full of attractive pictures as well as readable physical argument. Their 1972 paper includes a bibliography of earlier work. The Toomres have also made some beautiful movies showing what might happen in time to galactic structures when two passing galaxies interact tidally, and they compare what they have found with observed "bridges" and "tails" of some galaxies. Work of the same kind was done independently by A.E.Wright [109]. Have a look at some of the articles, and then see if you can resist this project! Several programs running this project are commercially available. One is included in the text *Astrophysical Simulations* [31].

Here we shall consider motion in two dimensions only. Generalization to three is not hard, but requires more storage and execution time; also extra decisions must be made on how the results should be viewed. A galaxy is, for the most part, a disk-like structure with a concentration of mass at the center. (Obviously, we are not talking about elliptic or irregular galaxies.) In this model each galaxy is represented by a point mass, one of them being initially surrounded by "stars" that constitute the disk. The two galaxies feel no gravitational effects from the stars, and move subject only to their mutual attraction. The stars, on the other hand, while not attracting each other, are attracted by both galaxies.

We shall not bother about units; it would be a useful exercise to consider realistic cases and actual units, but leave that until later. In particular, we shall take the gravitational constant $G = 1$. Let the galaxies have masses M_1 and M_2, and let M_1, initially, be the one with the disk of stars.

All motion will be considered relative to M_1. If the position vector of M_2 relative to M_1 is $\vec{r}$, then

$$\frac{d^2\vec{r}}{dt^2} = -(M_1 + M_2)\frac{\vec{r}}{r^3}, \tag{11.21.1}$$

where $r = \| \vec{r} \|$ is the magnitude of $\vec{r}$.

Each star is executing its own private version of the restricted problem of three bodies: itself and the two galactic nuclei. If the star S_i has position vector $\vec{r}_1$, relative to M_1, then

$$\frac{d^2\vec{r}_i}{dt^2} = -M_1\frac{\vec{r}_i}{r_i^3} + M_2\left(\frac{\vec{r} - \vec{r}_i}{\| \vec{r} - \vec{r}_i \|^3} - \frac{\vec{r}}{r^3}\right). \tag{11.21.2}$$

11.21.1 Initial Conditions.

The second galaxy.

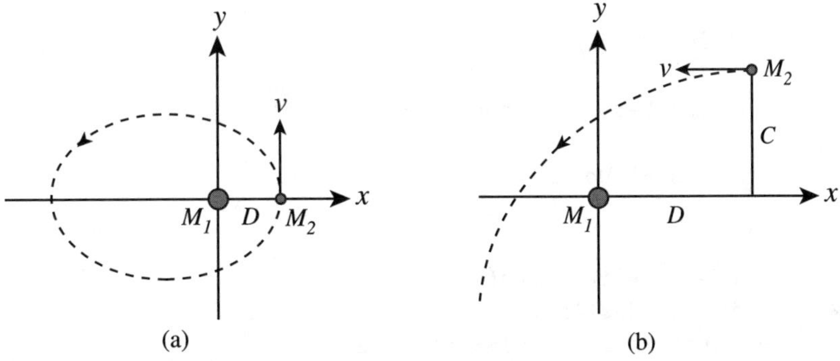

Figure 11.38: *Initial conditions for the galaxies.*

We first consider the initial conditions for the second galaxy, M_2. The simplest approach, shown in figure 11.38(a), is to start M_2 on the x-axis, distant D from M_1, moving perpendicularly to the line joining them. Then, initially,

$$t = 0;\ x = D,\ y = 0,\ \dot{x} = 0,\ \dot{y} = v.$$

There are two important speeds

$$v_c = \left(\frac{(M_1 + M_2)}{D}\right)^{1/2}, \text{ and } v_p = \sqrt{2}v_c. \tag{11.21.3}$$

If $v < v_p$, the orbit will be an ellipse. One end of the major axis will be distant D from M_1, and the distance of the other will be

$$D_1 = \frac{D}{2(M_1 + M_2)/(Dv^2) - 1}. \tag{11.21.4}$$

If $v < v_c$, $D_1 < D$. If $v = v_c$, $D_1 = D$, and the orbit is circular. If $v > v_c$, then $D_1 > D$. If $v = v_p$ the orbit is parabolic, and if $v > v_p$, it is hyperbolic.

A hyperbolic orbit would simulate a single encounter between the galaxies. In this case, the initial point of the calculation should not be at the closest relative position. A possible starting configuration is shown in figure 11.38(b). M_2 has coordinates (D, C) and velocity components $(-v, 0)$. For a hyperbolic orbit, v^2 should exceed $2(M_1 + M_2)/\sqrt{(D^2 + C^2)}$.

I recommend setting $M_1 = 1$, so M_2 is a parameter to be varied. Choose M_2. Then choose D. Then choose v to give the orbit for M_2 that you want.

The stars.

Consider a ring of radius R containing n stars. These will be equally spaced and will be initially moving in circles around M_1, with speed $\sqrt{M_1/R}$. I have found it best if the first star is placed randomly in the ring; this avoids the possibility of a symmetrical appearance when several rings are involved. So let ρ be a number randomly chosen between 0 and 2π. The i-th star will have initial conditions

$$\left.\begin{array}{lllll} x_i & = & R\cos\left(\frac{2\pi}{n}i+\rho\right), & \dot{x}_i & = -\sqrt{\frac{M_1}{R}}\sin\left(\frac{2\pi}{n}i+\rho\right), \\ y_i & = & R\sin\left(\frac{2\pi}{n}i+\rho\right), & \dot{y}_i & = \sqrt{\frac{M_1}{R}}\cos\left(\frac{2\pi}{n}i+\rho\right),\ i=1...n. \end{array}\right] \tag{11.21.5}$$

Suppose that the number of rings is `nRings`, and that the nth ring has radius `Radius(n)` and contains `nStars(n)` stars. The coordinates and velocities will be put into arrays `x(i), y(i), xv(i), yv(i)`. You might use something like the following code:

```
i = 0
For n = 1 To nRings Do
Begin
    Rho = random number between 0 and 2*Pi
    Angle = Rho
    For k = 1 To nStars(n) Do
    Begin
        i = i + 1
        Angle = Angle + 2*Pi/nStars(n)
        x(i) = Radius(n)*Cos(Angle)
        xv(i) = - Sqrt(M1/Radius(n)*Sin(Angle)
        y(i) = Radius(n)*Sin(Angle)
        yv(i) = Sqrt(M1/Radius(n)*Cos(Angle)
    End
End
```

11.21.2 Taking a step.

Each star will need to be individually moved. You will need to pick a time interval, Δt; each star will have had the time increased by this amount. Probably, you will pick a Δt so that unless a star moves close to M_1 or M_2, the natural stepsize will be larger than Δt. If this is the case, then consider this code for taking a step:

```
TimeCovered = 0
Repeat
    StepSize = DeltaT - TimeCovered
    Step(...)
    TimeCovered = TimeCovered + StepSize
Until Abs(DeltaT - TimeCovered) < Eps
```

If Δt is much greater than the natural stepsize, this procedure would be wasteful; it would then be more economical to take regular integration steps until Δt has been exceeded, and then to take one step backward to Δt. For instance:

```
TimeCovered = 0
```

```
Repeat
    Step(...)
    TimeCovered = TimeCovered + StepSize
Until TimeCovered > DeltaT
SaveStepSize = StepSize
StepSize = DeltaT - TimeCovered
Step(...)
StepSize = SaveStepSize
```

Before taking a step backward, always save the preceding **positive** stepsize.

How you move each star depends on how M_2 is moved. If it moves in a straight line or a circle, then a simple formula can be used for its position. Otherwise, unless you are prepared to spend some time learning computational methods for orbital dynamics, it is easiest to solve for the motion of a star and M_2 simultaneously. Each time, M_2 reverts to its original position in preparation for the next star; the exception is after the final star has been moved. So a system of eight equations is solved. Let

$$y_1 = x,\ y_2 = \frac{dx}{dt},\ y_3 = y,\ y_4 = \frac{dy}{dt},\ y_5 = x(i),\ y_6 = \frac{dx(i)}{dt},\ y_7 = y(i),\ y_8 = \frac{dy(i)}{dt}.$$

The equations to be solved are

$$\left.\begin{aligned}
r &= \sqrt{y_1^2 + y_3^2},\\
\frac{dy_1}{dt} &= y_2,\\
\frac{dy_2}{dt} &= -(M_1 + M_2)\frac{y_1}{r^3},\\
\frac{dy_3}{dt} &= y_4,\\
\frac{dy_4}{dt} &= -(M_1 + M_2)\frac{y_3}{r^3},\\
r_i &= \sqrt{y_5^2 + y_7^2},\\
D &= \sqrt{(y_1 - y_5)^2 + (y_3 - y_7)^2},\\
\frac{dy_5}{dt} &= y_6,\\
\frac{dy_6}{dt} &= -M_1\frac{y_5}{r_i^3} + M_2\left(\frac{y_1 - y_5}{D^3} - \frac{y_1}{r^3}\right),\\
\frac{dy_7}{dt} &= y_8,\\
\frac{dy_8}{dt} &= -M_1\frac{y_7}{r_i^3} + M_2\left(\frac{y_3 - y_7}{D^3} - \frac{y_3}{r^3}\right).
\end{aligned}\right] \qquad (11.21.6)$$

After a star is moved, set

$$x(i) = y_5,\ \dot{x}(i) = y_6,\ y(i) = y_7,\ \dot{y}(i) = y_8.$$

After the final, nth star is moved, set

$$x = y_1,\ \frac{dx}{dt} = y_2,\ y = y_3,\ \frac{dy}{dt} = y_4\ x(n) = y_5,\ \frac{dx(n)}{dt} = y_6,\ y(n) = y_7,\ \frac{dy(n)}{dt} = y_8.$$

11.22 If You Were on Venus, Could You See the Back of Your Head?

The answer is "No," and you would be most unwise to try! The idea for the project came from a suggestion that I read long ago that the atmospheric density was so high near the surface of Venus, that light rays could be refracted all the way around, leading to the unlikely effect of an observer seeing his back while looking forward. In this project, we shall investigate possible paths of a ray of light in a model planetary atmosphere. Absorption will be neglected, refraction being the only effect considered.

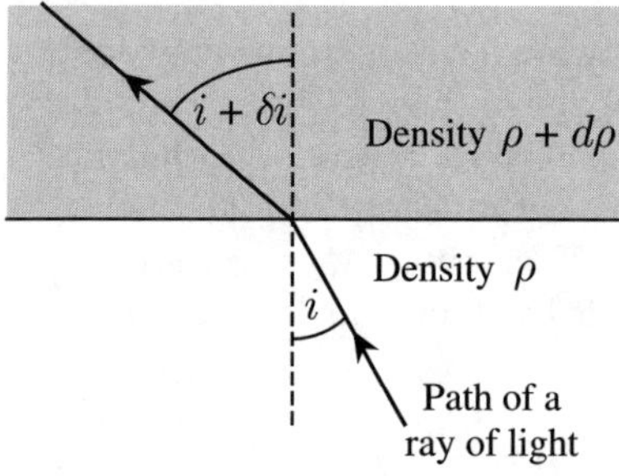

Figure 11.39: *Refraction between media of different densities.*

If a ray of light passes from one medium to another, then its path is bent by refraction. Figure 11.39 shows the path of a ray of light with *angle of incidence* i, and *angle of refraction* $i + \delta i$. The angles are measured from the line normal to the plane tangent to the media. Let the media have densities ρ and $\rho + d\rho$ and let the index of refraction be proportional to $1 + a\rho$ for some positive constant a. Then, from the law of refraction,

$$\frac{\sin(i + \delta i)}{\sin i} = \frac{1 + a\rho}{1 + a(\rho + d\rho)}. \tag{11.22.1}$$

Then, treating δi and $d\rho$ as differentials, we have

$$\delta i = -\frac{a \tan i}{1 + a\rho} d\rho. \tag{11.22.2}$$

This must be put into the context of a spherical atmosphere, as shown in figure 11.40. A ray of light passes through a spherical shell of radius r and thickness dr; the path of the ray through the shell subtends an angle $d\theta$ at the center of the shell. On leaving the shell, in preparation for its entering the medium outside, its incident angle is $i + di$, where, from the geometry of the figure,

$$di = \delta i - d\theta. \tag{11.22.3}$$

Also, since

$$\frac{\sin(i + di)}{r} = \frac{\sin(i + \delta i)}{r + dr}, \tag{11.22.4}$$

we have

$$\frac{dr}{d\theta} = r \cot i. \tag{11.22.5}$$

Let us assume an isothermal atmosphere, which leads to the formula

$$\rho = \rho_0 \exp\left(-(r - R)/h\right), \ r \geq R, \tag{11.22.6}$$

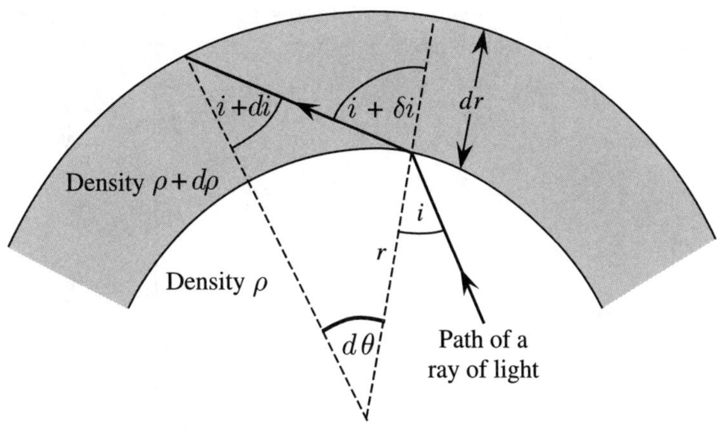

Figure 11.40: *Refraction in a spherical atmosphere.*

for the density at a point with altitude $r - R$, where R is the radius of the planet. ρ_0 is the density at the surface, and h is the *scale height* of the atmosphere. Then we have

$$\frac{d\rho}{dr} = -\frac{\rho}{h}. \tag{11.22.7}$$

From these formulas, we find that

$$\frac{di}{d\theta} = \frac{a\rho r}{h(1 + a\rho)} - 1. \tag{11.22.8}$$

This, together with equation (11.22.5), constitute the model.

One way of scaling the variables is to let

$$R = 1,\ \rho_0^{-1} = a,\ \text{and } b = 1/h.$$

Then equation (11.22.8) becomes

$$\frac{di}{d\theta} = br\left(e^{b(r-1)} + 1\right)^{-1} - 1. \tag{11.22.9}$$

I suggest that you start with $r = 1$ and $\theta = 0$ and vary the initial angle of the light ray. See whether it escapes to the outside, or "lands" again on the surface of the planet. Find out how different scale heights affect the situation. See if you can exactly manage the parameters so that you *will* see the back of your head!

11.23 Helium Burning in a Hot Star

Most stars, including the Sun, derive the energy that keeps them shining from the conversion of hydrogen into helium. After the hydrogen has been used up in the central core of the star, where temperatures were sufficiently high for hydrogen fusion to take place, the core heats up by gravitational contraction until, possibly, the temperature is high enough for helium "burning" to take place. Principally, carbon is formed by the collision of three helium nuclei; this is called the *triple alpha reaction.* Then oxygen is formed by collision between helium and carbon, and then neon, by collision between helium and oxygen. Considering only these reactions, V.C.Reddish [82] set up the following model.

Let Y, C, O, and Ne denote the number of atoms of each of the elements helium, carbon, oxygen and neon, respectively, per unit mass of stellar material. Then, if t is the time,

$$\left.\begin{aligned} \frac{dY}{dt} &= -3aY^2 - bYC - cYO, \\ \frac{dC}{dt} &= aY^2 - bYC, \\ \frac{dO}{dt} &= bYC - cYO, \\ \frac{dNe}{dt} &= cYO, \end{aligned}\right] \qquad (11.23.1)$$

where a, b and c are constants that are inversely proportional to the reaction times, and the factor 3 appears in the first equation because three helium nuclei join to form one carbon nucleus.

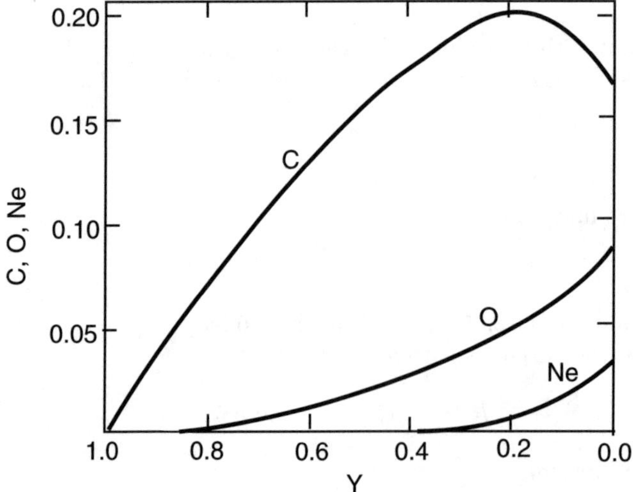

Figure 11.41: *From V.C.Reddish, "The R and N Stars." Observatory 74 (1954) Reproduced with permission.*

If the first equation of (11.23.1) is divided into the remaining three, then the time is eliminated, and the new independent variable is Y, or the remaining amount of helium. The new system is then

$$\left.\begin{aligned} \frac{dC}{dY} &= -\frac{aY - bC}{3aY + bC + cO}, \\ \frac{dO}{dY} &= -\frac{bC - cO}{3aY + bC + cO}, \\ \frac{dNe}{dY} &= -\frac{cO}{3aY + bC + cO}. \end{aligned}\right] \qquad (11.23.2)$$

Assuming only helium to be present at the start, initial conditions would be

$$t = 0;\ Y = 1,\ C = O = Ne = 0. \qquad (11.23.3)$$

If equations (11.23.2) are used, then the integration is *backward* with Y going from 1 to 0, with negative stepsizes.

Reddish assumed that at the temperatures of interest, the reaction times are nearly equal so that

$$\frac{a}{b} = \frac{a}{c} = 1.$$

By numerical integration, he derived the diagram reproduced (by permission) in figure 11.41. Reddish then used this diagram to try to explain the occurrence of relatively large amounts of carbon in giant cool stars in which helium burning has taken place.

For the project, first reproduce the figure. The model is too simplified to be of much practical use, but it does make possible some experimentation with parameters and initial conditions. Are the results very sensitive to the ratios a/b and a/c? What happens if small quantities of C and O are present initially? What then are the relative speeds at which the stages in the figure are reached?

11.24 An Approximate Model for a Star

To build a realistic model for a star is complicated, since a system of differential equations must be solved for which some of the "initial conditions" are at the center and some are on the surface. Also many of the numbers to do with energy production and transfer must be entered through tables. It is necessary to start with an approximate model and then to correct it until everything fits. For more information, and to see computer code for building models, see the section by R.Kouzes in the text *Astrophysical Simulations.* [31]

Here we shall build an approximate model called a *polytrope.* We assume that the star is nonrotating, is built up in concentric spherical layers, and exists in hydrostatic equilibrium. We also assume that the star is gaseous, with the gas obeying the laws for a perfect gas and the equation of state for an adiabatic gas; viz.,

$$\text{pressure} = \text{constant}\times(\text{density})^{\gamma}.$$

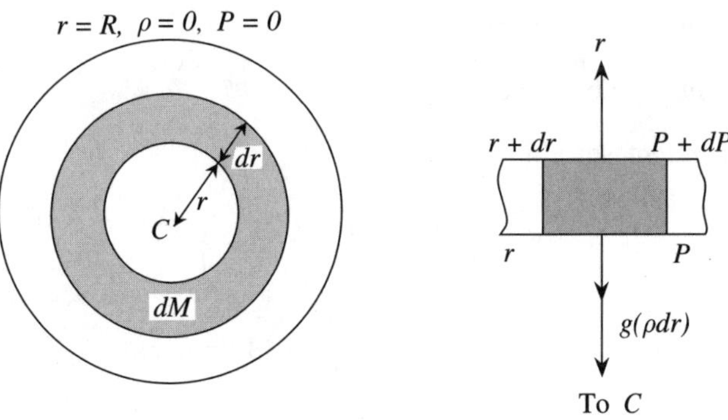

Figure 11.42: *Geometry for equilibrium in a star.*

Let r be the radial distance measured from the center C of the star. Consider a small lump of gas having unit cross-sectional area and thickness dr, bounded by r and $r + dr$. Let it have density $\rho = \rho(r)$; then it will have mass $dM = \rho dr$. See figure 11.42. Let the gas pressure at the face r be P, and that at the face $r + dr$ be $P + dP$. (Notice that dP will be negative.) Then the difference in pressures, dP, must be balanced by the weight of the lump, or $(\rho dr)g$, where $g = g(r)$ is the acceleration due to gravity at distance r from the center. Being careful with signs, we have

$$dP = -g\rho dr, \tag{11.24.1}$$

the condition for hydrostatic equilibrium. The gravitational force at a point distant r from the center is caused only by the stellar material *inside* the sphere of radius r. Let the mass of material inside this sphere be $M(r)$. Then from Newton's law of gravitation,

$$g(r) = G\frac{M(r)}{r^2}. \tag{11.24.2}$$

G is the constant of gravitation. Let the mass of a spherical shell having internal and external radii r and $r + dr$ be $dM(r)$. Then $dM(r) = 4\pi r^2 \rho dr$, so that

$$\frac{dM(r)}{dr} = 4\pi r^2 \rho. \tag{11.24.3}$$

But from (11.24.2),

$$M(r) = \frac{r^2 g}{G} = -r^2 \frac{dP}{dr}\frac{1}{G\rho}. \tag{11.24.4}$$

If we differentiate with respect to r, and combine with (11.24.3), we find that

$$\frac{d}{dr}\left(\frac{r^2}{\rho}\frac{dP}{dr}\right) = -4\pi G r^2 \rho. \tag{11.24.5}$$

From the adiabatic gas law,

$$P = K\rho^{\gamma}, \tag{11.24.6}$$

where γ is a constant greater than one but approaching one for complicated molecules. For a monatomic gas, $\gamma = 5/3$. K is called the polytropic temperature.

To derive the final, useful equation, we introduce dimensionless variables as follows:

- Let $\gamma = 1 + \frac{1}{n}$ define n, the *polytropic index.*
- Let the density at the center be called ρ_c.
- Let a new dependent variable θ be defined by $\rho = \rho_c \theta^n$.
- Let the new independent variable ξ be defined by

$$r = \left(\frac{(n+1)K}{4\pi G}\rho_c^{(1/n)-1}\right)^{1/2} \xi. \tag{11.24.7}$$

Then if you do not lose patience with the algebra, you will find that

$$\xi^{-2}\frac{d}{d\xi}\left(\xi^2 \frac{d\theta}{d\xi}\right) = -\theta^n. \tag{11.24.8}$$

This is the *Lane-Emden equation of index n.* Discussion of it can be found in many text books on astrophysics. An excellent reference is Chandrasekhar [24].

Equation (11.24.8) is to be solved subject to the following initial conditions at the center

$$\xi = 0,\ \theta = 1,\ \frac{d\theta}{d\xi} = 0. \tag{11.24.9}$$

For our purposes. we must first rewrite (11.24.8) as a system of two first-order equations. Let

$$y_1 = \theta,\ y_2 = \frac{d\theta}{d\xi} = \frac{d\theta}{dx}. \tag{11.24.10}$$

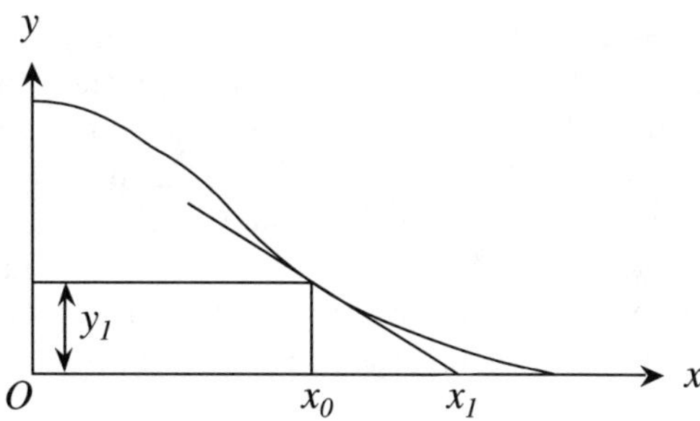

Figure 11.43: *A step in Newton's method for locating the boundary of a star.*

Then

$$\left.\begin{aligned}\frac{dy_1}{dx} &= y_2,\\ \frac{dy_2}{dx} &= -y_1^n - \frac{2y_2}{x},\end{aligned}\right] \tag{11.24.11}$$

where initially $x = 0,\ y_1 = 1$ and $y_2 = 0$.

For debugging purposes, we have the special solutions:

$$\begin{aligned} n &= 0,\ \theta_0 = 1 - \frac{1}{6}\xi^2, \text{ radius } \xi_1 = \sqrt{6}.\\ n &= 1,\ \theta_1 = \frac{\sin\xi}{\xi}, \text{ radius } \xi_1 = \pi.\\ n &= 5,\ \theta_5 = (1+\xi^2)^{-1/2}, \text{ radius infinite.}\end{aligned}$$

So in practice we shall be concerned with values of n between 0 and 5. The case $n = 3$, called *Eddington's model*, has been of special interest in astrophysics.

Beware! The very first step in the solution cannot be taken using regular numerical integration, because of the appearance of x in the denominator. A good way to deal with this situation is to use the series

$$y_1 = 1 - \frac{1}{6}x^2 + \frac{n}{120}x^4 \tag{11.24.12}$$

to approximate y_1 and y_2 for some small value of x, say $x = 0.05$, and then start the integration from there.

When $y_1 = 0$, the density is zero and we have reached the boundary of the star. But we have to find this point precisely. Newton's method is appropriate here. Since we are solving the equation $y_1(x) = 0$ for x, an iteration using Newton's method is

$$x_1 = x_0 - y_1(x_0)/y_1'(x_0) = x_0 - y_1/y_2. \tag{11.24.13}$$

So a stepsize during the iteration is $-y_1/y_2$. You might use code similar to the following:

```
Repeat  StepSize = - y(1)/y(2)
    Step(...)
until Abs(y(1)) < Eps
```

A complication arises in deciding when to start this iteration. If you overstep the point where $y_1 = 0$, then y_1 becomes negative, the term y_1^n will probably become undefined, and the program will crash — maybe with an impolite diagnostic, which you richly deserve. So whenever you call the procedure for calculating the derivatives, check **first** to see if y_1 is negative; if it is, abandon the current integration step and start Newton's method. During the use of Newton's method there should be no trouble (unless you try to get very high accuracy), since the graph of y_1 as a function of x is concave up near the boundary of the star. See figure 11.43.

See if you can find a sequence of models for different n, noting the values of ξ_1 and the shapes of the curves of θ graphed as a function of ξ. Chandrasekhar shows how physical information on quantities such as radius, mass, pressure, etc. can be derived from the integration. As an example, the ratio of the central density over the mean density for the star is

$$\frac{\rho_c}{\bar{\rho}} = -\xi \Big/ \left(3\frac{d\theta}{d\xi}\right)\Bigg|_{\xi=\xi_1}. \tag{11.24.14}$$

11.25 The Limiting Mass of a White Dwarf

Stars form, evolve and die. A star such as the Sun derives its energy for shining through fusion reactions that change hydrogen into helium. The radius of the Sun is essentially constant because the pressure of outward flowing radiation helps to balance the inward gravitational force. Eventually, the hydrogen will become exhausted, and the star may contract. One possibility is that the contraction continues until the star becomes a white dwarf. This is a small body, comparable in size to the planet Mercury, having density around $10^5 - 10^6$ gm/cm^3. One of the most important discoveries in the history of astronomy was made in the 1930s by S.Chandrasekhar, when he demonstrated that there was an upper limit to the mass of a white dwarf. For a star made up primarily of helium, this limit is approximately 1.44 times the mass of the Sun. Chandrasekhar showed that the white dwarfs could be classified by their mass, and that as the mass approached the limiting value, the radius approached zero. Initially some astronomers were unable to believe that physical matter could behave in this way. The "Chandrasekhar limit" was one of the great discoveries of this age. Chandrasekhar was awarded the Nobel prize for physics in 1983.

In this project we shall compute models for white dwarfs and will follow them to the limiting mass. Some derivation will be needed, although you can skip to the final equations if you wish. The structure of a white dwarf cannot be explained by classical physics, so some of the principles of quantum mechanics are needed. However, the derivation described here (following Chandrasekhar [24]) is elementary. I recommend that you try at least to follow the principles involved.

11.25.1 Degenerate Matter

The particles in a gas will be moving in different directions and at different speeds. A way to describe this is to use a *velocity distribution function.* Consider a cubic centimeter containing N particles of the same type. In a Cartesian reference system let the velocity components be (v_x, v_y, v_z). Let the number of particles with the x-component of velocity lying in the interval $(v_x,\ v_x + dv_x)$ be $dN(v_x)$. If we have a perfect gas, then

$$dN(v_x) = N\left(\frac{m}{2k\pi T}\right)^{1/2} e^{-mv_x^2/2kT} dv_x. \tag{11.25.1}$$

This is a *Maxwellian* velocity distribution. T is the temperature, m is the mass of the particle and $k = 1.38 \times 10^{-16}$ ergs/deg is Boltzmann's constant. Similarly, we can say that the number of particles with velocity components in the intervals $(v_x,\ v_x + dv_x)$, $(v_y,\ v_y + dv_y)$, and $(v_z,\ v_z + dv_z)$ is

$$N(v)dv_x\, dv_y\, dv_z = N\left(\frac{m}{2k\pi T}\right)^{3/2} e^{-mv^2/2kT} dv_x\, dv_y\, dv_z, \tag{11.25.2}$$

where $v = \sqrt{v_x^2 + v_y^2 + v_z^2}$.

If the density is sufficiently high, the *Pauli exclusion principle* prevents the randomness that is essential for a perfect gas. We shall need to discuss the position of a particle in *phase space.* This has six dimensions. Here we shall use components of position and momentum, $p = mv$:

$$x,\ y,\ z,\ p_x,\ p_y,\ p_z.$$

A volume element in this space is

$$d\tau = dx\, dy\, dz\, dp_x\, dp_y\, dp_z. \tag{11.25.3}$$

Next we introduce *Planck's constant,* $h = 6.6256 \times 10^{-27}$ erg·sec. This has dimensions $\mathrm{ML^2T^{-1}}$; $d\tau$ has dimensions $\mathrm{M^3L^6T^{-3}}$, or the same dimensions as h^3. Let the phase space be divided into cells, each having volume h^3. The Pauli exclusion principle states that in any one cell at most two particles of the same type can be found; these will have anti-parallel spins, shown formally by $s = \frac{1}{2}$ and $s = -\frac{1}{2}$ in figure 11.44

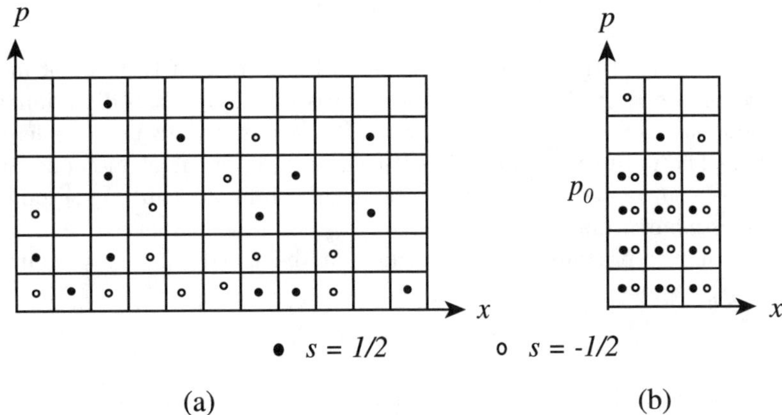

Figure 11.44: *Comparison between a perfect and a degenerate gas.*

In a perfect gas there is plenty of room for the particles to be distributed according to Maxwell's formula. This is illustrated in figure 11.44(a). But if the material is compressed, as in figure 11.44(b), the cells with the lower values of the momentum are filled up; some particles are forced to have higher momenta, and the gas is degenerate.

Suppose that in a volume of 1 cm^3 every cell is filled up to a threshold p_0. (Here $p = \sqrt{p_x^2 + p_y^2 + p_z^2}$.) For $0 \le p \le p_0$, the volume $(1)dp_x dp_y dp_z$ in phase space contains $(2/h^3)dp_x dp_y dp_z = (2m^3/h^3)dv_x dv_y dv_z$ particles. So the velocity distribution function will be

$$N_D(v)dv_x dv_y dv_z = (2m^3/h^3)dv_x dv_y dv_z. \tag{11.25.4}$$

Comparing this with equation (11.25.2), we see that there will be degeneracy if

$$N\left(\frac{m}{2k\pi T}\right)^{3/2} > 2\frac{m^3}{h^3}, \tag{11.25.5}$$

or if the quantity $\rho T^{-3/2} m^{-3/2}$ is too great, where ρ is the density. It follows that degeneracy will first occur with electrons, and it is electron degeneracy that is considered below. (Neutron degeneracy is the next type of importance in astronomy; it occurs in neutron stars.) Note that degeneracy can be relieved by decreasing the density or pressure, as would be expected, but also by *increasing* the temperature.

Let N_e be the electron density, and H be the mass of a particle of unit atomic weight. Define μ_e by

$$\mu_e H = \frac{\rho}{N_e}. \quad (11.25.6)$$

For a completely ionized helium gas, $\mu_e = 4/2 = 2$. Then condition (11.25.5) becomes

$$\rho > (2/h^3)(2\pi mkT)^{3/2}\mu_e H \approx 8.1 \times 10^{-9}\mu_e T^{3/2}. \quad (11.25.7)$$

We shall assume complete degeneracy. Let the number of electrons having momentum in the interval $(p, p + dp)$ be $N(p)dp$. The volume of a shell bounded by spheres of radii p and $p + dp$ is $4\pi p^2 dp$. So

$$N(p) = \begin{cases} (2/h^3)4\pi p^2, & p < p_0, \\ 0, & p > p_0. \end{cases} \quad (11.25.8)$$

p_0 is called the *Fermi threshold.* It can be determined by

$$N_e = \int_0^\infty N(p)dp = \int_0^{p_0} N(p)dp = \frac{8\pi p_0^3}{3h^3}. \quad (11.25.9)$$

The pressure exerted by the degenerate particles is the rate of transfer of momentum across unit area. We assume isotropy (i.e., the configuration is the same in all directions) and locate the unit area perpendicular to the x-axis. One third of the particles can be considered to be moving in the x-direction. The number of particles with the x-component of momentum in the interval $(p_x, p_x + dp_x)$ is $N(p_x)dp_x$, and the number crossing the unit area in one second is $N(p_x)dp_x v_x$. Each particle carries momentum p_x.

Before calculating the pressure, we need to look at the speeds that may be involved. We have $\rho/\mu_e H = N_e = 8\pi p_0^3/3h^3$, so

$$v_0^3 = p_0^3/m^3 = (\rho/\mu_e H)(3h^3/8\pi m^3).$$

If $\mu_e = 2$, then $v_0 = 2.4 \times 10^8 \rho^{1/3}$ cm/sec. So, for high densities, effects of special relativity must be considered.

For given speed v, the mass is $m(v) = m(1 - v^2/c^2)^{-1/2}$, and the momentum is $p = mv(1 - v^2/c^2)^{-1/2}$. Then

$$v = (p/m)(1 + p^2/m^2c^2)^{-1/2}.$$

We can now derive the formula for the pressure P.

$$\begin{aligned} P &= \int_0^\infty N(p_x)v_x p_x\, dp_x \\ &= \int_0^\infty N(p_x)\left[(p/m)(1 + p^2/m^2c^2)^{-1/2}\right] p_x\, dp_x \\ &= \frac{8\pi}{3mh^3}\int_0^{p_0} p^4(1 + p^2/m^2c^2)^{-1/2} dp. \end{aligned} \quad (11.25.10)$$

This is expressed using a parameter $x = p_0/mc$. Then

$$\rho = Bx^3, \quad P = Af(x), \quad (11.25.11)$$

with

$$f(x) = x(2x^2 - 3)(x^2 + 1)^{1/2} + 3\sinh^{-1} x, \quad (11.25.12)$$

and

$$\left.\begin{aligned} A &= \pi m^4 c^5/3h^3 \approx 6.01 \times 10^{22}, \\ B &= (8\pi m^3 c^3 H/3h^3)\mu_e \approx 9.82 \times 10^5 \mu_e. \end{aligned}\right] \quad (11.25.13)$$

11.25.2 The Structure of a White Dwarf

We shall follow the sequence of substitutions developed by Chandrasekhar. The equation for the equilibrium of the star is

$$\frac{1}{r^2}\frac{d}{dr}\left(\frac{r^2}{\rho}\frac{dP}{dr}\right) = -4\pi G\rho. \tag{11.25.14}$$

Into this we must introduce the equations of state, equations (11.25.11), making x the dependent variable

$$\frac{A}{B}\frac{1}{r^2}\frac{d}{dr}\left(\frac{r^2}{x^3}\frac{df(x)}{dr}\right) = -4\pi GBx^3. \tag{11.25.15}$$

Now

$$\frac{df(x)}{dr} = \frac{df(x)}{dx}\frac{dx}{dr} = \frac{8x^4}{(x^2+1)^{1/2}}\frac{dx}{dr},$$

so

$$\frac{1}{x^3}\frac{df(x)}{dr} = \frac{8x}{(x^2+1)^{1/2}}\frac{dx}{dr} = 8\frac{d(x^2+1)^{1/2}}{dr}.$$

So equation (11.25.15) can be written as

$$\frac{1}{r^2}\frac{d}{dr}\left(r^2\frac{d(1+x^2)^{1/2}}{dr}\right) = -\frac{\pi GB^2}{2A}x^3. \tag{11.25.16}$$

Next, let

$$y^2 = 1 + x^2. \tag{11.25.17}$$

Then equation (11.25.16) becomes

$$\frac{1}{r^2}\frac{d}{dr}\left(r^2\frac{dy}{dr}\right) = -\frac{\pi GB^2}{2A}(y^2-1)^{3/2}. \tag{11.25.18}$$

At the center of the star, let $x = x_c$ and $y = y_c$. Introduce the new variables η and ϕ, defined by

$$r = \alpha\eta, \quad y = y_c\phi, \tag{11.25.19}$$

where

$$\alpha = \left(\frac{2A}{\pi G}\right)^{1/2}\frac{1}{By_c} = \frac{7.71\times 10^8}{\mu_e y_c}\ \text{cm}, \quad y_c^2 = 1 + x_c^2. \tag{11.25.20}$$

Then we have, finally,

$$\frac{1}{\eta^2}\frac{d}{d\eta}\left(\eta^2\frac{d\phi}{d\eta}\right) = -\left(\phi^2 - \frac{1}{y_c^2}\right)^{3/2}. \tag{11.25.21}$$

Initial conditions at the center of the star are

$$\eta = 0, \quad \phi = 1, \quad \frac{d\phi}{d\eta} = 0. \tag{11.25.22}$$

At the surface of the star, the density is zero, so $x = 0$ and $y = 1$. So we have

$$\eta = \eta_1, \text{ where } \phi(\eta_1) = \frac{1}{y_c}. \tag{11.25.23}$$

Equation (11.25.21) is singular at $\eta = 0$, so the numerical integration cannot start at $\eta = 0$. Instead, a power series development is used to calculate $\phi(\eta)$ for small η. Chandrasekhar gives the series

$$\left.\begin{aligned}\phi \;=\; & 1 - \frac{q^3}{6}\eta^2 + \frac{q^4}{40}\eta^4 - \frac{q^5(5q^2+14)}{7!}\eta^6 + \frac{q^6(339q^2+280)}{3\times 9!}\eta^8 \\ & - \frac{q^7(1425q^4+11436q^2+4256)}{5\times 11!}\eta^{10} + \ldots,\end{aligned}\right] \tag{11.25.24}$$

where $q^2 = (y_c^2 - 1)/y_c^2$. y_c is the parameter of the model.

The variables involved have no immediate physical interpretation. So we need to see how some of the quantities of interest, such as density, are changing as the integration proceeds. Let's take density first. The central density is

$$\rho_c = Bx_c^3 = B(y_c^2 - 1)^{3/2}. \tag{11.25.25}$$

The density for intermediate points is given by

$$\rho(\eta) = \rho_c \frac{y_c^3}{(y_c^2 - 1)^{3/2}} \left(\phi^2 - \frac{1}{y_c^2}\right)^{3/2}. \tag{11.25.26}$$

The mass, inside a sphere specified by η, (where the actual radius is $r = \alpha\eta$) is

$$\begin{aligned} M(\eta) &= 4\pi \int_0^r \rho r^2\, dr \\ &= 4\pi\alpha^3 \int_0^\eta \rho\eta^2\, d\eta \\ &= 4\pi\rho_c \frac{\alpha^3 y_c^3}{(y_c^2 - 1)^{3/2}} \int_0^\eta \left(\phi^2 - \frac{1}{y_c^2}\right)^{3/2} \eta^2\, d\eta \\ &= -4\pi\rho_c \frac{\alpha^3 y_c^3}{(y_c^2 - 1)^{3/2}} \eta^2 \frac{d\phi}{d\eta}. \end{aligned} \tag{11.25.27}$$

Here we used equation (11.25.26), for ρ, and equation (11.25.21). Substituting for α from equation (11.25.20) and ρ_c from equation (11.25.25), we have

$$M(\eta) = -4\pi \left(\frac{2A}{\pi G}\right)^{3/2} \frac{1}{B^3} \eta^2 \frac{d\phi}{d\eta}. \tag{11.25.28}$$

The mass of the entire star is

$$M = -4\pi \left(\frac{2A}{\pi G}\right)^{3/2} \frac{1}{B^3} \left(\eta^2 \frac{d\phi}{d\eta}\right)_{\eta=\eta_1}. \tag{11.25.29}$$

Finally, the ratio of the mean density $\overline{\rho}$ to the central density is

$$\frac{\overline{\rho}}{\rho_c} = -3 \frac{y_c^3}{(y_c^2 - 1)^{3/2}} \frac{1}{\eta_1} \left(\frac{d\phi}{d\eta}\right)_{\eta=\eta_1}. \tag{11.25.30}$$

The numbers quoted here are in cgs units. To convert to stellar values, in terms of the mass and radius of the Sun, note that $M_\odot = 2 \times 10^{33}$ gm, and $R_\odot = 6.9672 \times 10^{10}$ cm.

To help with numerical checks, note that for $1/y_c^2 = 0.5$, Chandrasekhar finds $\eta_1 = 3.5330$, $\overline{\rho}/\rho_c = 0.13605$, $\rho_c/B = 1$, $M\mu_e^2/M_\odot = 2.02$, $R = 1.93 \times 10^9$ cm.

Chapter 12

Pendulums

12.1 The Simple Pendulum 

Pendulums appear in many places. They are interesting in themselves, and have many applications. In particular, they are often used to approximate physical systems. So, although the variety in the chapter is intended partly to entertain, I hope that you will find the experience of getting to know the models to be of practical use. We start with the simplest pendulum of all.

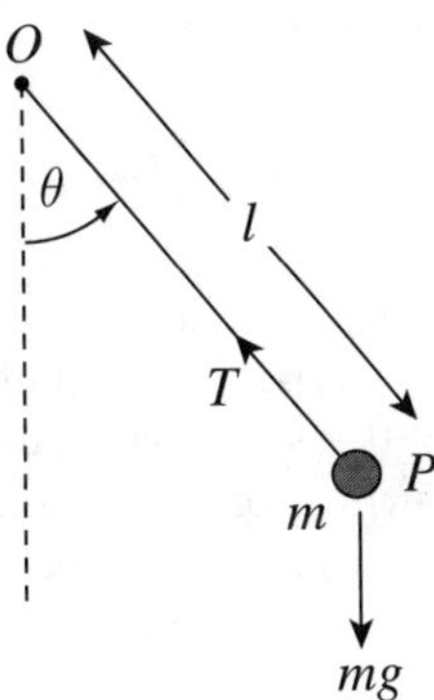

Figure 12.1: *The simple pendulum.*

A light, rigid rod of length l has a mass m attached to one end, at P. The other end, O, is attached to a fixed, frictionless pivot. The rod and mass are free to move in a vertical plane through O. The only force on the system is due to gravity, which causes a constant downward acceleration g. All resisting forces are neglected. The rod makes the angle θ with the downward vertical, as shown in figure 12.1. The independent variable is the time t.

The forces on m are its weight, mg, acting downward, and the tension, T, in the rod. If we resolve perpendicularly to the rod, T makes no contribution, and the component of the weight (in the direction θ increasing) is $-mg\sin\theta$. The component of velocity in this direction is $l\dot{\theta}$, and that of acceleration is $l\ddot{\theta}$. (A "dot" implies differentiation with respect to the time.) See figure 12.2. So, from Newton's second law of motion,

$$ml\frac{d^2\theta}{dt^2} = -mg\sin\theta,$$

or

$$\frac{d^2\theta}{dt^2} = -\frac{g}{l}\sin\theta, \tag{12.1.1}$$

showing that the value of the mass m does not influence the motion.

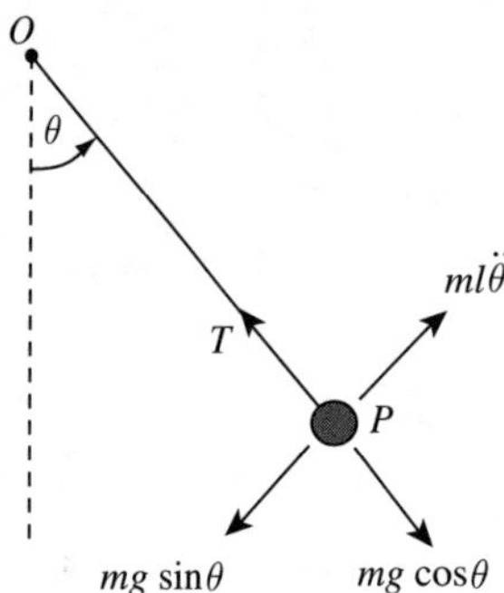

Figure 12.2: *Forces and acceleration.*

When θ remains small, $\sin\theta \approx \theta$ and we have the well-known approximation

$$\frac{d^2\theta}{dt^2} + \frac{g}{l}\theta = 0. \tag{12.1.2}$$

This is the equation of a harmonic oscillator with frequency $\sqrt{g/l}$ and period $2\pi\sqrt{l/g}$. These are independent of the (small) amplitude of the swing, a fact that is helpful in those clocks that use pendulums. If the frequency is called ω_0, then

$$\omega_0 = \sqrt{\frac{g}{l}}, \tag{12.1.3}$$

and it is called the *natural frequency* of the system.

Return to the nonlinear model for this project, equation (12.1.1). There are two equilibrium positions, one vertically down with $\theta = 0$ and stable, and the other vertically up with $\theta = \pi$ and unstable. The motion may consist of swings or "librations" about $\theta = 0$, when $-\pi < \theta < \pi$; or there may be "circulation," when the motion continues clockwise or counter-clockwise, and θ is unbounded. When you run the model, try to think in terms of an actual pendulum rather than computer output.

In order to run the model, the single second-order differential equation (12.1.1) must be expressed as two first-order equations. Let

$$y_1 = \theta, \quad \text{and} \quad y_2 = \frac{d\theta}{dt}. \tag{12.1.4}$$

Then we can write

$$\left.\begin{aligned} \frac{dy_1}{dt} &= y_2, \\ \frac{dy_2}{dt} &= -\frac{g}{l}\sin y_1. \end{aligned}\right] \tag{12.1.5}$$

The two right-hand sides of these equations must be entered into a procedure called, let's say, Fun. For instance, if the right-hand sides are put into an array, z, then the procedure should contain the lines:

```
z(1) = y(2)
z(2) = - (GravAccel/Length)*Sin(y(1))
```

Remember at all times, that all calculations must be done in radians. If you enter initial conditions using degrees (which is quite a good idea), convert them **instantly** to radians in the program. When entering initial conditions think of actually, physically, starting a real pendulum in motion. Make this as close to a "hands-on" project as you can. Take runs far enough so that you see complete swings, or circulations.

You might present results by plotting θ and $\dot{\theta}$ as functions of the time. In general, the best way to describe the action is in a *phase-plane* diagram, when the horizontal axis is θ and the vertical axis is $\dot{\theta}$. Figures 12.3 and 12.4 show librational and circulatory motion, respectively, as they appear in phase-plane diagrams. Try to act them out yourself, perhaps swinging an arm.

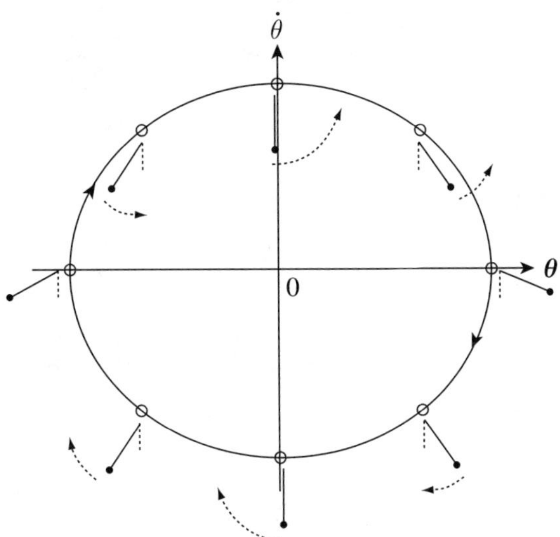

Figure 12.3: *Phase-plane diagram for librational motion.*

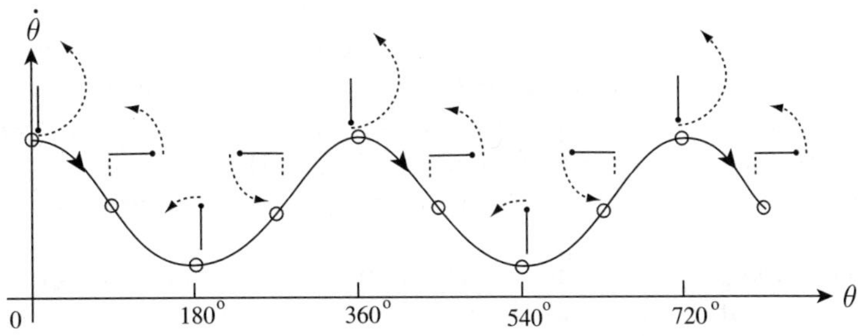

Figure 12.4: *Phase-plane diagram for circulatory motion.*

A phase-plane diagram combining many different solutions is shown in figure 12.5. Observe the different types of motion. You are likely to see similar diagrams in many texts, but it is good experience to generate several for yourself. That is the most important part of the project.

An advantage of a phase-plane diagram is that it can contain information about solutions with a variety of initial conditions. A disadvantage is that the time dependence of the motion is lost. Figure 12.6 shows a plot of θ versus the time. This shows periodic swinging that moves close to the unstable equilibrium at $\theta = \pi$; as it approaches its highest point, the motion slows down. If the starting value of θ were to approach π, with initial $\dot{\theta}(0) = 0$, then the period of oscillation would tend to infinity.

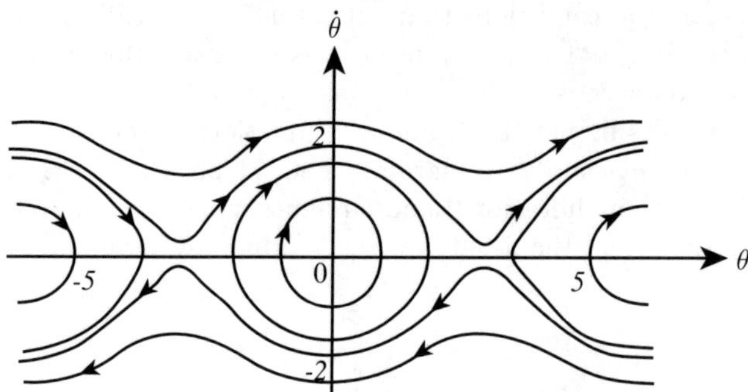

Figure 12.5: *Phase-plane diagram for* $\ddot{\theta} + \sin\theta = 0$. *Units are rad and rad/sec.*

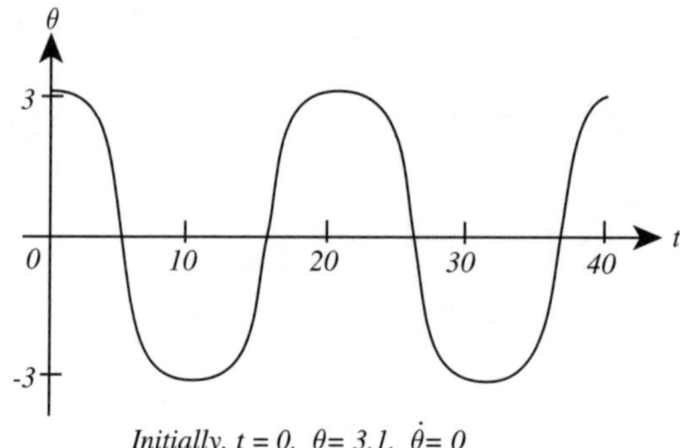

Figure 12.6: *A plot of* θ *versus the time for* $\ddot{\theta} + \sin\theta = 0$. θ *is measured in radians.*

12.2 The Period of a Simple Pendulum 

We have just seen that the period of oscillation does in fact depend on the amplitude of the swing. As the amplitude approaches π, the period tends to infinity. For this project get data so that you can make a plot of the period with changing amplitude. Increase the initial value of θ for each run, but always start out with the rate of change of θ equal to zero. This way, you will start at the top of a swing, and the initial value of θ is the amplitude. Now you need to find the corresponding period.

You might judge the period from interpolation in a table from a printout. But we shall look at two much better ways that will be useful later.

1. Find the point at which the pendulum first reaches its lowest point, $\theta = 0$; the time to this point is one quarter of the total period of oscillation.

2. Find the point at which the pendulum first reaches the opposite highest point; the time to this point is one half of the total period of oscillation.

Consider the first case. We shall use Newton's method. For solving $f(t) = 0$, by this method, we generate a sequence $\{t_i\}$, $i = 0, 1, 2, ...$ where

$$t_{i+1} = t_i - f(t_i) \Big/ \left(\frac{df}{dt}\right)\Bigg|_{t=t_i}. \tag{12.2.1}$$

We use notation from the preceding project. Each time you take an integration step, test to see if y_1 has changed its sign. As soon as this happens, the current value of t becomes t_0 in the iteration.

Newton's method then takes over in choosing the stepsize. The first stepsize is the quantity $t_1 - t_0$. Suppose that you have a variable called `y1Sign` which is equal to +1 if $y_1 > 0$ and −1 if $y_1 < 0$. If you started with a positive initial value of y_1 (with $y_2 = 0$), then you would initially set `y1Sign = +1`. Then, to check on whether you have passed over the bottom of the swing, have code such as:

```
Step(...)
if y1Sign*y(1) < 0 then FindBottom
```

The derivative of y_1 is y_2, in the notation used above, so the procedure `FindBottom` might contain code like

```
Repeat
    StepSize = - y(1)/y(2)
    Step(...)
Until Abs(y(1)) < Eps
```

`Eps` is a small number for you to choose.

Later, we may want to find the lowest point when the pendulum has been circulating; then `y1Sign` will not be helpful, since θ may not be passing through the value zero; instead, use $\sin\theta$ or `sin(y(1))` (no pun intended) in place of `y1` (for the test).

Finding the top of the swing is similar. Now we shall need to find the value of t when $\dot{\theta} = 0$, or $y_2 = 0$. Define a variable `y2Sign` which is equal to +1 if $y_2 > 0$ and −1 if $y_2 < 0$. Each time you take an integration step, test to see if y_2 has changed its sign. As soon as this happens, the current value of t becomes t_0 in the iteration. If you started with a positive initial value of y_1 (with $y_2 = 0$), then you would initially set `y2Sign = -1`. Then, to check on whether you have passed over the top of the swing on the other side, have code such as

```
Step(...)
if y2Sign*y(2) < 0 then FindTop
```

In the notation used above, the derivative of y_2 is z_2, so the procedure `FindTop` might contain code like

```
Repeat
    Call procedure Fun to calculate z(1) and z(2), which are the
        derivatives of y(1) and y(2).
    StepSize = - y(2)/z(2)
    Step(...)
Until Abs(y(2)) < Eps
```

Select a value of g/l; plot the period as a function of the amplitude. How does the shape of this curve change when g/l is changed? If the linear approximation is defined as acceptable if the error is less than 5%, then what is the maximum allowable amplitude? Does this depend on the value of g/l?

One further approach should be mentioned. It need not involve any iteration, so can be faster to compute, but it involves additional coding. The principle is that the equations are transformed so that the independent variable is the variable that is to be made equal to zero. Suppose that we want to make $\theta = 0$. Let

$$z_1 = t,\ z_2 = \dot{\theta},\ \tau = \theta. \tag{12.2.2}$$

Then, noting that equation (12.1.1) can be written as two first-order equations

$$\frac{d\theta}{dt} = \dot{\theta},\ \text{and}\ \frac{d\dot{\theta}}{dt} = -\frac{g}{l}\sin\theta,$$

so that

$$\frac{dt}{d\theta} = \frac{1}{\dot\theta}, \text{ and } \frac{d\dot\theta}{d\theta} = -\frac{g}{l}\frac{\sin\theta}{\dot\theta},$$

we can write

$$\left.\begin{aligned} \frac{dz_1}{d\tau} &= \frac{1}{z_2}, \\ \frac{dz_2}{d\tau} &= -\frac{g}{l}\frac{\sin\tau}{z_2}. \end{aligned}\right] \tag{12.2.3}$$

As soon as θ, or y_1, has changed sign, then these new equations are to be solved, with initial stepsize, for τ equal to the current value of θ; only one step should be needed.

In the same way, if $\dot\theta$ is to be made zero, write (12.1.1) as

$$\frac{dt}{d\dot\theta} = -\frac{l}{g\sin\theta}, \text{ and } \frac{d\theta}{d\dot\theta} = -\frac{l\dot\theta}{g\sin\theta}.$$

Let

$$z_1 = t,\ z_2 = \theta,\ \tau = \dot\theta. \tag{12.2.4}$$

Then

$$\left.\begin{aligned} \frac{dz_1}{d\tau} &= -\frac{1}{g\sin z_2}, \\ \frac{dz_2}{d\tau} &= -\frac{l\tau}{g\sin z_2}. \end{aligned}\right] \tag{12.2.5}$$

12.3 The Pendulum with Linear Damping

The preceding model exhibits perpetual motion, which is hardly realistic. The simplest way to introduce a damping force is to assume that the dissipative forces create a torque that is proportional to the angular velocity. Then the model becomes

$$ml\frac{d^2\theta}{dt^2} = -K\frac{d\theta}{dt} - mg\sin\theta, \tag{12.3.1}$$

where K depends on the magnitude of the resistance. This can be simplified as

$$\frac{d^2\theta}{dt^2} = -k\frac{d\theta}{dt} - \frac{g}{l}\sin\theta. \tag{12.3.2}$$

Here $k = K/(ml)$. This shows that the influence of the resistance is diminished if the mass is increased.

Equations (12.1.5) become

$$\left.\begin{aligned} \frac{dy_1}{dt} &= y_2, \\ \frac{dy_2}{dt} &= -ky_2 - \frac{g}{l}\sin y_1. \end{aligned}\right] \tag{12.3.3}$$

The lines in a procedure for calculating the right-hand sides might look like

```
z(1) = y(2)
z(2) = - Friction*y(2)- (GravAccel/Length)*Sin(y(1))
```

As expected, since all motion is damped, circulatory motion eventually becomes librational, and the amplitude of librational motion decreases to zero. Two phase diagrams are shown in figure 12.7.

As with the preceding project, make yourself familiar with the properties and possibilities of the model through your own computation. For a game, start the motion off with fast circulation, and see if you can guess in advance how many circuits will be described before librational motion takes over.

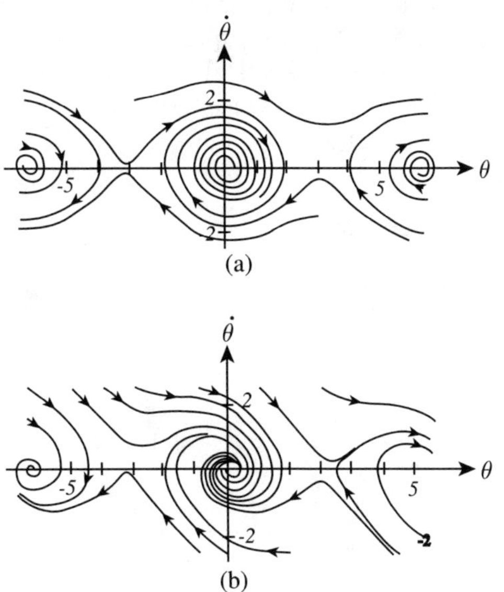

Figure 12.7: *Phase diagrams for: (a)* $\ddot{\theta} + 0.1\dot{\theta} + \sin\theta = 0$, *(b)* $\ddot{\theta} + 0.5\dot{\theta} + \sin\theta = 0$.

12.4 The Pendulum with Dry Friction

If the surface of contact between two solids is dry, then the force resisting the motion of one relative to the other is called *dry* or *Coulomb* friction. We shall look at two models for this. In the first, the resisting force is constant in magnitude (with no dependence on the relative velocity between the surfaces). The resulting model may be expressed as

$$\frac{d^2\theta}{dt^2} = -kSgn\left(\frac{d\theta}{dt}\right) - \frac{g}{l}\sin\theta, \tag{12.4.1}$$

where

$$Sgn(x) = \begin{bmatrix} +1, & x > 0, \\ 0, & x = 0, \\ -1, & x < 0. \end{bmatrix} \tag{12.4.2}$$

This function may be part of the programming language that you are using, or you might write a procedure for it. You are fairly safe in using `Sgn(x) = Abs(x)/x`, (but not if you initialize the starting angular velocity to be zero!). Alternatively, use the variable `y2Sign`, as in project 12.2. Initialize this in accordance with the starting conditions, (be careful!) and change its sign after each upper position has been reached.

There are several ways to approach the integration of (12.4.1). Using the transformation (12.1.4), the right-hand sides of the two resulting equations might be calculated by

```
z(1) = y(2)
z(2) = - Friction*Sgn(y(2))- (GravAccel/Length)*Sin(y(1))
```

Close to the top of a swing, $y_2 = \dot{\theta}$ will change its sign during the calculation of a step; assuming that you are using an integration method with adaptive stepsize, this will result in the drastic reduction of the stepsize, until one step is only on one side and the next step is only on the other side of the top of the swing. If you do this, it is interesting, at least once, to print out the changing stepsizes; once the top has been crossed over, the stepsizes rapidly return to an efficient size. This procedure has not failed me yet; it should not be used if it is driving animation.

The second way, which I prefer, is to find the top of each swing as we did in project 12.1. After each step, test to see if the product `y2Sign*y(2)` is negative:

```
Step(...)
if y2Sign*y(2) < 0 then FindTop
```

The derivative of y_2 is z_2, in the notation used above, so the procedure `FindTop` might contain code like

```
SaveStepSize = StepSize
Repeat
    Call procedure Fun to calculate z(1) and z(2), which are the
        derivatives of y(1) and y(2).
    StepSize = - y(2)/z(2)
    Step(...)
Until Abs(y(2)) < Eps
y2Sign = - y2Sign
StepSize = SaveStepSize
```

Note that the integration will proceed using the same stepsize used before the interation. This is important; at the end of the iteration the stepsize will be very small and may be negative.

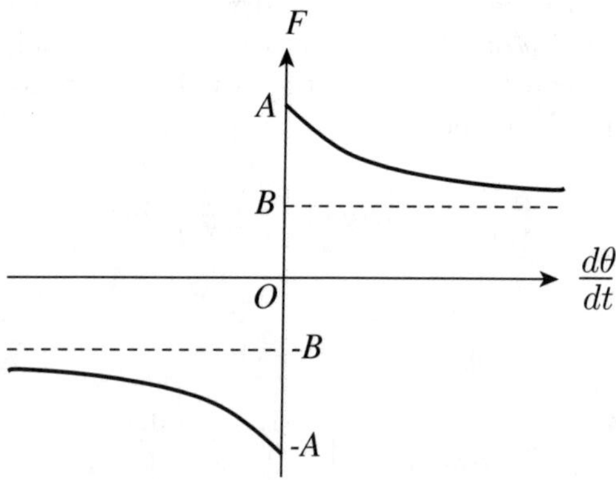

Figure 12.8: *The force F of dry friction as it depends on angular velocity.*

A more realistic representation of dry friction is to recognize a velocity dependence which has the property that the friction is greater with lower relative speeds. If the differential equation for the model is written as

$$\frac{d^2\theta}{dt^2} = -F - \frac{g}{l}\sin\theta, \tag{12.4.3}$$

then the function F depends qualitatively on $\dot{\theta}$ as shown in figure 12.8. A simple way to represent F is by

$$\left.\begin{aligned} F(\dot{\theta}) &= \frac{A + B\dot{\theta}}{1+\dot{\theta}}, \quad \dot{\theta} > 0; \quad A > 0,\ B > 0, \\ F(-\dot{\theta}) &= -F(\dot{\theta}). \end{aligned}\right] \tag{12.4.4}$$

Experiment with all of these methods, and generate phase-plane diagrams. They will be qualitatively similar to those in figure 12.7.

For a contrast with dry friction, you might play with the case where the frictional term is proportional to the square of the relative speed. This condition would give

$$F = k\dot{\theta}^2 Sgn(\dot{\theta}). \tag{12.4.5}$$

In the non-dry cases the resisting force goes to zero with $\dot{\theta}$. Again, you must be careful to control the transition when the sign of $\dot{\theta}$ changes.

12.5 The Pendulum of a Clock

This model consists of a pendulum with damping and an energy source. Energy is transmitted impulsively to the pendulum each time it passes through its lowest point. This model is discussed by A.A.Andronow and C.E.Chaikin [3].[1]

Two models for friction are considered, (a) linear damping and (b) dry friction. Also, two models are considered for the way in which the impulse acts: (c) an impulsive increase in angular speed, by a fixed amount, when

$$\dot{\theta}_{\text{new}} - \dot{\theta}_{\text{old}} = \text{constant}, \tag{12.5.1}$$

and (d) an impulsive increase in kinetic energy, by a fixed amount, when

$$\dot{\theta}^2_{\text{new}} - \dot{\theta}^2_{\text{old}} = \text{constant}. \tag{12.5.2}$$

For dry friction a formula such as (12.4.4) should be used. The only combination found to be satisfactory in the reference cited is that of (b) with (d). Preference for (d) is certainly reasonable, since, in the case of a clock, the energy may come from potential energy gained from the descent of a hanging weight.

To control the force of dry friction, you will need the variable `y2Sign` and a procedure like `FindTop` of the preceding project.

Care needs to be taken if the impulse is to be given at the lowest point. Following the method used in project 12.2 to find the bottom of a swing, you might use `y1Sign`, which takes the sign of $y_1 = \theta$. After any step, test to see whether the lowest point has been passed: this will be the case if the product `y(1)*y1Sign < 0`. As soon as this is the case, call a procedure `FindBottom`, say, that would contain lines such as:

```
SaveStepSize = StepSize
Repeat
    StepSize = - y(1)/y(2)
    Step(...)
Until Abs(y(1)) < Eps
y1Sign = - y1Sign
StepSize = SaveStepSize
Increase y(2) using (12.5.1) or (12.5.2)
```

This uses Newton's method to solve for $y_1(t) = 0$. y_2 is the derivative of y_1.

As part of the project, you might locate a grandfather clock and experiment with it. Any successful model must include a stable limit cycle. Initial oscillations that are greater than or less than the oscillations of the limit cycle are quickly changed so that they soon become indistinguishable from those of the limit cycle. But if the initial oscillation is too small, then it will die out.

[1] A.A.Andronov and C.E.Chaikin, *Theory of Oscillations*, trans. edited by Solomon Lefschetz. Copyright ©1949, 1976 by Princeton University Press. Excerpt 118-126, adapted with permission of Princeton University Press.

The principal parameters of the model are those for the friction and the increase in energy. Balance these to produce a realistic limit cycle. See if you can model an actual clock, and calculate the kinetic energy needed to keep it going for a week. What weight would be required to produce the potential energy needed, assuming that it descends a reasonable amount?

12.6 The Simple Pendulum in a Stiff Wind

Our pendulum is outdoors, with a wind blowing. With the x-axis horizontal and the y-axis pointing vertically upward, let the velocity of the wind have components (w_x, w_y). The velocity of the mass at the end of the pendulum has components $(l\dot{\theta}\cos\theta, l\dot{\theta}\sin\theta)$, so its velocity relative to the air has components

$$(w_x - l\dot{\theta}\cos\theta, w_y - l\dot{\theta}\sin\theta).$$

The unit vector in the direction of increasing θ has components $(\cos\theta, \sin\theta)$, so the component of the relative velocity in this direction is

$$w_x \cos\theta + w_y \sin\theta - l\dot{\theta}.$$

Finally the differential equation for θ is

$$ml\frac{d^2\theta}{dt^2} = -mg\sin\theta + K\left(w_x\cos\theta + w_y\sin\theta - l\frac{d\theta}{dt}\right). \tag{12.6.1}$$

If $g/l = \omega_0^2$, $k = K/m$, $v_x = Kw_x/(mg)$, and $v_y = Kw_y/mg$, this can be written as

$$\frac{d^2\theta}{dt^2} + k\frac{d\theta}{dt} + \omega_0^2(\sin\theta - v_x\cos\theta - v_y\sin\theta) = 0. \tag{12.6.2}$$

I recommend that you play with this model using phase-plane diagrams. Introduce v_x and v_y one at a time, and gradually. The positions of equilibrium can do interesting things.

12.7 The Simple Pendulum With Added Constant Load

The equation of this model is

$$\frac{d^2\theta}{dt^2} + k\frac{d\theta}{dt} + \omega_0^2\sin\theta = L, \tag{12.7.1}$$

where L represents a constant torque; there is no loss of generality if it is assumed to be nonnegative. Notice that for small L, the equilibria, given by

$$\omega_0^2\sin\theta = L,$$

are shifted. They approach one another with increasing L and coincide when $L = \omega_0^2$. For greater values of L, there is no equilibrium. Linear damping is assumed; you are welcome to substitute other models.

Two phase-plane diagrams are shown in figure 12.9, one without damping and one with. For this project, construct similar diagrams and find out what they look like when L is just less than, equal to and greater than ω_0^2.

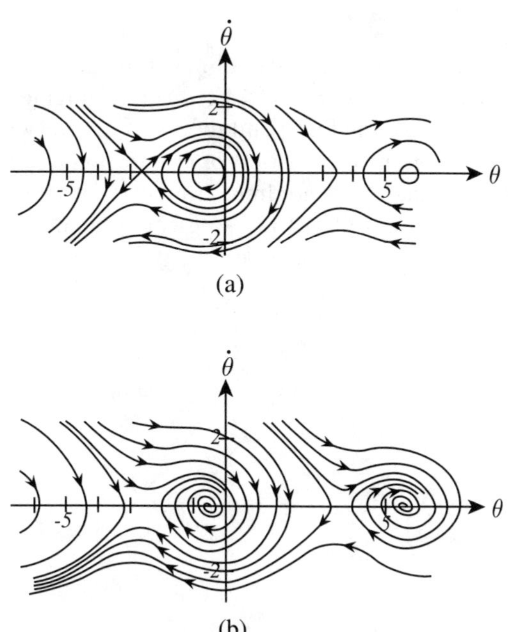

Figure 12.9: *(a) Phase diagram for* $\ddot{\theta} + \sin\theta = -0.5$*; (b) Phase diagram for* $\ddot{\theta} + 0.2\dot{\theta} + \sin\theta = -0.5$.

12.8 Pull-out Torques of Synchronous Motors

The project is an application of the preceding one. A synchronous motor has two components, a fixed armature and a rotor. The fixed armature creates a rotating field in space; it has a set of coils fed by an alternating current such that if α is the angle of the coils, then the phase angle for the alternating currents in the coils would differ by α. Then the period of rotation of the field is the same as the period of the alternating current.

In equilibrium motion, the rotor is in phase with the armature. Suppose that θ is the angle between the two fields. For varying θ, we have, for a first approximation,

$$\frac{d^2\theta}{dt^2} + k\frac{d\theta}{dt} + a\sin\theta = L. \tag{12.8.1}$$

The term $k\dot{\theta}$ is necessary to encourage synchronization; it is the damping term that makes an equilibrium asymptotically stable. Physically, the term arises from copper bars attached to the surface of the rotor, connected electronically. If the rotor were at rest in the field of the armature, then a torque would result, causing the rotor to turn in the direction of the rotating field.

Our problem is as follows. Suppose that the motor is running in equilibrium with a fixed load L_0. Suddenly a load L_1 is added. If L_1 is just large enough for the new motion to reach the unstable equilibrium, then the motor may fall too far out of phase and cease to operate. Here I suggest that you tackle the problem numerically. Put $a = 1$ and decide on a numerical value for k (you may want to experiment with this later). Then choose L_0 and find the equilibrium. Take initial conditions corresponding to this equilibrium, but with the term on the right-hand side of (12.8.1) equal to $L = L_0 + L_1$. Experiment with L_1 and see if you can find the critical value that sends the motor out of synchronization.

You will find a detailed discussion of this problem in a text by J.J.Stoker [92], pp. 66-80.

12.9 A Gravity Pendulum

It was once suggested that if two simple pendulums were close to one another, but mechanically independent, and if initially one was at rest and the other swinging, then gravitational attraction between the two masses would cause the first pendulum to start to swing. The measure of this effect could then lead to a determination of the constant of gravitation G. In fact, the effects are so small, and the difficulties of truly isolating the pendulums from each other so that there are no mechanical effects linking them (apart from gravitation) are so great, that nothing practical ever came of the suggestion. But we can still turn it into a project.

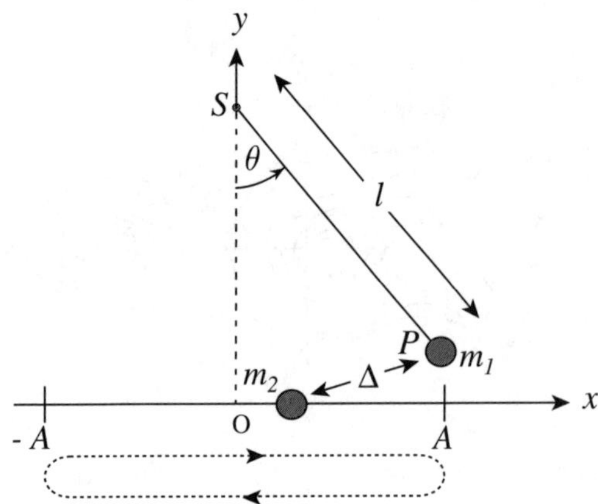

Figure 12.10: *A gravity driven pendulum.*

Let a mass m_2 be mechanically driven along the x-axis so that its coordinates at time t are $x_0 = A\sin(\omega t)$ and $y_0 = 0$. Let a mass m_1 hang from a pendulum of length l suspended at the point S with coordinates $(0, h)$. Without m_2 this configuration would be the usual model for the simple pendulum. The pendulum makes the angle θ with the downward vertical. See figure 12.10. Then m_1 will have coordinates

$$x = l\sin\theta, \quad y = h - l\cos\theta,$$

and the force of gravitational attraction exerted by m_2 and m_1 is be

$$\vec{F} = \frac{Gm_1m_2}{\Delta^3}\left[(A\sin(\omega t) - l\sin\theta)\hat{x} + (-h + l\cos\theta)\hat{y}\right], \tag{12.9.1}$$

where

$$\Delta^2 = (A\sin(\omega t) - l\sin\theta)^2 + (-h + l\cos\theta)^2. \tag{12.9.2}$$

Δ is the distance between m_1 and m_2. Here we have used Newton's law of gravitation.

The unit vector perpendicular to the pendulum, in the x-y plane, and in the direction of increasing θ, is $\hat{x}\cos\theta + \hat{y}\sin\theta$. So the component of the gravitational force in this direction is

$$R = \frac{Gm_1m_2}{\Delta^3}[A\sin(\omega t)\,\cos\theta - h\sin\theta]. \tag{12.9.3}$$

Then the differential equation for the motion of the pendulum is

$$m_1 l\frac{d^2\theta}{dt^2} + m_1 G\sin\theta = R. \tag{12.9.4}$$

(Include a damping term if you like, but make it very small.) Equations (12.9.3) and (12.9.4) define the model. Equation (12.9.4) is to be expressed as two first-order differential equations, in the usual way. For initial conditions, the time $t = 0$, and, since the pendulum is at rest, $\theta = \dot{\theta} = 0$.

For a start, I suggest numerically choosing the length $l = g$ so that the natural frequeny $\omega_0 = 1$. Then you should use $\omega = 1$ in order to set up possible resonance. The choice of masses is up to you. If you are working with high enough precision, you might use realistic numbers, just to see how small the effects might be; in this case, $G = 6.672 \times 10^{-11}\text{m}^3\text{kg}^{-1}\text{s}^{-2}$. Otherwise, it does no harm to put in a much larger value of G so that the swings will become perceptible more quickly. Once you have some results, investigate the effects if ω is not close to one, in order to assess the influence of resonance on the motion.

Do you agree that the method would not provide a practical way to estimate G? As a variation, replace m_1 and m_2 by magnets. Look for chaos.

12.10 A Magnetic Pendulum in Two Dimensions

Two small magnets are fixed on the x-axis at $(\pm A, 0)$ with their north poles directed upward, in the y-direction. The pivot of a pendulum of length l is attached at the point S with coordinates $(0, h)$. At the free end of the pendulum, P, another small magnet is attached; this has its south pole pointing downward. The pendulum is free to move in the x-y plane. See figure 12.11

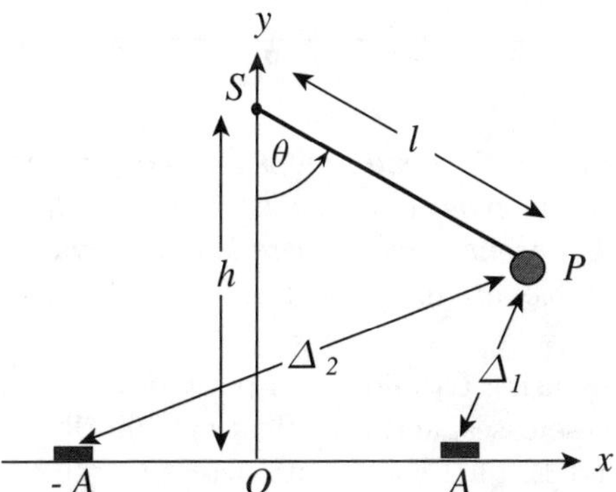

Figure 12.11: *A magnetic pendulum.*

If SP makes the angle θ with the downward vertical, and if P is distant Δ_1 and Δ_2 from the magnets, as shown, then

$$\left.\begin{aligned} \Delta_1^2 &= (A - l\sin\theta)^2 + (h - l\cos\theta)^2, \\ \Delta_2^2 &= (A + l\sin\theta)^2 + (h - l\cos\theta)^2. \end{aligned}\right] \tag{12.10.1}$$

Then, assuming that the two fixed magnets have equal strength, the differential equations for the motion of P follow from an analysis similar to that of the preceding project.

$$\frac{d^2\theta}{dt^2} + k\frac{d\theta}{dt} + \omega_0^2 \sin\theta = \frac{C}{\Delta_1^3}(A\cos\theta - h\sin\theta) + \frac{C}{\Delta_2^3}(-A\cos\theta - h\sin\theta). \tag{12.10.2}$$

There are three possibilities for equilibria: (1) one stable, one unstable; (2) two stable, two unstable; (3) three stable, three unstable. First, confirm in your mind how these might occur. If h is kept fixed (you might set it equal to one) then the three parameters are the length of the pendulum, l; half of the distance between the magnets, A; and C which depends on the strength of the magnets. It is best to vary these one at a time. Plot solutions in the phase-plane, first with $k = 0$ and later using a small value for k. Look for changes that separate any two of the three cases just listed.

One or both of the magnets on the x-axis might be inverted, so that they repel the swinging magnet, instead of attracting it; this is easily achieved by changing the sign of one or both terms

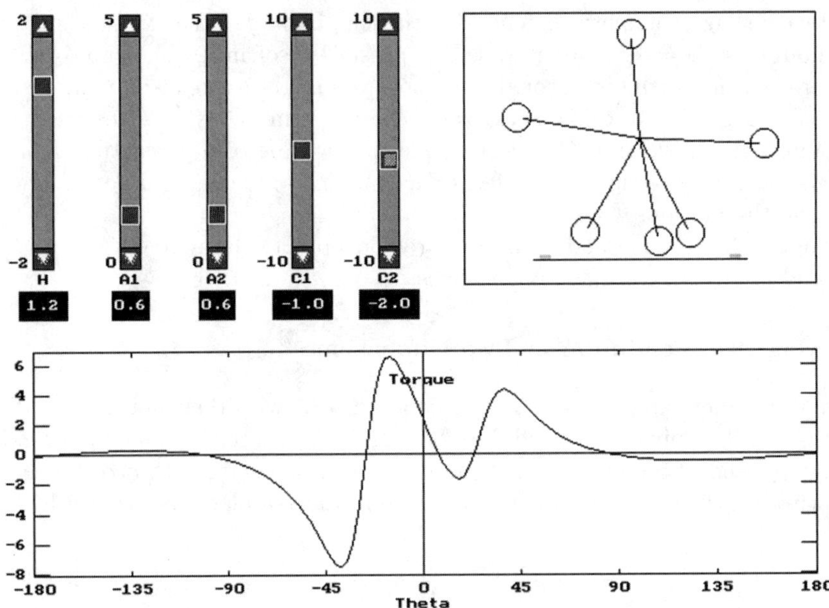

Figure 12.12: *The torque acting on the pendulum is plotted as a function of θ, the displacement of the pendulum from the vertical. The polarity of the fixed magnets has been chosen so that they repel the swinging magnet. When the torque is zero, there is a position of equilibrium. These positions, which alternate stable and unstable, are drawn at the top of the figure.*

on the right of 12.10.2. Also, by using C_1 and C_2 in place of C, you can make the strengths of the magnets unequal. Look into these cases, and investigate equilibria.

For figures 12.12, 12.13 and 12.14, I chose parameters $h = 1.2$, $A = 0.6$ units of length. The magnets are inverted, so that the swinging magnet experiences repulsion, with parameters $C_1 = -1$ and $C_2 = -0.2$. In figure 12.12 the torque (that is, the right-hand side of (12.10.2)) is plotted as a function of the angular displacement θ; where the torque is zero, there is an equilibrium. Positions of equilibrium, which alternate stable and unstable, are also drawn. Figure 12.13 shows solutions in the phase-plane; there is no friction. For figure 12.14 the value of the friction parameter was taken as $k = 0.3$.

12.11 A Child on a Swing: 1

A child pumps energy into the motion of a swing by synchronizing body movements with the motion of the swing. On the computer we are denied the instincts of the juvenile swinger, and will resort, instead, to physical guidelines. Basically, there are two of these.

- The motion of the body should be periodic, with period equal to one half the period of the swing. (This period will, of course, depend on the amplitude.)

- At the lowest point of the swing the center of mass should be lowered, and, at the highest point, the center of mass should be raised toward the point of suspension.

In this project it will be assumed that the change in center of mass is achieved by standing or crouching. (This means that you will need to give the kid a push to start him off.) It will also be assumed that the change is made instantaneously. This leads to simple computer code. The model provides a simple example of the effects of resonance and of a limit cycle.

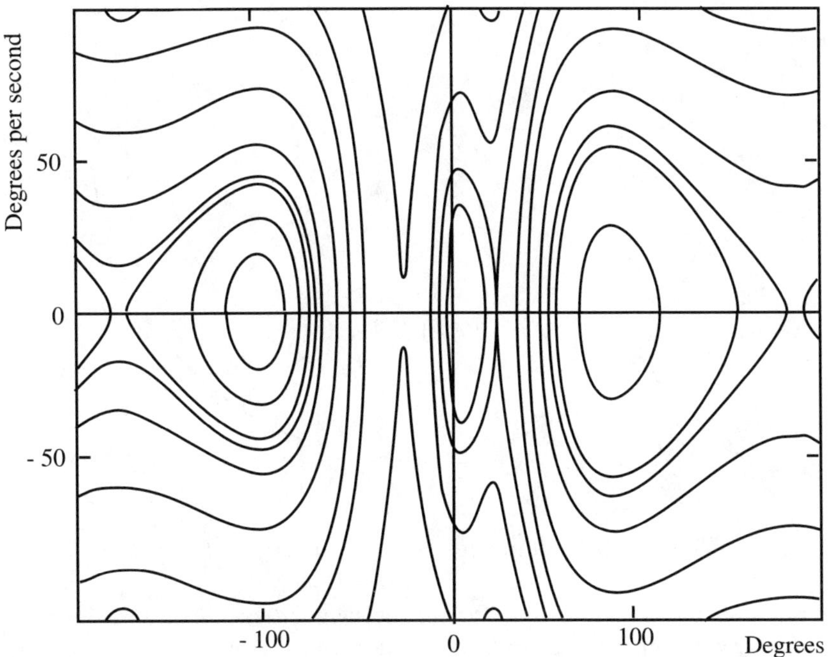

Figure 12.13: *Solutions plotted in the phase-plane using the parameters of figure 12.12. There is no friction. The three stable and three unstable equilbria are apparent.*

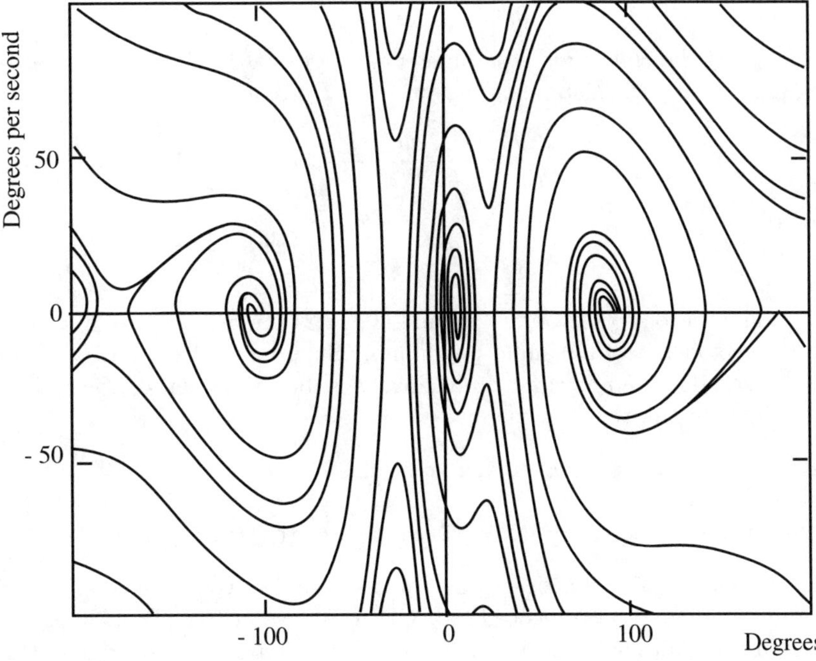

Figure 12.14: *Solutions plotted in the phase-plane using the parameters of figure 12,12. The value of the friction parameter was taken as $k = 0.3$.*

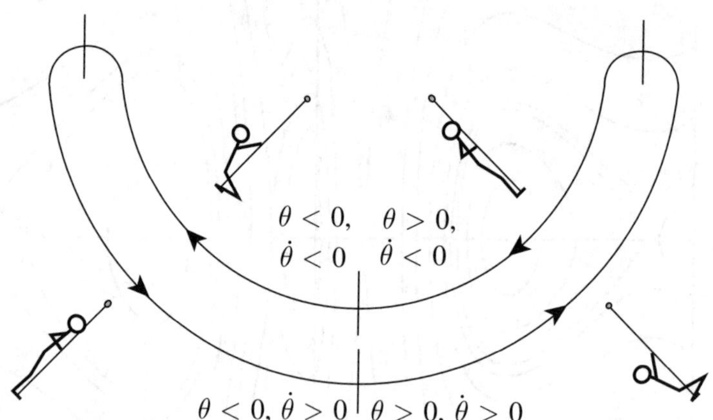

Figure 12.15: *Postures at different stages of a cycle.*

Following the rules just stated, the posture of the swinger should vary as shown in figure 12.15. θ is the angle measured counter-clockwise from the downward vertical; $\dot\theta$ is the rate of change of θ; so we see that if the product $\theta\,\dot\theta$ is positive, the child should crouch, and if it is negative, he should stand.

At its simplest, we can represent the model by a simple pendulum with variable length. So

$$mL\frac{d^2\theta}{dt^2} = -k\frac{d\theta}{dt} - mg\sin\theta, \tag{12.11.1}$$

where m is the mass of the child, k is a parameter proportional to the air resistance, and $L = L_1$ when crouching and $L = L_2$ when standing, where $L_1 > L_2$. Then

$$\frac{d^2\theta}{dt^2} = -\frac{K}{L}\frac{d\theta}{dt} - \frac{g}{L}\sin\theta. \tag{12.11.2}$$

Here $K = k/m$. Let

$$y_1 = \theta, \text{ and } y_2 = \frac{d\theta}{dt}. \tag{12.11.3}$$

In a program, y_1 and y_2 become `y(1)` and `y(2)`, and (12.11.2) is written as two first-order differential equations, as in the model for the simple pendulum. Suppose that we have a Boolean variable `Standing`, true for standing and false for crouching. A subroutine `Fun` for the right-hand sides of these equations might contain the following code:

```
If Standing Then Length = L2 Else Length = L1
z(1) = y(2)
z(2) = - (Resistance/Length)*y(2) - (Gravity/Length)*Sin(y(1))
```

There is no special need to find the critical points precisely, unless you want to. (Does the swinger?) If you do, then use the methods of project (12.2). Otherwise, you can make a change after a regular integration step. In the main program, immediately after a step has been taken, `Standing` should be updated by

```
If Sin(y(1))*y(2) < 0 Then Standing = True Else Standing = False
```

If there is no resistance, so that $K = 0$, then the amplitudes of the swings will increase until the swing will begin to circulate — not very safe! For sufficiently large K, the motion will approach a limit cycle. Note that a heavier child will result in a smaller value for K and a larger amplitude for this cycle.

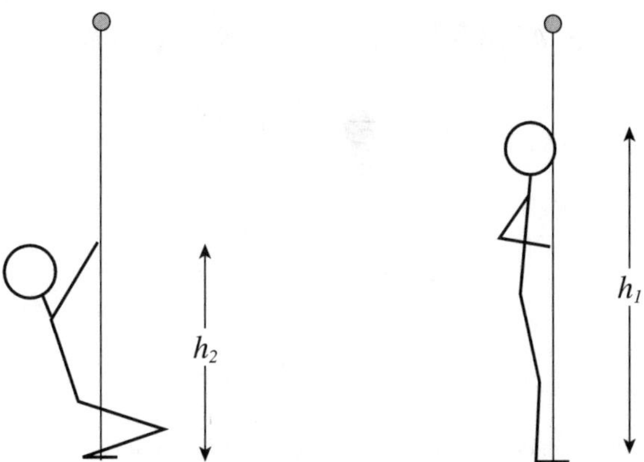

Figure 12.16: *Crouching and standing on a swing.*

This discussion is unsatisfactory if we want to model an actual child. Suppose the child has height $h = h_1$ standing and $h = h_2$ crouching, as shown in figure 12.16. For simplicity, assume that in either state, the body can be represented by a homogeneous cylinder. Let the child have weight W lb. If the swing has length L and the child has height h, his moment of inertia about the pivot at the top of the swing is

$$I = \int_{L-h}^{L} \frac{m}{h} x^2 \, dx = m(L^2 - Lh + \frac{1}{3}h^2), \tag{12.11.4}$$

where $m = W/g$. Assuming that the torque exerted by the resisting force is given by a force acting $L - h/2$ from the pivot, and that this force is proportional to h, we have

$$I\frac{d^2\theta}{dt^2} = -kh\left(L - \frac{h}{2}\right)\frac{d\theta}{dt} - \left(L - \frac{h}{2}\right) mg\sin\theta. \tag{12.11.5}$$

Then we can write

$$\frac{d^2\theta}{dt^2} = -\frac{kh}{m\lambda}\frac{d\theta}{dt} - \frac{g}{\lambda}\sin\theta, \tag{12.11.6}$$

where

$$\lambda = \frac{L^2 - Lh + h^2/3}{L - h/2}. \tag{12.11.7}$$

For example, if $L = 8$ ft and $h = h_1 = 4$ ft, then $\lambda = \lambda_1 = 6.2222$ ft. If $h = h_2 = 2$ ft then $\lambda_2 = 7.0476$ ft. So we see that λ is the length of an equivalent simple pendulum. So the simple model described at the start of this section can be used, with a modification to the resisting term, which contains the factor h.

In running the model, first choose numerical values for L, h_1 and h_2. Then take K as a parameter to vary. Plot phase-plane diagrams, of $\dot{\theta}$ vs θ. Start at the lowest point, $\theta = 0$, with a small initial value of $\dot{\theta}$. Follow the build-up of the amplitude of oscillation. Look for values of K so that you find a limit cycle.

Here is a mathematical justification of the tactics set out at the start of this project. Note that if

$$\frac{d^2\theta}{dt^2} = -\frac{g}{L}\sin\theta, \tag{12.11.8}$$

then

$$\frac{1}{2}\left(\frac{d\theta}{dt}\right)^2 = \frac{g}{L}\cos\theta + \text{ Const.} \tag{12.11.9}$$

Let us start at the lowest point, $\theta = 0$, with $L = L_1$ and $\dot{\theta} = \dot{\theta}_0$. Then

$$\frac{1}{2}\left(\frac{d\theta}{dt}\right)^2 = \frac{g}{L_1}\cos\theta + \frac{1}{2}\dot{\theta}_0^2 - \frac{g}{L_1}. \tag{12.11.10}$$

At the next highest point, $\dot{\theta} = 0$ and $\theta = \theta_1$ where

$$0 = \frac{g}{L_1}\cos\theta_1 + \frac{1}{2}\dot{\theta}_0^2 - \frac{g}{L_1}. \tag{12.11.11}$$

So

$$\cos\theta_1 = 1 - \frac{1}{2}\frac{L_1}{g}\dot{\theta}_0^2. \tag{12.11.12}$$

From this position, we start a descent with a new value for the length, L_2, so that

$$\frac{1}{2}\left(\frac{d\theta}{dt}\right)^2 = \frac{g}{L_2}\cos\theta + \text{ constant} \tag{12.11.13}$$

$$= \frac{g}{L_2}\cos\theta - \frac{g}{L_2}\cos\theta_1. \tag{12.11.14}$$

Now at the next lowest point let $\dot{\theta} = \dot{\theta}_1$, where

$$\frac{1}{2}\dot{\theta}_1^2 = \frac{g}{L_2} - \frac{g}{L_2}\cos\theta_1. \tag{12.11.15}$$

But using (12.11.12), we find

$$\dot{\theta}_1^2 = \frac{L_1}{L_2}\dot{\theta}_0^2. \tag{12.11.16}$$

So since $L_1 > L_2$, $\dot{\theta}_1 > \dot{\theta}_0$. This means that for successive passages through the lowest point, the angular velocity increases, and so will the amplitudes of the oscillations. This analysis takes no account of the resisting term. To account for this, we need numerical calculation.

12.12 A Child on a Swing: 2

In this model the child is seated, and either leans back or sits upright, with the body remaining straight. Figure 12.17 shows the geometry. O is the point of suspension of the swing and S is the seat. The rope of the swing, OS, has length L ft, and makes an angle θ with the downward vertical. The child is modeled by a uniform rod, length $h = 2l$, of mass m_1 and three masses: m_2 for the head, m_3 for the tail and m_4 for the feet. The child makes an angle ϕ with OS.

There will be two types of motion. In the first, the orientation of the body with respect to the swing will be changing. In the second, the swing will be "coasting" with the body fixed relative to the swing. We start by deriving equations for the first type.

The masses have coordinates

$$\begin{aligned}
m_2 &: \ (L\sin\theta - l\sin(\theta+\phi),\ -L\cos\theta + l\cos(\theta+\phi)),\\
m_3 &: \ (L\sin\theta,\ -L\cos\theta),\\
m_4 &: \ (L\sin\theta + l\sin(\theta+\phi),\ -L\cos\theta - l\cos(\theta+\phi))
\end{aligned}$$

and velocities

$$\begin{aligned}
m_2 &: \ (L\dot{\theta}\cos\theta - l(\dot{\theta}+\dot{\phi})\cos(\theta+\phi),\ L\dot{\theta}\sin\theta - l(\dot{\theta}+\dot{\phi})\sin(\theta+\phi)),\\
m_3 &: \ (L\dot{\theta}\cos\theta,\ L\dot{\theta}\sin\theta),\\
m_4 &: \ (L\dot{\theta}\cos\theta + l(\dot{\theta}+\dot{\phi})\cos(\theta+\phi),\ L\dot{\theta}\sin\theta + l(\dot{\theta}+\dot{\phi})\sin(\theta+\phi)).
\end{aligned}$$

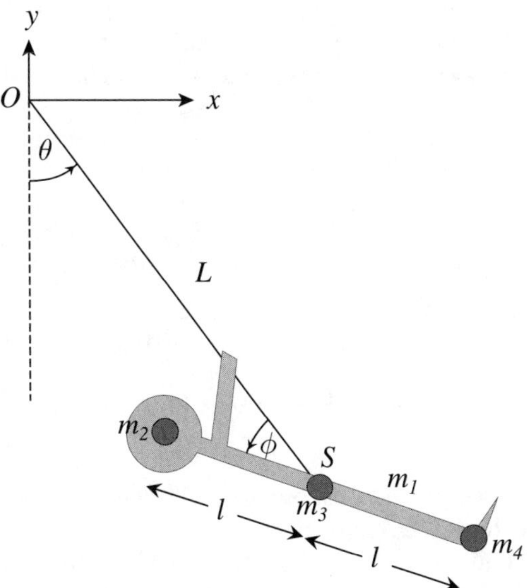

Figure 12.17: *Model for a seated swinger.*

The rod has moment of inertia $m_1 l^2/3$. The kinetic energy is T, where

$$\begin{aligned} 2T &= m_1\left(L^2+\frac{1}{3}l^2\right)\dot\theta^2 \\ &\quad +m_2\left(L^2\dot\theta^2+l^2(\dot\theta+\dot\phi)^2-2Ll\dot\theta(\dot\theta+\dot\phi)\cos\phi\right) \\ &\quad +m_3L^2\dot\theta^2 \\ &\quad +m_4\left(L^2\dot\theta^2+l^2(\dot\theta+\dot\phi)^2+2Ll\dot\theta(\dot\theta+\dot\phi)\cos\phi\right) \\ &= I_1\dot\theta^2+I_2(\dot\theta+\dot\phi)^2-2I_3\dot\theta(\dot\theta+\dot\phi)\cos\phi, \end{aligned}$$

where

$$\left.\begin{aligned} I_1 &= L^2M+m_1l^2/3, \\ I_2 &= l^2\,(m_2+m_4)\,, \\ I_3 &= Ll\,(m_2-m_4)\,, \\ M &= m_1+m_2+m_3+m_4. \end{aligned}\right] \tag{12.12.1}$$

The potential is

$$V=-MgL\cos\theta+(m_2-m_4)gl\cos(\theta+\phi),$$

so the Lagrangian is

$$\begin{aligned} L &= T-V \\ &= \frac{1}{2}(I_1\dot\theta^2+I_2(\dot\theta+\dot\phi)^2-2I_3\dot\theta(\dot\theta+\dot\phi)\cos\phi)+MgL\cos\theta \\ &\quad -(m_2-m_4)gl\cos(\theta+\phi). \end{aligned} \tag{12.12.2}$$

Then the differential equation for the motion is

$$\begin{aligned} (I_1+I_2-2I_3\cos\phi)\ddot\theta &= -I_2\ddot\phi-2I_3\sin\phi\dot\theta\dot\phi+I_3\cos\phi\,\ddot\phi-I_3\sin\phi\,\dot\phi^2 \\ &\quad -MgL\sin\theta+(m_2-m_4)gl\sin(\theta+\phi). \end{aligned} \tag{12.12.3}$$

To allow for resistance, a term $-k\dot{\theta}$ should be added to the right-hand side.

The change in ϕ will take place rapidly. It will continue until a maximum value, ϕ_m is reached, when ϕ is increasing, or until $\phi = 0$, when ϕ is decreasing. If change has duration Δt, and is made with constant acceleration a, then

$$\text{for } \phi \text{ increasing, } a = 2\phi_m/(\Delta t)^2, \quad \ddot{\phi} = a, \quad \dot{\phi} = a\tau, \quad \phi = a\tau^2/2, \tag{12.12.4}$$

and

$$\text{for } \phi \text{ decreasing, } a = -2\phi_m/(\Delta t)^2, \quad \ddot{\phi} = a, \quad \dot{\phi} = a\tau, \quad \phi = \phi_m + a\tau^2/2. \tag{12.12.5}$$

Here τ is the time measured from the start of the change.

When coasting, $\dot{\phi} = 0$. If there is a resistance proportional to $\dot{\theta}$, then

$$(I_1 + I_2 - 2I_3\cos\phi)\ddot{\theta} = -k\dot{\theta} - MgL\sin\theta + (m_2 - m_4)gl\sin(\theta + \phi), \tag{12.12.6}$$

where $\phi = 0$ or ϕ_m.

I suggest that you write two procedures, one for rising and one for descending. Each phase will begin and end exactly as in the preceding project. I find it simplest to initialize the time to be zero at the start of each phase. Then equation (12.12.3) must be solved until $t = \Delta t$. Since Δt will not be large (probably in the range 0.1-0.2), a reasonable way to implement this is:

```
Time = 0
Initialize Phi, PhiVel, PhiAcc
Repeat
    StepSize = DelTime - Time
    Step(...)
    Phi = ...  from (12.12.4) or (12.12.5)
    PhiVel = ...
Until Abs(DelTime - Time) < Eps
```

After this, set $\dot{\phi}$, or `PhiVel`, and $\ddot{\phi}$, or `PhiAcc`, equal to zero, and continue until the end of the particular phase.

12.13 A Pendulum with Varying Length

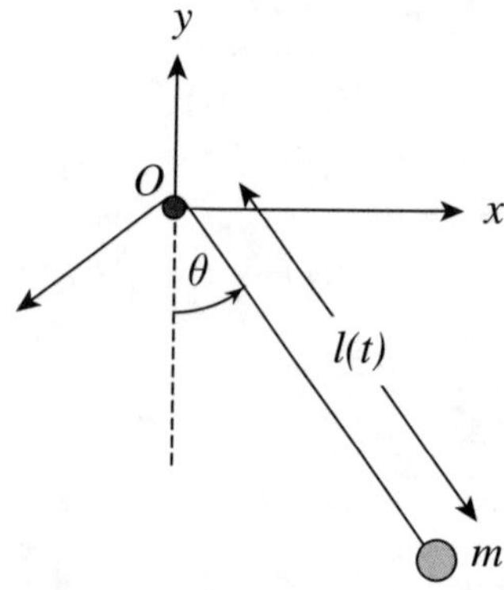

Figure 12.18: *A pendulum with varying length, $l(t)$.*

A mass m is attached to a light inextensible string that passes over a thin horizontal rod at O. The other end of the string is manipulated so that the length of the string, $l(t)$, is a function of the time. The pendulum makes an angle θ with the downward vertical, or negative y-axis, as shown in figure 12.18. The coordinates of the mass are

$$x = l(t)\sin\theta, \quad y = -l(t)\cos\theta,$$

and the components of the velocity are

$$\dot{x} = \dot{l}\sin\theta + l\dot{\theta}\cos\theta, \quad \dot{y} = -\dot{l}\cos\theta + l\dot{\theta}\sin\theta.$$

Then the Lagrangian is

$$\begin{aligned} L &= T - V \\ &= \frac{1}{2}m\left(\dot{l}^2 + l^2\dot{\theta}^2\right) + mgl\cos\theta. \end{aligned} \tag{12.13.1}$$

Lagrange's equation is, then,

$$\frac{d}{dt}\frac{\partial L}{\partial \dot{\theta}} = \frac{\partial L}{\partial \theta},$$

or

$$\frac{d}{dt}\left(ml^2\dot{\theta}\right) = -mgl\sin\theta.$$

So finally, we have

$$l\frac{d^2\theta}{dt^2} + 2\frac{dl}{dt}\frac{d\theta}{dt} + g\sin\theta = 0. \tag{12.13.2}$$

A resisting term can be included with the modification

$$l\frac{d^2\theta}{dt^2} + 2\frac{dl}{dt}\frac{d\theta}{dt} + k\frac{d\theta}{dt} + g\sin\theta = 0. \tag{12.13.3}$$

If this were to be due to air resistance to the string, you might make the resistance coefficient, k, proportional to l.

You can experiment with the system in several ways. l might be oscillatory, so that

$$l = l_0 + l_1 \sin\omega t. \tag{12.13.4}$$

Here l_1 should be less than l_0. The system could then be investigated in the manner of the forced pendulum. Play with values of ω close to the "natural frequency" $\omega_0 = \sqrt{g/l_0}$.

Another use of this model is to illustrate the action in Edgar Allen Poe's short story, "The Pit and the Pendulum." Here the mass m is replaced by a sharp knife, $l(t)$ is steadily increasing and there is a victim trapped underneath. In your model you can give the story whatever ending you please.

12.14 A Swinging Censer

A censer is a container in which incense is burned; the incense is distributed through the swinging of the censer. In some instances, a large area is to be covered, and the censer is suspended from the vault of a chapel. The censer is too heavy for one push to provide an adequate swing; so it hangs from a rope passing over a pulley; the other end is given small pulls in rhythm with the swing of the censer. As a consequence, the amplitude of the swings increases until it is adequate for the distribution of the incense. The principle used here is similar to the second model for the child on a swing, but the details are different.

We shall use the equations of the model for the pendulum with varying length. Let the length be L, and let the pendulum make the angle θ with the downward vertical. Then, if resistance is neglected,

$$L^2\frac{d^2\theta}{dt^2} = -2L\frac{dL}{dt}\frac{d\theta}{dt} - gL\sin\theta. \tag{12.14.1}$$

Here t is the time, and g is the acceleration due to gravity. For computation, let

$$\theta = y_1 \quad \text{and} \quad \frac{d\theta}{dt} = y_2. \tag{12.14.2}$$

Then

$$\left.\begin{aligned} \frac{dy_1}{dt} &= y_2, \\ \frac{dy_2}{dt} &= -\frac{2}{L}\frac{dL}{dt}y_2 - \frac{g}{L}\sin y_1. \end{aligned}\right] \tag{12.14.3}$$

The procedure Fun for calculating the right-hand sides of these equations might contain the lines:

```
z(1) = y(2)
z(2) = - (Gravity/Length)*Sin(y(1)) - 2*(LengthRate/Length)*y(2)
```

There will be two types of motion: a rapid pull to decrease the length, followed by coasting with constant length, and then a rapid release to increase the length, again followed by coasting. To pump energy into the swinging, the pulls will be initiated at the highest points, and the releases, at the lowest.

During a pull or a release, let the length of the pendulum be changed in the interval

$$L_0 - \Delta L < L < L_0 + \Delta L.$$

Also let L be changed with constant acceleration, $\pm a$. Consider the case of a pull, when the censer is ascending and the acceleration is $-a$. Let τ be the time measured from the start of the pull. Then

$$\frac{dL}{dt} = -a\tau, \text{ and } L = L_0 + \Delta L - \frac{1}{2}a\tau^2.$$

During a pull or a release, the length must change by $2\Delta L$, so the time taken is $\Delta\tau = 2\sqrt{\Delta L/a}$.

During coasting, the length is constant, so $dL/dt = 0$.

As in the second project for the child on the swing, we might have separate procedures for pulling or releasing. Consider possible code for pulling. The censer is descending, so the product $\theta\frac{d\theta}{dt}$ is negative; as before, we shall use $\sin\theta\frac{d\theta}{dt}$.

```
Time = 0
Repeat
    Length = MaxLength - LengthAcceleration*Time*Time/2
    If Length > MinLength Then LengthRate = - LengthAcceleration*Time
    Else
    Begin
        LengthRate = 0
        Length = MinLength
    End
    Step(...)
Until Sin(y[1])*y[2] > 0
```

Here MinLength and MaxLength are $L_0 - \Delta L$ and $L_0 + \Delta L$, respectively. The corresponding code for a release might be

```
Time = 0
Repeat
    Length = MinLength + LengthAcceleration*Time*Time/2
```

```
        If Length < MaxLength Then LengthRate = LengthAcceleration*Time
        Else
        Begin
            LengthRate = 0
            Length = MaxLength
        End
        Step(...)
    Until Sin(y[1])*y[2] < 0
```

A resisting term could be added to the expression for z[2] if desired. It will be needed if you want to find a limit cycle. In practice, of course, the pulling would stop when the amplitude of the swing was considered sufficient.

As with the swing, there is no special need to solve precisely for the times at which pulling or releasing start.

12.15 A Pendulum with Moving Pivot

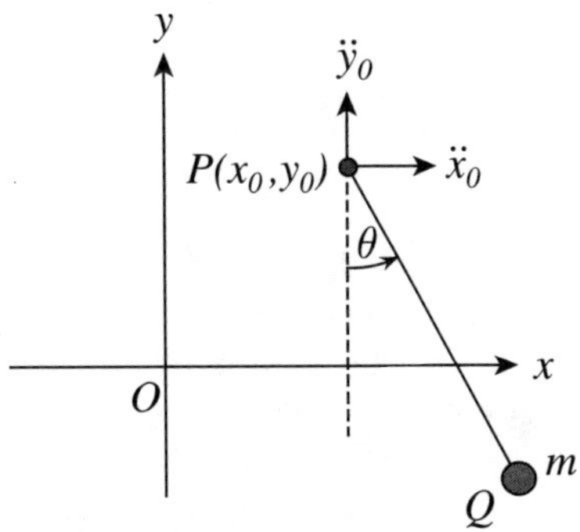

Figure 12.19: *A pendulum with moving pivot.*

A simple pendulum, with length l, has its pivot at the moving point P, with coordinates $(x_0(t), y_0(t))$ and a mass m at Q. The x- and y-axes are horizontal and vertical, respectively, as in figure 12.19. The pendulum makes an angle θ with the downward vertical. Let the components of acceleration of the pivot be $\ddot{x}_0$ and $\ddot{y}_0$. Then, by resolving accelerations along the pendulum, we can derive the following differential equation for the motion

$$ml\frac{d^2\theta}{dt^2} + k\frac{d\theta}{dt} + m\ddot{x}_0 \cos\theta + (mg - m\ddot{y}_0)\sin\theta = 0, \tag{12.15.1}$$

where we assume resistance proportional to the angular velocity.

There are many ways in which this model can be interpreted and run. For instance, the motion of the pivot might be controlled, with tactics similar to those of a child on a swing, or the swinging censer, so that small initial oscillations will increase in amplitude. In contrast, imagine that you are operating a "wrecking ball," and that you want to damp out an initially large swing. Operators of cranes know how to do this — do you?

For the principal interpretations, I suggest that you make $\ddot{x}_0$ and $\ddot{y}_0$ periodic, with frequency ω. Three types of oscillation are to be considered:

1. Vertical motion: $x_0 = 0,\ y = A_y \cos(\omega t)$.

2. Horizontal motion: $x = A_x \sin(\omega t),\ y = 0.$

3. A combination: $x = A_x \sin(\omega t),\ y = A_y \cos(\omega t).$

In type 3 it would make sense to have $A_x = A_y$, when the pendulum is on the rim of a wheel rotating with constant angular speed.

Note that we are talking about chaotic systems. The second type has already been considered in the discussion of the forced pendulum. The first type has received a lot of discussion in the literature. In particular, you should look at back-to-back papers by J.A. Blackburn, et al. [12] and by H.J.T. Smith and J.A. Blackburn [90]. These deal with theoretical discussion of small oscillations (not easy) and experimental verification of some of the predictions. You will also find a bibliography listing other articles on this subject. The principal conditions to look for are those for which the *upright* equilibrium becomes stable. It is also possible for the equilibrium with $\theta = 0$ to become unstable.

First, I shall change the notation so that it conforms with that in the cited papers. For generality, I shall consider the third type of motion. Let

$$s = \omega t,\ \omega_0 = \sqrt{\frac{g}{l}},\ \Omega = \frac{\omega}{\omega_0},\ Q = \frac{ml\omega_0}{k},\ \epsilon_x = A_x\frac{\omega_0^2}{g},\ \epsilon_y = A_y\frac{\omega_0^2}{g}. \tag{12.15.2}$$

Then

$$\frac{d^2\theta}{ds^2} + \frac{1}{Q\Omega}\frac{d\theta}{ds} - \epsilon_x \sin s \cos\theta + \frac{1}{\Omega^2}\sin\theta - \epsilon_y \cos s\, \sin\theta = 0. \tag{12.15.3}$$

For comparison with the references, put $\epsilon_x = 0$ and $\epsilon_y = \epsilon$.

All the methods described for the investigation of the forced pendulum can be used here. You can follow motion that tends (i) toward the lower equilibrium, or (ii) toward the upper equilibrium, or (iii) a uniform rotation, or (iv) is chaotic. Period-doubling can be followed along the road to chaos.

For a general categorization of where certain types of motion might be looked for, Blackburn et al., consider the parameters ϵ and Ω, and they give equations to three curves in the ϵ-Ω plane:

$$\left.\begin{array}{lcl} 1.\ \epsilon & = & \sqrt{2}/\Omega, \\ 2.\ \epsilon & = & 0.45 - 1.799/\Omega^2, \\ 3.\ \epsilon & = & 0.45 + 1.799/\Omega^2. \end{array}\right] \tag{12.15.4}$$

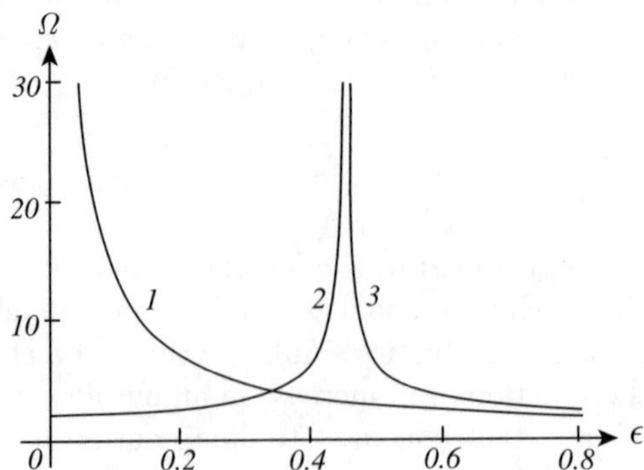

Figure 12.20: *Boundaries for some possible types of motion.*

These are drawn in figure 12.20. They are a helpful guide in looking for numerical values of the parameters. Motion of type (i) can be expected for values between the vertical Ω axis and curve 2. Motion of type (ii) is possible between curves 1 and 3.

The phase-plane, with or without Poincaré maps, is a good location for following the development of a solution. Treat ϵ as a parameter to vary. It has been claimed that the resisting force has little to do with the stability of the special solutions. You might test this hypothesis.

When you have a set of good solutions with just vertical motion of the pivot, introduce a small value of ϵ_x and see what effect this may have. Then increase ϵ_x.

12.16 A Pendulum Wrapped Around a Peg

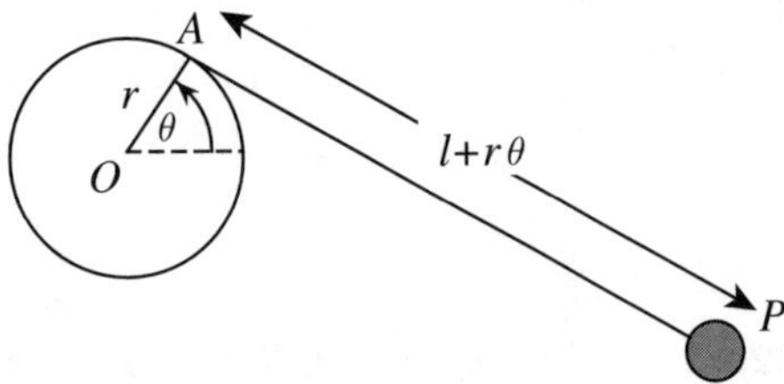

Figure 12.21: *A pendulum suspended from a cylindrical peg of radius r.*

A mass m is attached to a light string that is wound around a fixed horizontal cylinder, of radius r, as shown in figure 12.21. Let the length of the string hanging vertically downward, when the system is in equilibrium, be l.

If the pendulum makes an angle θ with the downward vertical, then the length of the hanging string will be $l + r\theta$. With origin at the center of the cylinder, O, x-axis horizontal and y-axis pointing vertically upward, the coordinates of the mass are

$$(r\cos\theta + (l + r\theta)\sin\theta,\ r\sin\theta - (l + r\theta)\cos\theta)\,.$$

The kinetic energy of the mass is T, where $2T = m(l + r\theta)^2\dot{\theta}^2$, and the potential energy is $V = -mg(l + r\theta)\cos\theta + mgr\sin\theta$. So the Lagrangian is

$$L = \frac{1}{2}m(l + r\theta)^2\dot{\theta}^2 + mg(l + r\theta)\cos\theta - mgr\sin\theta. \tag{12.16.1}$$

Then the differential equation for the motion is

$$(l + r\theta)\frac{d^2\theta}{dt^2} + r\left(\frac{d\theta}{dt}\right)^2 + g\sin\theta = 0. \tag{12.16.2}$$

A resisting term might be included. This might simply be proportional to $\dot{\theta}$, or might, in addition, be proportional to the length of the string. Then

$$(l + r\theta)\frac{d^2\theta}{dt^2} + r\left(\frac{d\theta}{dt}\right)^2 + g\sin\theta + k(l + r\theta)\frac{d\theta}{dt} = 0. \tag{12.16.3}$$

If

$$y_1 = \theta, \text{ and } y_2 = \frac{d\theta}{dt},$$

then

$$\left.\begin{aligned}\frac{dy_1}{dt} &= y_2,\\ \frac{dy_2}{dt} &= -(ry_2^2 + g\sin y_1)/(l + ry_1) - ky_2.\end{aligned}\right] \tag{12.16.4}$$

In running the model, assume that it is OK to have the string pointing upward. The motion must stop when $l + r\theta \leq 0$, so make sure that your dimensions allow for a variety of motions to be investigated. The motion is most easily described by the use of phase-plane diagrams.

12.17 The Motion of a Sliding Pendulum 1

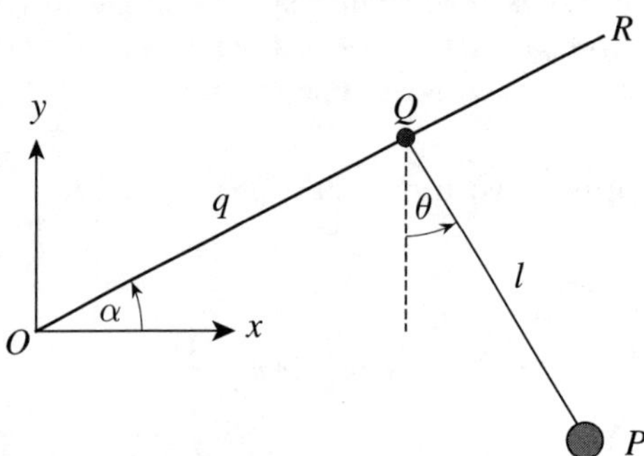

Figure 12.22: *A pendulum with sliding point of suspension.*

The point of suspension Q of a simple pendulum, QP, with length l and mass m slides on a wire, OR, that is inclined at an angle α to the horizontal. In this model the motion of Q has constant acceleration, a, so that if the length of OQ is q, then

$$\ddot{q} = a, \quad \dot{q} = at, \quad q = \frac{1}{2}at^2. \tag{12.17.1}$$

If OP makes the angle θ with the downward vertical, then the coordinates of P are

$$(q\cos\alpha + l\sin\theta,\ q\sin\alpha - l\cos\theta),$$

and its velocity has components

$$(at\cos\alpha + l\dot{\theta}\cos\theta,\ at\sin\alpha + l\dot{\theta}\sin\theta).$$

The kinetic energy is T, where

$$2T = m\left(a^2t^2 + l^2\dot{\theta}^2 + 2alt\dot{\theta}\cos(\theta - \alpha)\right).$$

The potential energy is

$$V = mg(q\sin\alpha - l\cos\theta).$$

So the Lagrangian is

$$L = \frac{1}{2}m\left(a^2t^2 + l^2\dot{\theta}^2 + 2alt\dot{\theta}\cos(\theta - \alpha)\right) - mg(q\sin\alpha - l\cos\theta). \tag{12.17.2}$$

The differential equation of the motion is, therefore,

$$l^2\frac{d^2\theta}{dt^2} + al\cos(\theta - \alpha) + gl\sin\theta = 0. \tag{12.17.3}$$

A resisting term can be included, if wanted. One way to work with this model is to fix the ratio g/a and to vary α between $\pm\pi/2$. Follow motion in the phase-plane. The character of the equilibria changes according to whether g/a is greater than or less than one.

12.18 The Motion of a Sliding Pendulum 2

The notation for this model follows that of the preceding one. But now the point Q is allowed to move freely, so that q joins θ as a generalized variable. In addition, we must allow the ring that slides along the wire to have mass M. The Lagrangian is now

$$L = \frac{1}{2}m\left(\dot{q}^2 + l^2\dot{\theta}^2 + 2l\dot{q}\dot{\theta}\cos(\theta-\alpha)\right) + \frac{1}{2}M\dot{q}^2 - (M+m)gq\sin\alpha + mgl\cos\theta. \qquad (12.18.1)$$

Then the differential equations for the motion are

$$\left.\begin{aligned}(M+m)\ddot{q} + ml\ddot{\theta}\cos(\theta-\alpha) - ml\dot{\theta}^2\sin(\theta-\alpha) &= -(M+m)g\sin\alpha,\\ ml^2\ddot{\theta} + ml\ddot{q}\cos(\theta-\alpha) &= -mgl\sin\theta.\end{aligned}\right] \qquad (12.18.2)$$

If we define

$$\mu = \frac{m}{M+m} \quad \text{and} \quad \phi = \theta - \alpha, \qquad (12.18.3)$$

and solve for $\ddot{q}$ and $\ddot{\phi}$, we find

$$\left.\begin{aligned}\frac{d^2q}{dt^2}(1-\mu\cos^2\phi) - \mu l\left(\frac{d\phi}{dt}\right)^2\sin\phi &= -g\sin\alpha + g\mu\sin(\phi+\alpha)\cos\phi,\\ l\frac{d^2\phi}{dt^2}(1-\mu\cos^2\phi) + \mu l\left(\frac{d\phi}{dt}\right)^2\sin\phi\cos\phi &= -g\sin\phi\cos\alpha.\end{aligned}\right] \qquad (12.18.4)$$

Start with small α, and look for situations where the motion does not, on the average, involve the point Q sliding downward. The system is conservative, with two degrees of freedom, and has the energy integral

$$h = \frac{1}{2}m\left(\dot{q}^2 + l^2\dot{\theta}^2 + 2l\dot{q}\dot{\theta}\cos(\theta-\alpha)\right) + \frac{1}{2}M\dot{q}^2 + (M+m)gq\sin\alpha - mgl\cos\theta. \qquad (12.18.5)$$

Consider setting up Poincaré maps, to find out if the system is chaotic. For instance, you might plot values of q and $\cos\theta$ when $\dot{q} = 0$. Fix h; for initial conditions, pick values of q and θ, with $\dot{q} = 0$; then solve (12.18.5) for $\dot{\theta}$.

12.19 The Swinging Atwood Machine

An Atwood machine consists of a light flexible string with masses M and m attached to its ends. These hang from two horizontal pulleys. There are no dissipative forces. The masses move vertically. This is surely one of the most predictable and boring models in existence. But, as its name implies, the "swinging" Atwood machine is a lot of fun. The "swing" is introduced by letting one mass, m, act as a pendulum. Then the motion is far from predictable; it is, in fact, chaotic. A good discussion of this model is given by N.B. Tufillaro [99]. A great hunting ground for papers on this subject is the *American Journal of Physics*.

Let m swing from the pulley at O, as a pendulum with varying length r making an angle θ with the downward vertical. The depth of M below the horizontal line of pulleys is $h = k - r$ where k is constant, depending on the length of the string and the separation of the pulleys. The square of the velocity of M is $\dot{r}^2$, and of m is $\dot{r}^2 + r^2\dot{\theta}^2$. So the kinetic energy of the system is

$$T = \frac{1}{2}\left(M\dot{r}^2 + m(\dot{r}^2 + r^2\dot{\theta}^2)\right) \qquad (12.19.1)$$

and the potential is

$$V = -mgr\cos\theta - Mg(k-r). \qquad (12.19.2)$$

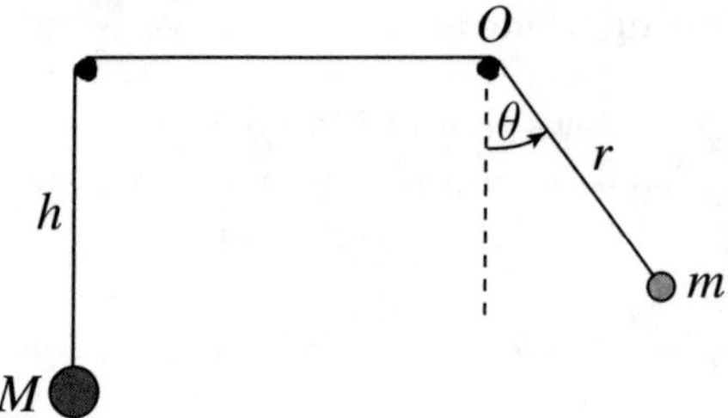

Figure 12.23: *The swinging Atwood machine.*

So the Lagrangian is

$$L = T - V = \frac{1}{2}\left((M+m)\dot{r}^2 + mr^2\dot{\theta}^2\right) + mgr\cos\theta + Mg(k-r). \tag{12.19.3}$$

The differential equations of motion are

$$\left.\begin{aligned}(M+m)\ddot{r} &= mr\dot{\theta}^2 + mg\cos\theta - Mg,\\ mr^2\ddot{\theta} + 2mr\dot{r}\dot{\theta} &= -mgr\sin\theta.\end{aligned}\right] \tag{12.19.4}$$

Let $\mu = M/m$; also, assume that the time is scaled, so that $g = 1$. The equations become

$$\left.\begin{aligned}\frac{d^2r}{dt^2} &= \frac{1}{1+\mu}\left(r\left(\frac{d\theta}{dt}\right)^2 + \cos\theta - \mu\right),\\ \frac{d^2\theta}{dt^2} &= -\frac{1}{r}\left(2\frac{dr}{dt}\frac{d\theta}{dt} + \sin\theta\right).\end{aligned}\right] \tag{12.19.5}$$

The integral $T + V =$ constant can then be written as

$$\frac{1}{2}(1+\mu)\dot{r}^2 + \frac{1}{2}r^2\dot{\theta}^2 - r\cos\theta + \mu r = E. \tag{12.19.6}$$

A boring feature of the non-swinging Atwood machine is that any motion is unbounded. We need to look for conditions in which r is bounded. From equation (12.19.6) we have

$$\frac{1}{2}(1+\mu)\dot{r}^2 + \frac{1}{2}r^2\dot{\theta}^2 = r\cos\theta - \mu r + E \geq 0 \tag{12.19.7}$$

so that

$$r(\mu - \cos\theta) \leq E. \tag{12.19.8}$$

So the integral is isolating, meaning that it can divide the $r-\theta$ space into regions where the motion is possible or impossible. On the boundary of such a region,

$$r = \frac{E}{\mu - \cos\theta}. \tag{12.19.9}$$

This is the polar equation of a conic. μ must be positive; suppose that it is less than one. Then equation (12.19.9) will represent a hyperbola (since if $\theta = \arccos\mu$, r will be infinite), and r is unbounded. So $\mu \geq 1$. Since $r > 0$, then $E > 0$. If $\mu > 1$, then the inequality (12.19.8) means that $0 \leq r \leq E/(\mu - 1)$. In the case $\mu = 1$, equation (12.19.9) represents a parabola, and the motion is unbounded.

If $r = 0$, then the equations become singular. This case is called a "collision." Conversely, if a run starts from $r = 0$, it is called an "ejection." A collision ends the run.

A factor that simplifies the discussion of this model is that the numerical value of E does not affect the properties of the dynamics. To see this, suppose that we know all about what happens for a given value of E. Now we start to worry about what happens for a new value, $E_1 = kE$, with $k > 0$. Let $\rho = r/k$ and $\tau = t/\sqrt{k}$. Then the integral in terms of r, t and E_1 will become an integral in terms of ρ, τ and E similar to equation (12.19.6). So changing E is equivalent to rescaling r and t. Accordingly, set $E = 1$, and stop worrying about it. The parameter that really matters is μ.

From equation (12.19.9), with $E = 1$, r must lie inside an ellipse having eccentricity $e = 1/\mu$. The semimajor axis of the ellipse is $a = \mu/(\mu^2 - 1)$. So as μ increases, the region in which r is confined shrinks, and approaches a circular shape.

For computation, let

$$y_1 = r,\ y_2 = \dot{r},\ y_3 = \theta,\ y_4 = \dot{\theta}. \tag{12.19.10}$$

Then the system to be integrated is

$$\left.\begin{aligned} \dot{y}_1 &= y_2, \\ \dot{y}_2 &= (y_1 y_4^2 + \cos y_3 - \mu)/(1+\mu), \\ \dot{y}_3 &= y_4, \\ \dot{y}_4 &= -(2y_2 y_4 + \sin y_3)/y_1. \end{aligned}\right] \tag{12.19.11}$$

There are two principal ways to enjoy this model. One of the best is to see the motion in animation. Or plot the (r, θ) polar coordinates of m. Various types of attractive figures can be derived. Of particular interest are paths that eventually repeat themselves, so that the solution is periodic. Hunting down such periodic solutions can be an enjoyable activity; once you have found one for a particular value of μ, see if you can discover how it evolves when μ is changed. You will be following a "family" of periodic orbits, with parameter μ. Families can begin, end and interact with one another.

Another way is to plot Poincaré maps. In the integral given by equation (12.19.6), set $E = 1$. Consider motion in the space of $r, \dot{r}$ and θ, with $\dot{\theta}$ given by

$$\dot{\theta}^2 = \left(2 + 2r\cos\theta - 2\mu r - (1+\mu)\dot{r}^2\right)/r^2. \tag{12.19.12}$$

The surface of section will be taken to be $\theta = 0$, with points $(r,\ \dot{r})$ mapped. Then we must have

$$2 + 2r - 2\mu r - (1+\mu)\dot{r}^2 \geq 0. \tag{12.19.13}$$

This defines a region bounded by a parabola illustrated in figure 12.24. The maximum value of r is $r_{\max} = 1/(\mu - 1)$, and the extreme values of $\dot{r}$ are $\pm\dot{r}_{\max}$ where $\dot{r}_{\max} = \sqrt{2/(\mu+1)}$.

A mapping is started by selecting initial value of $r = y_1$ and $\dot{r} = y_2$, with $\theta = y_3 = 0$ and $\dot{\theta} = y_4$ calculated from equation (12.19.12). You might as well choose the positive root, in which case the parameter `SignTheta` (or whatever you want to call it) would be set equal to +1. After each step, test to see if `y(3)*SignTheta` is negative; if it is, call a procedure for finding the mapped point. This might contain the lines:

```
Count = 0
SaveStepSize = StepSize
Repeat
    Count = Count + 1
    StepSize = - y(3)/y(4)
    Step(...)
```

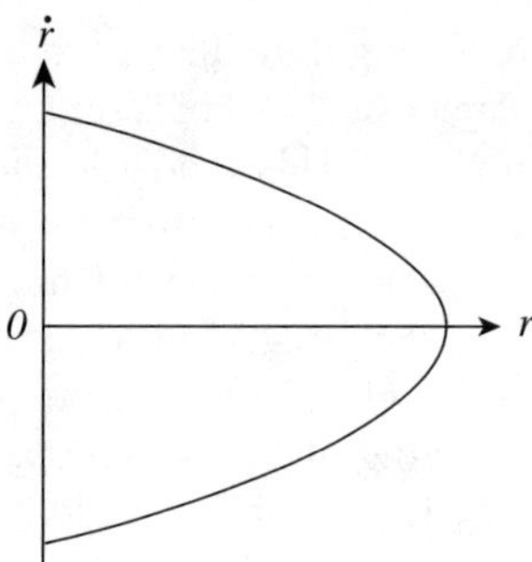

Figure 12.24: *Boundary for points in the Poincaré map.*

```
Until (Abs(y(3)) < Eps) Or (Count = 5)
If Count < 5 Then store the values of (y(3), y(4))
SignTheta = - SignTheta
StepSize := SaveStepSize
```

Tufillaro recommends changing the independent variable from `t` to `y(3)` and then taking one step with stepsize equal to the negative of `y(3)`. (But allowance must be made, when using as program with variable stepsize, in case this is not a "good" stepsize.) If you want to do this, the equations (which are only used for finding the Poincaré crossing-points) are

$$\left.\begin{aligned} y_1' &= y_2/y_4, \\ y_2' &= \left((y_1 y_4^2 + \cos y_3 - \mu)/(1+\mu)\right)/y_4, \\ t' &= 1/y_4, \\ y_4' &= -(2y_2y_4 + \sin y_3)/(y_1y_4), \end{aligned}\right] \qquad (12.19.14)$$

where the primes denote derivatives with respect to y_3. Although more coding is needed, this has the computational advantage of added speed, if you are to find crossing-points many thousands of times.

For a given value of μ choose a variety of initial conditions in order to look for as much structure as you can find. If possible link your interpretation with computations of periodic orbits done earlier. These will show up as sets of isolated and repeated points. Around them, if the orbit is stable, you should be able to find "island" structures. For $\mu = 3$ the chaos should disappear. For this value of μ, an analytical solution to the problem can be found.

12.20 The Motion of a Pendulum Connected to a Mass Moving on a Table

A mass m lies on a smooth horizontal table. It is connected by a light, flexible, inextensible string, which passes through a frictionless hole in the table, to a mass M. The mass M is free to move in a vertical plane. The total length of the string is l.

If m were initially at rest, then it would head straight for the hole, and the motion would have no interest. But if m is given nonzero angular momentum, then in the subsequent motion it can be bounded away from the hole. In the simplest example of this, M moves vertically, and this is a special case that can be discussed using the equations that we shall derive.

Let the hole be at O, the mass m at Q and the mass M at P, as shown in figure 12.25. Let OQ have length r. Let OQ make the angle ϕ with a fixed direction on the table, and let OP make the

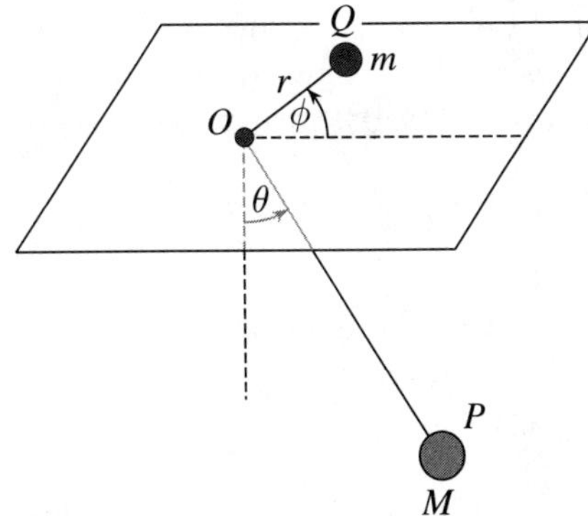

Figure 12.25: *A pendulum connected to a mass moving on a table.*

angle θ with the downward vertical. Then the kinetic energy of m is T_1 where

$$2T_1 = m(\dot{r}^2 + r^2\dot{\phi}^2).$$

Since the length of OP is $l - r$, M has kinetic energy T_2, where

$$2T_2 = M\left(\dot{r}^2 + (l-r)^2\dot{\theta}^2\right),$$

and potential energy

$$V = -Mg(l-r)\cos\theta.$$

Then the Lagrangian of the system is

$$L = \frac{1}{2}\left(m(\dot{r}^2 + r^2\dot{\phi}^2) + M\left(\dot{r}^2 + (l-r)^2\dot{\theta}^2\right)\right) + Mg(l-r)\cos\theta. \quad (12.20.1)$$

Lagrange's equations are

$$\left.\begin{aligned} \frac{d}{dt}\left(mr^2\dot{\phi}\right) &= 0, \\ \frac{d}{dt}\left((M+m)\dot{r}\right) &= mr\dot{\phi}^2 - M(l-r)\dot{\theta}^2 - Mg\cos\theta, \\ \frac{d}{dt}\left(M(l-r)^2\dot{\theta}\right) &= -Mg(l-r)\sin\theta. \end{aligned}\right] \quad (12.20.2)$$

From the first of these we can write

$$r^2\dot{\phi} = c. \quad (12.20.3)$$

c can be specified along with the initial conditions; then $\dot{\phi}$ need not appear in the equations, and we have the reduced system

$$\left.\begin{aligned} \frac{d\phi}{dt} &= \frac{c}{r^2}, \\ (M+m)\frac{d^2r}{dt^2} &= \frac{mc^2}{r^3} - M(l-r)\left(\frac{d\theta}{dt}\right)^2 - Mg\cos\theta, \\ (l-r)\frac{d^2\theta}{dt^2} - 2\frac{dr}{dt}\frac{d\theta}{dt} &= -g\sin\theta. \end{aligned}\right] \quad (12.20.4)$$

The first equation is only used if we want to follow the history of ϕ. The remaining equations define a conservative dynamical system having two degrees of freedom. This has an integral for the conservation of energy; using equation (12.20.3), it can be written as

$$\frac{1}{2}\left(m\left((\dot{r}^2+\frac{c^2}{r^2}\right)+M\left(\dot{r}^2+(l-r)^2\dot{\theta}^2\right)\right)-Mg(l-r)\cos\theta=h. \tag{12.20.5}$$

For a start, consider the model with $\theta=0$ and $\dot{\theta}=0$. From equation (12.20.5) we can write

$$(M+m)\dot{r}^2=2h-\frac{mc^2}{r^2}+2Mg(l-r)\geq 0. \tag{12.20.6}$$

Provided that h is large enough, r will have maximum and minimum values. The system

$$\left.\begin{aligned}\frac{d\phi}{dt}&=\frac{c^2}{r^2},\\(M+m)\frac{d^2r}{dt^2}&=\frac{mc^2}{r^3}-Mg\end{aligned}\right] \tag{12.20.7}$$

can be solved to show non-chaotic motion. The solution is best seen by polar coordinates r and ϕ.

Now, more generally, consider computing Poincaré maps with the coordinates r, $\dot{r}$, θ, $\dot{\theta}$, with $\dot{\theta}$ calculated from equation (12.20.5). Start with a value of h only slightly greater than that used in the runs with $\dot{\theta}\equiv 0$. Retain the same value for c, and start with initial values for r and $\dot{r}$, with $\theta=0$. For the Poincaré map, find points in the r-$\dot{r}$ plane, where $\theta=0$. The approach is similar to that used in the swinging Atwood machine. But there are more possibilities to be considered and enjoyed.

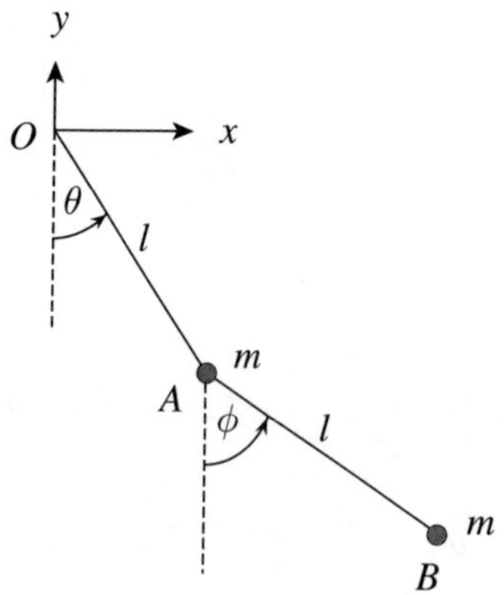

Figure 12.26: *A double pendulum.*

12.21 A Double Pendulum

A simple pendulum has a second pendulum suspended at its end. The combined system is free to move in a vertical plane. This simple apparatus is easy to construct. The system is chaotic, as is easily demonstrated.

For simplicity we shall assume that the two masses are both equal to m, and that the lengths of the pendulums are both equal to l. A generalization is messy, but not complicated. Let the pendulums make angles θ and ϕ with the downward vertical, as shown in figure 12.26. The origin is at the fixed point of suspension with the x- and y-axes horizontal and vertical, as shown.

The mass at A has coordinates $(l\sin\theta,\ -l\cos\theta)$, and velocity $(l\dot\theta\cos\theta,\ l\dot\theta\sin\theta)$.
The mass at B has coordinates $(l(\sin\theta+\sin\phi),\ -l(\cos\theta+\cos\phi))$,
and velocity $\left(l(\dot\theta\cos\theta+\dot\phi\cos\phi),\ l(\dot\theta\sin\theta+\dot\phi\sin\phi)\right)$.
The kinetic energy is T where

$$2T = ml^2\left(2\dot\theta^2+\dot\phi^2+2\dot\theta\dot\phi\cos(\theta-\phi)\right).$$

The potential is

$$V = -mgl\cos\theta - mgl(\cos\theta+\cos\phi).$$

So the Lagrangian is

$$L = \frac{1}{2}ml^2\left(2\dot\theta^2+\dot\phi^2+2\dot\theta\dot\phi\cos(\theta-\phi)\right) + mgl(2\cos\theta+\cos\phi). \quad (12.21.1)$$

Lagrange's equations each contain both $\ddot\theta$ and $\ddot\phi$. They must be solved for these separately. To simplify the notation, write

$$C = \cos(\theta-\phi) \quad \text{and} \quad S = \sin(\theta-\phi).$$

Then the equations can be written as

$$\begin{aligned} 2\ddot\theta + C\ddot\phi &= -S\dot\phi^2 - 2\omega^2\sin\theta, \\ C\ddot\theta + \ddot\phi &= S\dot\theta^2 - \omega^2\sin\phi, \end{aligned}$$

where we have set $g/l = \omega^2$. From these, we find

$$\left.\begin{aligned} \ddot\theta &= \left(-\dot\theta^2CS - \dot\phi^2S - 2\omega^2\sin\theta + C\omega^2\sin\phi\right)/(2-C^2), \\ \ddot\phi &= \left(2\dot\theta^2S + \dot\phi^2SC + 2C\omega^2\sin\theta - 2\omega^2\sin\phi\right)/(2-C^2). \end{aligned}\right] \quad (12.21.2)$$

These are the equations of the model.

Let

$$y_1 = \theta,\ y_2 = \dot\theta,\ y_3 = \phi,\ y_4 = \dot\phi. \quad (12.21.3)$$

Then

$$\left.\begin{aligned} C &= \cos(y_1-y_3),\ S = \sin(y_1-y_3), \\ \frac{dy_1}{dt} &= y_2, \\ \frac{dy_2}{dt} &= \left(-y_2^2CS - y_4^2S - 2\omega^2\sin y_1 + C\omega^2\sin y_3\right)/(2-C^2), \\ \frac{dy_3}{dt} &= y_4, \\ \frac{dy_4}{dt} &= \left(2y_2^2S + y_4^2SC + 2C\omega^2\sin y_1 - 2\omega^2\sin y_3\right)/(2-C^2). \end{aligned}\right] \quad (12.21.4)$$

This model is spectacular if observed in animation. One way to record a run is to plot θ and ϕ as functions of the time. A better way is to construct Poincaré maps.

The system has two degrees of freedom. It has the integral

$$T + V = E, \quad (12.21.5)$$

or

$$\frac{1}{2}ml^2\left(2\dot{\theta}^2+\dot{\phi}^2+2\dot{\theta}\dot{\phi}\cos(\theta-\phi)\right)-mgl(2\cos\theta+\cos\phi)=E, \tag{12.21.6}$$

so it is conservative. Let's take units so that $ml^2=1$ and $mgl=1$. Then we can follow motion in the space of θ, $\dot{\theta}$ and ϕ. A good choice of surface in this space for recording successive crossings is the plane $\theta-\phi=0$, or a multiple of 2π, since the configuration frequently straightens out during the motion. If we start with a point in this plane, with given values of θ and $\dot{\theta}$, then $\dot{\phi}$ can be found from

$$\dot{\phi}=-\dot{\theta}+\sqrt{6\cos\theta-\dot{\theta}^2+2E}, \tag{12.21.7}$$

from (12.21.6). Now choose a value for E. Then choose values for θ and $\dot{\theta}$ (so that the square root on the right-hand side of (12.21.7) is real), set $\phi=\theta$, and calculate $\dot{\phi}$. Integrate the equations of motion, finding points where $\sin(\theta-\phi)=0$ and where $\dot{\theta}+\dot{\phi}>0$ (to be consistent with the sign before the square root in (12.21.7)). On the θ-$\dot{\theta}$ plane, plot values of θ and $\dot{\theta}$. Alternatively, you might plot values of $\cos\theta$ and $\dot{\theta}$.

Suppose you have a variable `Crooked` which is equal to $+1$ if $\sin(\theta-\phi)>0$ and -1 if $\sin(\theta-\phi)<0$. Set its value when entering initial conditions. Then if `Crooked*Sin(`$\theta-\phi$`) < 0` at the conclusion of a step, an alignment has taken place. Then you need to call a subroutine or procedure that will change the sign of `crooked`, test to see whether this is an alignment that is to be found, and, if so, solve for $\sin(\theta-\phi)=0$. The code for finding the alignment using Newton's method might contain the following logic:

```
Count = 0
SaveStepSize = StepSize
Repeat
    Count = Count + 1
    Stepsize = - Sin(y(1) - y(3))/((y(2) - y(4))*Cos(y(1) - y(3)))
    Step(...)
Until (Abs(Sin(y(1) - y(3))) < Eps) or (Count = 5)
If Count < 5 then store y(1) and y(2)
StepSize = SaveStepSize
```

Figures 12.27(a) and (b) show maps for $E=-2.5$ and -1.5. Coordinates are $\cos\theta$ and $\dot{\theta}$. In figure 12.27(a) all motion appears to be non-chaotic. In figure 12.27(b), with $E=-1.5$, some chaotic structure can be seen, but most motion is now chaotic.

An alternative approach was taken by Richter and Scholz [84]. They show that the analysis may be made independently of the value of E. For given E, let us rescale the variables so that

$$l=\lambda\frac{E}{m}\text{ and }t=\tau\sqrt{\frac{E}{m}}. \tag{12.21.8}$$

Then, with a prime indicating differentiation with respect to τ,

$$\frac{1}{2}\lambda^2\left(2\theta'^2+\phi'^2+2\theta'\phi'\cos(\theta-\phi)\right)-g\lambda(2\cos\theta+\cos\phi)=1. \tag{12.21.9}$$

The parameter has become the quantity g. This is a measure of the ratio of the strength of gravity relative to the total energy of the system; so the smaller the value of g, the higher the energy, and the greater probability of chaos. If we let $\lambda=1$ then the new equations for the motion are identical to (12.21.4) but with ω^2 replaced by g and all derivatives taken with respect to τ. Then the methods just outlined can be applied: primes replace dots.

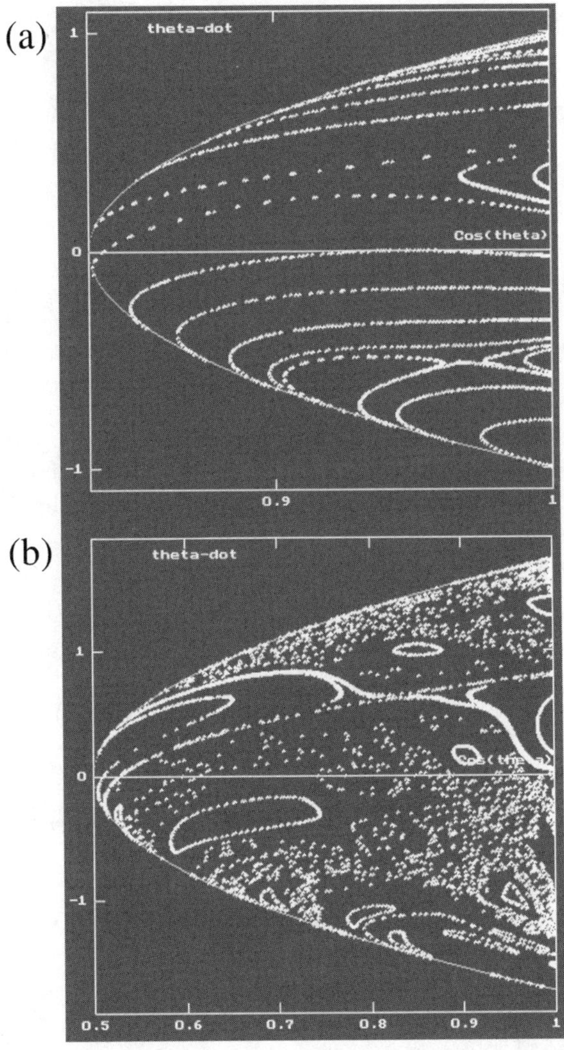

Figure 12.27: *The upper and lower pendulums make angles θ and ϕ with the downward vertical, and the rates of change of these angles are $\dot{\theta}$ and $\dot{\phi}$. There is a relation for the conservation of energy of the form $f(\theta, \phi, \dot{\theta}, \dot{\phi}) = E$, a constant. To investigate the motion, using the method of Poincaré maps, we calculate several solutions, each having the same value of E. Following each solution, we find configurations when both pendulums are aligned. At each of these points we record the values of $\cos\theta$ and $\dot{\theta}$, and plot them in the $\cos\theta$-$\dot{\theta}$ plane. (We use $\cos\theta$ rather than θ because θ may increase indefinitely during the motion, while $\cos\theta$ remains bounded.) In (a), with $E = -2.5$, all motion appears to be non-chaotic. In (b), with $E = -1.5$, some chaotic structure can be seen, but most motion is now chaotic.*

12.22 The Motion of a Pendulum Attached to a Freely Spinning Wheel

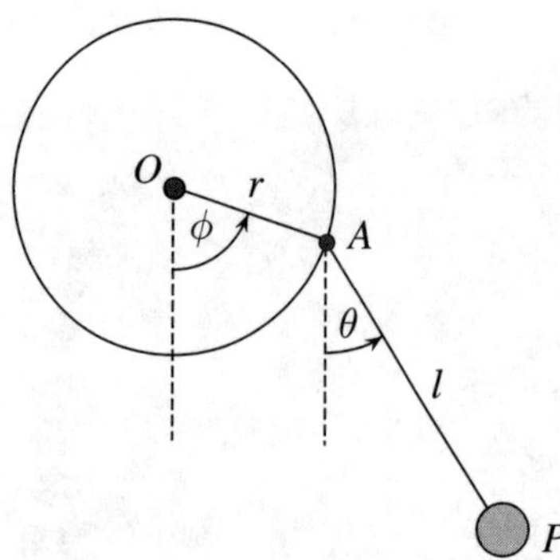

Figure 12.28: *A pendulum attached to a freely spinning wheel.*

A wheel, with radius r is free to spin in a vertical plane about its center, O. The moment of inertia of the wheel about its axis is $I = Mr^2$. A simple pendulum, AP, is attached to a point on the circumference of the wheel. The pendulum has length l, and the mass of its bob at P is m.

Let AP and OA make the angles θ and ϕ, respectively, with the downward vertical, as shown in figure 12.28. If coordinates x and y are measured horizontally and vertically, with origin at O, then the coordinates of P are

$$(r\sin\phi + l\sin\theta,\ -r\cos\phi - l\cos\theta),$$

and its velocity has components

$$(r\dot{\phi}\cos\phi + l\dot{\theta}\cos\theta,\ r\dot{\phi}\sin\phi + l\dot{\theta}\sin\theta).$$

The Lagrangian is

$$L = \frac{1}{2}\left(Mr^2\dot{\phi}^2 + m\left(r^2\dot{\phi}^2 + l^2\dot{\theta}^2 + 2rl\dot{\phi}\dot{\theta}\cos(\theta-\phi)\right)\right) + mg\left(r\cos\phi + l\cos\theta\right). \qquad (12.22.1)$$

Let

$$C = \cos(\theta-\phi),\ S = \sin(\theta-\phi).$$

The differential equations of motion are

$$\left.\begin{aligned} (m+M)r^2\ddot{\phi} + mrl\ddot{\theta}C - mrl\dot{\theta}^2 S &= -mgr\sin\phi, \\ ml^2\ddot{\theta} + mrl\ddot{\phi}C + mrl\dot{\phi}^2 S &= -mgl\sin\theta. \end{aligned}\right] \qquad (12.22.2)$$

Let

$$\frac{m}{M+m} = \mu,\ \text{and}\ \frac{l}{r} = \lambda. \qquad (12.22.3)$$

Then

$$\left.\begin{aligned} \ddot{\phi} + \lambda\mu\ddot{\theta}C - \lambda\mu\dot{\theta}^2 S + \frac{\mu g}{r}\sin\phi &= 0, \\ \ddot{\phi}C + \lambda\ddot{\theta} + \dot{\phi}^2 S + \frac{g}{r}\sin\theta &= 0. \end{aligned}\right] \qquad (12.22.4)$$

These can be solved for $\ddot{\phi}$ and $\ddot{\theta}$ to give

$$\left.\begin{aligned} \ddot{\phi}\left(1-\mu C^2\right) - \lambda\mu\dot{\theta}^2 S - \mu\dot{\phi}^2 CS + \frac{\mu g}{r}\left(\sin\phi - C\sin\theta\right) &= 0, \\ \lambda\ddot{\theta}\left(1-\mu C^2\right) + \dot{\phi}^2 S + \lambda\mu\dot{\theta}^2 CS + \frac{g}{r}\left(-\mu C\sin\phi + \sin\theta\right) &= 0. \end{aligned}\right] \qquad (12.22.5)$$

The integral for the conservation of energy is

$$\frac{1}{2}\left(Mr^2\dot{\phi}^2 + m\left(r^2\dot{\phi}^2 + l^2\dot{\theta}^2 + 2rl\dot{\phi}\dot{\theta}\cos(\theta - \phi)\right)\right) - mg\left(r\cos\phi + l\cos\theta\right) = h. \tag{12.22.6}$$

As with the double pendulum (which the present model resembles), the animation is spectacular. To document solutions, graphs of θ and ϕ as functions of the time can be helpful. But, again, the best way to investigate the model systematically is by the use of Poincaré maps. You can make your own choice of variables to use in the map.

12.23 A Magnetic Pendulum in Three Dimensions

This model is more complicated than that for the magnetic pendulum moving in a fixed vertical plane, but offers some wonderful chaotic motion. The geometry is shown in figure 12.29. Two equal magnets, of the same polarity, are fixed at points $(\pm d, 0, 0)$. The point of suspension of a pendulum is at S$(0, 0, h)$. A magnet, with polarity opposite to that of the other two, is attached to the end of the pendulum at P, which has length l. (The model is easily generalized to allow for different polarities or relative strengths.) The coordinates of P are (x, y, z), where

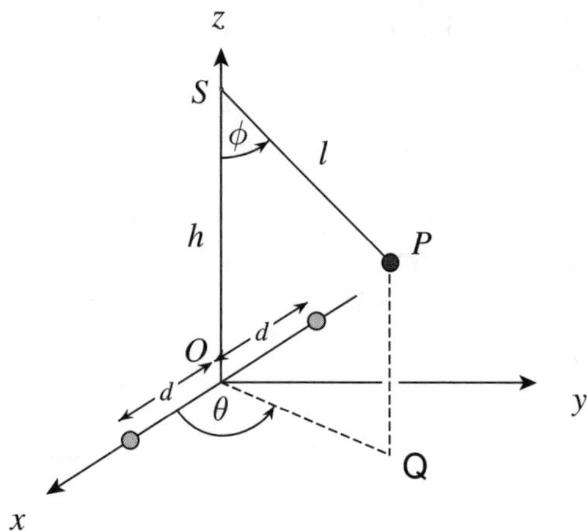

Figure 12.29: *Geometry for the pendulum.*

$$\left.\begin{aligned} x &= l\sin\phi\cos\theta, \\ y &= l\sin\phi\sin\theta, \\ z &= h - l\cos\phi. \end{aligned}\right] \tag{12.23.1}$$

The angles θ and ϕ are illustrated in figure 12.29. Q lies in the $x - y$ plane such that the angle $OQP = \pi/2$. The distances of P from the magnets at $(d, 0, 0)$ and $(-d, 0, 0)$ are D_1 and D_2, respectively, where

$$\begin{aligned} D_1^2 &= (l\sin\phi\cos\theta - d)^2 + (l\sin\phi\sin\theta)^2 + (h - l\cos\phi)^2 \\ &= l^2 + d^2 + h^2 - 2ld\sin\phi\cos\theta - 2lh\cos\phi. \end{aligned} \tag{12.23.2}$$

Similarly,

$$D_2^2 = l^2 + d^2 + h^2 + 2ld\sin\phi\cos\theta - 2lh\cos\phi. \tag{12.23.3}$$

The generalized variables are θ and ϕ. If we differentiate the expressions in equation (12.23.1), then we find

$$\dot{x}^2 + \dot{y}^2 + \dot{z}^2 = l^2\dot{\theta}^2\sin^2\phi + l^2\dot{\phi}^2.$$

Let the magnet at P have mass m. The potential can be written as

$$V = -mgl\cos\phi + K/D_1 + K/D_2,$$

where K will depend on the magnetic strengths. So the Lagrangian is

$$L = \frac{1}{2}m\left(l^2\dot{\theta}^2\sin^2\phi + l^2\dot{\phi}^2\right) + mgl\cos\phi - K/D_1 - K/D_2. \tag{12.23.4}$$

The differential equations of motion are

$$\left.\begin{aligned}
\ddot{\phi} &= \dot{\theta}^2\sin\phi\cos\phi - \frac{g}{l}\sin\phi \\
&\quad + \frac{K}{mlD_1^3}\left(-d\cos\phi\cos\theta + h\sin\phi\right) + \frac{K}{mlD_2^3}\left(d\cos\phi\cos\theta + h\sin\phi\right), \\
\ddot{\theta} &= -2\dot{\theta}\dot{\phi}\frac{\cos\phi}{\sin\phi} + \frac{2Kd\sin\theta}{ml\,\sin\phi}\left(\frac{1}{D_1^3} - \frac{1}{D_2^3}\right).
\end{aligned}\right] \tag{12.23.5}$$

The model does not allow for any dissipative forces. These could be included if the terms $-f\dot{\phi}$ and $-f\dot{\theta}\sin\phi$ are included in the first and second equations, respectively. There is a potential danger of a division by zero if $\phi = 0$; but this has not happened to me yet. In fact, $\phi = 0$ can correspond to an unstable or a stable equilibrium. If you have trouble in animation, then when ϕ falls below some small number, give the pendulum a small push; add π to θ and reverse the sign of $\dot{\phi}$.

The model is spectacular in animation, as it is in reality. One way to record a run is to plot the position of the end of the pendulum, P, as seen from above. This would be equivalent to plotting x and y, as shown in figure 12.29 and equation (12.23.1).

Another way is to plot Poincaré maps. The system is conservative, with two degrees of freedom, and the integral for the conservation of energy is

$$\frac{1}{2}m\left(l^2\dot{\theta}^2\sin^2\phi + l^2\dot{\phi}^2\right) - mgl\cos\phi + K/D_1 + K/D_2 = h. \tag{12.23.6}$$

You might find points where $\dot{\phi} = 0$ and then plot the points x and y.

12.24 A Dumbbell Satellite

This is a pendulum in orbit. A dumbbell satellite consists of two equal masses m connected by a light rigid rod of length $2d$. If the center of the rod is at C, and the center of the Earth is at E, then C moves around E in an elliptic orbit, with E at one focus of the ellipse. The rod holding the masses oscillates around C. See figure 12.30. For the model considered here, the oscillations will take place only in the plane of the orbit.

Let the perigee of the orbit of C (that is, the point in the orbit closest to the Earth) lie on the positive x-axis. Let the polar coordinates of C be (r, v), where the angle v is called the *true anomaly* of C in its orbit. Let the rod joining the masses make an angle θ with the x-axis. Then the angle between the rod and the radius vector EC is

$$\phi = \theta - v. \tag{12.24.1}$$

The gravitational effect of the Earth on the configuration of the satellite is tidal. To derive the equation of motion, consider the notation of figure 12.31. The masses at the ends of the satellite are at P_1 and P_2, and the vectors from the center of the Earth to P_1, C and P_2 are $\vec{\Delta}_1$, $\vec{r}$ and $\vec{\Delta}_2$. The gravitational force exerted on the mass m at P_1 is

$$\vec{F}_1 = -\frac{mEG}{\Delta_1^3}\vec{\Delta}_1\,. \tag{12.24.2}$$

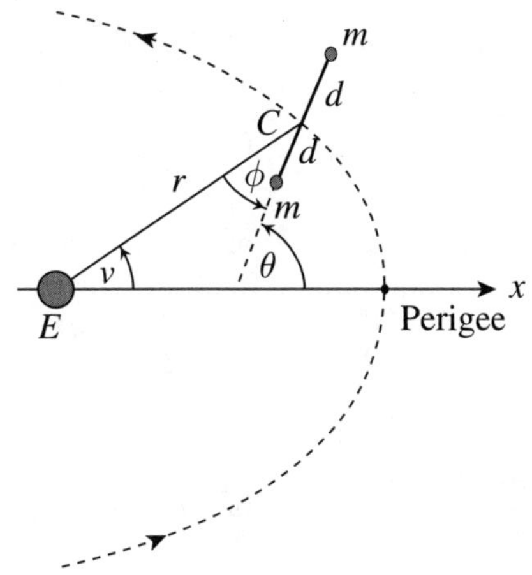

Figure 12.30: *A dumbbell satellite in orbit.*

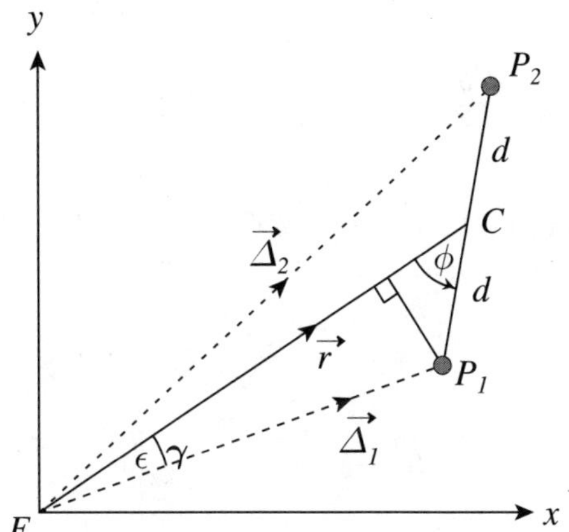

Figure 12.31: *Geometry for the force resolution.*

E is the mass of the Earth and G is the constant of gravitation. Now $d \ll r$; we shall ignore powers of d/r greater than the first. Then

$$\Delta_1^2 = r^2 + d^2 - 2rd\cos\phi = r^2\left(1 - 2(d/r)\cos\phi + (d/r)^2\right) \approx r^2\left(1 - (d/r)\cos\phi\right).$$

So

$$\frac{1}{\Delta_1^3} = \frac{1}{r^3}\left(1 - 2\frac{d}{r}\cos\phi\right)^{-3/2} = \frac{1}{r^3}\left(1 + 3\frac{d}{r}\cos\phi\right). \tag{12.24.3}$$

Then

$$\vec{F}_1 = -\frac{mEG}{r^3}\left(1 + 3\frac{d}{r}\cos\phi\right)\vec{\Delta}_1. \tag{12.24.4}$$

The moment of the force $\vec{F}_1$ about C is

$$\vec{\mu}_1 = -\vec{r} \times \vec{F}_1 = \frac{mEG}{r^3}\left(1 + 3\frac{d}{r}\cos\phi\right)\vec{r} \times \vec{\Delta}_1. \tag{12.24.5}$$

Now from the geometry of the triangle ECP_1, $\Delta_1 \sin\epsilon = d\sin\phi$. So

$$\vec{r} \times \vec{\Delta}_1 = -\hat{z}(r\Delta_1 \sin\epsilon) = -\hat{z}(rd\sin\phi).$$

Then

$$\vec{\mu}_1 = -\hat{z}\frac{mEG}{r^3}\left(1 + 3\frac{d}{r}\cos\phi\right) rd\sin\phi. \tag{12.24.6}$$

In the same way, the moment of the force of attraction of the Earth on the mass at P_2 is

$$\vec{\mu}_2 = \hat{z}\frac{mEG}{r^3}\left(1 - 3\frac{d}{r}\cos\phi\right) rd\sin\phi. \tag{12.24.7}$$

Adding these, we find the net moment to be

$$\vec{\mu}_1 + \vec{\mu}_2 = -\hat{z}\frac{mEG}{r^3}\left(6\frac{d}{r}\cos\phi\right) rd\sin\phi = -\hat{z}\frac{3mEGd^2}{r^3}\sin 2\phi. \tag{12.24.8}$$

The moment of inertia of the masses about C is $2d^2m$. So the differential equation of motion for θ is

$$2d^2m\frac{d^2\theta}{dt^2}\hat{z} = \vec{\mu}_1 + \vec{\mu}_2,$$

or

$$\frac{d^2\theta}{dt^2} + \frac{3EG}{2r^3}\sin(2\theta - 2v) = 0, \tag{12.24.9}$$

where we have used (12.24.1).

We state some properties of the elliptic orbit of C about E. Details can be found in Danby [30]. Let a be the semimajor axis of the ellipse and e be eccentricity. Then

$$r = \frac{a(1-e^2)}{1 + e\cos v}, \tag{12.24.10}$$

and

$$r^2\frac{dv}{dt} = \sqrt{EGa(1-e^2)}. \tag{12.24.11}$$

The first equation is the polar equation of the orbit; the second expresses the conservation of angular momentum about E.

For modeling purposes, we shall now take units such that

$$EG = 1, \text{ and } a = 1. \tag{12.24.12}$$

Rather than use formulas for the position of C, it will be easier to integrate equation (12.24.11) along with (12.24.9). Then if

$$y_1 = \theta,\ y_2 = \frac{d\theta}{dt},\ y_3 = v, \tag{12.24.13}$$

we have the system

$$\left.\begin{aligned} r &= \frac{1-e^2}{1+e\cos y_3}, \\ \frac{dy_1}{dt} &= y_2, \\ \frac{dy_2}{dt} &= -\frac{3}{2r^3}\sin(2y_1 - 2y_3), \\ \frac{dy_3}{dt} &= \frac{\sqrt{1-e^2}}{r^2}. \end{aligned}\right] \tag{12.24.14}$$

For plotting or display purposes, it may be convenient to calculate

$$\phi = \theta - v = y_1 - y_3.$$

First, consider circular orbits with $e = 0$. In this case, $\ddot{v} = 0$, so (12.24.9) can be written as

$$\frac{d^2\phi}{dt^2} + \frac{3}{2}\sin(2\phi) = 0. \tag{12.24.15}$$

This is similar to the equation for the simple pendulum, but the stable equilibria are at $\phi = 0,\ \pi$, and the unstable equilibria are at $\phi = \pi/2,\ 3\pi/2$. Phase-plane plots of ϕ against $\dot{\phi}$ are like those for the simple pendulum, with the one change in the horizontal scale. You should confirm this.

For $e > 0$ the model is equivalent to that of a forced pendulum, and is chaotic. Any of the methods described in section 5.4 can be applied. It can be especially rewarding to see the motion in animation, where the orbital motion around the Earth is included.

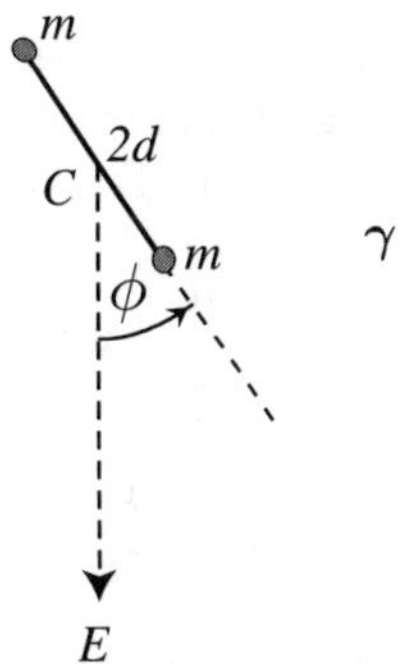

Figure 12.32: *Geometry of the "pendulum" relative to the Earth.*

For a start, I suggest that you look for conditions such that the satellite points, on average, toward the center of the Earth. Then the period of revolution in the orbit and the average period of rotation of the satellite are the same, or *synchronous*. This implies oscillations around $\phi = 0$. So think of the pendulum as shown in figure 12.32. To follow these oscillations, you must follow the variables

$$\phi = y_1 - y_3, \text{ and } \frac{d\phi}{dt} = \frac{d\theta}{dt} - \frac{dv}{dt} = y_2 - \frac{\sqrt{1-e^2}}{(1-e^2)^2}(1 + e\cos y_3)^2, \tag{12.24.16}$$

from (12.24.14). For initial conditions, start at perigee, where $v = y_3 = 0$, (so $r = (1-e)$), with $\phi = \dot{\phi} = 0$. So

$$t = 0,\ y_1 = 0,\ y_2 = \frac{\sqrt{1-e^2}}{(1-e)^2},\ y_3 = 0. \tag{12.24.17}$$

For values of e gradually increasing from $e = 0$ you might plot ϕ as a function of the time until you can confirm either periodicity (with period 2π) or chaotic behavior. Repeat with initial conditions (12.24.17) slightly changed to allow ϕ or $\dot{\phi}$ to be nonzero.

Phase-plane plots in the ϕ-$\dot{\phi}$ plane can be helpful. When these become too confusing, just sample ϕ and $\dot{\phi}$ at regular intervals of time, producing Poincaré maps. The usual time interval is 2π, the period of revolution of the satellite. Initial conditions can now be any values of ϕ and $\dot{\phi}$. You will need to plot values of ϕ mod 2π; alternatively, plot values of $\sin\phi$. (Some applications of this model plot Poincaré maps in the θ-$\dot{\theta}$ plane.)

It is possible that the satellite is initially oscillating about the position $\phi = 0$ because of launch conditions. Suppose a stabilizing force is applied so that a term $-k\dot{\phi}$ is added to the right of

(12.24.9). Include this damping term in your analysis. Start with a circular orbit, and look for a value of k so that oscillations, with initial amplitude of one radian, might become small after ten revolutions. Use this value of k to play with orbits of higher eccentricity.

For a major project, generate bifurcation diagrams for this system.

12.25 The Rotation of the Moon

The rotation of the Moon in space follows, on the average, three kinematic laws, known as *Cassini's laws.* For a statement of these and a dynamical justification of them, consult a textbook such as Danby [30]. The only one of the laws to concern us here, since we shall be keeping to two dimensions, is the first, which states that the period of rotation of the Moon about its axis is the same as the period of its orbital revolution around the Earth.

Think of the Moon as being approximated by an ellipsoid, with the longest axis pointing toward the Earth, and the shortest perpendicular to the orbital plane. We shall assume that the axis of rotation of the Moon is also perpendicular to this plane. Let the principal moments of inertia be A, B, and C, with $A < B < C$. Then A corresponds to the longest axis. We shall use the geometry of figure 12.30, with the longest axis replacing the line of the dumbbell. A derivation of the differential equation for θ can be found in Danby [30] chapter 14. It is

$$\frac{d^2\theta}{dt^2} + \frac{p}{r^3}\sin(2\theta - 2v) = 0, \tag{12.25.1}$$

where

$$p = \frac{3EG}{2}\frac{B-A}{C}. \tag{12.25.2}$$

A major difference between this project and the preceding one is that $(B - A)/C$ is small, around 10^{-4}. The average eccentricity of the Moon's orbit around the Earth is about 0.055.

For a start, I suggest that you link the two projects together. Use the scaling of equation (12.24.12). Consider equation (12.25.1) with adjustable parameters p and e. Gradually reduce the value of p from 1.5 to 10^{-4}, and find out what happens to the critical value of the eccentricity at which the librations become unstable.

As you follow your results, note the oscillations of ϕ. On the average, the Moon turns the same face toward the Earth; but with ϕ nonzero, part of the eastern or western side is turned towards us. This is the phenomenon of *libration in longitude.*

12.26 The Rotation of Hyperion

Hyperion is a satellite of Saturn, with a period of 21 days. An inhabitant of Saturn (or, less unlikely, another of the satellites) would enjoy sights unique in the solar system, because the rotation of Hyperion (in contrast to our boring Moon) is chaotic. (An inhabitant of Hyperion would have a very rough existence.) For a contrast with the Moon, Hyperion can be approximated by an ellipsoid with principal axes $a = 190$, km $b = 145$, km $c = 114$ km. The eccentricity of the orbit is approximately $e = 0.1$. If the unit of time is the day, and the notation is that of project 12.24, then the differential equation for the motion can be written as

$$\frac{d^2\theta}{dt^2} + n^2\frac{B-A}{C}\frac{3}{2}\left(\frac{a}{r}\right)^3\sin(2\theta - 2v) = 0, \tag{12.26.1}$$

where

$$n = \frac{1}{21}, \text{ and } \frac{a}{r} = \frac{1 + e\cos v}{1 - e^2}. \tag{12.26.2}$$

The moments of inertia are given by

$$A = \frac{1}{5}M(b^2 + c^2),\ B = \frac{1}{5}M(c^2 + a^2),\ C = \frac{1}{5}M(a^2 + b^2), \tag{12.26.3}$$

where M is the mass of the satellite. (Actually, the chaotic toppling is in three dimensions, but the equations given should provide you with quite enough to handle.)

Investigate this system with various initial conditions. How important is the value of the eccentricity?

12.27 The Rotation of Mercury

Until 1965 it was thought that, on the average, Mercury turned the same face toward the Sun, and it was accepted that Mercury was in synchronous rotation with respect to the Sun, as the Moon is with respect to the Earth. If so, then the kind of work we have been performing in the last two projects would also apply to Mercury. The eccentricity of Mercury's orbit around the Sun is approximately 0.2056. But in 1965 it was discovered through radar observations that Mercury's rotation period is two thirds of its orbital period. As this must have been going on for a long time, we are obviously observing some condition of stable equilibrium.

Let us normalize units as before. The average angular rate of revolution in the orbit will be equal to one. Then the average rate of increase of the angle θ in figure 12.30 will be equal to 1.5, so that the quantity $(1.5t - \theta)$ executes stable oscillations. Up to now, we have been essentially looking at oscillations of $(t - \theta)$; these exist for $e = 0$ and continue for larger e until they become unstable. But oscillations of $(1.5t - \theta)$ do not exist for $e = 0$. Then how can they arise?

The answer is that such oscillations can only take place (using the present model) for a narrow range of e. The object of this project is to explore such a range numerically. For a start, you might verify that for $e = 0.2716$ and p less than 0.09, such stable oscillations do indeed exist. See if, for a given value of p, you can find a range of e within which stable oscillations can take place. Start the motion off with initial conditions

$$t = 0;\ y_1 = 0,\ y_2 = 1.5,\ y_3 = 0. \tag{12.27.1}$$

Integrate the equations and look for stable patterns. When instability strikes, it is usually obvious, but of course, in an apparently stable situation we can never be absolutely sure that instability is not waiting around the corner. Numerical exploration is not the same as mathematical proof. You might construct a phase-plane plot for the coordinates

$$1.5t - \theta \quad \text{versus} \quad 1.5 - \dot{\theta}.$$

These coordinates are the libration angle of the oscillations and its time rate of change, respectively.

Try sampling output at regular values of the time, to generate Poincaré maps. The increment of time used should be $4\pi/3$. In the actual case of Mercury, the oscillations are small. But don't be limited by actuality. Invent your own planet.

What we are observing for Mercury is a "resonance" between the rotational and orbital periods; they are related by a factor m/n where m and n are integers. Resonances of various kinds are quite common in the solar system. For Mercury, what is special about 2/3? Why not 3/4, or 1/2? How about picking a fraction m/n (using small integers) and seeing if you can find e and p such that $(mt/n - \theta)$ has stable oscillations?

12.28 The Rotation of the Moon and Mercury, Including Effects of Tidal Friction

When tides sweep over the outer regions of a deformable body, some energy is lost. Tidal friction between the Earth and the Moon is slowing down the rate of rotation of the Earth, as well as causing the orbit of the Moon gradually to recede from the Earth. Maybe in the past the Moon rotated faster than it does now, but tidal forces slowed it down until it became trapped in its present resonance, 1/1, between its rotational and orbital periods. Maybe the same happened to Mercury. Was it just luck that Mercury was caught in the 2/3 resonance?

These matters are not completely understood. But we can fairly easily include terms in the equations that might model tidal forces and see what effects they might have. Several forms for these terms have been suggested; the one that I have picked presents a minimum of programming difficulty. It, and some other possibilities as well as references, can be found in a paper by W.T.Kyner [63]. The new differential equation for θ is

$$\frac{d^2\theta}{dt^2} + \frac{p}{r^3}\sin(2\theta - 2v) + \frac{q}{r^6}\left(\frac{d\theta}{dt} - \frac{dv}{dt}\right) = 0, \tag{12.28.1}$$

where p is defined as before, and q is a small (*very* small) positive number. The model now contains parameters p, q, e, and the order of the resonance to be considered. To avoid becoming swamped with too many possibilities, I suggest that you look at a few very special cases.

1. We saw in the preceding project that the 2/3 resonance was possible with $e = 0.2716$. Show that the introduction of the tidal term can stabilize the resonance when $e = 0.2056$. To do this, you might start without the tidal terms, and then introduce q.

2. Change your initial conditions to

$$t = 0;\ y_1 = 0,\ y_2 = 1.5 + K,\ y_3 = 0, \tag{12.28.2}$$

where K is positive and, to start with, small. Be cautious. The idea is to start off with a rotation that is too fast for the resonance and see whether the tidal terms will slow down the rotation so that it is trapped into resonance. At present it is considered that there is a *chance* that it will be trapped, but there is also a chance that the slowing down will simply continue, and the 2/3 resonance will be bypassed. You will need to use parameters that are too large to represent the real Mercury, but you may still learn something about how the model can act.

3. Now look at the case of the Moon and its 1/1 resonance. Start it rotating more rapidly than is needed for synchronization, and watch it slow down. Will it be trapped into the resonance?

4. Finally, start Hyperion with non-chaotic rapid rotation. Can you follow the motion so that it becomes chaotic?

Similar experiments can be made using the model of project (12.24).

Chapter 13

Springs

13.1 Non-Linear Springs

For a mass m hanging at the end of a spring, obeying Hooke's law and having spring, constant k, the equation of motion is

$$m\frac{d^2x}{dt^2} + kx = 0, \tag{13.1.1}$$

where t is the time, and x is the displacement of m from the equilibrium. In this case we have no need of the computer to tell us about the possible motion.

For *nonlinear* springs there are two types of restoring force:

$$\begin{aligned} \textit{Hard spring}: \quad \text{Force} &= kx(1 + a^2x^2). & (13.1.2)\\ \textit{Soft spring}: \quad \text{Force} &= kx(1 - a^2x^2). & (13.1.3) \end{aligned}$$

Clearly, in practice, the deflection x and the parameter a should not be too large.

If (13.1.1) is modified for a nonlinear spring, the resulting equation can be solved in terms of elliptic functions, but it is more easily investigated numerically. Consider the phase-plane diagram for x and $\dot{x}$. Start with $a = 0$; then introduce small a and compare the two cases of the hard and soft spring. Finally, increase a.

For the soft spring, we have

$$m\frac{d^2x}{dt^2} + kx(1 - a^2x^2) = 0. \tag{13.1.4}$$

Don't worry about physical interpretation now. Show that there are three equilibria; construct phase-plane diagrams and investigate their stability.

13.2 Duffing's Equation

The equation

$$\frac{d^2x}{dt^2} + kx + lx^3 = A\cos(\omega t) \tag{13.2.1}$$

is called *Duffing's Equation.* It describes a system with a nonlinear spring and a periodic forcing term. The equation is the subject of considerable discussion in textbooks. Here we can only chew a little at the periphery of the subject, but I hope that what you sample may whet your appetite for more.

The principal parameter to vary is ω, the applied frequency. If $l = 0$, or the spring is linear, then it is well known that the amplitude of the forced oscillations is a function of ω, and that it becomes infinite (mechanical resonance occurs) when the imposed and the natural frequencies are the same. A system with damping added is

$$\frac{d^2x}{dt^2} + D\frac{dx}{dt} + kx + lx^3 = A\cos(\omega t), \tag{13.2.2}$$

where D is a positive constant. With $l = 0$ this can still show a sharp (but finite) peak near this point. A plot of the amplitude of oscillations as a function of ω is sketched in figure 13.1(a). Parts (b) and (c) of this figure show similar sketches for the cases of hard and soft springs.

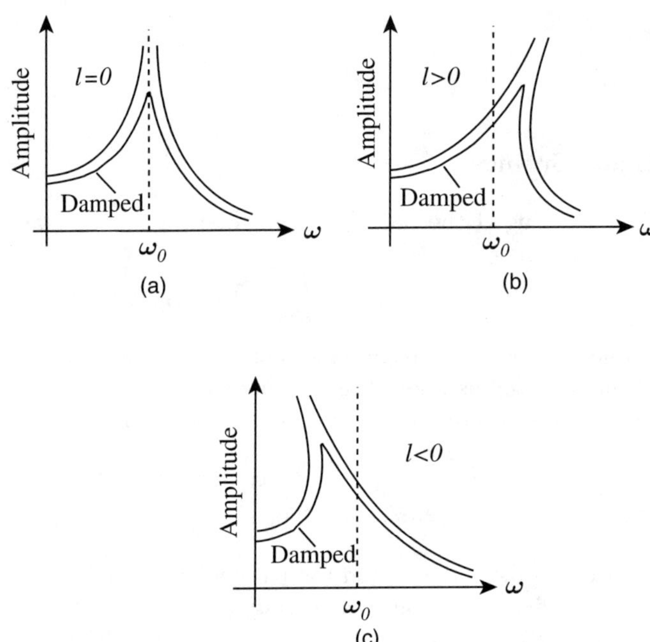

Figure 13.1: *Variation of amplitude with applied frequency, for different values of l.*

For the project, you should start by confirming the nature of the figures. Remember that the amplitudes refer to steady-state oscillations, so that the integrations will have to be maintained until transient effects can be ignored. Start with $l = 0$ before introducing small nonzero values.

Now try the following experiment. For the case of the hard spring, start with ω small and gradually allow it to increase. The amplitude of the steady-state oscillations will also start to increase, as is clear from the figure. But eventually there will be a stage when the amplitude can increase no further; this will correspond to the end of the loop leaning to the right in figure 13.1(b). After this occurs, an increase in ω will cause the amplitude to jump to a much lower value. Alternatively, you might run the experiment with large ω to start with, and let ω diminish. Then you will witness an upward jump. In each case, you might try running the system with ω varying slowly with the time.

This is a forced chaotic system. So you can use any of the methods of the model of the forced pendulum to investigate its properties.

13.3 Van der Pol's Equation, and Friends

Van der Pol's differential equation is

$$\frac{d^2x}{dt^2} + \epsilon(x^2 - 1)\frac{dx}{dt} + x = 0. \tag{13.3.1}$$

This equation arises in several contexts; once again, I hope that you will look it up in textbooks for interpretations and ideas for experiment. A feature of the solutions is the presence of limit cycles. Find these, and investigate their stability. Try graphing x as a function of the time when ϵ is equal to one or more; it has a remarkably jerky appearance.

A related equation is *Rayleigh's equation*,

$$\frac{d^2x}{dt^2} + \epsilon \left[\left(\frac{dx}{dt} \right)^3 - \frac{dx}{dt} \right] + x = 0. \tag{13.3.2}$$

Verify that this has some characteristics in common with (13.3.1).

To see several limit cycles, you might look at

$$\frac{d^2x}{dt^2} + a \sin \left(\frac{dx}{dt} \right) + x = 0. \tag{13.3.3}$$

Find and investigate its limit cycles; some are stable and some unstable. For cases like this, you may tire of numerical work; then you should look up and learn *Liénard's method* for investigating limit cycles.

13.4 Variation of Parameters and Van der Pol's Equation

We consider equation (13.3.1), and try to represent the solution in the form

$$\left.\begin{aligned} x &= A\cos(t-\phi), \\ \frac{dx}{dt} &= -A\sin(t-\phi). \end{aligned}\right] \tag{13.4.1}$$

If $\epsilon = 0$, then this is the correct solution, with A and ϕ arbitrary constants; they represent amplitude and phase, respectively. In the more general case, A and ϕ become variables. Differentiating equations (13.4.1) and substituting into (13.3.1), we find

$$\left.\begin{aligned} \frac{dA}{dt}\cos\psi + A\frac{d\phi}{dt}\sin\psi &= 0, \\ -\frac{dA}{dt}\sin\psi + A\frac{d\phi}{dt}\cos\psi &= \epsilon A\sin\psi(A^2\cos^2\psi - 1), \end{aligned}\right] \tag{13.4.2}$$

where

$$\psi = t - \phi. \tag{13.4.3}$$

Then

$$\left.\begin{aligned} \frac{dA}{dt} &= -\epsilon A^2\sin^2\psi(A^2\cos^2\psi - 1), \\ A\frac{d\phi}{dt} &= \epsilon A^2\sin\psi\cos\psi(A^2\cos^2\psi - 1). \end{aligned}\right] \tag{13.4.4}$$

These equations are no harder to solve numerically than are the equations for x and $\dot{x}$ that result from solving (13.3.1) in the usual way. The merit of the equations for the variation of the parameters A and ϕ is that these variables have more immediate physical meaning than do x and $\dot{x}$. Solve them for some of the cases already investigated in the preceding project.

You might also consider applying the method of variation of parameters to Duffing's equation and looking at some solutions when the motion is chaotic.

13.5 A Dynamic Model for the Buckling of a Column

The model for this project appears in a text by J.J.Stoker [92].[1] A thin elastic column is subjected to compressive forces along its axis. For forces above a critical limit, the column will bend or buckle. Before setting up the dynamical model, we shall look briefly at the conventional static treatment.

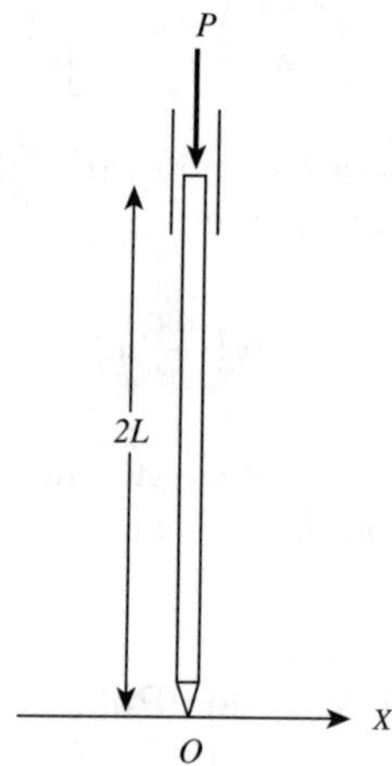

Figure 13.2: *A column with vertical force P.*

Set up the column, of length $2L$, on the y-axis, with its ends at $(0,0)$ and $(0,2L)$, as shown in figure 13.2. Any displacement will be confined to the x-y plane. Suppose the column to be smoothly pivoted at the origin and subjected to a downward vertical force P at the other end; this end is under constraint so that it cannot move horizontally. If the column were to bend, then the differential equation for its shape would be

$$EI\frac{d^2x}{dy^2} = -Px, \tag{13.5.1}$$

where E is *Young's modulus* and I is the moment of inertia of the column about its axis. This equation must be subject to the end-point conditions,

$$x(0) = x(2L) = 0. \tag{13.5.2}$$

If we write $(P/EI) = k^2$, then the general solution of (13.5.1) is

$$x = c_1 \cos(ky) + c_2 \sin(ky).$$

Applying the end-point conditions, we have

$$\begin{aligned} x(0) &= 0 \rightarrow c_1 = 0. \\ x(2L) &= 0 \rightarrow c_2 \sin(2kL) = 0. \end{aligned}$$

In order that x have any solution that is not identically zero, k must take one of the special values $\pi/2L$, $2\pi/2L$, $3\pi/2L$,.... If $k < \pi/2L$, or, equivalently, if $P < EI(\pi/2L)^2$, then the solution for x must be identically zero. But when $P = EI(\pi/2L)^2$, called the *critical Euler load,* there is a nonzero solution for x; so the column is able to bend and perhaps buckle.

[1] From J.J.Stoker, *Nonlinear Vibrations in Mechanical and Electrical Systems.* Copyright ©1950, John Wiley & Sons, Inc.

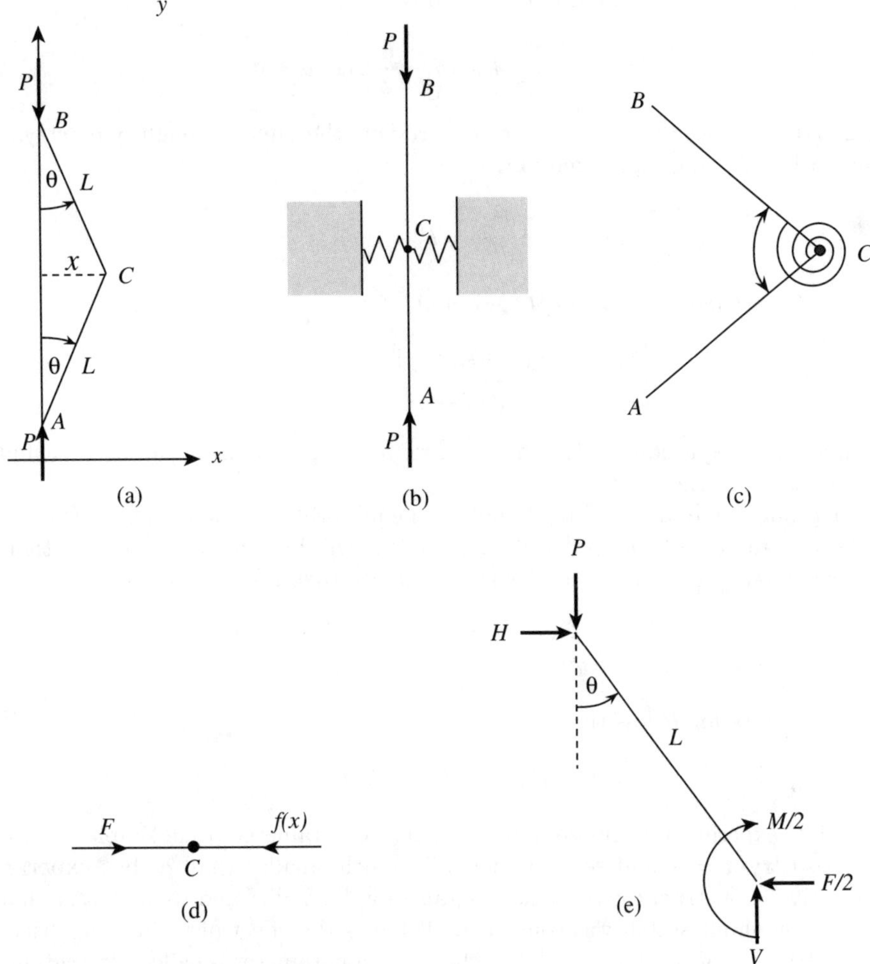

Figure 13.3: *Forces for the dynamical motion of the column.*

The dynamic model is shown in figure 13.3(a). The column is replaced by two light rods, each of length L, jointed at C, where a mass m is attached. The other ends, A and B, are free to move vertically along the y-axis. Vertical forces P are applied at both A and B, as shown. We assume symmetry so that C moves only horizontally. To model the elasticity and stiffness of the column, two kinds of spring are applied to C. Horizontal springs at each side (see figure13.3(b)) produce a net restoring force

$$f(x) = ax + bx^3. \tag{13.5.3}$$

A coil spring at C (see figure13.3(c)) exerts a force that tries to straighten out the configuration. If the angle between the rods is $\pi - 2\theta$, this restoring force has moment about C equal to

$$M = 2k\theta. \tag{13.5.4}$$

The mass at C will experience two horizontal forces: $f(x)$ due to the springs, and F due to other effects. We need to find F. Pay attention just to the upper rod, BC. The forces acting on this rod are shown in figure 13.3(e). Refer to that figure for the notation. Resolving vertically, we have

$$P = V, \tag{13.5.5}$$

since there is no acceleration. Taking moments about B,

$$-\frac{M}{2} + VL\sin\theta - \frac{F}{2}L\cos\theta = 0. \tag{13.5.6}$$

(We use $M/2$ and $F/2$ since the forces on the other rod are the same, through symmetry.) Combining these formulas with the equation of motion,

$$m\frac{d^2x}{dt^2} = F - f(x), \tag{13.5.7}$$

and eliminating θ, through $\theta = \sin^{-1}(x/L)$, we find

$$m\frac{d^2x}{dt^2} = 2\frac{Px - k\sin^{-1}(x/L)}{\sqrt{L^2 - x^2}} - (ax + bx^3). \tag{13.5.8}$$

This is the differential equation for the model. Friction might be introduced by including a term proportional to dx/dt on the right.

$x = 0$, corresponding to a straight column, is an equilibrium of the model. If P is small enough, this equilibrium is stable, but for a critical value of P it will become unstable, and then two stable equilibria appear at each side of $x = 0$. If x is very small, then approximately

$$m\frac{d^2x}{dt^2} = -\left(a + \frac{2k}{L^2} - \frac{2P}{L}\right)x, \tag{13.5.9}$$

which suggests stability for P less than

$$P_{\text{crit}} = aL/2 + k/L. \tag{13.5.10}$$

For numerical experiments, choose units so that the parameters take simple values. So $m = 1$ and $L = 1$. Also try $a = 1$ and set b numerically much smaller than a, but experiment with b positive or negative. Construct phase-plane diagrams for P smaller and then greater than P_{crit}, and see if the prediction about stability is confirmed. What is the effect of including a frictional force? This type of splitting up of equilibria with the change of a parameter is called *bifurcation*, a common feature of many dynamical systems.

The present model is not chaotic. However, if you were to include a periodic force in the model, you would introduce possible chaos. You might choose a frequency for this term that was the same, or close to, the frequency in the solution of equation (13.5.9), and see what happens when the amplitude of the term is gradually increased.

13.6 Zeeman's Catastrophe Machine

The basic model for this project was invented by Zeeman to demonstrate some aspects of "catastrophic" change. It is fairly easily constructed and demonstrated, but has generated some nontrivial mathematics. A circular disk, with radius r, is free to rotate about its center O. A peg is attached to a point R on its rim, and two equal elastic bands, RP and RQ, are looped around the peg, as shown in figure 13.4. The point P is fixed on the x-axis at $(-d, 0)$, where d is sufficiently large so that $d - r$ is greater than the unstretched length of the band; then the band is in tension, whatever the orientation of OR. The point Q, at (x, y), can be moved — but slowly. As envisaged by Zeeman, the motion of the disk is overdamped. As Q is moved, the orientation of the disk may change in a smooth manner, or it may snap from one position to another.

Suppose that Q is on the positive x-axis and far from O, so that the tension in OQ is much greater than that in OP. We can expect to have two equilibrium positions, a stable one with $x > 0$ and an unstable one with $x < 0$. (An equilibrium is stable if, after a small displacement

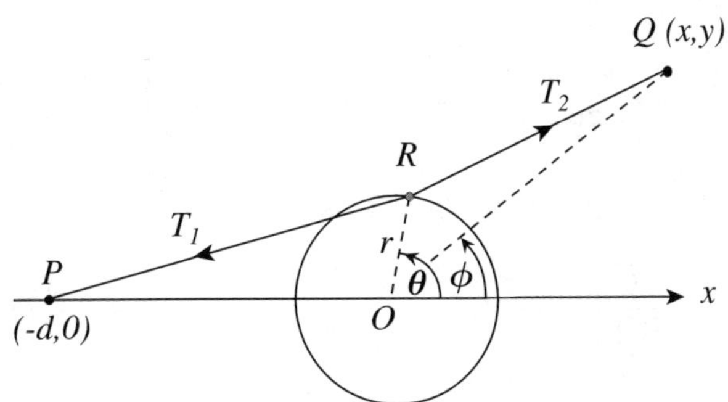

Figure 13.4: *Zeeman's catastrophe machine.*

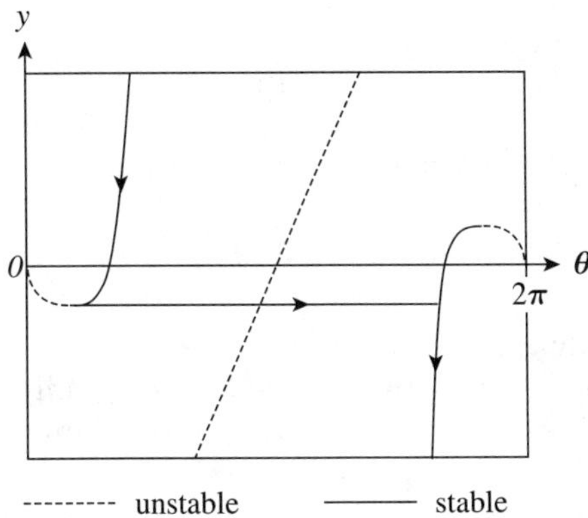

Figure 13.5: *Positions of equilibrium with diminishing* y.

away from it, the configuration returns to the equilibrium. It is unstable, if a small displacement is followed by further drifting away from the equilibrium.) Now bring Q closer to O. As the relative tensions become closer in magnitude, the equilibrium with $x > 0$ will eventually become unstable, and two stable equilibria appear, with positive x, symmetric about the x-axis. So the model includes bifurcation.

Now move Q, changing y, while keeping x fixed. The variations in equilibrium positions as y changes are shown in figure 13.5. For y sufficiently large, there will be just two equilibria, one stable and one unstable. Eventually, there will be four equilibria. For negative values of y, the active equilibrium will approach the base of the hook-like structure on the left. As y decreases further, the disk will eventually have to snap over so that it passes to the other stable branch.

For this project we shall assume only small damping, and observe the oscillation before and after bifurcation. To derive the equations for the model, note that the coordinates of P, Q and R are

$$\mathrm{P} : (-d, 0), \quad \mathrm{Q} : (x, y), \quad \mathrm{R} : (r\cos\theta,\, r\sin\theta).$$

Let the lengths of RP and RQ be ρ_1 and ρ_2, respectively. Then

$$\rho_1 = \sqrt{r^2 + d^2 + 2rd\cos\theta} \text{ and } \rho_2 = \sqrt{(r\cos\theta - x)^2 + (r\sin\theta - y)^2}. \tag{13.6.1}$$

Let the unstretched lengths of the elastic bands be l. The tensions in PR and RQ are T_1 and T_2, where

$$\begin{aligned} T_1 &= k(\rho_1 - l); \\ T_2 &= \left[\begin{array}{ll} k(\rho_2 - l), & \rho_2 > l, \\ 0, & \rho_2 < l. \end{array}\right] \end{aligned} \tag{13.6.2}$$

k is the spring constant. The torque of $T2$ about O is

$$\begin{aligned} \overrightarrow{\mathrm{OR}} \times \frac{\overrightarrow{\mathrm{RQ}}}{\mathrm{RQ}} T_2 &= \overrightarrow{\mathrm{OR}} \times \frac{\overrightarrow{\mathrm{RO}} + \overrightarrow{\mathrm{OQ}}}{\rho_2} T_2 = \overrightarrow{\mathrm{OR}} \times \frac{\overrightarrow{\mathrm{OQ}}}{\rho_2} T_2 \\ &= \frac{T_2}{\rho_2} \left(ry\cos\theta - rx\sin\theta\right)(\hat{x} \times \hat{y}). \end{aligned}$$

Similarly, the torque of T_1 about O is

$$\frac{T_1}{\rho_1} rd\sin\theta(\hat{x} \times \hat{y}).$$

Then if I is the moment of inertia of the disk about O, the equation of motion is

$$I\frac{d^2\theta}{dt^2} = \frac{T_2}{\rho_2}(ry\cos\theta - rx\sin\theta) + \frac{T_1}{\rho_1} rd\sin\theta - f\frac{d\theta}{dt}, \tag{13.6.3}$$

where f is a parameter depending on the strength of the damping.

The model is best viewed through the phase-plane diagram, with θ as horizontal and $\dot{\theta}$ as vertical. Interpretation of the output requires locating equilibrium positions. This can be done with sufficient accuracy by calculating the torque, for values of θ between 0 and 360°, and noting where the sign changes. The motion should be followed by varying the position of Q to see what can happen before and after bifurcation. Alternatively, allow one coordinate, say x, to change slowly to see transitions between different types of motion. Or keep the length OQ fixed, and vary the angle ϕ in figure 13.4.

13.7 Two Attracting Wires

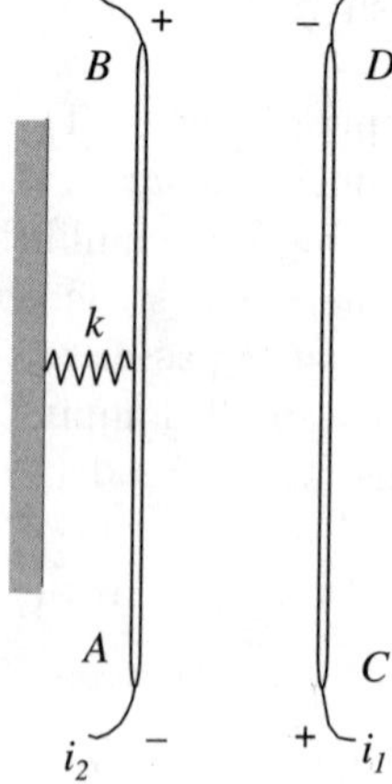

Figure 13.6: *Two attracting wires.*

A fixed straight wire, CD, carrying a current i_1 attracts a parallel straight wire, AB, carrying a current i_2. The wire AB, which has mass m, is attached to one end of a spring, with spring constant

k; the other end of the spring is fixed, as shown in figure 13.6. Each wire has length l. If the two wires are separated by the distance d, then the force of attraction between them is

$$\frac{2i_1 i_2}{d} l.$$

We shall investigate equilibria and possible oscillations of AB.

Let the separation when the system is in equilibrium with $i_2 = 0$ be D. For general motion, let AB be displaced by x from that equilibrium. Then the differential equation for x is

$$m\frac{d^2x}{dt^2} = \frac{2i_1 i_2}{D - x} l - kx. \tag{13.7.1}$$

The parameter to be varied is i_2. Choose suitable values for the other parameters, and start with i_2 small. It is best to follow possible motion in the phase-plane $x - \dot{x}$. For sufficiently small i_2 there will be two equilibria, one stable and one unstable. These combine into one unstable equilibrium for a critical value of i_2; for larger values of i_2 there are no equilibria.

13.8 The Action Between a Violin Bow and a String

To begin with, this model will evoke neither visions of a violin, nor echoes of its sound; but be patient.

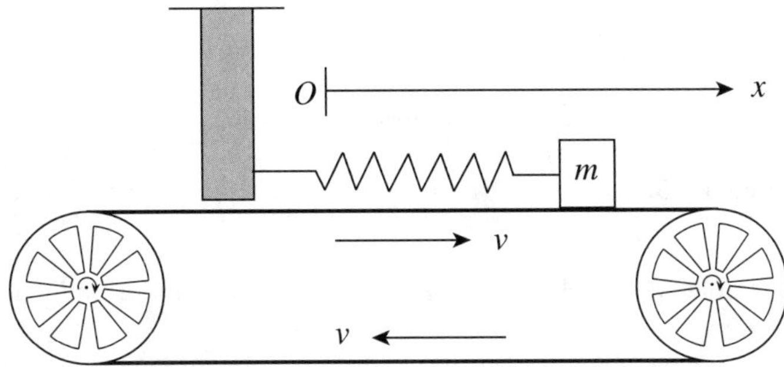

Figure 13.7: *A mass m attached to a spring and in contact with a moving belt.*

A rough belt moves at constant speed v between two wheels. A mass m rests on the belt and is connected by a spring to a fixed block, as illustrated in figure 13.7. The action of friction between the mass and the belt will be of the "dry" type. The motion of m will be horizontal, and the position of m will be given by the coordinate x, defined so that $x = 0$ when the spring is unstretched.

The motion can be qualitatively considered as follows. The mass will be carried to the right, remaining at the same place on the belt, until the tension in the spring is equal to the maximum force that can be balanced by the friction. At this point, the mass will start to return toward the block, executing part of an oscillation, until, on the "rebound," its speed matches that of the belt. Then it will come to rest relative to the belt and be carried forward once more.

The parallel with the violin bow moving across a string may now seem to be more reasonable. The bow has on its strings some rosin, which is rather hard and a bit sticky. Dependence of friction on relative speed is sketched in figure 13.8. An important characteristic is that the force becomes larger with small speeds, being greatest when the relative speed is zero. By contrast, the same function for a *waxed* bow is shown, demonstrating the utterly different characters of dry friction and linear damping. Try to persuade a violinist to show what happens if he puts wax on his bow (if you can afford to pay to have his bow re-haired). Notice that with different sorts of rosin, more or less

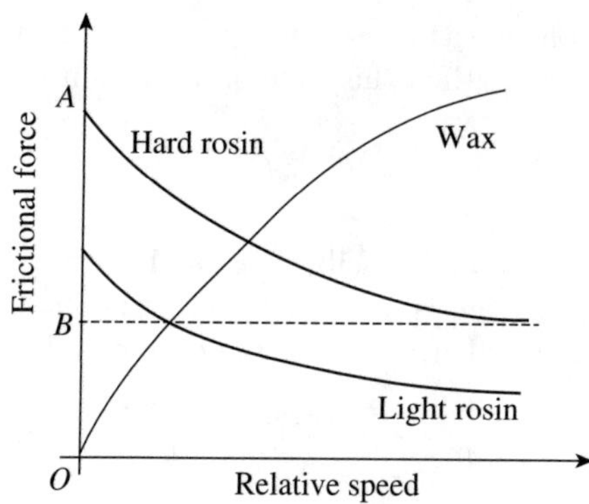

Figure 13.8: *The dependence of friction on relative speed.*

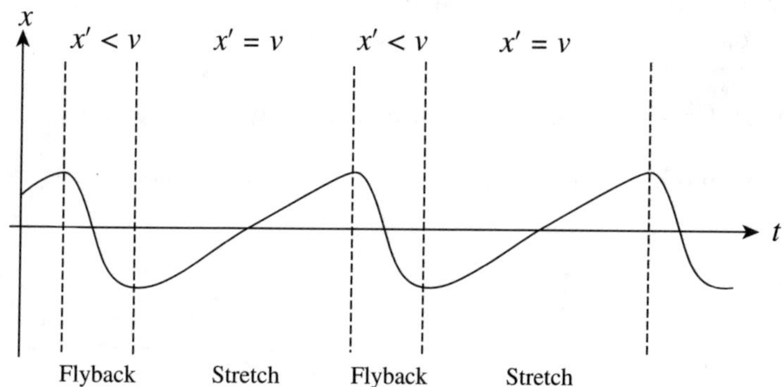

Figure 13.9: *Motion of the mass m with respect to the time.*

friction can be made possible. A sketch of what a solution for the model might look like is shown in figure 13.9.

Dry friction of this type has been used to model various phenomena, many of them unpleasant, like the screeching of chalk on a blackboard or the squealing of brakes. (If these should remind you of the violin, you have my pity!) But to learn more about this area, and the many ways in which science and music can combine, you should read the text *Fundamentals of Musical Acoustics* by A.H.Benade [10].

The first requirement for setting up a quantitative model is to define a formula for the frictional force. Our formula, considered in the fourth section of the chapter on pendulums, is the simplest function that has the basic properties required. Note that during the stretching, $\dot{x} = v$, since m moves with the belt, whereas during flyback, $\dot{x} < v$; we never have $\dot{x} > v$. So in figure 13.8 the horizontal argument is

$$z = v - \dot{x}. \tag{13.8.1}$$

The frictional force is

$$F(z) = \frac{A + Bz}{1 + z}. \tag{13.8.2}$$

For the computations I recommend that you choose simple values for the parameters; set the spring constant equal to one, for instance, and $m = 1$. The program must be divided into two stages. First,

Fly-back.

$$\left.\begin{aligned} \frac{d^2x}{dt^2} &= -x - F, \\ z &= v - \frac{dx}{dt}, \; z > 0, \\ F &= \frac{A + Bz}{1 + z}. \end{aligned}\right] \tag{13.8.3}$$

This part ends when the inequality for z is no longer true. So it is necessary to locate the time when $z = 0$. This will be discussed shortly. Then the second stage starts:

Stretch. z remains zero during the duration of the stretch, so that

$$\frac{dx}{dt} = v.$$

Stretching continues until the tension in the spring (for which I have assumed a spring constant equal to one) is equal to A, the greatest force that the friction can exert. This will happen when $x = A$. During the stretch no numerical integration is needed. Suppose that t_{start} and x_{start} are the values of t and x at the start of the stretch; then the values of the variables at the end of the stretch are

$$t = t_{\text{start}} + (A - x_{\text{start}})/v, \; x = A, \; \frac{dx}{dt} = v. \tag{13.8.4}$$

After these values are found, fly-back begins again.

Let us look at the problem of finding the value of t during fly-back for which $z = v - \dot{x} = 0$. At each step of the integration you should test for the sign of z; as soon as it becomes negative, start to use Newton's method to determine the stepsize. Suppose that the first value of t for which $z < 0$ is t_0. Then Newton's method generates a sequence $\{t_i\}$, $i = 1, 2, 3...$, where

$$t_{i+1} = t_i - z(t_i) \Big/ \left(\frac{dz}{dt}\right)\Bigg|_{t_i}, \; i = 0, 1, 2, \ldots. \tag{13.8.5}$$

So the stepsize for an integration step is given by

$$t_{i+1} - t_i = \frac{z(t_i)}{\ddot{x}(t_i)} = -\frac{z(t_i)}{x(t_i) + F(t_i)}. \tag{13.8.6}$$

In transforming the second-order equation of the model into two first-order equations, suppose you introduce the variables

$$y_1 = x, \; y_2 = \frac{dx}{dt}. \tag{13.8.7}$$

The equations for the model become

$$\left.\begin{aligned} z &= v - y_2, \\ F &= \frac{A + Bz}{1 + z}, \\ \frac{dy_1}{dt} &= y_2, \\ \frac{dy_2}{dt} &= -y_1 - F. \end{aligned}\right] \tag{13.8.8}$$

If $z < 0$ after a step, then call a procedure that will find the time when $z = 0$, and then find the conditions for the start of the next fly-back. This might contain code similar to the following:

```
SaveStepSize = StepSize
Repeat
    z = v - y(2)
    F = (A+Bz)/(1+z)
    StepSize = - z/(y(1) + F)
    Step(...)
Until Abs(v - y(2)) < Eps
t = t + (A - y(1))/v
y(1) = A
y(2) = v
StepSize = SaveStepSize
```

The motion can be followed in the phase-plane or x can be plotted as a function of the time. Two parameters that you might vary in your experiments are the speed v of the bow across the string and the pressure of the bow on the string; this latter quantity can be varied by multiplying F in (13.8.2) by some factor. Does increasing the speed have the same effect as increasing the pressure? See what you think, and then check your conclusions with a violinist.

13.9 Landing an Airplane on an Aircraft Carrier

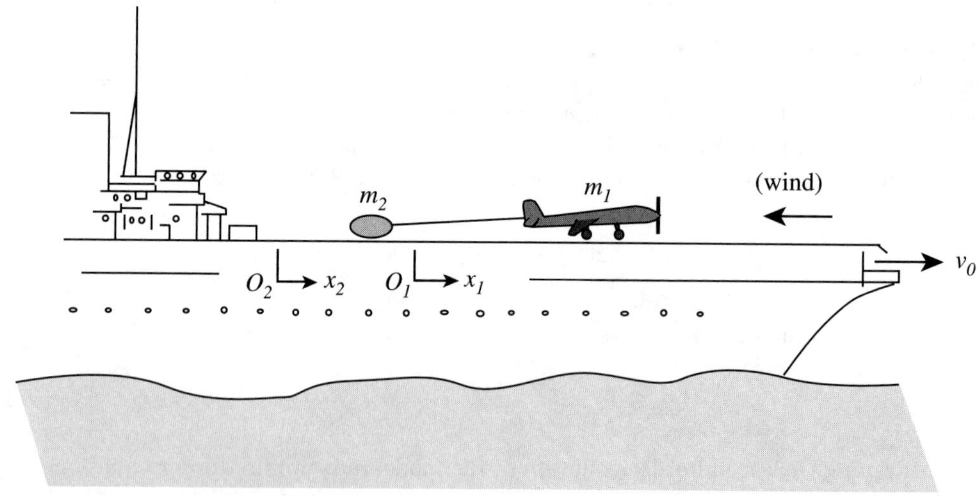

Figure 13.10: *Adapted from R.H.Cannon, Jr., Dynamics of Physical Systems. New York: McGraw-Hill Book Company, 1967.*

This model can be found in a text by R.H.Cannon [21].[2] We are referring to the early (the *very* early) days of flight. Immediately when an aircraft touched down on the deck of an aircraft carrier, a hook under its tail snared a wire connected to sandbags. The dragging of the sandbags along the deck then stopped the airplane. When you play with this model, you will be relieved to know that nowadays they use hydraulics.

In this model the motion is in one dimension only, and there is just one sandbag. The forces acting on the plane, which has mass m_1, are (1) drag from air resistance, proportional to the square of the relative speed between the plane and the air, and (2) the tension in the wire. The wire is

[2]R.H.Cannon, Jr., *Dynamics of Physical Systems.* New York: McGraw-Hill Book Company, 1967. With permission from McGraw-Hill Book Company.

assumed to be elastic, obeying Hooke's law with spring constant k. The forces on the sandbag, which has mass m_2, are (1) the tension in the wire, and (2) dry friction with the deck of the carrier.

We refer to figure 13.10. At the instant of landing, the sandbag is at O_2 and the hook on the airplane is at O_1, so the length O_1O_2 is the unstretched length of the wire. At later times, let the sandbag have coordinate x_2 relative to O_2, and the hook have coordinate x_1 relative to O_1. If $x_1 > x_2$, the wire is stretched and the tension is equal to $k(x_1 - x_2)$. Let the carrier have speed v_0 to the right and the wind have speed v_1 to the left, each of these being measured with respect to a fixed reference. Then the relative speed between the airplane and the air is $(\dot{x}_1 + v_0 + v_1)$, and the force of air resistance is $a(\dot{x}_1 + v_0 + v_1)^2$.

Three types of motion can take place in this model:

1. Stretching. The sandbag is at rest, and the tension, $k(x_1 - x_2)$, is less than the maximum possible force of dry friction between the sandbag and the deck: call this f. During this time,

$$\left.\begin{aligned} m_1\frac{d^2x_1}{dt^2} &= -a\left(\frac{dx_1}{dt} + v_0 + v_1\right)^2 - k(x_1 - x_2), \\ \frac{d^2x_2}{dt^2} &= \frac{dx_2}{dt} = 0. \end{aligned}\right] \tag{13.9.1}$$

This phase will end when $k(x_1 - x_2) = f$.

2. The wire is stretched and both bodies are moving. Then

$$\left.\begin{aligned} m_1\frac{d^2x_1}{dt^2} &= -a\left(\frac{dx_1}{dt} + v_0 + v_1\right)^2 - k(x_1 - x_2), \\ m_2\frac{d^2x_2}{dt^2} &= -f + k(x_1 - x_2), \quad x_1 > x_2. \end{aligned}\right] \tag{13.9.2}$$

Because $m_1 \gg m_2$, the acceleration of the sandbag will increase its speed until it exceeds that of the airplane. This phase ends when $x_1 = x_2$, after which the wire becomes slack.

3. The wire is slack, and the bodies move independently. Then

$$\left.\begin{aligned} m_1\frac{d^2x_1}{dt^2} &= -a\left(\frac{dx_1}{dt} + v_0 + v_1\right)^2, \\ m_2\frac{d^2x_2}{dt^2} &= -f, \quad x_1 < x_2. \end{aligned}\right] \tag{13.9.3}$$

This phase ends when $x_1 = x_2$. If the sandbag has come to rest, then the first phase is resumed; if it is still moving, then the second phase takes over.

Let's discuss possible code. Let

$$y_1 = x_1, \; y_2 = \frac{dx_1}{dt}, \; y_3 = x_2, \; y_4 = \frac{dx_2}{dt}. \tag{13.9.4}$$

Then equations (13.9.2) would become

$$\left.\begin{aligned} \frac{dy_1}{dt} &= y_2, \\ \frac{dy_2}{dt} &= \left[-a(y_2 + v_0 + v_1)^2 - k(y_1 - y_3)\right]/m_1, \\ \frac{dy_3}{dt} &= y_4, \\ \frac{dy_4}{dt} &= \left[-f + k(y_1 - y_2)\right]/m_2, \quad y_1 > y_3. \end{aligned}\right] \tag{13.9.5}$$

If the four right-hand sides of these equations are put into an array z_i, $i = 1..4$, then the following code might take care of phases 2 and 3:

```
If y(1) > y(3) Then Tension = 1 Else Tension = 0
z(1) = y(2)
z(2) = (- AirResistance(y(2) + AirSpeed)^2 -
    Tension*SpringConstant*(y(1) - y(3)))/AircraftMass
z(3) = y(4)
z(4) = (- Friction + Tension*SpringConstant*(y(1) - y(3)))/SandbagMass
```

To allow for the sandbag coming to rest requires care, since it is moving subject to a negative frictional force which should go to zero when the speed of the sandbag, or y_4, is zero. Take care that the program does not start to propel the sandbag *backwards*. One way to control this is to say that if y_4 is less than some small quantity (taken to be 0.01, below), then the sandbag has come to rest: then set y_4 and z_3 equal to zero. While $y_4 = 0$, $z_4 = 0$ until the tension in the wire builds up to exceed the friction; allowance is made for this in the pseudo code below.

```
If y(1) > y(3) Then Tension = 1 Else Tension = 0
z(1) = y(2)
z(2) = (- AirResistance(y(2) + AirSpeed)^2 -
    Tension*SpringConstant*(y(1) - y(3)))/AircraftMass
If y(4) < 0.01 Then
Begin
    y(4) = 0
    z(3) = 0
    z(4) = (- Friction + Tension*SpringConstant*(y(1) - y(3)))/SandbagMass
    If z(4) < 0 Then z(4) = 0
End
Else
Begin
    z(3) = y(4)
    z(4) = (- Friction + Tension*SpringConstant*(y(1) - y(3)))/SandbagMass
End
```

(My aim is to try to present the issues as clearly as possible, rather than to suggest optimal code.)

Cannon suggests the following numerical values:

$$\begin{aligned}
a &= 0.0363 \text{ lb}/(\text{ft}/\text{sec})^2, \\
f &= 200 \text{ lb}, \\
m_1 &= 3{,}000 \text{ lb}, \\
m_2 &= 400 \text{ lb}, \\
k &= 40{,}000 \text{ lb}/\text{ft}, \\
v_0 &= 24 \text{ knots} = 40.6 \text{ ft}/\text{sec}, \\
v_1 &= 9 \text{ knots},
\end{aligned}$$

and the initial speed of the airplane relative to the air as 48 knots. Remember that mass is weight/g, where $g = 32$ ft/sec^2.

If you are printing output, include information about which phase is currently active. There are a lot of parameters to vary; it is best to consider one at a time. For instance, how does the stopping distance depend on the initial speed?

13.10 A Pendulum with Sprung Pivot

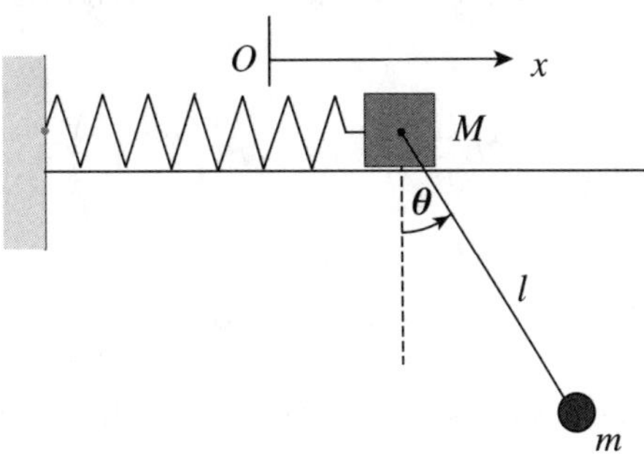

Figure 13.11: *A pendulum with pivot in a horizontal spring.*

This model was suggested as a means of investigating a simple pendulum with an unsteady pivot. A block with mass M moves, without friction, on a horizontal plane. It is attached to a spring, with spring constant k. Its displacement, x, is measured from the position, O, of the end of the unstretched spring. The pivot of a pendulum is attached to the block. The pendulum has length l, and has a mass m attached to its end. It makes an angle θ with the downward vertical. The system is free to move in a fixed vertical plane. See figure 13.11

The coordinates of m are $(x + l\sin\theta,\ -l\cos\theta)$, so the kinetic energy of the system is T where

$$2T = M\left(\frac{dx}{dt}\right)^2 + m\left(\frac{dx}{dt} + l\cos\theta\frac{d\theta}{dt}\right)^2 + m\left(l\frac{d\theta}{dt}\sin\theta\right)^2,$$

and the potential energy is

$$V = \frac{1}{2}kx^2 - mgl\cos\theta.$$

The Lagrangian is

$$L = \frac{1}{2}M\left(\frac{dx}{dt}\right)^2 + \frac{1}{2}m\left(\left(\frac{dx}{dt}\right)^2 + 2l\frac{dx}{dt}\frac{d\theta}{dt}\cos\theta + l^2\left(\frac{d\theta}{dt}\right)^2\right) - \frac{1}{2}kx^2 + mgl\cos\theta. \qquad (13.10.1)$$

Let $\mu = \dfrac{m}{M+m}$ and $K = \dfrac{k}{M+m}$. Then the equations of motion can be written as

$$\left.\begin{aligned} l\frac{d^2\theta}{dt^2} + \frac{d^2x}{dt^2}\cos\theta &= -g\sin\theta, \\ \frac{d^2x}{dt^2} + \mu l\frac{d^2\theta}{dt^2}\cos\theta &= \mu l\left(\frac{d\theta}{dt}\right)^2\sin\theta - Kx. \end{aligned}\right] \qquad (13.10.2)$$

These equations must be solved for the accelerations $\ddot{x}$ and $\ddot{\theta}$ to give

$$\left.\begin{aligned} \frac{d^2x}{dt^2} &= \left(\mu l\left(\frac{d\theta}{dt}\right)^2\sin\theta + \mu g\sin\theta\cos\theta - Kx\right)\Big/(1-\mu\cos^2\theta), \\ \frac{d^2\theta}{dt^2} &= \left(-\mu\left(\frac{d\theta}{dt}\right)^2\sin\theta\cos\theta + K\frac{x\cos\theta}{l} - \frac{g\sin\theta}{l}\right)\Big/(1-\mu\cos^2\theta). \end{aligned}\right] \qquad (13.10.3)$$

The animated motion for this model can be very entertaining. Results can be especially rewarding if the frequencies of the spring and pendulum are comparable. The motion can be chaotic. One way to construct a Poincaré map is to find times when $\dot{x} = 0$ and then plot $(\theta,\ \dot{\theta})$. The expression for the conservation of energy is

$$h = \frac{1}{2}M\left(\frac{dx}{dt}\right)^2 + \frac{1}{2}m\left(\left(\frac{dx}{dt}\right)^2 + 2l\frac{dx}{dt}\frac{d\theta}{dt}\cos\theta + l^2\left(\frac{d\theta}{dt}\right)^2\right) + \frac{1}{2}kx^2 - mgl\cos\theta. \tag{13.10.4}$$

So

$$h - \frac{1}{2}kx^2 + mgl\cos\theta \geq 0. \tag{13.10.5}$$

Pick a value for h. Then choose values of θ and $\dot{\theta}$, set $\dot{x} = 0$ and use equation (13.10.4) to solve for x, choosing $x > 0$.

13.11 A Spring Pendulum

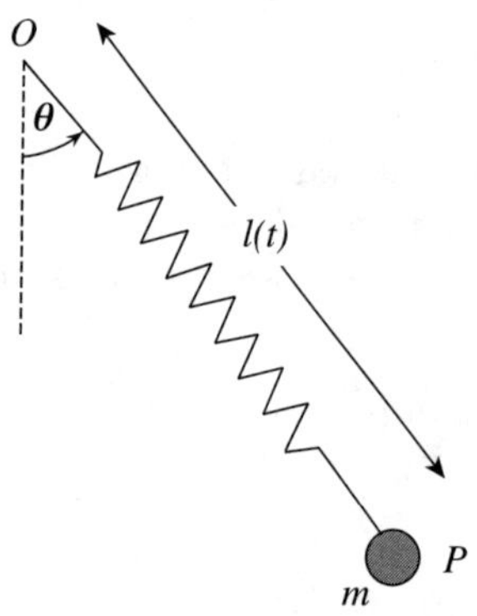

Figure 13.12: *A spring pendulum.*

In this model the light rod of the simple pendulum is replaced by a light spring. This has unstretched length l_0 and the tension in the spring obeys Hooke's law, with spring constant k. The mass m is attached to one end of the spring; the other end is attached to a fixed point of suspension, O. During the motion, which takes place in a vertical plane, the spring remains straight. At any time t let the pendulum have length $l(t)$, and let it make an angle θ with the downward vertical. See figure 13.12. The tension in the spring is $k(l(t) - l_0)$. Resolving the forces and accelerations along and perpendicular to the spring, we have

$$\left.\begin{aligned} m\frac{d^2l}{dt^2} &= ml\left(\frac{d\theta}{dt}\right)^2 + mg\cos\theta - k(l - l_0), \\ ml^2\frac{d^2\theta}{dt^2} + 2ml\frac{dl}{dt}\frac{d\theta}{dt} &= -mgl\sin\theta. \end{aligned}\right] \tag{13.11.1}$$

(See Appendix A for a derivation of these equations using Lagrangian mechanics.)

There are two "natural frequencies" in the model. $\omega_1 = \sqrt{g/l_0}$ corresponds to the pendulum without the spring, and $\omega_2 = \sqrt{k/m}$ corresponds to the spring without the pendulum. The vibrations in l and θ can exchange energies in interesting ways, and this can be especially noticeable if the ratio ω_1/ω_2 is close to a rational number like 1, 2 or 1/2. Then we can observe phenomena arising from conditions close to resonance. For instance, the motion might be started by pulling the spring down (with just the smallest sideways displacement). Then a swinging motion will start to develop at the expense of the spring oscillations, which might almost stop. Then the swinging diminishes, and the spring oscillations increase again, and so on.

For numerical integration, the system (13.11.1) must be expressed as a system of four first-order differential equations. Let

$$y_1 = l,\ y_2 = \frac{dl}{dt},\ y_3 = \theta,\ y_4 = \frac{d\theta}{dt}. \tag{13.11.2}$$

Then

$$\left.\begin{aligned} \frac{dy_1}{dt} &= y_2, \\ \frac{dy_2}{dt} &= y_1 y_4^2 + g\cos y_3 - \frac{k}{m}(y_1 - l_0), \\ \frac{dy_3}{dt} &= y_4, \\ \frac{dy_4}{dt} &= -2\frac{y_2 y_4}{y_1} - g\frac{\sin y_3}{y_1}. \end{aligned}\right] \tag{13.11.3}$$

With the system at rest, $y_1 = l = l_0 + mg/k$, with the other variables zero. You might set $g = 1$ and $l_0 = 1$ and treat k/m as a parameter. Start with small differences from the stable equilibrium. Vary k/m to see what effect resonance may have. Stop the integration if $l(t)$ becomes too small.

With two degrees of freedom, just one phase-plane diagram will not tell the whole story of the motion. But you might consider having two: one for y_1 and y_2, and one for y_3 and y_4, running at the same time. Or plot, simultaneously, l and θ, each as a function of the time.

The integral for the conservation of energy can be written as

$$\dot{l}^2 + l^2\dot{\theta}^2 - 2gl\cos\theta + (k/m)(l - l_0)^2 = h. \tag{13.11.4}$$

So

$$\dot{l}^2 + l^2\dot{\theta}^2 = 2gl\cos\theta - (k/m)(l - l_0)^2 + h \geq 0. \tag{13.11.5}$$

Then

$$2gl\cos\theta - (k/m)(l - l_0)^2 + h = 0 \tag{13.11.6}$$

provides a boundary for the motion as it is observed in the polar coordinates l and θ. Try plotting the locus of the mass at P to confirm this.

You will soon see that the model is chaotic. So the properties of the model can be investigated by calculating Poincaré maps. For instance, you might plot values of l and $\dot{l}$ whenever $\sin\theta = 0$.

First, select numerical values for g, l_0 and k/m. Pick a value for the energy, h; you may need trial and error to find a value large enough. For this value of h, run solutions with different initial conditions. Each time, start with numerical values of l, $\dot{l}$, with $\theta = 0$; substitute into equation (13.11.4) and solve for $\dot{\theta}^2$; if this is negative, try different l and $\dot{l}$; otherwise, take the positive square root to find $\dot{\theta}$. Integrate the orbit, plotting l and $\dot{l}$ whenever $\sin\theta = 0$.

Repeat for a new value of h. As h is increased, look for patterns of changing chaos.

Figures 13.13(a) and (b) show maps for $h = 0$ and 4. The length l and its rate of change, $\dot{l}$, are recorded when $\sin\theta = 0$. For numerical values, $k/m = 10$, $l_0 = 1$ and $g = 9.81$. Values of h are 0 for figure 13.13(a) and 4 for figure 13.13(b). The chaotic outer points were generated by just one starting condition. Notice that even in the chaotic regions there are isolated oases of non-chaos.

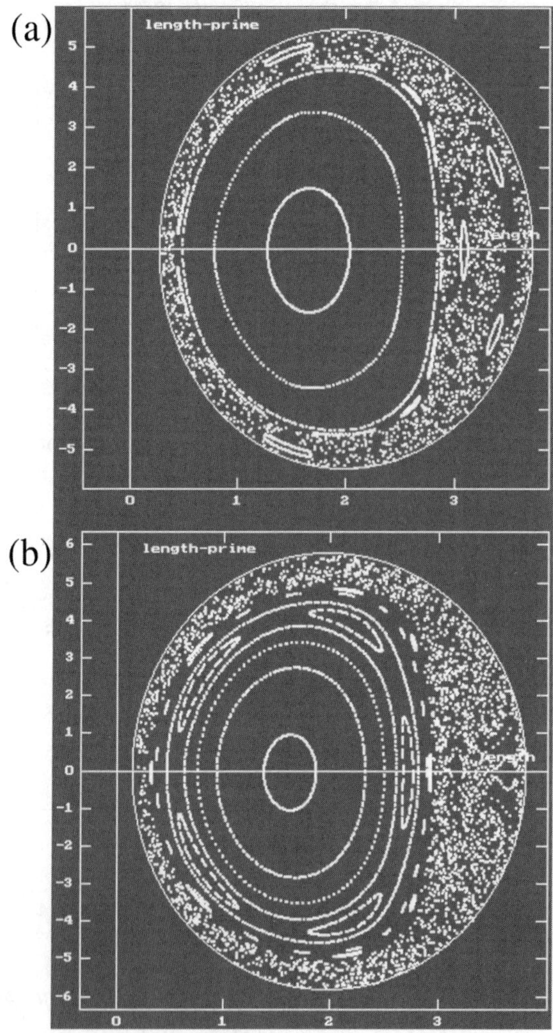

Figure 13.13: *The pendulum has length l and makes the angle θ with the downward vertical. The rates of change of these quantities are $\dot{l}$ and $\dot{\theta}$ There is an equation expressing the conservation of energy of the form $f(l, \theta, \dot{l}, \dot{\theta}) = h$, a constant. To investigate the motion, using the method of Poincaré maps, we calculate several solutions, each having the same value of h. Following each solution, we find configurations when the pendulum is vertical. At each of these points we record the values of l and $\dot{l}$, and plot them in the l-$\dot{l}$ plane: in (a), with $h = 0$, and (b), with $h = 4$. In each case the chaotic outer points were generated by just one starting condition. Notice that even in the chaotic regions there appear to be isolated oases of non-chaotic motion.*

13.12 A Chaotic Driven Wheel

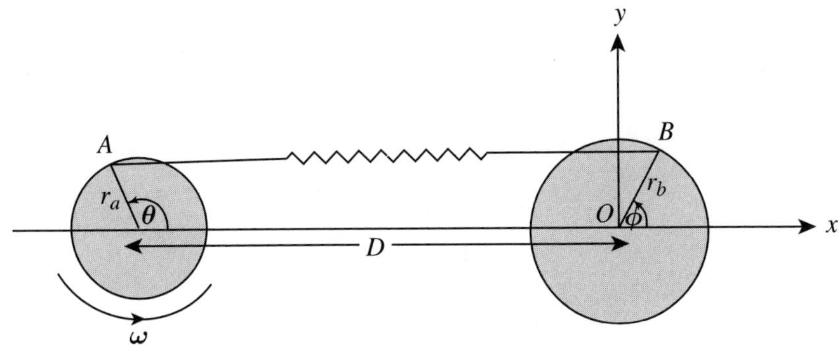

Figure 13.14: *The wheel on the left turns at a constant rate, ω.*

I first saw this model at an exhibition showing simply constructed models for physics demonstrations. It looks good in animation on a computer: even better, construct it yourself! It is shown in figure 13.14. The wheel on the left, with radius r_A rotates at a constant angular rate ω. A second wheel has radius r_B; the distance between the centers of the wheels is D. A and B are points on the circumferences of the wheels, and are attached to opposite ends of a spring. With suitable conditions, the motion of the second wheel is chaotic.

Let the origin be at the center of the second wheel, as shown, with the center of the first wheel at $x = -D$. Let the radii to A and B make angles θ and ϕ, respectively, with the x-axis. Then coordinates of A and B are

$$x_A = -D + r_A \cos\theta,\ y_A = r_A \sin\theta,\ \text{and}\ x_B = r_B \cos\phi,\ y_B = r_B \sin\phi.$$

Then

$$AB = \left(r_A^2 + r_B^2 + D^2 + 2D(-r_A\cos\theta + r_B\cos\phi) - 2r_Ar_B\cos(\theta-\phi)\right)^{1/2}. \tag{13.12.1}$$

Let the unstretched length of the spring be l_0, where $l_0 < D - r_A - r_B$, so that the spring is always in tension. If the spring constant is k, the potential energy of the stretched spring is

$$V = \frac{1}{2}k(AB - l_0)^2. \tag{13.12.2}$$

Then the Lagrangian for the system is

$$L = \frac{1}{2}I\dot{\phi}^2 - \frac{1}{2}k(AB - l_0)^2, \tag{13.12.3}$$

where I is the moment of inertia of the second wheel about its axis. Lagrange's equation follows as

$$I\frac{d^2\phi}{dt^2} = -k(AB - l_0)\frac{-Dr_B\sin\phi - r_Ar_B\sin(\theta-\phi)}{AB}, \quad \text{where}\ \ \theta = \omega t. \tag{13.12.4}$$

Friction can be included by adding a term proportional to $\dot{\phi}$, giving

$$I\frac{d^2\phi}{dt^2} = -k(AB - l_0)\frac{-Dr_B\sin\phi - r_Ar_B\sin(\theta-\phi)}{AB} - f\frac{d\phi}{dt}. \tag{13.12.5}$$

This model can be played with using any of the methods for the forced pendulum, which, in many ways, it resembles. There are many more parameters to be considered, but it is best to experiment by varying one only — the spring constant, k, for instance, or ω.

Chapter 14

Chemical and other Reacting Systems

14.1 The Decomposition of a Molecule

Suppose that the number of "normal" molecules of a particular kind is a molecules per unit volume. Let the number of "activated" molecules be b per unit volume. Activation depends on collisions between normal molecules, so the rate of activation is proportional to a^2. Deactivation is proportional to the product ab since it involves collisions between normal and activated molecules. Then

$$\frac{da}{dt} = -ka^2 + rab. \tag{14.1.1}$$

The activated molecules dissociate at a rate proportional to b, so

$$\frac{db}{dt} = ka^2 - rab - db. \tag{14.1.2}$$

Investigate these equations. For instance, take

$$k = 0.2, \quad r = 0.1.$$

See what happens when $d = 0$; investigate equilibria. Let $a = 1$ and $b = 0$ initially; then introduce small nonzero d.

14.2 Enzyme Kinetics

In a typical enzyme reaction, we start with an enzyme E and a "substrate" S. ρ molecules of S combine reversibly with one molecule of E to form a "complex," $E.S$. This complex then irreversibly produces a "product" P, an enzyme E, and some other stuff. The reaction is illustrated in figure 14.1. In more sophisticated notation, it is written as

$$\rho S + E \underset{k_-}{\overset{k_+}{\rightleftharpoons}} E.S \xrightarrow{k_2} P + E. \tag{14.2.1}$$

Let $[S]$ denote the concentration of S (the quantity per unit volume); the same notation will apply to the other molecules. The first reaction rate will be proportional to the product of the quantity E that is present and the quantity of S that is present counted ρ times. The constant of proportionality is k_{+1}. The reverse reaction will depend on the amount of $E.S$ that is present, with a constant of proportionality k_{-1}. The resulting differential equation is

$$\frac{d[S]}{dt} = -k_{+1}[E][S]^\rho + \rho k_{-1}[E.S]. \tag{14.2.2}$$

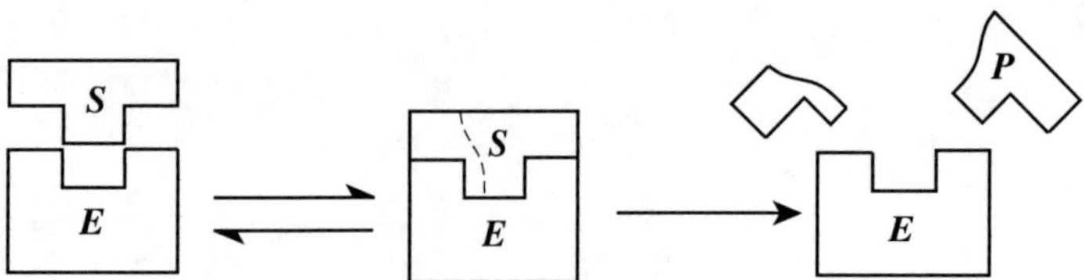

Figure 14.1: *Schematic of an enzyme reaction.*

In the final reaction the rate is k_2. This leads to the equations

$$\frac{d[E]}{dt} = -k_{+1}[E][S]^\rho + k_{-1}[E.S] + k_2[E.S], \tag{14.2.3}$$

$$\frac{d[E.S]}{dt} = k_{+1}[E][S]^\rho - (k_{-1} + k_2)[E.S] = -\frac{d[E]}{dt}, \tag{14.2.4}$$

$$\frac{d[P]}{dt} = k_2[E.S]. \tag{14.2.5}$$

From these we find that

$$S_T = [S] + \rho[E.S] + \rho[P] = \text{constant}, \tag{14.2.6}$$

and

$$E_T = [E] + [E.S] = \text{constant}. \tag{14.2.7}$$

With advantage taken of (14.2.6) and (14.2.7), the system can be reduced to two first-order differential equations. Let

$$x = [P] \quad \text{and} \quad y = [E.S]. \tag{14.2.8}$$

Then

$$\left.\begin{aligned} \frac{dx}{dt} &= k_2 y, \\ \frac{dy}{dt} &= k_{+1}(E_T - y)(S_T - \rho x - \rho y)^\rho - (k_{-1} + k_2)y. \end{aligned}\right] \tag{14.2.9}$$

Two approximations are associated with this reaction. For the *Briggs-Haldane* approximation, it is assumed that after a short while the rate of formation of the complex is small compared with the changes in the concentrations of S and P. Then

$$\frac{dy}{dt} = \frac{d[E.S]}{dt} \approx 0. \tag{14.2.10}$$

Putting $dy/dt = 0$ into the equations, we find that

$$0 = k_{+1}\left(E_T - [E.S]\right)[S]^\rho - (k_{-1} + k_2)[E.S],$$

from which it follows that

$$[E.S] = \frac{E_T[S]^\rho}{K' + [S]^\rho}, \tag{14.2.11}$$

where

$$K' = \frac{k_{-1} + k_2}{k_{+1}}. \tag{14.2.12}$$

Also,

$$\frac{d[P]}{dt} = k_2 \frac{E_T[S]^\rho}{K' + [S]^\rho}. \tag{14.2.13}$$

For the *Michaelis-Menten* approximation, assume that the substrate molecules greatly outnumber the enzymes, so that $[S] \gg [E]$. Then $S_T \approx [S]$, so that $[S]$ is nearly constant. Neglecting the derivative of $[S]$ in (14.2.2), we have

$$0 = -k_{+1}\left(E_T - [E.S]\right)[S]^\rho + k_{-1}[E.S].$$

This equation corresponds to the equilibrium $E + \rho S \rightleftharpoons E.S$; so in this approximation it is also assumed that $k_2 \ll k_{-1}$. Solving for $[E.S]$, we have

$$[E.S] = \frac{E_T[S]^\rho}{K_1 + [S]^\rho}, \quad K_1 = \frac{k_{-1}}{k_{+1}}, \tag{14.2.14}$$

and so

$$\frac{d[P]}{dt} = k_2 \frac{E_T[S]^\rho}{K_1 + [S]^\rho}. \tag{14.2.15}$$

The purpose of this project is to solve the system (14.2.9) completely and to compare results with the approximations. I recommend that you take a rather academic approach to the equations, getting to know their properties and not worrying too much about numbers for realistic reactions.

14.3 An Application of Enzyme Kinetics

Consider the following reactions:

$$\left.\begin{array}{l}
\text{DNA} + \text{NTP} \underset{k_{-1}}{\overset{k_{+1}}{\rightleftharpoons}} \text{DNA.NTP} \xrightarrow{k_2} \text{DNA} + m\text{RNA} \\
m\text{RNA} + \text{AA} \underset{k_{-3}}{\overset{k_{+3}}{\rightleftharpoons}} m\text{RNA.AA} \xrightarrow{k_4} m\text{RNA} + \text{protein} \\
\text{DNA} + \text{protein} \underset{k_{-5}}{\overset{k_{+5}}{\rightleftharpoons}} \text{DNA.protein}, \quad \text{which is inactive.}
\end{array}\right] \tag{14.3.1}$$

Assume that there are excess quantities of the substrates NTP and AA, so that their concentrations remain constant. Also assume that mRNA and the protein decay linearly, with rates d_1 and d_2, respectively. Let

$$g = [\text{DNA}],\ m = [m\text{RNA}],\ p = [\text{protein}],$$

$$c_a = [\text{DNA.NTP}],\ c_m = [m\text{RNA.AA}],\ c_i = [\text{DNA.protein}],$$

$$n_0 = [\text{NTP}] = \text{constant},\ a_0 = [\text{AA}] = \text{constant}.$$

Then

$$\left.\begin{aligned}
\frac{dg}{dt} &= -k_{+1} g n_0 + k_{-1} c_a + k_2 c_a + k_{-5} c_i - k_{+5} g p, \\
\frac{dm}{dt} &= k_2 c_a - k_{+3} m a_0 + k_{-3} c_m + k_4 c_m - d_1 m, \\
\frac{dp}{dt} &= k_4 c_m - k_{+5} g p + k_{-5} c_i - d_2 p, \\
\frac{dc_a}{dt} &= k_{+1} g n_0 - (k_{-1} + k_2) c_a, \\
\frac{dc_m}{dt} &= k_{+3} m a_0 - (k_{-3} + k_4) c_m, \\
\frac{dc_i}{dt} &= k_{+5} g p - k_{-5} c_i.
\end{aligned}\right] \tag{14.3.2}$$

From these we have the equation for the conservation of the total amount of DNA,

$$g_T = g + c_a + c_i = \text{constant}. \tag{14.3.3}$$

Assume steady states for the three complexes. Then the right-hand sides of the final three equations of (14.3.2) are set to zero. Solving them respectively for c_a, c_m and c_i gives

$$\left.\begin{aligned} c_a &= \frac{k_{+1}n_0}{k_{-1}+k_2}g = K_1 g, \\ c_m &= \frac{k_{+3}a_0}{k_{-3}+k_4}m = K_3 m, \\ c_i &= \frac{k_{+5}}{k_{-5}}gp = K_5 gp. \end{aligned}\right] \tag{14.3.4}$$

Then

$$g = \frac{g_T}{1 + K_1 + K_5 p}.$$

Finally, substitute into the equations for m and p to give

$$\left.\begin{aligned} \frac{dm}{dt} &= \frac{k_2 K_1 g_T}{1 + K_1 + K_5 p} - d_1 m, \\ \frac{dp}{dt} &= k_4 K_3 m - d_2 p. \end{aligned}\right] \tag{14.3.5}$$

These equations can be written in the simpler form

$$\left.\begin{aligned} \frac{dm}{dt} &= \frac{a}{1 + kp} - d_1 m, \\ \frac{dp}{dt} &= bm - d_2 p. \end{aligned}\right] \tag{14.3.6}$$

Equations (14.3.6) are the equations to be investigated. Show that there is one equilibrium. Investigate its stability. Calculate solutions starting close to it, and also further away.

If the final stage of (14.3.1) is modified so that ρ proteins combine with DNA to produce the inactive complex, then equations (14.3.6) become

$$\left.\begin{aligned} \frac{dm}{dt} &= \frac{a}{1 + kp^{\rho}} - d_1 m, \\ \frac{dp}{dt} &= bm - d_2 p. \end{aligned}\right] \tag{14.3.7}$$

Try an analysis for this system similar to the one given for equations (14.3.6). Note that by suitably rescaling the variables m, p and t, equations (14.3.7) can be written as

$$\left.\begin{aligned} \frac{dM}{d\tau} &= \frac{1}{1 + P^{\rho}} - AM, \\ \frac{dP}{d\tau} &= M - BP. \end{aligned}\right] \tag{14.3.8}$$

14.4 More Enzyme Kinetics

A more interesting system than those so far presented is derived as follows. Consider

$$\left.\begin{array}{l}
\text{DNA} + \text{NTP} \underset{k_{-1}}{\overset{k_{+1}}{\rightleftharpoons}} \text{DNA.NTP} \xrightarrow{k_2} \text{DNA} + m\text{RNA}, \\
m\text{RNA} + \text{AA} \underset{k_{-3}}{\overset{k_{+3}}{\rightleftharpoons}} m\text{RNA.AA} \xrightarrow{k_4} m\text{RNA} + \text{E}, \\
\text{E} + \text{L} \underset{k_{-5}}{\overset{k_{+5}}{\rightleftharpoons}} \text{E.L} \xrightarrow{k_6} \text{E} + \text{P}, \\
\text{DNA} + \rho\text{P} \underset{k_{-7}}{\overset{k_{+7}}{\rightleftharpoons}} \text{DNA.P}, \quad \text{which is inactive.}
\end{array}\right] \tag{14.4.1}$$

Assume that there are excess quantities of the substrates NTP, AA, and L, so that

$$[\text{NTP}] = n_0, \ \text{AA} = a_0. \ [\text{L}] = l_0 \tag{14.4.2}$$

are all constant. Also assume that mRNA, the protein P and the enzyme E decay linearly. Let

$$\left.\begin{array}{c}
g = [\text{DNA}], \ m = [m\text{RNA}], \ e = [\text{E}], \ p = [\text{P}], \\
c_1 = [\text{DNA.NTP}], \ c_2 = [m\text{RNA.AA}], \ c_3 = [\text{E.L}] \\
\text{and} \\
c_4 = [\text{DNA.P}].
\end{array}\right] \tag{14.4.3}$$

Then

$$\left.\begin{array}{rcl}
\dfrac{dg}{dt} &=& -k_{+1}gn_0 + (k_{-1} + k_2)c_1 + k_{-7}c_4 - k_{+7}gp^{\rho}, \\
\dfrac{dm}{dt} &=& k_2c_1 - k_{+3}ma_0 + (k_{-3} + k_4)c_2 - d_1m, \\
\dfrac{de}{dt} &=& k_4c_2 - k_{+5}el_0 + (k_{-5} + k_6)c_3 - d_2e, \\
\dfrac{dp}{dt} &=& k_6c_3 + \rho k_{-7}c_4 - \rho k_{+7}gp^{\rho} - d_3p, \\
\dfrac{dc_1}{dt} &=& k_{+1}gn_0 - (k_{-1} + k_2)c_1, \\
\dfrac{dc_2}{dt} &=& k_{+3}ma_0 - (k_{-3} + k_4)c_2, \\
\dfrac{dc_3}{dt} &=& k_{+5}el_0 - (k_{-5} + k_6)c_3, \\
\dfrac{dc_4}{dt} &=& k_{+7}gp^{\rho} - k_{-7}c_4.
\end{array}\right] \tag{14.4.4}$$

d_i are decay rates. The total amount of DNA is conserved, so that

$$g_T = g + c_1 + c_4 = \text{constant}. \tag{14.4.5}$$

Assuming steady states for the complexes, the system can be written as

$$\left.\begin{aligned} \frac{dm}{dt} &= k_2c_1 - d_1m, \\ \frac{de}{dt} &= k_4c_2 - d_2e, \\ \frac{dp}{dt} &= k_6c_3 - d_3p, \\ c_1 &= \frac{k_{+1}}{k_{-1}+k_2}gn_0 = K_1gn_0, \\ c_2 &= \frac{k_{+3}}{k_{-3}+k_4}ma_0 = K_2ma_0, \\ c_3 &= \frac{k_{+5}}{k_{-5}+k_6}el_0 = K_3el_0, \\ c_4 &= \frac{k_{+7}}{k_{-7}}gp^\rho = K_4gp^\rho, \\ g &= \frac{g_T}{1+K_1n_0+K_4p^\rho}. \end{aligned}\right] \tag{14.4.6}$$

The system can now be reduced to the three differential equations

$$\left.\begin{aligned} \frac{dm}{dt} &= \frac{k_2K_1n_0g_T}{1+K_1n_0+K_4p^\rho} - d_1m, \\ \frac{de}{dt} &= k_4K_2a_0m - d_2e, \\ \frac{dp}{dt} &= k_6K_3el_0 - d_3p. \end{aligned}\right] \tag{14.4.7}$$

These are the equations of the model. They can be written more simply as

$$\left.\begin{aligned} \frac{dm}{dt} &= \frac{a_1}{1+kp^\rho} - d_1m, \\ \frac{de}{dt} &= a_2m - d_2e, \\ \frac{dp}{dt} &= a_3e - d_3p. \end{aligned}\right] \tag{14.4.8}$$

With rescaling, they can be further simplified to

$$\left.\begin{aligned} \frac{dM}{d\tau} &= \frac{1}{1+P^\rho} - D_1M, \\ \frac{dE}{d\tau} &= M - D_2E, \\ \frac{dP}{d\tau} &= E - D_3P. \end{aligned}\right] \tag{14.4.9}$$

There is always one equilibrium, given by

$$0 = \frac{1}{1+P^\rho} - D_1D_2D_3P. \tag{14.4.10}$$

For low values of ρ, which must be an integer, this equilibrium is unstable; but it becomes stable for higher values. Investigate this situation numerically. Plot M, E and P as functions of the time.

14.5 Still More Enzyme Kinetics

Consider the reactions

$$\left.\begin{array}{l}\mathrm{DNA.P} + \mathrm{NTP} \underset{k_{-1}}{\overset{k_{+1}}{\rightleftharpoons}} \mathrm{DNA.P.NTP} \xrightarrow{k_2} \mathrm{DNA.P} + m\mathrm{RNA}, \\ m\mathrm{RNA} + \mathrm{AA} \underset{k_{-3}}{\overset{k_{+3}}{\rightleftharpoons}} m\mathrm{RNA.AA} \xrightarrow{k_4} m\mathrm{RNA} + \mathrm{E}, \\ \mathrm{E} + \mathrm{L} \underset{k_{-5}}{\overset{k_{+5}}{\rightleftharpoons}} \mathrm{E.L} \xrightarrow{k_6} \mathrm{E} + \mathrm{P}, \\ \mathrm{DNA} + \rho\mathrm{P} \underset{k_{-7}}{\overset{k_{+7}}{\rightleftharpoons}} \mathrm{DNA.P.} \end{array}\right] \tag{14.5.1}$$

Assume that there are excess quantities of the substrates NTP, AA, and L, so that

$$[\mathrm{NTP}] = n_0, \ \ \mathrm{AA} = a_0, \text{ and } [\mathrm{L}] = l_0 \tag{14.5.2}$$

are all constant. Also assume that mRNA, the protein P and the enzyme E decay linearly. Let

$$\left.\begin{array}{r}g = [\mathrm{DNA}], \ h = [\mathrm{DNA.P}], \ m = [m\mathrm{RNA}], \\ e = [\mathrm{E}], \ p = [\mathrm{P}], \ c_1 = [\mathrm{DNA.P.NTP}], \\ c_2 = [m\mathrm{RNA.AA}], \ c_3 = [\mathrm{E.L}]. \end{array}\right] \tag{14.5.3}$$

Then

$$\left.\begin{array}{rcl}\dfrac{dh}{dt} &=& -k_{+1}hn_0 + (k_{-1} + k_2)c_1 - k_{-7}h + k_{+7}gp^\rho, \\ \dfrac{dm}{dt} &=& k_2c_1 - k_{+3}ma_0 + (k_{-3} + k_4)c_2 - d_1m, \\ \dfrac{de}{dt} &=& k_4c_2 - k_{+5}el_0 + (k_{-5} + k_6)c_3 - d_2e, \\ \dfrac{dp}{dt} &=& k_6c_3 + \rho k_{-7}h - k_{+7}\rho gp^\rho - d_3p, \\ \dfrac{dg}{dt} &=& -k_{+7}gp^\rho + k_{-7}h, \\ \dfrac{dc_1}{dt} &=& k_{+1}hn_0 - (k_{-1} + k_2)c_1, \\ \dfrac{dc_2}{dt} &=& k_{+3}ma_0 - (k_{-3} + k_4)c_2, \\ \dfrac{dc_3}{dt} &=& k_{+5}el_0 - (k_{-5} + k_6)c_3. \end{array}\right] \tag{14.5.4}$$

The d_i are decay rates. The total amount of DNA is conserved, so that

$$g_T = g + h + c_1 = \text{constant}. \tag{14.5.5}$$

Again, we assume a steady state for the complexes, so the time derivatives of c_1, c_2, c_3, and g are put equal to zero. Then

$$\left.\begin{aligned}
\frac{dm}{dt} &= k_2c_1 - d_1m,\\
\frac{de}{dt} &= k_4c_2 - d_2e,\\
\frac{dp}{dt} &= k_6c_3 - d_3p,\\
h &= \frac{k_{+7}}{k_{-7}}gp^\rho = K_1gp^\rho,\\
c_1 &= \frac{k_{+1}}{k_{-1}+k_2}n_0h = K_2n_0h = K_2n_0K_1gp^\rho,\\
c_2 &= \frac{k_{+3}}{k_{-3}+k_4}a_0m = K_3a_0m,\\
c_3 &= \frac{k_{+5}}{k_{-5}+k_6}l_0e = K_4l_0e.
\end{aligned}\right] \tag{14.5.6}$$

So

$$\begin{aligned}
g_T &= g + K_1gp^\rho + K_1K_2n_0gp^\rho\\
&= g\,(1 + (K_1 + K_1K_2n_0)p^\rho)\\
&= g(1 + Kp^\rho).
\end{aligned} \tag{14.5.7}$$

Now we can write the three differential equations

$$\left.\begin{aligned}
\frac{dm}{dt} &= k_2K_1K_2n_0g_T\frac{p^\rho}{1+Kp^\rho} - d_1m,\\
\frac{de}{dt} &= k_4K_3a_0m - d_2e,\\
\frac{dp}{dt} &= k_6K_4l_0e - d_3p.
\end{aligned}\right] \tag{14.5.8}$$

These can be written as

$$\left.\begin{aligned}
\frac{dm}{dt} &= \frac{a_1p^\rho}{1+Kp^\rho} - d_1m,\\
\frac{de}{dt} &= a_2m - d_2e,\\
\frac{dp}{dt} &= a_3e - d_3p.
\end{aligned}\right] \tag{14.5.9}$$

Once more, suitable rescaling can lead to simpler equations, such as

$$\left.\begin{aligned}
\frac{dM}{d\tau} &= \frac{P^\rho}{1+P^\rho} - D_1M,\\
\frac{dE}{d\tau} &= M - D_2E,\\
\frac{dP}{d\tau} &= E - D_3P.
\end{aligned}\right] \tag{14.5.10}$$

For equilibria,

$$D_1 D_2 D_3 P = DP = \frac{P^\rho}{1 + P^\rho}. \tag{14.5.11}$$

If $\rho = 1$, there is either one equilibrium (the origin) or two. Investigate their stability. For ρ greater than one, the graph of $y = P^\rho/(1 + P^\rho)$ is S-shaped, passing through the origin and asymptotic to $y = 1$. There may then be one equilibrium or three equilibria. Verify that for $\rho = 2$ there are three equilibria if D is less than $1/2$, and investigate their stability. (One is stable and two are unstable.) The case of $\rho = 2$ is illustrated in figure 14.2.

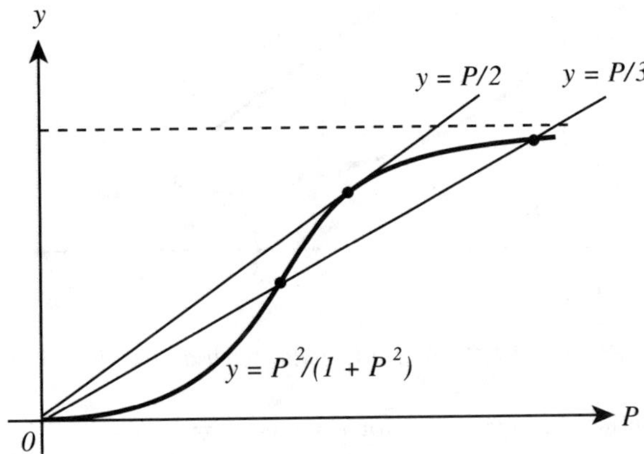

Figure 14.2: *Equilibria for the case* $\rho = 2$.

14.6 Limit Cycles in Chemical Reactions: The "Brusselator"

This model first appeared in a paper [80] by I.Prigogine (a Nobel Laureate) and R.Lefever in 1968. It is a model reaction, the chemical stages of which are given formally by

$$\left.\begin{array}{rcl} A & \longrightarrow & X + B, \\ X & \longrightarrow & Y + C, \\ 2X + Y & \longrightarrow & 3X + D, \\ X & \longrightarrow & E + F. \end{array}\right] \tag{14.6.1}$$

The chemicals X and Y are the ones of interest; A is assumed to have a fixed concentration, and the other products are inactive. If x and y are the concentrations of X and Y, then the differential equations for them follow according to the usual procedures, and they can be scaled to give the equations

$$\left.\begin{array}{rcl} \dfrac{dx}{dt} & = & a - (b + 1)x + x^2 y, \\ \dfrac{dy}{dt} & = & bx - x^2 y. \end{array}\right] \tag{14.6.2}$$

These are the equations of the model.

There is just one equilibrium point given by

$$x_e = a, \quad y_e = b/a. \tag{14.6.3}$$

A linear analysis shows that this point is unstable if $b > 1 + a^2$. Also, there is spiralling motion close to the equilibrium if

$$1 - a + a^2 < b < 1 + a + a^2. \tag{14.6.4}$$

I suggest that you fix the quantity a at, say, $a = 1$, and look at the results as b is varied. Start with b small, and then gradually increase it.

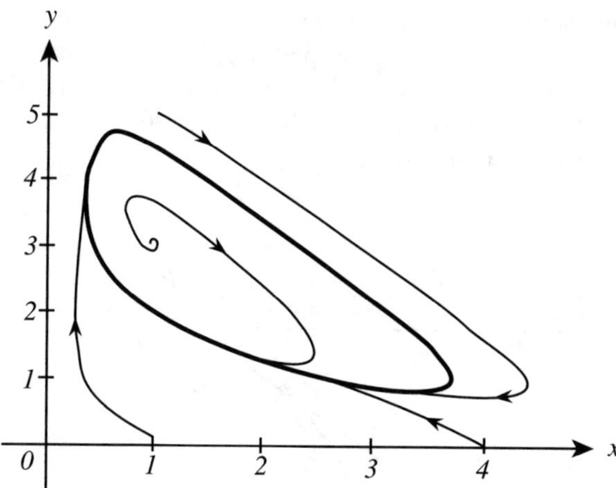

Figure 14.3: *A limit cycle, with* $a = 1,\ b = 3$.

Some solutions are shown in figure 14.3 for the case $a = 1,\ b = 3$. The equilibrium is unstable, but the solutions starting nearby spiral outward toward a stable limit cycle. This cycle is also the limit for solutions starting outside it. Find out to what extent this behavior depends on the value of b.

14.7 Limit Cycles in Chemical Reactions: The "Oregonator"

This model refers to an actual chemical reaction. An oscillatory chemical reaction was discovered in 1958 by B.P.Belousov and further developed in 1964 by A.M.Zhabotinskii. It involves cyclical changes in color and changes in spatial structure as well as in time. We consider oscillations in time in a model due to R.J.Field and R.M.Noyes [39] called the "Oregonator." Read it if possible, and don't omit a glance at the Acknowledgments. This model and the preceding one are discussed in several texts. See, for instance, the article by L.N.Howard [56].

The reactions and details of the model are complicated. Here only the barest details are mentioned, but they should be sufficient to set up the model. The variables that are followed in the oscillations are the concentrations of $HBrO^2$ (bromous acid), BR^- (bromide ion), and the cerium ion, Ce(IV). These concentrations are denoted by x, y and z, respectively. These are treated as products of the reaction and as reactants. Other substances are assumed to be supplied at constant concentrations when they are reactants, and to be inert when they are products. The model is made up of the five stages

$$\left.\begin{aligned} A+Y &\xrightarrow{k_1} X,\\ X+Y &\xrightarrow{k_2} P,\\ B+X &\xrightarrow{k_3} 2X+Z,\\ 2X &\xrightarrow{k_4} Q,\\ Z &\xrightarrow{k_5} Y. \end{aligned}\right] \tag{14.7.1}$$

From the law of mass action, we have

$$\left.\begin{aligned} \frac{dx}{dt} &= k_1 ay - k_2 xy + 2k_3 bx - 2k_4 x^2, \\ \frac{dy}{dt} &= -k_1 ay - k_2 xy + k_5 z, \\ \frac{dz}{dt} &= k_3 bx - k_5 z. \end{aligned}\right] \qquad (14.7.2)$$

Numerical constants used in the cited paper were

$$\left.\begin{aligned} k_1 &= 1.34 \text{ M}^{-1} \text{ sec}^{-1}, \\ k_2 &= 1.6 \times 10^9 \text{ M}^{-1} \text{ sec}^{-1}, \\ k_3 &= 8 \times 10^3 \text{ M}^{-1} \text{ sec}^{-1}, \\ k_4 &= 4 \times 10^7 \text{ M}^{-1} \text{ sec}^{-1}, \\ k_5 &= 1 \text{ sec}^{-1}. \end{aligned}\right]$$

The last of these is a parameter that can be varied, with differing effects on the model.

The variables can be made dimensionless by the transformations

$$\left.\begin{aligned} x &= (k_1 a/k_2)\alpha = 5.025 \times 10^{-11}\alpha, \\ y &= (k_3 b/k_2)\beta = 3.000 \times 10^{-7}\beta, \\ z &= (k_1 k_4 ab/k_2 k_3)\gamma = 2.412 \times 10^{-8}\gamma, \\ \text{time } t &= (k_1 k_3 ab)^{-1/2}\tau = 0.1610\tau. \end{aligned}\right] \qquad (14.7.3)$$

Then the equations become

$$\left.\begin{aligned} \frac{d\alpha}{d\tau} &= s(\beta - \alpha\beta + \alpha - q\alpha^2), \\ \frac{d\beta}{d\tau} &= s^{-1}(-\beta - \alpha\beta + \gamma), \\ \frac{d\gamma}{d\tau} &= \omega(\alpha - \gamma), \end{aligned}\right] \qquad (14.7.4)$$

where

$$\left.\begin{aligned} s &= (k_2 b/k_1 a)^{1/2} = 77.27, \\ w &= k_5 (k_1 k_3 ab)^{-1/2} = 0.1610, \\ q &= (2k_1 k_4 a)/(k_2 k_3 b) = 8.375 \times 10^{-6}. \end{aligned}\right]$$

There is an equilibrium for

$$\alpha_e = 488.68, \quad \beta_e = 0.99796.$$

Verify this.

Results of a numerical integration taken from [39] are shown in figure 14.4. You will find these results hard to reproduce: we have what is called a "stiff" system. There is a long stretch when α is close to one, and its derivative is close to zero. But β is large, and round-off error from β can corrupt the first equation of (14.7.4), leading to instability in the numerical part of the program. Special codes exist for stiff systems. Using a method with variable stepsize, and requiring high precision,

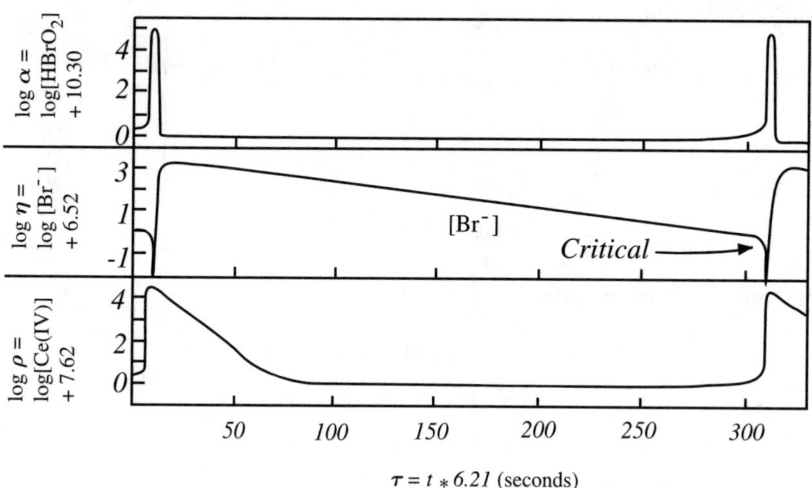

Figure 14.4: *Reproduced with permission from Field and Noyes, (1974), "Oscillations in Chemical Systems. IV. Limit cycle behavior in a model of a real chemical reaction," J. Chem. Phys, 60, 1877-1884 (1974), Figure 1. Reproduced with kind permission from the authors.*

see what you can do to reproduce these results. Notice that for a reasonable diagram you need to plot the logarithms of the variables.

Experiment with initial conditions close to the equilibrium. Since there are three dependent variables, you can choose any two for a phase-plane diagram. Look for the limit cycle.

It is stated in [39] that for k_5 above a certain value, oscillations are halted; also, when $k_5 = 0$, that y tends to zero and there are no oscillations. Can you confirm these results numerically?

Finally, for the system (14.7.4), conduct some investigations when the coefficients are not so disparate in magnitude.

14.8 Chemical-Tank-Reactor Stability

This project is based on an example given in *Applications of Undergraduate Mathematics in Engineering* by Ben Noble [75]. Put this book on your reading list.

A chemical C reacts in a tank of fixed volume V in the following way:

Flow rate = q Concentration = c_0 Temperature = T_0	in→	Volume V	out→	Flow rate = q Concentration = c Temperature = T

For the reactor, we have the following relation:

Rate of change of amount of C in the reactor	=	Rate at which C flows in	−	Rate at which C flows out	−	Rate at which C disappears due to the reaction

These can be written analytically as

$$\frac{d}{dt}(Vc) = qc_0 - qc - VK(T)c,$$

or

$$\frac{dc}{dt} = \frac{q}{V}(c_0 - c) - K(T)c. \tag{14.8.1}$$

By Arrhenius's law,

$$K(T) = Ae^{-B/T}. \qquad (14.8.2)$$

Also,

Rate of change of heat content	=	Heat brought in	−	Heat flowing out	−	Heat removed by cooling	+	Heat generated by the reaction

So

$$VC_p\frac{dT}{dt} = qC_pT_0 - qC_pT - VS(T) + HVK(T)c,$$

or

$$\frac{dT}{dt} = \frac{q}{V}(T_0 - T) - \frac{1}{C_p}S(T) + \frac{H}{C_p}K(T)c, \qquad (14.8.3)$$

where H is a constant and C_p is the constant specific heat.

The following formula and numerical values have been used in this project:

$$S(T) = C_p(T - TCOOL)(q/V), \qquad (14.8.4)$$

where $TCOOL$ is the temperature of the coolant. The time t is in minutes, c is in moles per unit volume, T is in °K, and q is in (minutes/unit volume)$^{-1}$.

	1	2	3	4
c(initial)	3.5	3.5	3.5	3.5
T(initial)	315	315	315	315
q	50	50	50	50
V	50	50	50	50
c_0	3.5	5	5	5
T_0	315	350	350	350
A	6.46	6.46	7.5	9
B	1,300	1,300	1,300	1,300
C_p	1.4	1.4	1.4	1.4
H	600	600	700	900
$TCOOL$	290	290	290	290

These give an interesting progression of results. Try them, and experiment further.

For further information and ideas, see the text *Elementary Chemical Reactor Analysis* by R.Aris[4].

14.9 Temperature and Volume Control in a Tank

I am indebted to my colleague, Dr. D.Marsland, for suggesting this project.[1] A vertical cylindrical tank with cross-section A in^2 is filled with water to a variable depth h in. The tank contains a heat source, and the water is assumed to be well stirred, so that the temperature T°F is uniform throughout the tank. The operation of the heat source and the depth of the water are subject to control.

The rate at which heat is supplied is a function of the temperature, and is $Q(T)$ kw. The rate at which water enters the tank, a function of the depth h, is $W_i(h)$ lb/min. The rate at which water leaves the tank is a prescribed function of the time, and is $W_o(t)$ lb/min.

[1] Dr. David Marsland is a member of the Chemical Engineering faculty at North Carolina State University.

If ρ is the density of the water, then

$$\frac{d}{dt}(\rho A h) = W_i(h) - W_o(t),$$

so

$$\rho A \frac{dh}{dt} = W_i(h) - W_o(t). \tag{14.9.1}$$

Let the entering water have the constant temperature T_i. Then if c is the heat capacity of the water and T_{ref} is some constant reference temperature, it follows that

$$\frac{d}{dt}\left[(\rho A h)c(T - T_{\text{ref}})\right] = W_i(h)c(T_i - T_{\text{ref}}) - W_o(t)c(T - T_{\text{ref}}) + Q(T). \tag{14.9.2}$$

The terms factored by T_{ref} cancel, by virtue of (14.9.1). Then

$$\rho A c \frac{d}{dt}(hT) = W_i(h)cT_i - W_o(t)cT + Q(T).$$

Differentiating the product, and using (14.9.1) for dh/dt, we have, finally,

$$\rho A c h \frac{dT}{dt} = W_i(h)c(T_i - T) + Q(T). \tag{14.9.3}$$

Equations (14.9.1) and (14.9.3) are the differential equations of the model.

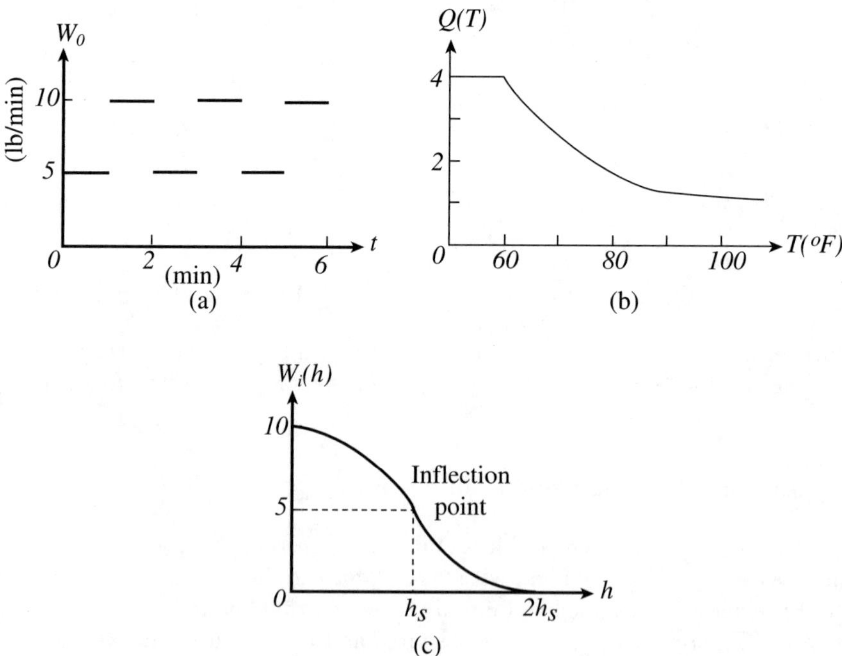

Figure 14.5: *Control functions for the model.*

The control functions of the model are graphed in figure 14.5. Possible analytical expressions for these functions are

$$Q(T) = \begin{bmatrix} 4, & T < 60, \\ \\ 1 + \dfrac{(T-90)^2}{300}, & 60 < T < 90, \\ \\ 1, & T > 90. \end{bmatrix} \qquad (14.9.4)$$

$$W_i(h) = \begin{bmatrix} 10 - 5(h/h_s)^2, & 0 < h < h_s, \\ \\ 5(2 - h/h_s)^2, & h_s < h < 2h_s. \end{bmatrix} \qquad (14.9.5)$$

For other numerical values, take $c = 1$ Btu/lbF, $\rho = 62$ lbm/ft^3. Try $A = 200$ in^2, $T_i = 60$°F, $h_s = 10$ in.

Find out how the system works. Find the equilibrium, and start with small deviations away from this. Then vary some of the numbers and controls. With the type of function involved in W_o, it will probably be best to use a constant stepsize for the integration; if possible, keep track of the estimated local truncation error, so that you can choose an effective stepsize.

14.10 The Dynamics of a Reservoir System

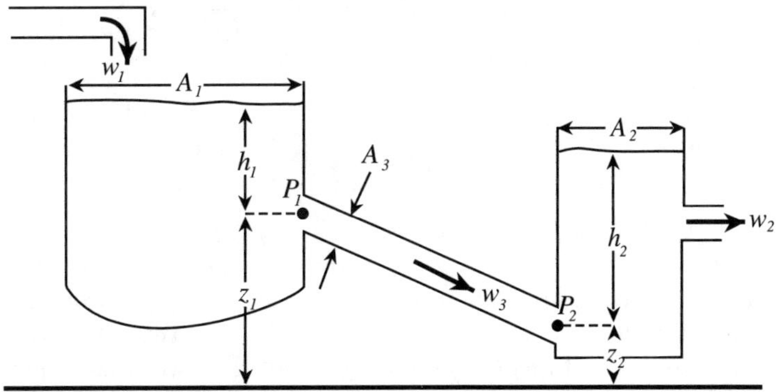

Figure 14.6: *A reservoir, connecting pipe and tank. Adapted from R.H.Cannon, Jr., Dynamics of Physical Systems. New York: McGraw-Hill Book Company, 1967.*

This project comes from the text by Cannon [21].[2] A reservoir is connected to a storage tank by a pipe, as illustrated in figure 14.6. The reservoir and tank are modeled by cylinders having cross-sectional areas A_1 and A_2, and the pipe has cross-sectional area A_3. Water is added to the reservoir, flows through the pipe, and is withdrawn from the storage tank at the rates w_1, w_3, and w_2 gallons per second, respectively. The motion of water in the tanks is ignored, and the pipe is represented by the extreme points P_1 and P_2. The lowest horizontal line in the figure represents some reference level, and P_1 and P_2 have heights z_1 and z_2 above this level. The water levels in the reservoir and tank are at heights h_1 and h_2, respectively, above P_1 and P_2. If ρ is the density of

[2]R.H.Cannon, Jr., *Dynamics of Physical Systems.* New York: McGraw-Hill Book Company, 1967. With permission from McGraw-Hill Book Company.

water, we have

$$\left.\begin{aligned} \rho A_1 \frac{dh_1}{dt} &= w_1 - w_3, \\ \rho A_2 \frac{dh_2}{dt} &= w_3 - w_2. \end{aligned}\right] \tag{14.10.1}$$

If the distance $P_1P_2 = l$, then the mass of water in the pipe is $m_3 = \rho A_3 l$, and it moves with average speed $v_3 = w_3/(\rho A_3)$. The dynamics of the flow in the pipe is modeled as follows:

$$\begin{aligned} m_3 \frac{dv_3}{dt} = \;& \text{(Force due to pressure at } P_1) \\ & - \text{(Force due to pressure at } P_2) \\ & + \text{(Component of the weight of the water in the pipe} \\ & \qquad \text{resolved along the pipe)} \\ & - \text{(Frictional force resisting the flow).} \end{aligned}$$

The pressures at P_1 and P_2 are $\rho g h_1$ and $\rho g h_2$, respectively. The frictional force is proportional to v_3^α, where α is a constant that depends on the type of flow. Take $\alpha = 2$, representing turbulent flow in a rough pipe. The constant of proportionality, c, will be discussed later. We now have

$$(\rho A_3 l) \frac{d}{dt}\left(\frac{w_3}{\rho A_3}\right) = (\rho g h_1) A_3 - (\rho g h_2) A_3 + (\rho A_3 l) g \frac{z_1 - z_2}{l} - c\left(\frac{w_3}{\rho A_3}\right)^\alpha. \tag{14.10.2}$$

Simplifying, we end up with

$$\frac{dw_3}{dt} = \frac{\rho g A_3}{l}(h_1 - h_2 + z_1 - z_2) - \frac{c}{l}(\rho A_3)^{-\alpha} w_3^\alpha. \tag{14.10.3}$$

Together with equations (14.10.1), this completes the model.

Cannon suggests that dw_3/dt can be neglected; in this case, (14.10.3) can be solved for w_3, and the result substituted into the equations (14.10.1), leading to a simplification of the system. But in experimenting numerically, there is no special advantage; in fact, the assumption that dw_3/dt is negligible can be tested. However, if dw_3/dt were to be zero, then we would have the equilibrium value

$$w_{3e} = \left[g\rho^{1+\alpha} A_3^{1+\alpha} c^{-1}(h_1 - h_2 + z_1 - z_2)\right]^{1/\alpha}, \tag{14.10.4}$$

for w_3, and this value can, in general, be used as an initial condition for w_3.

For numerical values for this system, take $\alpha = 2$ and $\rho = 2$ lb $\cdot$ sec^2/ft^4. Mathematically, z_1 and z_2 can be absorbed into h_1 and h_2; consequently, z_1 and z_2 can be ignored. Notice that the system has an equilibrium; effects of departures from this equilibrium will be important for the community that receives the water supply. You can, of course, design your own system. But for a start, suppose that in equilibrium $h_1 - h_2 = 100$ ft, and that $w_1 = w_2 = w_3 = 2$ slugs/sec, or 2 lb $\cdot$ sec/ft, or about 8 gallons per second. Let $A_2 = 1{,}000$ ft^2, and $A_1 = 1{,}000 A_2$, making the reservoir a small lake. Let $A_3 = 1$ ft^2. Notice that these data enable you to calculate the value of c, from (14.10.4); you need to do this.

You are now ready to experiment with the model. Verify first that your program "recognizes" the equilibrium — that is, that for the equilibrium initial conditions, all derivatives are zero and nothing varies. (Warning: if your program has an adaptive stepsize, and it calculates the estimated local truncation error to be zero, this may lead to division by zero in the calculation of the following stepsize. Run the test by making one calculation of the right-hand sides of the equations.) Then start to create small changes. The supply of water in the reservoir might diminish or even stop.

The demand for water will change. Having observed fluctuations about the equilibrium, consider more drastic changes. If there is a sudden surge in demand (everyone has a shower in the morning), how quickly can the system recover? Suppose that w_1 is negative, corresponding to evaporation in a drought — how serious could this be?

Chapter 15

Bits and Pieces

15.1 Fireflies

Fireflies can provide beautiful entertainment on a warm summer evening. Behind the display is the serious business of the males literally flashing to attract the opposite sex: OK with fireflies. In the U.S. we are accustomed to see sporadic flashing; roving males may flash every six seconds or so, and females are likely to reply within two seconds. But in some parts of southeast Asia, there are species which can flash in unison, with tens of thousands of insects involved. It is with this possible synchronization that we shall be mainly concerned.

For some good references see the text *Nonlinear Dynamics and Chaos* by Strogatz [93], and papers by Mirollo and Strogatz [73], Buck [19] and Ermentrout [35]. As mentioned by Mirollo and Strogatz, synchronization occurs in many contexts, including the chirping of crickets and pacemaker cells in the heart. See these papers for further references.

For a firefly we assume a dependent variable θ that will be always increasing. When $\theta = 0,\ 2\pi,\ 4\pi, \ldots$ a flash occurs. In our first model we shall consider two fireflies, one of which flashes at regular intervals of time, so that he ignores the other. The frequency of his flashes is ω_1, so that their period is $2\pi/\omega_1$. Then

$$\frac{d\theta_1}{dt} = \omega_1. \tag{15.1.1}$$

t is the time. If the second firefly were alone, then his variable θ_2 would increase according to

$$\frac{d\theta_2}{dt} = \omega_2, \tag{15.1.2}$$

where ω_2 is the "natural frequency" of his flashes. In company with the other firefly, this is modified to

$$\frac{d\theta_2}{dt} = \omega_2 + A\sin(\theta_1 - \theta_2). \tag{15.1.3}$$

So if he is flashed at in the interval $(0, \pi)$ after his own flash, he tends to slow down, and if he is flashed at in this interval before his own flash, he tends to speed up.

To play with this equation (which can, if you like to do so, be solved analytically), you might let $\omega_1 = 1$. Start with ω_2 close to ω_1, and look for a range of values of A so that the periods of θ_1 and θ_2 become the same, or the flashes are "entrained." This does not mean that the flashes are simultaneous. Move ω_2 further away from ω_1, and look for values where entrainment no longer occurs.

Now suppose that each firefly reacts to the other. Then we will have the system of equations

$$\left.\begin{aligned} \frac{d\theta_1}{dt} &= \omega_1 + A_2\sin(\theta_2 - \theta_1), \\ \frac{d\theta_2}{dt} &= \omega_2 + A_1\sin(\theta_1 - \theta_2). \end{aligned}\right] \tag{15.1.4}$$

If one equation is subtracted from the other, then the resulting equation for $\phi = \theta_1 - \theta_2$ is similar to (15.1.3), so no new mathematics is involved. But now consider three fireflies

$$\left.\begin{aligned} \frac{d\theta_1}{dt} &= \omega_1 + A_2\sin(\theta_2 - \theta_1) + A_3\sin(\theta_3 - \theta_1), \\ \frac{d\theta_2}{dt} &= \omega_2 + A_3\sin(\theta_3 - \theta_2) + A_1\sin(\theta_1 - \theta_2), \\ \frac{d\theta_3}{dt} &= \omega_3 + A_1\sin(\theta_1 - \theta_3) + A_2\sin(\theta_2 - \theta_3). \end{aligned}\right] \tag{15.1.5}$$

More parameters are involved; but all three are likely to be of the same species, so the ω_i will be equal or nearly equal, as will the A_i. Start with equality. Vary initial conditions and look for patterns of entrainment. Then allow some inequality; how are the patterns affected?

The model considered above allows entrainment but not synchronization. Synchronization is possible in a model given by Ermentrout [35]. A firefly has a *natural* frequency of flashing, ω_{nat}, and also maximum and minimum possible frequencies, ω_{max} and ω_{min}. Left to itself, the variable θ will follow the equations

$$\frac{d\theta}{dt} = \omega, \text{ and } \frac{d\omega}{dt} = \epsilon(\omega_{\text{nat}} - \omega). \tag{15.1.6}$$

ϵ is a parameter controlling how rapidly the frequency ω decays to ω_{nat}.

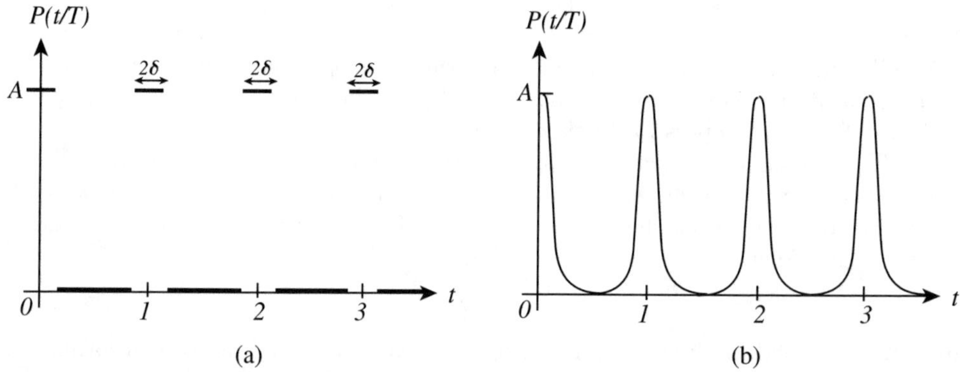

Figure 15.1: *Possible forms for the stimulating function $P(t/T)$.*

Now let the firefly be stimulated by flashing with constant period T. This is represented by a *stimulating function* $P(t/T)$. Possible forms for this function are shown in figure 15.1. The response to this stimulus is given by the *response function* $R(\omega, \theta)$; Ermentrout suggests the form

$$R(\omega, \theta) = \left[\begin{array}{ll} \omega_{\text{min}} - \omega, & 0 < \theta < \pi, \\ \omega_{\text{max}} - \omega, & \pi < \theta < 2\pi. \end{array}\right. \tag{15.1.7}$$

The equations are now

$$\left.\begin{aligned} \frac{d\theta}{dt} &= \omega, \\ \frac{d\omega}{dt} &= \epsilon(\omega_{\text{nat}} - \omega) + P(t/T)R(\omega, \theta). \end{aligned}\right] \tag{15.1.8}$$

The simplest form for the function $P(t/T)$ is that of figure 15.1(a). Then it is easiest to use a fixed stepsize equal to δ or 2δ. If you use a method with variable stepsize, prescribe an upper limit, since when $P(t/T) = 0$ the program will try to take large stepsizes. A function like that of figure 15.1(b) might be a set of curves such as

$$P_k = Ae^{-(t/T-k)^2/\delta^2}, \; k = 0, 1, 2, \ldots$$

where you would switch from one to the next for $t/T = 1/2,\ 3/2,\ 5/2, \ldots$. δ should be small, around 0.1. Diminishing it makes the peaks narrower. The period of synchronized flashing is typically between 0.5 and 0.9 seconds. If you fix ω_{nat}, then the remaining parameters are ω_{min}, ω_{max}, ϵ, A, T and δ. A satisfactory first approach is to vary T only, starting with $T = 2\pi/\omega_{\mathrm{nat}}$, to see entrainment and, perhaps, synchronization.

Now consider two fireflies. Assume that a flash has constant magnitude and lasts for a short interval, centered on $\theta = 0,\ 2\pi,\ 4\pi, \ldots$. One way to model this is by stimulating functions

$$P_i(\theta) = \begin{bmatrix} A_i, & \sin(\theta_i/2) < \delta_i, \\ 0, & \text{otherwise}. \end{bmatrix} \tag{15.1.9}$$

Response functions, $R_i(\omega_i, \theta_i)$, will have the same form as that given in (15.1.7). Then

$$\left.\begin{aligned} \frac{d\theta_1}{dt} &= \omega_1, \\ \frac{d\theta_2}{dt} &= \omega_2, \\ \frac{d\omega_1}{dt} &= \epsilon_1(\omega_{\mathrm{nat},1} - \omega_1) + P_2(\theta_2)R_1(\omega_1, \theta_1), \\ \frac{d\omega_2}{dt} &= \epsilon_2(\omega_{\mathrm{nat},2} - \omega_2) + P_1(\theta_1)R_2(\omega_2, \theta_2). \end{aligned}\right] \tag{15.1.10}$$

Since the fireflies will be of the same species, their parameters will be the same, or very nearly equal. Start them off asynchronously (different initial values of ω_i) and see how long entrainment takes.

The model can be simply generalized, in principle, to any number of fireflies, depending on your computer capacity and your patience in dealing with the output. For a system of n fireflies,

$$\left.\begin{aligned} \frac{d\theta_i}{dt} &= \omega_i, \\ \frac{d\omega_i}{dt} &= \epsilon_i(\omega_{\mathrm{nat},i} - \omega_i) + \left(\sum_{\substack{j=1 \\ j \neq i}}^{n} P_j(\theta_j) \right) R_i(\omega_i, \theta_i), \\ & i = 1, 2, \ldots, n. \end{aligned}\right] \tag{15.1.11}$$

15.2 Curves of Pursuit

You are chasing someone. As you run, you are always facing in the direction of your target. Your path is called a *curve of pursuit.* In some cases, (when the target moves in a straight line at constant speed, for instance) it is possible to solve mathematically for your path; but the mathematics is not much fun, and the solution does not give immediate insight into the time history of your chase. But a numerical computation of your path is easy.

Let the motion take place in the x-y plane. (But you can do it equally easily in three dimensions.) Let the target be at $(x_p(t),\ y_p(t))$ at time t. If you are at $(x(t),\ y(t))$, and are moving with speed V, then the differential equations for your path are

$$\frac{dx}{dt} = V\frac{x_p - x}{D}, \quad \frac{dy}{dt} = V\frac{y_p - y}{D}, \tag{15.2.1}$$

where $D = \sqrt{(x_p - x)^2 + (y_p - y)^2}$.

One possible application is in football. An opponent has the ball and is running to score a touchdown. You can set up the initial geometry, and the speed (assumed constant) of your target. If you always run toward him, how much faster must you run in order to catch him in time? Of course, in this case, running in your opponent's direction is not the most efficient tactic. (It is, in point of fact, stupid.) Define a tactic that would secure the approval of your coach (and any calculus students among the spectators), and compare efficiencies.

When a dog chases a bicycle he (she?) always runs toward the rider. Here, if you want to be sporting, assume that the dog runs a little faster than you can ride. Invent functions $(x_p(t), y_p(t))$ and see how long you can evade him. You are allowed to vary your speed.

A classic problem involves a dog, a duck and a circular pond. The duck swims around the edge of the pond, while the dog, starting at the center of the pond, swims toward the duck. Assume that the swimming speeds are constant. If the dog swims no faster than the duck, then look for limit cycles. What happens when the speeds are equal?

Actually, the preceding two paragraphs are unfair to one breed of dogs: sheepdogs. In this model you are the sheep. The dog wants you to pass through a gate. You start to run away from the gate, but, while keeping the same speed, accelerate in a direction opposite to that of the dog. If the dog remains still, where should he stand so that you eventually pass through the gate?

In another application, you are a farmer, of limited intelligence, trying to catch a pig (or any other animal of your choice). You always run in the direction of the pig. Unfortunately for you, you both run at the same speed. But to help matters, you are in a rectangular field; the pig acts as if he bounces off each boundary, like a perfectly elastic billiard ball. Will you catch him?

Suppose the field is defined by $0 \le x \le A$ and $0 \le y \le B$. Suppose that the pig's position is currently found from $x_p = x_0 + \alpha t$, $y_p = y_0 + \beta t$. Before taking an integration step, starting at time t, with stepsize h, check to see whether the time $t + h$ would put the pig outside the field; if so, then reduce h to put him on an edge, and take a step with that reduced stepsize. If that puts the pig on the x-axis, at $(x_1, 0)$, then the pig's position would be found (until the next collision) from $x_p = x_1 + \alpha t$, $y_p = -\beta t$, t being measured from the instant of collision. Similar formulas would follow from collisions with the other boundaries.

More than two participants can be involved in a pursuit. Suppose the farmer wants to kill the pig, but his wife wants to save it. So she chases the farmer, while the farmer chases the pig. Will she catch him in time? Maybe she doesn't run as fast as her husband. If the coordinates of the pig, the farmer and his wife are, respectively, (x_p, y_p), (x_f, y_f), (x_w, y_w), then the equations are

$$\left.\begin{aligned} \frac{dx_f}{dt} &= V\frac{x_p - x_f}{D_1}, & \frac{dy_f}{dt} &= V\frac{y_p - y_f}{D_1}, \\ \frac{dx_w}{dt} &= V_w\frac{x_f - x_w}{D_2}, & \frac{dy_w}{dt} &= V_w\frac{y_f - y_w}{D_2}, \end{aligned}\right] \tag{15.2.2}$$

where

$$\left.\begin{aligned} D_1 &= \sqrt{(x_p - x_f)^2 + (y_p - y_f)^2}, \\ D_2 &= \sqrt{(x_f - x_w)^2 + (y_f - y_w)^2}. \end{aligned}\right] \tag{15.2.3}$$

I leave you to invent other scenarios.

15.3 Low-level Bombing

A bomb with mass m moves with constant downward gravitational acceleration, and air resistance proportional to the square of its speed. If it moves in the x-z plane, with the z-axis pointing

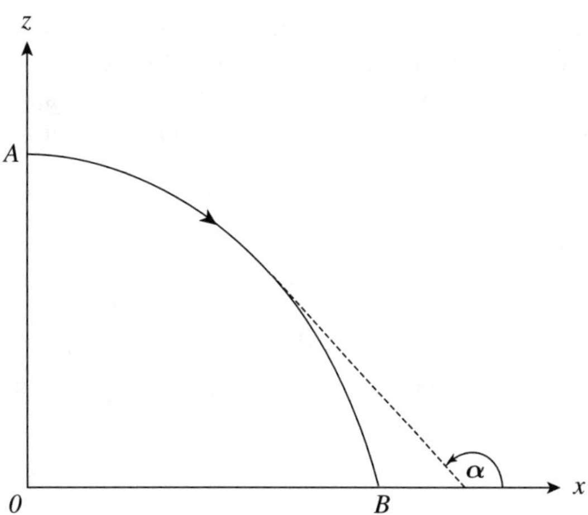

Figure 15.2: *The path of a falling bomb.*

vertically upward, then the equations of motion can be written as

$$\left.\begin{aligned} v &= \sqrt{\left(\frac{dx}{dt}\right)^2 + \left(\frac{dz}{dt}\right)^2}, \\ \frac{d^2x}{dt^2} &= -kv\frac{dx}{dt}, \\ \frac{d^2z}{dt^2} &= -kv\frac{dz}{dt} - g. \end{aligned}\right] \tag{15.3.1}$$

k is a constant measuring the resistance and g is the acceleration due to gravity. k can be varied considerably, since the bomb might be attached to a parachute. If we let

$$y_1 = x, \; y_2 = \frac{dx}{dt}, \; y_3 = z, \; \text{and} \; y_4 = \frac{dz}{dt},$$

then

$$\left.\begin{aligned} v &= \sqrt{y_2^2 + y_4^2}, \\ \frac{dy_1}{dt} &= y_2, \\ \frac{dy_2}{dt} &= -kvy_2, \\ \frac{dy_3}{dt} &= y_4, \\ \frac{dy_4}{dt} &= -kvy_4 - g. \end{aligned}\right] \tag{15.3.2}$$

These are the equations of the model. What can we do with them?

Suppose that you are flying horizontally with altitude h and speed v_0. At the point A $(0, h)$, you release a bomb. Find where it lands. Alternatively, if the target is fixed, find the point A where the bomb should be released. What is the effect of increasing k? On a computer this project can easily be turned into a game, with the bomb release operated by pressing a key. An added touch here is to make the target move. During the descent an interesting angle to follow is α, given by

$$\tan\alpha = -\frac{dz}{dx} = -\frac{y_4}{y_2}. \tag{15.3.3}$$

What is the angle at the point of impact? (See figure 15.2.) You might also investigate how sensitive the position of the point of impact is to small errors in the conditions of the bomb release.

If you don't like bombs, try releasing a parachutist. After release, she or he will count up to ten, and during that time the resisting force will be low. Then the parachute will open and the value of k will greatly increase.

15.4 A Carbon Microphone Circuit

This project is based on an example given in *Introduction to Nonlinear Analysis* by W.J.Cunningham [27]. It illustrates a case where elementary methods of solution (for solving a first-order linear differential equation in this case) *can* be used, but provide no coherent information about the nature of the solution.

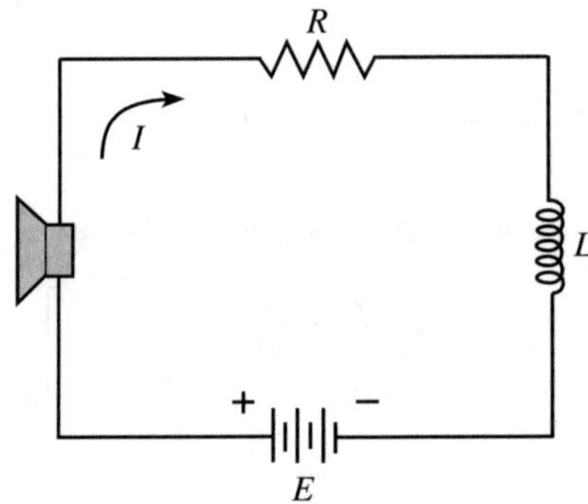

Figure 15.3: *A carbon microphone circuit.*

The circuit illustrated in figure 15.3 consists of a constant voltage E and a constant inductance L, in series with a constant and a variable resistance. The variable resistance comes from a carbon microphone which contains carbon granules coupled to a diaphragm which is exposed to the air. If a sound wave strikes the diaphragm, the density of the granules will vary, and so will the resistance. We consider a sound wave consisting of just one frequency ω. Then if the combined resistance is given by

$$R + Rm \sin \omega t,$$

the differential equation for the circuit is

$$L\frac{dI}{dt} + R(1 + m \sin \omega t)I = E. \tag{15.4.1}$$

The solution will include transient terms and, in addition to these, a response to the incoming sound. If this response were a term of the form $A \sin(\omega t + \delta)$, then there would be no distortion. But what is the actual situation? Trying to solve the equation analytically will not help you, so let's look at some numbers. The important parameter is m, so for a start you might take ratios $R/L = E/L = 1$. With no sound input, so that the resistance is $R(1+m)$, the steady-state current is then numerically equal to $1/(1+m)$; this will be the initial condition with sound included. Now take the numerical integration far enough so that transient terms cease to matter and you can observe the regular steady-state response. How does its distortion depend on m? What happens when you vary ω? Finally, see what effects follow if some of the other parameters are varied.

15.5 The Motion of a Ball in a Rotating Circular Ring: 1

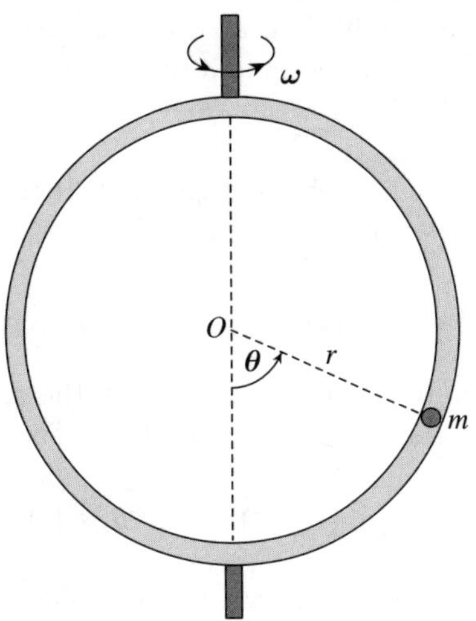

Figure 15.4: *A ring, mass m, sliding on a rotating hoop.*

A circular hollow ring, radius r and center O, is rotating about a vertical axis through O with constant angular velocity ω. A ball, mass m, slides inside the ring; it moves subject to its weight and the reaction with the ring. For now, friction is neglected.

Let the line joining the ball to O make an angle θ with the downward vertical. The velocity of the ball has a component $r\dot{\theta}$ tangential to the hoop, and $r\sin\theta\,\omega$ perpendicular to the ring (since it is instantaneously moving in a circle with radius $r\sin\theta$). The kinetic energy of the ball is T, where

$$2T = m\left(r^2\dot{\theta}^2 + r^2\sin^2\theta\,\omega^2\right),$$

and the potential energy is

$$V = -mgr\cos\theta.$$

So the Lagrangian is

$$L = \frac{1}{2}m\left(r^2\dot{\theta}^2 + r^2\sin^2\theta\,\omega^2\right) + mgr\cos\theta. \tag{15.5.1}$$

The differential equation of motion is

$$mr^2\frac{d^2\theta}{dt^2} = mr^2\omega^2\sin\theta\,\cos\theta - mgr\sin\theta. \tag{15.5.2}$$

Let

$$y_1 = \theta, \quad y_2 = \frac{d\theta}{dt}. \tag{15.5.3}$$

Then

$$\left.\begin{aligned} \frac{dy_1}{dt} &= y_2, \\ \frac{dy_2}{dt} &= \omega^2\sin y_1\cos y_1 - \frac{g}{r}\sin y_1. \end{aligned}\right] \tag{15.5.4}$$

The best way to run this project is to look at phase-plane diagrams; i.e., plot output in the θ-$\dot{\theta}$ plane. When $\omega = 0$, we have the familiar diagrams of the simple pendulum, and for small ω these do not change, in a qualitative sense: there are two equilibria, stable for $\theta = 0$ and unstable for $\theta = \pi$.

For oscillatory motion, the closed curve becomes "pinched" at the top and bottom. This pinching increases until, for a critical value of ω, what was a closed curve is divided into two lobes; there are two new stable equilibria, and the equilibrium at $\theta = 0$ is now unstable. If you start with initial conditions $\theta = 0$, $\dot{\theta} = 0$, then you should observe a horizontal figure eight. As ω increases, the two new equilibria approach $\theta = \pm\pi/2$. The critical value of ω depends on the ratio g/r; for $g/r = 1$, the critical value is $\omega_c = 1$.

This splitting should be expected on physical grounds. It is an example of *bifurcation*, which is a common feature of dynamical systems when some parameter is changed.

15.6 The Motion of a Ball in a Rotating Circular Ring: 2

This project is similar to the preceding one, but now the angular spin ω can vary freely. Let this spin be $\dot{\phi}$, where θ and ϕ are the generalized variables. The Lagrangian is

$$L = \frac{1}{2}I\dot{\phi}^2 + \frac{1}{2}m\left(r^2\dot{\theta}^2 + r^2\sin^2\theta\,\dot{\phi}^2\right) + mgr\cos\theta, \tag{15.6.1}$$

where I is the moment of inertia of the ring about the axis of rotation. If the mass of the ring is M, then $I = Mr^2/2$. Lagrange's equations are

$$\left.\begin{aligned} \frac{d}{dt}\left(I\frac{d\phi}{dt} + mr^2\sin^2\theta\frac{d\phi}{dt}\right) &= 0, \\ mr^2\frac{d^2\theta}{dt^2} &= mr^2\sin\theta\,\cos\theta\left(\tfrac{d\phi}{ds}\right)^2 - mgr\sin\theta. \end{aligned}\right] \tag{15.6.2}$$

Then

$$\left(I + mr^2\sin^2\theta\right)\frac{d\phi}{dt} = c, \tag{15.6.3}$$

a constant. If this is determined from initial conditions, then the remaining equation of (15.6.2) can be written as

$$\frac{d^2\theta}{dt^2} = \frac{c^2\sin\theta\,\cos\theta}{(I + mr^2\sin^2\theta)^2} - \frac{g}{r}\sin\theta. \tag{15.6.4}$$

Compare results with those of the preceding project. If the mass of the ring is a lot less than that of the ball, then things can become interesting since $\dot{\phi}$ may become very large when the ball is close to the top and bottom points in the ring.

15.7 A Compass Needle in an Oscillating Magnetic Field

A compass needle, with dipole moment m, moves in a horizontal plane in a magnetic field that oscillates in time. If the needle makes the angle θ with the direction of the field, then the torque on the needle is $mB\sin\theta$, where $B = B_0\sin\omega t$ is the field strength. Then the differential equation for θ is

$$I\frac{d^2\theta}{dt^2} = mB_0\sin\omega t\,\sin\theta - k\frac{d\theta}{dt}, \tag{15.7.1}$$

where I is the moment of inertia of the needle, and k is a coefficient for a resisting force. This equation can be written as

$$\frac{d^2\theta}{dt^2} = A\sin t\,\sin\theta - B\frac{d\theta}{dt}, \tag{15.7.2}$$

where the time is scaled to make $\omega = 1$.

This system is chaotic, and can be discussed in any of the ways described for the forced pendulum. It is not so easy to find chaos. For one range of values, take $B = 1$ and let A range from 1.4 to 5.4. You will encounter several regimes of periodic, then chaotic, then periodic motion. Since the needle rotates, on average, with the field, it is not a good idea to plot θ against the time. An alternative is to plot $\sin\theta$ or $\dot\theta$ against the time. Similarly, for phase-plane diagrams, plot $\dot\theta$ against $\sin\theta$, to give figures that remain bounded.

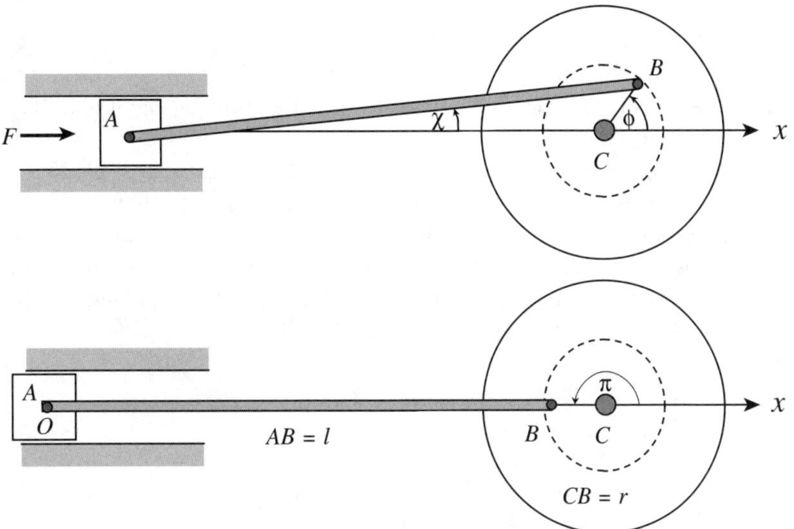

Figure 15.5: *A piston and flywheel.*

15.8 The Motion of a Piston and Flywheel

The mechanism illustrated in figure 15.5 shows a piston, mass M, free to move along the x-axis. A rod AB is connected to the piston and to a flywheel, centered at C, on the x-axis. AB has length l, and the distance CB is r, where the ratio r/l is sufficiently small so that its square can be neglected. The rod AB is uniform and has mass m. The moment of inertia of the flywheel about its axle is I. There may be a force with magnitude F acting on the piston.

Let CB and AB make angles ϕ and χ, respectively, with the x-axis. Then we are assuming that $\cos\chi = 1$. Let x measure the displacement of the piston, such that $x = 0$ when $\phi = \pi$. In general, then,

$$x = r + r\cos\phi + l - l\cos\chi = r + r\cos\phi \text{ and } \dot{x} = -r\dot{\phi}\sin\phi. \tag{15.8.1}$$

Now $l\sin\chi = r\sin\phi$, so $l\dot{\chi}\cos\chi = r\dot{\phi}\cos\phi$. Therefore $\dot{\chi} = (r/l)\dot{\phi}\cos\phi$.

The moment of inertia of AB about A is $\frac{1}{3}ml^2$. So the kinetic energy of the system is T, where

$$2T = M\dot{x}^2 + m\dot{x}^2 + \frac{1}{3}ml^2\dot{\chi}^2 + I\dot{\phi}^2 = (M+m)r^2\dot{\phi}^2\sin^2\phi + \frac{1}{3}mr^2\dot{\phi}^2\cos^2\phi + I\dot{\phi}^2.$$

The potential energy is

$$V = \frac{1}{2}mgl\sin\chi - Fx = \frac{1}{2}mgr\sin\phi - F(r + r\cos\phi).$$

Then the Lagrangian is

$$L = \frac{1}{2}(M+m)r^2\dot{\phi}^2\sin^2\phi + \frac{1}{6}mr^2\dot{\phi}^2\cos^2\phi + \frac{1}{2}I\dot{\phi}^2 - \frac{1}{2}mgr\sin\phi + F(r + r\cos\phi). \tag{15.8.2}$$

The differential equation for the motion is, therefore,

$$\left((M+m)r^2\sin^2\phi + \frac{1}{3}mr^2\cos^2\phi + I\right)\ddot{\phi} + \left(M + \frac{2}{3}m\right)r^2\sin\phi\,\cos\phi\,\dot{\phi}^2$$

$$= \quad -\frac{1}{2}mgr\cos\phi - Fr\sin\phi. \tag{15.8.3}$$

Finally, a resisting force acting on the axle of the flywheel should be included. This could be dry friction, or it could be proportional to $\dot{\phi}$.

There are a lot of parameters in this model, but the dominant terms in (15.8.3) are F and I, and I recommend that you experiment primarily with these. Alone, they would furnish a model equivalent to the simple pendulum, with oscillations or circulation possible. This assumes that F remains constant. It might be more realistic to make $F = 0$ when $\dot{x} < 0$. Then energy would be pumped into the motion, in a way similar to the model for a child on a swing. Then, depending on the resisting term, a limit cycle should be reached.

15.9 Watt's Governor

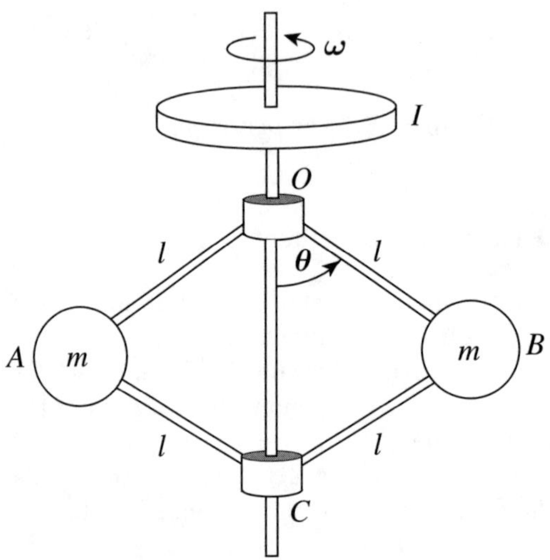

Figure 15.6: *Watt's Governor.*

A vertical spindle is connected to an engine that rotates at the variable angular velocity ω. To represent the inertia of the engine, we shall assume that a flywheel is attached to the spindle about which its moment of inertia is I. At a point O on the spindle, two light rigid rods, OA and OB, each of length l, are jointed so that they are free to move in the vertical plane OAB. Each of the ends A and B is connected to a ball of mass m. Each ball is then connected by two more light, rigid rods of length l to a sleeve that is free to move up and down the spindle. The weight of the spindle will be neglected, as, for the present, will all frictional forces.

The angle between an arm and the vertical is θ, as shown in figure 15.6. Suppose that it is desired that in operation the system should be in a stable equilibrium for which $\omega = n$ and $\theta = \alpha$. If during the operation ω exceeds n, then the balls will fly out further, θ will exceed α and the sleeve C will be moved upward. In the reverse situation the sleeve will be moved down as the balls move in. In either case the motion of the sleeve is communicated to a control that will operate to diminish or increase ω. This control will take the form of a torque, $T(\theta - \alpha)$, a function of the difference between the two angles.

To find the differential equation for θ, consider the motion of the ball A. The forces acting on A are its weight, mg, acting vertically downward, and the centrifugal force, $m\omega^2 l \sin\theta$, acting horizontally, away from the spindle. Resolving these forces perpendicular to OA in the plane OAB, and applying Newton's second law, we find

$$ml\frac{d^2\theta}{dt^2} = -mg\sin\theta + m\omega^2 l\sin\theta\cos\theta. \qquad (15.9.1)$$

The moment of inertia of the entire system about the spindle is

$$I + 2ml^2\sin^2\theta,$$

so the equation for the rate of change of angular momentum about the spindle gives

$$\frac{d}{dt}\left[(I + 2ml^2\sin^2\theta)\omega\right] = T(\theta - \alpha). \qquad (15.9.2)$$

The equilibrium angle α is found by substituting $\omega = n$ into (15.9.1) and putting $\ddot{\theta} = 0$. Then

$$\cos\alpha = g/ln^2. \qquad (15.9.3)$$

These equations and a discussion can be found in *Advanced Dynamics of a System of Rigid Bodies* by E.J.Routh [87]. Routh discusses the case

$$T(\theta - \alpha) = -k(\theta - \alpha), \qquad (15.9.4)$$

for constant k, and shows from a linear analysis that the equilibrium for this system is unstable.

To start the project the equations (15.9.1) and (15.9.2) must be written as three first-order differential equations. Let

$$y_1 = \theta,\ y_2 = \frac{d\theta}{dt},\ y_3 = \omega. \qquad (15.9.5)$$

Then

$$\left.\begin{aligned}\frac{dy_1}{dt} &= y_2,\\ \frac{dy_2}{dt} &= y_3^2\sin y_1\cos y_1 - \frac{g}{l}\sin y_1,\\ \frac{dy_3}{dt} &= \left(-4ml^2 y_2 y_3\sin y_1\cos y_1 + T(y_1 - \alpha)\right)/(I + 2ml^2\sin^2 y_1).\end{aligned}\right] \qquad (15.9.6)$$

Choose simple numerical values. You might pick an equilibrium angle α and then calculate n from (15.9.3). Find out what happens close to the equilibrium. A phase-plane diagram with θ and $\dot{\theta}$ will omit information about ω, but will show clearly if something terrible is happening to the system. Or try plotting θ and ω as functions of the time. Remember that $0 < \theta < \pi/2$.

Consider different expressions for the torque $T(\theta - \alpha)$, such as $(\theta - \alpha)^{1/2}$. Any form will do, provided that the torque is zero when the angles are equal.

The effect of damping can be modeled if the term

$$-ml^2 q\frac{d\theta}{dt} \qquad (15.9.7)$$

is added to the right-hand side of (15.9.1), or

$$-Iqy_2 \qquad (15.9.8)$$

is added to the right-hand side of the second equation in (15.9.6). Using the form (15.9.4), Routh states that this leads to stability if

$$nq\left[1 + 3\cos^2\alpha + I/(2ml^2)\right] > k\cot\alpha/(ml)^2. \tag{15.9.9}$$

(The model considered here is slightly simpler than that of Routh, and the notation is different. Routh omits the factor n from the left-hand side of (15.9.9).) Using q as a parameter, vary it so that you can follow effects on either side of this inequality.

Rather than having damping proportional to the rate of change of θ, it might be more logical for it to be proportional to the velocity of the sleeve, C, since that might be connected to a dashpot mechanism. In this case, in place of (15.9.8), use

$$-q\frac{d\theta}{dt}\sin\theta = -qy_2\sin y_1. \tag{15.9.10}$$

How does this modify the results?

15.10 A Dynamo System with Magnetic Reversal

This model has been considered in relation to the reversals of the magnetic field of the Earth. It has been discussed in detail by Robbins [85]. A good description can be found in the text by Jackson [60]

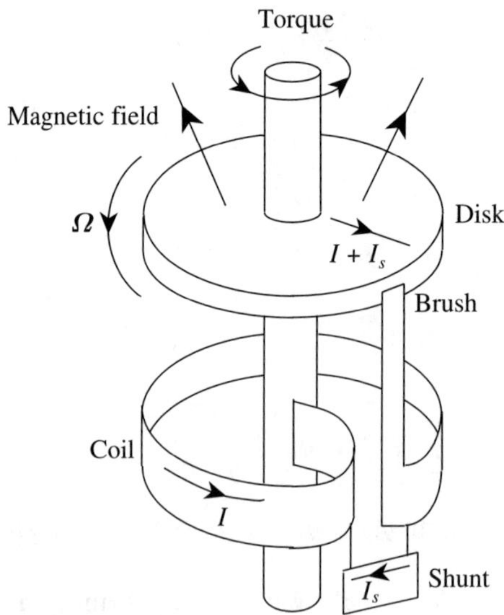

Figure 15.7: *A disk dynamo.*

A conducting disk is acted on by a constant torque, T; the disk has angular velocity Ω about a conducting axle. A magnetic field normal to the disk induces a radial electromagnetic force, and the current flowing in the disk is removed by a brush and fed to a coil and external load. The current in the coil produces a magnetic field that reinforces the original field. This is illustrated in figure 15.7. The model can feature reversals of the current in the coil, and hence reversals of the magnetic field.

Let I be the current in the coil, and I_s, the current in the shunt; then the current flowing in the disk is $I + I_s$. Let C be the moment of inertia of the disk about the axis of rotation, and $2\pi M$ be the mutual inductance between the coil and the disk. Then

$$C\dot{\Omega} = T - MI(I + I_s) - k\Omega, \tag{15.10.1}$$

where $k\Omega$ is a resisting force due to friction. Let L and R be the inductance and resistance of the coil, with L_s, R_s and L_b, R_b referring, similarly, to the shunt and the brush. For the coil we have

$$L\dot{I} + RI + L_b(\dot{I} + \dot{I}_s) + R_b(I + I_s) = M\Omega I, \tag{15.10.2}$$

and for the shunt,

$$L_s\dot{I}_s + R_sI_s + L_b(\dot{I} + \dot{I}_s) + R_b(I + I_s) = M\Omega I. \tag{15.10.3}$$

Robbins found that if $L/R > L_s/R_s$ and $L_b/R_b > L_s/R_s$, then there would be irregular reversals of I. The simplest way to achieve this is to set $L_s = 0$. Now if we let

$$I_1 = I + I_s, \tag{15.10.4}$$

equations 15.10.1 to 15.10.3 can be written as

$$\left.\begin{aligned} C\dot{\Omega} &= T - MII_1 - k\Omega, \\ L\dot{I} &= R_sI_1 - (R + R_s)I, \\ L_b\dot{I}_1 &= (R_s + M\Omega)I - (R_b + R_s)I_1. \end{aligned}\right] \tag{15.10.5}$$

Robbins simplifies these equations with the following changes of variables:

$$t = \gamma\tau,\ \Omega = \delta\omega - \frac{R_s}{M},\ I_1 = \alpha z,\ I = \beta y, \tag{15.10.6}$$

where

$$\left.\begin{aligned} \gamma &= \frac{L_b}{R_b + R_s}, & \delta &= \frac{(R + R_s)(R_b + R_s)}{R_sM}, \\ R &= \frac{\gamma k}{c\delta}\left(\frac{T}{k} + \frac{R_s}{M}\right), & & \\ \alpha^2 &= \frac{\delta C(R + R_s)}{MR_s\gamma}, & \beta &= \frac{R_s\alpha}{R + R_s}, \\ \nu &= \frac{k\gamma}{C}, & \sigma &= \frac{R + R_s}{L}\gamma. \end{aligned}\right] \tag{15.10.7}$$

The transformed equations are

$$\left.\begin{aligned} \frac{d\omega}{d\tau} &= R - yz - \nu\omega, \\ \frac{dy}{d\tau} &= \sigma(z - y), \\ \frac{dz}{d\tau} &= \omega y - z. \end{aligned}\right] \tag{15.10.8}$$

These are similar to the Lorenz equations. The model is chaotic. Plots of y against the time show the reversal very plainly; but x or z can be similarly plotted to show chaotic motion. An effective way to show results is to take any two of x, y, z as coordinate axes. This will result in a "butterfly" diagram. You will be seeing projections of a three-dimensional curve; this curve lies on a surface that is warped in a complicated way. If you have facilities for generating three-dimensional plots of this curve, you can see interesting views of this surface.

Numerical values for some runs showing interesting results are

$$\sigma = 5,\ \nu = 1,\ R = 14.25,\ \text{then } R = 14.255,\ \text{then } R = 14.26.$$

Try some others.

15.11 A Two-Magnet Toy

In a toy illustrating chaotic motion, two bar magnets of equal dimensions and strength are attached at their centers to vertical pins on a horizontal board. The magnets are free to rotate in a horizontal plane. When one or both are given an initial twirl, demonstrably chaotic motion ensues.

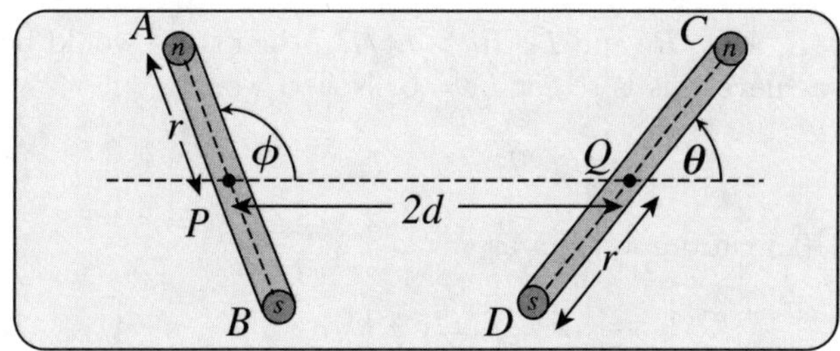

Figure 15.8: *A two-magnet toy.*

Let the magnets have length $2r$ and separation $2d$. Then if they lie on the x-axis, with the origin centered between them, they will be at points $\mathrm{P}(-d, 0)$ and $\mathrm{Q}(d, 0)$. See figure 15.8. We consider their poles to be located at points A, B, C and D, as shown. A and C have the some polarity, which is opposite to the polarity of B and D. Let APB and CQD make angles ϕ and θ, respectively, with the x-axis.

The torque about Q due to the forces from A and B on the poles at C and D is

$$k\overrightarrow{\mathrm{QC}} \times \left(\frac{\overrightarrow{\mathrm{AC}}}{AC^3} - \frac{\overrightarrow{\mathrm{BC}}}{BC^3}\right) + k\overrightarrow{\mathrm{QD}} \times \left(-\frac{\overrightarrow{\mathrm{AD}}}{AD^3} + \frac{\overrightarrow{\mathrm{BD}}}{BD^3}\right)$$

$$= k\overrightarrow{\mathrm{QC}} \times \left(\frac{\overrightarrow{\mathrm{AC}}}{AC^3} - \frac{\overrightarrow{\mathrm{BC}}}{BC^3} + \frac{\overrightarrow{\mathrm{AD}}}{AD^3} - \frac{\overrightarrow{\mathrm{BD}}}{BD^3}\right)$$

$$= k\overrightarrow{\mathrm{QC}} \times \left(\frac{\overrightarrow{\mathrm{AC}}}{AC^3} + \frac{\overrightarrow{\mathrm{CB}}}{BC^3} + \frac{\overrightarrow{\mathrm{AD}}}{AD^3} + \frac{\overrightarrow{\mathrm{DB}}}{BD^3}\right), \tag{15.11.1}$$

where k depends on the strength of the magnets. Similarly, the torque about P due to the forces from C and D on the poles at A and B is

$$k\overrightarrow{\mathrm{PA}} \times \left(\frac{\overrightarrow{\mathrm{CA}}}{CA^3} - \frac{\overrightarrow{\mathrm{DA}}}{DA^3}\right) + k\overrightarrow{\mathrm{PB}} \times \left(-\frac{\overrightarrow{\mathrm{CB}}}{CB^3} + \frac{\overrightarrow{\mathrm{DB}}}{DB^3}\right)$$

$$= k\overrightarrow{\mathrm{PA}} \times \left(\frac{\overrightarrow{\mathrm{CA}}}{CA^3} - \frac{\overrightarrow{\mathrm{DA}}}{DA^3} + \frac{\overrightarrow{\mathrm{CB}}}{CB^3} - \frac{\overrightarrow{\mathrm{DB}}}{DB^3}\right)$$

$$= k\overrightarrow{\mathrm{PA}} \times \left(\frac{\overrightarrow{\mathrm{CA}}}{AC^3} + \frac{\overrightarrow{\mathrm{AD}}}{AD^3} + \frac{\overrightarrow{\mathrm{CB}}}{CB^3} + \frac{\overrightarrow{\mathrm{BD}}}{BD^3}\right). \tag{15.11.2}$$

If the moment of inertia of a magnet about its center is I, then the equations of motion are

$$\left.\begin{aligned} I\frac{d^2\theta}{dt^2}\hat{z} &= k\overrightarrow{\mathrm{QC}}\times\left(\frac{\overrightarrow{\mathrm{AC}}}{AC^3}+\frac{\overrightarrow{\mathrm{CB}}}{BC^3}+\frac{\overrightarrow{\mathrm{AD}}}{AD^3}+\frac{\overrightarrow{\mathrm{DB}}}{BD^3}\right), \\ I\frac{d^2\phi}{dt^2}\hat{z} &= k\overrightarrow{\mathrm{PA}}\times\left(\frac{\overrightarrow{\mathrm{CA}}}{AC^3}+\frac{\overrightarrow{\mathrm{AD}}}{AD^3}+\frac{\overrightarrow{\mathrm{CB}}}{CB^3}+\frac{\overrightarrow{\mathrm{BD}}}{BD^3}\right). \end{aligned}\right] \tag{15.11.3}$$

To compute the right-hand sides, first find the coordinates of the poles as

$$x_a = r\cos\phi - d,\ y_a = r\sin\phi;\ x_b = -r\cos\phi - d,\ y_b = -r\sin\phi;$$

$$x_c = r\cos\theta + d,\ y_c = r\sin\theta;\ x_d = -r\cos\theta + d,\ y_d = -r\sin\theta.$$

Next, find the mutual distances, using

$$AC = \sqrt{((x_c - x_a)^2 + (y_c - y_a)^2)},$$

etc. Next compute the sums of the four fractions on the right of equations (15.11.3). Each will be a vector; call them $\langle x_t, y_t\rangle$ and $\langle x_p, y_p\rangle$. $\overrightarrow{\mathrm{QC}} = \langle r\cos\theta, r\sin\theta\rangle$ and $\overrightarrow{\mathrm{PA}} = \langle r\cos\phi, r\sin\phi\rangle$. So the two cross-products will be

$$r\cos\theta\cdot y_t - r\sin\theta\cdot x_t,\ \text{and}\ r\cos\phi\cdot y_p - r\sin\phi\cdot x_p.$$

Multiply these by k/I to obtain the second derivatives of θ and ϕ.

One way to follow the chaotic motion is to plot θ and ϕ as functions of the time. Changing d can control the onset of chaos, but the best parameter to use is the energy of the system. The model has the energy integral

$$E = K\left(-\frac{1}{AC}-\frac{1}{BD}+\frac{1}{AD}+\frac{1}{BC}\right)+\frac{1}{2}(\dot{\theta}^2+\dot{\phi}^2). \tag{15.11.4}$$

So the best way to investigate the model systematically is to plot Poincaré maps. For instance, when $\sin\phi = 0$, plot θ and $\dot{\theta}$ where these are treated as polar coordinates, $\dot{\theta}$ being the radial coordinate and θ being the angular coordinate. Fix E, and choose initial values for θ and $\dot{\theta}$, while setting $\phi = 0$, and solving equation (15.11.4) for $\dot{\phi}$.

15.12 Bernoulli's Problem

The title of this section comes from a discussion in the text *Advanced Dynamics of a System of Rigid Bodies* by E.J.Routh [87]. A balance in equilibrium consists of a horizontal arm, pivoted at its center, and two scales hanging from its ends, as shown in figure 15.9. In some experiments D.Bernoulli pulled aside one scale so that it started to swing to and fro, with the other scale undisturbed. Shortly after, the second scale began to move, and to oscillate with increasing amplitude, while the first scale gradually lost its oscillatory motion, eventually almost coming to rest. Then the oscillations were exchanged once more, in the same way. A theoretical explanation of this is given by Routh; he states that earlier attempts to do this included two papers by Euler which contained errors. (Euler? Errors?) Routh uses a linear analysis, involving the phenomenon of beats, which is only valid for very small displacements. Dynamically, the system is chaotic. It is a shame that Bernoulli only observed small oscillations; if he had thumped the balance really hard, then the science of chaos might now be several hundred years old!

The balance considered here is simplified so that the principal pivot is on the horizontal arm. (Normally they are joined by a short vertical rod.) Nothing is lost through this assumption, except

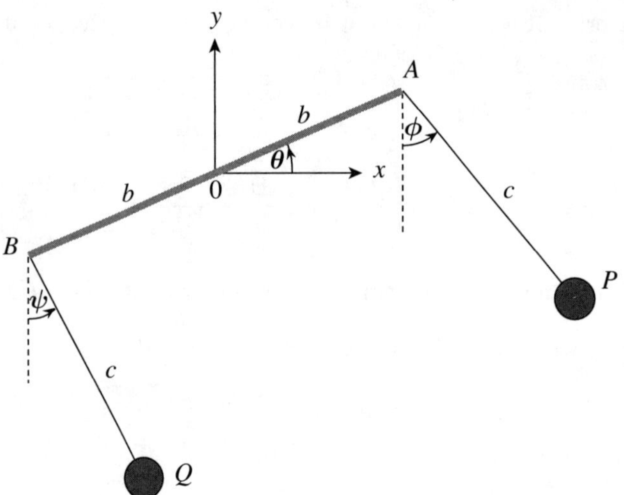

Figure 15.9: *Displacement of a balance.*

a bunch of extra terms in the equations. In figure 15.9 a rod AB is pivoted at its center at the point O. Friction is neglected at this and the other pivots. The rod is free to move in a vertical plane, the x-y plane in the figure; it makes the angle θ with the horizontal x-axis. The rod has length $2b$ and its moment of inertia about a direction through O, perpendicular to the x-y plane, is Mk^2, M being the mass of the rod. If the rod is uniform, then $k^2 = b^2/3$. The scales, with masses m, at P and Q are suspended from the ends A and B by weightless rods of length c; they make angles ϕ and ψ, respectively, with the downward vertical, or negative y-axis.

The coordinates of P and Q are

$$P(b\cos\theta + c\sin\phi,\ b\sin\theta - c\cos\phi) \text{ and } Q(-b\cos\theta + c\sin\psi,\ -b\sin\theta - c\cos\psi).$$

These must be differentiated with respect to the time t, and squared to build up the expression for the kinetic energy. The potential energy is

$$V = -mgc(\cos\phi + \cos\psi),$$

and the Lagrangian for the system is

$$\begin{aligned} L &= \frac{1}{2}Mk^2\dot{\theta}^2 + \frac{1}{2}m\left[2b^2\dot{\theta}^2 + c^2\left(\dot{\phi}^2 + \dot{\psi}^2\right) + 2bc\dot{\theta}\left(-\sin(\theta-\phi)\dot{\phi} + \sin(\theta-\psi)\dot{\psi}\right)\right] \\ &\quad + mgc(\cos\phi + \cos\psi). \end{aligned} \tag{15.12.1}$$

Lagrange's equations can now be derived, as usual. They can be written more simply if we define

$$\beta = \frac{b}{c}, \quad \gamma = \frac{g}{c} \quad \mu = \frac{Mk^2 + 2mb^2}{mbc} > 2\beta. \tag{15.12.2}$$

Then

$$\left.\begin{array}{rcl} \mu\dfrac{d^2\theta}{dt^2} - \sin(\theta-\phi)\dfrac{d^2\phi}{dt^2} + \sin(\theta-\psi)\dfrac{d^2\psi}{dt^2} & & \\ +\cos(\theta-\phi)\left(\dfrac{d\phi}{dt}\right)^2 - \cos(\theta-\psi)\left(\dfrac{d\psi}{dt}\right)^2 & = & 0, \\ \dfrac{d^2\phi}{dt^2} - \beta\sin(\theta-\phi)\dfrac{d^2\theta}{dt^2} - \beta\cos(\theta-\phi)\left(\dfrac{d\theta}{dt}\right)^2 & = & -\gamma\sin\phi, \\ \dfrac{d^2\psi}{dt^2} + \beta\sin(\theta-\psi)\dfrac{d^2\theta}{dt^2} + \beta\cos(\theta-\psi)\left(\dfrac{d\theta}{dt}\right)^2 & = & -\gamma\sin\psi. \end{array}\right] \tag{15.12.3}$$

The second and third equations must be used to eliminate $\ddot{\phi}$ and $\ddot{\psi}$ from the first. The result is

$$\begin{array}{rcl} \left[\mu - \beta\sin^2(\theta-\phi) - \beta\sin^2(\theta-\psi)\right]\dfrac{d^2\theta}{dt^2} & & \\ -\beta\left[\sin(\theta-\phi)\cos(\theta-\phi) + \sin(\theta-\psi)\cos(\theta-\psi)\right]\left(\dfrac{d\theta}{dt}\right)^2 & & \\ +\cos(\theta-\phi)\left(\dfrac{d\phi}{dt}\right)^2 - \cos(\theta-\psi)\left(\dfrac{d\psi}{dt}\right)^2 & & \\ +\gamma\left[\sin(\theta-\phi)\sin\phi - \sin(\theta-\psi)\sin\psi\right] & = & 0. \end{array} \tag{15.12.4}$$

To code these equations, let

$$y_1 = \theta,\ y_2 = \frac{d\theta}{dt},\ y_3 = \phi,\ y_4 = \frac{d\phi}{dt},\ y_5 = \psi,\ y_6 = \frac{d\psi}{dt}. \tag{15.12.5}$$

Then

$$\left.\begin{array}{rcl} s_1 & = & \sin(\theta-\phi),\ c_1 = \cos(\theta-\phi),\ s_2 = \sin(\theta-\psi),\ c_2 = \cos(\theta-\psi), \\ \alpha & = & \mu - \beta s_1^2 - \beta s_2^2, \\ \dfrac{dy_1}{dt} & = & y_2, \\ \dfrac{dy_2}{dt} & = & \left(\beta(s_1c_1 + s_2c_2)y_2^2 - \gamma s_1\sin y_3 + \gamma s_2\sin y_5 - c_1y_4^2 + c_2y_6^2\right)/\alpha, \\ \dfrac{dy_3}{dt} & = & y_4, \\ \dfrac{dy_4}{dt} & = & \beta s_1\dfrac{dy_2}{dt} + \beta c_1y_2^2 - \gamma\sin y_3, \\ \dfrac{dy_5}{dt} & = & y_6, \\ \dfrac{dy_6}{dt} & = & -\beta s_2\dfrac{dy_2}{dt} - \beta c_2y_2^2 - \gamma\sin y_5. \end{array}\right] \tag{15.12.6}$$

To run the project, first choose values for b and c. Pick a value for μ and take initial conditions, as did Bernoulli, with y_1 small and the other $y_i = 0$. Do your observations agree with those of

Bernoulli? Vary the parameter μ; this is equivalent to adding or removing equal weights from the scales. What is the effect of this? When you get tired of small oscillations, increase the initial displacement, or give one scale a large thump (with the initial value of y_2 large, perhaps) and look for the wonderful chaos that Bernoulli missed.

Appendix A

Lagrange's Equations

A.1 Introduction

"Lagrange's equations" are taught in upper level classes in physics, and are consequently seen by many as being "advanced" and therefore difficult. In fact, for the simple cases of concern in this text, they involve no more than the concepts of kinetic and potential energy, and can make life a lot easier. The differential equations of motion of a dynamical system may be derived through careful analysis of all forces and the application of Newton's second law of motion; but the use of Lagrange's method may be more direct. For instance, in the model on Bernoulli's problem, section 15.12, Lagrange's method is used for an elementary derivation of the equations. But, according to Routh, Euler actually made mistakes in attempting to derive the equations by analysing forces.

We consider dynamical systems with no dissipative forces. There will be a set of variables or *coordinates* that can describe the configuration of the system at any time. For example:

1. For the simple pendulum, 12.1, one coordinate, θ: the angle made with the downward vertical.

2. For the spring pendulum, 13.11, two coordinates, r and θ: the length of the pendulum and the angle made with the downward vertical.

3. For Bernoulli's problem, 15.12, three coordinates, θ, ψ and ϕ: The angle that the balance makes with the horizontal and the angles that the rods from the ends of the balance to the scales make with the vertical.

These three models are said to have, respectively, one, two and three degrees of freedom.

These are examples of *generalized coordinates* written traditionally as q_1, q_2, q_3, ... It is necessary to derive the kinetic energy of the system, T, in terms of these coordinates and their derivatives. Here we shall only work with dynamical systems in which the forces can be derived from the gradient of a potential. The potential energy, V, must also be expressed in terms of the coordinates. Then the forces are found from the **negative** gradient of V.

The *Lagrangian* is

$$L = T - V. \tag{A.1.1}$$

L is a function of q_1, q_2, q_3, ..., $\dot{q}_1$, $\dot{q}_2$, $\dot{q}_3$, ... and perhaps the time, t. *Lagrange's equations* are

$$\frac{d}{dt}\left(\frac{\partial L}{\partial \dot{q}_k}\right) = \frac{\partial L}{\partial q_k},\ k = 1,\ 2,\ 3, \dots. \tag{A.1.2}$$

In several of the models of this text the Lagrangian does not depend explicitly on the time t. Then the total energy is conserved. This can usually be expresed as

$$T + V = h, \tag{A.1.3}$$

a constant.

We shall not derive these equations. But we will discuss their implementation for the simple pendulum and the spring pendulum. In the text the equations are found more directly; these demonstrations provide alternative derivations.

A.2 The Simple Pendulum

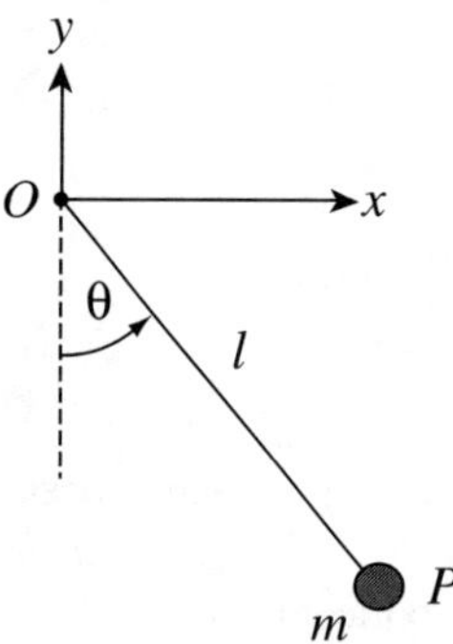

Figure A.1: *The simple pendulum.*

Figure A.1 resembles figure 12.1 of section 12.1, with the omission of the forces, but the inclusion of an inertial reference system, $0xy$. The generalized coordinate is θ. The (constant) length of the pendulum is l; m is the mass at the end of the pendulum.

The first step is to write down the coordinates of m

$$x = l\sin\theta, \quad y = -l\cos\theta. \tag{A.2.1}$$

Next, write down their derivatives,

$$\dot{x} = l\dot{\theta}\cos\theta, \quad \dot{y} = l\dot{\theta}\sin\theta. \tag{A.2.2}$$

The square of the velocity of m is, then,

$$v^2 = \dot{x}^2 + \dot{y}^2 = l^2\dot{\theta}^2, \tag{A.2.3}$$

so the kinetic energy is

$$T = \frac{1}{2}mv^2 = \frac{1}{2}ml^2\dot{\theta}^2. \tag{A.2.4}$$

The potential energy of m increases as m is raised. It is

$$V = mgy = -mgl\cos\theta, \tag{A.2.5}$$

from (A.2.1) (Just between you and me, let's admit that half of the time, we write down V with the wrong sign. When this happens, it will be pretty obvious from inspection of the final equations. The stable equilibrium will be at the top. Just change the sign quietly, and don't tell anyone.) Then

$$L = T - V = \frac{1}{2}ml^2\dot{\theta}^2 + mgl\cos\theta. \tag{A.2.6}$$

To generate Lagrange's equation, first find

$$\frac{\partial L}{\partial \dot{\theta}} = ml^2\dot{\theta}.$$

Finally, from (A.1.2),

$$\frac{d}{dt}(ml^2\dot{\theta}) = \frac{\partial L}{\partial \theta},$$

or

$$ml^2\ddot{\theta} = -mgl\sin\theta. \tag{A.2.7}$$

The conservation of energy, from (A.1.3), is expressed as

$$T + V = \frac{1}{2}ml^2\dot{\theta}^2 - mgl\cos\theta = h. \tag{A.2.8}$$

This is equivalent to (12.1.1) derived in Chapter 12. But we did not have to discuss forces or their resolution. Whether in this particular example this is an advantage or not, I leave to you.

A.2.1 The Spring Pendulum

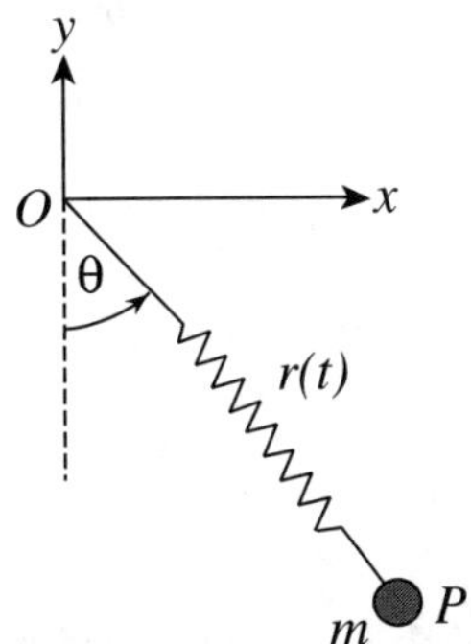

Figure A.2: *The spring pendulum.*

Figure A.2 resembles figure 13.12 in section 13.11. With the point of suspension at O and the mass m at P, the distance $OP = r$, a function of the time t. The generalized coordinates are θ and r. The coordinates of m are

$$x = r\sin\theta, \quad y = -r\cos\theta. \tag{A.2.9}$$

Their derivatives are

$$\dot{x} = \dot{r}\sin\theta + r\dot{\theta}\cos\theta, \quad \dot{y} = -\dot{r}\cos\theta + r\dot{\theta}\sin\theta. \tag{A.2.10}$$

The square of the velocity of m is, then,

$$v^2 = \dot{x}^2 + \dot{y}^2 = \dot{r}^2 + r^2\dot{\theta}^2, \tag{A.2.11}$$

so the kinetic energy is

$$T = \frac{1}{2}mv^2 = \frac{1}{2}m(\dot{r}^2 + r^2\dot{\theta}^2). \tag{A.2.12}$$

The potential depends on the displacement θ, which contributes

$$V_1 = -mgr\cos\theta,$$

and on the extension of the spring. Let the unstretched length be L, and the spring constant be k. The potential energy stored in the spring increases as $|r - L|$ increases, and is

$$V_2 = \frac{1}{2}k(r - L)^2.$$

To see that the sign is right, note that

$$\frac{\partial}{\partial r}(-V_2) = -k(r - L),$$

which is the correct expression for the restoring force, using Hooke's law. Then the total potential is

$$V = V_1 + V_2 = -mgr\cos\theta + \frac{1}{2}k(r - L)^2. \tag{A.2.13}$$

The Lagrangian is

$$L = T - V = \frac{1}{2}m(\dot{r}^2 + r^2\dot{\theta}^2) + mgr\cos\theta - \frac{1}{2}k(r - L)^2. \tag{A.2.14}$$

To derive Lagrange's equations, first note that

$$\frac{\partial L}{\partial \dot{\theta}} = mr^2\dot{\theta}, \text{ and } \frac{\partial L}{\partial \dot{r}} = m\dot{r}.$$

Then

$$\frac{d}{dt}(mr^2\dot{\theta}) = \frac{\partial L}{\partial \theta}.$$

or

$$m(r^2\ddot{\theta} + 2r\dot{r}\dot{\theta}) = -mgr\sin\theta. \tag{A.2.15}$$

Similarly,

$$m\ddot{r} = mr\dot{\theta}^2 + mg\cos\theta - k(r - L). \tag{A.2.16}$$

These are equivalent to (13.11.1).

The conservation of energy, from (A.1.3), is expressed as

$$T + V = \frac{1}{2}m(\dot{r}^2 + r^2\dot{\theta}^2) - mgr\cos\theta + \frac{1}{2}k(r - L)^2 = h. \tag{A.2.17}$$

Appendix B

Software

These programs have been written using Borland/Turbo Pascal, and a set of utilities developed by William MacDonald and Jaroslaw Tuszynski. These utilities were used in the Consortium for Upper-level Physics Software, or CUPS, which produced nine sets of software with accompanying textbooks, published by John Wiley & Sons. I wrote a set of programs dealing with dynamical astronomy, which received an award in 1996 from the Journal *Computers in Physics*, in their sixth annual educational software contest. I am indebted to John Wiley & Sons for their permission to use the CUPS utilities in the development of this software.

The programs are written to be run on MS-DOS platforms. The minimum hardware configuration is an IBM compatible 386-level machine with math coprocessor, mouse and VGA color monitor. The programs require 8.5 Mb of disk space and consist of executable files. Pascal code is also included for the user's information. To obtain the CUPS utilities, I suggest that you purchase one of the CUPS publications such as *Astrophysics Simulations*[31].

Most programs include help files accessed through the menu item `<walk-through}`. They are intended to provide advice and hints to a first-time user. The text of the files can be found in the file `walkthru.txt`.

B.1 Introduction

1. Direction Fields and Euler's Method

   This is designed to supplement the material in chapters 1, 2 and section 3.2. You are prompted to enter the right-hand side of a first-order differential equation of the type $\frac{dy}{dx} = f(x, y)$. You can then plot direction fields, superimpose solution curves, and run Euler's and the improved Euler's methods, with emphasis on the influence of different stepsizes on the errors.

2. Testing Runge-Kutta-Fehlberg

   This follows the projects for "debugging, testing and understanding" the program described in chapter 3. You can enter your own first-order differential equation.

3. Richardson's Arms Race

   Section 4.2. The variables describing "war preparedness," x, y, of two countries are plotted in the x-y plane as the time changes. Various types of stable and unstable situations can be followed.

B.2 Chaotic Systems

1. The System of Hénon and Heiles

Section 5.2. You can choose a value for the "energy" of the system (h in the text), and can then construct Poincaré maps. Chaos develops as h increases. The starting point for a mapping, and its color, can be selected using the keyboard or the mouse. The dependent variables for the model are x, y, dx/dt, dy/dt. In a mapping, values of y and dy/dt are plotted when $x = 0$. You have the option of seeing the orbit in the three-dimensional space of x, dx/dt, dy/dt, with points marked when it crosses the plane $x = 0$.

2. The Lorenz Equations

   This utility deals with the Lorenz equations, section 5.3, but includes, as options, Rossler's equations (section 5.3) or those for the chaotic dynamo (section 15.10). You can also enter your own system. The variables are x, y, z, dependent, and t, independent. You can plot solutions projected in any of the planes: t-x, t-y, t-z, x-y, x-z and y-z, or view three-dimensional motion in x-y-z space.

   You can also plot "Lorenz maps." If p is any one of the coordinates, and if $p(t)$ has maxima at p_1, p_2, p_3, p_4, ..., then points with coordinates (p_1, p_2), (p_2, p_2), (p_3, p_4), ... are plotted. Although the motion may be chaotic, these points are restricted to well-defined locations.

3. A Periodically Forced Pendulum

   Section 5.4. A pendulum moves subject to gravity, a resisting term, with parameter k, and a forcing term $c\cos(\omega t)$, with period $P = 2\pi/\omega$. Depending on values of k, c, and ω, the motion may be chaotic. You can view the chaos in a variety of ways: observe the swinging pendulum; plot angular displacement, θ, or its derivative, as a function of the time; follow the motion in a phase-plane plot with axes θ-$d\theta/dt$. In the phase-plane you can see a smooth curve, or you can see points plotted only for times t_0, $t_0 + P$, $t_0 + 2P$, $t_0 + 3P$, ... (Such a plot is called, by some, a Poincaré map.)

   There are also two utilities that may be very slow. The first is to plot a bifurcation diagram. For different values of c, within a given range, Poincaré maps are calculated; the first 30 (or however many you select) are ignored and the values of $d\theta/dt$ are plotted for the following 30. This illustrates the history of non-chaotic behavior merging into chaos as c increases. The second uses a grid of points in the θ-$d\theta/dt$ plane; each is used as initial conditions, with the subsequent run taken until the pendulum settles down to regular oscillations (or fails to do so); the starting point is then colored according to the net number of complete revolutions made before settling down.

4. One-Dimensional Maps

   Sections 5.5.1 to 5.5.5. You can choose from a selection of maps, including quadratic and logistic, or you can enter your own. Then you can follow the mapping in various ways discussed in the text: cobwebs, bifurcation diagrams, etc.

5. Two-Dimensional Maps

   Sections 5.5.7, 5.5.8. You have a choice of maps, or you can enter your own. The maps take $x(n)$, $y(n)$ into $x(n+1)$, $y(n+1)$, and depend on a parameter, c. You can choose a value for c and then generate maps in the x-y plane for varied starting conditions.

6. Newton's Method

   Sections 5.5.7, 5.5.8. Newton's method is used for solving two nonlinear equations $f(x, y) = 0$, $g(x, y) = 0$. Depending on the starting conditions, the iteration may converge to one of several possible solutions, or may fail to converge. You can choose from some given functions, $f(x, y)$, $g(x, y)$, or enter your own. Then you can follow iterations. Or you can use a grid of points in the x-y plane; each point is a starting condition, and can be colored in one of two ways. In the first way, it is colored according to the final point of convergence; in the second, it is colored according to the number of iterations needed for convergence, regardless of the final value. In each case you can see fractal patterns; then you can select smaller and smaller regions in the plane to see how these patterns are replicated for smaller scales.

B.3 Predator-Prey Models

1. Sections 6.1 to 6.7. This utility covers the models of Volterra, Volterra with fishing, logistic growth for either species, Holling's model for predation and May's model. You can also enter your own; this makes it possible to investigate models such as 6.8 to 6.10. You have the option of making the birthrate of the prey periodic.

   You can display the models as time plots, plots in the three-dimensional predator-prey-time-space and in the predator-prey phase-plane. In the last case, if you have periodic birthrate for the prey, you have the option of plotting a continuous curve, or just plotting points at instants of time separated by one period of the birthrate (i.e., a Poincaré map), since the solution may be chaotic.

B.4 Sickness and Health

1. Spread of Disease

   Sections 7.1, 7.2, 7.4, 7.7 and 7.8. You can choose any combination of the basic model and vaccination, incubation, birth and death and periodic rate of infection. The results can be displayed as time plots or as plots in the S-I plane. (S is the number susceptible to, and I is the number infected by the disease.) In the latter case, if you have periodic infection rate, so that the solution may be chaotic, you have the option of plotting a continuous curve, or just plotting points at instants of time separated by one period of the infection rate (i.e., a Poincaré map).

2. The Epidemiology of Malaria

   Section 7.9. This model follows the spread of malaria in the two species: humans and mosquitos. Options include logistic growth models for the species and periodic birthrate for the mosquitos. Numbers infected and total populations are displayed as functions of the time.

3. The Spread of Gonorrhea

   Section 7.10. The two species in this model are promiscuous, heterosexual males and females. Birth and death are not included. Parameters are the populations, cure rates and infection rates. These can be varied to see ways in which the disease may approach an equilibrium or may die out. The dependent variables are the numbers of infected males, x, and females, y. The progress of the disease is followed in the x-y phase-plane. During this progress any of the six parameters can be changed by moving sliders at the sides of the screen.

4. Zeeman's Model for the Heartbeat.

   Section 7.13. The variables of the model represent muscle fiber length and electrochemical activity. The principal parameter is the overall tension of the system. The model cycles between two states; the relaxed state is called diastole, and the contracted state is called systole. You can follow, in detail, the dynamics of the contraction, or you can view complete cycles. If the tension is too high, then you can produce a "heart attack." Also, by plotting the electrochemical activity versus the time, you can generate an "EKG."

B.5 Sports

1. Pitching in Baseball.

   Sections 9.2 and 9.3. As the pitcher, you can vary the initial height of the pitch, the initial velocity and the three components of the spin. The trajectory can be viewed from the side, from above or from the view of the catcher. You can also pitch a knuckleball.

   The default values of the parameters for the drag and lift forces are set to apply to a baseball. You have the option of varying these, (something that might land a real pitcher into deep trouble!).

2. Driving a Golf Ball.

   Section 9.6. Drives can be viewed from three different directions, as with the baseball pitch. The initial velocity and the components of backspin and sidespin can be varied. One option is to view simultaneously trajectories (a) with no drag or lift, (b) with drag but no lift and (c) with both drag and lift. The parameters controlling drag and lift can also be varied.

3. Serving at Tennis.

   The initial height, velocity and topspin can be varied. Motion can be viewed from three different directions. Parameters relating to drag and lift can be varied, as can the coefficient of restitution, controlling the bounce of the ball.

4. Bowling in Cricket.

   Sections 9.9 and 9.10. Initial conditions and viewing directions are similar to those for the baseball pitch. But since the ball usually bounces, the effect of the spin on the trajectory after the bounce is more important than its effect on the flight through the air. Parameters for the forces of drag and lift can be varied, along with the coefficient of restitution. One option is to bowl a "swinger," for which there is a sideways drag on a non-spinning ball, caused by the orientation of the seam of the ball.

5. Shuttlecock Trajectories in Badminton.

   Section 9.11. The dominant force in the model is drag. Initial position and velocity can be varied, and also the drag coefficient. Motion is followed in two dimensions, and viewed from the side.

6. The Path of a Discus.

   Section 9.15. The motion of a discus is followed in two dimensions. Wind can be included. You can see how the range can increase when the discus is thrown against the wind, leading to increased lift, and, consequently, increased range.

7. The Motion of a Javelin.

   Section 9.16. The motion of a javelin, translational and rotational, is followed in two dimensions. Many quantities can be varied, including the initial conditions and the design of the javelin.

B.6 Spaceflight and Astronomy

1. A Trip to the Moon.

   Section 11.2. A space vehicle is launched from a circular parking orbit around the Earth. Motion is followed in two dimensions. The radius of the parking orbit, position in the parking orbit and the speed of launch are quantities to be entered. Possible motion includes orbits passing close to the Moon and then returning to the Earth, orbits that hit the Moon and orbits that gain extra energy from an encounter with the Moon, and then escape from the Earth-Moon system (the "slingshot" effect).

2. The Descent of Skylab.

   Section 11.5. The model follows the motion of an artificial satellite in its final revolutions before it falls to Earth. Motion is followed in two dimensions. The cross-sectional area of the satellite (assumed constant) and its mass can be varied; so also can the drag coefficient. Initial conditions should be chosen with care, in case the satellite falls instantly or takes too many revolutions for the patience of the operator. The motion is seen in animation; then you have the option of viewing a plot of the altitude as it varies with time.

3. The Range of an ICBM.

   Sections 11.6 and 11.7. The model is the same as that for the descent of Skylab, but launch (or burnout) takes place close to the surface of the Earth. Properties of the orbits, such as the influence on range of the velocity and angle of launch, can be investigated.

4. Jupiter and a Comet.

   Section 11.16. The comet can start from the outer reaches of the solar system, depending on the initial conditions selected; the conditions also include the position of Jupiter in its orbit at the initial time. The motion is followed in two dimensions. If the comet passes sufficiently close to Jupiter, its orbit will be radically changed. It might be expelled from the solar system. Or it might have its orbit changed into a small ellipse (i.e., a "short period" comet). After such a capture, later encounters between the comet and Jupiter can lead to large changes, such as expulsion.

5. Motion close to L4 or L5.

   Sections 11.3 and 11.4. In the restricted problem of three bodies, two bodies, such as the Sun and Jupiter, move around each other in circular orbits, and a third body, with negligible mass, moves subject to the gravitational attraction of the others. All motion takes place in a plane. L4 and L5 are locations in the plane of motion that make up the corners of equilateral triangles with the first two masses. If the third body is placed at one of these positions, with no relative velocity, then, mathematically, it will remain there in equilibrium.

   In fact, these positions are usually unstable, in that a displacement, however small initially, will be magnified. But if the ratio of the masses of the first two bodies is small enough, then the positions can be stable. Such is the case with the Sun-Jupiter-Trojan asteroid system.

   In this utility, orbits of the third body can be followed, and the influence of the mass ratio investigated. The dynamical system is chaotic; an option is to investigate this using the method of Poincaré maps.

6. Aerobraking a Spacecraft.

   Section 11.8. A spacecraft approaches a planet in a hyperbolic orbit. One way by which it can be "captured" by the planet is to lose kinetic energy through atmospheric drag when passing through the planetary atmosphere. This is "aerobraking." You can design your planet and its atmosphere. You can also specify the mass and cross-sectional area of the spacecraft, and the initial position and velocity of the approach.

B.7 Pendulums

1. The Simple Pendulum.

Sections 12.1 to 12.4. The motion can be followed in animation, in plots of angular displacement versus the time, or in the phase-plane. Resisting forces can be proportional to the angular velocity, or can be of the "dry" or Coulomb category.

2. A Magnetic Pendulum in Two Dimensions.

   Section 12.10. Two magnets are fixed on a horizontal surface, and a pendulum, with a magnet attached to its free end, swings above them. The magnets can be oriented such that the swinging magnet is attracted or repelled; also their strengths and positions can be varied. The motion takes place in two dimensions. Depending on the values of the parameters, several positions of equilibrium may be possible. One utility plots the net torque acting on the pendulum as a function of its angle of displacement, showing where the equilibria are located. Motion can be followed in animation or in the phase-plane.

3. A Child on a Swing.

   Section 12.11. This particular child pumps energy into the swinging by standing up or crouching. You can enter parameters describing the swing and the child and the frictional forces (which are proportional to the angular velocity and the cross-sectional area of the child). Then you have the option of controlling the action of the child, using hotkeys. Alternatively, you can let the child (or the program) make the decisions. In the latter case, unless you have been unwise in your choices, and the child makes complete revolutions, the motion approaches a limit cycle, which will depend in part on the frictional force and the mass of the child.

   The motion can be followed in animation or in the phase-plane.

4. A Spring Pendulum.

   Section 13.11. A mass is suspended from a fixed point by a spring; the tension in the spring is given by Hooke's law. Like the double pendulum, this system is chaotic and can be followed in animation or through the method of Poincaré maps.

5. A Double Pendulum.

   Section 12.21. In this chaotic model one simple pendulum is suspended from another. The motion can be seen in animation, when it can be spectacular, or the chaos can be followed through the method of Poincaré maps.

6. The Dumbbell Satellite.

   Sections 12.24 to 12.28. A dumbbell satellite consists of two masses joined by a light rigid rod. This is a pendulum in orbit around the Earth. If the orbit is circular, the satellite is in stable equilibrium if the rod points to the Earth's center, and the satellite is in synchronous motion (i.e., it rotates once for every revolution around the Earth). If the eccentricity of the orbit is increased, synchronous motion is still possible, but for high enough eccentricity, the motion becomes unstable and is, in fact, chaotic. Its motion can be investigated using Poincaré maps, with points in the phase-plane of the pendulum's motion plotted at the start of each revolution around the Earth.

   Synchronous motion is an example of resonance: one-to-one. Other kinds of resonance, such as three rotations for two revolutions (which applies to the planet Mercury), are possible for ranges of the eccentricity not including zero. These can also be investigated by Poincaré maps, suitably modified.

   If frictional forces are included, then the model can be applied to a satellite with de-spinning torque. It can also be applied to a planet subject to such a torque through tidal forces. (But the actual time scale of billions of years is not to be addressed.) Then ask such questions as: Why was Mercury captured into a three-to-two resonance, as its spin slowed down? Why did it not continue to slow down until it ended in a one-to-one resonance, like the Moon?

This utility enables some of these questions to be investigated. You can see the motion in animation, or plot Poincaré maps.

7. A Swinging Censer.

   Section 12.14. This model is similar to that for a child on a swing. A censer contains incense which is to be scattered over a large area; the censer is at the end of a rope, the length of which is changed in rhythm with the swings, so that the amplitude of the swings is increased.

8. The Pit and the Pendulum.

   Section 12.13. An enactment of the scenario described by Edgar Allen Poe. A blade at the end of a rope, with gradually increasing length, swings over a hapless victim.

B.8 Bits and Pieces

1. Production and Exchange.

   Section 8.2. The model concerns two people who produce goods, keep some and give some away. You can control the rates at which goods are produced and exchanged, while the animated solution is displayed.

2. The Economics of Fishing.

   Section 8.3. A population of fish varies logistically. The rate at which it is fished, or harvested, depends on the effort, or cost of fishing, and the price that the catch will command in the market. The population of the fish can be followed, while the parameters are varied. One option is to make the birthrate of the fish and the effort involved in fishing periodic functions of the time.

3. The Motion of a Yo-yo.

   Section 10.7. In the motion of a descending yo-yo the linear velocity may approach zero toward the end, while the angular velocity should be made as large as possible. Important parameters are the diameters of the central spindle when fully wound and fully unwound, and the moment of inertia of the yo-yo about the central axis; the more the mass is concentrated around the edge, the better the yo-yo may perform. You can design your yo-yo and control the starting speed of descent. Only vertical motion is followed.

4. The Action Between a Violin Bow and String.

   Section 13.8. The bow is represented by a belt moving at constant speed. The string is represented by a mass attached to a fixed point by a spring. The mass can be dragged along the belt until the tension in the spring becomes too large for the friction, and the mass springs back. The speed of the bow and the parameters describing the dry friction can be varied.

5. Landing an Aircraft on an Aircraft Carrier.

   Section 13.9. The aircraft is attached to a sandbag by an elastic cable. The sandbag experiences dry friction with the deck of the carrier. The aircraft is slowed down by wind resistance and the tension in the cable. You can control parameters for the masses, friction, elasticity of the cable, speed of the carrier and the wind, and also the landing speed. You are safer at the computer than in the aircraft.

6. Pitching and Rolling at Sea.

   Section 10.3. The two modes of motion are coupled together so that energy can be exchanged between them. The forcing terms in the motion are provided by a "regular" sea, with waves of constant amplitude and frequency. You can vary the frequency of the waves and the natural frequencies of pitching and rolling, as well as the damping that might be provided by the ship's stabilizers. Look for exchanges of energy between the two modes.

7. The Motion of a Ball in a Rotating Circular Ring.

   Section 15.5. A hollow ring is rotating about a vertical axis attached to the ends of a diameter. A ball moves inside the ring. The principal parameter for the model is the angular velocity of rotation about the vertical axis. For slow values the lowest position of the ball is a stable equilibrium; as the rate is increased, this position becomes unstable and two new stable equilibria appear.

8. The Swinging Atwood Machine.

   Section 12.19. Two masses are attached to the ends of a string which passes over two pulleys at the same horizontal level. One mass moves vertically; the other is free to swing in a vertical plane. The motion is chaotic. It can be followed in animation, or through the construction of Poincaré maps.

9. A Chaotically Driven Wheel.

   Section 13.12. A wheel rotates at a constant rate. A point on its circumference is connected, by a spring, to a point on the circumference of a second wheel. The motion of the second wheel can be chaotic. This motion can be seen in animation, plotted as a function of the time, plotted in the phase-plane or recorded by the method of Poincaré maps. It is also possible to generate bifurcation diagrams, as can be done in the program for the forced pendulum.

10. Bernoulli's Problem.

    Section 15.12. This model is that of a pair of scales with weights hanging from each end. Bernoulli noticed that if one mass was slightly deflected, then its oscillations would gradually decrease in amplitude, while the other mass would begin to move. You can observe this effect. But the principal attraction of the model, which Bernoulli unfortunately missed, is that it is chaotic. You can design the scales and enjoy the chaos in animation.

Bibliography

[1] Adair, R.K. "The Physics of Baseball," *Physics Today,***48** (1995) 26–31.

[2] Adair, R.K. *The Physics of Baseball*, Harper Collins, New York, (1991).

[3] Andronov, A.A. and Chaikin, C.E. *Theory of Oscillations*, Princeton University Press, Princeton, NJ, (1949).

[4] Aris, R. *Elementary Chemical Reactor Analysis*, Prentice-Hall, Englewood Cliffs, NJ, (1969).

[5] Bachman, R.A. 1984. "Idealized dynamics of balloon flight," *Am. J. Physics* **52** (1984) 309–312.

[6] Bailey, N.T.J. *The Mathematical Theory of Infectious Diseases and it Applications*, Hafner Press, New York, (1975).

[7] Baker, G.L. and Gollub, J.P. *Chaotic Dynamics — An Introduction,* Cambridge University Press, NY, (1990).

[8] Ball, K.J and Osborne, G.F. *Space Vehicle Dynamics*, Oxford University Press, U.K., (1967).

[9] Bearman, P.W. and Harvey, J.K. (1976) "Golf ball aerodynamics," *Aeronaut. Quarterly* **27** (1976) 112–122. Also reprinted in *Physics of Sports*, ed. Frohlich, C.

[10] Benade, A.H. *Fundamentals of Musical Acoustics*, Oxford University Press, New York, (1976).

[11] Best and Bartlett. "Aerodynamic Characteristics of New Rules Javelin," Proc. Inst. Mech. Engineers Conference Report, Leeds, Sept (1987).

[12] J.A. Blackburn, H.J.T. Smith, N. Grønbech-Jensen. "Stability and Hopf bifurcations in an inverted pendulum,"*Am. J. Physics* **60** (1992) 903–908.

[13] Blatt, J.M. *Dynamic Economic Systems*, Armonk, New York, (1983).

[14] Brancazio, P.J. "Rigid-body Dynamics of a Football," *Am. J. Physics*, **55** (1987) 415–420.

[15] Brancazio, P.J. "Physics of Basketball," *Am. J. Physics*, **49** (1981) 356–365. Also reprinted in *Physics of Sports*, ed. Frohlich, C.

[16] Brancazio, P.J. (1984) *Sport Science*, Simon and Schuster, New York. (1984).

[17] Braun, M. *Differential Equations and their Applications*, Springer-Verlag, New York (1983). An excellent text; enjoyable to read.

[18] L.J. Briggs. "Effect of spin and speed on the lateral deflection (curve) of a baseball; and the Magnus effect for smooth spheres," *Am. J. Physics.* **27** (1959) 589–596. Also reprinted in *Physics of Sports*, ed. Frohlich, C.

[19] Buck, J. "Synchronous rhythmic flashing of fireflies," *Quart. Rev. Biol.* **63** (1988) 265–289.

[20] Burns, J.A., Lamy, P.L. and Soter, S. " Radiation forces on small particles in the Solar System," *Icarus* **40** (1979) 1–48.

[21] Cannon, R.H.,Jr. *Dynamics of Physical Systems*, McGraw Hill, New York, (1967).

[22] Casti, J.L. *Connectivity, Complexity and Catastrophe in Large-Scale Systems*, John Wiley & Sons. New York, (1979).

[23] Caton, C. and Shell, K. "An exercise in the theory of heterogeneous capital accumulation," *Review of Economic Studies* **38** (1970) 13–21.

[24] Chandrasekhar, S. *An Introduction to the Study of Stellar Structure*, Dover, New York, (1958).

[25] Cornille, H.J. "A method of accurately reducing the spin rate of a rotating spacecraft," *NASA TN* **D-1676** (1962).

[26] Cunningham, C.J. *Introduction to Asteroids*, Willmann-Bell, Richmand, VA, (1988).

[27] Cunningham, W.J. *Introduction to Nonlinear Analysis*, McGraw-Hill, New York. (1955).

[28] Curry, J.H. "On the Hénon transformation," *Communications of Mathematical Physics* **68** (1979) 129–140.

[29] Daish, C.B. *The Physics of Ball Games*, English Univ. Press, London, (1972).

[30] Danby, J.M.A. *Fundamentals of Celestial Mechanics*, Willmann-Bell, Richmand, VA, (1992).

[31] Danby, J.M.A., Kouzes, R. and Whitney, C. *Astrophysical Simulations*, John Wiley & Sons, Inc, New York, (1995).

[32] J.M.Davies. "The aerodynamics of golf balls," *J. Appl. Phys.* **20** (1949) 821–28.

[33] de Mestre, N. *The Mathematics of Projectiles in Sport*, Cambridge University Press, New York, (1990).

[34] Devaney, R.L. *A First Course in Chaotic Dynamical Systems*, Addison Wesley, (1993).

[35] Ermentrout, G.B. "An adaptive model for synchrony in the firefly *Pteroptyx malaccae*," *J. Math. Biol.* **29** (1991) 571–585.

[36] Fedor, J.V. "Analytical theory of the stretch yo-yo for de-spin of satellites," *NASA TN* **D-1676** (1963).

[37] Fehlberg, E. "Classical fifth-, sixth-, seventh- and eighth-order Runge-Kutta formulas with stepsize control," *NASA TR* **287** (1968).

[38] Fehlberg, E. "Low order classical Runge-Kutta formulas with stepsize control and their application to some heat transfer problems," *NASA TR* **315** (1969).

[39] Field, R.J., and Noyes, R.M. 1974. "Oscillations in Chemical Systems. IV. Limit cycle behavior in a model of a real chemical reaction," *Journal of Chemical Physics* **60** (1974) 1877–1884.

[40] Frohlich, C. *Physics of Sports. Selected reprints*, Frohlich, C,. Ed. American Association of Physics Teachers, College Park, Md. (1986).

[41] Frohlich, C. "Do springboard divers violate angular momentum conservation?" Am. J. Physics **47** (1979) 583–592. Also reprinted in *Physics of Sports*, ed. Frohlich, C.

[42] Frohlich, C. "Aerodynamic effects on discus flight," *Am. J. Physics*, **49** (1981) 1125–1132.

[43] Furusawa, K, Hill, A.V. and Parkinson, J.L. "The dynamics of sprint running," *Proc. R. Soc.* **B 102** (1927) 29–42.

[44] Furusawa, K, Hill, A.V. and Parkinson, J.L. "The energy used in sprint running," *Proc. R. Soc.* **B 102** (1927) 43–50.

[45] Gandolfo, G. *Economic Dynamics: Methods and Models*, North Holland Publishing Company, New York, (1980).

[46] Gause, G.F. *The Struggle for Existence*, Dover New York, (1964).

[47] Goodwin, R.M. "A growth cycle," pp 54–58. In Feinstein, G.H. *Socialism, Capitalism and Economic Growth.* Cambridge, U.K., (1967).

[48] Griner, M. (1984) "A parametric solution to the elastic pole-vaulting problem," *J. Appl. Mech.* **51** (1984) 409–414.

[49] Gwinn, E.G. and Westervelt. R.M. (1986) "Fractal basin boundaries and intermittency in the driven damped pendulum," *Phys. Rev. A.* **33** (1986) 4143–4155.

[50] Hart, D. and Croft, T. *Modelling with Projectiles*, John Wiley and Sons, New York, (1988).

[51] Heithaus, R.E., Colver, D.C., and Beattie, A.J. "Models of some Ant-Plant mutualisms," American Naturalist **116** (1980) 347–361.

[52] Hénon, M. "Numerical study of quadratic area-preserving mappings," *Q. Appl. Math,* **27** 219–312 (1969).

[53] M.Hénon and C.Heiles. "The application of the third integral of motion: some numerical experiments," *Astronomical Journal* **69** (1964) 73–79.

[54] Hénon, M. (1976) "A two-dimensional mapping with a strange attractor," *Communications in Mathematical Physics.* **50** (1976) 69–77.

[55] Holling, C.S. "The fundamental response of predators to prey density and its role in mimicry and population regulation," *Memoirs of the Entomological Society of Canada* **45** (1965) 1–60.

[56] Howard, N.L. "Nonlinear oscillations." In *Nonlinear Oscillations in Biology,* F.C.Hoppensteadt, ed., American Mathematical Society, Providence, RI, (1979).

[57] Hubbard, M. "Dynamics of the pole vault" *J. Biomech,* **13** (1980) 965–976.

[58] M.Hubbard and H.J. Rust. "Simulation of javelin flight using experimental aerodynamic data," *J. Biomech.*, **17**, (1984), 769–776.

[59] M.Hubbard. "Optimal javelin trajectories," *J. Biomech.*, **17**, (1984), 777.

[60] Jackson, E.A. *Perspectives of Nonlinear Dynamics*, vol 2, section 7.6. Cambridge University Press, New York, (1990).

[61] Jones, D.S., and Sleeman, B.D. *Differential Equations and Mathematical Biology,* Allen and Unwin, UK, (1983).

[62] Kautz, R.L. and Huggard, B.M. "Chaos at the Amusement Park: Dynamics of the Tilt-a-Whirl," *Am. J. Physics* **62** (1994) 59–66.

[63] Kyner, W.T. "Passage through resonance." pp 501–514 in *Periodic Orbits, Stability and Resonance,* G.Giacaglia, ed. Reidel, Dordrecht, Holland, (1970).

[64] Lanchester, F.W. *Aircraft in Warfare, The Dawn of the Fourth Arm.* Tiptree, Constable and Co, Ltd. U.K., 1916.

[65] Leslie, P.H. "Some further notes on the use of matrices in population mathematics," *Biometrika* **35** (1948) 213–245.

[66] Lorenz, E.N. "Deterministic nonperiodic flow," *J. Atmos, Sci.* **20** (1963) 130–141.

[67] Ludwig, D,. Jones, D.D., and Holling, C.S. "Qualitative analysis of insect outbreak systems: the spruce budworm and forest," *Journal of Animal Ecology* **47** (1978) 315–332.

[68] Margaria, R. *Biomechanics and Energetics of Muscular Exercise*, Clarendon Press. Oxford, UK, (1976).

[69] May, R.M. *Stability and Complexity in Model Ecosystems*, Princeton University Press, (1974). The introduction and the first few chapters are very highly recommended.

[70] May, R.M. "Biological populations with non-overlapping generations: stable points, stable cycles and chaos," *Science* **186** (1974) 645–647.

[71] Mehta, R.D. "Aerodynamics of sports balls," *Ann. Rev. Fluid Mech.* **17** (1985) 151–189.

[72] R.W.McCarley and J.A.Hobson. "Neuronal Excitability Modulation over the Sleep Cycle: A Structural and Mathematical Model," *Science* **189** (1975) 58–60.

[73] Mirollo, R.E , Strogatz, S.H. "Synchronization of pulse-coupled biological oscillators," *SIAM J. Appl. Math* **50** (1990) 1645–1662.

[74] Nayfeh, A.H., Mook, D.T., and Marshall, L.R. "Nonlinear coupling of pitch and roll modes in ship motions," *Journal of Hydronautics* **7** (1973) 145–152.

[75] Noble, B. *Applications of Undergraduate Mathematics in Engineering*, MacMillan, New York, (1967).

[76] Peastrel, M., Lynch, R. and Armenti, A., Jr. "Terminal velocity of a shuttlecock," *Am. J. Physics*, **48** (1980) 511–513.

[77] Poincaré, H. *Les Méthodes Nouvelles de la Méchanique Céleste*, Gauthier-Villars, France, (1892).

[78] Post, W.M., Travis, C.C., and DeAngelis, D.L. "Evolution of mutualism between species." pp 183–201 in *Differential Equations and Applications in Ecology, Epidemics and Population Problems*, Busenderg, S.N., and Cooke, K.L., eds. Academic Press, New York, (1981).

[79] Poynting, J.H. *Phil. Trans. Roy. Soc.,* A, **202** (1903) 525.

[80] Prigogine, I, and Lefever, R. "Symmetry breaking instabilities in dissipative systems, II," *Journal of Chemical Physics* **48** (1968) 1695–1700.

[81] Rapoport, A. *Fights, Games and Debates.* Univerity of Michigan Press, Ann Arbor, (1960).

[82] Reddish, V.C. "The R and N Stars," *Observatory* **74** (1954) 216–218.

[83] Richardson, L.F. "Generalized Foreign Policy," *British Journal of Psychology Supplements* **23** (1939).

[84] Richter, P.H. and Scholz, H.-J. "Chaos in Classical Mechanics: The Double Pendulum." pp 86–97 in *Stochastic Phenomena and Chaotic Behaviour in Complex Systems,* Ed. Schuster, P. Springer-Verlag. New York, (1984).

[85] Robbins, K.A. "A new approach to subcritical instability and turbulent transitions in a simple dynamo," *Math. Proc. Camb. Phil. Soc.* **82** (1977) 309–325.

[86] Robertson, H.P. "Dynamical effects of radiation in the Solar System," *Monthly Notices of the Royal Astronomical Society*, **97** (1937) 423–438.

[87] Routh, E.J. *Advanced Dynamics of a System of Rigid Bodies*, Dover, New York. (1955).

[88] Ruppe, H.O. *Introduction to Astronautics*, Academic Press, New York, (1966).

[89] A.C.Segal. "A Linear Diet Model," *College Mathematics Journal* **18** (1987) 44–45.

[90] Smith, H.J.T. and Blackburn. J.A. "Experimental study of an inverted pendulum," *Am. J. Physics* **60** (1992) 909–911.

[91] Sparrow, C. *The Lorenz Equations: Bifurcations, Chaos and Strange Attractors*, Appl. Math. Sci. **41**, Springer, New York, (1982).

[92] Stoker, J.J. 1950. *Nonlinear Vibrations in Mechanical and Electrical Systems*, Interscience Publishers, Inc, New York, (1950).

[93] Strogatz, S.H. *Nonlinear Dynamics and Chaos: with Applications to Physics, Biology, Chemistry and Engineering*, Addison-Wesley Publishing Company, New York, (1994).

[94] Stuhlinger, E. "Flight Path of an Ion-Propelled Spaceship," *Jet Propulsion* **27** (1957) 410.

[95] Thomson, W.T. *Introduction to Space Dynamics*, John Wiley & Sons, New York, (1963).

[96] Thomson, J.J. (1910) "The dynamics of a golf ball," *Nature* **85** (1910) 2151–2157. Also reprinted in *Physics of Sports*, ed. Frohlich, C.

[97] Toomre, A. and Toomre, J. "Galactic Bridges and Tails," *Astrophysical Journal* **178** (1972) 623–666.

[98] Townend, M.S. *Mathematics in Sport*, John Wiley and Sons, New York. (1984).

[99] Tufillaro, N.B. "Motions of a swinging Atwood machine," *Journal De Physique* **46** (1985) 1495–1500.

[100] Vinh, N.X., Busemann, A, Culp, R.D. *Hypersonic and Planetary Entry Flight Mechanics*, University of Michigan Press, Ann Arbor, (1980).

[101] Walker, H.S and Kirmser, P.G. "Computer modeling of pole vaulting." pp 131–142 from *Mechanics and Sport*, Bleustein, J.L., ed. The American Society of Mechanical Engineers, Applied Mathematics Division. New York. (1973).

[102] Ward-Smith, A.J. "A mathematical theory of running, based on the first law of thermodynamics, and its application to the performance of world-class athletes," *Journal of Biomechanics*, **18** (1985) 337–349. Also reprinted in *Physics of Sports*, Ed. Frohlich, C.

[103] Ward-Smith, A.J. and Clements, D. "Numerical evaluation of the flight mechanics and trajectory of a ski jumper," *Acta Applic. Math.*, **1** (1983) 301–314.

[104] Watts, R.G. and Baroni, S. "Baseball-bat collisions and the resulting trajectories of spinning balls," *Am. J. Physics*, **57** (1989) 40–45.

[105] Watts, R.G. and Bahill, A.T. *Keep your Eye on the Ball*, W.H.Freeman and company, New York, (1990).

[106] Watts, R.G. and Sawyer, E. "Aerodynamics of a knuckleball," *Am. J. Physics*, **43** (1986) 960–963.

[107] Whittaker, E.T. (1959). *A Treatise on the Analytical Dynamics of Particles and Rigid Bodies*, Cambridge University Press, New York, (1959).

[108] Wiesel, W.E. *Spaceflight Dynamics*, McGraw Hill, New York. (1989).

[109] Wright, A.E. "Computational models of gravitationally interacting galaxies," *Monthly Notices of the Royal Astronomical Society* **157** (1971) 309–333.

[110] Zeeman, E.C.,"Differential equations for the heartbeat and nerve impulse." pp. 8–67 in *Towards a Theoretical Biology, Vol 4*, Waddington, C.H., ed. Aldine Publishing Company, Chicago, (1972).

Index